BUSINESS ESSENTIALS
(SUPPORTING HNC/HND AND FOUNDATION DEGREES)

Human Resource Management

Course Book

In this September 2007 first edition

- full and comprehensive coverage of the key topics within the subject

- activities, examples and quizzes

- practical illustrations and case studies

- index

- fully up to date as at August 2007

- coverage mapped to the Edexcel Guidelines for HND/HNC Business Specialist Units 21-24

BPP
LEARNING MEDIA

BUSINESS ESSENTIALS

First edition September 2007

ISBN 9780 7517 4484 2

British Library Cataloguing-in Publication Data

A catalogue record for this book is available from the British Library

Printed in Great Britain by WM Print

45-47 Frederick Street

Walsall, West Midlands

WS2 9NE

Published by

BPP Learning Media Ltd

BPP House, Aldine Place

London W12 8AA

www.bpp.com/learningmedia

We are grateful to Edexcel for permission to reproduce the Guidelines for the
BTEC Higher Nationals in Business.

CONTENTS

INTRODUCTION

This is the first edition of BPP Learning Media's dynamic new **Business Essentials** range. It is the ideal learning solution for all students studying for business-related qualifications and degrees, and the range provides concise and comprehensive coverage of the key areas that are essential to the business student.

Qualifications in Business are traditionally very demanding. Students therefore need learning resources which get straight to the core of the topics involved, and which build upon students' pre-existing knowledge and experience. The BPP Learning Media Business Essentials range has been designed to meet exactly that need.

Features include:

- In depth coverage of essential topics within business-related subjects
- Plenty of activities, quizzes and topics for class discussion to help retain the interest of students and ensure progress
- Up to date practical illustrations and case studies that really bring the material to life
- A full index

In addition, the contents of the chapters are comprehensively mapped to the **Edexcel Guidelines**, providing full coverage of all topics specified in the HND/HNC qualifications in Business.

Each chapter contains:

- An introduction and a list of specific study objectives
- Summary diagrams and signposts to guide you through the chapter
- A chapter roundup, quick quiz with answers and answers to activities.

Further resources

Lecturers whose colleges adopt the Business Essentials range (minimum of 10 copies for each relevant unit) are entitled to receive **free practice assignments and answers** for the units concerned. While remaining under the copyright of BPP Learning Media, these can be copied and distributed to students as desired.

BPP Learning Media CD Roms will also be available early in 2008 to complement some titles within the series. These provide interactive learning modules for the key topics in the subject.

BPP Learning Media
2007

Other titles in this series:

Generic titles

Economics *

Accounts *

Business Maths *

Core units for the Edexcel HND/HNC Business qualification

Unit 1	Marketing
Unit 2	Managing Financial Resources and Decisions
Unit 3	Organisations and Behaviour
Unit 4	Business Environment
Unit 5	Business Law *
Unit 6	Business Decision Making
Unit 7	Business Strategy
Unit 8	Research Project

Specialist units (endorsed title routes) for the Edexcel HND/HNC Business qualification

Units 9-12	Finance
Units 13-16	Management
Units 17-20	Marketing
Units 21-24	Human Resource Management
Units 25-28	Company and Commercial Law *

* CD Roms available spring 2008.

For more information, or to place an order, please call 0845 0751 100 (for orders within the UK) or +44(0)20 8740 2211 (from overseas), e-mail learningmedia@bpp.com, or visit our website at www.bpp.com/learningmedia.

If you would like to send in your comments on this Course Book, please turn to the review form at the back of this book.

STUDY GUIDE

This course book includes features designed specifically to make learning effective and efficient.

(a)   Each chapter begins with a summary diagram which maps out the areas covered by the chapter. There are detailed summary diagrams at the start of each main section of the chapter. You can use the diagrams during revision as a basis for your notes.

(b)   After the main summary diagram there is an introduction, which sets the chapter in context. This is followed by learning objectives, which show you what you will learn as you work through the chapter.

(c)   Throughout the text, there are special aids to learning. These are indicated by symbols in the margin,

Signposts guide you through the course book, showing how each section connects with the next.

Definitions give the meanings of key terms. The *glossary* at the end of the course book summarises these.

Activities help you to test how much you have learnt. An indication of the time you should take on each is given. Answers are given at the end of each chapter.

Topics for discussion are for use in seminars. They give you a chance to share your views with your fellow students. They allow you to highlight holes in your knowledge and to see how others understand concepts. If you have time, try 'teaching' someone the concepts you have learnt in a session. This helps you to remember key points and answering their questions will consolidate your knowledge.

Examples relate what you have learnt to the outside world. Try to think up your own examples as you work through the course book.

Chapter roundups present the key information from the chapter in a concise format. Useful for revision.

Weblinks indicate useful websites for your own research.

(d)   The wide **margin** on each page is for your notes. You will get the best out of this book if you interact with it. Write down your thoughts and ideas. Record examples, question theories, add references to other pages in the course book and rephrase key points in your own words.

(e)   At the end of each chapter, there is a **chapter roundup**. Use this to revise and consolidate your knowledge. The chapter roundup summarises the chapter.

(f)   At the end of the course book, there is a glossary of key terms and an index.

PART A

HUMAN RESOURCES MANAGEMENT

Chapter 1:
THE DEVELOPMENT OF HRM

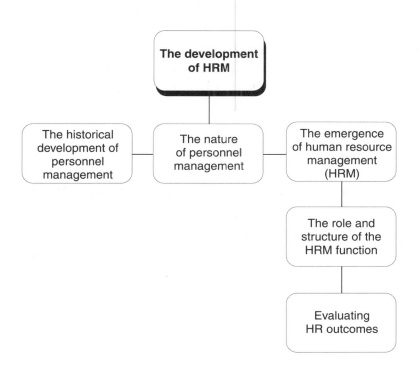

Introduction

It can be argued that people are an organisation's most important resource: after all, organisations are made up of people, and the way money, technology, information and other resources are used depends on human decisions. So it is generally recognised that the success of any business is greatly influenced by the calibre and attitude of the people who work for it.

It is therefore also commonly recognised that *someone* in every organisation will need to be responsible for the many matters that arise in connection with the recruitment, selection, training, motivation, payment and movement of staff through the organisation, as well as compliance with the various laws relating to employment. This is traditionally the role of the personnel function.

However, as the pace of social and technological change has quickened, there has been a growing recognition that thought must be given to managing the vital human resource at an earlier stage and at a higher level of organisational planning than has previously been the case. This has encouraged a longer-term, more proactive and strategic approach to people management, known as 'Human Resource Management' or HRM. In this chapter, we trace the development of this approach, while in Chapter 8, we explore its implications further, as an introduction to some key issues in HRM.

Your objectives

In this chapter you will learn about the following.

(a) The historical development of personnel management
(b) The shift towards 'human resource management' as an alternative approach
(c) The role and tasks of the human resource management (HRM) function
(d) The involvement of line managers in human resource practices

1 THE NATURE OF PERSONNEL MANAGEMENT

1.1 The nature of personnel management

The main professional body for personnel managers in the UK is the Chartered Institute of Personnel and Development (CIPD). The CIPD defined the function of personnel management as follows.

Definition

> **'Personnel management'** is that part of management concerned with people at work and with their relationships within an enterprise...'

'[Personnel management's] aim is to bring together, and develop into an effective organisation, the men and women who make up an enterprise, having regard for the well-being of the individual and of working groups, to enable them to make their best contribution to its success.

'In particular, personnel management is concerned with the development and application of policies governing:

- Human resources planning, recruitment, selection, placement and termination

- Education and training; career development

- Terms of employment, methods and standards of remuneration

- Working conditions and employee services

- Formal and informal communication and consultation both through the representatives of employers and employees and at all levels throughout the enterprise

- Negotiation and application of agreement on wages and working conditions; procedures for the avoidance and settlement of disputes.

'Personnel management must also be concerned with the human and social implication of change in internal organisation and methods of working, and of economic and social changes in the community.'

This statement highlights a number of useful – and potentially controversial – ideas about personnel management.

- It is centrally concerned with **people and relationships**. It is founded on attempts to understand and manage human behaviour: we will encounter some of these attempts – in the form of theories of learning, motivation and so on – in later chapters of this Course Book. It also involves a moral or ethical dimension: the employment relationship has 'human and social implications', raising issues of human dignity, fairness and corporate social responsibility.

- It embraces not only 'soft' values to do with the well-being of people at work, but also 'hard' values to do with the **success of the enterprise**: the role of people and relationships in fostering efficiency, effectiveness and contribution. (These 'soft' and 'hard' perspectives, and HRM's role in seeking a 'fit' between them, are discussed in Part B of this Course Book.)

- It is a '**part of management**'. Organisation of the personnel function may require a specialist department or departments, but it has been suggested that a separate function need not exist: *all* managers in an organisation need to achieve results through the efforts of other people, and must therefore manage the employment relationship.

Activity 1   **(30 minutes)**

Check out the websites of two or three Professional HR associations, such as:

www.cipd.co.uk	Chartered Institute of Personnel & Development (UK)
www.shrm.org	Society for Human Resource Management (USA)
www.jshrm.org	Japan Society for Human Resource Management

Browse through their home and mission statement pages, noting any useful definitions of 'personnel management' and 'Human Resource Management', and any statements of the philosophy underlying these concepts. How (and why) are people seen as important to the success of business? What cultural differences (if any) can you notice? What kinds of activity are seen as part of the personnel/HR professional's role?

---

2 THE HISTORICAL DEVELOPMENT OF PERSONNEL MANAGEMENT

Tyson & Fell (1986) suggest that personnel management has its roots in four traditions, arising from developments in the employment environment over the last 150 years.

- The welfare tradition
- The industrial relations tradition
- The control of labour tradition
- The professional tradition

2.1 The personnel practitioner as welfare worker

It is generally agreed that the personnel function can be traced back to the benevolent attempts by some employers in the latter half of the nineteenth century to improve the working conditions and circumstances of workers, who had been hard hit by the first wave of industrialisation and urbanisation. Victorian entrepreneurs in the UK like Rowntree, Cadbury and Lever initiated programmes providing such facilities as company housing, basic health care, canteens and education for workers' families, managed on behalf of the employer by 'industrial welfare workers'.

There was a dual motivation for these measures.

- They reflected a wider programme of **social reform and philanthropy**, led by political and religious movements of the day. Groups such as the Quakers, who in the USA were leaders in the abolition of slavery, strove to integrate successful business performance with the social, moral and spiritual betterment of their workers. (This may seem unduly paternalistic today, but at the time brought much-needed improvements in the quality of working life and the legal protection of workers.)

- Improved health and education, and the appreciation of their beneficiaries, secured an on-going pool of **suitable and willing labour** for the employer. Cadbury considered welfare and efficiency as 'two sides of the same coin' at his model factory at Bournville.

Nevertheless, the **welfare tradition** of personnel management arose from the time when much of the work and responsibility of the personnel officer was directed to the benefit of the employees, rather than to the strategic concerns of the enterprise and its management. Personnel management was in a sense the 'soft' or person-centred part or side of management. In specialised areas of personnel management today, such as occupational health, employee assistance schemes, workplace counselling services and so on, elements of this tradition persist with some force. However, as we will see below, the personnel officer is not in any formal sense the representative of the workforce: (s)he is paid to be part of the organisation's management team, as both representative and adviser.

2.2 The personnel practitioner as industrial relations negotiator

From the mid 19th century, the newly industrialised workers were also becoming increasingly organised. The legalisation of trade unions in 1871 raised the need for systematic frameworks for negotiation, conflict resolution and the management of relations between labour and employers.

The increasingly active role taken by labour organisations was reflected in political recognition. The Labour Party was formed in 1906, largely out of, and funded by, the trades union movement.

The industrial relations tradition of personnel management arose in response to the growing power of trade unions through to the 1960s and '70s, when much of the work and responsibility of the personnel officer involved mediating between the sides in industrial disputes, facilitating collective bargaining and negotiation and ensuring compliance with industrial relations law and regulation.

Elements of this tradition may persist in the modern era in the perceptions of personnel officers and other parties to negotiations, conflict resolution, discipline and grievance procedures and so on. The 'diplomatic' role of personnel may also pose a dilemma of dual allegiance – particularly where there is lack of trust in the relationship between the personnel function and other members of the management team.

Activity 2   **(20 minutes)**

Whose 'side' is the personnel practitioner on? From your own experience or current knowledge of what a personnel officer does, suggest three examples of the conflict which might exist between his or her position as a member of the management team and his or her special relationship with the workforce, and discuss what you feel are the issues involved. Where would *you* stand on these issues?

2.3 The personnel practitioner as bureaucrat

Meanwhile, in the boom following the industrial revolution, businesses had been growing larger and more complex. The **'control of labour'** tradition of personnel management arose in response to the increasing pace of organisational growth and change. The primary responsibility of the personnel officer came to be seen as supporting management by standardising, monitoring and controlling the range and complexity of workplace activity. This involved a range of activities such as: job allocation and performance monitoring; time-keeping and control of absenteeism; recording sick leave and holidays; administering pay and benefits, training and promotion; devising rules, regulations and compliance checklists; preparing workforce-related reports and returns and so on.

This is an essentially bureaucratic tradition, which is still evident in many personnel departments. It has been perpetuated, in part, by the ambiguity of personnel's perceived role and authority in the management team: where a department lacks direct positional or 'line' authority, the application of rules, regulations, procedures and forms is one of the key methods of exercising influence.

2.4 The personnel practitioner as professional

The latter half of the 20th century saw a period of intense legislation in all areas of employment: health and safety, employment protection, equal opportunities and so on. (This has continued in the early 2000s, largely driven by the requirement to implement European social policy and EU Directives.)

The increasing complexity of legislation and regulation, together with the development of increasingly sophisticated behavioural and managerial theory, fostered **specialism** within the personnel function. The need for a specialised body of knowledge – drawing on law, economics, administrative management and the social sciences (sociology, psychology and so on) led to the establishment of a scheme of education and qualification, and the professionalisation of the work of the personnel practitioner.

Personnel management became recognised as a discipline in its own right, broadly applicable to all fields of employment. The Institute of Personnel Management (now the CIPD) made determined efforts to establish personnel management as a profession, through a programme of learning and examinations leading to qualification; opportunities for professional communication and networking; and requirements for continuing professional development.

According to the CIPD's *Code of Professional Practice in Personnel Management*, the personnel practitioner has three principle areas of responsibility.

NOTES

- 'A personnel manager's primary responsibility is to his **employer**.'

- He will 'resolve the conflict which must sometimes exist between his position as a member of the **management team** and his special relationship with the **workforce** in general and with individual **employees**.'

- He will 'use his best endeavours to enhance the standing... of his **profession**' in dealing with other bodies.

EXAMPLE

TEAM PLAYERS WITH ENERGY AND VISION

Resource manager

You will have overall management for the movement of resources within projects, be an active member in negotiations with departmental heads and project managers, have close links with other offices in order to utilise international resources, be responsible for defining yearly recruitment targets and identify detailed skill sets within each competence.

You must have 2+ years of resource or project-management experience. New media knowledge is desirable as well as knowledge of other European languages.

Training adviser

You will co-ordinate all aspects of the training cycle from identifying training needs to drawing up and implementing plans, sourcing external providers in order to develop enthusiastic and passionate employees. Working alongside department heads, HR and recruitment, you will be driving the development strategy together with the company.

You must be CIPD-qualified (full or part) with at least two years' experience in a training environment.

HR officer

You will be an integral part of this dynamic company by providing the day-to-day HR function, defining resource requirements, tracking employees, ensuring appraisal objectives are met, assisting with the induction process.

You need to be CIPD part-qualified, have good time management skills, computer literacy and excellent communication skills.

(Recruitment advertisements in *People Management*, September 2000)

Activity 3 (20 minutes)

Analyse the recruitment advertisements shown in the example above, in terms of the four 'traditions' of personnel management discussed above. What elements of each tradition can be seen, if any? What key words stand out as foreign to these traditions, and what do they suggest about the organisation, its environment and the role of personnel management within it?

2.5 A shift in perception of the personnel management role

By the 1950s, the personnel function appeared to have developed as 'a collection of incidental techniques without much internal cohesion': 'partly a file clerk's job, partly a housekeeping job, partly a social worker's job and partly "fire-fighting" to head off union trouble or to settle it.' (Drucker, 1955).

There was a widespread perception of personnel management as an essentially **reactive** – even defensive – role: avoiding or settling industrial disputes, preventing accidents and ill-health (and their associated costs) and so on.

Figure 1.1 illustrates this traditional perception of the role of the personnel function in the organisation.

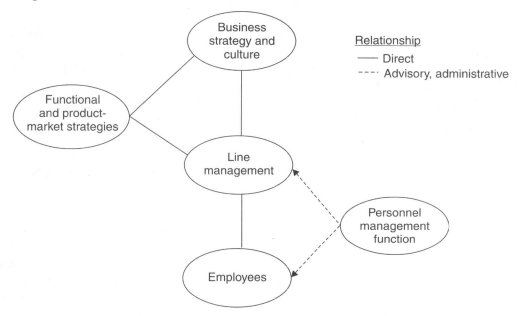

Figure 1.1 The personnel function in the organisation

The profession was becoming increasingly aware, however, that as long as personnel policy and practice were divorced from the strategy of the business, and failed to be proactive and constructive, personnel management would continue to be perceived by line management as having little to do with the 'real' world of business management and the 'bottom line' (profitability). Personnel specialists were commanding scant respect as business managers, and their influence continued to be limited to areas of little strategic impact.

A typical call, from the professional literature of the 1980s and '90s, was:

'The real requirement is **proactive** and **constructive**, rather than **defensive** and **reactive**. To discharge their true role, personnel managers must anticipate the needs of the organisation in the short and the long term. They must develop the policies to produce solutions to anticipated problems resulting from the external and internal environment, whilst influencing and creating the attitudes amongst employees needed for the enterprise's survival and success.' (Livy, 1988)

FOR DISCUSSION

'People may be regarded as a vital resource – at least plenty of lip service is paid to this concept by company chairmen in their annual statement – but many managers find it difficult to appreciate where the personnel department fits in, except in the simplest terms as a procurement (recruitment) and fire-fighting function.'

Role-play a discussion between the company CEO or line manager (in a field of your choice: say, Marketing or IT) and the personnel manager: what is the personnel function really *for*, from their respective points of view?

We have highlighted some of the key sources of discontent with the role of the traditional personnel function: its reactive/defensive (rather than proactive/ constructive) nature, and its perceived irrelevance to the strategic and performance concerns of the business. We will now look at some further factors which prompted a re-evaluation of the role of personnel management, and the emergence of the new term 'human resource management'.

3 THE EMERGENCE OF HUMAN RESOURCE MANAGEMENT (HRM)

3.1 Context for a shift in perspective

Throughout the 20th century, new models and theories of **organisation and management** had been emerging to reflect the accelerating page of change in the business environment, the diversity and expectations of workers and consumers, and the increasing sophistication of work psychology. The commitment, involvement and flexibility of the workforce was increasingly recognised as a key to organisational survival, challenging the personnel function to become involved in concerns of broader relevance to the business and its objectives:

- The management of change and changing organisational forms (including the globalisation of business, and the advent of 'virtual organisations' enabled by Information and Communications Technology (ICT) development such as the Internet).

- Planning for long-term demographic challenges, such as the falling birthrate and skill shortages in the pool of available labour

- Creating attractive 'employer brands' in the labour marketplace

- Empowering workers; facilitating team-working and flexible working methods

- Managing increasing diversity in the workforce: supporting equality of opportunity, developing family-friendly policies and so on

- Creating and adapting organisational culture as a key to mobilising employee loyalty, commitment and creativity.

Intensifying business competition was likewise demanding that personnel management justify itself in terms of **contribution** to the organisation's goals for growth, competitive gain and the improvement of bottom line performance. The payroll costs of many organisations today are of such magnitude (30-80% of total expenses) that senior managers must be concerned with human resources!

In the **social environment,** advances in education, technological skills and general affluence had raised employees' expectations of the quality of working life and awareness of their rights within the employment relationship. The need to compete in innovative, technology– and quality-sensitive markets put a premium on skilled **knowledge workers,** altering the balance of power in the employment relationship. Coercive and controlling psychological contracts of employment are no longer the norm (other than in very stable markets and/or areas of high unemployment): employees expect to have access to influence, responsibility and information related to their work. There has been a shift from **compliance** to **commitment** as the core of the psychological contract.

Definition

> A **psychological contract** is the set of values that determines what an organisation expects of its employees, and what they expect of it, in the employment relationship.

Politically, the UK government of the 1980s encouraged a shift away from trade union power and collective bargaining, instead emphasising entrepreneurialism, individualism and a 'unitary' perspective (discussed in detail in Part D of this Course Book) which assumed that management and employees shared a common interest in the success of the enterprise. It seemed possible that industrial conflict and collective negotiation could be pre-empted – and ultimately replaced – by pro-active people-focused personnel strategies such as participation and information-sharing.

Meanwhile, the popularity of the American anecdotal literature focusing on 'excellence' (for example, *In Search of Excellence* by Peters and Waterman) associated the success of high-performing companies with enlightened, people-focused management practices.

> 'All the **value** of this company is in its people. If you burnt down all of our plants and we just kept our people and information files, we would soon be as strong as ever. Take away our people and we might never recover.'
> (Tom Watson, former president of IBM, quoted in Peters and Waterman, 1982)

This represented a conceptual shift away from regarding employees as a cost to be managed and controlled, and towards regarding them as an **asset** (or 'human **capital**') to be nurtured and developed. A former IBM President, Barry Curnow, further noted in the late 1990s that: 'We've moved through periods when money has been in short supply and when technology has been in short supply. Now it's the people who are in short supply. So personnel directors are better placed than ever before to make a real difference – a bottom line difference. The **scarce resource**, which is the people resource, is the one that makes an impact at the margin, that makes one firm competitive over another.'

A variety of research studies have attempted to support the anecdotal evidence with hard data. Although the link to **business performance** is by no means clear cut, there is broad agreement that a greater use of 'human resource practices' (notably those focused on securing employee skills, motivation/commitment and flexible working) is associated with positive employee attitudes, higher levels of productivity and higher quality of service.

3.2 The emergence of Human Resource Management (HRM)

Definition

> **Human Resource Management (HRM)** may be defined as: 'a strategic approach to managing employment relations which emphasises that leveraging people's capabilities is critical to achieving sustainable competitive advantage, this being achieved through a distinctive set of integrated employment policies, programmes and practices.'   (Bratton & Gold, 2007)

As this definition suggests, the term HRM is often associated with both:

- An orientation towards **personnel management**, viewing its role as proactive, system-wide interventions, linking HRM with strategic planning and cultural change; and

- An orientation towards the **employment relationship**, embracing distinctive people-centred values such as trust, commitment, involvement and collaboration.

The term Human Resource Management (HRM) gained recognition in the USA in early 1980s as a label for the way certain blue-chip companies such as IBM, Xerox and Hewlett Packard were managing their people. The terms and its implications were subsequently explored by UK writers including David Guest, Karen Legge and John Storey, in the late 1980s and early 1990s. Despite heated debate about the nature, impact and morality of HRM (discussed briefly in Paragraph 3.5 below), the term has had widespread adoption in the last few years, and many of its underlying assumptions are now being incorporated into personnel management policy and practice.

3.3 Characteristics of HRM

The main features of HRM may be summed up as follows (Armstrong, 2003).

(a) The attempt to achieve **strategic 'fit'** or integration between HR and business planning: HR policy should be formulated at the strategic level, and directly related to the organisation's competitive and value-adding objectives. (This may be called '*vertical*' integration.)

(b) The development of coherent, mutually-supporting **HR policies and practices**: the strategic management of people will be reflected in all areas and systems of HRM. (This may be called '*horizontal*' integration.)

(c) An orientation towards **commitment**: securing employee identification with the organisation's goals and values, not mere compliance with directives. This is often associated with management practices such as flexibility, teambuilding, empowerment, involvement and the creation of strong cultural values.

(d)   The **treatment of people as assets** rather than costs: regarding employees 'as a source of competitive advantage and as **human capital** to be invested in through the provision of learning and development opportunities'. This is often associated with a strong emphasis on the delivery of quality and customer satisfaction, and on rewarding performance, competence, contribution and added value.

(e)   A **unitarist approach to employee relations,** which assumes that there need be no inherent conflict of interest between employers and employees. This is often reflected in a shift from collective/representative to more individual employee relations.

(f)   The responsibility of **line management** for delivery of HRM objectives.

EXAMPLE

'The **Selfridges** story is one of reinvention and growth, in which people management has played a vital role in creating a highly successful retail chain... One of the [new management] team's first critical choices was to decide what sort of retailer it should be – and how its people management should support that identity.

'Selfridges now markets itself as the "house of Brands", with its own strong image based on that presumption. In transforming its employment culture to complement the change, it adopted a series of new HR initiatives. It conducted culture surveys, organised focus groups and replaced its old Hay job evaluation scheme with a broadbanding pay arrangement. The Trafford Park store in Manchester... put great emphasis on communication, training and development.

'Behind all these innovations, Selfridges made an explicit effort to model the underlying stakeholder values required in its dealings with customers, employees, the local community, suppliers and other stakeholders. These values were expressed under four goals: to be "aspirational, friendly, accessible and bold"...

'Staff turnover, particularly in the first few years [of the Manchester store] was high... but the company did cut it from 78% in 2000 to 40% in 2001. There is a heavy reliance on part-time staff, making it more expensive to develop a sophisticated HR system, and another complication is that a large number of the sales associates are concession staff. The values matrix includes the statement "My concession staff are treated well and made to feel welcome". In practice, this means that they join the Selfridges sales teams, take the same training and are included in company communications...

'Staff at Selfridges displayed one of the highest levels of commitment out of the 12 organisations in our research. The factors they particularly linked to job satisfaction, motivation and commitment were challenging work; job security; teamwork; career opportunities; appraisal; and, most of all, communication, involvement and the way their managers managed.'

(Purcell *et al*, 2003)

In his influential work, Guest (1989) defined the four key policy goals of HRM as follows.

(a) **Strategic integration** – 'the ability of organisations to integrate HRM issues into their strategic plans, to ensure that the various aspects of HRM cohere and for line managers to incorporate an HRM perspective into their decision-making.' This can be depicted as shown in Figure 1.2: compare this model with that shown in Figure 1.1.

(b) **High commitment** – people must be managed in a way that ensures both their genuine 'behavioural' commitment to pursuing the goals of the organisation and their 'attitudinal' commitment, reflected in strong identification with the enterprise.

(c) **Flexibility** – HRM policies must be structured to allow maximum flexibility for the organisation, so it can respond to ever-changing business needs: for example, by encouraging functional versatility in employees and by creating 'an adaptable organisational structure with the capacity to manage innovation'. (This has since been further supported by technological developments such as laptops and the Internet, allowing widely dispersed units and individuals to collaborate 'virtually' and on the move.)

(d) **High quality** – the notion of quality must run through everything the organisation does, 'including the management of employees and investment in high-quality employees, which in turn will bear directly on the quality of the goods and services provided.'

The main conceptual difference between HRM and personnel management is, arguably, its focus on strategic integration.

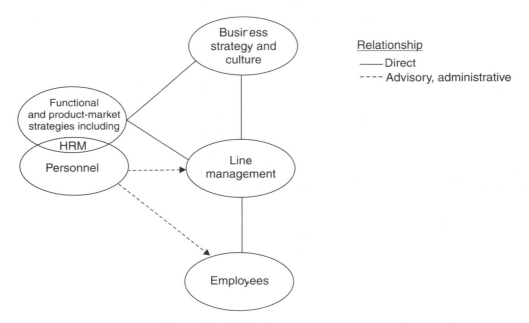

Figure 1.2 HRM: the strategic integration of personnel management

However, some commentators (Armstrong, 2003; Guest, 1989; Legge 1989) have suggested that that there are more similarities than differences between personnel

management and HRM – and that HRM should perhaps been seen rather as a particular orientation to personnel management than an alternative approach.

We will discuss different perspectives on HRM itself in Chapter 8, where the ambiguities of the approach are explored in more detail.

Activity 4   **(30 minutes)**

Think of the business context(s) you are familiar with, or arrange to conduct a brief informal or telephone interview with any personal contacts you may have in the HR/Personnel field. Activity text

(a) What label is given to the personnel management function in the organisation?

(b) Is the term 'HRM' used – and if so, what is it understood to mean?

(c) If the name 'HRM' was adopted in place of 'Personnel Management' (or something similar), how was this reflected in changes of philosophy, policy and practice?

(d) Why do you think the name of the function might matter?

3.4 21st century HRM?

Tyson (2006) suggest that the first decade of the 21st Century has seen further – and more pronounced – changes to the way HR work is conducted, including:

- The adoption of the **business partner** model (Figure 1.3), requiring HR specialists to operate effectively across a range of dimensions, as the desirable position for HR.

- An increasing **consultancy orientation**, seeking to balance HR's roles in supporting – but also, where necessary challenging and changing – corporate strategy and practice. Among other effects, this has placed a premium on skills in organisational diagnosis, facilitation and coaching.

The business partner model (Figure 1.3) represents HR as operating across four key business dimensions: strategic and operational, processes and people.

Strategic

HR as: Strategic Partner	*HR as:* Change Agent
HR as: Administrative Experts	*HR as:* Employee Champions

Processes ———————————————— **People**

Operational

Figure 1.3: The business partner model (adapted from Tyson, 2006)

'A business process focus with a strong strategic intent, coupled with the capacity to act as change agents may be one determinant, but HR specialists must show they can perform at the operational level as well, or they will never be given the chance to play the bigger strategic game.' (Tyson, *ibid*.)

FOR DISCUSSION

Tyson raises some interesting questions about this model.

- Is it the role of HR to act as 'employee champions' – or is this only applicable in a North American context (where trade unions have less power than in Western Europe, say)?

- Can an HR director be both a 'strategic partner' and a 'change agent'? What if it is the corporate strategy that needs changing?

Tyson summarises the **range of models** now embraced within HRM (which also reflect variation in the extent to which firms have adopted a full-blown HRM approach as follows (showing progressive development from left to right).

	Administration	*IR Systems*	*Business manager*	*Consultancy*
Role	• Support to line management	• Policy	• Strategic	• Internal consultancy service
Focus	• Welfare • Personnel services • Records/ procedures • Unitary relations	• Industrial relations • Procedures/ systems • Rules • Pluralist relations	• Integration with corporate strategy • Business case/ relevance	• Service agreements • Projects • OD/change • External networks • Balanced interests
Objectives	• Service need of managers/ individuals	• Harmony • Legal compliance	• Results • Employee commitment	• Enable change • Organisational flexibility
Job title	• Welfare officer • Employment manager	• IR manager • Labour officer • Personnel manager	• HR manager (or director)	• Change manager • HR director

3.5 On-going debate about 'HRM'

The concept and terminology of HRM have fuelled on-going debate among academics and practitioners.

- **Is HRM (in practice) really different from 'personnel management'?** The terms are often used interchangeably. One point of view is that 'HRM' is a term which practitioners have seized upon and applied to themselves, in the interests of their individual and professional status – whether or not they are in fact doing anything more than traditional personnel management: 'old wine in new bottles'. Another point of view, however, is that by continually focusing debate on the nature of the employment relationship and its role in business performance, HRM – whatever terminology is used – has helpfully altered both the orientation and practice of management and the expectation and experience of working life.

- **Is HRM a fair and ethical way to manage people?** One viewpoint is that HRM policies are merely a more subtle, psychologically-based form of manipulation than authoritarian or bureaucratic control. Another reservation is that acknowledging the importance of people in business success may simply be a more acceptable 'spin' on using or exploiting employees as a means to an end. 'Sadly, in a world of intensified competition and scarce resources, it seems inevitable that, as employees are used as a means to an end, there will be some who will miss out.' (Legge, 1998) On the other hand, 'it could be argued that if organisations exist to achieve ends, which they clearly do, and if those ends can only be achieved through people, which is clearly the case, the concern of managements for commitment and performance from those people is not unnatural. What matters is *how* managements treat people as ends and *what* managements provide in return.' (Armstrong, 2000)

- **Does it really make a difference to organisational performance?** Major research for the CIPD by Purcell, Kinnie and Hutchinson (2003) argued that 'organisations that support their employees by developing effective policies based on ability, motivation and opportunity will create higher levels of organisational commitment, motivation and job satisfaction', which in turn 'give (employees) the chance to help make their team, section and company better'. However, research has also shown 'a disjunction between rhetoric and reality... between HRM theory and HRM practice; between what the HR function says it is doing and that practice as perceived by employees; and between what senior management believes to be the role of the HR function, and the role it actually plays' (Gratton *et al*, 1999)

FOR DISCUSSION

(Set up a discussion or debate about any one of the three questions cited above, and justify the alternative points of view given (or your own viewpoints on the questions).

Having explored the nature of HRM, we can now gather together some ideas on what HR practitioners typically do in practice, and how they operate within the organisation.

4 THE ROLE AND STRUCTURE OF THE HRM FUNCTION

4.1 Operational tasks and activities

The range of tasks and activities commonly carried out by human resource practitioners include the following.

Organisation	• *Organisational design:* structuring the organisation, by grouping activities, assigning accountabilities and establishing communication and authority relationships
	• *Organisational development:* planning and implementing interventions in the organisation's social processes to improve effectiveness through techniques such as structural change, team-building, process consultancy, interpersonal skill development and role negotiation.
	• *Job/role design and definition:* structuring the content and size of jobs (for efficient task performance, flexibility and worker satisfaction) and defining their component tasks, conditions and competency requirements (for recruitment, appraisal, reward and a number of other HR processes)
	• *Flexible working:* planning and implementing flexible structures and procedures to maximise the efficiency and adaptability of the organisation
Human resource planning and resourcing	• *Human resource planning:* forecasting the organisation's future requirements for labour, skills and competence, and planning to meet them through subsidiary plans for recruitment, deployment, development, retention and so on
	• *Recruitment:* Attracting employment applications from the number, type and calibre of people required by the HR plan
	• *Selection:* Assessing and selecting suitable employees from applicants
	• *Retention:* Planning rewards and incentives to control labour turnover and retain high quality staff
	• *Exit management:* managing the termination of contracts, retirements, resignations, dismissals and redundancies, in such a way as to comply with legal requirements and minimise human and organisation costs

Performance management	• *Objective and competence requirement setting:* developing and agreeing frameworks of organisational, unit and individual goals to direct and motivate performance
	• *Performance monitoring and appraisal:* on-going monitoring and periodic assessment of performance within agreed requirements
	• *Discipline handling:* managing informal and formal processes to confront employee behaviour or performance which falls below organisational rules and standards
	• *Grievance handling:* managing informal and formal processes to address individual employee grievances or complaints
	• *Identifying learning and development needs:* as part of continuous improvement of performance
Reward management	• *Pay systems:* developing and managing salary structures, systems and scales that are equitable, fair and compliant with equal pay legislation.
	• *Performance pay systems:* developing and managing ways of relating pay progression or bonuses to results, attainments (eg competence or skill), effort and other measures of performance
	• *Benefit schemes:* developing and managing employee entitlements (eg pensions, maternity and sick pay, annual leave) and 'fringe' benefits (eg allowances and services)
	• *Non-financial rewards:* building non-monetary rewards (such as recognition, challenge, personal development) into job design and management style, as part of a 'total reward' package
Human resource development	• *Learning organisation:* creating a culture and systems to support individual and organisational learning, information gathering and sharing and so on
	• *Education and training:* planning, implementing and evaluating on– and off-the-job learning opportunities and programmes to meet identified gaps in the skills required by the HR plan
	• *Personal development:* facilitating individual learning plans and opportunities, beyond the immediate job (eg for general employability)
Human resource development cont'd	• *Career management:* identifying potential and planning career development opportunities; succession and promotion planning; guiding and mentoring individuals in career planning
	• *Managerial development:* providing education, training and opportunities to develop managerial competencies and support enhanced contribution

NOTES

Health, safety and welfare	• *Occupational health and safety:* monitoring and managing work environments, practices and culture to ensure that employees are protected from health hazards and accidents; complying with relevant legislation; actively promoting health, fitness and 'work-life balance' to improve the wellbeing and performance of staff • *Welfare services:* providing services such as catering or recreational facilities, individual counselling and support (eg for illness, forthcoming redundancy or retirement, personal health problems)
Employee relations	• *Industrial relations:* managing informal and formal relationships with employee representatives (trade unions and staff associations); collective bargaining on terms and conditions; resolving collective disputes; implementing consultative committees and partnership agreements • *Employee communication:* informing employees about matters relevant to their work or of interest or concern to them • *Employee voice:* creating consultation opportunities for employees to contribute to decision-making in matters affecting them and their work
HR services	• *Managing the employment relationship:* contract management • *HR policies and procedures:* developing and administering guidelines and systems for all the above, to guide line managers and employees • *HR information systems:* developing and operating integrated systems for preparation of employee record-keeping, management reporting, statistical reports and returns and so on • *Compliance:* Assuming that all HR policies and practices are compliant with relevant law, regulation and codes of practice (and ideally, best practice) in areas such as employment protection, health and safety, equal opportunity and diversity, data protection and so on.

Graham and Bennett (1998) classify these activities into three dimensions of management.

(a) The **utilisation of people at work**: recruitment, selection, transfer, promotion, separation, appraisal, training and development

(b) The **motivation of people at work**: job design, remuneration, consultation, participation, negotiation and justice

(c) The **protection of people at work**: working conditions, welfare services, safety, implementation of appropriate legislation.

If this seems too employee-centred a classification, it must be added that the overall objective of these dimensions of management is maintained or enhanced **business performance**.

We will be covering many of these tasks and activities in detail, in the following chapters of this Course Book.

Another way of thinking about what HR practitioners do is to consider the various **processes** that are involved in performing the various activities and tasks listed above.

Definition

A **process** is a sequence of activities (often crossing functional and organisational boundaries) involved in achieving goals, delivering services or adding value.

Armstrong (2003), for example, identifies a broad set of processes underpinning the HRM approach.

(a) **Strategic HRM** – 'defining intentions and plans for the development of HRM practices, and ensuring that HR strategies are integrated with the business strategy and one another'.

(b) **Policy making** – formulating and implementing HR policies which set guidelines on how personnel issues should be handled.

(c) **Competency, job and role analysis** – developing content and competency frameworks to support various activities such as organisation and job design, recruitment, appraisal, training and reward.

(d) **Change management** – advising on and facilitating the process of change in organisational structures and systems.

(e) **Knowledge management** – developing systems for obtaining and sharing knowledge, to foster organisational learning, innovation and performance.

Activity 5   **(no time limit)**

Use whatever online, work or personal contact sources you have at your disposal to obtain a copy of a job or role description of an HR manager. Such a document may be available – without breaching organisational confidentiality – as part of a job application package, on a careers/recruitment website, on a corporate Internet or intranet site, or via your own business contacts.

Assess:

(a) the objectives/outcomes of the role, as stated in the description
(b) the tasks, activities and responsibilities set out in the description
(c) any relationships with other roles in the organisation which are mentioned

4.2   Roles of HR management

HR practitioners may fulfil a range of roles, depending on the organisational context.

(a) **Guidance role** – offering specialist recommendations and policy frameworks to guide line management decisions: for example, in regard to emerging HR issues, and the consistent and effective implementation of HR procedures.

(b) **Advisory role** – offering specialist information and perspectives to line managers (and individual employees) on employment matters. Managers, for example, may be advised on training options, legislative provisions or how to handle specific people problems. Employees may be advised on their legal rights or development options, or counselled in relation to work or personal problems.

(c) **Service role** – providing services to a range of internal customers. This includes administrative services (in areas such as payroll administration, employee records, reports and returns) and delivery of HRM programmes (recruitment and selection, training, health and welfare and so on).

(d) **Control/auditing role** – analysing personnel indices (such as wage costs or labour turnover), monitoring performance, carrying out benchmarking or a local government review, say. This role has traditionally caused conflict with line managers, who felt they were being 'policed' – but line managers' discretion must be balanced with the need for consistency in applying HR policy, compliance with legal obligations, and ensuring that the strategic aims of HRM are being met.

(e) **Planning/organising role** – for example, in human resource forecasting and planning, developing flexible working methods and so on.

At a more strategic and proactive level of HRM, HR practitioners may also take on role as:

(a) **Strategists**: helping to fulfil the business objectives of the organisation through strategic management of the human resource *and* influencing business planning by highlighting the human resource implications of objectives and strategies.

(b) **Business partners**: sharing responsibility with senior and line management for the success of the enterprise, through the identification and exploitation of opportunities and the seeking of competitive advantage.

(c) **Internal management consultants**: working alongside line managers in analysing business processes and systems, diagnosing and exploring problems, recommending solutions that the 'client' can own and implement, or implementing solutions and delivering services.

4.3 Shared responsibility for HRM

Definition

> **Centralisation** and **decentralisation** refer to the degree to which the authority to make decisions is held centrally by a particular group of people *or* delegated and spread to a number of individuals and groups within the organisation.

Centralised control over human resource management generally implies the existence of an HR officer or department with authority over (or advisory input to) all personnel management tasks in the organisation.

De-centralised control over human resource management generally implies the delegation to line managers and team leaders of the authority for personnel management tasks affecting their own staff and activities.

In practice, there is a need for a mix of both, in order to gain the benefits of co-ordination and consistency as well as flair and flexibility.

FOR DISCUSSION

'Managers, if one listens to the psychologists, will have to have insights into all kinds of people. They will have to be in command of all kinds of psychological techniques. They will have to understand an infinity of individual personality structures, individual psychological needs, and individual psychological problems... But most managers find it hard enough to know all they need to know about their own immediate area of expertise, be it heat-treating or cost accounting or scheduling.' (Drucker, 1955)

What does this say about the respective roles of line managers and HR specialists in managing people at work?

As the role of the HR function has become more strategic/proactive, rather than welfare/administrative/reactive, the following areas have commonly been retained as the responsibility of a centralised HR function.

(a) **Strategic issues**, such as change management programmes and human resources planning, and all aspects of HR at the strategic level, including the formulating and communication of organisational policy. This ensures that the impact of human factors on strategic plans (and vice versa) is taken into account.

(b) **Organisation-wide** communication and employee relations management. Centralisation has the advantage both of special expertise and a wider organisational viewpoint.

(c) Provision of **specialist services** and **advice/consultancy**, where up-to-date specialist knowledge or input, or extra-departmental perspective, is required.

(d) **Researching and auditing** of HR systems. This helps to co-ordinate and control HR functions across the organisation, to ensure that line departments are complying with policy and that policies are effective and relevant to the needs of line departments.

Such centralised functions create a coherent and integrated framework of policies, plans, systems and rules, developed by HR specialists, which help to maintain consistent practice and minimise redundant problem-solving and 're-inventing the wheel' by line managers. Within such a framework, a number of aspects of personnel management could be devolved to line departments.

> **Activity 6**   **(30 minutes)**
>
> You are a sales manager in Mpower Ltd, an organisation which develops and markets software and services for Internet users: web page design, Internet connection, browser programmes and so on. You are responsible for a team of 12 salespeople who work more or less 'independently' from home and 'on the road' and who service a remote rural area with a widely dispersed population.
>
> What personnel management tasks would you wish to be *your* responsibility? What areas would you wish to have specialised or centralised help with? What other options might you consider?
>
> (You might like to do this activity with a fellow student who can take the role of Mpower's head office HR manager. See what conflicts of interest come up, and how they might be resolved.)

4.4 The role and responsibilities of line managers in human resource practices

Most commentators observe a trend toward greater **decentralisation** of personnel management roles, in line with 'slimmer' head office staffs, flatter management structures and the fostering of flexibility by giving greater autonomy to local business units.

The increase in the white-collar 'knowledge-based' workforce, with its mobility and higher expectations, has also supported a move toward individualism in career development, reward negotiation and other areas, which may be more flexibly managed by line managers and team leaders than by centralised personnel departments.

Meanwhile, integrated business process and HR information systems have facilitated HR decision-making, on a day-to-day basis, by line managers.

The responsibility of line managers for delivering HR outcomes is a distinctive feature of the HRM approach, but even in a traditional personnel management model, line managers would often have responsibility for activities immediately concerned with the manager-team relationship: team selection, interviewing, and timekeeping management, performance appraisal, team motivation and so on.

EXAMPLE

'A key finding [of CIPD-funded research into 12 organisations to investigate how effective HRM creates competitive advantage] was the role of line managers in bringing HR policies to life... Their managerial behaviour – in implementing HR policies; in showing leadership by involving staff and responding to their suggestions; and in controlling quality, timekeeping and absence – makes a real difference to employees' attitudes...

'Looking at the information from our employee interviews, we found that there were frequent and statistically significant associations between people's approval of their managers' leadership style and a range of HR policies and practices. The way in which managers brought these HR policies to life and exercised leadership was strongly related to positive employee views on such areas as involvement, worker-management relations, communication, openness, coaching and guidance, performance appraisal, reward and recognition, training, job influence and quality control.

'Three of the case-study organisations made significant changes to the roles and competence profiles of their line managers after our first-year survey. One of these was Selfridges, where performance has continued to improve. We found similar remarkable results at the Royal United Hospital at Bath. Despite difficulties at the top of the organisation, at ward level a new manager was appointed, a revised appraisal scheme was implemented and a stronger focus on work-life balance was achieved. Employee attitudes improved markedly and what once had been a retention blackspot ended the second year with no job vacancies.

'This was also true at Clerical Medical, now the life insurance arm of HBOS. We asked a manager in charge of a department that had achieved great progress which HR policies he had found most helpful. His answer was instructive: "It is the quality of team leaders that's important. If they take a close interest in people, it makes a big difference."'

(Purcell *et al*, 2003)

FOR DISCUSSION

Which 'side' do you naturally relate to: the line managers trying to get things done but hedged in by personnel rules and policies – or the HR manager having to beat his or her head against a brick wall to convince line managers of hard-won insights into people at work? Do you feel that as a line manager, you would be glad of expert help with complex people issues? Or as an HR manager, would you be glad that line managers are prepared to get on with their jobs, leaving you to more 'global' perceptions of the organisation's needs?

Set up a discussion between line and 'staff/advisory' functions: 'Why should we/you listen to the HR department?'

4.5   A shared services approach

Shared services are support functions that are used by many different line departments or units in an organisation. A **shared service unit (SSU)** is a centralised, dedicated provider of such services to internal customers – on a quasi-'outsourced' basis. Functions such as HR (like procurement and IT) may be 'outsourced' by business units (such as regional divisions of a company) to the SSU, which:

- Employs its own dedicated resources,

- Is responsible for managing the costs/quality of its services (like any external service provider), and

- Is often bound by contractual agreements with its internal customers, to provide guaranteed or target levels of service (via service level agreements or consultancy contracts).

Advantages claimed for the SSU approach include:

- Consistency of practice and standards across the organisation

- Strengthening of core competences

- Significant cost savings (since there may be economies of scale and a reduction in the cost of back-office processes through centralisation eliminating duplication in individual units).

As with any form of centralisation, however, care must be taken to avoid the SSU from becoming isolated from end users and 'local' demands. Service level agreements must also be flexible enough to avoid the tendency to stifle innovation, initiative and above-specified performance.

EXAMPLE

Tyson (2006) outlines how: 'companies such as IBM have pioneered the division of HR activity into three areas: the senior strategic role; the policy-making and consulting role; and the transactional/administrative role. This latter role, and some of the consulting work, can then be conducted through an HR call centre [or SSU] where there are HR staff who are fluent in appropriate European languages, to deal with employee queries, or to refer them to the internal consultant.'

4.6 Outsourcing HR tasks

The need for organisational flexibility has supported the concept of the **core** organisation: focusing in-house resources and expertise on the distinctive value-adding and competitive advantage-gaining competences and functions of the organisation, and purchasing non-core support services and functions from a range of 'peripheral' sources. We will discuss the 'core-periphery' model in Chapter 9 of this Course Book, but for now, it may be sufficient to note that a number of HR activities may be regarded as 'peripheral' or complementary to the primary functions of the business, and outsourced to external consultants or service providers.

The main areas identified as amenable to effective outsourcing include:

- Training and development

- Recruitment (and some aspects of selection, such as screening or testing)

- Health and safety monitoring and advice (and related health and fitness promotion and services, if provided)

- Employee welfare and counselling

- Payroll management (and related benefit schemes, pensions administration and so on)

- Legal advice on compliance.

Activity 7   **(20 minutes)**

Why might it be beneficial to outsource the particular activities listed above? What sort of external service providers would be suitable to take on each activity?

In addition, the HR function may have *de facto* responsibility for a range of ancillary activities – such as on-site catering, security, office/facility management, child care, company care fleet management and so on – which could be more effectively outsourced to external specialists.

The advantages and disadvantages of outsourcing may be summarised as follows.

Advantages	Disadvantages
• HR costs are reduced by downsizing the HR function and potentially cheaper provision of services by specialists	• External advisers/providers must be carefully chosen, contracted and managed, in order to maintain standards and organisational values
• HR specialists are freed up to focus on core value-adding and business-specific tasks and knowledge	• External advisers/providers may lack understanding or flexibility to be able to tailor their offering to reflect the organisation's objectives, culture or brand
• Specialist knowledge and expertise may be easier to buy in than to develop within the organisation	
• External specialists may have access to infrastructure development (eg website or application software, purpose-built facilities) that the business lacks	• Outsourcing may be carried out for short-term cost saving without defining which activities are (or may become) 'core' to the business or role of HRM in the organisation
• The objectivity of external service/advice providers may improve the quality of solutions and their acceptability to members of the organisation	• The horizontal integration and consistency of application across the range of HR policy and practice may be lost

4.7 Summary

As we have suggested, HRM is perhaps most helpfully seen as a broadly distributed organisational competence or orientation, rather than a 'function' in the sense of a department of specialists. The HR function may be thought of as the integration of people management systems throughout the organisation, rather than a particular set of roles and activities.

The diagram on the following page (Figure 1.4), loosely based on the work of Shuler *et al* (1995) may be read from the bottom up (following the classical planning hierarchy) or from the top down (from a functional perspective).

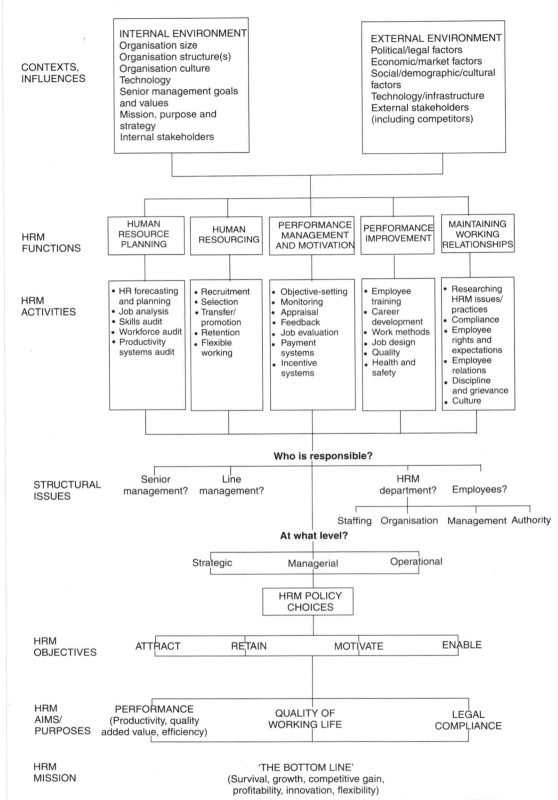

Figure 1.4: HRM in context

5 EVALUATING THE HR OUTCOMES

5.1 The problem of evaluation

If HRM is to be taken seriously at a strategic level as a contributor to bottom line business performance, it must be subject to evaluation. However, there are considerable difficulties attached to the evaluation of the HR function.

(a) While some performance-based criteria (profitability, productivity, error reduction, compliance and so on) are relatively easy to measure and compare, having to do with units and monetary values, others are not (for example, innovation or flexibility).

(b) Effective HRM should, over the long term, measurably impact on improved business performance. However:

    (i) Its short-term activities may not show such effects

    (ii) It is difficult to attribute these effects to HR activity alone: organisational performance involves many other variables, including technology, management effectiveness, market conditions, competitor initiatives and so on.

(c) Subjective criteria such as the quality of working life, employee motivation, team spirit, openness to change, job satisfaction, the quality of employee relations and so on are notoriously difficult to measure, let alone to attach monetary values to, as a means of comparison.

(d) Benchmarking (standard-setting on the basis of best practice in other organisations) is difficult because of the wide differences in the environmental and internal variables affecting different organisations.

(e) HRM itself is a wide-ranging activity, and therefore requires a wide range of criteria for evaluation.

5.2 Cost-benefit analysis

Despite these difficulties, there are certain criteria, both quantitative and qualitative, which allow HR managers to demonstrate their effectiveness in the way that other managers do: by cost-benefit analysis. Assessing the costs of their activities against the benefits resulting from them, HR managers can determine:

(a) Whether the costs are justified by equal or greater benefits

(b) Whether costs and/or benefits are increasing or decreasing over time

(c) How the costs and/or benefits compare to competitor or benchmark organisations

---

Activity 8   **(15 minutes)**

Activity text Before we proceed, see if you can brainstorm ten examples each of benefit criteria and cost criteria relevant to HR management.

You may have noted that benefit criteria – such as 'legal compliance' or 'improved productivity' – may apply to all HRM activities, while costs tend to be more specific to each activity: the cost of training, for example, which might include training resources, teacher payroll, coaches' and trainees' time in lost production and so on. Costs are more easily measurable, because they have a monetary value attached, but benefit criteria can usually be given a monetary value, if required: 'reduced accidents and illness', for example, can be expressed as a saving of the potential costs of lost production, benefits and compensation payments, training of replacement workers and so on.

5.3 Quantitative measures

Quantitative or statistical indices of the HR function's activities may be available in relation to areas such as the following.

(a) Staff turnover/labour wastage (or labour stability) ratios

(b) Absenteeism rates

(c) Unit labour costs (useful in comparison to previous periods and/or competing businesses)

(d) Incidences of grievance procedures, disciplinary procedures, appeals to industrial tribunals, compensation claims, proceedings for non-compliance and so on

(e) Number of days production (and associated costs) lost through accidents, sickness, industrial disputes and so on

(f) Number of applications attracted by recruitment methods and/or lead time to recruit an employee

(g) Number of selected recruits remaining in the job, achieving performance targets, achieving promotion and so on

(h) Number of staff (including HR staff) achieving professional or other qualifications, or undertaking training programmes

(i) Success of training (and other) programmes in achieving their objectives

(j) Number of requests for information handled by the HR department, lead time in responding to requests, ability to answer technical personnel questions on demand and so on

(k) The costs of any and all of the above

We will look at means of evaluating specific HR activities, such as recruitment and training, in relevant chapters.

5.4 Qualitative measures

Qualitative, or subjective, criteria may be harder to measure, but may be equally important in the field of HRM. Examples include the following.

(a) Employee motivation, team spirit, job satisfaction, acceptance of change and so on – as gauged by attitude surveys, interviews, psychological testing and other tools of behavioural science, as well as presumed observed effects on productivity, communication, absenteeism and so on

(b) The extent to which HR proposals, policies, documentation and so on are accepted by line managers – as suggested by implementation rates, questions and objections

(c) The perception of the HR function's value, service, expertise, quality of advice, professionalism and so on by its internal customers: senior management, line managers and employees

5.5 The Four Cs

The Four Cs model was developed by researchers at the Harvard Business School as a means of investigating HRM issues (Beer *et al*, 1984). It suggests that the effectiveness of the outcomes of HRM should be evaluated under four headings.

(a) **Commitment** – that is, employees' identification with the organisation, loyalty and personal motivation in their work. This, like the qualitative criteria mentioned above, may be assessed through methods such as attitude surveys, exit interviews and analysis of presumed effects (such as absenteeism and labour turnover).

(b) **Competence** – that is, employees' skills and abilities, training needs and potential for performance improvement and career development. This may be measured through skill audits, competency testing and performance management systems.

(c) **Congruence** – that is, the harmonisation of the goals, values and efforts of management and employees (or at least the *perception* by employees that they have a mutual vision and purpose, to mutual benefit). This may be estimated by the quality of employee/industrial relations, the incidence of grievance and disciplinary action, conflict and communication and so on.

(d) **Cost-effectiveness** – that is, efficiency, whereby HRM objectives are met and benefits obtained at the lowest input cost.

The Harvard model does not solve the problems of the accurate measurement of qualitative criteria; nor of the incompatibility of varying criteria (cost-effectiveness achieved by downsizing, for example, might not encourage commitment or congruence); nor of the sheer variety of HR activity and contexts (since there are organisations and areas of organisational activity in which low-skilled monotonous jobs and authoritarian management styles, for example, are still possible and indeed appropriate). However, it does offer a simple framework for thinking about HR effectiveness.

Activity 9 (30 minutes)

Think about your own work organisation, or an organisation you know well.

(a) How would you go about assessing the effectiveness of its HRM, according to the Four Cs model?

(b) Without doing a detailed assessment, how do you estimate it would rate on each of the Four Cs?

5.6 Internal service and consultancy agreements

The effectiveness of HR projects and services may also be measured ore explicitly against defined **performance indicators** and service standards set out in contractual agreements with internal customers.

- **Service agreements** may be used by HR departments (or external providers) which provide day-to-day HR administration and operations to business units. They establish clear agreement on the nature and level of service to be provided – acting as an incentive to HR performance *and* as a way of managing user expectations! Service-level issues may include: how often the service is to be provided; during what hours it is to be available; what number and grade of staff will be available; how far the service does (and does not extend); and what speed of response can be guaranteed.

- **Consultancy agreements** may be appropriate where an HR practitioner or project team acts in an internal consultancy capacity to a line department or business unit. An **internal consultant** works inside one part of an organisation to help another part. Although this is a complex role – since the consultant is working within the same system and culture as the client – they both have the same *external* customers and share goals; the increased effectiveness of the organisation.

Internal (and external) consultants may be called in to propose or design something, or solve a problem, outside the expertise of the client unit, or to introduce and manage change in the client unit. (Examples of potential consultancy projects in HR include reorganisation, training, introduction of flexible working or performance management or employee relations problem-solving.)

A consultancy agreement may therefore include matters such as:

- The clients' expectation, needs and wants

- An agreed definition of the problem

- Specific objectives outcomes or deliverables

- A working approach that will suit both parties (what will be reported back, how, how often and to whom? What co-operation and access to the information will be supplied by the client? and so on)

- A preliminary time (and where appropriate, cost) schedule for the process

NOTES

Chapter roundup

- The personnel function may take different forms in different organisations. Traditionally, it has been regarded as a primarily administrative, reactive, problem-handling function, concerned with hiring and firing, employee welfare and industrial relations.

- Four traditions colour perceptions of personnel management: the welfare tradition, the industrial relations tradition, the control of labour tradition and the professional tradition.

- Human Resource Management (HRM) is a concept which seeks to recognise employees as an asset to be nurtured, rather than a cost to be controlled, and which views the sourcing, deploying and developing of these human resources as a key integrated element of business strategy.

- HRM developed out of influences such as: the increased complexity of business processes and their dependence on employee flexibility and commitment; the need for competitive advantage; the increased power and expectations of highly-skilled knowledge workers; and the identification of human relations policy as the key to management effectiveness and business 'excellence'.

- Key areas of operational HR activity include: organisation; human resource planning and resourcing; performance management; reward management; human resource development; health, safety and welfare; employee relations; HR services

- One of the distinctive characteristics of an HRM orientation is the devolution of responsibility for delivering HRM outcomes to line management. In practice, strategic, specialised and organisation-wide activities are often centralised under the control of an HR function, while day-to-day aspects of people management are often devolved to line managers, who are able to manage the employment relationship in a more individualised and flexible way. Other options are the outsourcing of peripheral HR functions or the adoption of a shared services approach.

- The HR function can only establish credibility by systematic evaluation of its activities in the light of business objectives, and any internal service or consultancy agreements drawn up with internal customers/clients.

BPP
LEARNING MEDIA

Quick quiz

1. List the four 'traditions' of personnel management.

2. To what groups of people does the HR practitioner have responsibilities?

3. List a number of factors which contributed to the shift towards an HRM orientation.

4. What are the main features of HRM?

5. What, according to Guest, are the four key policy goals of HRM?

6. List eight broad areas into which the operational activities of HRM may be grouped.

7. List the possible roles of HR practitioners.

8. What is the role of line managers in delivering HR outcomes?

9. Summarise the arguments for and against outsourcing HR activities.

10. What are the Four Cs of the Harvard model?

Answers to quick quiz

1. Welfare, industrial relations, control of labour, professional   (para 2)

2. To the employer, to the workforce (in part), to the profession   (para 2.4)

3. Dissatisfaction with the reactive role of personnel management; developments in organisation/management theory; competition putting pressure on contribution; social changes raising employee expectations of the psychological contract; political support for pro-active employee relations; focus on the value of people as a scarce resource and source of value.   (paras 2.5, 3.1)

4. Strategic fit; integrated HR policies and practices; commitment orientation; people as assets; unitarist employee relations; involvement of line managers.   (para 3.3)

5. Strategic integration, high commitment, flexibility, high quality   (para 3.3)

6. Organisation; HR planning and resourcing; performance management; reward management; human resource development; health, safety and welfare; employee relations; HR services.   (para 4.1)

7. Guidance, advice, service, control/auditing, planning/auditing, strategy, business partnership, internal consultancy.   (para 4.2)

8. Delivering HR policies to employees (explicit in HRM orientation); interpersonal processes of team management and motivation; specific devolved personnel management tasks at the interface between the employer and the team (eg team selection, individual discipline, absence management, motivation).   (para 4.4)

9. See Paragraph 4.6 for a complete answer

10. Commitment, congruence, competence, cost-effectiveness   (para 5.5)

Answers to activities

1   There is no suggested answer to this activity: it is intended to stimulate your awareness of:

      (a)   some of the research sources available to you in exploring this topic further

      (b)   the variety of ways in which HRM concepts are expressed

      (c)   cultural, legal and other variations in HRM principles and practices in different parts of the world.

2   Examples of conflicts of interest might include the following.

      (a)   The need for downsizing or delayering for organisational efficiency. The workforce may well see this as a betrayal, yet it is part of resource management to know when to liquidate assets: organisational survival may even depend on increased efficiency/flexibility or cost reduction.

      (b)   The negotiation of reward packages. As a member of management, you may wish to minimise increases in the cost of labour, or rationalise them in some other way. The workforce perceives pay rises as a 'right' or as an indication of the value the organisation puts on its services, and may be disappointed.

      (c)   Disciplinary procedures. The interests of management may best be served by 'clamping down' on absenteeism, poor time-keeping and so on in order to keep general discipline and efficiency – but the workforce, or particular individuals, will often feel that rules are unfair or unfairly applied.

      Broadly, these are issues of the way power is used in organisations. The personnel function can go a long way to minimising the potential hurt and conflict caused by applying and communicating the decisions of management fairly and sensitively.

3   *Welfare tradition*: very little sign of such an orientation in the job descriptions – except perhaps in the HR officer's responsibility for 'assisting with the induction process': even this seems more likely to be performance-oriented rather than for the psychological comfort of the recruits.

      Industrial relations tradition: very little of this either, in the traditional sense. The word 'negotiations' crops up (Resource Manager), but more in the sense of collaborative responsibility for project resourcing. The phrase 'enthusiastic and passionate employees' (Training Advisor) suggests a unitarist perspective on the employment relationship: no inherent conflict anticipated.

      Control of labour tradition: targets, competence frameworks, plans, co-ordination, the 'tracking' (monitoring) of employees against appraisal objectives, the requirement for computer literacy: this suggests the presence of administrative control systems in the organisation. However, these elements are tempered with more 'dynamic' elements.

      Professional tradition: the Training Adviser and HR officer are required to have CIPD qualifications and the Training Adviser additionally requires specific specialist experience. However, more general managerial skills and experience are also mentioned: time management, languages, communication and so on.

Non-traditional concepts: the key word seems to be integration. 'In negotiation with departmental heads and project managers... links with other offices... overall management...' (Resource Manager). 'Driving the development strategy together with the company' (Training Adviser). 'Integral part' (HR Officer).

4   Terminology clearly matters to some of the people who perform the function, for their own sense of self-esteem and the status of their profession. An important consideration is whether the employees view the idea of themselves as 'resources' positively or negatively, and whether practice justifies the more 'enlightened' sounding title, or is indeed viewed cynically as the same 'old wine' in 'fancy new bottles'. Adoption of the title may be a sign of conflict and power struggles within the organisation (with HR trying to boost its status, credibility and influence) or it may enhance the organisation's reputation or 'brand' as an employer in the labour market.

5   This is a research activity. (Keep written evidence of your information search for your portfolio or assignment bibliographies!)

6   The answer to this activity is personal to you. However, the case scenario suggests some areas for consideration.

(a)   As sales manager, you are responsible for staff who have particular needs: notably for motivation, encouragement and supervision while 'on the road'. You need to think about whether team-building would be best served by *your* maintaining contact with them on HR matters (such as appraisal, reward, training) or through a (possibly anonymous) personnel department. On the other hand, you might like some expert briefing on how to manage 'virtual teams', on problems suffered by team members (eg suffering isolation or stress) and so on.

(b)   You have quite specific requirements for your staff. They need to be technically aware (in order to advise customers), highly knowledgeable about the company's products, proactive sales people (since the customers are dispersed, and likely to be a bit traditional – although ideal candidates for the products). You might feel, given the difficulties of team building, that you would like to retain responsibility for selection and training – or you may prefer a more organisation-wide perspective: perhaps it would be good to have centrally selected/trained people who are close to the product and its technical possibilities – and then train them in sales?

These are just some suggestions to show you how widely and deeply an organisation needs to think through these issues.

7   *Training:* specialist facilities/equipment/resources, specialist knowledge of learning techniques, suitable for 'off-the-job' training. Providers: eg colleges, training companies, online campuses, publishers of books and software

Recruitment: specialist techniques (eg in psychometric testing), networks of contacts, savings in advertising media buying, online facilities (e-recruitment), removes routine pre-screening etc. Providers: eg recruitment consultants, e-recruitment sites, Job Centres, careers officers

Health/safety: specialist knowledge of law/regulation, removes perception of 'policing' from team leaders, special facilities (medical testing, fitness etc). Service providers: consultants, fitness/medical facilities

Welfare/counselling: specialist training, access to networks/referrals, removes 'personal' issues from workplace. Providers: counsellors, welfare agencies, Employee Assistance providers

Payroll/benefits/pensions: specialist software/knowledge, removes routine peripheral tasks, avoids legal responsibility for financial advice. Providers: specialist agencies, financial service providers

Legal advice: specialist knowledge, removes 'policing' on compliance from the HR department. Providers: law firms

8   Some examples are as follows.

(a)   **Benefit criteria**: increased productivity, increased quality/reduced error/wastage, reduced absenteeism, reduced labour turnover, increased job satisfaction, legal compliance, reduced accidents/ illness, reduced employee stress, increased job involvement, increased innovation, reduced costs of fines, reduced grievance/ disciplinary actions, reduced industrial disputes, enhanced response to recruitment, enhanced community goodwill

(b)   **Cost criteria**: costs of health and safety activity, training, recruitment, consultancy, remuneration, HR department training, welfare provision, computerisation, HR salaries, ergonomic improvements, compliance

9   Suggested methodologies include attitude surveys, questionnaires, observation, interviews (eg exit interviews, counselling interviews, appraisal interviews), and analysis of the presumed effects of more or less 'C' factors (positive or negative labour stability, absenteeism rates, incidence of conflict and so on).

In terms of the evaluation of your chosen organisation's HRM function, you are on your own! Do attempt this exercise, however, even if it is just a brief mental survey of your college, your favourite fast food outlet or whatever. This will get you thinking not just about how to evaluate the success of HRM policy and practice, but about how HRM goes about fostering, maintaining and increasing the 'C' factors in the organisation.

NOTES

Chapter 2:
HUMAN RESOURCE PLANNING

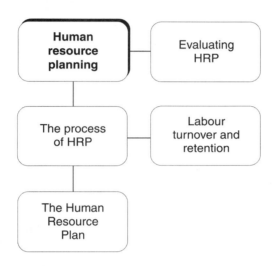

Introduction

As we saw in Chapter 1, human beings are one of the resources that a business must obtain and manage in pursuit of its objectives. Human resource (previously 'manpower') planning is the task of assessing and anticipating the skill, knowledge and labour time requirements of the organisation, and initiating action to fulfil or 'source' those requirements. If the organisation (or a particular area of its activity) is declining, it may need to plan a reduction or redeployment of the labour force. If it is growing, or moving into new areas of activity, it will need to find and tap into a source of suitably skilled labour.

It may already have occurred to you that this cannot be as easy as it sounds! External factors – particular over the long term – create fluctuations in the demand for and supply of labour. So do internal factors, such as individual and team productivity, training, and labour turnover through retirements, resignations, maternity leaves and so on.

If anything, as we shall see, the uncertainties of human resource planning make it even more important – and certainly, it becomes more important to approach it systematically: in this chapter, we consider how this can be done.

Your objectives

In this chapter you will learn about the following.

   (a)   The purpose of human resource planning

   (b)   The processes and stages involved in human resource planning

   (c)   The need for human resource planning and the difficulties involved in accurately predicting manpower requirements

   (d)   Limiting factors in the external environment, and changes in the external environment, which influence the human resource planning process

1 HUMAN RESOURCE PLANNING

1.1 'Manpower planning' and HRP

Definition

> **Human resource planning** may be defined as 'a strategy for the acquisition, utilisation, improvement and retention of the human resources required by the enterprise in pursuit of its objectives.'

The traditional 'manpower planning' model may be broadly outlined as follows.

- Forecast **demand** for specific skills, competences or grades of employee.

- Forecast **supply** of these skills, competences or grades, both within and outside the organisation.

- Plan to remove any *discrepancy* between demand and supply. If there is a shortage of labour, for example, you would need to reduce demand (say, through improved productivity), or improve supply (through training and retention of current staff, or recruitment from outside, for example).

Apart from the sexist connotations of this term, this traditional model has, in the light of HRM, come to seem too narrow in three key respects.

(a) It is heavily reliant on calculations of employee numbers, with insufficient attention to skills, competences and other factors in productivity or value.

(b) It is insufficiently integrated with other key factors in the management of the human resource: motivation and productivity; organisational culture and systems; job and organisation design; and so on.

(c) It is based on matching people with 'jobs', in an era when traditional job designs are being eroded by the emphasis on functional, temporal and numerical flexibility in the workforce.

Liff (2000) notes that 'there has been a shift from reconciling numbers of employees available with predictable, stable jobs, towards a greater concern with skills, their development and deployment'.

(a) **Recruiting** the required number and type/quality of staff

(b) **Retaining** the required number and type/quality of staff – and therefore letting go those who are not required (by natural labour turnover and/or by planned downsizing)

(c) **Utilising** staff in the most efficient and effective manner: increasing productivity, introducing multi-skilling and other forms of flexibility and so on

(d) **Improving** the skills, capabilities and motivation of staff, so that they become a more flexible resource capable of fulfilling new requirements.

It is arguable that forecasting staff and skill requirements has become more *difficult* in recent times because of the increasing uncertainty and rate of change in the business environment. However, it has also arguably become more *necessary*, because the risks of 'getting it wrong' are correspondingly greater.

Human resource planning (HRP) is a form of **risk management**. It involves realistically appraising the present and anticipating the future (as far as possible) in order to get the **right people** into the **right jobs** at the **right time** *and* managing employee behaviour, organisational culture and systems in order to **maximise the human resource** in response to anticipated opportunities and threats.

Activity 1 (15 minutes)

We have noted that the supply (and demand) of skilled human resources is subject to a number of factors outside and within the organisation. Suggest three possible reasons why a business might find itself experiencing a shortage of a particular skill or type of employee.

1.2 HRP and corporate planning

As suggested in Chapter 1, human resources are one element of the overall corporate strategy or plan, and the two are mutually inter-dependent. If the corporate plan envisages a cut in output, for example, or the closure of a particular plant, then the human resource plan will need to consider redeployment of staff, redundancies and so on. If the corporate plan specifies a move into a new product market, the human resource plan will have to source the required labour from outside or within the organisation, through recruitment, training or sub-contracting.

In turn, the availability of labour resources can act as a constraint on, or spur to, the achievement of corporate goals. If there are skill shortages and employees cannot be recruited or developed cost-effectively, plans for expansion or diversification may have to be curtailed. The availability of multi-skilled or expert teams, on the other hand, my inspire innovative strategies for growth and change.

Lam and Schaubroeck (cited in Torrington *et al*, 2002) argue that HR planning is critical to organisation strategy, because it is able to identify:

- **Shortfalls in organisational capability** (skills, knowledge, people) which would *prevent* the corporate plan from being implemented successfully

- **Surpluses in organisational capability** which might *shape* the corporate plan by suggesting opportunities to capitalise on currently under-utilised resources

- **Poor utilisation of people** in the organisation, which would highlight the need to add value through *revised HR practices*

Some people might still argue that proactive forward planning to meet human resource requirements is a waste of time, especially for small to medium-sized businesses. Why does it have to be so complicated? Surely, if you are short of staff, you hire some – or train or promote some of your existing staff? And if business declines and you find yourself with superfluous staff, you make some redundancies? In fact, it is not quite so simple. We will suggest why.

1.3 Why is HRP necessary?

An attempt to look beyond the present and short-term future, and to prepare for contingencies, is increasingly important. Some manifestations of this are outlined below.

> Manpower planning has maintained its imperatives for several reasons: (i) a growing awareness of the need to look into the future, (ii) a desire to exercise control over as many variables as possible which influence business success or failure, (iii) the development of techniques which make such planning possible.
>
> Livy (1988)

(a) Jobs in innovative and fast-changing contexts may require experience and skills which cannot easily be bought in the market place, and the more complex the organisation, the more difficult it will be to supply or replace highly specialised staff quickly. The need will have to be anticipated in time to initiate the required development programmes.

(b) Employment protection legislation and increasing public demand for corporate social responsibility make downsizing, redeploying and relocating staff a slow and costly process.

(c) Rapid technological change is leading to a requirement for manpower which is both more highly skilled and more adaptable. Labour flexibility is a major issue, and means that the career and retraining **potential** of staff is at least as important as their actual qualifications and skills. ('Trainability' is now a major criterion for selection.)

(d) The scope and variety of markets, competition and labour resources are continually increased by environmental factors such as the expansion of the European Union, the globalisation of business and the explosive growth of e-commerce.

(e) Information and Communication Technology (ICT) has made available techniques which facilitate the monitoring and planning of human resources over fairly long time spans: accessing of demographic and employment statistics, trend analysis, 'modelling' of different scenarios and variables, and so on.

Armstrong (2003) sums up the aims of HRP as follows.

- To attract and retain the number of people required, with the skills, expertise and competences required.

- To anticipate potential surpluses or shortfalls which will need to be adjusted.

- To develop a well-trained and flexible workforce which will support organisational adaptation to external changes and demands.

- To reduce dependence on external recruitment to meet key skill shortages (by formulating retention and development strategies).

- To improve the utilisation of people (most notably by developing flexible working systems).

Activity 2   **(15 minutes)**

To what extent would HRP be possible and desirable for:

(a) A company designing, manufacturing and selling personal computers?

(b) A large local government authority?

(c) An international airline?

1.4 A contingency approach to HRP

We have suggested that **long-range, detailed human resource planning** is a necessary form of risk management, preparing businesses for foreseeable contingencies. However, there has been some disillusionment about the feasibility and value of such planning, given the rapidly evolving and uncertain business environment and the kinds of highly flexible organisational structures and cultures that have been designed to respond to it.

(a) The trend in **organisation and job design** is towards functional feasibility (multi-skilling), team working, decentralisation (or empowerment) and flexibly-structured workforces (discussed later in this Course Book), to facilitate flexible deployment of labour. Peters (1994) cites successful US businesses like McKinsey, CNN and Titeflex as examples of 'unglued' structures made up of small, functionally versatile units that come together and disband constantly, according to task requirements; that find their own customers, set up their own networks and generate their own projects; that continuously re-educate themselves to meet new demands. Such structures are entirely flat, output/customer-focused, business-generating, information-seeking, continuously learning and shifting. They sweep aside traditional barriers to innovation, customer service and creative problem-solving – but also effectively abolish 'jobs' and predictability of labour utilisation.

(b) Within flexible structures and markets, where manipulating information – not making things – is the primary business activity, the traditional concepts of 'job' and 'career' are being eroded. Bridges (1995), for example, foresaw a workforce made up of '**vendor workers**' who sell their services to a variety of clients and work for them on a project basis. This fundamentally changes the nature of 'job vacancies' and of the labour pool.

(c)   With new emphasis on continuous improvement, customer service and product innovation, organisations are striving to be more adaptive, visionary, fluid in their structures and holistic in their thinking. The **'learning organisation'** embraces learning at all levels and in all areas, focusing on the process of learning and adapting to what is learned: HRP is thus seen as an opportunity to explore different scenarios, without pre-conceived requirements or solutions.

In such environments, a different, less prescriptive approach to HRP may be required. Recent literature suggests three broad alternatives.

(a)   **The staff replacement approach.** Staff are recruited or promoted to fill a vacancy as and when it occurs – if it is still required – with little formal planning. While this is essentially reactive, and does not provide for much change in the knowledge and skill base of the organisation, it allows a degree of flexibility on an *ad hoc* basis. Organisations or units with relatively stable environments may have little difficulty filling vacancies as they arise, while in volatile environments and organisations with high staff mobility and turnover, it may be recognised that longer-range projections of labour requirements are in any case meaningless.

(b)   **Short-term Human Resource Strategy.** In environments where long-term forecasting of future requirements is quickly rendered obsolete by change and uncertainty, yet the ability to adapt the skills and knowledge of the workforce is required, a short-term strategic model may be more suitable. This approach has a 'key issues' orientation: HR and line managers collaborate to determine what the organisation's **key HR issues** are in the short term, emphasising flexibility and speed of response to emerging threats and opportunities. HR plans are thus more likely to be:

•   Focused on short-term action planning and implementation
•   Based on simpler data analysis
•   Owned by line managers.

(c)   **Vision-driven Human Resource Development.** This approach is long-term in its orientation, but is driven by organisational vision, mission and core values, rather than detailed staffing forecasts and targets. Such an approach is often employed where a major cultural shift is required, calling for corresponding shifts in employee attitudes, skills and behaviours.

The process of choosing the appropriate approach may be shown as follows (adapted from Kane and Stanton (1994): Figure 2.1.

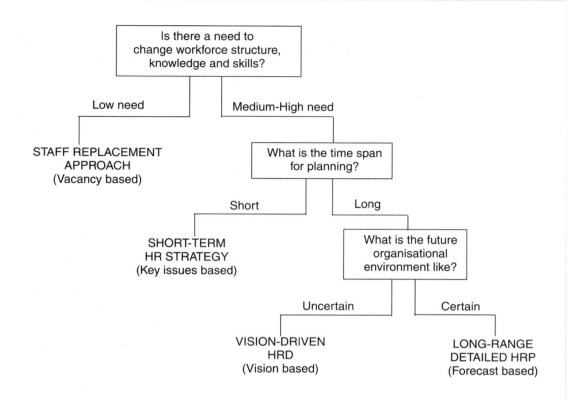

Figure 2.1: Approaches to human resource planning

Let us now look at the HR planning process in more detail. We have already suggested that it is a form of 'supply and demand management', aiming to minimise the risk of either surplus (and therefore inefficiency) or shortage (and therefore ineffectiveness) of the labour resource. We shall now see how that works in practice.

2   THE PROCESS OF HRP

2.1   Forecasting demand

The **demand** for labour, competencies and productivity levels may be forecast by considering several factors.

(a)   The **objectives** of the organisation, and the long and short-term plans in operation to achieve those objectives. Where plans are changed, the effect of the changes must be estimated: proposed expansion, contraction, innovation or diversification of the organisation's activities will affect the demand for labour in general or for particular skills. This may be estimated by market research, competitive analysis, trends in technological advances and so on, (although sudden changes in market conditions complicate the process: the effect of global terrorism on defence spending, for example).

(b)   **Staff utilisation** – how much labour will be required, given the expected productivity or work rate of different types of employee and the expected volume of business activity. Productivity in turn will depend on a range of factors, such as capital expenditure, technology, work organisation, employee motivation, management style and negotiated productivity deals.

(c) **The cost of labour** – including overtime, training, benefits and so on – and therefore what financial constraints there are on the organisation's manpower or skill levels.

(d) **Environmental factors** and trends in technology and markets that will require organisational change in response to emerging demands, threats or opportunities. Economic recession and developments in ICT, for example have encouraged downsizing and delayering. At the same time, ICT developments have created new markets, products and business processes creating demand for new skills (such as network management or website design).

EXAMPLE

NatWest: an integrated approach to HR planning

'The knowledge and skills of the workforce are crucial and difficult to change quickly, so it is important to plan ahead to identify the skills required to deliver business plans (demand) compared with those that are currently available (supply), to find out where potential skill gaps may lie and how these might be filled.'

NatWest has approached this process as follows.

(a) Demand for skills was assessed through a systematic, top-down approach, driven from the corporate centre. The central HR function held a series of meetings with line managers and HR leaders in each of five core businesses to consider the implications of their strategic plan in the light of their existing skills mix.

(b) A shared model was developed, which highlighted likely demand for skills, and provided an initial perspective on potential skill gaps, as a basis for exploring ways of filling gaps, and discussing the specific concerns of each business.

(c) A bottom-up skills audit was then implemented, to validate the findings of the top-down analysis, and to give a 'better feel' for the likely future supply of skills.

  (i) Because of the size and variety of the workforce, NatWest 'needed to establish a common language between businesses to describe skills', and chose a broad-based 'job family' approach. An agreed set of job families (such as 'project manager') was drawn up: each family included characteristic competency profiles for different levels of staff. Gaining agreement on the families and profiles was the major challenge of the exercise, given 'the need to establish a common language and framework, while still recognising differences of interpretation between businesses'.

  (ii) A range of different auditing techniques were used, such as sampling the performance of staff from each of the job families.

(d) Recognising the importance of flexibility to environmental factors, NatWest devolved responsibility for assessing demand for skills back to line managers in individual businesses, based on their own job family frameworks, tailored to their particular business environments. However, 'there is still a need to take an overview of the results of the business' analysis, to build an organisational picture of the changes in core or generic skills.'

(e) Such broad-based thinking has led to HR plans such as the introduction of annualised-hours contracts, thought to be the biggest arrangement of its kind for employees in a retail environment. The 'Hours by Design' system is based on what cover is required, which hours staff want to work and how long branches are open: managers set out the expected workflow demands and the staffing levels these require, and employees work out staffing rosters four weeks in advance. In effect, this is on-going human resource planning at the micro-level.

Activity 3 **(30 minutes)**

Bratton and Gold (2007) note that many HR departments practice 'e-HR': using the Internet and related ICT systems (including internal networks or intranets) to support their activities.

(a) How might e-HR be used in HR planning?

(b) What other sources of information can you brainstorm, that might be used in supply and demand forecasting for HRP?

2.2 Forecasting supply

The available **supply** of labour, competencies and productivity levels may be forecast by considering the following factors.

(a) The competencies, skills, trainability, flexibility and current productivity level of the existing work force.

(b) The structure of the existing workforce in terms of age distribution, skills, hours of work, rates of pay and so on.

(c) The likelihood of changes to the productivity, size and structure of the workforce. Such changes may come through:

(i) Wastage (turnover through resignations and retirements), promotions and transfers, absenteeism and other staff movements; this will require information on:

- The age structure of staff (forthcoming retirement or family start-up)

- Labour turnover for a comparable period

- The promotion potential and ambitions of staff

(ii) Employee trainability, morale and motivation, which may influence productivity and flexibility

(iii) Organisational, technological, cultural, managerial and other changes which may positively or negatively affect employee productivity, loyalty and so on.

(d) The present and potential future supply of relevant skilled labour in the environment – that is, the **external labour market**. The HR planner will have to assess and monitor factors such as:

(i) **Skill availability**: locally, nationally and also internationally (for example, within the European Economic Area)

(ii) **Changes in skill availability**, due to education and training trends, resources and initiatives (or lack of these)

(iii) **Competitor activity**, which may absorb more (or less) of the available skill pool

(iv) **Demographic changes**: areas of population growth and decline, the proportion of younger or older people in the workforce in a particular region, the number of women in the workforce and so on

(v) **Wage and salary rates** in the market for particular jobs. ('Supply' implies *availability:* labour resources may become more or less affordable by the organisation.)

FOR DISCUSSION

Select an organisation you are familiar with. Is its need for labour growing, shrinking, or perhaps moving into new skill areas? What, if anything, is the organisation doing about this? What other key strategic issues is the organisation facing – and what challenges do they present for human resource management?

2.3 Closing the gap between demand and supply

Shortfalls or surpluses of labour/skills/productivity which emerge may be dealt with in various ways, in accordance with the organisation's specific HR and business objectives and policies (for example, equal opportunities), cultural values (for example about encouraging commitment, quality focus or developing people within the organisation) and available structures and technologies. Detailed action programmes may be drawn up for the following strategies.

Shortfalls may be met by:

Internal transfers and promotions, training and development (including individual career management and succession/promotion planning)

External recruitment or improvement of recruitment methods (eg diversity programmes to encourage more applicants)

The extension of temporary contracts, or the contracts of those about to retire

Reducing labour turnover, by reviewing possible causes (including pay and conditions), improving induction/ socialisation measures

The use of freelance/temporary/ agency staff to cover fluctuating demand

Outsourcing appropriate activities to external contractors

The development of flexible (or otherwise more productive) working methods and structures: multi-skilling, project structures, delayering

Productivity bargaining encouraging overtime working or offering bonuses and incentives to increase productivity

Review and adjustment of corporate culture, management style and organisation to increase productivity

New technology (increasing productivity, and/or reducing the need for human labour)

Adjustment of corporate objectives: contracting in recognition of the constraints

Surplus may be met by:

Running down manning levels by natural wastage or 'accelerated wastage' (encouraging labour turnover by with-holding incentives to loyalty: eg pay freezes or barriers to promotion)

Restricting or 'freezing' recruitment

Redundancies (voluntary and/or compulsory)

Early retirement incentives

Short-contract and flexible-hours (eg annual hours contracts) to cover fluctuating demand

Eliminating overtime and 'peripheral' workforce groups (freelance and temporary workers)

Retraining and/or redeployment of staff to other areas of skill/productivity shortage. This may involve diversification by the organisation, to utilise existing skills/knowledge; retraining of employees in newly-needed skill areas; and/or multi-skilling, so that the workforce can be flexibly deployed in areas of labour shortage as and when they emerge

Bear in mind that there are also **external constraints** on HR planners in considering any or all of the above: UK legislation and EU directives, regulations and court rulings, the organisation's employer brand (reputation in the labour market) and other factors must be taken into account when planning to hire, 'fire', or alter working terms and conditions.

Note that the sources of labour are both internal (the current workforce and its future potential) and external (people in the 'labour pool'). We will discuss the external labour market and the internal labour market (and related issues of promotion and succession) in Chapter 3. Another key issue of HRP– flexibility – is discussed in detail in Part B of this Course Book. Here we will look at a major factor in forecasting the internal supply of labour: turnover and retention.

NOTES

3 LABOUR TURNOVER AND RETENTION

3.1 Measuring labour turnover

Definition

Labour turnover is the number of employees leaving an organisation and being replaced. The rate of turnover is often expressed as the number of people leaving as a *percentage* of the average number of people employed, in a given period. The term 'natural wastage' is used to describe a 'normal' flow of people out of an organisation through retirement, career or job change, relocation, illness and so on.

There are different ways of measuring labour turnover. Most simply, actual gross numbers of people leaving may provide a basis for recruitment/replacement – but this statistic does not say anything about whether or not these people need replacing! To measure labour turnover in a more systematic and useful way, an index such as the following may be used.

(a) **Crude labour turnover rate** (*the BIM Index, British Institute of Management, 1949*)

Here we express turnover as a percentage of the number of people employed.

$$\frac{\text{Number of leavers in a period}}{\text{Average number of people employed in the period}} \times 100 = \% \text{ turnover}$$

This is normally quoted as an annual rate and may be used to measure turnover per organisation, department or group of employees. The *advantage* of this index is that it can alert HR planners to unusually high percentages of the workforce leaving – compared with the HR plan, or with the industry average, say – which would suggest that something is wrong, or that more effort is needed to retain employees. The *disadvantage* of this index is that it does not indicate *who* is leaving the department or organisation: even a high turnover rate may not reflect any real instability if the core of experienced staff consistently remains. (In fact, most wastage occurs among young people and those in the early stages of their employment in an organisation: stability tends to increase with length of service.)

(b) **Labour stability**

Here we try to eliminate short-term employees from our analysis, thus obtaining a better picture of the significant movements in the workforce.

$$\frac{\text{Number of employees with one or more years' service}}{\text{Number of employees employed at the beginning of the year}} \times 100\% = \% \text{ stability}$$

Particularly in times of rapid expansion, organisations should keep an eye on stability, as a meaningful measure.

(c) The labour stability index ignores new starts during the year and does not consider actual length of service, which may be added to the measurement via **length of service analysis**, or **survival rate analysis**. Here, the organisation calculates the proportion of employees who are engaged within a certain period who are still with the firm after various periods of time. There may be a survival rate of 70% after two years, for example, but only 50% in year three: the distribution of losses might be plotted on a survival curve to indicate trends.

Activity 4   **(20 minutes)**

Suppose a company has 20 employees at the beginning of 2007, and 100 at the end of the year. Disliking the culture created by the expansion, 18 of the original experienced labour force resign.

Calculate:

(a) The crude labour turnover rate
(b) The stability rate

Comment on the significance of your results.

3.2   Causes of labour turnover

Some reasons for leaving will be largely unavoidable, or unforeseeable. '**Natural wastage**' occurs through:

(a)   Illness or accident (although transfer to lighter duties, excusing the employee from shiftwork or other accommodations might be possible)

(b)   A move from the locality for domestic, social or logistical reasons

(c)   Changes to the family situation, for example, when an individual changes job or gives up work to accommodate child-rearing responsibilities

(d)   Retirement

(e)   Career change

Other causes of labour turnover, however, may be to do with the organisation, management, terms and conditions and so on: in other words, **job dissatisfaction**.

Activity 5   **(15 minutes)**

Suggest a number of factors that might contribute to labour turnover, which might broadly be grouped under the heading of 'job dissatisfaction'.

Which of these factors would be sufficient to make you leave an organisation: (a) in a market where you were reasonably sure of finding other employment and (b) in a market where other employment was scarce?

Labour turnover is also influenced by the following factors.

(a) **The economic climate and the state of the job market.** When unemployment is high and jobs are hard to find, labour turnover will be much lower.

(b) **The age structure and length of service of the work force.** An ageing workforce will have many people approaching retirement. However, it has been found in most companies that labour turnover is highest among:

(i) Young people, especially unmarried people with no family responsibilities

(ii) People who have been in the employment of the company for only a short time.

The employment life cycle usually shows a decision point shortly after joining, when things are still new and perhaps difficult. This is called the **'first induction crisis'**. There is then a period of mutual accommodation and adjustment between employer and employee (called the **'differential transit'** period): in the settling of areas of conflict, there may be further turnover. A second (less significant) induction crisis occurs as both parties come to terms with the new status quo. Finally, the period of **'settled connection'** begins, and the likelihood of leaving is much less.

So far, you may have got the impression that 'labour turnover' equals 'instability', and that, since it is caused by job dissatisfaction, it must be a bad thing for the organisation. But remember: earlier in this chapter we noted that an organisation may from time to time have a surplus of labour or particular skills, which it would like to be able to 'lose' through natural wastage instead of costly redundancies. And some organisations may be constantly creating and disbanding projects: forming loose, temporary or 'virtual' networks of people – without tying themselves to expectations of 'jobs' or 'carers'. So should organisations fight to retain employees – or not?

3.3 Is turnover a 'bad thing'?

The following table puts labour turnover in perspective.

Potential advantages of labour turnover	Potential disadvantages of labour turnover
(a) Opportunities to inject 'new blood' into the organisation: new people bringing new ideas and outlooks, new skills and experience in different situations.	(a) Broken continuity of culture and succession, where continuity could offer stability and predictability, which may be beneficial to efficiency.
(b) Balance in the age structure of the workforce. Absence of labour turnover would create an increasingly aged workforce, often accompanied by an increasing wage/salary cost.	(b) There is bound to be an hiatus while a replacement is found and brought 'on line' to the level of expertise of the previous job-holder.
(c) The creation of opportunities for promotion and succession which offers an important incentive to more junior employees.	(c) Morale problems. Turnover may be perceived by other employees as a symptom of job dissatisfaction, causing the problem to escalate.
(d) The ability to cope with labour surpluses, in some grades of job, without having to make redundancies.	(d) The costs of turnover, including:
	(i) **Replacement costs**: recruiting, selecting and training; loss of output or efficiency
	(ii) **Preventive costs**: the cost of retaining staff, through pay, benefits and welfare provisions, maintaining working condi-tions or whatever

It is common to hear that turnover is bad when it is high – but this cannot be assessed in isolation. What is an acceptable rate of turnover and what is excessive? There is no fixed percentage rate of turnover which is the borderline between acceptable and unacceptable. Labour turnover rates *may* be a signal that something is wrong when:

(a) They are higher than the turnover rates in another similar department of the organisation; for example, if the labour turnover rate is higher at branch A than at branches B, C and D in the same area, something might be wrong at branch A

(b) They are higher than they were in previous years or months; in other words, the situation might be deteriorating

(c) The costs of labour turnover are estimated and are considered too high – although they will be relative to the costs of preventing high turnover by offering employees incentives to stay.

Otherwise, the organisation may live with high rates because they are the norm for a particular industry or job: (think about call centres, for example), because the organisation culture accepts constant turnover; (as in a project-based or 'virtual' network organisation) or because the cost of keeping employees is greater than the cost of replacing them!

NOTES

So, if an organisation does decide that it needs to control or reduce its labour turnover rate, what can it do?

3.4 Retention planning

A systematic **investigation** into the causes of unusually or undesirably high turnover will have to be made, using various methods.

(a) Information given in **exit interviews** with leaving staff, which should be the first step after an employee announces his/her intention to leave. (It must be recognised, however, that the reasons given for leaving may not be complete, true, or those that would be most useful to the organisation. People may say they are 'going to a better job', for example while the real reason for the move is dissatisfaction with the level of interest in the current job.)

(b) **Attitude surveys**, to gauge the general climate of the organisation, and the response of the workforce as a whole to working conditions, management style and so on.

(c) Information gathered on the number of (interrelated) **variables** which can be assumed to **correlate** with labour turnover – such as an ageing workforce, higher rates of pay outside the organisation and so on.

The causes of turnover should be addressed by HR planning, where it is practical and cost-effective to do so.

(a) If particular managers' practices or styles are creating significant dissatisfaction, performance improvement measures may be implemented.

(b) Coherent policies may be introduced (or more consistently applied) with regard to training and development and promotion from within the organisation.

(c) Induction or orientation programmes for new recruits should address the issues that cause problems at the 'first induction crisis' stage.

(d) Selection programmes should be reviewed to ensure that future recruits are made aware of (and ideally are compatible with) the demands of the job and culture of the organisation.

(e) Problems with working conditions should be solved – especially if they also concern health and safety.

(f) Pay levels and structures may be reviewed in the light of perceived fairness and/or market rates.

FOR DISCUSSION

'Accelerated wastage' is the practice of allowing (or using) job dissatisfaction to encourage people to leave in higher numbers than they would by 'natural wastage', in order to reduce a labour surplus.

How do you respond to this concept? Do you think it has a place in an ethical HRM policy? How would you justify it?

The apparently simple 'supply and demand' equation discussed in Section 2 above makes HRP look scientific – but there are so many 'messy' human factors involved that its feasibility and reliability have been questioned. This raises the further question of how the success and value of HRP can be measured by the organisation. We will look at some of these issues below.

4   EVALUATING HRP

4.1   How reliable is HRP?

Human resource planning is regarded as a scientific, statistical exercise, but it is important to remember that statistics in themselves are limited in value.

Forecasting is not an exact science. Few exponents of even the most sophisticated techniques would claim that they are wholly accurate, although:

(a)   The element of guesswork has been substantially reduced by the use of computer models to test various assumptions and to indicate trends

(b)   The general principles can still be applied to indicate problems and stimulate control action.

Activity 6   **(15 minutes)**

HR planners are human beings, and so are the resources or people-assets themselves: what might be the major limitations on the reliability or objectivity of statistical methods in HR planning?

Statistical methods can be used to create a more accurate model of the future than simple subjective estimates. Computerisation has greatly enhanced the speed, ease and accuracy with which they can be applied, and many PC-based HR software packages are now available. Even so, there are a number of assumptions involved, and the results are purely **quantitative** – for example, numbers of staff required – where **qualitative** information may be required for meaningful decision-making: the effects of change, re-staffing or management style on the culture of the organisation and individual/group behaviour and so on.

Weblink

If you are curious about PC-based HR software, you might like to check out software source, a site established by the CIPD to provide information on HR software suppliers and products.

▶▶ **http://softwaresource.co.uk**

Where end products are measurable, **work-study techniques** can offer a reasonably accurate forecast of staffing requirements. In service sectors and 'knowledge work', however, end products and output may not be easily subject to standard-setting. For example, the number of telephone calls, interviews, customers served, or ideas generated is likely to fluctuate widely with the flow of business and the nature of particular transactions.

Definition

Work study methods break down and measure the elements of a given task in order to define the standard number of staff hours per unit of output.

Managerial estimates form the simplest and cheapest method of assessment. As such, they may be the most appropriate – and are the most common – method for small organisations. At the best of times, however, this method has the disadvantage of a high degree of subjectivity, and although this can be controlled to an extent (by requiring managers to support their estimates with reasons and to reconcile their estimates with those of senior management), it is a source of potential risk.

A measure of flexibility will need to be built into any HR plan, so that it can be adapted to suit likely or even unforeseen contingencies. Above all, it should not be seen or communicated as an inflexible plan, as if it were based on certainty.

> 'Clearly, the more precise the information available, the greater the probability that HR plans will be accurate. But, in practice, they are subject to many imponderable factors, some completely outside an organisation's control... international trade, general technological advances, population movements, the human acceptance of or resistance to change, and the quality of leadership and its impact on morale. The environment, then, is uncertain, and so are the people whose activities are being planned. HR plans must therefore be accepted as being continuous, under constant review, and ever-changing. Since they concern people, they must also be negotiable.'
>
> *Cuming* (1993)

4.2 Is HRP working?

Definition

A **human resource audit** is an investigation designed to:

(a) Give a picture of the current structure, size and productivity of the organisation's labour force

(b) Check that HR plans, systems, policies and procedures have been and are being carried out

The best test of the accuracy and effectiveness of HRP is to check whether the reality has in fact conformed to the forecasts and plans: a basic system of control.

    (a)   **Actual staffing levels and trends** should be checked against budgets.

         (i)   If HR planners have allowed for reductions in staffing levels through natural wastage, it is important to ensure that such wastage is allowed to happen. (It is a natural tendency for managers to seek replacements for any staff losses, even those which have been budgeted for.)

(ii) The budgets themselves may be (or may have become) inappropriate. The HR plan must constantly be reviewed and revised in the light of changes and actual (unanticipated) events.

(b) **HR records** should be checked to identify that any change (promotion, transfer, redundancy, recruitment, etc) has been properly approved, in line with the HR plan.

This process may uncover:

(i) Inadequate authorisation of particular types of change; for example, it may be common to transfer employees within the same department without proper approval or reference to the overall staffing plan.

(ii) Unauthorised or unnecessary use of agency or temporary personnel.

(c) **Staff utilisation** should be reviewed: how efficiently is the human resource employed? This process may uncover a need for fundamental change (such as a complete restructure or automation of work). Under-utilisation of a skill category is an inefficient use of the organisation's resources as well as a common source of personal dissatisfaction among staff.

4.3 Is HRP cost-effective?

Although labour costs in many manufacturing companies are falling as a proportion of total costs, as more expensive technology is used, HR costs are still significant and may form a large proportion of total costs in labour-intensive sectors such as services.

The organisation should therefore assess the **cost** effect of any HR plan – recruitment drive, training initiative or indeed downsizing exercise – in proportion to the **expected benefits** to be derived from it.

Definition

> A **cost-benefit analysis** is a comparison of the cost of an actual or proposed measure with an evaluation or estimate of the benefits gained from it. This will indicate whether the measure has been, or is likely to be, cost-effective – or 'worthwhile'.

There are a number of reasons why a cost-benefit analysis of the HR plan might be useful.

(a) It emphasises the **total cost** of the plan, including wages and related costs, in relation to gains in efficiency or effectiveness.

(b) It allows costs of the plan to be **compared** with other options. For example, once the cost of recruitment has been evaluated, the organisation can assess the merits of alternative plans such as:

(i) Outsourcing the activity

(ii) Developing and multi-skilling existing staff

 LEARNING MEDIA

Part A: Human Resources Management

(iii) Buying capital equipment or altering work processes in other ways to enhance productivity.

(c) It emphasises that **cost-effectiveness** – not cost-minimalisation – is the aim. For example, temporary or part-time workers may be 'cheaper' for the organisation – but if long-term gains in stability, expertise, management succession, knowledge preservation and motivated output are lost (compared with employing full-time, permanent staff), this would be a false economy.

FOR DISCUSSION

Do a cost-benefit analysis of your present studies. Is education and training a good investment – and if so, for whom?

It should be clear that HRP, at the stage of closing the gap between supply and demand, actually involves planning in a number of areas of HRM. We will end this chapter with a summary of the Human Resource Plan.

5 THE HUMAN RESOURCE PLAN

Once the analysis of human resource requirements has been carried out, and the various options for fulfilling them considered, the **human resource plan** will be drawn up. This may be done at a strategic level (and indeed, as we saw in section 1.2 above, it will have strategic impact). It will also involve tactical plans and action plans for various measures, according to the strategy that has been chosen. Typical elements might include the following.

(a) **The resourcing plan**: approaches to obtaining skills/people within the organisation, and by external recruitment

(b) **Internal resource plan**: availability of skills within the organisation; plans to promote/redeploy/develop

(c) **The recruitment plan**: numbers and types of people, and when required; sources of candidates; the recruitment programme; desired 'employer brand' and/or recruitment incentives

(d) **The training plan**: numbers of trainees required and/or existing staff who need training; training programme

(e) **The re-development plan**: programmes for transferring or retraining employees

(f) **The flexibility plan**: plans to use part-time workers, jobsharing, homeworking, outsourcing, flexible hour arrangements and so on.

(g) **The productivity plan**: programmes for improving productivity, or reducing manpower costs; setting productivity targets

(h) **The downsizing plan**: natural wastage forecasts; where and when redundancies are to occur; policies for selection and declaration of redundancies; redevelopment, retraining or relocation of employees; policy on redundancy payments, union consultation and so on

(i)   **The retention plan:** actions to reduce avoidable labour wastage

The plan should include budgets, targets and standards. It should allocate responsibilities for implementation and control (reporting, monitoring achievement against plan).

Chapter roundup

- HRP is a strategy for the acquisition or reduction, utilisation, improvement and retention of an enterprise's human resources in response to the requirement of the organisation's strategic plan.

- A systematic approach to HRP would be as shown in the diagram below.

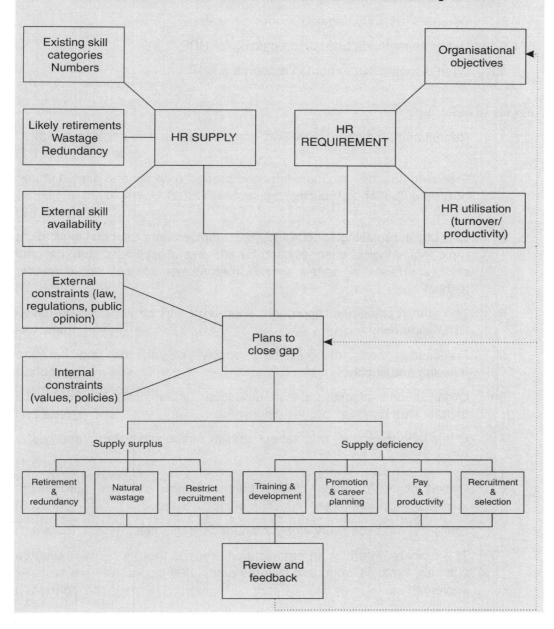

Quick quiz

1   List the elements of human resource planning.

2   Outline the items commonly contained in an organisation's corporate or strategic plan as they affect HRP.

3   List the reasons why human resource planning has increased in importance in recent years.

4   List three basic approaches to HRP in a changing environment

5   Outline the three major stages involved in the human resource planning process.

6   What are the major areas of information required by the human resource planner?

7   How is labour turnover measured?

8   What are the *advantages* of labour turnover?

9   List three methods used in forecasting for HRP.

10   What is meant by the human resource audit?

Answers to quick quiz

1   Recruitment, retention, utilisation, improvement and downsizing of staff.
(see paragraph 1.1)

2   Predicted financial situation; intended product markets and market share; desired output and productivity; changes in location; employee numbers.
(para 1.2)

3   Difficulty in replacing specialised staff; employment protection legislation; rapid technological change; need for effective utilisation of staff; national skills shortages in certain areas; international competition; computer technology.
(para 1.3)

4   The staff replacement approach; short-term; HR strategy; vision-driven HRD approach.
(para 1.4)

5   Forecasting demand; forecasting supply; closing the gap between demand and supply.
(section 2)

6   Organisational objectives; staff utilisation; labour costs; environmental factors; staff turnover; production levels.
(para 2.1)

7   Crude labour turnover rate; labour stability index; survival rate analysis.

(para 3.1)

8   Opportunities for 'new blood'; balanced age structure; promotion/ succession opportunities; reduction of labour surplus.
(para 3.3)

9   Statistical methods; work study; managerial estimates.
(para 4.1)

10   The process whereby an organisation ensures that its human resource planning systems work, and that the plans they incorporate are properly implemented.
(para 4.2)

Answers to activities

1   A skill shortage might be caused by:

   (a)   long-term declines in education and training, or in population (nationally or in the local area)

   (b)   the immediate effects of a competitor entering the market or area and employing some of the pool of skilled labour

   (c)   increases in demand for the product or service for which the skill is required; or the relocation, resignation or demotivation of key skilled people – for all sorts of personal and circumstantial reasons

2   (a)   The computer company is operating in an extremely volatile and changing market, which will present HRP difficulties. The technology, and associated skills, are constantly changing, along with competitive pressures: an innovative competitor could 'steal' the market. This is also a highly-skilled business, however, with skill shortages in the labour market, and long training times: despite the difficulties, long-term planning will be important.

   (b)   Some years ago, the local authority would have represented a fairly stable (not to say 'ponderous') bureaucratic structure, with fairly rigid, predictable HR plans. Reductions in funding, and the contracting out of services, have made HRP more difficult and desirable: workforce reduction and flexibility, and the use of HRP to change organisational culture, will be key issues.

   (c)   The airline is a business which is potentially volatile, and sensitive to barely controllable factors such as price wars. Political/terrorist action, industrial action, airspace restrictions, crashes affecting image and so on. At the same time it is dependent on several categories of employees (airline pilots, aerospace engineers) who are scarce and have long training cycles: planning ahead for selection and retention will be crucial.

3   (a)   The Internet is a rich source of statistical, environmental, benchmarking and other relevant information for HRP. Internal corporate databases (possibly integrated into Human Resource Information Systems) should provide data on current skills, workforce structure, productivity and so on. Expert and decision-support software is also available for manpower and 'Enterprise Resource Planning' (ERP). (You may like to do a web search on 'ERP' or 'Human Resource Planning' and check out some of the resources for yourself.)

   (b)   This may be useful as the beginnings of a research/information database. There are many potential sources of labour and environmental information. Just a few suggestions:

   •   CIPD and other HR journals (and their websites)

   •   News media

   •   Employment and industry journals (*Employment Gazette, Employment Digest,* specific industry journals, *Industrial Relations Review, Labour Market Quarterly*)

   •   Government statistical publications (census information, *Social Trends*)

- Publications, websites and contacts of relevant bodies: trade unions, trade associations, employers' associations, training bodies and so on.

- Competitors and other employers (websites, annual reports and accounts, personal contacts)

4   At the end of 2007, the company works out that it has:

BIM Index: $\dfrac{18\,\text{leavers}}{60\,(\text{average})\,\text{employees}} \times 100 = 30\%$ **turnover**

This is not uncommon, and would cause no undue worries. However:

Stability index: $\dfrac{2\,\text{year servers}}{20} \times 100 = 10\%$ **stability**

Only 10% of the labour force is stable (and therefore offering the benefits of experience and acclimatisation to the work and culture of the organisation). A crude turnover rate has disguised the significance of what has happened.

5   Common factors include the following.

(a)   **Incompatibilities with the organisation climate or culture, or its style of leadership**. An organisation might be formal and bureaucratic, where employees are expected to work according to prescribed rules and procedures. Other organisations are more flexible, and allow more scope for individual expression and creativity. Individuals will prefer – and stay with – one system or the other.

(b)   **Unsatisfactory pay and conditions of employment.** If these are not good enough according to people's needs (or in comparison with others), people will leave to find better terms elsewhere, or will use this as a catalyst to express their discontent in other areas.

(c)   **Poor physical working conditions.** If working conditions are uncomfortable, unclean, unsafe, or noisy, say, people will be more inclined to leave.

(d)   **Lack of career prospects and access to training.** If the chances of advancement before a certain age are low, an ambitious employee is likely to consider leaving to find a job where promotion is likely to come more quickly. The same may be true where an employee wants training for a qualification or skill development, and opportunities are limited in his/her current job.

The second part to this activity is personal to you.

6   (a)   Statistics are not the only element of the planning process, and are subject to interpretation and managerial judgements that are largely qualitative and even highly speculative (involving future growth, say, or potential for innovation).

(b)   Trends in statistics are the product of social processes, which are not readily quantifiable or predictable. Staff leave for various social reasons in (unpredictable) individual cases, to get married, relocate or whatever. The growth of the temporary and freelance workforce is a social trend, as are the buying patterns which dictate demand for goods and services.

Chapter 3:
RECRUITMENT

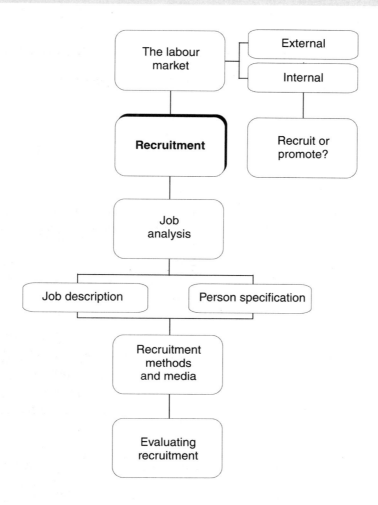

Introduction

In Chapter 2 we noted that there were sources of labour supply both **inside** the organisation and in its **environment**. In this chapter, we look briefly at the labour market (external and internal) and at some of the issues affecting the **resourcing and recruitment plan**.

Recruitment is the process whereby an organisation communicates opportunities and information to the labour market in order to attract the quantity and quality of potential employees it requires to fulfil its human resource plan. This chapter outlines a systematic approach to this task.

The process of deciding which of the candidates short-listed by the recruitment process are suitable is called **selection**: this will be discussed in Chapter 4.

Your objectives

In this chapter you will learn about the following.

    (a)   The structured approach to recruitment (highlighting 'best practice')

    (b)   Recruitment policies and procedures, including job analysis, job description and person specification

    (c)   Recruitment methods and media, including job advertisements, application forms and e-recruitment

    (d)   The legislative framework and benchmark evidence guiding recruitment policy and practice

1   THE LABOUR MARKET

1.1   Changes in the labour market

Definition

> The **labour market** is the sphere in which labour is 'bought' and 'sold', and in which market concepts such as supply, demand and price operate with regard to human resources.

The **labour market** has changed dramatically in the last few decades. Writers on manpower planning (as it was then called) in the 1970s suggested that a 'seller's market' had been established, as technology increased the skills and therefore scarcity value of employees in certain jobs, and as the scale of state benefits blunted the fear of unemployment: the initiative seemed to be with the employee, or with organised groups of employees.

The decline of manufacturing, the increase of women in employment, the globalisation of business (allowing offshoring of production and service provision to low-cost labour countries) and the more general application of technology, among other factors, have changed that situation. A 'buyer's market' for labour now gives employers considerable power, with a large pool of available labour created by unemployment and non-career (temporary, freelance) labour.

On the other hand, even in conditions of high overall employment, particular skill shortages still exist and may indeed be *more* acute because of economic pressures on education and training. Engineers and software designers, among other specialist and highly trained groups, are the target of fierce competition among employers, forcing a re-evaluation of recruitment and retention policies.

We will be discussing the labour market in other contexts in this Course Book: as a spur to flexibility (in Chapter 9) and as a globalised phenomenon (in Chapter 12).

Here we will note some of the key labour market trends that may affect the recruitment plan.

The following have been identified (Torrington *et al*, 2002) as the three major trends in the UK labour market as a whole:

- Demographic trends
- Diversity
- Skills and qualifications

1.2 Demographic trends

Definition

> **Demography** is an analysis of statistics on birth and death rates, the age structure of populations, ethnic groups within communities, population movements and so on.

(a) The **number of people who are economically active** in the UK is still increasing, principally due to immigration and expanding the number of women returning to and remaining in paid work (supported by diversity and family-friendly HR policies). Over the long term, however, the proportion of the population that is available for work is expected to shrink: birth-rates continue to fall, and life-expectancy to lengthen, creating an increasing retired population in proportion to those of working age.

(b) As a result, the **age profile of the workforce** is also changing: the population as a whole is getting older, with fewer young people entering the workforce (especially as a greater proportion of them remain longer in full-time education). This has been reinforced by the introduction of age diversity legislation in the UK in 2000, encouraging the selection and retention of mature workers.

Activity 1 (10 minutes)

What can you see as the main implications for employers of the demographic changes identified above, in terms of challenges in attracting and retaining quality workers?

1.3 Diversity

The workforce is becoming increasingly diverse in its make-up, in several respects.

(a) **Gender diversity**. Increased female participation in the workforce has been a significant social trend since the Second World War. The employment rate for women of working age is currently just under 70%. Although a majority of managerial posts are still occupied by men, and there is a continued gender gap in overall pay levels, there has been an increase in the representation of women at all levels. There is still significant segregation in terms of the types of work performed, with particular areas of work dominated by either men or women. Women currently account for over 80% of part-time workers in the UK, which is in itself a growth sector.

(b) **Ethnic diversity**. Multi-racial representation has greatly increased in the UK workforce. The Workplace Employee Relations Survey 2004 suggests that over 50% of workplaces are multi-racial compared to only 30% in 1980.

Major implications for employee resourcing include:

- The need to take account of anti-discrimination legislation and best practice in recruitment (discussed further in Paragraph 2.4 below). As well as legal protection for groups which are traditionally been under-represented in the workplace, heightened sensitivity to such matters means that positive equal opportunity and diversity policies play an important part in building an employer brand which will enable organisations to attract quality labour.

- The need to take account of the needs of increasingly diverse family shapes and circumstances, in order to attract and retain people. Legislation has begun to address the needs of dual income families (eg parental leave and time off for emergencies) but proactive HR initiatives – such as career breaks and childcare support – contribute importantly to a 'family-friendly' employer brand.

FOR DISCUSSION

There has been a change in the gender balance within HRM as well. 61% of HRM managers at the most senior level were female in 2003 (compared to 49% in 1999 and 34% in 1995).

What do you think accounts for this shift?

And what further affects do you think it might have?

Other issues in the management of diversity will be covered in detail in Chapter 10 of this Course Book.

1.4 Skills and qualifications

There has been a steady decline in the demand for skills in the manufacturing and agricultural sectors, and a corresponding growth in managerial and professional occupations and in service industries. A new premium has been placed on interpersonal skills (such as team-working, customer service and communication) and on personal skills (such as flexibility, time-management and self-motivation).

Since the early 1990s, there has been an increase in the number of **graduates** entering the labour market. However:

(a) The number of 'graduate jobs', despite strong demand, has not kept pace with the increase in supply (Bratton & Gold, 2007), making it difficult for new graduates to find employment on advantageous terms.

(b)   There remain specific skill shortages, creating difficulties for recruiters in filling vacancies. 'There are still too few people with high-level IT and scientific qualifications entering the labour market and far too many people lacking basic numeracy and literacy skills' (Torrington *et al*, 2002), despite on-going policy initiatives (discussed in Chapter 16) to improve the skill base.

The implications for recruiters may be:

- The need to compete more aggressively for skilled candidates

- The need to re-define jobs to maximise the use of scarcer (or more expensive) skills

- The need to recruit (or relocate work) overseas

- The need to 'lower' recruitment requirements for specific skills and qualifications and invest in employee training and development in the required skills.

FOR DISCUSSION

Select an organisation or business sector that you know well, and identify the key issues facing human resourcing in that organisation or sector.

(Alternatively, you may wish to interview a contact in business, and write a report on the recruitment issues in his or her firm.)

Activity 2	**(45 minutes)**

Outline a simple HRP procedure (refer to Section 2 of Chapter 2 if you need to) which will take into account demographic and educational trends in the country of your choice.

When forecasting the supply of labour and skills available to the organisation to meet the demands of its activities and objectives, the HR planner must take into account:

- *The current skill base, size and structure of its existing workforce*
- *The potential for change in that skill base, size and structure.*

This constitutes an **internal labour market.**

1.5   Internal sources of labour

If the organisation faces a demand for a particular skill, that demand may be satisfied from within the existing labour force by:

(a)   **Retaining** skilled individuals, against the flow of labour turnover

(b) **Transferring** or deploying individuals with the relevant skills from their current job to the job where those skills can more effectively be utilised

(c) **Training and developing** individuals in the required skills and abilities

(d) **Exploiting contacts** with present employees, friends and family of employees, and former external applicants, who might be referred (and to an extent, pre-appraised) for vacancies.

If the organisation experiences **fluctuating** demand for a particular skill or for numbers of workers, it may need to approach the above strategies somewhat differently, in order to be able to deploy labour flexibly. If a retail business requires extra sales people in the pre-Christmas period, for example, or a factory requires trained specialists in a particular field only at certain stages of a project – or in the event of problems – what do they do? Train, retain and transfer sufficient people for the busiest scenario? You should be able to see that this would be costly and inefficient – and unlikely to enhance the credibility of the HR planner! This is in essence what **labour flexibility** – in terms of numbers and skills deployed – is about.

Retention was discussed in Chapter 2. Training and development are covered in detail in Part C of this Course Book. Flexibility is discussed in Chapter 9. Here we will briefly discuss promotion *as a form of internal 'recruitment'.*

1.6 Promotion and succession

Definition

> **Succession** is the act, process or right by which one person 'succeeds to' or takes over the office or post of another person. In a business organisation, there may be a policy whereby a 'successor' is developed to replace a more senior manager who retires or leaves.

Promotion and succession policies are a vital part of the human resource plan, as a form of risk management associated with the internal supply of labour. The planned development of staff (not just skills training, but experience and growth in responsibility) is essential to ensure the **continuity of performance** in the organisation. This is particularly so for **management succession planning**: the departure of a senior manager with no planned or 'groomed' successor could leave a gap in the organisation structure and the lead time for developing a suitable replacement may be very long.

A comprehensive **promotion programme**, as part of the overall HR plan will include:

(a) Establishing the relative significance of jobs by analysis, description and classification, so that the line and consequences of promotion are made clear

(b) Establishing methods of assessing staff and their potential for fulfilling the requirements of more senior positions

(c) Planning in advance for training where necessary to enhance potential and develop specific skills

(d)   Policy with regard to internal promotion or external recruitment and training

A coherent **promotion policy** may vary to include provisions such as the following.

(a)   All promotions, as far as possible, and all things being equal, are to be made from within the firm. (For the argument for this, see our answer to Activity 4.)

(b)   Merit and ability (systematically appraised) should be the principal basis of promotion, rather than seniority (age or years of service) – although this may vary in cultures where seniority is a key value.

(c)   Vacancies should be advertised and open to all employees.

(d)   There should be full opportunities for all employees to be promoted to the highest grades.

(e)   Training should be offered to encourage and develop employees of ability and ambition in advance of promotion.

(f)   Scales of pay, areas of responsibility, duties and privileges of each post and so on should be clearly communicated so that employees know what promotion means – in other words, what they are being promoted *to*.

Activity 3   **(15 minutes)**

What problems with line/departmental managers can you foresee for an HR Manager who attempts to implement a policy such as the one outlined above?

1.7   Internal or external recruitment?

Promotion is useful from the firm's point of view, in establishing a management succession, filling more senior positions with proven, experienced and loyal employees. It is also one of the main forms of reward the organisation can offer its employees.

The decision of whether to promote from within or fill a position from outside will hinge on many factors. If there is simply no-one available on the current staff with the expertise or ability required (say, if the organisation is venturing into new areas of activity, or changing its business processes), the recruitment manager may have to seek qualified people outside. If there is time, a person of particular potential in the organisation could be trained in the necessary skills, but that will require an analysis of the costs as compared to the possible (and often less quantifiable) benefits.

Activity 4   **(15 minutes)**

Outline what you think would be the advantages of promoting from within the organisation, instead of recruiting someone from outside. What would be the main disadvantages?

2   RECRUITMENT

Definition

Recruitment is the part of the human resourcing process concerned with finding the applicants: it is a positive action by management, going into the labour market, communicating opportunities and information, and encouraging applications from suitable candidates.

2.1   A systematic approach

The overall aim of the recruitment process in an organisation is to obtain the quantity and quality of candidates required to fulfil the objectives of the organisation.

A systematic approach to recruitment will involve the following stages.

(a)   Detailed **human resource planning** defining what resources the organisation needs to meet its objectives.

(b)   **Job analysis** (or variants), so that for any given job or role there is a definition of the skills, knowledge and attributes required to perform the job.

  (i)   A **job description**: a statement of the component tasks, duties, objectives and standards of the job

  (ii)   A **person specification**: a reworking of the job description in terms of the kind of person needed to perform the job

  (iii)   Some other appropriate definition of the requirement, such as a **competence or role definition**.

  If such documents already exist, they may need to be updated or confirmed.

(c)   An identification of **vacancies**, from the requirements of the human resource plan or by a job requisition from a department, branch or office which has a vacancy, and subsequent approval or **authorisation** for engagement. Seeking authorisation to refill a vacancy is a means of ensuring that the need for recruitment, and the criteria for recruitment, are in line with departmental and organisational requirements, timely and cost-effective. It may also provide an opportunity to review other options.

(d)   Evaluation of the **sources of skills,** which again should be identified in the human resource plan. Internal and external sources, and media for reaching them (eg through **job advertisement** or e-recruitment, say) will be considered.

(e)   Preparation and publication of recruitment **information**, which will:

  (i)   Attract the attention and interest of potentially suitable candidates

  (ii)   Give a favourable (but accurate) impression of the job and the organisation

  (iii)   Equip interested candidates to make an application (how and to whom to apply, desired skills, qualifications and so on).

(f) **Processing applications** prior to the selection process. This may include:

    (i)   Screening replies at the end of the specified period for application

    (ii)   Short-listing candidates for initial consideration

    (iii) Advising applicants of the progress of their application

    (iv) Drawing up a programme for the selection process which follows.

Activity 5   **(30 minutes)**

Which features of the recruitment process suggest that it might be most efficient and effective if *centralised* within the HR function, rather than delegated to line managers in their own departments? (Refer back to Chapter 1 if you need some hints.) Suggest five advantages of centralised recruitment.

Trends towards flexibility and multi-skilling have encouraged a slightly different approach, which is oriented more towards 'fitting the job to the person' than 'fitting the person to the job'. In a highly innovative market, technological environment or organisational culture, for example, rigid job descriptions would not be suitable. In order to creatively exploit the opportunities or such environments, organisations should be able to look at the skills and attributes of the people they employ, and those of gifted outsiders, and ask: 'What needs doing, that this person would do best?'

In a relatively informal environment, where all-round knowledge/skills and experience are highly valued and suitable external labour resources are scarce (say, in management consultancy), this approach would give much-needed flexibility. The organisation would try to recruit excellent, flexible, motivated and multi-skilled personnel, without reference to any specific job, as defined by a job description. They would form an available resource for any tasks or requirement that arose on a project or 'virtual project team' basis.

However, the **'selection' approach** ('fitting the person to the job') is still by far the most common, and is suitable for most organisations with fairly defined goals and structures.

2.2 Recruitment policy and best practice

Detailed procedures for recruitment should only be devised and implemented within the context of a coherent **policy**, or code of conduct.

A typical recruitment policy might deal with:

    (a)   Internal advertisement of vacancies

    (b)   Efficient and courteous processing of applications

    (c)   Fair and accurate provision of information to potential recruits

    (d)   Selection of candidates on the basis of qualification, without discrimination on any grounds

    (e)   Recruitment of local labour where possible (supporting **sustainability** targets, eg in the public sector)

Detailed **procedures** should be devised in order to make recruitment activity systematic and consistent throughout the organisation (especially where it is devolved to line managers). Apart from the resourcing requirements which need to be effectively and efficiently met, there is a **marketing** aspect to recruitment, as one 'interface' between the organisation and the outside world: applicants who feel they have been unfairly treated, or recruits who leave because they feel they have been misled, do not enhance the organisation's reputation in the labour market.

Activity 6   **(1 hour)**

Find out what the recruitment and selection procedures are in an organisation of your choice. This may be stated on the corporate website, or you may be able to ask a recruitment or HR officer. (Alternatively, do a web search on the phrase 'Recruitment Code of Practice' – and browse some of the varied examples of good practice...)

If you are employed, get hold of and examine some of the documentation your organisation uses. We show specimens in this chapter, but practice and terminology varies.

2.3 Influences on recruitment policy

Recruitment policy will be influenced by the following considerations.

(a) The organisation's **image** in the community, market-place and labour market: its '**employer brand**' and identity as an employer. Recruitment advertising, in particular, is a public relations exercise: it must reflect the organisation's values and professionalism – and, where appropriate, its marketing message (quality, products/services and so on)

(b) The **human resource plan** and subsidiary plans

(c) **Fairness, courtesy and professionalism** in dealing with applicant, as defined by 'best practice' benchmark evidence.

(d) **Legislation and regulations** affecting:

    (i) **Terms and conditions** able to be offered to (or imposed on) potential employees (for example, minimal wage, working hours, holiday entitlements)

    (ii) **Equal opportunities** – the prevention of direct and indirect discrimination by:

        • The wording and placing of recruitment advertisements which imply or tend towards a preference for a particular group

        • Indicating or implying intention to discriminate in internal planning, advertising or instructions to recruitment agencies.

    This will be discussed further below.

(iii) **Labour mobility** – for example, discrimination on the basis of nationality or national origin against candidates from the European Economic Area.

(e) The **cultural values** of the organisation, as well as national culture. These are often reflected in the attributes considered essential or desirable in candidates: the importance attached to educational, vocational or professional qualifications; and/or identification with the organisation's self-image (responsible, fun, fast-paced, flexible or whatever).

2.4 The legislative framework on recruitment

We will be discussing **equal opportunity** and the **management of diversity** in detail in Chapter 10 of this Course Book, as one of the key HRM issues. The key points in relation to recruitment, however, are as follows.

Sex and race

- The **Sex Discrimination Act 1975** (amended 1986) makes it unlawful to discriminate – directly or indirectly – between the sexes in recruitment policy, job advertisements and application forms. This includes discrimination on the grounds of change of sex and marital status.

- The **Race Relations Act 1976** (amended 1996, 2000 and 2003) makes similar provisions in regard to colour, race, nationality or ethnic or national origin.

- The **Employment Equality Regulations** 2003, make similar provision in regard to sexual orientation and religious belief.

Direct discrimination occurs when one group is treated less favourably than another. This may be implied by job titles and terminology in recruitment documentation. Recruiters should avoid terms potentially perceived as sexist, such as 'salesman': neutral alternatives (such as 'sales representative') or amplifications (such as 'salesman or saleswoman') should be used. Similarly, references to the sex of the desired candidate should be avoided by the use of terms such as 'the applicant', 'the candidate' or 'man or woman', 'he or she' and so on. Armstrong (2003) suggests that, in regard to the Race Relations Act, 'as long as race is never mentioned or implied in an advertisement, you should have no problem in keeping within the law'.

Indirect discrimination occurs when an employer applies a provision, criterion or practice in such a way as to put one group at a particular disadvantage without justification. For example, a requirement that applicants be over six feet tall would prohibit more women than men from applying. The employer must, if challenged, justify the conditions on non-racial or non-sexual grounds.

There are, however, strictly defined exceptions ('genuine occupational requirements') which justify stated preference for a particular group.

(a) In relation to women, these include reasons of physiology (*not* 'strength'), decency/privacy, special welfare consideration and international law or customs which would prevent women operating effectively in a foreign context.

NOTES

(b)   In relation to race, they include special welfare considerations and authenticity criteria (eg in dramatic or photographic roles).

Disability

The **Disability Discrimination Act 1995** makes it unlawful to discriminate against a disabled person in deciding whom to interview or whom to employ or in the terms of an employment offer.

A disabled person is defined as a person who has a physical or mental impairment that has a substantial and long-term (more than 12 months) effect on his or her ability to carry out normal day-to-day tasks. (This effect may include: mobility; manual dexterity or physical co-ordination; and impaired ability to lift, speak, hear, see, remember, concentrate, learn or understand.)

Age diversity

The **Employment Equality (Age) Regulations 2006** ban unjustified direct and indirect discrimination on the basis of age in recruitment.

It is *not* unlawful to treat candidates differently on the basis of their age if:

(a)   There is an **objective justification** for doing so (eg it may be necessary to fix a maximum recruitment age to reflect the training requirement of the post, or the need for a reasonable period of employment before retirement).

(b)   The candidate is older than, or within six months of, the employer's normal retirement age (or 65 if the employer doesn't have one).

(c)   There is a 'genuine occupational requirement' (eg dramatic roles for older or younger characters).

In its publication *'Age and the Workplace'*, ACAS advises employers: 'Base your decision about recruitment on the skills required to do the job. Provide training to help those making judgements to be objective and avoid stereotyping people because of their age.'

FOR DISCUSSION

'For those employers who ignore or fail to comply with [diversity and equal opportunity] legislation, the consequences will be severe,' says [employment lawyer] Richard Lister.

'Damage can also be inflicted on a company's reputation, according to [diversity manager for financial services group, HBOS] Jones. "Forget about legal claims: it is about treating people with respect."

'It's also about the war for talent. Employers will also miss out on a talented and diverse workforce and lose their competitive edge if they ignore this legislation, believes Dinah Warman, CAP adviser, diversity. "These new legal obligations will help employers stamp out the kinds of prejudices that stop organisations from accessing the talent they need and that keep talented people out of the job," she said.'

(Higginbottom, 2003)

What are the HRM values behind each of these three statements? You might like to take each of the three positions and argue them against opposing or resistant viewpoints.

We will now discuss some of the recruitment procedures listed in Paragraph 2.1 in more detail.

3 JOB ANALYSIS

Definitions

> **Job analysis** is 'the determination of the essential characteristics of a job', the process of examining a job to identify its component parts and the circumstances in which it is performed (*British Standards Institute*).
>
> The product of the analysis is usually a **job specification** – a detailed statement of the activities (mental and physical) involved in the job, and other relevant factors in the social and physical environment.

3.1 Uses of job analysis

Job analysis, and the job specification resulting from it, may be used by managers:

(a) In **recruitment and selection** – for a detailed description of the vacant job to provide a source of information for the preparation of job descriptions and personnel specifications

(b) For **appraisal** – to assess how well an employee has fulfilled the requirements of the job

(c) In devising **training programmes** – to assess the knowledge and skills necessary in a job

(d) In establishing **rates of pay** – this will be discussed later in connection with job evaluation

(e) In eliminating **risks** – identifying hazards in the job

(f) In re-organisation of the **organisational structure** – by reappraising the purpose and necessity of jobs and their relationship to each other.

3.2 Content of job analysis

Information which should be elicited from a job appraisal is both task-oriented information, and also worker-oriented information, including:

(a) **Initial requirements of the employee:** aptitudes, qualifications, experience, training required; personality and attitudinal considerations

(b) **Duties and responsibilities of the job:** physical aspects; mental effort; routine or requiring initiative; difficult and/or disagreeable features; degree of independence of discretion; responsibilities for staff, materials, equipment or cash etc; component tasks (where, when, how frequently, how carried out); standards of output and/or accuracy required; relative value of tasks and how they fit together

(c) **Environment and conditions of the job:** physical surroundings, with notable features such as temperature or noise; hazards; remuneration; other conditions such as hours, shifts, benefits, holidays; career prospects; provision of employee services – canteens, protective clothing etc

(d) **Social factors of the job:** size of the department; teamwork or isolation; sort of people dealt with – senior management, the public; amount of supervision; job status.

3.3 Methods of job analysis

Opportunities for analyses occur when jobs fall vacant, when salaries are reviewed, or when targets are being set, and the HR department should take advantage of such opportunities to review and revise existing job specifications.

Job analysis can be carried out by:

(a) **Observation of working practice**, where jobs are relatively routine and repetitive. The analyst watches and records the job holder's activity, task times and performance standards, working conditions and so on. A proforma question sheet listing the factors to be recorded would normally be used, incorporating range statements (circumstances in which each task is carried out and standards to which competence is required) and rating scales

(b) **Questionnaires and interviews**, for jobs with longer task cycles and invisible work (planning, problem-solving and so on). The job holder would be asked to explain, describe and quantify (as far as possible) the job. His or her manager, and other third parties, may be asked to complete the same exercise

(c) **Diaries, time sheets and other self-recording techniques.** The job holder may be asked periodically to record activity, or may include **critical incidents** highlighting key aspects of the job.

Activity 7 (15 minutes)

The fact that a job analysis is being carried out may cause some concern among employees: they may fear that standards will be raised, rates cut, or that the job may be found to be redundant or require rationalisation.

How might the analyst need to carry out his or her work in order to gain their confidence?

4   JOB DESCRIPTION

Definition

> A **job description** is a broad description of a job or position at a given time (since jobs are dynamic, subject to change and variation). 'It is a written statement of those facts which are important regarding the duties, responsibilities, and their organisational and operational interrelationships.' (Livy, 1988)

4.1   Uses of job description

In **recruitment,** a job description can be used:

(a)   To decide what skills (technical, human, conceptual, design or whatever) and qualifications are required of the job holder. When formulating recruitment advertisements, and interviewing an applicant for the job, the interviewer can use the resulting job specification to match the candidate against the job.

(b)   To assess whether the job will efficiently utilise the abilities and provide scope for the aspirations of the prospective job holder

(c)   To determine a rate of pay which is fair for the job, if this has not already been decided by some other means

4.2   The contents of a job description

A job description should be clear and to the point, and so ought not to be lengthy. Typically, a job description would show the following.

(a)   **Job title** and department and job code number; the person to whom the job holder is responsible; possibly, the grading of the job.

(b)   **Job summary** – showing in a few paragraphs the major functions and tools, machinery and special equipment used; possibly also a small organisation chart.

(c)   **Job content** – list of the sequence of operations that constitute the job, noting main levels of difficulty. In the case of management work there should be a list of the main duties of the job, indicating frequency of performance – typically between 5 and 15 main duties should be listed. This includes the degree of initiative involved, and the nature of responsibility (for other people, machinery and/or other resources).

(d)   The extent (and limits) of the jobholder's authority and responsibility.

(e)   Statement showing relation of job to other closely associated jobs, including superior and subordinate positions and liaison required with other departments.

(f)   Working hours, basis of pay and benefits, and conditions of employment, including location, special pressures, social isolation, physical conditions, or health hazards.

(g)   Opportunities for training, transfer and promotion.

(h)   Possibly, also, objectives and expected results, which will be compared against actual performance during employee appraisal – although this may be done as a separate exercise, as part of the appraisal process.

EXAMPLE

MIDWEST BANK PLC

1   *Job title*:   Clerk (Grade 2)

2   *Branch*:   All branches and administrative offices

3   *Job summary*:   To provide clerical support to activities within the bank

4   *Job content*:   Typical duties will include:

    (a)   Cashier's duties
    (b)   Processing of branch clearing
    (c)   Processing of standing orders
    (d)   Support to branch management

5   *Reporting structure*:

Administrative officer/assistant manager

Supervisor (Grade 3)

Clerk (Grade 2)

6   *Experience/Education*: Experience not required, minimum 3 GCSEs or equivalent.

7   *Training to be provided*: Initial on-the-job training plus regular formal courses and training.

8   *Hours*: 38 hours per week

9   *Objectives and appraisal*: Annual appraisal in line with objectives above.

10   *Salary*: Refer to separate standard salary structure.

Job description prepared by: Head office HR department (October 2007)

4.3   Limitations of job descriptions

Townsend (1985) suggested that job descriptions are of limited use.

(a)   They are only suited for jobs where the work is largely repetitive and therefore performed by low-grade employees.

(b)   Jobs are likely to be constantly changing as turbulent business environments impact upon them, so a job description is constantly out of date or limiting.

(c)   Job descriptions stifle flexibility and encourage demarcation disputes, where people adhere strictly to the contents of the job description, rather than responding flexibly to task or organisational requirements.

Where job descriptions are used, it should be remembered that:

    (a)   A job description is like a photograph, an image 'frozen' at one point in time

    (b)   A job description needs constant and negotiated revision

    (c)   A job description should be secondary in importance to a customer requirement, quality improvement or problems solved

4.4 Alternatives to job description

It has been suggested that work requirements should be defined in terms of the contribution or outcomes expected of the job holder.

Some organisations are therefore moving towards:

- **Goal, competence or accountability profiles,** setting out the outputs and performance levels expected of the individual (or team). We will look at competence profiles a bit later.

- **Role definitions,** defining the part played by the job holder in meeting organisational and departmental objectives. A role definition is therefore wider than a job description, focusing less on 'content' than on how the job holder contributes to business processes and results through competent and flexible performances.

    A role profile of definition will therefore specify: the overall purpose of the role; what role holders are expected to achieve (key results) and what they will be accountable for; and the behavioural/technical competences required to achieve the defined level of contribution.

5 PERSON SPECIFICATION

Definition

A **person specification** profiles the type of person the organisation should be trying to recruit for a given position, that is, the 'ideal' candidate.

Professor Alec Rodger was a pioneer of the systematic approach to recruitment and selection in the UK. He suggested that:

> If matching *[ie of demands of the job and the person who is to perform it]* is to be done satisfactorily, the requirements of an occupation (or job) must be described in the same terms as the aptitudes of the people who are being considered for it.

This was the basis for the formulation of person specification as a way of matching people to jobs on the basis of comparative sets of data: defining job requirements and personal suitability along the same lines.

5.1 Models for person specification

Two influential models were adopted as the basis of person specification.

The Seven Point Plan (Rodger, 1970)	Five Point Pattern of Personality (Munro Fraser 1971)
(a) Physical attributes (such as neat appearance, ability to speak clearly and without impediment)	(a) Impact on others, including physical attributes, speech and manner
(b) Attainment (including educational qualifications)	(b) Acquired knowledge or qualifications, including education, training and work experience
(c) General intelligence	(c) Innate ability, including mental agility, aptitude for learning
(d) Special aptitudes (such as neat work, speed and accuracy)	(d) Motivation: individual goals, demonstrated effort and success at achieving them
(e) Interests (practical and social)	
(f) Disposition (or manner: friendly, helpful and so on)	(e) Adjustment: emotional stability, tolerance of stress, human relations skills
(g) Background circumstances	

Each feature in the specification may helpfully be classified as:

(a) **Essential** – for instance, honesty in a cashier is essential whilst a special aptitude for conceptual thought is not

(b) **Desirable** – for instance, a reasonably pleasant manner should ensure satisfactory standards in a person dealing with the public

(c) **Contra-indicated** – some features are actively disadvantageous, such as an inability to work in a team when acting as project leader.

EXAMPLE

PERSON SPECIFICATION: CUSTOMER ACCOUNTS MANAGER

	ESSENTIAL	DESIRABLE	CONTRA-INDICATED
Physical attributes	Clear speech Well-groomed Good health	Age 25-40	Age under 25 Chronic ill-health and absence
Attainments	2 'A' levels GCSE Maths and English Thorough knowledge of retail environment	Degree (any discipline) Marketing training 2 years' experience in supervisory post	No experience of supervision or retail environment
Intelligence	High verbal intelligence		

	ESSENTIAL	DESIRABLE	CONTRA-INDICATED
Aptitudes	Facility with numbers Attention to detail and accuracy Social skills for customer relations	Analytical abilities (problem solving) Understanding of systems and IT	No mathematical ability Low tolerance of technology
Interests	Social: team activity		Time-consuming hobbies 'Solo' interests only
Disposition	Team player Persuasive Tolerance of pressure and change	Initiative	Anti-social Low tolerance of responsibility
Circumstances	Able to work late, take work home	Located in area of office	

5.2 Limitations of person specifications

As our example suggests, a wide number of variables may be included in a person specification. If it is not used flexibly, however, and the specification fails to evolve as business and employment conditions change, it may swiftly lose its relevance. For example:

(a) Attainments are often focused on educational achievements, since there has traditionally been a strong correlation between management potential and higher education. However, this does not necessarily reflect the range of learning and experience available, nor the increasing diversity of educational backgrounds and qualification standards in a global labour market.

(b) 'Physical attributes' and 'background circumstances' may suggest criteria which can now be interpreted as discriminatory, to the disabled (in the case of a speech impairment, say) or to women (for example, the ability of women with family responsibilities to undertake full-time employment).

(c) The category of 'general intelligence' has traditionally been based on 'IQ', a narrow definition of intelligence as mental dexterity. It is now accepted that there are at least seven different intelligences, not least of which are emotional, intuitive, practical and interpersonal intelligence, which are key factors in the new fluid, horizontal business world.

NOTES

FOR DISCUSSION

'Forget loyalty and conformity. We can't afford narrow-skill people' (Rosabeth Moss Kanter). What does this say about the concept of the desirable **disposition** for an employee? What kind of characteristics may now take the place of loyalty and conformity as desirable attributes for success and contribution in today's business environment (or in an industry or occupation of your choice)?

5.3   Competency profiles

Definition

> **Competency** may be defined as 'the set of behaviour patterns that the incumbent needs to bring to a position in order to perform its tasks and functions with competence'. (Woodruffe, 1992)

Competency frameworks, definitions or profiles are based on **key success factors** in a given business or sector (through benchmarking exercises or definitions formulated by standard-setting lead bodies). They may also be developed within organisations, linked to their specific strategic objectives, cultural values and task requirements.

The advantage of competence-based profiles include the following.

(a)   They can be linked directly to the strategic objectives of an organisation.

(b)   They reflect best practice in the relevant occupation or profession (if defined by standard-setting bodies).

(c)   They are flexible in the face of changing conditions are requirements, as they are menu-driven and non-prescriptive about job/organisational specifics.

(d)   They can be applied at all levels of the organisation (although the behaviours expected will obviously vary), which helps to foster core values and consistent practice in the organisation.

(e)   They directly relate candidates' attainments and attributes to the demands of the job, and should therefore be both accurate (in predicting job performance) and non-discriminatory.

> **Activity 8**   **(5 minutes)**
>
> Think of an example of competencies which are (a) likely to have been demonstrated in candidates' academic or working life; (b) likely to predict successful job performance; and (c) readily assessable in an interview or other selection test.

6 RECRUITMENT METHODS AND MEDIA

6.1 External recruitment

A number of methods are available to organisations to contact (and attract) potential candidates. These can be summarised as follows.

Method	Evaluation	
(a) Unsolicited requests: Write-ins or walk-ins (Media: word-of mouth, recommendation, previous recruitment advertising, general employer branding)	**Advantages:** **Disadvantages:**	Inexpensive. Pre-selected for enthusiasm, initiative Open **walk-in** policy may encourage application where job difficult to fill Needs control and systematic application handling
(b) Existing contacts: Previous (re-employable) em-ployees; retirees; career break; previous applicants of suitable general quality held on file.	**Advantages:** **Disadvantages:**	Work behaviour/attributes known; may be amenable to part-time, temporary or flexible working Needs systematic database manage-ment
(c) Referrals: Registers of members seeking employment, kept eg by trade unions and professional bodies	**Advantages:** **Disadvantages:**	Pre-selection at low cost Indirectly discriminative
(d) Agencies **Job centres:** Network of agencies provided by central government: particularly for manual and junior positions in admin/clerical/retail	**Advantages:** **Disadvantages:**	Free Local and national Socially responsible (not-for-profit) Register limited to unemployed Require relationship/selection management
Resettlement services: Finding civilian positions for armed forces personnel at end of service	**Advantages:** **Disadvantages:**	Can be highly trained/experienced Inexperience in civilian culture?
Careers services: Placing graduates of schools and training institutions	**Advantages:** **Disadvantages**	Potential for young unsocialised recruits Potential for preview through work placements Financial incentives (government schemes such as YT, Apex) Potential for strong relationship – selection preference, curriculum influence Recruits may lack experience Administration of work-experience Possible indirect discrimination
Employment agencies: Wide range of specialising agencies; temporary agencies for one-off requirements and short-term cover	**Advantages:** **Disadvantages:**	May undertake pre-screening Temp agencies facilitate flexible working Quality can vary Cost

Method	Evaluation	
(e) **Consultancies** **Selection consultants:** Recruit and select for positions; may cover clerical/admin staff, specialist staff (media, financial etc), or managerial	Advantages:	Reduces administration for employer Specialist selection skills Wide-ranging contacts
	Disadvantages:	Cost May lack awareness of organisation's culture, values, detailed criteria Excludes internal applicants Lack of accountability
Outplacement consultants: Registers, retraining etc to help redundant and early-retired employees	Advantages:	Perceived socially responsible Provide some training
	Disadvantages:	Quality varies
Search consultants: 'Head hunters'. Networking to track highly employable individuals: candidates proactively approached	Advantages:	Selects for high employability networking, exploration opportunity
	Disadvantages:	Cost Limited range Organisation may be victim as well as beneficiary!
(f) **Direct to source:** Schools, colleges, universities (Media: advertisement, 'milk-round' presentation)	Advantages:	Networking relationships Opportunities to preview via work placement, 'gap' year etc Access to graduates in desirable (scarce) disciplines
	Disadvantages:	Local catchment area Tends to be annual 'season' Recruits lack experience Potential for indirect discrimination
(g) **The Internet:** Wide range of recruitment databases, plus web advertising/application	Advantages:	IT-literate users Pre-selection by database, low cost World-wide catchment
	Disadvantages:	Difficulty of verification Competition

EXAMPLE

A survey reported in *People Management* (31 May 2007) showed that only 18% of employers used recommendations from employees as a recruiting tool – and thereby 'throw away millions of pounds on recruitment advertising'.

A company hiring 250 people a year could save £80,000 if 10% of hires came from referrals by employees of people they know – even if a £250 reward was offered for a successful referral!

Activity 9 (1 hour)

We have already mentioned some of the 'media' by which an organisation can advertise or make known its staffing needs by the methods listed above. Brainstorm as a full list as you can of advertising/information media relevant to recruitment. For each of the media you mention, add any advantages or disadvantages you can think of.

Weblink

Virgin Group

Check out the 'Jobs' section of this (and other corporate sites) for examples of e-recruitment. The virgin site has helpful information on the recruitment process, equality and diversity policies and so on.

►► http://www.virgin.com

6.2   E-recruitment

E– (or Internet) recruiting has exploded in recent years, having been used mainly for IT jobs in the early stages of Internet adoption. The Internet is a useful tool in a number of ways.

- To post or advertise vacancies, either on the employer's own website (or intranet, for internal advertising) or on specialist online recruitment sites.

- To provide information about the employer, recruitment policies and jobs (often available on the employer's own website, as well as recruiter databases).

- To allow database searches, matching employers' requirements and job seekers' CVs.

- To facilitate communication (via e-mail) between enquirers/applicants and employers.

- To complete recruitment applications electronically (online application forms, computerised screening of essential matching criteria, online psychometric tests and so on).

Advantages of e-recruitment

- Its ability to reach a wide and geographically dispersed (even global) audience of potential candidates.

- Its cost-effectiveness, compared to traditional forms of advertising.

- Its ability to offer more information (for self-selection) about the organisation and the job, potentially in a more attractive (interactive, multi-media) format.

- Its demonstration of basic computer literacy (where desired) by applicants.

- Electronic support for application, CV matching, short-listing and so on – more swiftly and cost-effectively than by human agency.

- The provision of application information for use in Human Resource Information Systems, eg to analyse applications received, monitor equal opportunities and so on.

- The ability to monitor traffic (hits on the site, pages views etc) to derive information on the effectiveness of the site, levels of interest and so on.

However, many applications through e-recruitment may be irrelevant (especially if the organisation only wants to recruit locally or nationally). Screening and short-listing software relies heavily on matching keywords, and can disqualify suitable candidates on this basis. Despite the increasing take-up of Internet technology, e-recruitment may still screen out otherwise suitable applicants for whom it is not the preferred job-seeking tool: there are still security concerns about transmitting personal data via the web, for example.

EXAMPLE

'Is the HR function really taking online recruitment and its accompanying technology to heart? Are recruitment managers genuinely enthusiastic about the savings and quality increases it can lead to? Or, with half of all FT500 firms having no corporate website recruitment, is there another side to the story?

'Ask many of the top companies in the UK, and they are enthusiastic about online recruitment. They say they have their current vacancies online, they have e-mail links, they may even have online forms and a system to scan them. It is, they say, a cheap and easy method of gathering more applications from a wider pool.

'Yet the first major benchmarking study of the top 500 companies' own online recruitment efforts show that the effects permeate no further. Only a tiny fraction of those that recruit online back this up with fully automated recruitment systems to manage the process ... Is it the money? Or the real ability of the tools to deliver? Or something deeper ...

' "We expected a big spread in the levels of performance – but not this big," says Colin Farrow, managing director of consultancy The Driver Is, which ... combed each FT500 site to find if it fulfilled nine simple recruitment criteria ...

' "The overriding criterion was 'as a user – what would I expect to find?' We were not looking for leading-edge technology," Farrow insists, "just assistance and information – an existing career profile, an impression of working there. These are indicators of above-average empathy with the user." ...

'One firm that can feel proud of its recruitment website is engineering services provider Amec. Coming joint first in the corporate website benchmarking study, the site offers taster job profiles, latest jobs and help during studies and internships.'

The nine criteria; How e-savvy is your firm?

- [ ] Are current vacancies listed?
- [ ] Can people apply online?
- [ ] Can potential candidates see an existing employee's career profile?
- [ ] Are company business principles referred to?
- [ ] Can people register for e-mail alerts?
- [ ] Do they actually receive e-mail alerts?
- [ ] Is there a graduate section?
- [ ] Is there an 'experience of hires' section?
- [ ] Are HR contacts featured?

Welch (2003)

Weblink

For more results of the benchmarking study by The Driver Is, visit:

▶▶**www.ukcorporatewebrankings.com**

Activity 10 **(1 hour)**

Use the Internet to appraise the e-recruitment strategies of two or more firms, using the checklist suggested by the benchmarking study cited above.

(a) Start with your own organisation or place of study.

(b) Browse the sites of Amec, or any other top companies you are interested in.

(c) Browse the 'jobs' or 'careers' channels of your preferred Internet portal (Yahoo! or MSN, say), or the specialist careers/jobs agencies/sites advertised.

6.3 The recruitment advertisement

The object of recruitment advertising is to home in on the target market of labour, and to attract interest in the organisation and the job.

In a way, it is already part of the **selection** process. The advertisement will be placed where suitable people are likely to see it (say, internally only – immediately pre-selecting members of the organisation – or in a specialist journal, pre-selecting those specialists). It will be worded in a way that further weeds out people who would not be suitable for the job (or for whom the job would not be suitable). Be aware however, that some such forms of pre-selection may be construed as discriminatory if they disadvantage some groups more than others. (Advertising internally only, where the current workforce is overwhelmingly male, may be construed as indirectly discriminatory to women, for example.)

The way in which a job is advertised will depend on the type of organisation and the type of job.

A factory is likely to advertise a vacancy for an unskilled worker in a different way to a company advertising for a CIPD-qualified person for a senior HR position. Managerial jobs may merit national advertisement, whereas semi– or un-skilled jobs may only warrant local coverage, depending on the supply of suitable candidates in the local area. Specific skills may be most appropriately reached through trade, technical or professional journals.

The advertisement, based on information set out in the job description, (or variants) and recruitment policy, should contain the following information.

    (a)   The organisation: its main business and location (at least)

    (b)   The job: title, main duties and responsibilities and special features

    (c)   Conditions: special factors affecting the job

    (d)   Qualifications and experience (required, and preferred); other attributes, aptitudes and/or knowledge required

    (e)   Rewards: salary and benefits (negotiable, if appropriate), opportunities for training and career development, and so on

    (f)   Application: how to apply, to whom, and by what date.

The advertisement should encourage a degree of **self-selection**, so that the target population begins to narrow itself down. (The information contained in the advertisement should deter unsuitable applicants as well as encourage potentially suitable ones.) It should also reflect the desired image of the organisation in the outside world: its employer brand.

AT MILTON KEYNES
'NO' ISN'T A WORD WE LIKE TO USE

We'd much rather give the thumbs up to new ideas and new innovations. And in our forward-thinking HR department, that's exactly what we're doing.

It's all part of the Council's wider aims to change the way local government operates. Embracing new legislation and bringing our services closer to internal and external clients alike, we're adopting a real business focus - and shaping some bold plans for the future. If you're MCIPD qualified, have a record of continued professional development and you're aware of the wider issues confronting a Council like ours, they're plans you could share in.

HUMAN RESOURCES OFFICER
- OPERATIONS

£22,194 - £26,091 REF: R01331

You'll be part of our central HR operation, ensuring that all our services run smoothly and effectively - as well as contributing to the overall development of the department. We'll also look to you to provide Council-wide advice on everything from employment legislation to HR procedure, calling on at least 3 years' generalist human resources experience, a background in trade union liaison and proven communication skills. Requests for full/part-time or term-time only are welcome.

HUMAN RESOURCES OFFICER
- EMPLOYEE RELATIONS

£22,194 - £26,091 REF: R01332

You'll be reviewing, developing and undertaking briefings on HR policies; advising managers and HR colleagues on policies and employment legislation; trade union consultation; reviewing and monitoring the Occupational Health contract. You will have at least 3 years' human resources experience.

CLOSING DATE: 16 OCTOBER 2000.

Further information and application forms are available by telephoning (01908) 253344 or 253462 (answerphone service available 24 hours per day) or by writing to HR Recruitment Team, Milton Keynes Council, Saxon Court, 502 Avebury Boulevard, Milton Keynes MK9 3HS. Minicom (01908) 252727 (office hours only) or e-mail: Helen.Davey@milton-keynes.gov.uk

PLEASE QUOTE THE APPROPRIATE REFERENCE.

MILTON KEYNES COUNCIL

POSITIVE ABOUT DISABLED PEOPLE

The Council is an Equal Opportunities Employer. Applications are invited from candidates with the necessary attributes regardless of gender, colour, ethnic origin, nationality, creed, disability or sexual orientation. Many Council jobs are suitable for job sharing.

The aim of the recruitment process is **applications** *by suitably qualified candidates.* *What form might an application take, in order for it to be fed into the selection process?*

BPP LEARNING MEDIA

6.4 Applications

Applications for a particular advertised (or unadvertised) vacancy, or for employment in the organisation as and when vacancies arise, may be received in various forms.

(a) **Unsolicited letter, e-mail, 'walk-in' or other enquiry**. This would normally be responded to with a request for the following.

(b) **Application form**

    (i) For lower-level, relatively standardised jobs, for which a high volume of applicants is expected, this may be a brief, directly targeted form (focusing on qualifications and experience considered essential to the job) in order to facilitate ruthless weeding out of unsuitable applicants, and requiring minimal discretion, self-expression and time in both completion and interpretation.

    (ii) For managerial, specialist or culturally-driven jobs, a more complex application form or package may be used, in order to elicit more complex responses: biographical/psychological ('biodata') questionnaires, guided self-expression, samples for hand-writing analysis, preliminary testing (description of previous work-related problem-solving, or response to case-study scenarios, say) and so on. Such in-depth tools for pre-selection save time and effort at the interview stage, but are time-consuming to prepare and analyse, and should be subjected to cost-benefit considerations.

(c) **Curriculum vitae (CV) or résumé**, usually accompanied by a **covering letter** drawing the recruiter's attention to specific aspects of the applicants' CV which are relevant to the vacancy or organisation. The CV is essentially a brief, systematic summary of the applicant's qualifications, previous work experience and relevant skills/interests/requirements, plus details of individuals willing to vouch for his or her performance, character and employability (**referees**).

The application form or CV will be used to find out relevant information about the applicant, in order to decide, at the initial sifting stage:

(a) Whether the applicant is obviously unsuitable for the job, or

(b) Whether the applicant might be of the right calibre, and worth inviting to interview.

The application form will be designed by the organisation (or recruitment agency) fulfil the following criteria.

(a) It should elicit information about the applicant which can be directly compared with the requirements of the job.

(b) For managerial, interpersonal and culturally-driven jobs – requiring particular values, orientations and attributes – it should give applicants the opportunity to describe (briefly) their career ambitions, why they want the job, perceived strengths and weaknesses and so on.

(c) It should convey a professional, accurate and favourable impression of the organisation, a public relations and employer branding tool.

(d) It should elicit any information required to enable the organisation subsequently to monitor and evaluate the success of its recruitment procedures (in regard to numbers of female, minority and disabled applicants, number of applications per source and so on).

An example of a basic application form is given here.

AOK PLC	Page 1
APPLICATION FORM	

Post applied for ….

PERSONAL DETAILS

Surname Mr/ Mrs/ Miss/Ms

First name

Address

Post code

Telephone   (Daytime)   (Mobile)

Date of birth

Nationality

Marital status

Dependants

Education (latest first)

Date		Institution	Exams passed/qualifications
From	To		

TRAINING AND OTHER SKILLS

Please give details of any specialised training courses you have attended.

Please note down other skills such as languages (and degree of fluency), driving licence (with endorsements if any), keyboard skills (familiarity with software package).

NOTES

EMPLOYMENT

Dates		Employer name and address	Title and duties
From	To		

Current salary and benefits …

INTERESTS

Please describe your leisure/hobby/sporting interests.

YOUR COMMENTS

Why do you think you are suitable for the job advertised?

ADDITIONAL INFORMATION

Do you have any permanent health problems? If so, please give details.

When would you be able to start work?

REFERENCES

Please give two references. One should be a former employer.

Name

Address

Name

Address

Position

Position

Signed

Date

Activity 11   **(20 minutes)**

Suggest four ways in which an application form could be *badly* designed (both in appearance and content). You may be able to do this from personal experience.

6.5 Internal recruitment

Internal advertising of vacancies may be a requirement for some organisations, under agreements negotiated with trade unions. Advertising media include noticeboards (paper and electronic – for example via corporate intranet), in-house journals, memoranda to supervisors/managers soliciting recommendations and observation and word-of-mouth (the **grapevine**).

Methods of **internal recruitment** include:

    (a)   Advertising for self-applicants
    (b)   Soliciting recommendations from supervisors/managers and training officers
    (c)   Soliciting referrals by existing employees to family, friends and contacts
    (d)   Formal succession, promotion and transfer planning.

Most of these methods incur little extra cost, being based on existing or easily accessible information about the candidate's abilities, attitudes and so on.

7 EVALUATING RECRUITMENT

An evaluation of recruitment (and selection) procedures will aim to determine whether the procedures succeeded in getting a *suitable* person into a job, at the *time* when the person was required and at an acceptable *cost*. At a more strategic level, it determines whether recruitment is succeeding in achieving the organisation's overall manpower plan.

Connock (1991) suggests that the recruitment process can be audited at four levels.

    (a)   **Performance indicators** should be established and measured at each stage of the process including:

        • Total numbers of applications received
        • Time taken to locate applicants
        • Cost per applicant
        • Time taken to process applications/per application
        • Number of female/minority/disabled applicants
        • Number of qualified applicants (matching advertised criteria)
        • Number of qualified female/minority/disabled applicants

        These basically assess the effectiveness and cost-efficiency of recruitment advertising, equal opportunities policy and recruitment administration. Post-entry criteria – such as number of offers extended per source/method or in relation to applications received, cost and time of training recruits, subsequent job performance and length of service of recruits and so on – may only be applied after the selection process but still reflect on recruitment.

(b)   **Cost-effectiveness** of the various methods used should be measured. It may be that a certain advertising medium is too costly for the number of worthwhile responses it generates, for example.

Activity 12   **(20 minutes)**

What kind of information would you need to record in order to appraise the cost-effectiveness of a recruitment method/medium? Aim to end up with a meaningful figure for the cost per person appointed (and actually entering employment).

(c)   **Monitoring the make up of the workforce** and the impact of new recruits is essential as part of an equal opportunities policy to identify areas where certain groups are under-represented.

(d)   An **attitude survey** may be conducted amongst recruits to measure satisfaction and gather feedback: did the job advertisement give a fair idea of the job, were they frustrated by the length of time they had to wait for a decision and so on? and so on.

Other methods of evaluating recruitment and selection include **'benchmarking'**: comparing the organisation's systems with known example of good practice used in other organisations. Where the HR department has adopted the concept of the **'internal customer'**, it can also gather feedback from internal customers (line managers) and users (job applicants and recruits).

Chapter roundup

• The labour market consists of potential employees, both internal and external to the organisation.

• Demographic trends have important implications for HR planning, especially the falling number of young people in the workforce, the rising number of female and older workers, increasing ethnic diversity and national/regional education trends.

• Recruitment is concerned with defining job requirements and attracting suitable applicants. Selection is concerned with fitting the person to the job.

• A systematic recruitment procedure can be summarised in diagrammatic form shown opposite.

Cont...

Chapter roundup cont.

The Recruitment Process

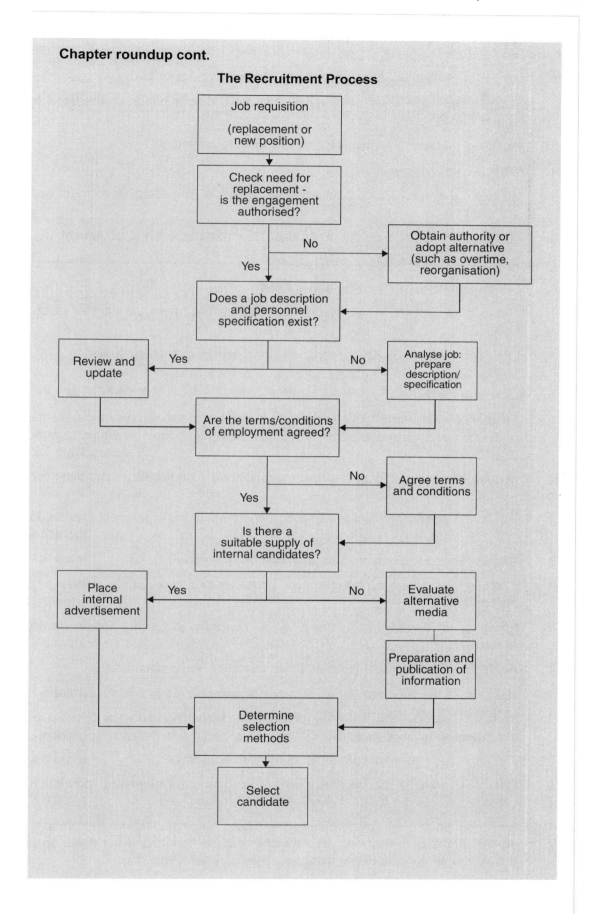

BPP
LEARNING MEDIA

Quick quiz

1   Why is the shift towards an ageing population important for HRP?

2   Suggest two ways in which recruiters can avoid discrimination on the basis of (a) sex and (b) age.

3   List three methods by which job analysis may be carried out.

4   What is a job description?

5   What three criteria make 'competencies' effective in guiding recruitment and selection?

6   List five methods of recruitment of candidates from the external job market.

7   What are the *drawbacks* of e-recruitment?

8   List four methods of receiving applications.

9   List four methods by which vacancies could be filled from the internal labour pool.

10   List three methods by which recruitment procedures may be evaluated.

Answers to quick quiz

1   Because the workforce will reflect the proportion of older workers, and because of the corresponding decline in the number of young people available to work.
(see paragraph 1.2)

2   (a) Avoid sexist terms. Avoid unjustifiable (indirectly discriminatory) requirements.

   (b) Avoid stating age limits. Avoid implying restrictions (eg 'recent graduate').
(para 2.4)

3   Observation, questionnaire/interview, diaries/self-recording   (para 3.3)

4   A broad description of the purpose, scope, duties and responsibilities of a particular job.   (para 4)

5   Focusing on demonstrable areas; likely to predict job performance; readily assessable.   (para 5.3)

6   Agencies, consultancies, Internet, direct to source, existing contacts.

(para 6.1)

7   Irrelevant applications. Difficulty of accurate screening. Lack of take up by potentially suitable applicants.   (para 6.2)

8   CV; application form; unsolicited enquiry; web application.   (para 6.4)

9   Retention, transfer or redeployment, training and development, promotion, exploiting employee contracts and/or flexible working methods.   (para 6.5)

10   By determining key performance indicators and monitoring performance against them; by measuring cost-effectiveness; by monitoring the make-up of the workforce; by conducting attitude surveys; by benchmarking.

(section 7)

Answers to activities

1 (a) The falling number of younger workers will make it increasingly difficult to recruit and retain skilled younger people, with intense competition – particularly among organisations that have traditionally recruited school leavers and new graduates. Organisations will either have to revise strategies to compete for younger workers – or change their resourcing policies and culture to accept older workers (a process supported by age diversity legislation).

   (b) In the UK, the ratio of people 65+ to those of working age is 21 : 100. By 2030, this is anticipated to be 25+ : 100, adding to the difficulties of the state to provide pensions for the retired population. Employers are likely to find the provision of occupational pension benefits an increasingly important tool in attracting and retaining employees.

2 Connock (1991) suggests six steps by which organisations can cope with these demographic and educational trends.

   (1) Establish what labour market the organisation is in.

   (2) Discover the organisation's catchment areas (ie location of potential recruits).

   (3) Discern the supply-side trends in the catchment area labour force. (For example, how many school leavers are expected? What is the rate of growth/decline of local population?)

   (4) Examine education trends in the location.

   (5) Assess the demand from other employers for the skills you need. (If there is a large concentration of, say, electronics companies in the region, they will be interested in hiring people with similar skills.)

   (6) Try to assess whether some of your demand can be satisfied by a supply from other sources.

3 It is often difficult to persuade departmental managers to agree to the promotion of a subordinate out of the department, especially if (s)he has been selected as having particular ability: the department will be losing an able member, and will have to find, induct and train a replacement. Moreover, if the manager's resistance were revealed, there might be a motivational issue to contend with. The HR manager will have to be able to justify a recommendation with sound policies for providing and training a replacement with as little impact on the department's efficiency as possible.

4 Where the organisation has the choice, it should consider the following points.

   (a) Management will be familiar with an internal promotee: there will be detailed appraisal information available from employee records. The outside recruit will to a greater extent be an unknown quantity – and the organisation will be taking a greater risk of unacceptable personality or performance emerging later.

   (b) A promotee has already worked within the organisation and will be familiar with its:

       (i) Culture, or philosophy; informal rules and norms as well as stated policy

(ii)   Politics; power-structures and relationships

    (iii) Systems and procedures

    (iv) Objectives

    (v)   Other personnel (who will likewise be familiar with him/her)

(c) Promotion of insiders is visible proof of the organisation's willingness to develop people's careers. This may well have an encouraging, motivating and loyalty-inducing effect.

(d) Internal advertisement of vacancies contributes to the implementation of equal opportunities policies. Many women are employed in secretarial and clerical jobs from which promotion is unlikely – and relatively few are in higher-graded roles. Internal advertising could become a route for opening up opportunities for women at junior levels.

(e) On the other hand, an organisation must retain its ability to adapt, grow and change, and this may well require new blood, wider views, fresh ideas. Insiders may be too socialised into the prevailing culture to see faults or be willing to 'upset the apple cart' where necessary for the organisation's health.

5   Some ideas:

(a) The overall priorities and requirements of the organisation will be more clearly recognised and met, rather than the objectives of sub-systems such as individual departments.

(b) There will be a central reference point for communication, queries and applications from outside the organisation.

(c) Communication with the environment will also be more standardised, and will be more likely to reinforce the overall corporate image of the organisation.

(d) Potential can be spotted in individuals and utilised in the optimum conditions – not necessarily in the post for which the individual has applied, if (s)he might be better suited to another vacant post.

(e) The volume of administration and the need for specialist knowledge (notably of changing legal and industrial relations requirements) may suggest a specialist function.

(f) Standardisation and central control should arguably be applied to, for example, equal opportunities, pay provisions and performance standards, where fairness and consistency must be seen to operate.

6   This task is intended to develop your research skills and your awareness of HR practice in a specific organisation. Make it an on-going assignment to gather case study information about the recruitment policies and practices of organisations that interest you…

7   The job analyst will need to gain their confidence by:

(a) Communicating: explaining the process, methods and purpose of the appraisal

(b) Being thorough and competent in carrying out the analysis

(c) Respecting the work flow of the department, which should not be disrupted

(d) Giving feedback on the results of the appraisal, and the achievement of its objectives. If staff are asked to co-operate in developing a framework for office training, and then never hear anything more about it, they are unlikely to be responsive on a later occasion

8 Competencies:

- Likely to be demonstrated: eg leadership, initiative, ability to work with others, ability to work under (or without) supervision

- Likely to predict job performance: eg motivation to achieve, specific technical skills related to the job (numeracy, computer use)

- Assessable: eg team building (asking candidates to describe when they have successfully built a team), problem analysis (asking candidates to analyse and suggest solutions to a case study scenario), conflict resolution (asking a candidate to role play a mediator in an industrial conflict scenario)

9 Some of the media you may have come up with include the following.

(a)	Newspapers and journals (trade, professional) – ie 'Press' media	• Journals better targeted, papers offer wider local or national coverage • Wider and more targeted coverage – higher cost: cost-effectiveness must be monitored, controlled • May offer opportunity to produce own artwork – may not (control required)
(b)	Cinema, radio, TV – ie 'broadcast' media	• Can offer general marketing opportunity • Powerful all-senses effect • Expensive (especially TV) • Mass coverage (option of local) • Appeal to young audience
(c)	Posters, leaflets, notices on notice boards (+ multi-media equivalents: cassettes, videos)	• Targeting through positioning only • Can be expensive, hit-and-miss, long timescale • Content/style controlled by organisation
(d)	Exhibitions, conferences, roadshows, open-days, presentations	• If well targeted location, can reach large number of relevant people • Opportunities for non-committal networking, exploration • Immediacy of face-to-face communication – but also a risk • Can be expensive to organise/delegate
(e)	Websites	• Untargeted (except to IT-literate) • Controllable • Relatively low-cost • Opportunity for general marketing

10 This is a research exercise. You may like to print out some of your findings for your portfolio or assignment bibliography.

11 (a) Answer spaces too small to contain the information asked for

(b) Forms which are (or look) so lengthy or complicated that prospective applicants either complete them perfunctorily or give up (and apply to another employer instead)

BPP
LEARNING MEDIA

(c) Illegal (eg discriminatory) or offensive questions

(d) Lack of clarity as to what (and how much) information is required

12 Connock suggests that a framework such as that shown below be used to determine the cost per person appointed for each method.

Source of application	Number of applications	Number of shortlisted candidates	Number offered job	Number commenced employment	Total cost	Cost per head appointed
Local press advert National press advert Specialist press advert Leaflet drop etc						
Total						

Chapter 4:
SELECTION

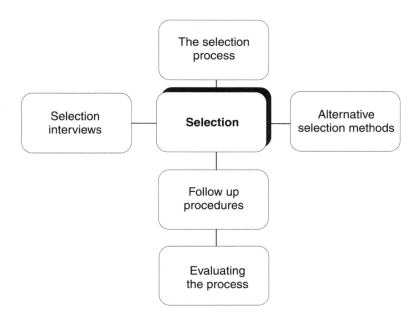

Introduction

The Introduction to Chapter 3 introduced the idea of selection. Selection: the part of the employee resourcing process which leads naturally on from recruitment. It involves identifying the most suitable of the candidates attracted by recruitment efforts. (In practice, this may be a negative process of weeding out people who are *unsuitable* for the job or organisation – or people for whom the job or organisation may be unsuitable.)

The selection of the right candidate(s) is of vital importance. No organisation would like to find a 'star' employee for a competing organisation on its rejection list, any more than it wants an employee who can't do the job and doesn't 'fit in' – however perfect they may have seemed in the interview! Various selection methods are used to try to reduce the risks of either event by gathering as much relevant information about the candidate as possible. In this chapter we look at how this can be done.

Your objectives

In this chapter you will learn about the following.

(a) The aims and objectives of the selection process

(b) The selection interview

(c) A range of alternative selection methods to supplement the interview

(d) The legislative framework and benchmark evidence guiding the selection process

1   THE SELECTION PROCESS

1.1   The aims and objectives of selection

The overall aim of the selection process is to identify candidates who are suitable for the vacancy or wider requirements of the HR plan (eg in regard to workforce diversity).

Within this aim, there may be a number of subsidiary goals.

(a)   To predict, as accurately as possible, the future or potential job performance of candidates.

(b)   To compare, as validly as possible, one candidate with another, to find 'best fit' between applicants and the organisation's needs.

(c)   To inform candidates, as accurately and attractively as possible, about the organisation, the job, the psychological contract of employment and likely future prospects, in order to:

    (i)   Facilitate self-selection by the candidates

    (ii)   Facilitate subsequent adjustment by the successful candidate, minimising disappointment and induction crisis and supporting retention.

(d)   To give the best possible impression of the organisation as a potential employer: creating a brand as 'employer of choice' in an industry or sector, or in competition with other potential employers.

(e)   To comply with legislation, policy and organisational values in regard to equal opportunity, fair treatment and professionalism in dealing with candidates.

(f)   To provide information for other HRM processes, such as employee induction and development, or the evaluation of the selection process itself.

1.2   A systematic approach to selection

A typical selection system will include the following basic procedures.

(a)   Take any **initial steps** required. If the decision to interview or reject cannot be made immediately, a standard letter of acknowledgement might be sent, as a courtesy, to each applicant. It may be that the job advertisement required applicants to write to the personnel manager with personal details and to request an application form: this would then be sent to applicants for completion and return.

(b)   Set each application against **key criteria** in the job advertisement and specification. Critical factors may include age, qualifications, experience or whatever.

(c)   **Sort applications** into 'possible', 'unsuitable' and 'marginal'.

(d)   'Possibles' will then be more closely scrutinised, and a **shortlist for interview** drawn up. Ideally, this should be done by both the HR specialist and the prospective manager of the successful candidate, who will have more immediate knowledge of the type of person that will fit into the culture and activities of the department.

(e) Invite candidates for **interviews** (requiring them to complete an application form, if this has not been done at an earlier stage).

(f) Interview potentially qualified candidates.

(g) Reinforce interviews with **selection testing** and other mechanisms where required.

(h) Check the **references** of short-listed candidates.

(i) Institute **follow-up procedures** for successful applicants.

    (i) Make an **offer of employment**, negotiating terms and conditions if appropriate.

    (ii) Draw up a **contract** or **written particulars of employment**.

    (iii) Arrange **work permits** and related issues of residency, if required by cross-border recruitment.

    (iv) Plan initial **induction** into the organisation and provide preparatory information.

(j) Review un-interviewed 'possibles', and 'marginals', and put potential future candidates on **hold** or in reserve.

(k) Send standard letters to **unsuccessful applicants**, informing them that they have not been successful.

(l) Keep **records** of criteria and processes used in decision-making, both for evaluation – and to provide evidence of fair dealing if required to counter a claim of discrimination.

1.3 The legal framework on selection

Discrimination

Detailed provisions in regard to equal opportunities will be discussed in Part B of this Course Book, since it is an area of relevance throughout HR policy and practice. However, in regard to selection, you should be aware of the following.

(a) **Application forms** should include no questions which are not work-related (such as marital or domestic details) unless they are asked of all applicants/groups.

(b) **Medical references** should not be required exclusively from older applicants.

(c) **Interview procedures** and documentation should be carefully controlled to avoid discrimination. For example:

    (i) A non work-related question must be asked of all candidates, if any, and even then, should not imply discriminatory intent (by asking only women about care of dependants, or about hormonal influences on moods, say)

    (ii) At least one representative of both sexes and all races of applicants should be invited for interview

(iii) Detailed notes of proceedings, criteria and decisions should be made in order to furnish justification in the event of a claim of discrimination.

(d) **Selection tests** should demonstrably avoid favouring particular groups (although this is a contentious area, as we will see in Paragraph 3.3 below).

Remember, as discussed in Chapter 3, that current UK legislation outlaws discrimination on the grounds of sex, or change of sex, sexual orientation and marital status; colour, race, nationality, ethnic or national origin; disability; religious belief and age. In the selection context, there is also legislation protecting offenders whose convictions have been 'spent' after a period of time (which varies according to the severity of the offence).

Activity 1   **(15 minutes)**

The following is a classic IQ test question.

'Which is the odd man out?

MEASLES, STEAMER, LEAVE, OMELETTE, COURAGE.'

(a) What is the answer?
(b) How might this question discriminate against certain tested groups?

Privacy and data protection

The gathering of data in the application and selection process is also a sensitive area. In the UK the Data Protection Act 1998 has been implemented in stages up to 2007 – but retrospectively affects all record systems set up on or after 24 October 1998. Major provisions include the following.

(a) The right of employees to access their personnel files, to be informed of the purpose for which data is being collected about them, and to approve the use of that data for any other purposes.

(b) Requirements for the adequacy, up-to-dateness and security of information (particularly if it is to be exported outside the European Economic Area).

(c) Additional safeguards on the collection of data about race, ethnic origin, religious or political beliefs, union membership, health, sexual orientation or criminal activities (except for the purposes of monitoring racial equality).

EXAMPLE

A US retailer testing some 2,500 applicants for security jobs, required applicants to answer intimate personal questions in a pre-employment psychological examination, but was later forced to pay more than $2 million to settle a lawsuit over the test, which included 'true or false?' questions such as:

- I have never indulged in any unusual sexual practices
- I am very strongly attracted by members of my own sex
- I believe my sins are unpardonable
- I feel sure there is only one true religion

The employer argued in court that the test was necessary to screen out applicants who are emotionally unstable, unreliable, and resistant to established rules, as well as applicants with addictive or violent tendencies who might put customers or other employees at risk.'...

(From *Bulletin to Management*, 1993, cited by Shuler, 1995)

FOR DISCUSSION

Aside from the actual outcome of the case example cited above, how far do you think a test of this kind is:

(a) Useful or effective (and with what intention)? and

(b) Ethically reprehensible (and on what grounds)?

To the extent that the employer's concerns are genuine, what other means of screening might or should they employ?

We will now go on to outline some of the methods by which selections can be made.

1.4 Selection methods

Various techniques are available, depending on the policy and criteria of selection in each case.

(a) **Interviews**. These may be variously structured (one-to-one, panel, sequential), and using various criteria of job relevance (application details, skills and competences, critical incident/situational questions) and scoring methods (general impressions, criteria ratings). As the most **popular** of methods, interviews will be considered in detail below.

(b) **Evaluation of education and experience**, comparing application data to job requirements.

(c) **Selection testing**. Written tests of ability and aptitude (cognitive and/or mechanical), personality and so on are increasingly used, alongside work sample tests which simulate job related activities (such as typing or copy writing tests) and examination of portfolios of work (eg for architects or photographers). Tests are also discussed in more detail below.

(d) **Background and reference checks**, in order to verify application claims as to qualifications, previous employment record and reasons for leaving and so on. References will be discussed in Section 5 of this chapter.

(e) **Biodata analysis**. Biodata (biographical data) is gathered via multiple choice questions on family background, life experiences, attitudes and preferences. The results are compared against an 'ideal' profile based on correlations with effective job performance.

(f) **Handwritten analysis,** or graphology. Handwriting is said to indicate up to 300 character traits of the individual. There is no scientific evidence of its predictive accuracy, but it is popular in Europe and to a lesser extent in the USA and Australia. (In general, handwritten covering letters are requested as a useful general indicator of orderly thinking, presentation and so on.)

(g) **Group selection methods,** or **assessment centres,** allowing the assessment of team-working, leadership, problem-solving and communication skills through the use of group discussions, role plays, business games and 'in-tray' simulations. These are discussed below.

(h) **Physical/medical testing**. Medical examinations are often one of the final steps in selection, to ensure fitness for work (and avoid compensation claims for pre-existing injuries or conditions). Specific tests – for example, testing for HIV/AIDS (subject to strict policy guidelines, and mindful of discrimination), drug and/or alcohol abuse or genetic sensitivity to workplace chemicals – may also be used for particular job categories: subject to privacy, data protection and equal opportunity (eg in regard to age) principles.

Activity 2 (20 minutes)

How accurate do you think the above-listed methods are at predicting job performance and suitability?

A number of research studies have attempted to measure how popular and how effective various techniques are.

- **Effectiveness** is measured according to the '**predictive validity**' scale, which ranges from 1 (the technique unfailingly predicts candidates' subsequent job performance) to 0 (the technique is no better than random chance at predicting candidates' subsequent job performance).

- **Popularity** is measured by the % of surveyed companies that use the technique.

  (a) Rank the following techniques in order from most popular to least popular, from what you might anticipate.

  (b) For each, add a number between 0.00 and 1.00 to indicate what you think their predictive validity might be.

Techniques: Personality tests, references, work sampling, interviews, assessment centres, cognitive tests, graphology, biodata.

We will now look at each of the three major techniques in turn.

2   SELECTION INTERVIEWS

2.1   Types of interview

Individual or **one-to-one interviews** are the most common selection method. They offer the advantages of direct face-to-face communication, and opportunity to establish **rapport** between the candidate and interviewer: each has to give his attention solely to the other, and there is potentially a relaxed atmosphere, if the interviewer is willing to establish an informal style.

The disadvantage of a one-to-one interview is the scope it allows for a biased or superficial decision.

(a)   The candidate may be able to disguise lack of knowledge in a specialist area of which the interviewer himself knows little.

(b)   The interviewer's perception may be selective or distorted (see Paragraph 2.4 below), and this lack of objectivity may go unnoticed and unchecked.

(c)   The greater opportunity for personal rapport with the candidate may cause a weakening of the interviewer's objective judgement.

Panel interviews are designed to overcome the above disadvantages. A panel may consist of two or three people who together interview a single candidate: most commonly, an HR specialist and the candidate's future boss. This may be more daunting for the candidate (depending on the tone and conduct of the interview) but it has several advantages.

(a)   The HR and line specialists can gather the information they each need about the candidate and give him or her the various information(s)he requires from each of them at one sitting.

(b)   The interviewers make a joint assessment of the candidate's abilities, and behaviour at the interview. Personal bias is more likely to be guarded against, and checked if it does emerge.

Large formal panels, or **selection boards,** may also be convened where there are a number of individuals or groups with an interest in the selection. This has the advantage of allowing a number of people to see the candidate, and to share information about him at a single meeting: similarly, they can compare their assessments on the spot, without a subsequent effort at liaison and communication.

Offsetting these administrative advantages, however, there are some drawbacks to selection boards.

(a)   Questions tend to be more varied, and more random. Candidates may have trouble switching from one topic to another so quickly, and may not be allowed time to expand their answers in such as way as to do justice to themselves.

(b)   Some candidates may not perform well in a formal, artificial situation such as a board interview, and may find such a situation extremely stressful. The interview will thus not show the best qualities of someone who might nevertheless be highly effective in the work context.

(c)   Board interviews favour individuals who are confident, and who project an immediate and strong image: those who are articulate, dress well and so on. First impressions of such a candidate may cover underlying faults or shortcomings.

> **Activity 3** (20 minutes)
>
> In some cases, there may be the option of **sequential interviewing**: instead of, say, four people on a panel spending an hour with each of four candidates, the members might each spend an hour alone with each candidate. The panel could then take its selection decision in the light of the information obtained at the separate interviews.
>
> What do you think would be the pros and cons of this approach?

2.2 Preparing interviews

In brief, the factors to be considered with regard to conducting selection interviews are:

(a) The impression of the organisation given by the interview arrangements

(b) The psychological effects of the location of the interview, seating arrangements and manner of the interviewer(s)

(c) The extent to which the candidate can be encouraged to talk freely (by asking open questions) and honestly (by asking probing questions), in accordance with the organisation's need for information

(d) The opportunity for the candidate to learn about the job and organisation

(e) The control of bias or hasty judgement by the interviewer

The interview is a two-way process, but the **interviewer** must have a clear idea of what it is intended to achieve, and must be in sufficient control of the process to cover the required ground.

The **interview** agenda and questions will be based on:

• The job description, competence profile and/or person specification setting out the job/role requirements

• The information supplied by the candidate in the application form, CV and covering letter

The interview process should be efficiently run to make a favourable impression on the candidates and to avoid unnecessary stress (unless ability to handle pressure is a selection criterion!). The interview room should be free from distraction and interruption.

2.3 Interviewer skills and questioning techniques

> **Activity 4**   **(30 minutes)**
>
> Think back to a selection interview you have had, for a job, school or place at your university/college.
>
> (a) What sort of interview did you have: one-to-one, panel, formal or informal?
>
> (b) What impression of the organisation did you get from the whole process?
>
> (c) How well-conducted was the interview, looking back on it?
>
> (d) What efforts (if any) were made to put you at your ease?

'Interviews are so common that they are often taken for granted. People view interviews as simply conversations during which information is gathered. While interviews are similar to conversations, there are important differences. An interview is a specialised form of conversation conducted for a specific task-related purpose.' (Whetton & Cameron, 2002).

Whetton & Cameron identify the following key skills for interviewers.

(a) Creating **effective questions**, arising out of a clear purpose and agenda, with the aim of eliciting the information required.

(b) Creating an **appropriate climate** for information sharing, using supportive communication techniques, such as:

   • Rapport building, establishing trust and relationship

   • Active listening, using attentive body language and responsive verbal behaviours (eg summarising, clarifying)

   • Introducing the interview in a way that establishes a positive tone and orients the candidate as to how the interview will be conducted.

(c) Using **question types** intentionally, in order to control the pace and direction of the interview, remaining responsive to the replies given by the candidate. (This is discussed further below.)

(d) Using and interpreting **non-verbal cues**, or 'body language' (dress, posture, eye contact, gestures, facial expressions).

(e) Being willing, and able, to identify shallow or unconvincing responses, and to **probe and challenge** when necessary: in other words, critically evaluating the candidate's responses.

(f) Being alert to the influence of first impressions, stereotypes and other forms of potential **bias**.

NOTES

EXAMPLE

Whetton & Cameron (2002) cite a six-step process used by a major firm (un-named) outlining an effective interview process.

'PEOPLE-oriented Selection Interview Process'

P   Prepare

   1   Review application, CV and other background information
   2   Prepare both general and individual-specific questions
   3   Prepare suitable physical arrangements

E   Establish Rapport

   1   Try to make applicant comfortable
   2   Convey genuine interest
   3   Communicate supportive attitude with voice and names

O   Obtain Information

   1   Ask questions
   2   Probe
   3   Listen carefully
   4   Observe the person (dress, mannerisms, body language)

P   Provide Information

   1   Describe current and future job opportunities
   2   Sell positive features of firm
   3   Respond to applicant's questions

L   Lead to Close

   1   Clarify responses
   2   Provide an opportunity for final applicant input
   3   Explain what happens next

E   Evaluate

   1   Assess match between technical qualifications and job requirements
   2   Judge personal qualities (leadership, maturity, team orientation)
   3   Make a recommendation

A variety of question styles may be used, to different effects.

   (a)   **Open questions** or open-ended questions ('Who...? What...? Where...? When...? Why...?') force interviewees to put together their own responses in complete sentences. This encourages the interviewee to talk, keeps the interview flowing, and is most revealing ('Why do you want to be in HR?')

   (b)   **Probing questions** are similar to open questions in their phrasing but aim to discover the deeper significance of the candidate's experience or achievements. (If a candidate claimed to have had 'years of relevant experience', in a covering letter, the interviewer might need to ask 'How many years?', or 'Which particular jobs or positions do you consider relevant and how?')

(c) **Closed questions** are the opposite, inviting only 'yes' or 'no' answers: ('Did you...?', 'Have you...?'). A closed question has the following effects.

  (i) It elicits answers only to the question asked by the interviewer. This may be useful where there are small points to be established ('Did you pass your exam?') but there may be other questions and issues that (s)he has not anticipated but will emerge if the interviewee is given the chance to expand ('How did you think your studies went?').

  (ii) It does not allow interviewees to express their personality, so that interaction can take place on a deeper level.

  (iii) It makes it easier for interviewees to conceal things ('You never *asked* me....').

  (iv) It makes the interviewer work very hard!

(d) **Multiple questions** are just that: two or more questions are asked at once. ('Tell me about your last job? How did your knowledge of HRM help you there, and do you think you are up-to-date or will you need to spend time studying?') This type of question can be used to encourage the candidate to talk at some length, but not to stray too far from the point. It might also test the candidate's ability to listen and handle large amounts of information, but should be used judiciously in this case.

(e) **Problem solving or situational questions** present candidates with a situation and ask them to explain how they would deal with it or how they have dealt with it in the past. ('How would you motivate your staff to do a task that they did not want to do?' or 'Can you tell us about a time when you were successful about setting a goal and achieving it?') Such questions are used to establish whether the candidate will be able to deal with the sort of problems that are likely to arise in the job, or whether (s)he has sufficient technical knowledge. Whetten and Cameron (2002) suggest asking negative questions as well as positive ('Now tell us about a time you *failed* to meet a goal you set. How could you have done better?') in order to expose hidden bias.

(f) **Leading questions** lead the interviewee to give a certain reply. ('We are looking for somebody who likes detailed figure work. How much do you enjoy dealing with numbers?' a 'Don't you agree that...?' 'Surely...?')

The danger with this type of question is that interviewees will give the answer they think the interviewer wants to hear, but it might legitimately be used to deal with highly reticent or nervous candidates, simply to encourage them to talk.

Activity 5   **(20 minutes)**

Identify the type of question used in the following examples, and discuss the opportunities and constraints they offer the interviewee who must answer them.

(a) 'So you're interested in a business studies degree, are you, Jo?'

(b) 'Surely you're not interested in business studies, Jo?'

(c) 'How about a really useful qualification like a Business Studies degree Jo? Would you consider that?'

(d) 'Why are you interested in a Business Studies degree, Jo?'

(e) 'Why *particularly* Business Studies, Jo?'

Candidates should also be given the opportunity to **ask questions**. Indeed, well-prepared candidates will go into an interview knowing what questions they want to ask. Their choice of questions might well have some influence on how the interviewers finally assess them. Moreover, there is information that the candidate will need to know about the organisation and the job, and about:

(a) Terms and conditions of employment (although negotiations about detailed terms may not take place until a provisional offer has been made) and

(b) The next step in the selection process – whether there are further interviews, when a decision might be made, or which references might be taken up.

Having said all this, why did interviews score so badly on the predictive validity scale? (See our answer to Activity 2, if you have not already done so.) Despite their popularity, they have a number of limitations...

2.4 Limitations of interviews

Interviews are criticised because they fail to provide accurate predictions of how a person will perform in the job. The main reasons why this might be so are as follows.

(a) **Limited scope**. An interview is necessarily too brief to 'get to know' candidates in the kind of depth required to make an accurate prediction of their behaviour in any given situation.

(b) **Limited relevance**. Interviews that lack structure and focus may fail to elicit information that is relevant to the candidate's likely future performance in the job and compatibility with the organisation.

(c) **Artificiality**. An interview is an artificial situation: candidates may be 'on their best behaviour' or, conversely, so nervous that they do not do themselves justice. Neither situation reflects what the person is 'really like'.

d) **Errors of judgement** by interviewers. These include:

  (i) The **halo effect** – a tendency for people to make an initial general judgement about a person based on a single obvious attribute, such as being neatly dressed, or well-spoken, which will colour later perceptions.

  (ii) **Contagious bias** – a process whereby an interviewer changes the behaviour or responses of the applicant by suggestion, through the wording of questions or non-verbal cues.

  (iii) **Logical error**. For example, an interviewer might place too much emphasis on isolated strengths or weaknesses, or draw unwarranted conclusions from facts (confusing career mobility with disloyalty, say).

(e) **Lack of skill and experience by interviewers.** For example:

  • Inability to take control of the direction and length of the interview

  • A reluctance to probe into facts and challenge statements where necessary.

3 SELECTION TESTING

3.1 Types of tests

In many job selection procedures, an interview is now supplemented by some form of selection test.

Cushway (1994) lists six criteria which such tests should satisfy.

1 A sensitive measuring instrument that discriminates between subjects.
2 Standardised, so that an individual's score can be related to others.
3 Reliable, in that it always measures the same thing.
4 Valid, in that the test measures what it is designed to measure.
5 Acceptable to the candidate.
6 Non-discriminatory.

The science of measuring mental capacities and processes is called 'psychometrics'; hence the term **'psychometric testing'**. There are five types of test commonly used in practice.

Intelligence or cognitive ability tests

These are tests of general cognitive ability which typically test memory, ability to think quickly (perceptual speed, verbal fluency) and logically (inductive reasoning), and problem solving skills. Reliance on such criteria has shown steady increase, perhaps because of uncertainty in UK employers' minds about the validity of A-level and GCSE results, the wide variation in degree classes between higher educational institutions and the difficulties of comparing international qualifications.

Most people have experience of IQ tests, and few would dispute their validity as good measures of general intellectual performance.

Aptitude tests

Aptitude tests are designed to predict an individual's **potential** for performing a job or learning new skills. There are various accepted areas of aptitude, as follows.

(a) **Reasoning** – verbal, numerical and abstract/visual (eg accuracy and speed in arithmetical calculations, naming or making words, identifying shapes)

(b) **Spatio-visual ability** – practical intelligence, non-verbal ability and creative ability (eg ability to solve mechanical puzzles)

(c) **Perceptual speed and accuracy** – eg clerical ability (identifying non-identical pairs of numbers)

(d) **'Psycho-motor' ability** – mechanical, manual, musical and athletic: ability to respond accurately and rapidly to stimuli (eg pressing lighted buttons), using controlled muscular adjustments and/or finger dexterity and so on.

With a few possible exceptions, most of the areas of aptitude mentioned above are fairly easily measurable: so long as it is possible to determine what particular aptitudes are required for a job, such tests are likely to be useful for selection.

Personality tests

Personality tests may measure a variety of characteristics, such as applicants' skill in dealing with other people, ambition, motivation or emotional stability. Probably the best known example is the 16PF, originally developed by Cattell in 1950 and was described (in *People Management*) as follows.

> The 16PF comprises 16 scales, each of which measures a factor that influences the way a person behaves.

> The factors are functionally different underlying personality characteristics, and each is associated with not just one single piece of behaviour but rather is the source of a relatively broad range of behaviours. For this reason the factors themselves are referred to as source traits and the behaviours associated with them are called surface traits.

> The advantage of measuring source traits, as the 16PF does, is that you end up with a much richer understanding of the person because you are not just describing what can be seen but also the characteristics underlying what can be seen.

> The 16PF analyses how a person is likely to behave generally, including, for example, contributions likely to be made to particular work contexts, aspects of the work environment to which the person is likely to be more or less suited, and how best to manage the person.

Other examples include the Myers-Briggs Type Indicator ®(mostly intended for self-development purposes), the Minnesota Multiphasic Personality Inventory (MMPI) and the FIRO-B personality profile. The validity of such tests has been much debated, but it seems that some have been shown by research to be valid predictors of job performance, so long as they are used and interpreted properly. A test may indicate that a candidate is introverted, has creative ability and is pragmatic – but this is only of use if this combination of characteristics can be linked to success or failure in the type of work for which the candidate is being considered.

Weblink

British Test Publishers Association

▶▶ http//www.btpa.org.uk

Another area of current interest (which falls somewhere between personality, aptitude and intelligence testing) is the concept of **emotional intelligence**.

Definition

> The capacity for **emotional intelligence (EQ)** is recognising our own feelings and those of others, for motivating ourselves, and for managing emotions well in ourselves and in our relationships.
> (Goleman, 1998)

Goleman argues that: 'the more complex the job, the more emotional intelligence matters – if only because a deficiency in these abilities can hinder the use of whatever technical expertise or intellect a person may have'. Emotional competence accounts for some 70% of the competences listed by an organisation as essential for effective performance. They also correlate strongly with managerial success, labour stability completion of training and promotability (Whetten & Cameron, 2002; Goleman, 1998).

Goleman (and others) have published **Emotional Competence Assessment** questionnaires for each of the fiver key domains of EQ: self awareness, self regulation, motivation, empathy and social skills.

Proficiency and attainment tests

Proficiency tests are perhaps the most closely related to an assessor's objectives, because they measure ability to do the work involved. An applicant for an audio typist's job, for example, might be given a dictation tape and asked to type it. This is a type of attainment test, in that it is designed to measure abilities or skills already acquired by the candidate.

Activity 6   **(30 minutes)**

What kind of work sample or proficiency tests would you devise for the following categories of employee? For each, state whether your test is a physical, verbal or mental test.

(a) Administrative assistants
(b) Construction supervisors
(c) Airline pilots
(d) Magazine editors
(e) Telephone operators

EXAMPLE

'A government agency has adopted innovative recruitment techniques by using psychometric tests to measure how well candidates fit in with the public-sector culture.

'And other public-sector organisations could soon follow suit, after the *Environment Agency* revealed the move had dramatically reduced staff turnover rates.

'The agency overhauled its recruitment for environmental officers, following retention problems. Candidates are now sent to assessment centres specifically to evaluate whether they have the "personality and qualities to work in the public sector" …

' "Understanding the public-sector ethos is being increasingly recognised as important and as necessary to getting the right skills … It is certainly harder to train people in those behavioural attributes than it is to train them in the technical side." '

Watkins (2003)(b)

3.2 Limitations of psychometric testing

Psychometric testing has grown in popularity in recent years, but you should be aware of certain drawbacks.

(a) There is not always a direct (let alone predictive) relationship between ability in the test and ability in the job: the job situation is very different from artificial test conditions.

(b) The interpretation of test results is a skilled task, for which training and experience is essential. It is also highly subjective (particularly in the case of personality tests), which belies the apparent scientific nature of the approach.

(c) Additional difficulties are experienced with particular kinds of test. For example:

(i) An aptitude test measuring arithmetical ability would need to be constantly revised or its content might become known to later applicants.

(ii) Personality tests can often give misleading results because applicants seem able to guess which answers will be looked at most favourably.

(iii) It is difficult to design intelligence tests which give a fair chance to people from different cultures and social groups and which test the *kind* of intelligence that the organisation wants from its employees: the ability to score highly in IQ tests does not necessarily correlate with desirable traits such as mature judgement or creativity, merely mental agility. In addition, 'practice makes perfect': most tests are subject to coaching and practice effects.

(d) It is difficult to exclude discrimination and bias from tests. Many tests (including personality tests) are tackled less successfully by women than by men, or by immigrants than by locally-born applicants because of the particular aspects chosen for testing. This may make their use indirectly discriminatory.

The most recent edition of the 16PF test, for example has been scrutinised by expert psychologists 'to exclude certain types of content, such as dated material, content that might lead to bias, material that might be unacceptable in an organisational setting and anything considered to be strongly socially desirable or undesirable'.

FOR DISCUSSION

'Among the qualities which neither the interview nor intelligence tests are able to assess accurately are the candidate's ability to get on with and influence his colleagues, to display qualities of spontaneous leadership and to produce ideas in a real-life situation.'

(Plumbley)

Why might this be a drawback? What can be done about it?

4   GROUP SELECTION METHODS

4.1   Techniques in group selection

Group selection methods or **assessment centres** might be used by an organisation as the final stage of a selection process for high-value jobs (since they are comparatively expensive to run). They consist of a series of tests, interviews and group situations over a period of two days, involving a small number of candidates (typically six to eight).

Group selection methods are appropriate for assessing the following.

(a)   **Social skills** such as sensitivity to the views and opinions of others, reaction to disagreement and criticism, and the ability to influence and persuade others

(b)   **Intellectual skills** such as the consideration of the merits and demerits of other arguments put forward and the ability to think clearly (particularly at short notice), situational problem-solving and so on

(c)   **Attitudes,** such as political, racial or religious views, and attitude to authority, particularly where these may be relevant to a potential employee's efficiency at work.

Typical techniques used in group selection include:

(a)   Group **role-play** exercises, in which candidates can explore (and hopefully display) interpersonal skills and/or work through simulated managerial tasks

(b)   **Case studies,** where candidates' analytical and problem-solving abilities are tested in working through described situations/problems, as well as their interpersonal skills, in taking part in (or leading) group discussions of the case study

(c)   **'In-tray' exercises,** simulating a typical work-load to be managed

BPP
LEARNING MEDIA

(d)   **Leaderless discussion groups** (LDGs), allowing leadership skills and issues to emerge freely.

Often what are termed 'leaderless group activities' will be conducted. Such activities can be used to assess the leadership potential of job applicants in uncertain situations with no formal power structure. The group is presented with a topic for discussion and given a defined period of time to reach a conclusion. The topic may be related to the job in question, and may either be of a problem-solving nature ('Should product X be developed given the following marketing and financial information?') or more general ('Is capital punishment an effective deterrent?'). The contribution made by individual candidates will be scored according to factors such as assertiveness, quality of thought and expression, analytical skill, and the ability to lead the group towards a decision.

Another method of assessment involves giving candidates a typical job problem to solve individually in a set time, at the end of which each candidate has to present and justify his or her solution to the other members of the group.

EXAMPLE

The **Virgin Atlantic** careers website outlines its selection methods for prospective candidates is as follows.

Assessment Centres

An Assessment Centre is a method of assessing the strengths and development needs of candidates. They generally last for all or part of a day and they're made up of a number of exercises.

For positions in Cabin Crew, In-Flight Beauty Therapist, Airports and Contact Centre there will be some kind of assessment centre, which will contain some of the following elements:

- Group decision
- Role plays
- Analysis presentation
- Ability tests, such as numerical reasoning
- Behavioural/biographical interview

Group discussions

These are useful in assessing candidates who are applying for roles with a strong element of teamwork.

Ability tests

These measure certain abilities or aptitudes and usually involve some kind of scoring that will indicate the level of your ability in the area being tested or your potential to lean more.

Behavioural/biographical interviews

In a behavioural interview you will be asked to give specific examples of situations that you have dealt with and what the outcomes were.

At a biographical interview you will be asked to discuss your CV and employent history, outlining what you have done, what your achievements are and how/why you have made your career choices.

4.2 Purposes of group selection

Group sessions might be useful because:

(a)   They give selectors a longer opportunity to study the candidates.

(b)   They reveal more than application forms, interviews and tests alone about the ability of candidates to persuade others, negotiate with others, and explain ideas to others and also to investigate problems efficiently. These are typically management skills.

(c)   They reveal more about how candidates' personalities and attributes will affect the work team and their own performance.

(d)   They achieve some measure of comparability between candidates.

(e)   The pooled judgement of the panel of assessors is likely to be more accurate than the judgement of a single interviewer.

We will now look at some of the later considerations in the selection process, bringing the candidate through to a contract of employment.

Activity 7   **(1 hour)**

For an organisation of your choice, find out:

(a) What selection methods are used, and for what kinds of jobs
(b) The policies or guidelines given for the use of these methods

---

5   FOLLOW UP PROCEDURES

5.1   Reference checking

References provide further confidential information about the prospective employee, although it may be of varying value: the reliability of all but the most factual information must be questioned. A reference should contain:

(a)   Straightforward factual information confirming the nature of the applicant's previous job(s), period of employment, pay, and circumstances of leaving.

(b)   Opinions about the applicant's personality and other attributes. These should obviously be treated with some caution. Allowances should be made for prejudice (favourable or unfavourable), charity (withholding detrimental remarks), and possibly fear of being actionable for libel (although references are privileged, as long as they are factually correct and devoid of malice).

At least two **employer** references are desirable, providing necessary factual information, and comparison of personal views. (**Personal** references tell the prospective employer little more than that the applicant has a friend or two.)

If a judgement of character and suitability is desired, it might be most tellingly formulated as the question: 'Would you re-employ this individual? (If not, why not?)'

Telephone references may be time-saving, if standard reference letters or forms are not available. They may also elicit a more honest opinion than a carefully prepared written statement. For this reason, a telephone call may also be made to check a very glowing or very reluctant reference...

(Note that when **giving** references, caution is also required. A landmark legal judgement in *Spring v Guardian Assurance plc 1995*, decided that an employer owes a duty of care to employees in relation to giving a reference, and in obtaining the information upon which the reference is based. On the other hand, an employer could face civil liability from a company which suffered economic loss as a result of hiring an employee on the basis of a false complimentary reference!)

Activity 8	(10 minutes)

At the end of a recent selection process one candidate was, in the view of everyone involved, outstanding. However, you have just received a very bad reference from her current employer. What do you do?

5.2 The offer of employment

Assuming that the 'right' candidate has by now been identified, an offer of employment can be made. Time may be sensitive, so it is common for an **oral offer** to be made, with a negotiated period for consideration and acceptance: this can then be followed up with a written offer, if appropriate.

(a) All terms, conditions and circumstances of the offer must at this point be clearly stated.

(b) Any provisos ('subject to... satisfactory references, medical examination, negotiation of contract terms', or whatever) must also be clearly set out.

(c) Negotiable aspects of the offer and timetables for acceptance should be set out, in order to control the closing stages of the process.

The organisation should be prepared for its offer to be rejected at this stage. Applicants may have received and accepted other offers. They may not have been attracted by their first-hand view of the organisation, and may have changed their mind about applying; they may only have been testing the water in applying in the first place, gauging the market for their skills and experience for future reference, or seeking a position of strength from which to bargain with their present employers. A small number of eligible applicants should therefore be kept in reserve.

5.3 Contracts of employment

Once the offer of employment has been confirmed and accepted, the contract of employment can be prepared and offered.

A contract of employment may be written, oral or a mixture of the two. Senior personnel may sign a contract specially drafted to include complex terms on matters such as performance-related pay, professional indemnity, confidentiality and restraint of trade.

Others may sign a standard form contract, exchange letters with the new employer or supply agreed terms orally at interview. Each of these situations, subject to the requirements (outlined below) as to written particulars, will form a valid contract of employment, as long as there is mutual agreement on essential terms.

5.4 Written particulars of employment

Although the contract need not be made in writing, the employer must give an employee (who works at least eight hours a week) a written statement of certain particulars of his or her employment, within two months of the beginning of employment (*Employment Rights Act 1996*).

The statement should identify the following.

- The names of **employer** and **employee**
- The **title** of the job which the employee is employed to do
- The **date** on which employment began
- Whether any service with a previous employer forms part of the employee's **continuous period** of employment (for calculation of entitlements)
- **Pay** and **hours of work**
- Any **holiday** and holiday pay, **sick leave** and sick pay entitlements
- **Pension** scheme provisions
- Length of **notice** of **termination** to be given on either side (or expiry date, if employed for a fixed term)
- Details of **disciplinary procedures** and **grievance procedures,** works rules, union of staff association membership
- Rules on **health and safety at work** (by custom only)

It is sufficient to refer to separate booklets or notices (on pension schemes, disciplinary/grievance procedures and so on) where the relevant details can be found: not all the information needs to go in the written statement! The point is to give employees clear, precise information.

6 EVALUATING THE PROCESS

6.1 Evaluating selection

Much the same method can be used to evaluate selection as recruitment: see Paragraph 7 of Chapter 3.

Selection procedures can further be evaluated by determining whether selection decisions seem to have been 'correct' in the light of subsequent job performance, cultural impact and service longevity of the successful candidate.

(a) If tests were used to assess likely potential to perform certain tasks, the retained test results can be compared against actual performance in the job. Regular discrepancies may suggest that the tests are flawed.

(b)   Similar comparisons may be made using interview ratings and notes. Interviewers who consistently fall short in the accuracy of their judgements should be trained accordingly.

Other performance criteria for evaluating selection procedures include:

(a)   Number of candidates (and/or minority/female/disabled candidates) interviewed in relation to applications

(b)   Number of offers made in relation to number of interviews (especially to minority/female/disabled candidates)

(c)   Number of acceptances in relation to offers made

(d)   Number of successful applicants subsequently appraised as competent in the job

(e)   Lead time for successful applicants to be trained to competence

(f)   Number of starters still employed after one year (two years or an appropriate period of measurement)

(g)   Cost of selection methods per starter employed one year later

Chapter roundup

- The contents of this chapter may again be summarised in diagrammatic form.

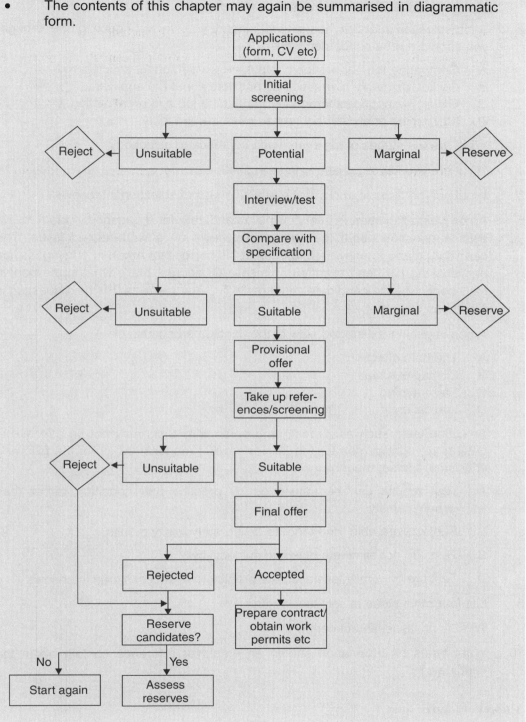

NOTES

Quick quiz

1   What are the aims of selection?

2   A job selection interview has several aims. If you were conducting one, though, you should **not** be concerned with:

    A   Comparing the application against the job/personnel specification
    B   Getting as much information as possible about the applicant
    C   Giving the applicant information about the job and organisation
    D   Making the applicant feel he has been treated fairly

    What are the stages of the systematic approach to selection?

4   What are two key legal issues in selection?

5   What can be done to improve the effectiveness of selection interviews?

6   Amon Leigh-Hewman is interviewing a candidate for a vacancy in his firm. He asks a question about the candidate's views on a work-related issue. The candidate starts to answer, and sees to his horror that Amon in pursing his lips and shaking his head slightly to himself. 'Of course, that's what some people say', continues the candidate, 'but I myself...' Amon smiles. His next question is 'Don't you think that...?

    Amon is getting a distorted view of the candidate because of:

    A   The halo effect
    B   Contagious bias
    C   Stereotyping
    D   Logical error

7   Selection tests such as IQ tests and personality tests may not be effective in getting the right person for the job for several reasons. Which of the following criticisms is false, though?

    A   Test results can be influenced by practice and coaching rather than genuine ability

    B   Subjects are able (and tend) to deliberately falsify results

    C   Tests do not eliminate bias and subjectivity

    D   Test are generally less accurate predictors of success than interviews

8   List four main types of selection testing.

9   What is an 'assessment centre'?

10 What types of information should an employer reference contain about the candidate?

Answers to quick quiz

1   Filling vacancies with best person; informing applicants (to facilitate self-selection and adjustment); creating employer brand; upholding values of fairness and professionalism. (see paragraph 1.1)

2   B. Information needs to be relevant (para 2.1)

3   Set key criteria; compare applications (forms, CV) against criteria; sort and shortlist; acknowledge all responses; invite candidates to interview/selection testing or other methods; check references; issue offer of employment; draw up

contract; obtain work permits (if necessary); plan induction; send standard letters to 'rejects' and 'reserves'. (para 1.2)

4   Discrimination/equal opportunity and privacy/data protection (para 1.3)

5   Planning; relevant criteria; interviewer training and appraisal; structured style of questioning; awareness of potential for bias. (paras 2.2-2.3)

6   B (para 2.4)

7   D. Interviews are generally less accurate. (para 3.1)

8   Cognitive, aptitude, personality, proficiency. (para 3.1)

9   A group selection process, using a series of tests, interviews and group situations and exercises over a period of two days, typically involving 6-8 candidates for a job. (para 4.1)

10   Factual information confirming the nature of the applicant's previous job, period of employment, pay and circumstances of leaving. Opinions (cautious) about the applicant's attributes and employability. (para 5.1)

Answers to activities

1   (a) 'Steamer'. (The others share national connotations: German measles, French leave, Spanish omelette, Dutch courage.)

     (b) The answer presupposes a knowledge of expressions which are rooted in a European context and, in some cases, are old-fashioned and dependent on a middle-class upbringing and education.

2   Influential research by Smith & Abrahamsen (1994) showed the following results.

Method	% use	Predictive validity
Interviews	92	0.17
References	74	0.13
Work sampling	18	0.57
Assessment centres	14	0.40
Personality tests	13	0.40
Cognitive tests	11	0.54
Biodata	4	0.40
Graphology	3	0.00

Employers appear to rely *most* heavily on the least *valid* selection methods!. Interviews, in particular, seem not much better than tossing a coin…

3   Rees (1991) suggested the following points. You may not agree with all of them.

     (a) The method need take no more time for the organisation: in fact single interviews may turn out to take less than an hour.

     (b) Candidates would have to spend more time being interviewed but 'might not mind this if they felt it was a more effective method of selection'.

     (c) It is normally easier to create rapport and coax information out of a person when you are seeing him or her alone.

     (d) However, inexperienced interviewers will be far more 'exposed' than they would have been in a panel interview. They may prefer merely to observe.

NOTES

(e) The method is liable to create more argument about the final decision: the interviewee may be flagging by the end of the session and give a totally different impression to later interviewers.

4 This is personal to your experience: it will help you develop the evidence to show your competence in investigating selection procedures in organisations.

5 (a) Closed. (The only answer is 'yes' or 'no', unless Jo is prepared to expand on it, at his or her own initiative.)

(b) Leading. (Even if Jo was interested, (s)he would get the message that 'yes' would not be what the interviewer wanted, or expected, to hear.)

(c) Leading closed multiple! ('Really useful' leads Jo to think that the 'correct' answer will be 'yes': there is not much opportunity for any other answer, without expanding on it unasked.)

(d) Open. (Jo has to explain, in his or her own words.)

(e) Probing. (Jo has to defend his or her decision.)

6 Here are some suggestions.

		Test
(a)	Admin assistants	Use of specific software or equipment (physical) Dictation (physical) Filing (physical) Letter proof-reading/correction (mental) Telephone answering (verbal)
(b)	Construction supervisors	Plan error recognition (mental) Role play dealing with worker problems (verbal)
(c)	Airline pilots	Rudder control, direction control (physical) Navigational reading (mental) Radio procedures (verbal)
(d)	Magazine editors	Writing headlines (mental) Proof-reading/correction (mental) Page-layout (mental/physical)
(e)	Telephone operators	Switchboard handling (physical/mental) Role play in-coming calls (verbal)

7 This is another investigation opportunity: keep a record for your portfolio.

8 It is quite possible that her current employer is desperate to retain her. Disregard the reference, or question the referee by telephone, and seek another reference from a previous employer if possible.

Chapter 5:
REWARD MANAGEMENT

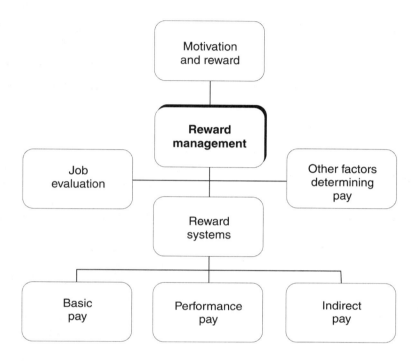

Introduction

'**Reward management** is concerned with the formulation and implementation of strategies and policies that aim to reward people fairly, equitably and consistently in accordance with their value to the organisation. It deals with the 'design, implementation and maintenance of reward practices that are geared to the improvement of organisational, team and individual performance.' (Armstrong, 2003)

Reward management strategies are designed to support the achievement of business objectives, by helping to ensure that the organisation can attract, retain and motivate competent and committed employees.

In this chapter, we will look briefly at the role of reward in the context of motivation theories (a topic of which you may already be aware from your other studies in (*Organisational Behaviour or Management*). We will then go on to explore some key aspects of reward management: how the value of work is determined (by job evaluation) and other determinants affecting pay. We will also look at a variety of financial and non-financial reward systems, as part of the 'total reward' concept.

This chapter discusses several ways in which people can be rewarded differentially according to their *performance*. This theme will be explored further in Chapter 6, where we cover the monitoring of performance – partly for the purposes of allocating rewards.

Your objectives

In this chapter, you will learn about the following.

- (a) The relationship between motivation theory and reward
- (b) The process of job evaluation
- (c) The main factors determining pay levels
- (d) Different types of reward systems, including performance-related pay
- (e) Flexible benefits

1 MOTIVATION AND REWARD

1.1 What is motivation?

The word 'motivation' is commonly used in different contexts to mean:

- (a) The **mental process** of choosing desired outcomes, deciding how to go about them, assessing whether the likelihood of success warrants the amount of effort that will be necessary, and setting in motion the required behaviours. This is sometimes called 'intrinsic motivation', as it arises from factors and processes within the individual.

- (b) The **social process** by which the behaviour of an individual is influenced by others. 'Motivation' in this sense usually applies to the attempts of organisations to maintain or increase workers' effort and commitment by using rewards and punishments. This is sometimes called 'extrinsic motivation', as it arises from actions done to or for the individual by others.

Theories of motivation are often categorised as 'content theories' and 'process theories'

Content theories assume that human beings have an innate package of motives (needs or desired outcomes) which they take action to pursue. They ask: '*What* motivates people?' Maslow's need theory and Herzberg's two-factor theory are two of the most important approaches of this type.

Process theories explore the psychological process through which outcomes become desirable and are pursued by individuals. They ask: '*How* are people motivated?' This approach assumes that people are able to select their goals and choose the paths towards them, by a conscious or unconscious process of calculation. Expectancy theory is a key example.

We will look briefly at these key motivational theories in turn, highlighting the nature of 'rewards' in each.

1.2 Need theory

Need theories suggest that individuals have certain innate needs. When a need is unsatisfied, the individual experiences tension – and acts in pursuit of goals that will satisfy the need.

Abraham Maslow (1954) developed the original and most famous need theory. He argued that Man has five innate needs, which he suggested could be arranged in a 'hierarchy of relative pre-potency': Figure 5.1.

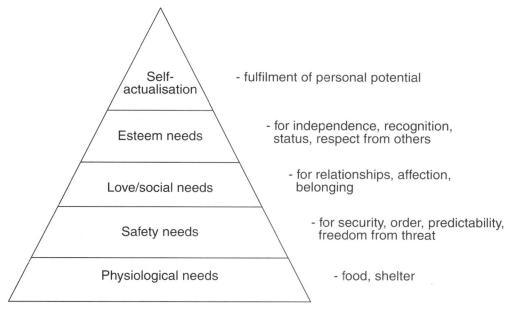

Figure 5.1: Maslow's Hierarchy of Needs

Each level of need is dominant until satisfied: only then does the next level of need become a motivating factor. Maslow regarded self-actualisation as the ultimate human goal: 'the desire to become more and more what one is, to become everything that one is capable of becoming'. It can never be satisfied in full.

Maslow's hierarchy is simple and intuitively attractive: you are unlikely to worry about respect if you are starving! However, it is only a theory, and not derived specifically from work psychology. Empirical verification of the hierarchy is hard to come by. Individuals may select any number of specific goals to satisfy their needs: for example, esteem needs may be satisfied by promotion, or a pay increase – or neither, depending on the individual's values and vocation. Research has also suggested that the hierarchy reflects UK and US cultural values, which may not transfer to other contexts.

Nevertheless, the hierarchy underpins later recognition that people can be motivated at work by **rewards which offer satisfaction of their 'higher order needs'**: esteem (competence, achievement, independence, confidence and their reflection in the perception of others: recognition, appreciation, status, respect) and self-actualisation (challenge, personal development, fulfilment).

1.3 Two factor theory

Frederick Herzberg (1966) interviewed Pittsburgh engineers and accountants about 'critical incidents' which made them feel good or bad about their work. He identified two basic need categories of individuals at work.

- The **need to avoid unpleasantness**, associated with fair treatment in compensation, supervision, working conditions and administrative practices. These needs are satisfied by what Herzberg called **'hygiene' factors**: they may minimise dissatisfaction and poor job performance, but have little ability to motivate the individual to higher levels of job satisfaction or extra performance. Hygiene factors are essentially extrinsic rewards, deriving from factors in the environment or context of work, and offering satisfaction of lower-level needs.

- The **need to develop in one's occupation**, as a source of personal growth, associated with factors such as advancement, recognition, responsibility, challenge and achievement. These needs are satisfied by what Herzberg called '**motivator**' **factors**, which are seen to be effective in motivating the individual to more positive attitudes, and greater effort and performance. Motivator factors are essentially intrinsic rewards, deriving from factors inherent in the content of the work itself, and offering psychological satisfaction of higher-level needs.

The two-factor model has been criticised as being based on an inadequately small sample size and a limited cultural context. In particular, the impact of job satisfaction on work performance has proved difficult to verify and measure: 'A satisfied worker is not necessarily a high producer, and a high producer is not necessarily a satisfied worker.' (Armstrong, 2003)

However, Herzberg's key assertion that 'dissatisfaction arises from environment factors: satisfaction can only arise from the job' confirmed the growing recognition of the value of **intrinsic rewards** – as opposed to extrinsic rewards – as motivating factors. Herzberg's work focused on job-design, as a means of building challenge, scope and interest into jobs: his concept of **job enrichment** ('the planned process of up-grading the responsibility, challenge and content of the work') became a cornerstone of the quality of working life and employee empowerment movements.

Today's '**total reward**' **concept** recognises that a reward system offering a mix of both extrinsic *and* intrinsic rewards is likely to be the most effective way of motivating employees.

Definition

> **Reward** refers to 'all of the monetary, non-monetary and psychological payments that an organisation provides for its employees in exchange for the work they perform.' (Bratton & Gold, 2007)

> **Activity 1** (30 minutes)
>
> What 'intrinsic' or internal satisfactions and rewards do you value in your own job (as opposed to the 'extrinsic' or external things the organisation can give you, like pay, comfortable working environment or likeable management)? Why do you work? What do you get out of your work that you most value? What would you miss most if you didn't work? (If you've never been employed, ask these questions of someone who has.)
>
> Try putting each of these satisfactions into (a) Maslow's categories of needs and (b) Herzberg's categories of hygiene and motivator factors.
>
> Did you have any hesitation about where to put 'pay' in these categories? If so, why?

1.4 Expectancy theory

The expectancy theory of motivation basically states that the strength of an individual's motivation to do something will be influenced by:

- The perceived link between individual effort, performance and particular outcomes (Will reward follow effort?) and

- The importance of those outcomes to the individual (Will the reward make the effort worthwhile?)

Vroom (1964) suggested a formula by which motivation could be assessed and measured, based on an expectancy theory model. In its simplest form it may be expressed as:

$$\textbf{F}\text{orce or strength of motivation to do x} = \textbf{V}\text{alence (Strength of the individual's preference for outcome y)} \times \textbf{E}\text{xpectancy (Individual's perception of the likelihood that doing x will result in outcome y)}$$

Valence is represented as a positive or negative number, or zero – since outcomes (or rewards) may be desired, avoided or considered with indifference. Expectancy is expressed as a probability (in the perception of the individual): any number between 0 (no chance) and 1 (certainty).

So, for example, an employee may have a high expectation that behaviour x (say, increased productivity) will result in outcome y (say, promotion) – because of a performance contract, perhaps – so E = 1. However, if she is indifferent to that outcome (say, because she doesn't want the responsibility), V = 0 (or less) and she will not be motivated to increase her productivity. Similarly, if the employee has a great desire for promotion – but doesn't believe that more productive behaviour will secure it for her (say, because she has been passed over previously), E = 0 and she will still not be highly motivated.

This model helps to explain why performance incentives and rewards work most effectively when:

- **The link between effort and reward is clear.** (This is a key criterion in designing performance-based pay schemes – but would also apply to the giving of non-financial rewards such as praise and recognition, for example.)

- **Intended results and goals are made clear,** and especially when individuals share in setting goals (so they can complete the calculation).

- **The reward is perceived to be worth the effort.** (This is part of the rationale for flexible benefit schemes, allowing employees to choose from a menu of incentives and rewards.)

NOTES

FOR DISCUSSION

These has been on-going debate about the role of job satisfaction in motivated performance. Some authorities have argued that 'Happy bees make more honey': others counter that this cannot be proved.

Huczynski & Buchanan (2001) note that:

'There is less talk about "the quality of working life" when there is little work to be had...'

What is your own view on how far employees need – and employers should offer – 'higher order' satisfactions at work?

What motivates *you*?

1.5 Pay as a motivator

Monetary reward has a central, but ambiguous, role in motivation theory. It is not mentioned explicitly in any need list, but it can offer the satisfaction of many of the various needs. According to Herzberg, it is the most important of the hygiene factors: valuable not only in its power to be converted into a wide range of other satisfactions, but also as a consistent measure of worth or value, allowing employees to compare themselves with other individuals or occupational groups. However, it is still only a hygiene factor: it gets taken for granted, and often becomes a source of dissatisfaction (particularly by comparison with others) rather than satisfaction.

Individuals may have needs unrelated to money, to which the pay system of the organisation is irrelevant or even conflicting (eg overtime bonuses conflicting with the need for work-life balance). Although the size of their income will affect their standard of living, most people tend not to be concerned to *maximise* their earnings. They may like to earn more but are probably more concerned to:

(a) Earn *enough* to meet their needs and aspirations

(b) Know that their pay is *fair* in comparison with the pay of others in comparable groups both inside and outside the organisation. This is sometimes known as the principle of distributive equity (Adams, 1963): it has been highlighted in recent decades by expectation and legislation in regard to equal pay for men and women (discussed later in the chapter).

'**Instrumentality**' is the concept that people will do one thing in order to achieve or bring about another. An 'instrumental orientation to work' is an attitude that sees work purely as a means to other ends: in other words, people basically work for money. The 'Affluent Worker' research of Goldthorpe, Lockwood *et al* (1968) illustrated this orientation to work in highly-paid Luton car assembly workers. Although they experienced their work as routine and dead-end, they had made a rational decision to enter employment offering high monetary reward rather than intrinsic interest. However, the research also suggested that people will seek a suitable balance of:

(a) The rewards that are important to them; and

(b) The deprivations they feel able to put up with in order to earn them.

Even those with an instrumental orientation to work have limits to their purely financial aspirations, and will cease to be motivated by money if the deprivations required to earn it – in terms of long working hours, poor conditions and so on – become too great.

Pay should be seen as only one of several intrinsic and extrinsic rewards offered by work. If it is used to motivate, it can only do so in a wider context of the job and other rewards. The significance in motivation theory of high-order needs, intrinsic rewards and subjective factors (such as expectancy and valance) suggests that HR managers need to:

- Develop reward systems which offer both financial and non-financial rewards, rather than relying on simplistic assumptions of instrumentality

- Support job re-design, employee involvement and on-going development planning which offer intrinsic satisfactions (particularly in the area of potential self-actualisation)

- Support an organisational and managerial culture which consistently values and expresses appreciation for employee contribution.

We will return to the influence of rewards on performance in Section 4 of this Chapter. First, we will look in more detail at 'pay' and how pay levels are determined.

2 JOB EVALUATION

Definition

Job evaluation is the process of analysing and assessing the content, worth or size of jobs within an organisation, in order to rank and group them as a basis for an equitable remuneration system.

2.1 The purpose and aims of job evaluation

Job evaluation is intended to create a rational and fair framework for job gradings and the pay decisions arising from them. It aims to:

(a) Assess the value of jobs to the organisation in relation to one another

(b) Support the development of job gradings and pay structures that are objective, balanced and equitable

(c) Ensure that the organisation is able to give (and demonstrate that it gives) equal pay for work of equal value, as required by law.

2.2 Arguments for and against formal job evaluation

Formal job evaluation fell out of favour in the 1980s, being seen as too bureaucratic and inflexible for business environments which increasingly emphasised flexibility and reward for individual performance. However, a renewed focus on equity – and specifically, on equal pay – has encouraged widespread adoption of formal job evaluation schemes in recent years.

The arguments for and against job evaluation may be summarised as follows.

Advantages	Disadvantages/limitations
• Job evaluation can offer a systematic approach to determining relative job values, without which it is difficult to justify the fairness of pay differentials.	• Job evaluation can be bureaucratic, inflexible and time-consuming.
• Job evaluation offers a framework for consistent on-going decision-making about job grades and rates of pay.	• Job evaluation can inhibit the development of a flexible, 'high-involvement' workplace (Bratton & Gold, 2007), because it adds 'rigidity' to the job and the pay structure, and imparts a 'top-down' ethos.
• A properly designed and applied job evaluation process is more likely to be *felt* to be fair by employees.	• Job evaluation ratings can be gender biased, eg if job factors to be valued are based on jobs dominated by men.
• An analytical job evaluation scheme is the only acceptable defence in equal pay cases, as a means of achieving equal pay for work of equal value.	• Job evaluation is at best 'systematic' rather than 'scientific': there is an element of subjective judgement.
	• Job evaluated salary structures get out-of-date, unless attention is given to periodic review and maintenance.

In general, the criticisms focus on badly designed or applied job evaluation, rather than the concept of job evaluation itself.

Activity 2   **(1 hour)**

Do you feel your salary is fair for the job you do, and in relation to others? (Remember, job evaluation concerns the content, size and value of the *job* to your organisation – not on how much you put into it or how well you perform it.) Do you know how your job is evaluated? Do you know how your salary is worked out? What could the organisation do to make the system (a) clearer and (b) fairer?

Either answer these questions yourself, or ask them of an employed person who is willing to be interviewed by you on this topic.

2.3 The process of job evaluation

The process of job evaluation covers four basic steps.

Step 1. **Select compensable factors**

Compensable factors represent the aspects of jobs for which the organisation is willing to pay. Armstrong (2003) suggests that effective factors should:

(a) Apply equally well to different types of work (including specialists and generalists, lower level and higher level jobs, and jobs performed by men and women)

(b) Refer to relevant and important differences between jobs, in order to allow comparison for ranking purposes

(c) Be understandable by, and acceptable to, all those who will be covered by the scheme

Examples of compensable factors include: knowledge and skills, judgement and decision-making, freedom to act and responsibility for financial resources.

Step 2. **Gather data on jobs**

Some information for evaluation may already be available in the form **of job descriptions,** or may have to be gathered by **job analysis** (see Chapter 3).

Step 3. **Evaluate jobs**

There are two basic types of job evaluation scheme.

(a) **Non-analytical schemes** make largely subjective judgements about the whole job, its difficulty, and its importance to the organisation relative to other jobs.

(b) **Analytical schemes** systematically analyse how far compensable factors are present in each job, in order to arrive at appropriate weightings and rankings.

These methods will be discussed further below.

Step 4. **Assign specific pay values to the job**

The output of a job evaluation scheme is a **pay structure:** a ranking or hierarchy of jobs in terms of their relative value to the organisation. The organisation must then make policy decisions to assign pay values to jobs or job grades within the structure. This is generally done with reference to market rates of pay, how the organisation's pay levels compare with those of its competitors, and how aggressively it must compete to attract and retain quality labour. (This will be discussed in Section 3 below.)

2.4 Job evaluation schemes

Non-analytical schemes

Job classification is most common non-analytical approach. The organisation decides what grades of pay there should be and defines the requirements of each grade. Jobs are allocated to an appropriate grade by matching job descriptions to grade definitions.

Job ranking compares jobs with one another and ranks them in accordance with their relative importance or contribution to the organisation. Having established a hierarchy of jobs, they can be divided into groups for grading purposes.

Analytical schemes

Analytical schemes break jobs down into their component elements, for more detailed analysis. The Equal Pay (Amendment) Regulations 1984 clearly state that job evaluations must use analytical methods in order to demonstrate that the organisation is offering equal pay for work of equal value. They must examine 'the demands on a worker under various headings (for instance, effort, skill, decision)'.

Points rating is currently the most popular method of formal job evaluation.

- It begins with the definition of about 8 – 12 compensable factors: these will vary according to the type of organisation and can be adapted to its changing needs and key values.

- A number of *points* is allocated to each compensable factor, as a maximum score, across a range of '*degrees*' which reflect the level and importance (or weighting) of the factors within a job.

- A comprehensive *points rating chart* is therefore established, covering a range of factors and degrees which can be applied to a variety of specific jobs. An example of such a chart is shown in Figure 5.2.

- Each *job* is then examined, analysed factor by factor according to the points rating chart, and a points score is awarded for each factor, up to the maximum allowed. The total points score for each job provides the basis for ranking the jobs in order of importance, for establishing a pay structure and for pricing the pay structure. An example of a job evaluation form for points rating is shown in Figure 5.3.

	Compensable factor	DEGREE (Weighting)				
		1	*2*	*3*	*4*	*5*
G E N E R A L	Job knowledge	10	25	50	70	-
	Practical experience	15	30	50	70	-
	Physical effort	5	10	15	-	-
	Complexity	15	20	25	30	-
	Judgement/initiative	15	20	30	40	50
	Job conditions	5	10	15	-	-
	Contact with peers	5	10	20	40	-
	Contact with clients	10	20	30	40	50
	Attention to detail	5	10	15	20	-
	Potential for error	5	10	20	40	-
	Confidential data	5	10	15	20	30
	.....	...	...	...	...	...
S U P E V I S O R Y	Nature of supervision	5	10	20	-	-
	Scope of supervision	10	15	25	-	-
	Resource allocation	10	15	25	30	-
	Trust	15	20	30	40	50
	Management reporting	10	15	25	30	-
	Quality	15	30	90	50	60
	.....	...	...	...	...	...

Degree definitions

- **Job knowledge**

1. Maintain basic procedures; operate and maintain basic machinery; undertake range of tasks under supervision; comply with rules and policies.

2. Administer a routine area of work, under supervision; operate and maintain basic machinery to proficient standard; understand purpose of rules and policies and be able to identify compliance issues.

3. Supervise a small number of staff in routine and non-routine tasks; be responsible for checking of working; manage own routine and non-routine workload; control maintenance of range of machinery and compliance with rules and policies, including coaching/briefing of staff; certificate-level qualification in job-related area

4. Supervise staff in routine and non-routine tasks; manage quality and customer service issues; plan and co-ordinate own and section workload; systematic view of rules and procedures, with ability to propose improvements; diploma-level qualification in job-related area

5. –

Figure 5.2: Points rating chart (excerpt)

Each **job** is then examined, analysed factor by factor according to the value chart, and a points score awarded for each factor, up to the maximum allowed. The total points score for each job is found by adding up its points score for each factor. The total points scored for each job provides the basis for ranking the jobs in order of importance, for grading jobs, if required, and for fixing a salary structure.

Job evaluation form

Key job code _____   Department _____

Job type _____   Job holder studied _____

Date _____   Employee number _____

Task number

Description

Factor	Rating			Comments
	Points	Weighting	Total	

Skills and knowledge
  Education/qualifications
  Experience
  Dexterity				

Skills sub-total				
Initiative				

Responsibility
  People
  Equipment
  Resources				

Responsibility sub-total				

Effort
  Mental
  Physical				

Effort sub-total				

Communication
  Oral
  Written				

Communication sub-total				
Interpersonal skills				

Conditions of work
  Hazards
  Isolation
  Monotony				

Conditions sub-total				
TOTAL				
RANKING				
COMMENTS				

Figure 5.3: Points rating form

Factor comparison involves the selection of key *benchmark jobs*, for which the rate of pay is considered to be fair (perhaps in comparison with similar jobs in other organisations).

- Each of these jobs is analysed, using compensable factors, to decide how much of the total salary is being paid for each factor. So if technical skill is 50% of a benchmark job paying £12,000, the *factor pay rate* for technical skill (within that job) is £6,000.

- When this has been done for every benchmark job, the various factor pay rates are correlated, to formulate a *ranking and pay scale* for each *factor*.

- Other (non-benchmark) jobs are then evaluated factor by factor, to build up a *job value*. For example, an analysis for a clerical job might be:

Factor	Proportion of job		Pay rate for factor (as established by analysis of benchmark jobs)	Job value £
Technical skills	50%	×	£12,000 pa	6,000
Mental ability	25%	×	£16,000 pa	4,000
Responsibility for others	15%	×	£10,000 pa	1,500
Other responsibilities	10%	×	£5,000 pa	500
				12,000

FOR DISCUSSION

The 'transparency' or openness of a job evaluation exercise is critical to its effectiveness. Why might employees and their representatives be suspicious, or feel threatened, by a job evaluation programme (particularly if it is being introduced for the first time)? What kinds of information and messages will the HR manager want to give them in order to support effective job evaluation and preserve employee relations? (You may like to role play this as a discussion between staff, union representatives and an HR manager.)

Job evaluation only determines a job's relative worth to the organisation, by ranking or grading. It does not reflect its monetary worth to the organisation. We will now consider a number of other factors influencing the setting of actual pay levels.

3 OTHER FACTORS DETERMINING PAY

3.1 Market rates of pay

In order to arrive at pay rates which support recruitment, retention and motivation, a pay structure should be a combination of:

- The results of job evaluation, based on relative worth of jobs to the organisation and internal equity *and*

- The results of market pay analysis, based on the 'absolute' worth of jobs to the organisation and competitiveness in the labour market.

The concept of the market rate is not exact: different employers will pay a range of rates for similar job titles – particularly in the case of managerial jobs, whose scope and nature will vary according to context and culture. However, most organisations use **pay surveys** of key or 'benchmark' jobs to get a broad indication of the 'going rate' of pay for a job. Sources of information on market rates include:

- Published surveys

- Surveys carried out by HR specialists or commissioned from management consultants

- Business network or 'club' surveys, where organisations exchange pay information on a regular basis

- General market monitoring and intelligence: recruitment advertising, government statistics, recruitment consultancies and so on.

Market rate information on benchmark jobs can be used to add monetary values to 'similar' jobs within the organisation's job-evaluated rankings. Other jobs can then be placed on the pay scale according to their relative positions in the ranking, and priced accordingly.

Activity 4	(30 minutes)

You may like to check out some of the sources of published pay surveys available online, such as the *Annual Survey of Hours and Earnings* (www.statistics.gov.uk) or www.salariesreview.com.

(a) How reliable do you think each of the sources of market rate data listed in Paragraph 3.1 would be?

(b) How would you go about 'job matching': comparing the jobs cited in market rate data with jobs in your own organisation, as 'like with like' in terms of the type and size of the job and the type of organisation?

The market rate of pay will vary with supply/demand factors such as:

(a) The **relative scarcity of particular skills** in the particular market from which the organisation draws its labour

(b) The **sensitivity of employees** to pay levels or differentials. Pay may or may not act as an incentive to change employers, depending on the availability of work elsewhere, the employee's loyalty and the non-financial rewards offered by the organisation or the job.

Market rates of pay will have most influence on pay structures where there is a standard pattern of supply and demand in the open labour market. If an organisation's rates fall below the benchmark rates in the local or national labour market from which it recruits, it may have trouble attracting and holding employees. Management has three basic policy choices:

- To **lead** the competition: often used for key or scarce skills, or to establish a leading employer brand as part of the organisation's competitive strategy

- To **match** what other employers are paying: the least-risk approach

- To **lag** behind the market: may be cost-effective where vacancies can be easily filled in the local labour market (minimising direct competition with other employers)

> **Activity 5**   **(45 minutes)**
>
> What are the arguments *for* and *against* an organisation's offering above-market rates of pay?

Other factors which may distort or dilute the effect of the forces of supply and demand on labour pricing (in addition to job-evaluated equity criteria) include:

(a)   **Affordability:** the organisation's ability to pay the market rate

(b)   The **culture and value system** of the organisation, which will influence the attitude of management towards the market rate, and whether age, length of service, motivation, employee aspirations and/or other factors are taken into account in the determination of pay, rather than fluctuations in supply and demand. (You may note from some of the International Comparisons in this chapter that national cultural differences also influences salary strategy.)

(c)   The bargaining strength of trade unions (where applicable) in **collective bargaining** negotiations. Pay scales, differentials and minimum rates may be negotiated at plant, local or national level.

(d)   **Government intervention**, including incomes policies and anti-inflationary measures (limiting the size of pay increases by pay controls). UK governments have often used control of public sector pay to influence general pay trends. The UK also has a national minimum wage (*National Minimum Wage Regulations 1999*) and equal pay legislation (discussed further below).

INTERNATIONAL COMPARISON

Reward policy in **Germany** is highly collectivised. Each trade union (organised on broad industry lines) negotiates with the employers' federation on a state by state basis – allowing for the relative prosperity of the region. Companies (such as Volkswagen) which are not part of a trade association may negotiate separately with the relevant trade union. Many HR managers will therefore not be involved in wage negotiation at all, but will simply implement the agreement locally.

The system of industrial democracy known as 'co-determination' gives a plant-level Works Council the right to co-determine company policy on matters including how wages and salaries are to be paid (method, time), the use of incentives (bonus schemes, piece work, performance-related pay) and so on. Traditionally popular elements of reward systems include holiday and long-service bonuses, suggestion schemes, incentive/merit pay (for manual grades) and profit sharing (for managerial grades), with employee share ownership schemes attracting tax incentives.

3.2 Individual performance

Job evaluated pay structures are generally designed to allow increasing rewards for seniority (eg by using incremented rates for age or length of service), competence (eg by applying competence-based bands) and/or performance (eg by applying merit or contribution bands). The **incentive** role of pay in motivating employees to higher levels of performance may also be built into the reward system through separate bonus schemes, performance-related pay, employee share ownership schemes and so on. We will discuss these aspects in detail later in the chapter.

3.3 Equal pay

The Equal Pay Act 1970 was the first major attempt 'to prevent discrimination as regards terms and conditions of employment between men and women.' Women were entitled to claim equal pay and conditions of service for:

- Jobs rated as equivalent under a job evaluation scheme, and

- Work that was 'the same as or broadly similar' to the work of a man in the same establishment, where job evaluation was not used.

The Equal Pay (Amendment) Regulations 1984 established the right to equal pay and conditions for work of equal value (that is, not necessarily 'similar' work, but work of equivalent evaluation). If job evaluation is not used in an organisation, the employee can apply to an Employment Tribunal for a (legally enforceable) order to have an evaluation carried out by an independent expert.

FOR DISCUSSION

Why do you think there has been continuing sensitivity in recent years to the issue of equal pay?

Why is it important for 21st Century business organisations to take this into account?

We will now look briefly at reward systems and how they can be structured.

4 REWARD SYSTEMS

Definition

> A **reward system** is 'the mix of extrinsic and intrinsic rewards provided by the employer... [It] also consists of the integrated policies, processes, practices and administrative procedures for implementing the system within the framework of the human resources (HR) strategy and the total organisational system.'
>
> (Bratton & Gold, 2007)

4.1 Objectives of the reward system

The key objectives of any reward system can be summed up as follows.

(a) **Recruiting and retaining quality labour** in line with the human resource plan. External competitiveness with market rates may be the strongest influence on recruitment, while internal equity may be the strongest influence on retention.

(b) **Motivating individual and team performance**, to maximise return on investment from the human resource. There are various forms of reward system which link reward to performance (discussed below).

(c) **Supporting organisational culture**, by conveying messages about the values, behaviours and outcomes that the organisation prizes and is willing to pay for.

(d) **Supporting flexibility**, by responding to changing organisational skill and performance requirements.

4.2 Components of the reward system

Three broad reward components can be identified within the reward system.

(a) **Direct or base pay**: a fixed salary or wage that constitutes a standard rate for the job, as defined by market pricing and job evaluation. This amount is paid at intervals of a week or month and reflects 'hours of work': the amount of *time* spent at the workplace or on the job. It is appropriate as a basic pay component in jobs where outputs are less meaningful or measurable. It also provides a relatively consistent and predictable basic income. Pay *progression* (increases in basic pay over time) may be related to age or length of service, or to performance-related criteria such as competence or skill attainment.

The key advantages of direct pay are that it is easy to implement and administer; it is generally felt to be fair (especially if established by job evaluation); and it helps to establish mutual commitment in the employment relationship.

(b) **Performance or variable pay**: a method or component of pay directly linked to work-related behaviour, such as performance or attainments. There are various types of variable pay, including:

(i) **Payment by results (PBR)**, which links pay directly to the quantity of output produced by the individual (or team): piecework, commission (usually a percentage of sales value generated) or output– or target-based bonuses

(ii) **Performance-related pay (PRP)**, offering additional payments for individual or team performance according to a range of possible performance criteria (quality, customer service, teamworking, innovation and so on)

(iii) **Organisation performance pay**, based on the profitability of the firm: eg value added schemes, profit-sharing schemes and employee shareholding.

The key advantage of such rewards (in theory) is that they motivate employees to higher levels of performance and foster a culture in which performance, competence and contribution (and specific criteria such as teamworking or innovation) are valued and rewarded. However, as we noted in Section 1 of this chapter, the assumption that people are motivated and managed solely by pay is simplistic.

(c) **Indirect pay or 'benefits':** non-cash items or services. These may include 'deferred pay' in the form of pension contributions, legal entitlements (for example, to sick pay, maternity pay, maternity/paternity leave, and annual leave), and so-called 'fringe' benefits such as company cars, housing assistance, medical insurance and allowances.

4.3 The 'total reward' concept

The sum of the components discussed above is known as '**total remuneration**'. The concept of '**total reward**' is based on the premise that monetary payments are not the only, or necessarily the most effective, form of reward and that financial and non-financial rewards should be linked together as an integrated reward package: Figure 5.4.

Figure 5.4: Total reward package

A total reward orientation seeks to integrate reward strategy both vertically (with business strategy) and horizontally (with a range of other HRM strategies).

Armstrong (2003) cites a study by WorldatWork which suggests the following benefits of a total reward approach:

- **Increased flexibility**: tailoring rewards to changing circumstances

- **Recruitment and retention**: offering employees the 'total value' of the employment package (and monitoring its true cost to the organisation)

- **Potential for low-cost reward solutions**

- **Heightened visibility in tight labour markets**: offering valued rewards

EXAMPLE: TOTAL REWARD AT ROYAL BANK OF SCOTLAND

'Total Reward describes the value of everything employees get in return for working for us. At the heart of their Total Reward is cash – their salary and benefit funding plus any bonuses, incentive payments or allowances they may receive.

'Retail and leisure

Discounted shopping vouchers for many major supermarkets and high street retailers are available through RB*Select* – these include Sainsburys, Asda, Somerfield, Marks & Spencer, GAP, John Lewis, Dixons and many more.

Lifestyle

Lifestyle benefits, often with great tax savings, are available through RB*Select*, these include: childcare vouchers, bikes, holidays, wine, mobile phones & telephone legal advice.

Well being

Employees can choose benefits including private medical cover, reimbursement for dental treatment, health screening and the Healthcare Cash Plan: generous cash benefits towards the cost of everyday health care expenses.

Savings and protection

We offer a range of options to enable employees to save and plan for the future. These include an employer funded flexible retirement savings plan (for eligible employees) and a choice of share ownership plans. Protection benefits vailbre through RB*Select* include, life cover, disability cover, personal accident assurance, life assurance – spouse/partner.'

(RBS website, 2007)

Weblink

> For more details, see:
>
> ▶▶ **http://www.rbs.com/careers**

We will now look at each of the three components of the total remuneration package in turn.

5   BASIC PAY

5.1   Salary and wage systems

The terms 'wages' and 'salaries' are sometimes used interchangeably to refer to monetary rewards, but there are traditional distinctions between them.

Wages	Salaries
• Manual/'blue collar' workers – historically on short contract terms	• White-collar workers – historically with greater security of tenure
• Paid weekly	• Paid monthly, as a proportion of an annual fixed sum
• Based on a weekly or hourly rate for time/output	• Related to seniority, qualifications, performance, with progression over time
• Premium rates paid for overtime	• Overtime not usually paid

In the UK and US, wage payment systems have increasingly been replaced by salaries as part of **single status** schemes. These represent an attempt to harmonise the payment systems operating in an organisation, and in the process to remove barriers between workers and management and to encourage commitment and co-operation.

Activity 6	(10 minutes)

What advantages and disadvantages for the organisation and its workers can you see from single status schemes?

EXAMPLE: INTERNATIONAL COMPARISON

Severn Trent Water introduced performance-related pay for all front-line staff in 2005, so they are assessed in the same way as managers and directors.

The new pay structure, introduced in 2006, linked total award to overall company performance based on profit, safety and attendance records.

Previously, the company had mixed pay practices, with staff on different rates. (And some rather outdated policies such as a 'Sheepdog allowance' for staff patrolling reservoirs!)

(*People Management*, 13 October 2005) (Example end)

5.2 Salary systems

A salary system generally consists of:

- A **grade structure,** consisting of a hierarchy of bands or levels ('grades') to which are allocated groups of jobs that are broadly comparable in value: Figure 5.5.

- A **pay structure**, defining pay ranges or scales for each grade, allowing scope for *pay progression* or increases according to length of service and performance.

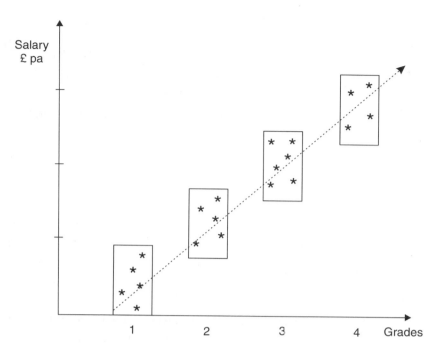

Figure 5.5: Grade structure

The grade structure will require careful design, because of the consequences for promotions and transfers between grades.

(a) **Differentials** between pay ranges should recognise increases in job value between one grade and another.

(b) The **range** of each grade should be wide enough to allow for progression offering rewards for lateral career development (where promotion opportunities are few) and competence development. 'Broad banding' (having few grades of 'bands', each spanning a wide range) also allows rates of pay to be more flexibly adapted to market rate fluctuations, individual performance and flexible roles.

(c) There should be some **overlap**, in recognition that an experienced person performing well in a given job may be of more value than a new or poor performer in the next grade up.

Progression or pay increases within a grade may be achieved by fixed increments linked to age or length of service (common in the public sector) or by various forms of performance-related increases.

Flexibility will be required: changes in job content or market rates should prompt re-grading. Individual growth in competence should also be allowed for: in the case of an individual whose performance is outstanding, but for whom there are no immediate openings for promotion, discretionary payment above the grade maximum may be made.

NOTES

Activity 7	(No time limit)

(a) Is there a salary policy and structure in your organisation (or an organisation of your choice?) Find out and record the salient details.

(b) If you had trouble finding out, what does this say about the political aspects of salary administration?

5.3 Wage systems

A typical wage structure will include:

(a) A basic (time or piecework) rate; *plus*

(b) Overtime premium rates for work done outside normal hours

(c) Shift pay at premium rates for employees who work unusual or socially disruptive hours or shift patterns (a form of *compensatory* pay)

(d) Compensatory payments for abnormal working conditions (eg 'danger money', 'dirt money', 'wet money'), although these may be built into basic rates during job evaluation

(e) Allowances (eg to employees living in high cost-of-living areas like London)

(f) Merit or length-of-service bonuses

(g) Payment by results bonuses and incentives (discussed below).

6 PERFORMANCE PAY

6.1 Effective performance pay systems

Effective performance (or 'contingent') pay systems should fulfil the following criteria.

- Targets and standards of performance required to earn the rewards must be made clear to the people involved.

- The formulae used to calculate rewards, and any conditions that apply, should be easily understood.

- The rewards should be – and perceived to be – significant enough to make the effort worthwhile (perhaps 10% of basic salary)

- Rewards should be related to performance indicators over which people have control or influence, through their own behaviour or decision-making.

- There should not be a lengthy time lag between performance and reward.

6.2 Performance-related pay (PRP)

Individual performance-related pay (IPRP) relates monetary bonuses and/or the rate and extent of pay progression (increases in basic pay over time) to the performance of individuals, assessed according to defined criteria.

For managerial and other salaried jobs, a form of **performance management** is usually applied so that:

(a) Key results can be identified and agreed, for which merit awards will be paid

(b) The exact conditions and amounts of awards can be made clear to employees

(c) Performance indicators can be regularly monitored and evaluated, in order to establish when targets have been reached and awards earned.

For service and other departments, a PRP scheme may involve **bonuses** for achievement of key results, or **points schemes**, where points are awarded for performance on various criteria (efficiency, cost savings, quality of service and so on) and a certain points total (or the highest points total in the unit, if a competitive system is used) wins cash or other awards.

PRP is not appropriate for all organisations. It requires an individualistic, performance-oriented culture, where individuals have an instrumental orientation to work, are able to control the outcomes of their work, and are supported by systematic goal setting, feedback and objective results measurement. (Torrington *et al*, 2002)

Advantages of IPRP	Disadvantages/limitations of IPRP
• Encourages the setting, clarification and communication of key task behaviours and performance criteria	• Based on over-simplistic belief in instrumentality: not all employees motivated by financial incentives
• Encourages the monitoring, gathering and sharing of feedback on current performance	• Fosters instrumentality: creates a culture where employees expect to be rewarded for everything
• Integrates organisational and individual priorities and objectives	• Fosters a manipulative management culture based on 'carrot and stick' rather than intrinsic rewards
• Promotes a results-focused culture and behaviours: flexibility, customer service, quality and 'entrepreneurial' thinking	• Undermines teamworking by focusing on individual effort
	• May focus on quantitative outputs, at the expense of quality
• Reduces the need for other types of managerial control (direct supervision, technology), fostering self-motivation	• May focus on established ways of doing things, inhibiting creativity and innovation
• Attracts and retains people who expect to be rewarded for delivering results	• May focus on short-term productivity gains rather than long-term strategic goals
	• May frustrate employees, where they are not able to control all factors in their performance
	• Relies heavily on effective performance management for objective performance definition and assessment

FOR DISCUSSION

'Managers who insist that the job won't get done right without rewards have failed to offer a convincing argument for behavioural manipulation. Promising a reward to someone who appears unmotivated is a bit like offering salt water to someone who is thirsty. Bribes in the workplace simply can't work.' (Kohn, cited by Torrington *et al*, 2002)

Do incentives only secure temporary compliance – or can they change underlying attitudes? (Example end)

INTERNATIONAL COMPARISON

A key feature of employment in **Japan** has traditonally been the seniority system, which links reward with length of service rather than with job or performance factors. This is a subtler distinction than it may appear, since length of service is equated with commitment, skill development and status. 'It is a scale of 'person-related' payments – as opposed to 'job related' payments... an intricate set of rules, based on the exponential principle that the higher you go, the faster you rise, designed to give recognition to both seniority and merit. The seniority principle requires that everybody goes up a notch every year' (Dore, cited by Beardwell and Holden, 1997). This concept of 'performance related pay' is very different from the Western concept of performance as individual achievement: it reflects the complexity of the relationship between the individual, the organisation, the job and socio-cultural values of status, commitment and belonging.

6.3 Suggestion schemes

Another variant on performance-based pay is the **suggestion scheme**, where payments or non-cash prizes are offered to staff to come up with workable ideas on improving efficiency or quality, new marketing initiatives or solutions to production problems. The theory is that there is in any case motivational value in getting staff involved in problem-solving and planning, and that staff are often in the best position to provide practical and creative solutions to their work problems or the customer's needs – but that an added incentive will help to overcome any reluctance on the part of staff to put forward ideas (because it is seen as risky, or doing management's job for them, or whatever).

Wherever possible, the size of the payment should be related to the savings or value added as a result of the suggestion – either as a lump sum or percentage. Payments are often also made for a 'good try' – an idea which is rejected but considered to show initiative, effort and judgement on the part of the employee.

Suggestion schemes usually apply only to lower grades of staff, on the grounds that thinking up improvements is part of the manager's job, but with the increase of worker empowerment and 'bottom up' quality initiatives, they are becoming more widespread in various forms.

6.4   Team-based pay

Group incentive schemes typically offer a bonus for a group (distributed equally, or proportionately to the earnings or status of each individual) which achieves or exceeds specified targets. Offering bonuses to a whole team may be appropriate for tasks where individual contributions cannot be isolated, workers have little control over their individual output because tasks depend on each other, or where team-building is required.

One key objective of team reward is to enhance team-spirit and co-operation as well as to provide performance incentives – but it may also create pressures or conflict within the group, if some individuals are 'not pulling their weight'.

Long-term, large-group bonus schemes may be applied plant– or organisation-wide. **Gain sharing** schemes allocate additional awards when there has been an increase in profits or a decrease in costs.

(a)   **Value-added** schemes, for example, work on the basis that improvements in productivity (indicated by a fall in the ratio of employment costs to sales revenue) increases value added, and the benefit can be shared between employers and employees on an agreed formula.

(b)   **Scanlon plans** pay frequent, plant-wide bonuses, based on improvements in productivity and reduction in labour costs which are brought about through collective bargaining and the participation of employee representatives.

Profit-sharing schemes offer employees current or deferred bonuses (paid in cash or shares) based on company profits. The formula for determining the amounts may vary, but in recent years, a straightforward distribution of a percentage of profits above a given target has given way to a value-added concept.

The link between individual effort and profitability is recognised to be remote, so profit sharing does not constitute a direct incentive. However, it is based on the belief that all employees can contribute to profitability, and that their contribution should be recognised. It may foster profit-consciousness and commitment to the future prosperity of the organisation. The greatest effect on productivity arising from the scheme may in fact arise from its use as a focal point for discussion with employees about the relationship between their performance and results, and areas and targets for improvement.

An **employee stock plan** or **employee share ownership scheme** (such as an *All Employee Share Ownership Plan* or *Savings-Related Share Option Scheme)* allows employees to acquire shares in their employing company. The key advantage of such systems may be to encourage employees to take 'ownership' of the long-term success of the business – although the notorious collapse of the Enron Corporation, in the United States, has highlighted the extent to which this may be a double-edged sword...

Activity 8	(15 minutes)

Are you motivated by monetary incentives? At what point would the offer of more money cease to motivate you to longer hours, greater efforts (or whatever)? Try and identify three likely problems with, or limitations of, cash/monetary incentives.

6.5 Non-cash incentives

Incentive and recognition schemes are increasingly focused not on cash, but on non-cash awards. Traditionally aimed at sales people, non-cash gifts and incentives are now widely used to add interest to quality and suggestion schemes, enabling managers to recognise staff contribution flexibly, informally and at relatively low cost. Incentive awards include vouchers, air miles, the choice of gift from a catalogue, travel experiences and so on.

EXAMPLES

Tulip (2003) suggests that incentive schemes need to be up-to-the-minute, fresh and flexible if they are to be effective.

'An incentive scheme has to be achievable, but people also have to be rewarded with the sort of things they want. Call centre workers, for example, tend to be a young market, often making a first home, and so tend to select electrical merchandise or kitchen goods. These are less likely to incentivise high-flyers, older workers and managers, who typically go for an "experience", whether that be a holiday or something more extreme.'

A wide range of fresh ideas for incentives is highlighted, including:

- Experience-based incentives (particularly effective as rewards for successful teams or team-based projects) such as snowboarding or dolphin watching events. The latest trend is to use learning and training in skills, sports and hobbies. ('If you are learning something, you are keeping your "skills to learn" alive, and probably gaining skills that can be transferred back into the workplace.')

- New variations on the gift vouchers traditionally backed by major retailers such as Marks & Spencer and John Lewis Partnership: the trend is towards vouchers offering a wider range of opportunities eg those offered by the Virgin brand (from CDs to hot air ballooning).

- New variations on the gift catalogue, notably web-based incentive sites: 'We can set up a virtual shopping site, tailored to the needs of a company, so that the experience is just like personal shopping, only without having to pay.' (www.LongService.com)

Such schemes can be regarded by some staff as manipulative, irrelevant or just plain gimmicky. However, they can be effective as team-building exercises and as part of a total reward programme.

FOR DISCUSSION

Which of the non-cash incentive examples mentioned above do you think would be a good investment for the organisation, and why? Which would you, as an employee, find most attractive? (Explore any personal and cultural differences in the answers from your discussion group.)

7 INDIRECT PAY

7.1 Benefits

Employee benefits consist of items or awards which are supplementary to normal pay. Some – such as pension provisions and sick pay, maternity/paternity leave and maternity pay – are legal entitlements, so the common term 'fringe' benefits is perhaps misleading. Other benefits are more in the nature of optional extras, and as such may be part of the total remuneration package.

Discretionary benefits which may be offered include the following.

(a) **Extended holiday entitlement**. This is a benefit which is often taken for granted, but it was only fairly recently (Working Time Regulations 1998) that any formal entitlement to annual leave was formulated.

(b) **Company cars** are a highly-regarded benefit in the UK, especially among managerial staff (despite the reduction in tax incentives over the years) and those whose work requires extensive road travel.

(c) **Employee assistance**, for example with transport (loans or discounted purchase of annual season tickets) or housing (allowances for transferred or relocated staff, bridging loans or preferential mortgage terms)

(d) **Insurance** – including private medical/dental insurance and life insurance/assurance.

(e) **Catering services** – eg subsidised food and drink at the workplace, or luncheon vouchers.

(f) **Recreational facilities** – the subsidy or organisation of social and sports clubs, or provision of facilities such as a gymnasium.

(g) **Allowances** for telephone costs, professional subscriptions, work-related reading matter or home computer/laptop purchase.

(h) **Discounts or preferential terms** on the organisation's own products/services.

(i) **Educational programmes** – in-house study opportunities, or sponsorship of external study (not necessarily work-related).

(j) **Family-friendly policies** such as workplace crèche, child-care vouchers, term-time hours contracts, career break schemes and generous maternity/paternity terms.

Activity 9 **(15 minutes)**

Which, of all the benefits mentioned, would you think were most valued by people?

You might like to check out the websites below for more information in this area.

Weblink

www.benefitslinks.com

www.benefits.org

7.2 Objectives of benefit packages

There are a number of reasons why organisations offer benefit packages.

(a) To attract and retain staff by the generosity and/or relevance of benefits offered, and by facilitating career longevity and work-life balance (eg by allowing career breaks and sabbaticals, flexible work hours and so on)

(b) To encourage commitment to (and consumption of) the organisation's own products (eg by offering employees discounted rates)

(c) To demonstrate corporate social responsibility (CSR) by giving above-statutory levels of sick pay, paternity leave, pension provisions, employee assistance and so on

(d) To promote desirable behaviours and values in employees (for example, by subsidising clothing, fitness programmes or learning/training experiences)

(e) To offer rewards of perceived high value to employees, ideally with discounted or marginal cost to the employer.

7.3 Flexible benefits

Increasing recognition that individuals have different needs and wants has led to the development of flexible benefit ('flex') or 'cafeteria' benefit programmes (CBP). A range of benefits with different values are on offer, and employees can choose from among them up to their budget, as allocated to a personal benefit account: the most common allowance for flexible benefits is 5-10% of basic salary.

This is not a new concept, having been accepted practice for some time in America, where there has been a relative lack of state-sponsored welfare benefits. However, is has caught on swiftly in the last few years in the UK, especially in medium-sized firms. (Large complex multinational structures make flex difficult to deliver consistently – while very small firms find it difficult to deliver cost-effectively.)

The Internet is increasingly recognised as an important tool, 'both in communicating the merits and values of the benefit scheme and in shifting part of the administrative burden on to the employees themselves as 'self-service'. New technologies may also support the outsourcing of the design, maintenance and management of flexible benefit schemes.

The **advantages** claimed for flexible benefits are, broadly, as follows.

(a) Choice allows employees to select benefits to meet their individual needs, increasing their appreciation of the benefit (especially where state-funded provision for sickness and retirement are increasingly uncertain).

(b) Choice supports the management of diversity, in meeting the needs of a diverse workforce (in terms of age, culture and personal preferences).

(c) Choices such as additional holidays, learning accounts, home PCs and childcare vouchers support (and are supported by) UK government initiatives in regard to work-life balance and skill development.

(d) The organisation only pays for the most highly-desired benefits, allowing it to capitalise cost-effectively on any motivational value accruing from them.

(e)   The system can help to reduce the total cost of compensation and specific future cost increases, through: savings on national insurance; better control of benefit spend; reduced premium costs for health and life insurance; and even reduction in payroll costs, if employees take more holiday.

However, it should also be noted that there are significant start up and administrative costs involved in flex schemes. There are also risks for the employer, especially in dealing with long-term financial benefits: the choice of benefits must be clearly the responsibility of the employee, and any financial advice (eg on life insurance or pensions) must be given by the benefit provider – *not* the employing organisation. The distinction between fixed benefits (laid down in the contract of employment) and variable benefits (linked to individual service or performance) must be made clear, to avoid benefits becoming taken for granted.

FOR DISCUSSION

Do flexible benefits meet the real needs of employees – or are they just a way for the organisation to try to buy commitment more cheaply?

BPP
LEARNING MEDIA

NOTES

Chapter roundup

- Reward management is concerned with the formulation and implementation of strategies and policies that aim to reward people fairly, equitably and consistently in accordance with their value to the organisation.

- Need theories of motivation (Maslow, Herzberg) suggest that intrinsic rewards (as well as extrinsic rewards) must be included in reward strategy. Process theories of motivation (Vroom) highlight the need for flexibility, clear communication and careful design of reward systems to support the motivation calculation. Instrumentality underpins monetary reward systems, but it is recognised that there are limitations to financial incentives.

- Job evaluation is the process of analysing and assessing the content of jobs, in order to place them in an acceptable rank order which can then be used as a basis for a remuneration system. Job evaluation methods may be non-analytical (job ranking, job classification) or analytical (points rating, factor comparison): only analytical methods provide a defence in equal pay claims.

- Other factors in determining pay levels include market rate analysis (using pay surveys), affordability, organisation strategy and culture, government intervention, collective bargaining, the need to offer performance incentives and rewards, and legal provisions on equal pay.

- Total remuneration includes basic (or direct) pay, performance (or contingent) pay and indirect pay (or benefits). Total reward is a wider concept still, embracing a range of intrinsic rewards available from the job.

- Salary structures are commonly graded, with a range (or scale) or salaries within each grade.

- Incentives may be built into graded salary systems on a limited basis. In addition, many organisations operate incentive or performance-related pay schemes, including IPRP, suggestion schemes, gain sharing schemes and profit-sharing.

- A range of benefits may be offered to employees in addition to basic entitlements. Flexible benefits have become particularly popular in the UK in recent years.

Quick quiz

1   Explain the formula $F = E \times V$ in terms of motivational theory.

2   What is 'instrumentality' and what is its relevance to reward management?

3   Outline the advantages and disadvantages of job evaluation.

4   List the four basic steps in job evaluation.

5   List four sources of information on market rates of pay.

6   What are the implications of the Equal Pay Act for setting pay levels?

7   Define a 'grade structure' and a 'pay structure' in a salary system.

8   What are the advantages and disadvantages of performance-related pay?

9   List three options for organisation-wide performance rewards.

10   What are the advantages of flexible benefits?

Answers to quick quiz

1   Force of motivation to do x = valence (important of outcome y) x expectancy (perceived probability that doing x will lead to y.   (see paragraph 1.4)

2   The concept that people will do something as a means to an end: eg work for money. Lies behind monetary/extrinsic reward systems, but is simplistic: instrumentality is not universal or straightforward as a motivating factor.

                                                                                       (para 1.5)

3   For a full answer, see the table in paragraph 2.2

4   Select compensable factors, gather data on jobs, evaluate jobs (using non-analytical or analytical methods), assign pay values to jobs.   (para 2.3)

5   Published surveys; special surveys; business network/club surveys; general marketing monitoring and intelligence.   (para 3.1)

6   Women are entitled to claim equal pay for work of equal value. This should be justified by analytical job evaluation, which uses both non-gender-biased compensable factors and non-gender-biased evaluation   (para 3.3)

7   Grade structure: a hierarchy of bands or levels ('grades') to which are allocated groups of jobs that are in the same value range.

        Pay structure: pay ranges or scales for each grade, allowing scope for pay progression within the grade.   (para 5.2)

8   For a full answer, see paragraph 6.2.

9   Gain sharing schemes, profit-sharing, employee share ownership.   (para 6.4)

10   For a full answer, see paragraph 7.3

Answers to activities

1   The answers to this activity will be personal to you, and should clarify your thinking about need theories and rewards. The issue of pay will be discussed in Paragraph 1.5 of the chapter.

2   Again, the answer to this activity will be personal to you, but remember to draw out the relevant learning. *Your* subjective experience of job evaluation (your own sense of the fairness of your salary *and* the transparency and perceived fairness of your organisation's job evaluation scheme) should highlight some of the issues for HR managers. You will also be building up your 'case study' file of examples of HR practices in the real world.

3   (a)   Subjectivity may take the following forms.

              (i)   The factors for analysis are themselves qualitative, not easy to define and measure. Mental ability and initiative are observable in job holders, but not easily quantifiable as an element of the job itself.

              (ii)   Assessment of the importance and difficulty of a job cannot objectively be divorced from the context of the organisation and job holder. The relative importance of a job is a function of the culture and politics of the organisation, the nature of the business and not least the personal power of the individual in the job. The difficulty of the job depends on the ability of the job holder and the favourability or otherwise of the environment/technology/work methods/management.

(iii) The selection of factors and the assignment of monetary values to factors remain subjective judgements.

(b) It is undoubtedly desirable to achieve objectivity, to reduce the resentment commonly felt at the apparent arbitrariness of pay decisions. If job evaluation were truly objective, it would be possible to justify differentials on a rational basis, the organisation would have a balanced and economical pay structure based on contribution, and employers would be safe from accusations of unfair pay decisions.

4 (a) Published surveys are quick and relatively inexpensive – but may not be relevant to the organisation's jobs, and may be out of date.

Special surveys may be time-consuming and costly, but they directly compare jobs in the market place with jobs in the firm.

Network/club surveys are a cost-effective way of accessing surveys, and are regularly updated.

Recruitment ads and consultancies may be misleading: the job descriptions are unlikely to be sufficient to match jobs accurately, and salaries offered/cited may not be reflected in practice.

(b) Job matching may be done by using job titles, but this is likely to be very misleading. Job descriptions are likely to offer greater accuracy in identifying directly comparable jobs: the fuller the description, the greater the comparability. Comparing full job evaluations of different jobs would be most valuable – if such data were available (eg through commissioned or published surveys).

5 One may list the general arguments for paying over market rate as follows.

(a) The offer of a notably higher remuneration package than market rate may be assumed to generate greater interest in the labour market. The organisation will therefore have a wider field of selection for the given labour category, and will be more likely to have access to the most skilled/experienced individuals. If the organisation establishes a reputation as a 'wage leader' it may generate a consistent supply of high-calibre labour.

(b) There may be benefits of high pay offers for employee loyalty, and better performance resulting from the (theoretically) higher calibre and motivation of the workforce.

(c) Even if a cheap supply of labour were available, and the employer could get away with paying a low rate, its ideology or ethical code of an organisation may make reluctant to do so. A socially responsible employer may wish to avoid the exploitation of labour groups, such as immigrants, who may not be aware of general market rates.

(d) An employer might adopt a socially responsible position not purely for ethical reasons but to maintain a respected image and good relations with government, interest groups, employee representatives and the general public (potential customers/ consumers).

(e) Survival and immediate profit-maximisation are not necessarily the highest objective of any organisation. Employers in growth markets, or hoping to diversify into new markets, cannot afford a low-calibre, high-turnover workforce. Notably innovative organisations can be seen to be offering higher than market rate on salaries (eg Mars) or remuneration packages including profit-related bonuses (eg Sainsbury's): moreover, their financial performance bears out their view that pay is an investment. To an extent, this pay strategy stems from the culture or value system of the organisation, the importance it attaches to loyalty, innovation and initiative, and its willingness to pay more to attract and retain such higher-level attributes: quantity may not be the prime employment criterion.

On the other hand, there are substantial cost savings in paying lower rates. It cannot be assumed that high remuneration inevitably leads to higher motivation and better performance. Not everybody has an instrumental orientation to work: money may not be the prime incentive – and pay is often a source of dissatisfaction rather than satisfaction, whatever its level.

If the organisation's ability to maintain high rewards in the future is in doubt, management ought also to be aware that the disappointment and culture shock of reversing a high-remuneration policy is very great.

6   Single status schemes can save an organisation administrative and overtime costs, and may improve employee flexibility and industrial relations. For manual workers, there are clear advantages in receiving a wider range of benefits and an annual salary (which at least improves their borrowing position).

However, there may be an increase in labour costs overall. For the workers, too, there is a drawback, in monthly – instead of weekly – payments. There is also a perceived loss of status for salaried workers, in the achievement of parity by previous wage-earners: this may affect their morale, although the organisation culture will have a lot to do with whether harmonisation is perceived as threatening or equitable and exciting.

7   If you are not employed in a work organisation, ask a salaried acquaintance. Do not neglect to think about part (b) of this activity: research has shown that in the absence of information about salaries, people become dissatisfied by what they *think* they are earning in relation to others. Some people seem genuinely not to want to know how their salary is determined, as long as it progresses year on year: what might the consequences of such an attitude be for loyalty, motivation and the salary bill of the organisation?

8   There are a number of difficulties associated with incentive schemes based on monetary reward.

(a) Increased earnings simply may not be an incentive to some individuals. An individual who already enjoys a good income may be more concerned with increasing his leisure time, for example.

(b) Workers are unlikely to be in complete control of results. External factors, such as the general economic climate, interest rates and exchange rates may play a part in *profitability* in particular. In these cases, the relationship between an individual's efforts and his reward may be indistinct.

(c) Greater specialisation in production processes means that particular employees cannot be specifically credited with the success of their particular products. This may lead to frustration amongst employees who think their own profitable work is being adversely affected by inefficiencies elsewhere in the organisation.

(d) Even if employees *are* motivated by money, the effects may not be altogether desirable. An instrumental orientation may encourage self-interested performance at the expense of teamwork: it may encourage attention to output at the expense of quality, and the lowering of standards and targets (in order to make bonuses more accessible).

Workers remain suspicious that if they achieve high levels of output and earnings, management will alter the basis of the incentive rates to reduce future earnings. Work groups therefore tend to restrict output to a level that they feel is 'fair' and 'safe'.

9   In a survey of 2,000 people in full-time employment in France, Britain, Germany and Italy, it was discovered that:

(a) Most workers think a staff restaurant is a more important benefit than a company car (84% of workers, in 'cuisine-conscious' France!)

(b) Company cars were also rated less important than pensions or private health insurance

Chapter 6:
MONITORING AND MANAGING PERFORMANCE

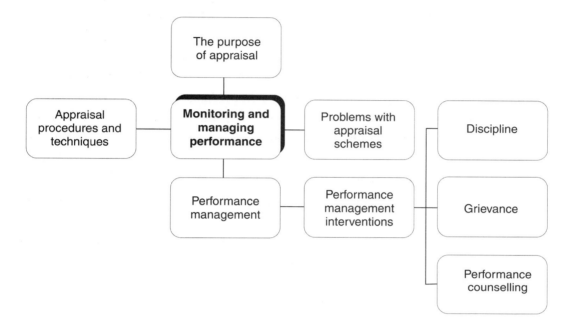

Introduction

The process of monitoring individual and group performance, and giving helpful feedback for improvement, is generally called **performance appraisal**. The purpose of appraisal was traditionally regarded as constructive criticism of an employee's performance by the line manager, but nowadays it has a more forward-looking approach.

(a) Helping the employee to overcome any problems or obstacles to performance

(b) Identifying where an employee's potential for improved performance and greater challenge could be better fulfilled

(c) Setting goals and priorities for further monitoring and development.

Your objectives

In this chapter you will learn about the following.

(a) Organisational approaches to monitoring performance, including appraisal and performance management

(b) The role, purpose and types of appraisal

(c) 360 degree feedback

(d) Skills in appraisal and giving feedback

(e) Performance management interventions including discipline, grievance and counselling

1 THE PURPOSE OF APPRAISAL

Definition

> **Performance appraisal** is the process whereby an individual's performance is reviewed against previously agreed goals, and where new goals are agreed which will develop the individual and improve performance over the forthcoming review period.

1.1 Role of appraisal

Monitoring and evaluating the performance of individuals and groups is an essential part of human resource management. It has several key aims.

(a) To identify individuals' learning/development and performance improvement needs

(b) To identify problems or barriers to performance which require intervention

(c) To identify people with potential for future promotion, supporting succession planning

(d) To provide a basis for reward decisions: eligibility for results-related bonuses, competence-related increments, merit awards and so on

(e) To improve communication about work issues, performance and development opportunities between managers and team members.

It may be argued that a particular, deliberate stock-taking exercise is unnecessary, since managers are constantly monitoring progress and giving subordinates feedback from day to day.

1.2 Why have a formal appraisal system?

It must be recognised that, if no system of formal appraisal is in place:

(a) Managers may obtain random impressions of subordinates' performance (perhaps from their more noticeable successes and failures), but not a coherent, complete and objective picture

(b) Managers may have a fair idea of their subordinates' shortcomings – but may not have devoted time and attention to the matter of improvement and development

(c) Different managers may be applying a different set of criteria, and varying standards of objectivity and judgement, undermining the value and credibility of appraisal

(d) Managers rarely give their subordinates systematic or constructive feedback on their performance.

Activity 1 (15 minutes)

List four disadvantages to the *employee* of not having an appraisal system.

1.3 The systematic approach to appraisal

A typical appraisal system would involve:

(a) Identification of **criteria** for assessment

(b) The preparation of an **appraisal report**

(c) An **appraisal interview**, for an exchange of views about the results of the assessment, targets for improvement, solutions to problems and so on

(d) The preparation and implementation of **action plans** to achieve improvements and changes agreed

(e) **Follow-up:** monitoring the progress of the action plan.

We will now look at each stage in turn.

2 APPRAISAL PROCEDURES AND TECHNIQUES

2.1 What should be monitored and assessed?

Assessments must be related to a common set of standards, so that comparisons can be made between individuals. On the other hand, they should be related to meaningful and specific performance criteria, which take account of the critical variables in each job.

Activity 2 (20 minutes)

Think of some criteria which you would want to use in assessment of some jobs – but which would not be applicable in others.

Personal qualities like reliability or outgoingness have often been used as criteria for assessing people. However, they are not necessarily relevant to job performance: you can be naturally outgoing, but still not good at communicating with customers, if your product knowledge or attitude is poor. Also, personality judgements are notoriously vague and unreliable: words like 'loyalty' and 'ambition' are full of ambiguity and moral connotations.

In practical terms, this has encouraged the use of **competence or results-based appraisals**, where performance is measured against specific, job-related performance criteria.

Most large organisations have pre-printed assessment forms setting out all the relevant criteria and the range of possible judgements. (We reproduce such a form later in this chapter.) Even so, a manager should critically evaluate such schemes to ensure that the criteria for assessment are relevant to his or her team and task – and that they remain so over time, as the team and task change.

Relevant criteria for assessment might be based on the following.

(a) **Job, role or competence descriptions** as a guide to what competences, responsibilities and results might be monitored and assessed.

(b) **Departmental or team plans, performance standards and targets**. If the plan specifies completion of a certain number of tasks, or production of a certain number of units, to a particular quality standard, assessment can be focused on whether (or how far) those targets have been achieved.

(c) **Individually negotiated goals and standards** for performance and/or improvement. This is a feature of 'performance management', discussed in Section 4 of this Chapter.

Let us now look at some of the performance monitoring and reporting methods used in organisations.

2.2 Reporting methods

Overall assessment

The manager writes in narrative form his or her judgements about the appraisee. There will be no guaranteed consistency of the criteria and areas of assessment, and managers may not be able to convey clear, effective judgements in writing.

Guided assessment

Assessors are required to comment on a number of specified characteristics and performance elements, with guidelines as to how terms such as 'application', 'integrity' and 'adaptability' are to be interpreted in the work context. This is a more precise, but still rather vague method.

Grading

Grading adds a comparative frame of reference to the general guidelines, whereby managers are asked to select one of a number of defined levels or degrees to which an individual displays a given characteristic. These are also known as rating scales, and have been much used in standard appraisal forms. (See Figure 6.2 on the following page.)

Numerical values may be added to gradings to give rating scores. Alternatively a less precise graphic scale may be used to indicate general position on a plus/minus scale, as in Figure 6.1.

Factor: job knowledge

High |————✓————| Average |————————| Low

Figure 6.1: graphics scale

Personnel Appraisal: Employees in Salary Grades 5-8

Date of review	Time on position		Age	S.G.	Name
	Yrs	Mths	Yrs		
Period of Review	Position Title				Area

Important : Read guide notes carefully before proceeding with the following sections

Section One — Performance Factors

Section Two — Performance Characteristics 1 2 3 4 5 6

Performance Factors columns: N/A U M SP E O

Section One
- Administrative Skills
- Communications - Written
- Communications - Oral
- Problem Analysis
- Decision making
- Delegation
- Quantity of Work
- Development of Personnel

Section Two
- Initiative
- Persistence
- Ability to work with others
- Adaptability
- Persuasiveness
- Self-confidence
- Judgement
- Leadership
- Creativity

Section Three Highlight Performance Factors and particular strengths/weaknesses of employee which significantly affect Job Performance

Development of Quality Improvements

Overall Performance Rating (Taking into account ratings given)

Prepared by: Signature ___ Date ___ Position Title ___

Section Four Comments by reviewing authority

Signature ___ Date ___ Position Title ___ IR Review Initial ___ Date ___

Section Five Supervisor's Notes on Counselling Interview

Signature ___ Date ___ Position Title ___

Section Six Employees Reactions and Comment

Signature ___ Date ___

Performance Classification

Outstanding performance is characterised by high ability which leaves little or nothing to be desired.
Personnel rated as such are those who regularly make significant contributions to the organisation which are above the requirements of their position. Unusual and challenging assignments are consistently well handled.

Excellent performance is marked by above-average ability, with supervision required.

Satisfactory Plus performance indicates fully adequate ability, without the need for excessive supervision.
Personnel with this ratings are able to give proper consideration to normal assignments, which are generally well-handled. They will meet the requirements of the position. '**Satisfactory plus**' performers may include those who lack the experience at their current level to demonstrate above-average ability.

Marginal performance is in instances where the ability demonstrated does not fully meet the requirements of the position, with excessive supervision and direction normally required.
Employees rated as such will show specific deficiencies in their performance which prevent them from performing at an acceptable level.

Unsatisfactory performance indicates an ability which falls clearly below the minimum requirements of the position.

'**Unsatisfactory**' performers will demonstrate market deficiencies in most of the major aspects of their responsibilities, and considerable improvement is required to permit retention of the employee in his current position.

Personal Characteristic Ratings

1.- Needs considerable improvement - substantial improvement required to meet acceptable standards.
2.- Needs improvement - some improvement required to meet acceptable standards
3.- Normal - meets acceptable standards
4.- Above normal - exceeds normally acceptable standards in most instances.
5.- Exceptional - displays rare and unusual personal characteristics.

4168B/1

Figure 6.2: Standard appraisal form

Behavioural incident methods

These concentrate on employee behaviour, which is measured against typical behaviour in each job, as defined by common **'critical incidents'** of successful and unsuccessful job behaviour reported by managers. The analysis is carried out for **key tasks**, which are identified as critical to success in the job and for which specific standards of performance *must* be reached. This makes scales highly relevant to job performance, and facilitates objective assessment because ratings are described in behavioural terms.

The behavioural equivalent of the graphic scale for a manager's key task of 'marketing initiative' might appear as follows:

| Produces no new ideas for marketing. Appears apathetic to competitive challenge | Produces ideas when urged by head office. Ideas not clearly thought out nor enthusiastically applied | Produces ideas when urged by head office and gives full commitment to new programmes | Spontaneously generates new ideas for marketing and champions them through head office approval. Ideas related to identified needs and effective in practice |

Figure 6.3: Critical incident scale

Results-orientated schemes

All the above techniques may be used with more or less results-orientated criteria. A wholly results-orientated approach sets out to review performance against specific targets and standards of performance, which are agreed in advance by a manager and subordinate together.

Key advantages of such an approach include the following.

(a) The subordinate is more involved in appraisal, and performance, because (s)he is able to evaluate progress in achieving clear, jointly-agreed measures.

(b) The manager is relived of the 'critic' role and becomes more of a 'counsellor', jointly defining solutions to performance issues.

(c) Clear and known targets are beneficial in motivation, especially in maximising the effectiveness of financial incentives.

(d) The emphasis of appraisal becomes forward-looking (focusing on improvements and incentives), rather than purely retrospective.

FOR DISCUSSION

Which of the above reporting methods would you consider:

(a) Fairest
(b) Most easily justified to the person being appraised
(c) Most suitable for determining performance pay awards?

In introducing 'performance management', we have raised the possibility that an employee might be involved in monitoring and evaluating his or her own performance. We will look at some of the sources of assessment feedback other than the appraisee's immediate boss.

2.3 Sources of performance feedback

Organisations have begun to recognise that the employee's immediate boss is not the only (or necessarily the best) person to assess his or her performance. Other options include:

(a) The employee him or herself (self appraisal)
(b) Peers and co-workers (peer appraisal)
(c) Subordinates (upwards appraisal)
(d) Or a combination of sources (360 degree feedback)

Self-appraisal

Self-appraisal allows individuals to carry out a self-evaluation as a major input to the appraisal process.

Advantages

(a) It **saves the manager time,** as the employee identifies the areas which are most relevant to the job and his/her relative strengths.

(b) It offers **increased responsibility** to the individual, which may improve motivation.

(c) It helps to integrate the goals of the individual with those of the organisation.

On the other hand, of course, people are often not the best judges of their own performance. They may deliberately over– (or under-) estimate their performance, in order to gain approval or reward – or to conform to group norms, say.

Upward appraisal

This is a notable modern trend, adopted in the UK by companies such as BP and British Airways.

The advantages of subordinates appraising their superiors might be as follows.

(a) Subordinates tend to know their superior (particularly in the area of leadership skills) better than anyone.

(b) Multiple ratings (from a group of subordinates) has greater statistical validity than a single view.

(c) Upward appraisal encourages subordinates to give feedback and raise problems they may have with their boss, which otherwise would be too difficult or risky for them.

(d) It supports upward communication in general, which may have knock-on benefits for creativity, problem-solving and employee relations.

NOTES

Activity 3	**(15 minutes)**

Imagine you had to do an upward appraisal on your boss, parent or lecturer. Suggest the two major problems that might be experienced with upward appraisal.

Customer appraisal

In some companies part of the appraisal process may take the form of feedback from 'customers' (internal or external). This may be taken further into an influence on remuneration: at Rank-Xerox, for example, 30% of a manager's annual bonus is conditional upon satisfactory levels of 'customer' feedback.

Feedback from customers (external and internal) is particularly valuable in:

(a) Encouraging and monitoring the customer care orientation of the organisation as a whole – in line with modern thinking about business processes, quality management and so on

(b) Showing a commitment to respond meaningfully to customer feedback

(c) Focusing areas of an employee's performance that are recognised to have real impact on the business

(d) Encouraging the 'internal customer' concept within the organisation, as an aid to co-ordination.

360 degree feedback

360 degree feedback (also known as 'multi-rater instruments' and 'multi-source assessment') is the most radical recognition of multiple **stakeholders** in an individual's performance. As described by Peter Ward (who introduced the system at Tesco):

> Traditional performance measurement systems have rarely operated on more than one or two dimensions. However, 360-degree feedback is designed to enable all the stakeholders in a person's performance to comment and give feedback. This includes the current (and perhaps previous) boss (including temporary supervisors), peers and co-workers, subordinates and even external customers. Finally, the employee's own self-assessment is added and compared.

Information is usually collected (anonymously) through questionnaires, either on paper or online.

The advantages of 360 degree feedback are as follows.

(a) It offers the opportunity to build up a rounded picture of an employee's performance: the more relevant parties contribute, the more complete the picture.

(b) Multiple appraisal may reduce or at least balance the element of subjectivity which inevitably enters appraisal of one individual by another.

(c) 360 degree feedback increases the amount and openness of multi-directional task and performance-related communication in the organisation. This is particularly beneficial in the case of cross-functional communication, creating opportunities for improved integration, co-ordination and knowledge/ideas sharing.

(d)   The extensive information-gathering process, and feedback from key performance areas and contacts (including customers and suppliers, where relevant), signals the seriousness with which appraisal is regarded by the organisation, reinforcing commitment to performance management and improvement.

The approach has a number of disadvantages, however.

(a)   Subjectivity is not eliminated by the process: a number of subjective viewpoints is arguably no fairer than just one!

(b)   There are still difficulties in gathering feedback from peers (fear of being 'disloyal' and subordinates (fear of reprisals).

(c)   It is not easy to define performance criteria that will be meaningful and measurable for each appraiser, nor to weight the evaluations of the different appraisers, nor to reconcile or prioritise contradictory evaluations by different appraisers.

(d)   There is extra organisation, paperwork and evaluation to be done, although this is now minimised by a range of software packages for the process, allowing computer or online 'form' filling, integration and reporting. (Do a web search on '360 degree appraisal' for a huge sampling of providers…)

EXAMPLE

W H Smith is often used as a case study for 360° appraisal. The company had operated upwards appraisal (covering some 1,200 managers) since 1990, but in 1996 it trialed a 360 degree system in its HR function.

'Between eight and fifteen people filled in forms covering each manager's competences and personal objectives. The appraisers were asked to rate them on a scale of one to five and give anecdotal examples to support the marks (ie 'critical incidents'). The forms were sent to an independent third party for collating.

The company found that the system sharpened the developmental aspects of its appraisal meetings, but that is also caused a significant administration load. Many appraisers found it hard to comment on the individual manager's performance objectives, and to come up with anecdotal evidence for ratings.

When the system was rolled out to the IT function, the processing was done in-house (to save costs). When it was extended to the rest of the organisation a computerised system was developed to reduce bureaucracy.

NOTES

> **Activity 4** (20 minutes)
>
> In a 360° feedback questionnaire a skill area like 'communicating' might be defined as the 'ability to express oneself clearly and to listen effectively to others'. Guiding descriptions might then include 'Presents ideas or information in a well-organised manner' or 'Allows you to finish what you have to say'; followed by rating scales.
>
> Rate yourself on the two descriptions mentioned here, on a scale of 1–10. Get a group of friends, fellow-students, even a tutor or parent, to write down (anonymously) *their* rating for you on the same two comments. Keep these notes in an envelope, unseen, until you have gathered a few.
>
> Compare them with your self-rating, if you dare... What drawbacks did you (and your respondents) find to such an approach?

Having reported on an individual's performance – whether in a written narrative comment, or on a prepared appraisal form – a manager must discuss the content of the report with the individual concerned.

2.4 The appraisal interview

There are basically three ways of approaching appraisal interviews (Maier, 1958).

(a) The **tell and sell** method. The manager tells the subordinate how (s)he has been assessed, and then tries to 'sell' (gain acceptance of) the evaluation and any improvement plans. This requires unusual human relations skills, in order to convey feedback in a constructive manner, and to motivate behavioural change.

(b) The **tell and listen** method. The manager tells the subordinate how (s)he has been assessed, and then invites comments. The manager therefore no longer dominates the interview throughout, and there is greater opportunity for counselling as opposed to pure direction. The employee is encouraged to participate in the assessment and the working out of improvement targets and methods. Change in the employee may not be the sole key to improvement, and the manager may receive helpful feedback about job design, methods, environment or supervision.

(c) The **problem-solving** approach. The manager abandons the role of critic altogether, and becomes a counsellor and helper. The discussion is centred not on assessment of past performance, but on future solutions to the employee's work problems. The employee is encouraged to recognise the problems, think solutions through, and commit to improvement. This approach is more involving and satisfying to the employee and may also stimulate creative problem-solving.

Many organisations waste the opportunity represented by appraisal for **upward communication**. If an organisation is development-focused, it should harness the aspirations and abilities of its employees by asking positive and thought-provoking questions such as: Could any changes be made in your job which might result in improved performance? Have you any skills, knowledge, or aptitudes which could be made better use of in the organisation?

2.5 Follow-up

After the appraisal interview, the manager may complete his or her report with an overall assessment and/or the jointly-reached conclusion of the interview, with recommendations for follow-up action. This may take the following forms.

(a) Informing appraisees of the results of the appraisal, if this has not been central to the review interview.

(b) Carrying out agreed actions on reward, training, problem-solving and so on

(c) Monitoring the appraisee's progress and checking that (s)he has carried out agreed actions or improvements

(d) Taking necessary steps to help the appraisee to attain improvement objectives, by guidance, providing feedback, upgrading equipment, altering work methods or whatever.

Activity 5   **(5 minutes)**

What would happen if there was no follow up action? (Think past the obvious.)

INTERNATIONAL COMPARISON

Some key cultural issues are involved in appraisal and its uses. Budwhar & Mellahi (2006), for example, highlight the inequitable application of promotion criteria in some Middle Eastern countries.

Nepotism, known usually as *wasta*, is perceived to be widespread in **Saudi Arabia**. Anecdotal evidence suggests that the promotion of people with tribal or family connections is very common… This is especially true in large and public sector organisations. This is a result of the tribal-based collectivist culture, where an individual's loyalty to the tribe, family and friends is valued over and above that to the organisation.

2.6 Skills in giving feedback

Giving feedback on performance is a key leadership skill. Many people find receiving positive feedback (compliments, praise) just as hard to receive as negative feedback. However, the purpose of feedback is to help people learn by increasing their awareness of what they do, how they do it and its impact on other people. There are two main types of feedback, both of which are valuable in enhancing performance and development.

(a) **Motivational feedback** is used to reward and reinforce positive behaviours, progress performance by praising and encouraging the individual. Its purpose is to increase *confidence*.

(b) **Developmental feedback** is given when a particular area of performance needs to be changed and how this might be done. Its purpose is to increase *competence*.

'Constructive' feedback (or either type) is designed to widen options and increase development. It does *not* mean giving only positive or 'encouraging' feedback about what a person did well: feedback about undesirable behaviours and their effects, given skilfully, is in many ways more useful.

The following are some brief guidelines on giving constructive developmental feedback.

(a) **Be intentional**. Emotions may be running high: feedback is best given calmly. There may be other people present: feedback is best given confidentially.

(b) **Start with positives**. People will more readily accept that criticism is objective and constructive if it is balanced with praise for positive aspects of their behaviour or performance.

(c) **Focus on the behaviour**. Feedback needs to refer clearly and objectively to behaviours, actions and results – *not* the person or their personality. ('Tough on the problem, soft on the person' is a good general rule.)

(d) **Be precise**. Feedback needs to be specific, avoiding vague and global statements: *not* 'you are always late' but 'on two occasions this week you have been more than five minutes late for meetings'.

(e) **Gain co-operation**. Try asking people first how *they* think they acted or handled a particular situation: you may find that, in giving feedback, you are able to confirm what they are already aware of. This encourages collaborative problem-solving.

(f) **Don't tackle everything at once**! Give the person one or two priority areas to deal with at a time.

(g) **Close with encouragement**. Balance negative feedback with positive encouragement that change is possible and will be supported.

FOR DISCUSSION

Consider a situation in the past when you had to give feedback to someone about their performance or behaviour.

(a) How did you feel about it?

(b) What do you think makes giving (i) positive feedback on good performance and (ii) negative feedback on poor performance difficult for you (and others)?

In theory, systematic appraisal schemes may seem fair to the individual and worthwhile for the organisation, but in practice the system often goes wrong. Let's see how, and what can be done.

3 PROBLEMS WITH APPRAISAL SCHEMES

3.1 Problems in practice

Lockett (1992) lists a number of reasons why appraisal may not always be effective in practice.

Appraisal barriers	Comment
Appraisal as confrontation	Many people use appraisals 'as a sort of show down, a good sorting out or a clearing of the air.' In this kind of climate: • There is little collaboration in problem-solving. • The feedback is subjective (often hostile). • The feedback is badly delivered. • Appraisals are 'based on yesterday's performance not on the whole year'. • There is lack of attention to positive development potential.
Appraisal as judgement	The appraisal 'is seen as a one-sided process in which the manager acts as judge, jury and counsel for the prosecution'. This puts the subordinate on the defensive. Instead, the process of performance management 'needs to be jointly operated in order to retain the commitment and develop the self-awareness of the individual.'
Appraisal as chat	The appraisal is conducted as if it were a friendly chat 'without ... purpose or outcome ... Many managers, embarrassed by the need to give feedback and set stretching targets, reduce the appraisal to a few mumbled "well dones!" and leave the interview with a briefcase of unresolved issues.'
Appraisal as bureaucracy	Appraisal is a form-filling exercise, to satisfy the personnel department. Its underlying purpose, improving individual and organisational performance, is forgotten.
Appraisal as unfinished business	Appraisal should be part of a continuing future-focused process of performance management, not a way of 'wrapping up' the past year's performance issues.

Activity 6	**(15 minutes)**
What would you anticipate the effects of appraisal on employee motivation to be?	

3.2 Evaluating appraisal

The appraisal scheme should itself be assessed (and regularly re-assessed), according to the following general criteria.

(a) **Relevance**

☐ Does the system have a useful purpose, relevant to the needs of the organisation and the individual?

☐ Is the purpose clearly expressed and widely understood by all concerned, both appraisers and appraisees?

☐ Are the appraisal criteria relevant to the purposes of the system?

(b) **Fairness**

☐ Is there reasonable standardisation of criteria and objectivity throughout the organisation?

☐ Has attention been given to the potential for direct or indirect discrimination in the criteria and methods of appraisal?

(c) **Serious intent**

☐ Are managers committed to the system – or is it just something the personnel department thrusts upon them?

☐ Who does the interviewing, and are they properly trained in interviewing and assessment techniques?

☐ Is reasonable time and attention given to the interviews – or is it a question of 'getting them over with'?

☐ Is there a genuine demonstrable link between performance and reward or opportunity for development?

(d) **Co-operation**

☐ Is the appraisal a participative, problem-solving activity – or a tool of management control?

☐ Is the appraisee given time and encouragement to prepare for the appraisal, so that he can make a constructive contribution?

☐ Does a jointly-agreed, concrete conclusion emerge from the process?

(e) **Efficiency**

☐ Is all the above achieved with a justifiable investment of time and cost?

> **Activity 7**   **(15 minutes)**
>
> Look up the procedures manual of your organisation, and read through the appraisal procedures – or ask someone about their organisation.
>
> How effective are these appraisal procedures? Measure them against the criteria given above.
>
> If you can get hold of an appraisal report form, have a go at filling one out for yourself – a good exercise in self-awareness!

4 PERFORMANCE MANAGEMENT

4.1 What is performance management?

Definition

> **Performance management** is an approach in which there is a dual emphasis: on setting key accountabilities, objectives, measures, priorities and time scales for the following review period *and* monitoring, appraising and adjusting performance on an on-going basis.

Torrington *et al* (2002) summarise a typical performance management system as follows: Figure 6.4.

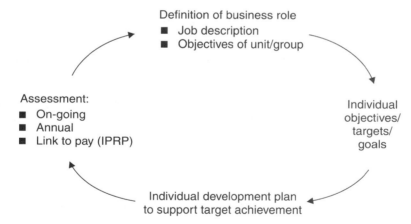

Figure 6.4: Typical performance management system

4.2 Why performance management?

In the late 1980s, the emphasis moved from (largely retrospective) performance appraisal to (on-going) performance management as increasing global competition created strong pressure for organisations to continually improve their performance and capabilities. The new focus on quality, customer service and added value meant that quality standards had to be set or refined – and this fed through to the performance management processes.

There are a number of advantages to a performance management orientation.

(a) Objective-setting gives employees the security and satisfaction of both understanding their jobs and knowing exactly what is expected of them. (A report by the Audit Commission, entitled '*Calling the Tune*', showed that local authorities who operated a comprehensive performance management system scored highly in staff attitude surveys on 'know how' and 'feel good' factors. In other words, objective-setting and appraisal help staff to feel that they understand more about their work, and 'feel good' about it.)

(b) Joint-objective setting and a developmental approach are positive and participatory, encouraging regular and frequent dialogue, a shared results focus; helping employees' to own and commit to change and improvement.

(c) Performance management focuses on future performance planning and improvement rather than retrospective performance appraisal, so it contributes to an output, customer flexibility and continuous improvement focus.

However, it should also be noted that such a system depends on the integration of goal-setting, development planning, appraisal and reward planning activities – and this appears (Torrington *et al*, 2002) not to be widespread in organisations using it. Performance management is also not immune to the problems of appraisal: inconsistent use of ratings, appraiser bias, lack of training by line managers implementing the scheme and so on.

FOR DISCUSSION

Armstrong (2003) describes the purpose of performance management as follows.

> Performance management is a means of getting better results from the organisation, teams and individuals by understanding and managing performance within an agreed framework of planned goals, standards and competence requirements. It is a process for establishing shared understanding about what *is* to be achieved, and an approach to managing and developing people in a way which increases the probability that it *will* be achieved in the short and long term. It is owned and driven by line management.

How is this different from performance appraisal? What are its implications for the HR function: recruitment, reward, training and development and its own role?

How does this work in practice?

4.3 Performance management activities

There are four key performance management activities.

- Preparation of performance agreements
- Preparation of performance and development plans
- Management of performance throughout the year
- Performance reviews

Preparation of performance agreements or contracts

These set out individual or team objectives; how performance will be measured; the knowledge, skills and behaviour needed to achieve the objectives; and the organisation's core values.

Objectives may be either:

(a)   Work/operational (results to be achieved or contribution to be made to the accomplishment of team, departmental and/or organisational objectives) or

(b)   Developmental (personal or learning objectives).

Performance measures should be objective and capable of being assessed: relevant data should be readily available. They should relate to results (not to effort) and those results should be within the individual's control.

Discussions should ensure that individuals fully understand what is expected of them and that if they fulfil those expectations they will be regarded as having performed well.

Preparation of performance and development plans

These set out detailed performance and personal development needs, and action plans to address them, in order to meet individual objectives.

Management of performance throughout the year

This involves the continuous process of providing feedback on performance, conducting informal progress reviews and dealing with performance problems as necessary. This may include the planning and implementation of:

(a)   Training interventions, to address competence gaps or other shortfalls (or opportunities)

(b)   Disciplinary action, to improve individual behaviours and attitudes

(c)   Counselling interventions, to guide individuals in defining and solving problems

(d)   Managerial intervention to improve resources, systems, work organisation or other barriers to performance.

Performance reviews

Performance reviews involve both taking a view of an individual's progress to date *and* reaching an agreement about what should be done in the future. The performance review provides the means by which:

(a)   Results can be **measured** against targets

(b)   The employee can be given **feedback**

(c)   An **agreement can be reached** on on-going development needs and future performance targets

(d)   The **link** between results and performance-related pay can be made

The area of individual performance management is vast, and covered by a vast literature on management and leadership. In this Course Book, we are focusing on the role of HR practitioners: disciplinary and grievance handling, performance counselling and training/development planning are key tasks in this area. We cover training in detail in Part C, so we will discuss the remaining aspects briefly here.

5 DISCIPLINE

Definition

> **Discipline** can be considered as: 'a condition in an enterprise in which there is orderliness, in which the members of the enterprise behave sensibly and conduct themselves according to the standards of acceptable behaviour as related to the goals of the organisation'.

Discipline is often imposed in organisations through the definition of rules and standards of conduct, and through the threat of sanctions for non conformance (this is sometimes called 'negative' discipline, although it need not be applied in a negative way.) Disciplinary action may be **punitive** (punishing an offence), **deterrent** (warning people not to behave in that way) or **reformative** (calling attention to the nature of the offence so that it will not happen again). Its goal is nevertheless always to improve the future behaviour of the employee and other members of the organisation.

5.1 Types of disciplinary situations

There are many types of disciplinary situations which may require intervention. The most frequently occurring are:

(a) Excessive absenteeism

(b) Repeated poor timekeeping

(c) Defective and/or inadequate work performance

(d) Poor attitudes which influence the work of others or which reflect on the public image of the firm.

> **Activity 8**   **(15 minutes)**
>
> Suggest five more reasons for management taking disciplinary action. (You might be able to draw on your own experience at work, school or college.)

In addition, managers might be confronted with disciplinary problems stemming from employee behaviour *off* the job: abuse of alcohol or drugs, or involvement in some form of law-breaking activity. If off-the-job conduct has an impact upon performance *on* the job, the manager must be prepared to deal with it.

5.2 Model disciplinary procedure

Many enterprises have accepted the idea of **progressive discipline**, which provides for increasing severity of the penalty with each repeated offence: a bit like the yellow card (warning), red card (sent off) system used in football. The following are the suggested steps of progressive disciplinary action.

(a) **The informal talk**

The manager simply discusses with the employee his or her behaviour in relation to the standards expected by the organisation, and tries to get a recognition that such behaviour is unacceptable, with a commitment that it will not be repeated.

(b) **Oral warning or reprimand**

The manager emphasises the undesirability of repeated violations, and warns the offender that it could lead to more serious penalties.

(c) **Written or official warning**

A written warning is a formal matter, and becomes a permanent part of the employee's record. (It may also serve as evidence in case of protest against the later dismissal of a repeated offender.)

(d) **Suspension without pay**

Disciplinary lay-offs may extend over several days or weeks, and may only be used if provided for in the contract of employment.

(e) **Dismissal**

This should be reserved for the most serious offences. For the organisation it involves waste of a labour resource, and potential loss of morale in the work team.

Regulations under the *Employment Act* 2002, sought to encourage the internal resolution of workplace disputes by introducing **statutory minimum requirements for internal discipline and grievance procedures**. The regulations (in force since 2004) impose a mandatory three-step procedure:

- The parties must put the issue in writing

- The parties must meet to discuss the issue (the employee being entitled to be accompanied by a trade union or staff association representative, if desired)

- An appeal must be held if required.

Steps must be taken without unreasonable delay; the timing and location of meetings must be reasonable; parties must be able to explain their cases; and the employer's representative at appeals should be more senior than the representative who attended the first meeting (in other words, the issue is referred upwards).

Failure to complete this basic procedure will currently make any subsequent dismissal of the employee on disciplinary grounds unfair.

Unfortunately, the Gibbons Review into these changes (published in April 2007) concluded that the procedures have instead exacerbated and accelerated employment disputes, partly by formalising those that could have been dealt with informally. The review has, among other things, recommended that the statutory procedures be **repealed** – and the Government has announced further consultation. *Watch this space!*

In the meantime, employers would do well to observe the clear, non-prescriptive guidelines on good practice represented by the *ACAS* (Advisory, Conciliation and Arbitration Service) *Code of Practice* 2002.

Good disciplinary procedures should:

- Be in writing

- Say to whom they apply

- Be non-discriminatory

- Allow for matters to be dealt with without undue delay

- Allow for information to be kept confidential

- Tell employees what disciplinary actions might be taken

- Say what the levels of management have the authority to take disciplinary action

- Require employees to be informed of the complaints against them, and supporting evidence, before a meeting

- Give employees a chance to have their say before management reaches a decision

- Provide workers with the right to be accompanied

- Provide that no employee is dismissed for a first breach of discipline except in cases of gross misconduct

- Require management to investigate fully before any disciplinary action is taken

- Ensure that employees are given an explanation for any sanction; and

- Allow employees to appeal against a decision

(ACAS Code of Practice 2002)

FOR DISCUSSION

How (a) accessible and (b) clear are the rules and policies of your college: do people really know what they are and are not supposed to do? Have a look at the student regulations. How easy is it to see them – or were you referred elsewhere? Are they well-indexed and cross-referenced, and in language that all students will understand?

How (a) accessible and (b) clear are the disciplinary procedures? Who is responsible for discipline?

The crucial interpersonal event in disciplinary action will be the interview. The following advice takes into account both procedural guidelines and interpersonal issues.

5.3 Disciplinary interviews

Preparation for the disciplinary interview will include the following.

(a)   Gathering facts about the alleged infringement.

(b)   Determination of the organisation's position: how valuable is the employee, potentially? How serious are the offences/lack of progress? How far is the organisation prepared to go to support or impose improvement?

(c)   Identification of the aims of the interview: punishment? deterrent to others? problem-solving? Specific standards for future behaviour/ performance need to be determined.

(d)   Notification of the employee concerned, with time to prepare for the disciplinary interview and seek representation if desired.

The disciplinary interview will then proceed as follows.

Step 1.   The manager will explain the purpose of the interview.

Step 2.   The manager will explain the organisation's position with regard to the issues involved and the organisation's expectations with regard to future behaviour/performance.

Step 3.   The employee should be given the opportunity to comment, explain, justify or deny.

Step 4.   Improvement targets should be jointly agreed (if possible).

(i)   They should be specific and quantifiable, performance related and realistic.

(ii)   They should be related to a practical but reasonably short time period. A date should be set to review progress.

(iii)   Measures should be proposed to help the employee where necessary (eg mentoring, extra supervision or coaching, counselling and so on).

Step 5.   The manager should explain any penalties imposed on the employee, the reasons behind them and, if the sanctions are ongoing, how they can be withdrawn (eg at what point and at what terms the employee could expect the removal of the formal warning from their record). There should be a clear warning of the consequences of failure to meet improvement targets or breaching expected codes of behaviour

Step 6.   The manager should explain the appeals procedure.

Step 7.   The manager should ensure the employee understands fully steps 1-6 above and then should briefly summarise the proceedings.

Records of the interview will be kept on the employee's personnel file for the formal follow-up review and any further action necessary, until such time as it is agreed they should be removed.

NOTES

6 GRIEVANCE

Definition

A **grievance** occurs when an individual feels that (s)he is being wrongly or unfairly treated by a colleague or supervisor: picked on, unfairly appraised, or discriminated against and so on.

6.1 Purpose of a grievance procedure

Ideally grievances should be solved informally by the individual's manager. However, if this is not possible, a formal grievance procedure should be followed.

(a) To allow objective grievance handling – including 'cooling off' periods and independent case investigation and arbitration.

(b) To protect employees from victimisation – particularly where a grievance involves their immediate superiors.

(c) To provide legal protection for both parties, in the event of a dispute resulting in claims before an Employment Tribunal.

(d) To encourage grievance airing – which is an important source of feedback to management on employee problems and dissatisfactions.

(e) To require full and fair investigation of grievances, enabling the employer-employee relationship to be respected and preserved, despite problems.

6.2 Grievance procedures

Formal grievance procedures, like disciplinary procedures, should be set out in **writing** and made available to all staff. These procedures should do the following things.

(a) State what **grades of employee** are entitled to pursue a particular type of grievance.

(b) **Distinguish between individual grievances and collective grievances** (which might be pursued through industrial relations processes).

(c) State the **rights of the employee** for each type of grievance: what actions and remedies may be claimed.

(d) State what the **procedures for pursuing a grievance** should be. They will typically involve appeal in the first instance to the line manager (or next level up, if the line manager is the subject of the complaint). If the matter cannot be resolved, the case will be referred to specified higher authorities. The assistance of the HR department may be required.

(e) Allow for the employee to be **accompanied** by a trade union or staff association representative or other colleague.

(f) **State time limits** for initiating certain grievance procedures and subsequent stages of them, such as appeals and communication of outcomes.

(g)   **Require written records** of all meetings concerned with the case to be made and distributed to all the participants.

(h)   Provide for right of **appeal**, and specify the appeals procedure.

As with disciplinary action, the focus of conflict resolution will be in an interview between the manager and the subordinate.

6.3   Grievance interviews

The dynamics of a grievance interview are broadly similar to a disciplinary interview, except that it is the subordinate who primarily wants a positive result or improvement in someone else's behaviour. (Remember *discipline* is where an employee does wrong: *grievance* is where an employee feels wronged.)

Prior to the interview, the manager should gain some idea of the complaint and its possible source. The meeting itself can then proceed through the following stages.

Step 1.   **Exploration.** What is the problem: the background, the facts, the causes (obvious and hidden)? At this stage the manager should simply try to gather as much information as possible, without attempting to suggest solutions or interpretations: the situation must be seen to be open.

Step 2.   **Consideration.** The manager should:

- Check the facts

- Analyse the causes – the problem of which the complaint may be only a symptom

- Evaluate options for responding to the complaint, and the implication of any response made.

It may be that information can be given to clear up a misunderstanding, or the employee will withdraw the complaint – having 'got it off his chest'. However, the meeting may have to be adjourned (say, for 48 hours) while the manager gets extra information and considers extra options.

Step 3.   **Reply.** The manager, having reached and reviewed various conclusions, reconvenes the meeting to convey (and justify, if required) his or her decision, and hear counter-arguments and appeals. The outcome (agreed or disagreed) should be recorded in writing.

Activity 9   **(20 minutes)**

Think of a complaint or grievance you have (or have had) at school or college. Have you done anything about it? If so, was it on your own, or through some kind of grievance procedure? If so, what happened: were you satisfied with the process and outcome? If not, why not? How could the procedure have been improved?

7 PERFORMANCE COUNSELLING

Where problems are identified in an individual's performance – whether through annual appraisal or on-going monitoring – a line manager may need to intervene.

7.1 Reasons for poor performance

Not all performance problems will be disciplinary in nature, or due to training/ competence gaps. Other factors the manager may need to consider include:

(a) Job changes which have left the job-holder less suited for the work

(b) Personality factors or clashes with team members

(c) Factors outside the work situation (eg marital or financial problems)

(d) Problems with job design, work layout, management style and other factors outside the individual's own control.

7.2 Performance counselling process

In order to deal with the issue, the following four-step process could be implemented.

(a) Counsel the individual through a basic problem-solving process.

   (i) **The facts.** The manager should help the individual to accept and define the problem, through constructive feedback and supportive questioning.

   (ii) **The causes.** The individual and the manager should explore and agree on the causes of the problem. A collaborative, problem-solving orientation is needed.

   (iii) **The remedies.** The individual and the manager should explore and agree on the remedies to the problem.

(b) Ensure the individual understands the consequences of persistent poor performance, where relevant; this might involve invoking the firm's disciplinary procedures.

(c) Set and agree clear improvement targets and action plans and agree a period of time over which performance is expected to improve.

(d) Support the individual with agreed follow-up action: training, coaching, specialist counselling and so on.

Workplace counselling, and the skills involved, will be considered further in Chapter 11 of this Course Book.

Chapter roundup

- Performance appraisal is the process whereby an individual's performance is reviewed against previously agreed goals, and where new goals are agreed which will develop the individual and improve performance over the forthcoming review period.

- Trends in appraisal include: the use of behavioural and results-oriented appraisal criteria; the use of multiple sources of feedback; and a problem-solving approach to interviewing.

- 360° feedback is designed to enable all the stakeholders in a person's performance to comment and give feedback.

- A **grievance** occurs when an individual feels that (s)he is being wrongly or unfairly treated by a colleague or supervisor: picked on, unfairly appraised, or discriminated against and so on.

- Performance management is a recent approach which emphasises *both* defining the knowledge, skills, behaviours and standards required to produce the desired results *and* the appraisal and comparison of performance against objectives for the purposes of on-going performance improvement. It is a forward-looking, on-going and collaborative approach.

- Performance management interventions which may be required to address identified problems in an individual's performance include:

  - Disciplinary action, to address problems of behaviour or attitude: a model procedure is set out in the ACAS Code of Practice

  - Grievance procedures, to address workplace conflicts

  - Performance counselling, to investigate and collaboratively attempt to solve a range of performance problems

  - Training and development planning (discussed in Part C of this Course Book)

Quick quiz

1   What are the purposes of appraisal?

2   What bases or criteria of assessment might an appraisal system use?

3   What is 360-degree feedback?

4   What follow-up should there be after an appraisal?

5   Distinguish between motivational and developmental feedback.

6   What kinds of criticism might be levelled at appraisal schemes by a manager who thought they were a waste of time?

7   How can appraisal be made more positive and empowering to employees?

8   What is the difference between performance appraisal and performance management?

9   What are the four key performance management stages?

10   Distinguish between discipline and grievance.

Answers to quick quiz

1   Identifying performance levels, improvements needed and promotion prospects; deciding on rewards; assessing team work and encouraging, communication between manager and employee.   (see paragraph 1.1)

2   Job analysis, job description, plans, targets and standards.   (para 2.1)

3   Appraisal by all the stakeholders in a person's performance.   (para 2.3)

4   Appraisees should be informed of the results, agreed activities should be undertaken, progress should be monitored and whatever resources or changes are needed should be provided or implemented.   (para 2.5)

5   Motivational: used to reward and reinforce positive behaviour, increase confidence.

        Developmental: given in order to guide and motivate change and improvement, to increase competence.   (para 2.6)

6   The manager may say that he or she has better things to do with his or her time, that appraisals have no relevance to the job and there is no reliable follow-up action, and that they involve too much paperwork.   (para 3.1)

7   Ensure the scheme is relevant, fair, taken seriously and co-operative.

                                                                               (para 3.2)

8   Appraisal is a backward-looking performance review. Performance management is a forward-looking results-orientated scheme.   (para 4.1)

9   Preparation of performance agreements or contracts, preparation of performance/development plans; on-going management of performance; performance reviews.   (para 4.3)

10   Discipline is the 'downward' process whereby a manager addresses the behaviours or performance of an employee which do not meet the firm's standards. Grievance is the 'upward' process by which employees can appeal to higher authority to address problems or conflicts affecting them.(sections   5 and 6)

Answers to activities

1   Disadvantages to the individual of not having an appraisal system include the following. The individual is not aware of progress or shortcomings, is unable to judge whether s/he would be considered for promotion, is unable to identify or correct weaknesses by training and there is a lack of communication with the manager.

2   You will have come up with your own examples of criteria to assess some jobs but not others. You might have identified such things as:

        (a) Numerical ability (applicable to accounts staff, say, more than to customer contact staff or other non-numerical functions)

        (b) Ability to drive safely (essential for transport workers – not for desk-bound ones)

(c) Report-writing (not applicable to manual labour, say)

(d) Creativity and initiative (desirable in areas involving design and problem-solving not routine or repetitive jobs in mass production or bureaucratic organisations)

3 Problems with upward appraisal include fear of reprisals or vindictiveness (or extra form-processing). Some bosses in strong positions might feel able to refuse to act on results, even if a consensus of staff suggested that they should change their ways.

4 Drawbacks to 360-degree appraisal include:

(a) Respondents' reluctance to give negative feedback to a boss – or friend

(b) The suspicion that management is passing the buck for negative feedback, getting people to 'rat' on their friends

(c) The feeling that the appraisee is being picked on, if positive feedback is not carefully balanced with the negative

5 If follow-up action is not taken, employees will feel that appraisal is all talk and just a waste of time, and that improvement action on their side will not be appreciated or worthwhile.

6 The effects of appraisal on motivation are a tricky issue.

(a) Feedback on performance is regarded as vital in motivation, because it enables an employee to make calculations about the amount of effort required in future to achieve objectives and rewards. Even negative feedback can have this effect – and is more likely to spur the employee on to post-appraisal action.

(b) Agreement of challenging but attainable targets for performance or improvement also motivates employees by clarifying goals and the value (and 'cost' in terms of effort) of incentives offered.

(c) A positive approach to appraisal allows employees to solve their work problems and apply creative thinking to their jobs.

However, people rarely react well to criticism – especially at work, where they may feel that their reward or even job security is on the line. In addition, much depends on the self-esteem of the appraisee. If s(he) has a high self-image, (s)he may be impervious to criticism. If s(he) has a low self-image, (s)he may be depressed rather than motivated by criticism.

7 Your own research.

8 Reasons for disciplinary action might include:

(a) Breaking rules regarding rest periods and other time schedules, such as leaving work to go home early.

(b) Improper personal appearance or dress.

(c) Breaking safety rules, such as failing to observe fire regulations, failing to wear protective clothing and so on.

(d) Other violations of rules, regulations and procedures, such as smoking in a non-smoking office, or abuse of expenses claims.

(e) Open insubordination: refusal to carry out a legitimate order.

(f) Fighting, sexual harassment, racial or religious abuse or other forms of unacceptable conduct towards others.

9 Assuming you did do something about your grievance, you probably found there were various stages of the procedure. Hopefully the first and second stages were sufficient to solve the problem, but you may have felt that the procedure was too cumbersome or long-winded.

Chapter 7:
EXIT RIGHTS AND PROCEDURES

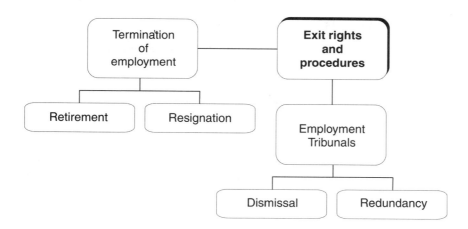

Introduction

So far, this Course Book has covered some of the processes by which the human resource is managed as it moves into and through or within the organisation. In this chapter, we look at some of the ways in which it must be managed on its way *out* of the organisation.

The exit of employees from the organisation requires careful management because of:

(a)   The need for compliance with the legal framework on employment protection (particularly in regard to dismissal and redundancy)

(b)   The need for sensitivity to the human issues involved (since the employment relationship, work and competence are so central to people's sense of their role and value in life)

(c)   The need for the organisation to gather feedback from voluntarily departing employees (resigners or early retirers) in order to identify retention problems.

We will consider these aspects in the context of each type of exit.

As you encounter law and regulation on various employment-related issues, remember: 'The law is a floor'. It sets minimum standards below which no organisational practice may fall without penalties. It does not set out 'best practice'. HR managers should ask themselves 'What *must* we do?' (compliance) – but also 'What *should* we do?' (best practice) and 'What *could* we do to enhance business performance *and* employee satisfaction and commitment?'

Your objectives

In this chapter you will learn about the following.

    (a)   The role and operation of Employment Tribunals

    (b)   Various form so termination of employment: resignation, retirement and termination of employment

    (c)   Wrongful, unfair and justified dismissal of employees

    (d)   The nature and procedures of redundancy

    (e)   Issues in the equitable and responsible management of exit

1 TERMINATION OF EMPLOYMENT

1.1 Termination of the employment contract

As we discussed in Chapter 4, the formation of a contract signals the beginning of an employment relationship. That relationship is finite: it comes to an end at some point.

Contracts of employment can be 'terminated' in the following ways.

    (a)   **By performance**

        The employee does what (s)he was hired to do, and the employer gives the agreed payment or consideration: the contract is fulfilled. This is common in fixed-term contracts and contracts for specific services. (It may also be said to apply in the case of retirement, where there is an agreed age at which employment ends.)

    (b)   **By mutual agreement**

        Both parties can agree that they are entitled to terminate the contract at any time, say in the event of 'irreconcilable differences'.

    (c)   **By notice**

        One party can terminate the contract, but must give adequate notice or warning to the other. This happens in the case of:

        (i)   Resignation by the employee and
        (ii)   Dismissal of the employee.

        There are strict rules on the periods of notice which must be given to protect both parties.

    (d)   **Breach of contract**

        If one party 'breaks' or fails to fulfil key terms of the contract, the other party has the option of considering the contract to have been terminated. (In addition, (s)he may seek legal remedies to compensate for, or minimise the effects of, the breach.) Failure by the employer to pay the agreed wage, say, or gross misconduct by the employee, would constitute breach of contract.

    (e)   **Frustration**

        A contract is 'frustrated' when it is prevented from being fulfilled – for example, because of the death, illness or imprisonment of one of the parties.

We will now go on to look at the HR department's role in managing the termination of employment contracts, looking in particular at the legislative and managerial frameworks that influence policy in this area. We will start by looking at employee-side reasons for leaving: retirement and resignation.

1.2 Retirement

The average age of the working population has been steadily increasing, with higher standards of living and health care. The problems of older workers, and the difficulties of adjusting to retirement, are therefore commanding more attention. The time at which an individual will experience difficulties in obtaining or retaining jobs because of age will obviously vary according to the individual, his/her lifestyle and occupation, and the attitudes of his/her society (including all diversity legislation where relevant) and employers. A 2003 CIPD survey (*Age, Pensions and Retirement*) suggested that, of employees in their fifties, 31% want to work beyond the age of 60, and 80% do not want to retire formally.

There are two basic approaches to retirement policy:

(a) **Flexible retirement,** whereby a stated retirement age is a minimum age at which the contract can be ended for retirement purposes: fit and capable employees are allowed to continue to work after this age.

(b) **Fixed retirement,** whereby retirement is enforced at the stated age.

The new **Employment Equality (Age) Regulations 2006** set the default retirement age at 65. If an organisation's normal retirement age is below this, the policy will have to be objectively justified. Employees also have the right to request to continue working beyond this age – and to have their request considered (if not accepted). We discuss these provisions in detail in Chapter 10.

> **Activity 1** (10 minutes)
>
> Employers can give not only financial assistance to retiring employees, but also practical help and advice. Suggest three ways in which the HR department could help older employees.

EXAMPLE

The **NHS** introduced a flexible retirement policy, made available to GPs in November 2002:

'This sits within a suite of flexible working policies designed to help improve productivity, developed by Debbie Mellor, head of employment. It encourages highly trained, highly skilled staff – who would otherwise leave – to remain within the service or return later, on flexible contracts …

'Unsurprisingly, Mellor says initial feedback suggests the intrinsic reward of the job features highly in doctors' motivations to stay on. "You don't go into the NHS simply to make lots of money like in the City". Many [doctors] feel their contribution to patient care can continue to offer great benefits to local communities and they are keen to remain active and use their skills for as long as possible. As one of them put it: "There's only so much golf you can play".'

'Mellor says performance management is paramount. "[Training] co-ordinators are in place to ensure that the pathway back to practice fits with an individual's training and development requirements." Alan Trickett, 67, is about to return as a GP after four years of retirement and says: "We live in an age of audit in every professional walk of life and we [doctors] should be no different." He cites cheaper, non-branded drugs as an area he must swot up on. "One of the most important aspects of being a GP is listening very carefully to patients and I think that is something which can often improve with age," he says.'

(Ball, 2003)

Weblink

> You may like to check out the Age Positive website for more information.
>
> ►► **http://www.agepositive.gov.uk**

1.3 Resignation

Definition

> **Resignation** is the process by which an employee gives notice of his or her intention to terminate the employment contract.

Employees may resign for any number of reasons, personal or occupational. Some or all of these reasons may well be a reflection on the structure, management style, culture or HR policies of the organisation itself. Management should attempt to find the real reasons why an employee is leaving in an **exit interview,** which may provide helpful feedback on its policies and practices: note, however, that there is no legal requirement for the employee to give reasons for leaving.

The principal aspect of any policy formulated to deal with resignations must be the length to which the organisation will go to try to dissuade a person from leaving. In some cases, the organisation may decide to simply let the person go, but when an employee has been trained at considerable cost to the firm, is particularly well qualified and experienced, or has knowledge of information and methods that should not fall into the hands of competitors, the organisation may try to keep him or her. Particular sources of employee dissatisfaction (eg salary) *may* sometimes be resolved, but there are dangers in setting precedents by giving special treatment.

FOR DISCUSSION

What issues are presented for an employer when a 'key talent' wants to leave the organisation? How can talent and knowledge be retained – or prevented from benefiting competitors?

Various arrangements will have to be made when an employee decides to leave. There will have to be co-operation and full exchange of information between the HR function and the leaver's immediate superior, so that procedures can begin when notice is given of an intended departure.

(a) If attempts to encourage the employee to stay have been unsuccessful, the exit interview will have to be arranged.

(b) The period of notice required for the employee to leave should be set out in the contract of employment, but some leeway may be negotiated on this, for example if the employee wishes to take up another position immediately. The statutory minimum notice period (Employment Rights Act 1996) is one week.

(c) Details of the departure have to be notified to the wages clerk, pension fund officer, security officer and so on, so that the appropriate paperwork and other procedures can be completed by the date of leaving. The organisation may have a departure checklist to ensure that all procedures are completed.

(d) The department head should complete a leaving report form: an overall assessment of the employee's performance in the organisation. This can then be used to provide references to his/her future employer(s).

It should be noted that during the notice period, all terms and conditions of the employment contract still apply: the employee still owes the employer duties of fidelity, obedience and care, while the employer still owes the employee duties of trust, care and provision of work. If there is any doubt that this kind of relationship will be possible during the notice period, due to the circumstances or feelings surrounding the resignation, it may be advisable to let the employee leave immediately with pay in lieu of notice: this may prevent loss of morale in the team from a disgruntled employee's behaviour, and indeed possible sabotage of work or customer relations by the outgoing employee, gathering of information for use by the new (competing) employer and so on.

Activity 2	(30 minutes)

Brainstorm the following issues.

(a) Reasons for resigning from a job .
(b) Procedures that should be included on an Employee Departure Checklist.

NOTES

Of course, not everybody leaves their organisation on a 'voluntary' basis. Where employees are required to leave employment, there is a clear need to protect their rights and livelihoods against injustice or exploitation by employers. After all, staff may be 'resources' and 'assets' – but they are also people. This is where employment protection legislation comes into force. We will start by looking at the key bodies enforcing employee rights.

2 EMPLOYMENT TRIBUNALS

Definition

> **Employment tribunals** are independent judicial bodies which arbitrate in employment matters including unfair dismissal, employment protection and claims in relation to sexual/racial discrimination and equal pay.

2.1 The composition of tribunals

The composition of an employment tribunal is governed by the Employment Tribunals Act (ETA) 1996. A tribunal usually has three members.

- A legally-qualified chairperson (solicitor or barrister)
- An employer representative
- An employee representative (usually from a trade union)

2.2 The powers of tribunals

Tribunals have powers to hear disputes or claims, and to:

(a) Order the disclosure and inspection of documents, or otherwise demand information relevant to the claim

(b) Set timescales for compliance with information requests

(c) Strike out applications and/or award costs, if a party does not comply with a directive order, or conducts proceedings in a disruptive or abusive fashion

(d) Make legally binding decisions and orders (eg to reinstate an employee who has been unfairly dismissed) and award compensation payments, within the boundaries of employment legislation.

In effect, the tribunal is a court, with jurisdiction in a wide range of matters derived from relevant statutory provisions.

The **Employment Appeal Tribunal (EAT)** hears appeals on the decisions of Employment Tribunals, but only on matters of law – not disputed facts of the case.

2.3 Tribunal procedures

A case is initiated when an employee presents an **application**, specifying the persons against whom relief is sought and the grounds on which it is sought.

LEARNING MEDIA

The application is registered, and a copy is sent to the respondent in the case, and to ACAS. Either party to the case (or the tribunal itself) may then require:

(a)   That the case go through **mediation and/or arbitration** by ACAS

(b)   That a **preliminary hearing** may be held to consider the merits of the case before proceeding to a full hearing

(c)   That the other party provide further or better **particulars** of any facts or contentions relevant to the claim, so that both parties are clear in advance what the nature of the case is. The tribunal may enforce this with orders for the disclosure and inspection of documents.

If the case proceeds to a **full hearing**, both parties must gather witnesses and documentation to support their case. Employees may be represented by a lawyer, trade union representative or other person of their choice: if they do not have a representative, the tribunal will assist them as far as possible (without bias) to comply with proper procedure.

At the hearing, witnesses are heard, or witness statements read out, and may be cross-examined by the other side and questioned by the tribunal.

Tribunal members then withdraw to consider their decision. If the employee is successful, further submissions may be made in regard to compensation or other forms of relief to be awarded.

3   DISMISSAL

3.1   Dismissal

An individual can be legally dismissed in three ways.

- Employment is terminated with or without notice (summary dismissal for gross misconduct).

- Employment under a fixed-term contract comes to an end and is not renewed on the same terms.

- Employee resigns (with or without notice) because of 'conduct [on the part of the employer] which is a significant breach of the contract of employment or which shows that the employer no longer intends to be bound by one or more of the essential terms of the contract' (*Western Excavating v Sharp 1978*). This is known as 'constructive dismissal'.

Dismissal with notice

In the UK, legislation sets out detailed requirements as to individual employee rights.

(a)   The statutory minimum period of notice that must be given (depending on length of service and contract terms)

(b)   Rights to waive notice periods, or accept payment in lieu

(c)   Rights to explanation of reasons for dismissal

(d)   Definitions of 'length of service' and 'continuous employment' (which qualify employees for many of the rights established by the Act) in regard to hours of work, periods of absence and transfer of the undertaking.

Dismissal without notice

In most cases, the statutory and/or contractual minimum notice of dismissal *must* be given to the employee. However, rare circumstances may justify '**summary**' **dismissal** without notice. The law protecting employees from unfair dismissal (discussed below) requires that summary dismissal be limited to cases of serious breach of contract, such as:

(a) **Gross misconduct** by the employee: theft, violence, serious refusal to obey reasonable instruction, endangerment of other staff

(b) **Serious neglect of duties**, or absence from work without permission or good cause

(c) **Serious breaches of trust** or **conflicts of interest** affecting the organisation's business.

Even then, with the onus on employers to justify fair dismissal, an organisation may prefer to use temporary suspension and other disciplinary measures, or dismissal by notice (with pay in lieu of notice if the employee must be removed immediately from the workplace).

FOR DISCUSSION

Debate for and against the proposition:

'An employer should have the right to fire incompetent, incompatible and dishonest employees without costly restrictions and red tape.'

Dismissal is clearly a bit of a political, legal and interpersonal minefield! Fortunately, there are two relatively clear definitions of circumstances in which an employee cannot legally be dismissed.

3.2 Wrongful dismissal

A claim for wrongful dismissal is open to employees at common law, if they can show they were dismissed in **breach of contract** (for example, with less than the required notice) and that they thereby suffered loss. They may then be able to claim damages compensating for the amount lost: accrued wages, payment for an entitlement to notice, or the balance of wages due under a fixed-term contract. In practice, such claims are less common now that **unfair dismissal** provisions offer wider remedies, but the common law remedy is still useful for those who cannot claim unfair dismissal (for example, because they have not been continuously employed for long enough to qualify).

Wrongful dismissal claims are taken to Employment Tribunals if they are for less than £25,000, and to the County Court for larger sums.

Wrongful dismissal is compensated under common law – but only to the amount lost by the employee. Employment protection legislation has widened the scope of protection and increased the range of remedies available. The concept of 'unfair dismissal' is an extremely important element of this legislation.

3.3 Unfair dismissal

Under the Employment Rights Act 1996 (and 1999 amendments) an employee currently has the right not to be unfairly dismissed if the following apply.

(a) Is under the normal retiring age applicable to his/her job, or under 65

(b) Has been continuously employed for 12 months (whether full-time or part-time)

(c) Lodges a claim with the tribunal office within three months of the date of dismissal.

Dismissal will *automatically* be deemed justified or unfair in the following cases.

Dismissal is justified where related to:	**Dismissal is unfair where related to:**
(a) **Redundancy** (provided that the selection for redundancy was fair).	(a) **Redundancy** where the selection is deemed unfair.
(b) **Legal impediment** – eg loss of driving licence or lack of work permit	(b) **Trade union membership** (actual or proposed) and activities, or refusal to join a trade union.
(c) **Incapability** (including ill health) or lack of qualifications.	(c) **Pregnancy**, maternity, dependant care or parental leave.
(d) **Misconduct**, provided that minimum disciplinary procedures have been followed (Employment Act 2002).	(d) **Spent conviction** (Rehabilitation of Offenders Act 1974).
(e) Some other **'substantial' reason**: for example, the employee marries a competitor, or refuses to accept a reorganisation made in the interests of the business and with the agreement of other employees.	(e) **Transfer of the undertaking** (unless economic, technical or organisational reasons justifying it).
	(f) **Assertion of a statutory right** (eg under Equal Pay or Working Time Regulations.
	(g) **Participation in official industrial action**, within the first twelve weeks (Employment Relations Act 2004)
	(h) **Refusal to work on a Sunday** (for shop or betting workers).
	(i) **Whistle blowing**: Disclosure of information believed to expose malpractice, injustice or health and safety dangers (Public Interest Disclosure Act 1998).
	(j) Carrying out **duties as a safety representative** or **pension fund trustee**.
	(k) **Discrimination** (on grounds of sex, marital status, sex change, sexual orientation, race, religious belief, disability or part-time status).

3.4 Remedies for unfair dismissal

An employee who believes (s)he has been unfairly dismissed may present a complaint to an Employment Tribunal, within three months of dismissal.

Before a case comes to tribunal, ACAS will often try to help the parties reach a settlement, rather than proceed to a full tribunal hearing.

Defending a claim successfully relies on the employer being able to demonstrate the following.

(a) That the real or principal reason for the dismissal was one of the **justifiable reasons** listed above, or was otherwise a '**substantial reason** of a kind such as to justify the dismissal of an employee' (rather than some lesser action), and

(b) That it was '**reasonable**' to dismiss in all the circumstances of the case (including any mitigating circumstances on behalf of the employee), and

(c) That a '**fair procedure**' was followed, eg in regard to warnings, investigation, appeals, acting in good faith and attempting lesser disciplinary measures where relevant and possible.

Points (b) and (c) highlight the importance of HR policy and practice – particularly disciplinary and grievance procedures (discussed in Chapter 6).

Activity 3 (20 minutes)

All other criteria being met, would the following cases constitute fair or unfair dismissal?

(a) Bernie is a van-driver for a carrier firm. After a number of driving infringements in his own car and in his own time – ie not on the job – Bernie has lost his driving licence. The carrier firm dismisses him.

(b) Berenice is a shop manageress, but after an period when it has been observed that she leaves the shop dirty and untidy, fails to maintain cash registers and does not put stock away, the chain of shops dismisses her.

(c) Bernadette worked in telecommunications. The global economy and internet usage requires increased staffing at night, and the company proposes a change in its shift-working, which is accepted by the trade union following a vote. Bernadette refuses to work night shifts. She is dismissed.

(d) Benedict has noticed that he is not getting an itemised pay statement, and believes that he is entitled to one by law. The HR department is evasive. Benedict consults the union representatives, who press the question. The HR department stalls. Benedict starts putting up posters and holding meetings. He is told to stop 'being a trouble maker'. He refuses, and continues lobbying his colleagues. He is dismissed for persistent trouble-making.

The Conciliation Officer or Employment Tribunal to whom a complaint of unfair dismissal is made may order various remedies.

(a) **Re-instatement** – giving the employee his old job back

(b) **Re-engagement** – giving him a job comparable to his old one

(c) **Compensation** – which may consist of:

   (i)   A **basic award** based on age and length of service. (If the employee is also entitled to redundancy pay, the lesser is set off against the greater amount.)

   (ii) A **compensatory award** (taking account of the basic award) for any additional loss (earnings, expenses, benefits) on common law principles of damages for breach of contract

   (iii) A **punitive additional award** if the employer does not comply with an order for re-instatement or re-engagement, and in cases of sex and race discrimination

   (iv) A **special award** in the case of health and safety, and trade union membership or activity.

In deciding whether to exercise its powers to order re-instatement or re-engagement, the Tribunal must take into account whether the complainant **wishes** to be reinstated, whether it is **practicable** for the employer to comply with such an order and, if the complainant contributed to any extent to his dismissal, whether it would be **just** to make such an order. (Such orders are very infrequent.)

Compensation payments may also be reduced if the ex-employee is deemed to have contributed to his or her own dismissal or loss. So, for example, an employee may be found to have been unfairly dismissed on grounds of poor work performance because no warnings were given – but the poor performance will still be taken into account.

The Employment Relations Act 1999 raised the ceiling for unfair dismissal awards to £50,000. It also provided that there should be *no* limit on compensation payouts for employees dismissed as 'whistleblowers', in order to protect the public interest.

3.5 Dismissal procedures

Procedures for dismissal should include the following.

(a) Ensuring that **standards** of performance and conduct are set, clearly defined and communicated to all employees.

(b) **Warning** employees where a gap is perceived between standard and performance, or where other legal impediments or 'substantial reasons' are foreseen to arise.

(c) Giving a clearly defined and reasonable **period for improvement** or adjustment – with help and training where necessary, and clear improvement targets.

(d) Ensuring that statutory **disciplinary procedures** (including appeal procedures, rights to representation and so on) are made clear and meticulously followed.

(e) Implementing fair and transparent procedures for **redundancy**, particularly in regard to selection (as discussed below).

(f) **Evaluating all decisions** and actions in the light of policy, legislation and the requirement to 'act reasonably' at all times.

One of the fair and justified reasons for dismissal (listed earlier) is 'redundancy' – provided that selection of employees for redundancy is fair. We will now go on to look at redundancy in detail.

4 REDUNDANCY

Definition

Redundancy is defined by the Employment Rights Act 1996 as dismissals for the following reasons.

(a) The employer has ceased (or intends to cease) to carry on the business for the **purposes** of which the employee was employed

(b) The employer has ceased (or intends to cease) to carry on the business in the **place** where the employee was employed

(c) The **requirements** of the business for employees to carry out work of a particular kind have ceased or diminished, or are expected to

(d) For reasons 'not related to the individual concerned.' (*The Trade Union Reform and Employment Rights Act 1993* says that all such dismissals shall be presumed to be for redundancy, for the purposes of statutory consultation with trade unions – though *not* for redundancy pay. This complies with the EU Directive on **collective redundancy**.)

4.1 Causes of redundancy

In simple terms, 'redundancy occurs when the employer closes down completely, moves premises, requires fewer people for particular jobs or requires no people for particular jobs' (Gennard & Judge, 2003).

Over the past few decades, economic and business conditions have given rise to increasing levels of redundancy.

(a) **Adverse trading conditions**, especially in recessionary phases of the economy. In recent years, though the UK economy has been perceived to be relatively strong and stable, there have been high-profile sector 'downturns' – such as the 'dot.com' collapse or the post-'9/11' downturn in air travel.

(b) **Increased global competition** across business sectors. Many organisations have 'delayered' (eliminated excess layers of management and supervision), or 'downsized' (reduced their labour force) in order to reduce labour costs. Armstrong (2003) notes that productivity and added-value objectives have increased the use of indices such as added value per £ of employment cost to measure business performance.

(c) The **introduction of information and communications (and manufacturing) technology** has reduced labour in unskilled and semi-skilled jobs. It has also permitted increased outsourcing of functions and replacement of customer service and other skilled jobs, notably through the development of e-commerce and 'virtual organisation' (linking dispersed employees and work units via the Internet).

Redundancies are therefore a fact of life for HR practitioners, and are central to many **change management** projects in HRM.

FOR DISCUSSION

'Organisations are becoming mean as well as lean.'

(Armstrong, 2003)

How far is this true in your experience?

Why might an organisation wish to minimise redundancies – or minimise their impact on employees, beyond statutory requirements?

4.2 HR responsibilities in regard to redundancy

The HR function have the following responsibilities in regard to redundancy.

(a) To establish a redundancy policy which clarifies the psychological contract, balancing the organisation's commitment to maintain employment (on the one hand) with clear recognition of the need to ensure the economic viability of the business (on the other).

(b) To develop appropriate redundancy procedures

(c) To conduct advance HR planning (see Chapter 2) in order to achieve downsizing, as far as possible, without involuntary redundancies.

(d) To advise on and/or implement other methods of avoiding or minimising involuntary redundancy.

(e) To advise on and/or take part in managing redundancy (in regard to consultation, outplacement, counselling, payment and other impact minimisation measures).

We will look at some of these matters in turn.

Activity 4 (5 minutes)

(a) A's job is abolished, and A is transferred to B's job, and B is dismissed. Is this a case of redundancy?

(b) An employer wishes to alter employees' contract terms in order to harmonise terms following a merger. It decides to do this by dismissing all employees and re-employing them all on new terms: no one effectively ceases to be employed, since everyone accepts the new terms. Has there been a redundancy?

4.3 Minimising involuntary redundancies

Unemployment can represent not only an economic threat to livelihood and lifestyle, but a source of stress, insecurity and loss of self-esteem. On grounds of social responsibility, therefore, as well as reduced cost and preserved morale, the organisation should attempt to minimise compulsory redundancy as far as possible. There are various ways by which this can be done.

(a) **Advance HR planning**, so that foreseen seasonal or other contractions in demand for labour can be taken into account, and natural wastage can be allowed to downsize the organisation.

(b) **Adjusting HR plans** to ban non-essential recruitment; reduce overtime working; develop job-sharing (people alternating or splitting days of work in the same job); encourage short-contract working; restrict the use of sub-contracted, temporary and casual staff; and, if necessary, implement temporary layoffs.

(c) Encouraging **voluntary redundancy**. People may be induced to volunteer to leave by offering financial incentives (above-statutory redundancy pay), offering outplacement training or counselling (to help them find work elsewhere) and so on.

(d) **Retraining and redeployment programmes**. This may be a solution where alternative jobs are available, employees have some of the skills (or at least aptitudes) required and retraining facilities are available. The organisation may use outplacement agencies, or liaison with other employers in the same industry, supply chain or area, with a view to securing redeployment within a network of organisations.

(e) Encouraging **early retirement**, or insisting on the retirement of employees over the normal retirement age. This may be felt to be fair, if careers are seen to 'wind down' in any case, but it may not be appropriate in a high loyalty/seniority culture such as that pertaining in Japan. It may also be a factor, in terms of social responsibility, that mature-aged employees will have greater difficulty in finding new employment if they wish to do so.

Most claims for unfair dismissal in respect of redundancy are for unfair selection and lack of consultation: we will look at these two areas next.

4.4   Selection for compulsory redundancy

There are two basic approaches for selection for redundancy, which have proved acceptable to tribunals and trade unions.

(a)   The least contentious and easiest method may be '**Last in, first out**' (**LIFO**): newcomers are dismissed before long-serving employees. This may be deemed 'reasonable' by tribunals, but in the case of *Blatchfords v Berger and Others*, the Employment Appeal Tribunal stated: 'It cannot be said with certainty either that selection on the basis of LIFO would always be reasonable or that no reasonable employer today would adopt LIFO as the sole criterion'. The method may be construed as indirectly discriminatory, if the recruitment of women and ethnic minorities is recent, for example. LIFO may sound fair (especially in a loyalty/seniority culture of employment) – but it may also mean that the organisation loses its youngest employees, those with the most up-to-date skills, or employees of particular merit.

(b)   **Point score systems** are an alternative favourably viewed by tribunals. These allow **retention by merit** – retaining good performers and dismissing less effective ones – while supporting the objectivity of the process.

   (i)   Clear criteria should be chosen, and ideally agreed in advance with trade unions. They may be based on aspects such as attendance records, disciplinary records, competence assessments, range of work experience and other objectively measurable factors.

   (ii)   Each employee is scored on each criteria to build up a points score.

   (iii)   Managers implementing the system should have clear definitions of criteria; points available for different degrees of fulfilment of each criterion; and weighting of criteria to reflect their relative importance and value to the organisation.

   (iv)   Once all scores have been calculated, employees with the lowest scores are selected for redundancy.

From the organisation's point of view, selection criteria should ensure that the skills needed for organisational survival and regrowth are not lost through redundancy, and if possible that the best people are retained in the most value-adding jobs.

Employees who are employed on special projects or who have special skills required by the organisation may need to be removed from the pool prior to selection, or this should be provided for in the selection criteria.

4.5   Employee rights and redundancy procedures

Armstrong (2003) notes that redundancy procedures have three key aims.

- To treat employees as fairly as possible,
- To reduce hardship as much as possible, and
- To protect management's ability to run the business effectively.

In addition, of course, any procedure must take into account the employee's legal rights in redundancy situations. Many large organisations provide services and benefits well in excess of the statutory minimum with regard to consultation periods, terms, notice periods, counselling and aid with job search and so on.

EXAMPLE: THE BODY SHOP

'How does a firm that prides itself on its ethical approach to its "employees, customers, franchisees, suppliers and shareholders" negotiate the process of making redundancies?'

'The Body Shop found itself in the potentially embarrassing situation of having to cut jobs in order to press ahead with restructuring and fight off competition from cheap suppliers ... An ethical employer cannot be seen to hand out redundancy notices without any thought for the people involved...

'The **entrepreneurs**' club was set up to try and reduce the impact of impending redundancies on the local area. As well as loans, it also provided coaching and mentoring, opportunities for networking and access to an IT business centre. Other new businesses set up by former staff included a payroll consultancy, a glass-staining business and a video and music soundtracking company...

'About 40 per cent of the redundancies were **voluntary**, although the head of HR believes some of those who were made compulsorily redundant were also happy to leave. **Outplacement support** was provided ...

'Special treatment was given to **staff aged over 50**. This was partly a result of pressure from the consultation and representation committee, made up of employee representatives (the firm is non-unionised). People over 50 who had not found a job by the end of their redundancy period were entitled to an extra 25% on top of their original redundancy payment – although only 4 out of the eligible 25 applied for any additional cash. Employees leaving the firm were also offered £1,000 to spend on **training** ... matched by a further £1,000 from Sussex Enterprise, a local training and enterprise council.

'Only 37 out of the 200 staff whose jobs were made redundant did not take up the training grant. It was later decided to extend the £1,000 offer to people who weren't leaving ... "There was a feeling at the time that people were leaving and being well supported, but that maybe **those who were staying** were not being given the same backing" ...

'Staff in the service centre (where the redundancies occurred) felt under pressure because of the length of time it took to decide who was going to be made redundant. The Head of HR admits that the **consultations**, which took up to three months in some cases, went on too long. Some managers failed to tell people what was happening ... These criticisms were initially made by ... a consultant on employee surveys who was asked to evaluate the consultation exercise.

'In an attempt to improve communication, the firm introduced a monthly **newsletter** for all employees, along with fortnightly **meetings** with managers from the service centre, so that people could be kept better informed ...'

Neil Merrick, *People Management*, 26 October 2000

Activity 5   **(1½ hours)**

Use your research skills to find one or more further accounts (written or oral) of a redundancy situation: HR journals, quality press and acquaintances who have experienced redundancy are good sources. The **redundancy policy** of a business organisation, including selection criteria and ethical aims, will also be useful if you can gain access to one (or more).

Consultation

From a social responsibility point of view, it is obviously desirable to consult with employee representatives and to give warning of impending redundancies and methods of selection as early as possible. The legal requirements in the UK (based on the Employment Protection Act 1975 and several subsequent amendments) are broadly as follows.

In the case of collective redundancies, affecting 20 or more employees, the employer must consult with '**appropriate representatives**'. If there is no recognised trade union in the workplace, employers are bound to make suitable arrangements for the fair election (by secret ballot) of employee representatives from among the affected workforce.

Consultation about proposed redundancies must begin 'at the earliest opportunity', as defined by the legislation.

(a) A minimum of 90 days before the first dismissal, if 100 or more employees are to be dismissed at any one establishment

(b) A minimum of 30 days before the first dismissal of 20–99 employees.

These rules are applied to the total number involved and cannot be evaded by making essential dismissals in small instalments!

Prior to consultation, employees or their representatives must have been provided with information about: the reason for redundancies; numbers to be dismissed; proposed methods of selection for redundancy; timescale and methods of the redundancy programme; and method to be used in calculating redundancy pay (if not the statutory formula). The consultation period is not deemed to have started until sufficient information is provided on all these matters.

Consultation must be 'genuine', with the intention of reaching agreement with the employee representatives. It has to explore whether there are other options open to the business.

(a) Are there ways of avoiding dismissals altogether?
(b) Can the numbers to be dismissed be reduced?
(c) How can the impact of redundancy on those who must be dismissed be minimised?

Failure to comply with consultation requirements entitles the union to bring a complaint before an Employment Tribunal. If the complaint is upheld, the tribunal may postpone the dismissals and order consultation to take place, or may make a 'protective award' of pay to employees concerned, based on the number of redundancies and the period over which they are carried out.

Redundancies and transfers are also regarded as 'decisions likely to lead to **substantial changes** in work organisation or contracts' and are therefore subject to the **Information and Consultation of Employees (ICE)** regulations. ICE regulations give employees the right to be informed and consulted on these among other issues – and will be discussed further in Chapter 18.

FOR DISCUSSION

'The obligation on the employer is only to consult before proposals become fixed decisions. The likely outcome of the consultation is that the employer's proposal will be implemented either unaltered or altered in a way that the employer finds acceptable.'

(Dalganna & Davies, 2003)

What do you think is the purpose and importance of consultation?

Redundancy pay

Redundant employees are entitled to compensation, in the form of redundancy pay:

(a)   For loss of security

(b)   To encourage them to accept redundancy without damage to employee relations.

The employee may not be entitled to redundancy pay if the employer has made an offer of 'suitable' alternative employment and the employee has 'unreasonably' rejected it.

The statutory minimum entitlement is half a week's pay for each year of employment under the age of 22; one week's pay for each year of employment between 22 and 40; and one-and-a-half weeks' pay for each year of employment above the age of 41. In practice this is often supplemented by voluntary payments by the employer.

Other employee rights

Redundant employees also have:

(a)   The right to 'reasonable' time off with pay to look for another job or arrange training

(b)   The right to accept alternative work offered by the employer for an agreed trial period, and to refuse that work (if unsuitable) at the end of the trial period without prejudice to the right of redundancy pay.

4.6   Compassionate exit management

A number of measures may be taken to alleviate the consequences of redundancy for employees.

(a)   **Informing employees** who are to be dismissed of their selection should be managed with as much sensitivity as possible. This is generally done by what is called a '**release interview**'. The interview is generally conducted by a line manager, but an HR specialist may also be present, in order to explain the basis of selection, the employee's entitlements and organisational support services that will be offered. Managers should be given training and/or guidance in how to handle the difficult situation sensitively. They should also be given information about any special circumstances that might make the employee react particularly badly.

(b) **Counselling** may be offered to employees, to aid their readjustment and job search. (Counselling is discussed in Chapter 11 of this Course Book.) The employee will be guided in reinforcing his or her sense of employability, redefining career objectives, devising strategies for job search, and working through personal issues (including anger and grief) around job loss.

(c) **Outplacement services** may be offered, often through external consultancies, to help redundant employees to find alternative work. The HR department or consultancy may offer services such as:

(i) Seeking specific job opportunities in the local area

(ii) Training employees in CV preparation, selection interview techniques and application filling

(iii) Helping employees to draw up skill or competence inventories, personal success/attainment inventories and other aids to applications

(iv) Carrying out psychometric assessments and helping employees to set career and job objectives

(v) Matching of employee details to advertised vacancies or network opportunities

(vi) Helping the employee to plan a focused job-search campaign

(d) **Information** on job, self-employment and retraining opportunities and funding should be made available. Individuals should be made aware of the role and accessibility of the Department of Employment's facilities, and private sector services for careers counselling, recruitment, CV preparation and so on.

Activity 6 (30 minutes)

Conduct a web search and develop your own source list of organisations and websites that provide outplacement support.

Note that the impact of redundancy is also felt by those who were *not* selected. 'Survivors' may suffer guilt and anxiety, insecurity about their own jobs and a loss of loyalty to the organisation: they may tend to identify more closely with fellow workers and less with the organisation. Efforts will have to be made to reinforce survivors' loyalty and morale by acknowledging their worth to the employer – particularly since, despite the concept underlying 'redundancy', remaining workers may in fact have to shoulder an increased workload!

NOTES

Definition

> The term **survivor syndrome** has been coined for a psychological state which involves long-term anxiety about job loss, increased loyalty to co-workers and reduced loyalty to the employer.

'Survivor syndrome' can lead to increased labour turnover, deliberately restricted output, risk-averse behaviour (suppression of feedback, new ideas, innovation) and industrial conflict. In order to avoid these effects, management's motives and intentions must be transparent and true, and fairness (even generosity, if possible) demonstrated. Positive values around the redundancies (better chances of corporate survival and success, 'heroism' of the lean-mean workforce, the value of retained employees) must be promoted.

EXAMPLE: THE ROYAL MAIL

'Having made a loss after tax of £940 million in 2001-02, the Royal Mail announced one of the biggest restructures in British corporate history. In 2002 around 30,000 redundancies were announced and more have been made since then.

'Andrew Kinder was, until recently, principal welfare co-ordinator and chartered occupational psychologist for the Royal Mail, and now provides the same services of agency Schlumberger Sema. Describing the impact of such large-scale change on Royal Mail staff, he says: "Many individuals find it hard to cope, some feeling that they have to work harder to secure their futures, others feeling deep concerns about why they kept their jobs. Royal Mail is committed to addressing these issues not only because they could have a negative effect on productivity but also because the organisation takes its legal duty of care to individuals very seriously. Reorganisations like this happen and we as humans can't control change but we can control how we respond to it. Counselling is one of the key aspects of the firm's efforts to empower employees to cope with change."

'Pauline Leech, head of information services in the Royal Mail's property division, has taken advantage of Kinder's counselling services. "The team in which I work has been going through so much change that we felt it would be useful to bring in a counsellor," she says. "Andrew ran a session helping us to develop a number of coping strategies. We talked about our feelings and behaviour, completed a questionnaire and discussed responses to situations. A drama triangle, involving three people playing the role of victim, persecutor and rescuer, was very interesting and gave an insight into different approaches to the same situation. It gave us good insight into the pressure felt by colleagues. For me it helped to know that the firm cared enough to offer this support." '

(Blyth, 2003)

Note: In June 2007, Royal Mail was still being threatened with industrial action in protest over further job cuts...

Chapter roundup

- Exit from employment takes several forms, voluntary and involuntary, including:

    - Retirement: termination of contract at a fixed, statutory or negotiated retirement age

    - Resignation: voluntary termination by notice on the part of the employee

    - Dismissal: termination, with or without notice, on the part of the employer, or (constructive dismissal) on the part of the employee where (s)he is entitled to assume that the employer has terminated the contract by breach

    - Redundancy: dismissal by reason of the ending of the work for which the employee was contracted

- Employment protection legislation and regulations set out employee rights with regard to:

    (a) Notice periods to be given for dismissal

    (b) Valid reasons for dismissal

    (c) Remedies in the event of dismissal being judged 'unfair'

    (d) Consultation with employee representatives over proposed redundancies

    (e) Redundancy pay

    (f) Time off to prepare for redundancy

    (g) Trial periods prior to acceptance of alternative employment

- In addition to statutory requirements, exit has ethical and employee relations implications. Attention is commonly given to:

    (a) Learning from resignations by means of exit interviews

    (b) Socially responsible polices surrounding progressive discipline, dismissal and redundancy

    (c) The motivation of 'surviving' employees

Quick quiz

1   In what five basic ways may a contract (including a contract of employment) be terminated?

2   What are the arguments for enforcing retirement?

3   What procedures should be carried out when an employee resigns from the organisation?

4   Who are the members of an Employment Tribunal?

5   What is the difference between wrongful dismissal and unfair dismissal?

NOTES

6   What reasons may an employer rely on in seeking to show that a dismissal was fair?

7   When is dismissal called 'redundancy'?

8   What measures can be used to avoid compulsory redundancies?

9   What are two potentially justifiable methods of selecting employees for redundancy?

10   Explain the term 'survivor syndrome'.

Answers to quick quiz

1   Performance, mutual agreement, notice, breach or frustration.

(see paragraph 1.1)

2   To open up promotion opportunities; to offer security to younger employees; to inject 'young blood'; to save money; to enhance efficiency.   (para 1.2)

3   Persuade to stay (if appropriate); exit interview; negotiate notice period; notify key people; complete performance assessment.   (para 1.3)

4   A legally-qualified chairperson, employer representative and employee representation.   (para 2.1)

5   Wrongful dismissal is where there are insufficient reasons to justify dismissal, whereas unfair dismissal is where law and internal policies have been breached.   (paras 3.2, 3.3)

6   Redundancy; legal impediment; non-capability; misconduct; some other substantial reason.   (para 3.3)

7   Cessation of the business; cessation of the business in a particular location; cessation of the need for work of a particular kind.   (para 4)

8   A full answer is provided in paragraph 4.3.

9   LIFO and point score systems.   (para 4.4)

10   A psychological state suffered by employees who have survived redundancy programmes, characterised by long-term anxiety, increased loyalty to co-workers and decreased commitment to the organisation.   (para 4.6)

Answers to activities

1   (a)   The burden of work in late years can be eased by shortening hours or a transfer to lighter duties.

       (b)   The final stage of employee training and development may take the form of courses, commonly run by local technical colleges, intended to prepare employees for the transition to retirement and non-work.

       (c)   The organisation may have, or may be able to put employees in touch with, social/leisure clubs and other facilities for easing the shock of retirement.

2   (a)   Reasons for leaving are many and various, but some of the ones you may have thought of are: relocation to another city/area; dissatisfaction with work conditions (or location, or workmates or scope for responsibility or any number of work-related factors); finding another (preferred) job; being head-

BPP
LEARNING MEDIA

hunted; change of career (or return to full-time education, or move to self-employment, or change of domestic circumstances/family responsibilities); clash of culture/values with the employer; ill-health; to pre-empt dismissal in order to save face.

(b) Procedures may include: return of keys, security passes and so on; handing of files to department head; completion or transfer of work-in-progress; removal of personal data/passwords from computer files; collection of final pay and leaving information; removal of personal effects.

3   (a) Bernie was fairly dismissed by reason of legal impediment.

(b) Berenice was fairly dismissed by reason of lack of 'capability': she is clearly incompetent compared to the standard of performance required by the job.

(c) Bernadette was fairly dismissed: failure to accept necessary reorganisation is a 'substantial' reason.

(d) Benedict was unfairly dismissed, because he was trying to enforce his employment rights in a reasonable manner.

4   (a) Yes – but it is **B** who has been made redundant.

(b) Yes – for the purposes of consultation with trade unions, since this fits the TURER '93 definition of collective redundancy: the reasons for dismissal were not related to the individuals concerned. The consultation requirements refer to 'proposals to dismiss': the employer presumably proposed to dismiss any employee who did not accept the new terms – even if this did not eventuate. The employer bound to consult – and to pay penalties if it had failed to do so. (This is based on an actual case before the EAT: *GMBV v Man Truck and Bus UK Ltd, 2000.*)

5   The answer is up to you!

6   A research activity. Find out more about outplacement – *and* the kind of information employees can be steered towards.

PART B

HRM ISSUES

BPP
LEARNING MEDIA

Chapter 8:
PERSPECTIVES ON HRM

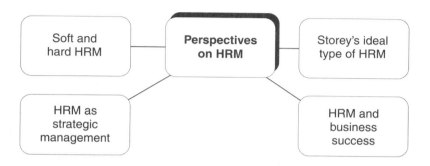

Introduction

In this chapter, we explore further some of the themes already discussed in Chapters 1 and 2, highlighting the ambiguities and dualities in the role of the Human Resource Management.

One of the key assumptions of HRM is that the employment relationship can be managed so that the needs of both organisation and employees are met, to mutual benefit. Ethical, people-friendly HR policies are intended to facilitate efficient and effective working as well as employee health, welfare and satisfaction. This dual emphasis will be reflected in the following chapters as we look at some of the major issues facing HR managers in the 21st Century workplace.

Your objectives

In this chapter you will learn about the following.

    (a) Guest's model of the hard-soft, loose-tight dimensions of HRM

    (b) Storey's model of the differences between HRM and personnel/industrial relations practices

    (c) HRM from a strategic perspective, and its implications for the role of the line manager and employees

    (d) How HRM impacts on the success of the business

BPP
LEARNING MEDIA

NOTES

1 SOFT AND HARD HRM

In Chapter 1, we defined HRM as 'a strategic approach to managing employment relations which emphasises that leveraging people's capabilities is critical to achieving sustainable competitive advantage' (Bratton & Gold, 2007).

We have so far suggested that the role of HRM is twofold (leading to some ambiguity): both business-oriented (concerned with performance) and people-oriented (concerned with the motivation and quality of working life of employees). However, key writers on HRM (Storey, 1989, Legge, 1998; Guest, 1999) have identified two distinct versions of HRM, which they characterise as 'hard' and 'soft'.

1.1 Hard HRM

Definition

Karen Legge (1998) defined the '**hard model**' of HRM as a process emphasising 'the close integration of human resource policies with business strategy which regards employees as a resource to be managed in the same rational way as any other resource being exploited for maximum return'.

The hard model of HRM may be summarised as follows.

(a) Its philosophy towards managing people is rational, quantitative and explicitly **business-oriented**: employees must be managed in such a way as to obtain value-adding performance, which will in turn give the organisation competitive advantage.

> The drive to adopt HRM is… based on the business case of a need to respond to an external threat from increasing competition. It is a philosophy that appeals to managements who are striving to increase competitive advantage and appreciate that to do this they must invest in human resources as well as new technology.

(Guest, 1999)

(b) It regards employees as a resource of the organisation, to be managed (exploited) in as rational and strategic a manner as any other economic resource: **human capital** from which a return can be obtained by adding value, through judicious investment in performance management and employee development.

(c) It emphasises the interests, role and authority of **management** 'over' those of employees.

(d) It is essentially a **pluralist** viewpoint, which maintains that the interests of the owners and managers of a business are inherently different from those of the workers: organisations are therefore political systems, within which there is competition for scarce power and resources. Workers must be controlled in order to ensure that they perform in the organisation's interests.

216

Features of hard HRM include:

(a) A close matching or integration of the strategic objectives of the HR function with the **business strategy** of the organisation. 'Hard strategic HRM' will emphasise the yield to be obtained by investing in human resources in the interests of the business (Storey, 1989)

(b) A focus on **quantitative, business-strategic objectives** and criteria for management

(c) An emphasis on the need for **performance management** and other forms of managerial control.

Activity 1	(10 minutes)

What HRM techniques (covered so far) would you expect to be adopted as a result of a hard HRM approach?

1.2 Soft HRM

Definition

Legge defined the **'soft'** version of HRM as a process whereby employees are viewed as 'valued assets and as a source of competitive advantage through their commitment, adaptability and high level of skills and performance.

The soft model of HRM may be summarised as follows.

(a) Its philosophy towards managing people is based in the human and neo-human relations schools of management thought which emphasised the influence of **socio-psychological factors** (relationships, attitudes, motivation, leadership, communication) on work behaviour.

(b) It views employees as 'means rather than objects' (Guest, 1999): 'treating employees as **valued assets,** a source of competitive advantage through their commitment, adaptability and high quality (of skills, performance and so on)' (Storey, 1989).

(c) It focuses on **'mutuality'**, a unitarist viewpoint which assumes that the interests of management and employees can and should coincide in shared organisational goals, working as members of an integrated team. Employees are viewed as key stakeholders in the organisation.

The main **features of soft HRM** are:

(a) A complementary approach to strategic HRM, in relation to the business strategies of the organisation. Brewster (1999) argues that a **stakeholder perspective** and environmental constraints (such as EU legislation) mean that HR strategies cannot be entirely governed by business strategy. **'Soft strategic HRM'** will place greater emphasis on the human relations aspect of people management, stressing security of employment, continuous development, communication, involvement and the quality of working life.

(b)   A focus on **socio-psychological and cultural objectives** and criteria for management.

(c)   An emphasis on the need to gain the **trust and commitment** of employees – not merely compliance with control mechanisms.

Activity 2   (10 minutes)

What HRM techniques (covered so far) would you expect to be adopted as a result of a soft HRM approach?

We will now look briefly at two early US models of HRM which reflect the roots of the soft and hard approaches respectively.

1.3   The Michigan model

The **matching model** of HRM was developed by the Michigan School (Fombrun *et al*, 1984). It suggested that HR systems should be managed in such a way as to 'match', or be congruent with, the organisation's business strategy: an essentially hard orientation. The **human resource cycle** consists of four basic functions which are performed in all organisations to drive business performance.

(a)   **Selection**: designed to match available human resources to jobs

(b)   **Performance management/appraisal**: designed to match performance to objectives and standards

(c)   **Rewards**: reinforcing short- and long-term achievements

(d)   **Development**: matching the skill quality of the human resource to future requirements

Fombrun *et al* suggest that the HR function should be linked to line management by:

(a)   Providing good HR databases

(b)   Ensuring that senior mangers give HR issues as much attention as they give to other functions

(c)   Measuring the contribution of the HR function at the strategic (long-term policies designed to encourage organisational 'fit' to its environment in the future), managerial (medium-term activities ensuring the acquisition, retaining and development of people) and operational (daily support of business activities) levels.

1.4   The Harvard Framework

The Harvard Framework (Beer *et al*, 1984) was based on the belief that the problems of historical personnel management could only be solved:

> When general managers develop a viewpoint of how they wish to see employees involved in and developed by the enterprise, and of what HRM policies and practices may achieve those goals... Today, many pressures are demanding... a longer-term perspective in managing people and consideration of people as potential assets rather than merely a variable cost.

The Harvard model was influential in emphasising the fact that:

(a)   'Human resource management involves **all management decisions** and actions that affect the nature of the relationship between the organisation and its employees'

(b)   Organisations involve a variety of **stakeholders** who have an interest in the practice and outcomes of HR policies: there is a 'trade-off' between the interests of owners and employees, as well as other stakeholders, with a view to mutuality and commitment

(c)   Strategic HRM choices are influenced by a broad range of **contextual factors**, including both product-market and socio-cultural factors

(d)   Line managers are at the **interface** between competitive strategy and HR policies and must take more responsibility for their alignment.

The Harvard framework can be illustrated as follows (Beer *et al* 1984): Figure 8.1.

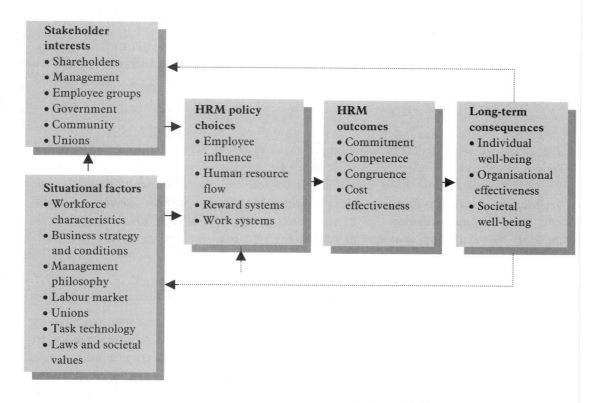

Figure 8.1 Map of the HRM territory

This is essentially a soft HRM model,

> composed of policies that promote **mutuality** – mutual goals, mutual influence, mutual respect, mutual rewards, mutual responsibility. The theory is that policies of mutuality will elicit commitment, which in turn will yield both **better economic performance** and **greater human development**.
> (Walton, cited by Armstrong, 2003)

FOR DISCUSSION

How do you respond intuitively to the 'hard' and 'soft' versions of HRM? What words and phrases connected with each strike you as positively or negatively loaded: where do your perceptions come from? Are 'soft' and 'hard' perspectives really as different as contrasting descriptions make them seem? Does your experience of organisations suggest that they operate under *either* one *or* the other?

1.5   Hard or soft?

In practice, there are likely to be times when a hard orientation (eg in the face of the need for organisational downsizing) directly conflicts with the more developmental and paternal philosophy of the soft approach. Many organisations operate a mix of soft-hard, loose-tight systems. One way of formalising this is to segment the labour force into a 'core' of permanent employees managed via soft HRM policies, and a 'periphery' of short-contract labour used as an exploitable commodity. As Kramer, McGraw and Shuler (1997) note, 'whether an organisation leans more towards the hard or soft version of HRM depends very much on the values of the organisation.'

In addition, research (cited by Armstrong, 2003) suggests that organisations in practice implement a mix of hard and soft approaches, so that the distinction may not always be precise or helpful.

The broad 'achieve success through people' focus of HRM may therefore be approached from two different perspectives, which imply very different techniques of management. These techniques have been classified, according to the amount of control each orientation assumes to be necessary to obtain job performance from workers, as 'tight' and 'loose'. Before we discuss the characteristics of tight and loose HRM, we will look at an early model of how managerial philosophy and assumptions set up the hard-soft, tight-loose continuum.

1.6   Theory X and Theory Y

The distinction between hard/tight and soft/loose management control was suggested by **Douglas McGregor,** an influential contributor to the neo-human relations school. In *The Human Side of Enterprise*, he discussed the way in which managers handle people according to the **assumptions** they have about them and about what kind of management style will obtain their efforts. He identified two extreme sets of assumptions (Theory X and Theory Y) and explored how management style differs according to which set of assumptions is adopted (McGregor, 1987).

(a)   **Theory X** holds that human beings have an inherent dislike of work and will avoid it if they can. People prefer to be directed, wishing to avoid responsibility. They have relatively little ambition and want security above all, resisting change. They are self-interested, and make little effort to identify with the organisation's goals. They must be coerced, controlled, directed, offered rewards or threatened with punishments in order to get them to put adequate effort into the achievement of organisation objectives: this is management's responsibility.

(b)   According to **Theory Y**, however, the expenditure of physical and mental effort in work is as natural as play or rest. The ordinary person does not inherently dislike work: according to the conditions, it may be a source of satisfaction or deprivation. A person will exercise self-direction and self-control in the service of objectives to which (s)he is committed. Management's responsibility is to create conditions and methods that will enable individuals to integrate their own and the organisation's goals.

You will have your own viewpoints on the validity of Theory X and Theory Y. In fact, McGregor intentionally polarised his theories as the extremes of a continuum along which most managers' attitudes fall at some point. However, he also recognised that the assumptions are self-perpetuating, even where the 'types' of employee described do not really exist. If people are treated according to Theory X (or Theory Y) assumptions, they will begin to act accordingly – thus confirming management in its beliefs and practices. Essentially, Theory X embodies the 'hard-tight' **control theory of management**, while Theory Y embodies the 'soft-loose' **commitment theory of management**.

Activity 3   **(45 minutes)**

The following was sent to the letter page of *Personnel Management.*

> Hark, I think I detect the first cuckoo of a recessionary spring on your pages ('Making time for productivity', March). Come on, all you personnel folk. Off with your HR nomenclature; away with all this nonsense about the 'success culture', 'employee involvement', 'maximising people power', 'establishing the right climate' and 'sharing gains' (all drawn from the CIPD's current national priorities). Get out your sticks and stopwatches, 'precisely time' those tea breaks, slash that overtime, enforce 'bell-to-bell working', put in a few more controls and 'disincentives'... Surely employee involvement is not just an illusion created by the 1980s boom which we can ignore now times are tough?

What are the characteristics of the approach to HRM which the letter identifies? Why might economic recession lead managers to adopt such an approach?

1.7   Tight and loose HRM

The distinction between tight and loose HRM may be characterised as the difference between a system based on compliance and a system based on commitment.

Definitions

Compliance means performing according to set rules and standards, according to what you are expected and asked to do.

Commitment has been defined as 'the relative strength of an individual's identification with and involvement in a particular organisation. It is characterised by at least three factors:

(a) A strong belief in and acceptance of an organisation's goals and values

(b) A willingness to exert considerable effort on behalf of the organisation

(c) A strong desire to maintain membership of the organisation.'

(Mowdray *et al*, 1982)

Compliance-based systems of control reflect a low level of trust and challenge: performance is expected to be no less than the set standard – but also no *more*, since there is little room for creative or exceptional input or effort, which may militate against tight managerial control. Such systems may be effective and efficient: in a highly stable market environment; where the task is low-tech and low-discretion, with little need to differentiate skills or abilities and little difference between compliant and committed performance; and where the managerial prerogative of superiority and control continue to have meaning because of cultural values to do with respect and conformity (eg in latino cultures and traditional family businesses).

Commitment-based systems of control reflect a high level of trust and mutuality, based on Theory Y assumptions that the work relationship can offer employees opportunities to meet their needs and aspirations as well as the organisation's needs. Such systems are effective in environments where customer demands and technologies are varied and changing, and employees are required to be flexible, creative and positive in contributing to the organisation's goals.

Guest (2001) set out the differences in HR policy in a compliance-based system of control and a commitment-based system of control, as follows.

Aspects of policy	Compliance	Commitment
Psychological contract of work	'Fair day's work for a fair day's pay'	Mutual/reciprocal commitment
Behavioural references	Norms, custom and practice	Values/mission
Source of control over workers' behaviour	External (rules, instructions)	Internal (goals, values, willingness)
Employee relations	Pluralist perspective ('Us' and 'Them') Collective Low trust	Unitarist ('Us') Individual Trust
Organising principles/ organisational design	Formal/defined roles Top down Centralised control Hierarchy Division of labour Managerial control	Flexible roles Bottom-up Decentralised control (delegation, empowerment) Flat structures Team-work/autonomy Self control
Policy goals	Administrative/efficiency Performance to standard Minimising cost	Adaptive/effectiveness Constantly improving performance Maximising utilisation for added value

Guest also identified these contrasting dimensions as distinguishing 'traditional industrial relations' and 'HRM' approaches.

Activity 4   **(10 minutes)**

Would you say you were compliant in your attitude to your studies, or committed? Think about how you approach the assignments set for you, the classes you attend and so on.

(a) What are (or would be) the benefits to you if you are/were committed rather than compliant?

(b) What are/would be the benefits to your trainers?

(c) What could (1) you and (2) your trainers do to increase your commitment to your studies?

EXAMPLE

When Levi Strauss & Co UK was beset by a loss of market share, the HR department drove the necessary change, as 'managers were the key resisters to change,' said Bruce Robertson, head of HR at the company.

Managers were so resistant that 'it resulted in senior leadership being removed'. When Robertson first saw the results of a customer survey that called service 'just abysmal', 'chaotic' and 'totally disorganised' he said, 'my blood went cold. I sent it to managers and the response at the UK head office was 'so?' '.

'In 2002, Robertson and his HR team led a series of changes. "We repositioned to a more adult/adult relationship between the company and employees," he said. "The old relationship had created a culture where many employees were too passive to make decisions and where little power struggles broke out," Robertson said. He spearheaded a new way of thinking, calling for employees to respect the Levi's heritage and be 'passionate about our brands'.

'Employees are now called upon to be committed to making things better and be more flexible and adaptable in their ways of working. "They need to be more positive. The glass needs to be half full more of the time," he said. "Be happy with us or be happy somewhere else".'

Employees are encouraged to take a solutions-oriented approach, to support co-workers and be more team-focused.

(Overman, 2003)

2 STOREY'S 'IDEAL TYPE' OF HRM

2.1 Storey's definitions

Storey (1992) regarded HRM as a 'set of interrelated policies with an ideological and philosophical underpinning'. A meaningful version of HRM involves:

(a) A particular cluster of beliefs and assumptions

(b) A strategic focus to decision-making about people management

(c) A central role for line managers in delivering HR outcomes

(d) The use of 'levers' to shape the employment relationship, which can be distinguished from those used under traditional industrial relations systems.

Storey put forward a theoretical 'ideal type' description of what a fully implemented model of HRM might look like, in contrast to a similarly abstracted description of the traditional personnel/industrial relations model. As you consider the differences tabulated in Figure 8.2 below, remember that this is an 'ideal': it is not meant to describe the current, typical state of affairs – since, as we have seen, the definition of HRM, and its application in practice, is by no means clear cut.

DIMENSION	PERSONNEL/IR APPROACH	HRM APPROACH
Beliefs and assumptions		
1 Contract	Careful delineation of written contracts	Aim to go 'beyond contract'
2 Rules	Importance of devising clear rules/mutuality	'Can do' outlook; impatience with 'rules'
3 Guide to management action	Procedures/consistency/ control	'Business-need'/flexibility/ commitment
4 Behaviour referent	Norms/custom and practice	Values/mission
5 Managerial task *vis-à-vis* labour	Monitoring	Nurturing
6 Nature of relations	Pluralist	Unitarist
7 Conflict	Institutionalised	De-emphasised
8 Standardisation	High (eg 'parity' an issue)	Low (eg 'parity' not seen as relevant)
Strategic aspects		
9 Key relations	Labour-management	Business-customer
10 Initiatives	Piecemeal	Integrated
11 Corporate plan	Marginal to	Central to
12 Speed of decision	Slow	Fast
Line Management		
13 Management role	Transactional leadership	Transformational leadership
14 Key managers	Personnel/IR specialists	General/business/line managers
15 Communication	Indirect	Direct
16 Prized management skills	Negotiation	Facilitation
Key levers (strongly-featured issues and techniques)		
17 Foci of attention for interventions	Personnel procedures	Wide ranging cultural, structural and personnel strategies
18 Selection	Separate, marginal task	Integrated, key task
19 Pay	Job evaluation (fixed grades)	Performance related
20 Job categories and grades	Many	Few
21 Conditions	Separately negotiated	Harmonisation
22 Labour management	Collective bargaining contracts	Towards individual contracts
23 Thrust of relations with union delegates	Regularised through facilities and training	Marginalised (with exception of some bargaining for change models)
24 Communication	Restricted flow	Increased flow
25 Job design	Division of labour	Teamwork
26 Conflict handling	Reach temporary truces	Manage climate and culture
27 Training and development	Controlled access to courses	Learning companies

Figure 8.2: Twenty-seven points of difference

NOTES

> **Activity 5** (10 minutes)
>
> What kinds of HR policies and practices might:
>
> (a) 'Institutionalise' or 'de-emphasise' conflict (point 7)?
> (b) 'Restrict' or 'increase' the flow of communication (point 24)?

2.2 Implications for the line manager's role

Transactional and **transformational** leadership (referred to in Storey's model) were terms coined by Burns (1978) for two different styles of leadership.

- **Transactional leaders** see the relationship with their followers in terms of a trade: they give followers the rewards they want, in exchange for services, loyalty and compliance.

- **Transformational leaders** see their role as inspiring and motivating others to work at levels beyond mere compliance. Transformational leadership is achieved through role modelling, articulating powerful goals, team-building, high expectations, two-way communication, empowering, developing and other such processes.

Transactional leadership can arguably be mediated via HR policies and practices. Transformational leadership is an essentially interpersonal process, underscoring the role of line managers and team leaders in delivering HRM.

2.3 Implications for the worker's role

The HRM viewpoint, as outlined above, is explicitly unitarist. It implies that employees can be willingly co-opted to the business task of competition, quality enhancement and problem-solving. Tight managerial control over workers is replaced by a culture of trust: performance is assumed to be largely self-regulating within a guiding framework of inspirational leadership and shared cultural values and aspirations.

Instead of power being used from the top down to **control** workers' performance, power is used to **support** workers' performance: performance (including quality, customer satisfaction, innovation and so on) becomes the guiding force of the organisation, not the wishes of senior management.

This has implications for the HR function, as illustrated in Figure 8.3.

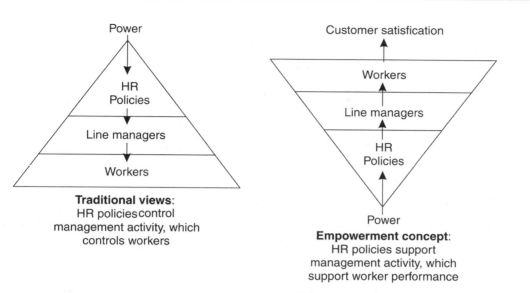

Traditional views:
HR policies control
management activity, which
controls workers

Empowerment concept:
HR policies support
management activity, which
support worker performance

Figure 8.3: From control to empowerment

Activity 6   **(10 minutes)**

What might be the consequences of empowerment for HR policy in the areas of (a) recruitment and selection and (b) training?

2.4 Implications for HR responsibilities

One of the key features of HRM is that 'its performance and delivery are integrated into line management' (Storey, 1989).

According to Armstrong (2000) the hard HRM approach, in particular,

> is claimed to be a central, senior management-driven strategic activity that is developed, owned and delivered by management as a whole to promote the interests of the organisation that they serve. It purports to be an holistic approach concerned with the total interests of the organisation – the interests of the members of the organisation are recognised but subordinated to those of the enterprise. Hence the importance attached to strategic integration and strong cultures, which flow from top management's vision and leadership, and which require people who will be committed to the strategy, who will be adaptable to change, and who will fit the culture. By implication, as Guest (1991) says: 'HRM is too important to be left to personnel managers.

Kramar, McGraw and Shuler (1997) note the ironic and paradoxical result:

> HRM has become more influential in company decision-making, yet has declined as a separate department within the organisation as HR tasks and decisions have been devolved to line managers. Many leading edge HR practitioners now see themselves more in an internal consultancy capacity assisting line managers to devise and implement more sophisticated ways of managing people, rather than implementing and managing those systems themselves. Such HR managers would also claim to be working towards the eventual removal of their own positions within the organisation.

HR specialists therefore increasingly share responsibility for delivering HR policy outcomes with:

(a)   **Top management**, who shape the aims, strategy and culture of the organisation supported by HR policies and consultancy. (We discussed the 'business partner' model, for example, in Chapter 1.)

(b)   **Line managers**, who take on a day-to-day leadership-oriented responsibility for people management (supported by HR advice and services).

(c)   **Employees themselves**. It is no longer uncommon for employees to appraise themselves (and their peers and superiors), write their own job descriptions, determine their own performance standards and improvement goals, and manage their own learning and career development.

We suggested in Chapter 1 that four key policy goals of an authentic HRM approach are: high commitment, flexibility, strategic integration and high quality. We have discussed commitment (above), and will be covering flexibility in detail in Chapter 9. Here, we will look briefly at some models for the strategic integration of HRM, and then at HRM as a quality issue.

3   HRM AS STRATEGIC MANAGEMENT

3.1   Strategic HRM

The term 'strategic human resource management' emerged in the 1980s to describe a variety of models which attempt to explain how human resource policies can be **integrated with business strategy**.

Definitions

> **Strategic management** 'denotes a specific pattern of decisions and actions undertaken by the upper echelon of an organisation in order to accomplish specific outcomes and/or performance goals'.
>
> **Strategic HRM** is 'the process of linking the human resource function with the strategic objectives of the organisation in order to improve performance'.
>
> (Bratton & Gold, 2007)

Bratton & Gold *(ibid)* note that the term 'strategic HRM' can be seen as:

•   An **outcome**: 'organisational systems designed to achieve sustainable competitive advantage through people' (Snell *et al*)

•   A **process**: 'the process by which organisations seek to link the human, social and intellectual capital of their members to the strategic needs of the firm' (Bamberger & Meshoulam).

Torrington *et al* (2002) note that strategic HRM may be achieved by the integration of HRM policy goals into business strategy and line management thinking, *or* by the involvement of the HR function in both organisational and HR strategy development. They argue that while there is a greater likelihood of involvement in strategy when the most senior HR person is a member of the Board of Directors, Board membership does not *guarantee* the involvement of specialists in strategy development – and is not necessarily *essential* to strategic involvement. In order to maximise opportunities to influence strategy, the HR function must:

(a)   Use the business and financial language shared by corporate management (elements of 'hard' HR)

(b)   Describe the rationale for HR activities in terms of business benefits, added value or competitive advantage

(c)   Appoint line-experienced managers into the HR function (to enhance credibility and relevance)

(d)   Concentrate on the priorities defined by business strategy

(e)   Offer well-developed change-management skills

(f)   Demonstrate an ability to think strategically, having its own mission, strategy and integrative approach (involving line management in the development of HR strategy).

EXAMPLE

'Four years ago Kim Reid was running British Aerospace's youth programmes, ranging from graduate development to schools liaison. Before that she was a pensions specialist. Now she sits round a boardroom table with 11 others, helping to run one of the main business divisions of what is now BAE Systems.

'Her views have fed into the business strategy for the customer solutions and support division (CS&S), a 14,000-strong business, and she has led the senior team through workshops to develop the vision and capabilities needed to support the strategy. She also chairs the group pensions committee. Reid is one of dozens of HR professionals at BAE 'Systems whose role has been transformed since the merger of British Aerospace and Marconi Electronic Systems in 1999.

'In many ways, what the company did is a textbook example of current thinking on HR and corporate strategy – what Richard Finn, of Penna Consulting, calls 'tiering'. It split off the **HR administration** into a **service centre**, run for BAE Systems by a joint venture company called Xchanging, which was set up for the purpose. Most of the remaining HR staff became **business partners** (although BAE doesn't use the term as a job title), working closely with line managers in the group's dozen or so divisions. John Whelan, now the company's HR director for resourcing and development, says: "We wanted people to take on an organisation development/consultancy type of role." '

(Pickard, 2003)

We will now look at some of the different approaches suggested for developing and integrating HR strategies.

According to Armstrong (2000):

> The fundamental aim of strategic HRM is to generate **strategic capability** by ensuring that the organisation has the skilled, committed and well-motivated employees it needs to achieve sustained competitive advantage. Its objective is to provide a **sense of direction** in an often turbulent environment so that the business needs of the organisation, and the individual and collective needs of its employees can be met by the development and implementation of coherent and practical HR policies.

3.2 Strategic integration or fit

The concept of strategic fit is central to strategic HRM. It suggests that to maximise competitive advantage, a firm must:

(a) Match its capabilities and resources to the opportunities and constraints of the **external environment** (**external fit**)

(b) Match the **macro features** of the organisation: its mission, strategy, structure, technology, products and services, culture and workforce (**internal fit**).

For Guest (1989), there are three aspects to strategic fit in HRM terms.

(a) Developing HR strategies that are integrated with the business strategy and support its achievement (**vertical integration or fit**)

(b) Developing integrated HR practices (resourcing, reward, development and so on) so that they complement and mutually reinforce one another (**horizontal integration or fit**), consistently encourage the quality, flexibility and commitment

(c) Encouraging line managers to **realise and internalise** the importance of human resources.

As one of the key policy goals of HRM specified by Guest, strategic integration ensures that HRM 'is fully integrated into strategic planning so that HRM policies cohere both across policy areas and across hierarchies and HRM practices are used by line managers as part of their everyday work.'

3.3 Approaches to developing strategic HRM

Guest identified various types of fit, which reflect different approaches to developing HR strategies.

(a) **Fit as strategic integration.** HR strategies are congruent with, or aligned to, the thrust of business competitive strategies (for innovation, quality and cost-leadership); appropriate to the stage of the business life-cycle reached by the business (start-up, growth, maturity, decline); adapted to organisational dynamics and characteristics and so on.

Employee expectations should also be aligned with strategic direction, by communication of the organisational vision, translating strategy into performance management, and developing a corresponding organisational culture.

(b)   **Fit as an ideal set of practices**: ensuring that internal practices reflect 'best practice'. The **best practice approach** is based on the belief that adopting certain broadly-applicable HRM practices will lead to superior **organisational performance**.

Several sets of best practices, based on benchmarking, have been developed, including elements such as: employment security; sophisticated recruitment and selection processes; self-managed teams; high compensation contingent on performance; high-level participation processes; information sharing; coherent appraisal; skill flexibility; motivating job design (including responsibility, flexibility and development); on-going training; use of quality improvement teams; and harmonised (single status) terms and conditions (Armstrong, 2003).

Armstrong himself notes that while 'these could all be regarded as 'good practice' … it is difficult to accept that they will universally constitute 'best practice'. What works well in one organisation will not necessarily work well in another.'

(c)   **Fit as contingency**: ensuring that internal practices suit the particular (and changing) context of the firm, and its business strategy. The **'best fit' approach** (or contingency approach) is based on the belief that there is no 'one best way' or set of universal prescriptions for strategy: it all depends. Benchmarked 'good practices' must be selected and adapted to fit specific needs identified by analysis of the firm's context both external (opportunities, threats and constraints) and internal (culture, structure, technology and processes). Purcell *et al* (2003) note that the contingencies or variables in HR decision-making are so complex that it is impossible to isolate them all: the important thing is to be sensitive to changing needs and circumstances.

(d)   **Fit as 'bundles'**: developing and implementing distinct **configurations** or 'bundles' of HR practices (such as quality management, performance management or competence frameworks) which can be used in multiple contexts to create coherence across a range of activities, ensuring that they complement and mutually reinforce each other.

In particular, practices designed to enhance employee **skills/competences** should be integrated with practices designed to enhance employee **motivation**, since both are essential to performance. So, for example, if the overall HR strategy is to improve performance, the sourcing strategies for competence-based recruiting will be integrated with development strategies for competence-based training and rewards strategies to offer competence-related pay. Likewise, to increase motivation, strategies will need to integrate motivation-based selection criteria with development opportunities, job design and other intrinsic motivating factors.

NOTES

Activity 7   **(20 minutes)**

What do you think might be the key HR policy issues and approaches of an organisation:

(a) Pursuing an innovation strategy?
(b) Pursuing a cost leadership strategy?
(c) In the growth stage of its life cycle?
(d) In the decline stage of its life cycle?

---

4   HRM AND BUSINESS SUCCESS

4.1   How does HRM impact on business performance?

Key research carried out by the Work and Employment Research Centre, University of Bath (Purcell *et al*, 2003) attempted to look inside 'the black box' which previously obscured the process by which people inputs are transformed into performance outputs. The researchers developed a complex 'People and Performance Model', which can be simplified as follows: Figure 8.4. This is primarily a **behavioural model**.

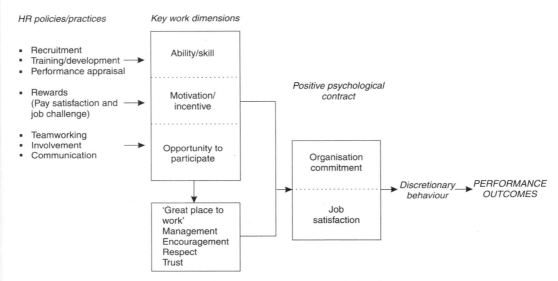

Figure 8.4: People and performance model (simplified and adapted by BPP)

A more **strategic model** was suggested by Guest *et al* (2000) as follows: Figure 8.5.

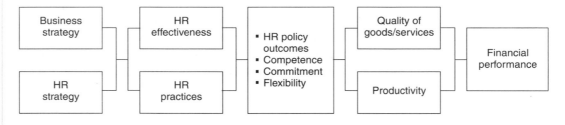

Figure 8.5: HRM and performance

> **Activity 8** (no time limit)
>
> Using whichever of the above models appeals to you, analyse the link between the HR practices of an organisation you know (or know about) and its economic performance (or fulfilment of other outcomes, if it is a not-for-profit organisation). See if you can trace the effects all the way through the 'black box'.

4.2 HR vision: a quality workforce

Connock (1991) saw a renewed focus on the need for a 'productive, trained, flexible and innovative workforce', which he summed up as 'a **quality** workforce'. He argued that HR managers should use vision and strategies to create and maintain this quality workforce in support of business objectives as HR's key contribution to added value.

Connock lists what he considers the **dimensions of quality** for employers.

(a) A customer services orientation
(b) Taking personal responsibility for quality output
(c) Well trained and developed staff to meet quality requirements
(d) Employee involvement in all aspects of quality
(e) Maintaining quality standards
(f) Communication and recognition programmes which reinforce quality
(g) Searching for continuous improvement
(h) Knowledge of and identification with quality from staff at all levels.

4.3 Human capital management

'Human capital' consists of the combined intelligence, knowledge, skills, abilities and energies of the people employed by a given organisation. These attributes have **value** as an organisational resource, and can have **value added** to them by investment.

- Organisations invest in human capital (through recruitment, retention, training, development, organisation and motivation) in order to enlarge their skill base, increase levels of competence, and foster knowledge acquisition and sharing. This in turn should reap returns in the form of productivity, flexibility, innovation and performance.

- Individuals invest in human capital (through acquiring skills, knowledge and experience) and reap returns in terms of higher earnings, enhanced cover (or employability) prospects, greater job satisfaction and so on.

'Human resource accounting' (or **'human asset accounting'**) is an attempt to quantify the financial value of human capital to the firm, as part of its market worth and asset base.

Under recommendations published in 2003 by the DTI's Accounting for People task force, employers are advised to report on human capital management (HCM) in their operating and financial reviews (FRs).

Following wide consultation with employers, investors and other stakeholders, the taskforce decided against a one-size-fits-all approach to HCM reporting. Instead, it

advised that employers should report on the aspects of HCM they see as key to business performance and strategy, including training, recruitment, diversity and leadership. Employers should show clearly how these policies affect business strategy and performance.'

EXAMPLE

The **Marks & Spencer** plc 'How Do We Do Business Report' (2007) has an 'Our Performance' section which sets out the company's 2006/07 targets *and* performance ('How we did') in areas including:

- Training
- Pension changes
- Career development
- Responding to the collapse of the Farepak Christmas savings scheme for employees
- Fire, health and safety
- Code of ethics
- Diversity and data (including Age Discrimination)

There is also a separate breakdown of workforce diversity including percentages of employers and managers among women, ethnic minority backgrounds and over 50 years of age.

Check out the Annual Reports and Accounts (downloadable from corporate websites) of organisations that interest you, and look for the 'Our People' or 'Our employees' sections...

The *Accounting for People* consultation paper highlighted four basic areas for Human Capital Reporting.

(a) The size and composition of the workforce – the numbers of people that the company relies on for its performance. This should include agency, contract staff and those on the payroll. Information should be produced in relation to age, gender and ethnicity.

(b) Employee motivation. As well as data on staff turnover and absentee rates, this should include information on arrangements for gathering employees' views.

(c) Staff training and development. This should include the match between the skills acquired and business objectives.

(d) Remuneration and fair employment – the organisation's approach to pay and incentives, and the means by which it satisfies itself that it does not discriminate unfairly.

FOR DISCUSSION

'The amount of information in a company's annual report about its employees, and on how the ways in which they are managed and developed add value to the business, is pathetically inadequate. Maybe there's a bland statement on people being our most important asset, a few pictures, a dozen pages on executives' rewards and perhaps total numbers employed in the notes – but that's about it. Hardly a "true and fair" view in our knowledge-, information– and service-based economy.'

(Brown & Baron, 2003)

What benefits can you see for organisations, employees and other stakeholders (shareholders, potential investors, potential employees) in having more rigorous human capital reporting?

Chapter roundup

- While HRM is about 'success through people', there are two different orientations of this view.

    - 'Hard' HRM emphasises the close integration of human resource policies with business strategy, and regards employees as a resource to be quantitatively measured and managed in the same rational way as any other resource being exploited for maximum returns.

    - 'Soft' HRM views employees as valued assets and as a source of competitive advantage through their commitment, adaptability and high level of skills and performance.

- The Michigan model stressed the matching of HR policy to business strategy (hard), while the Harvard model stressed development and neutrality (soft).

- HR policies may be categorised as tight or loose according to the extent of managerial control which they assume to be necessary to achieve performance goals. Guest identifies the contrast between (tight) systems of compliance and (loose) systems of commitment.

- Storey developed an ideal type model or HRM contrasted to the traditional personnel/industrial relations model of labour management. 27 points of difference (expressed as extremes) were identified in the areas of beliefs and assumptions, strategy, the line management role and key levers used to shape the employment relationship.

- Strategic HRM is the direction of HR policy in such a way as to achieve the strategic goals of the business. HR strategy may be developed using business strategy, 'best fit', 'best practice' or 'configuration/bundling' approaches.

- There is increasing emphasis on the need to report accurately on the value of human resources and their impact on business performance, with Human Capital Reporting requirements introduced in 2005. Various models have been devised to shed light on the 'black box' process whereby people inputs are transformed into performance outputs.

Quick quiz

1   What are the features of hard HRM?

2   What are the philosophical underpinnings of soft HRM?

3   What levels of management should HR be involved in, according to the Michigan model?

4   List four key ideas of the Harvard Framework.

5   Distinguish between:

(a) Theory X and Theory Y
(b) Compliance and Commitment

6   What is the difference between a personnel/IR approach and an HRM approach in the dimensions of:

(a)   The role of rules
(b)   The nature of relations
(c)   Prized managerial skills
(d)   The focus of attention for interventions

7   What does 'strategic fit' involve as applied to HRM?

8   Distinguish between a 'best fit' and 'best practice' approach to HR strategy.

9   Draw Guest's model of HRM and performance.

10   What is human capital?

Answers to quick quiz

1   Matching of HR and business strategy; focus on yield on human resources; focus on quantitative measures of management effectiveness; emphasis on the need for performance management and managerial control.

(see paragraph 1.1)

2   Human relations school of management; socio-psychology; view of employees as assets/means rather than costs/objects; unitarist ideology; stakeholder perspective.   (para 1.2)

3   Strategic (long-term, focus on future 'fit'), managerial (medium-term, focus on acquisition, retention and development), operational day-to-day, focus on supporting business activities.   (para 1.3)

4   HRM involves all management decisions affecting the employment relationship. Organisations are made up of stakeholders and there is a trade-off between their interests. HRM is influenced by a range of contextual factors. Line managers take responsibility for aligning HR policy and competitive strategy.

(para 1.4)

5   See paragraphs 1.6 and 1.7 for a full account.

6   (a)   Importance of rules v 'can do' outlook creating impatience with rules

(b)   Pluralist v unitarist

(c)   Negotiation v facilitation

(d)   Personnel procedures v wide-ranging cultural, structural and personnel strategies.   (para 2.1)

7   HR strategies integrated with business strategy to support its achievement (vertical fit). HR practices developed to complement and mutually reinforce one another with consistent results (horizontal fit). Line managers internalising the importance of human resources.   (para 3.2)

8   'Best practice' assumes there are universally effective HR practices; 'best fit' assumes that 'good practices' will need to be selected and adapted to fit the external and internal context of the organisation, and remain sensitive to change.   (para 3.3)

9   See paragraph 4.1., figure 8.5.

10   The combined intelligence, knowledge, skills, abilities and energies of people employed by an organisation.   (para 4.3)

Answers to activities

1   **Hard**: high levels of rules, procedures and instructions, and appropriate training; strong corporate culture/values for the purposes of selection, socialisation and 'weeding out'; selection on the basis of pre-determined job criteria; close supervision and work inspection; administrative controls on time-keeping, absence, hours worked and so on; performance management focused on monitoring of performance against imposed standards and targets; job descriptions; job evaluation based on standard measures of performance; payment by results (narrowly defined); short-term cost-benefit evaluation of HR policies; centralised control over HR functions; adversarial mechanisms for dealing with discipline, grievance and relationships with trade unions; 'need to know' communication policies; welfare to minimise costs/lost production; managerial status symbols and tiered terms and conditions.

2   *Soft:* articulation of goals and values; strong corporate culture/values for the purposes of inspiration – especially quality; flexible working methods; emphasis on teamwork; self-managed time-keeping and attendance; consultation and agreement on work targets and criteria; values– and outputs-driven criteria; consultation and agreement on issues affecting the workforce; delegation and empowerment; HR fulfilling and enabling rather than controlling role; training for development, employability, flexibility; personal development and improvement plans; employee relations based on communication and involvement; welfare based on well-being and enabled performance; reward systems and performance management based on collaboratively agreed criteria; harmonised terms and conditions.

3   The writer is describing a Theory X, tight-control approach. In a recession, organisations are likely to be faced with pressures to cut costs and improve productivity in order to remain competitive: managers may be tempted to adopt this approach towards HR issues to achieve these goals. Remember that 'loose-tight' is a continuum. According to a contingency view of strategic 'fit', there is nothing inherently right or wrong about loose or tight control strategies: the chosen approach must suit the business needs of the organisation and respond to changes in its environment.

4   This answer will be highly individual to you and your situation (which may indicate why commitment is not easy to pin down or foster in practice). Benefits to *you* (analogous to the employee) may have included enjoyment, sense of purpose, possibly extra effort resulting in better results, which in turn may lead

to further satisfaction and opportunities for development. Benefits for your *trainers* (analogous to employers) may have included the same, perhaps defined in different ways: better attendance and time keeping, more creative ideas put forward to improve the course, encouragement to other students from your positive attitude, better results. Ways of *increasing commitment* may have included: clearer instructions, linking your studies to your goals in HRM, more enjoyable or challenging teaching methods and activities, and perhaps your willingness to put effort in now for rewards later.

5   Some examples you may have thought of are:

    (a) *Institutionalise conflict* through strict procedures for disciplinary action, grievance handling, appeals mechanisms, conflict resolution, negotiation with union representatives. (These are all good and helpful in the event of conflict – but they do assume that conflict is going to occur...) *De-emphasise conflict:* interpersonal conflict resolution handled on a contingency basis by management; win-win approach (assuming mutuality of interests); emphasise and reward teamworking and co-operation.

    (b) *Restrict communication:* institutionalised communication avenues (eg house journal or bulletin); managerial control over in-house communication; hierarchical, functional channels of communication; 'need to know' policies; lack of training in communication skills; centralised information storage and retrieval; discouragement of social networking among employees (by job and work environment design). *Increase communication:* training in communication; cultural reinforcement of communication (management example, reward and appraisal on communication skills); encouragement of multi-functional teamworking and/or briefings; encouragement of informal networking; focus on quality/customer overriding procedure.

6   Empowerment might influence recruitment/selection in the following ways.

    (a) Empowered workers may wish to take over responsibility for recruiting new members of their teams.

    (b) Jobs (and therefore job descriptions and selection criteria) would need to reflect new ways of working such as multi-skilling, team-working and so on.

    (c) Communication, leadership and facilitation skills would become key selection criteria for managers.

    Empowerment might influence training as follows.

    (a) Training would be initiated and shaped by the job needs of empowered workers: relevant to the job, focused on areas such as responsibility, planning, teamworking and communication.

    (b) The trainer's role would be that of 'coach', reflecting the empowering/equipping philosophy towards training.

    (c) The manager may well take on the coaching/facilitating role: training will be seen to be a continuous on-the-job process and part of personal development by employees.

7   (a) For innovation, the organisation will require creative behaviour, long-term thinking, collaborative working, willingness to take risks and tolerance of unpredictability. HR practices that may help foster these qualities include:

teamworking, high communication flow, multi-skilling and flexible working; broader career/development paths allowing flexibility; longer-term, team-based performance appraisal; selection and reward for innovation values.

(b) For cost leadership, the organisation will need a focus on output quantity (with less concern for quality), a relatively short-term outlook, and controlled/low-risk performance. HR practices that may help foster these qualities include: narrow job design and explicit job descriptions; short-term, output-focused appraisal and reward; close monitoring of employee activities; little investment in training and development; focus on cost minimisation.

(c) In the growth stage, the organisation will require more progressive and sophisticated recruitment and selection (compared to start-up), training and development, performance management processes and reward systems, a focus on achieving high commitment and emphasis on developing stable employee relations.

(d) In decline, the organisation may have to shift to rationalisation, down-sizing by accelerated wastage or redundancy, curtailing of HR programmes (especially employee development) in order to cut costs, the attempt to marginalise or de-recognise trade unions.

8   This exercise is designed to help you build up case study material. It may also help you to realise how complex the relationships between all these variables are. In the 'People and Performance' model, for example, you might notice that the line management aspects (trust, respect) also *increase* the likelihood that HR policies (eg communication, teamworking, job satisfaction) will be successful. This underlines the key role of line managers in delivering HRM outcomes.

Chapter 9:
FLEXIBILITY

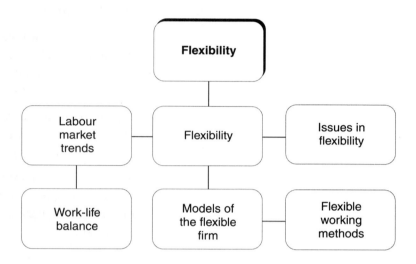

Introduction

In Chapters 2 and 3, we noted that sourcing labour requirements may be achieved from *within* the organisation as well as from the external labour market. The efficiency with which labour resources can be deployed and redeployed, at need, within the organisation depends on a measure of **flexibility**. Employees who are functionally versatile (or multi-skilled) and culturally flexible may be redeployed across the functional boundaries previously set by job descriptions and occupational demarcation zones. A numerically flexible workforce may be deployed at periods of peak workloads. Given the pace of change in technologies and market places, and the 'ungluing' of traditional organisational structures to meet changing customer demands, flexibility is one of *the* Hot Topics in HRM!

Your objectives

In this chapter you will learn about the following.

(a)   Labour market trends reinforcing the need for flexibility

(b)   Models of the flexible firm

(c)   Types of flexibility and flexible working methods

(d)   The advantages and disadvantages of flexible working practices

NOTES

1 FLEXIBILITY

1.1 Why flexibility?

Flexibility first emerged as a major issue in the 1980s, as the Western European economies were forced to respond to change. Increased global competition, international recession, uncertainty about future markets and the effects of new technology undermined historical expectations of stable economic growth and the pace and complexity of such changes has continued to increase into the 21st century.

(a) Increased competition has placed emphasis on quality, innovation and reducing the unit costs of production: job design and the organisation of work must both mobilise employees' energies for quality/innovation and reliable productivity.

(b) Increased market uncertainty means that organisations need to be more adaptable to changes in demand: able to vary the size and deployment of their workforces to meet demand as effectively and efficiently as possible.

(c) Technological change, particularly in the automation and computerisation of work processes and information flows, has eroded traditional demarcation boundaries between jobs: job design and the organisation of work must fit the new technology in order to secure its benefits for efficiency.

(d) Demographic (and related labour market) changes have highlighted the need for flexible job and career designs, in order to meet the needs of dual income families, women and older workers for 'work life balance'. (This is discussed in more detail below.)

The need for flexibility underpinned new working practices.

- Increasing managerial ability to adapt the size and deployment of the workforce in line with changing demand and supply

- Increasing scope for flexible working for individual employees

- Raising the quality and/or quantity of workforce output.

1.2 Labour market trends and flexibility

In Chapter 2, we discussed how HR planners need to take account of demographic and other factors in the internal and external labour markets, in order to meet the organisation's demand for skills. Specific pressures towards flexibility include the following.

(a) **Age structure**

Social Trends shows that the number of economically active people in the age group 16-24 is falling, while those aged 25-44 is rising. As well as the resourcing implications discussed in Chapter 2, this means that an increasing proportion of the workforce may have family and child-rearing responsibilities, or care of a dependent aged relative: focus on 'work life balance' (Paragraph 1.3 below) has created the need for flexibility in working hours and place of work to support these workers.

BPP
LEARNING MEDIA

(b) **Diversity**

The most recent *Workplace Employee Relations Survey* data (WERS 2004) shows (Bratton & Gold, 2007) that in the UK:

- Women's share of total employment has continued to increase

- In some 44% of workplaces that employ part-time staff, women make up all of these part-time staff.

- The majority of women workers are engaged in clerical, serving or cleaning work, but female participation has also increased in middle and senior management

Gender diversity in the workplace, and the need to recruit and retain female workers (in order to meet both skill/labour shortages *and* equal opportunity requirements) has reinforced the focus on work life balance. Organisations need to deploy labour flexibly in order to accommodate the demands made of working mothers (and fathers, given the related trend towards shared family responsibilities and dual career families) and the desire for career breaks and return after child-rearing.

(c) **The use of non-standard contracts**

The WERS 2004 data shows that the use of non-standard forms of employment has now become 'commonplace' in UK workplaces. 8.3% of workplaces employed part-time employees (less than 30 hours per week), up from 79% in 1998. Almost one third of workplaces had employees on temporary contracts. There has also been an increase in the contracting out or outsourcing of services such as cleaning, transport, security – and HR and training.

(d) **Differences in particular labour markets**

Employers may compete for labour and skills in a number of different markets: local, national and international.

- Particular factors in the local labour market (people living in the 'travel to work area' or within reasonable commuting distance) may create pressure for flexibility. For example: geographical dispersion or lack of public transportation may require flexible starting hours, or work from home options.

- National/regional skill shortages and wage costs may encourage the outsourcing of 'off-shoring' of operations to low-cost labour countries or the co-opting of overseas team-members through 'virtual' collaboration using ICT links.

- Different occupational structures and orientations (at local and national level) may also require different approaches to the employment relationship, career management and so on. Professionally and technically qualified staff, for example, may be treated differently (as 'core' employees) from lower-skilled and high-mobility workers (who may be more flexibly contracted).

(e) **Regulation of working hours**

The *Working Time Regulations 1998* sets (currently negotiable) limits on working hours per week and entitlement to rest breaks and days. In order to cover equivalent workloads, employers may have to implement job-sharing and other flexible work patterns.

Weblink

The Workplace Employment Relations Survey (WERS) 2004

▶▶ **http://www.dti.gov.uk/employment/research-evaluation/wers-2004**

Activity 1   **(30 minutes)**

Check out www.statistics.gov.uk, or the WERS 2004 website. (Alternatively, there are government publications such as *Social Trends* or the *Department of Employment Gazette.*)

See if you can locate the following information.

- The percentage of the UK labour force in permanent employment in the current year.

- The percentage of women in the UK labour force in the current year.

- The percentage of women in part-time work in the current year.

1.3   Work life balance

Work-life balance is a concept which recognises the need for employers to support workers in achieving a balance between the demands of their work and the demands of home and family responsibilities (including the care of children, older people and sick family members).

Flexible working policies, designed to give employees options in regard to their hours and/or locations of work, have been supported in recent years by **equal opportunity** and **family-friendly** rights law. These have provided a package of entitlements including: annual leave, maximum working hours, parental leave and time off for dependent care; maternity/paternity leave and adoption leave; equal rights for part-time workers and so on.

The *Employment Act 2002* provided for an additional package of rights in relation to **flexible working**.

(a) Any employee with 26 weeks' service, who is the parent or legal guardian of a child under six (under 18 if the child is disabled) has the right to request flexible working arrangements: to change the total numbers of hours contracted to work; when those hours are worked; and/or where the work is done.

(b) Requests must be written/emailed, and include details of the applicant's eligibility, the nature and timetable of the requested change, and consideration of the impact of the change on the business. A number of on-line resources is available to help applicants think the issues through: eg www.flexrequest.co.uk.

(c) The employer has 28 days to consider the request and approve – or at least meet with the applicant to discuss the application. Employees are entitled to be accompanied by a work colleague at any discussion.

(d) If the application is declined, the employee may appeal. Justified reasons for refusal include: the burden of extra costs; negative impact on productivity, quality or performance; inability to reorganise or redistribute work; or inability to recruit extra staff to make up lost hours.

(e) If the employer refuses to consider a request, or fails to follow the statutory procedure, the employee has three months to bring a complaint before an Employment Tribunal.

'For years, best-practice organisations have taken an informal approach to fielding flexible working requests, with local line managers making decisions that best fit an individual or department, by involving other team members in the matter. In many cases, this method will continue to be the most effective in driving a flexible work culture while avoiding red tape' (Cartwright, 2003).

Weblinks

> For more information on work life balance, you may like to check out the following websites.
>
> **TUC**
> ► ►http://www.tuc.org.uk/changingtimes
>
> *People Management* **online**
> ► ►http:// www.peoplemanagement.co.uk/work-life
>
> **Parents at Work**
> ► ►http:// www.parentsatwork.org.uk
>
> **Flex Request**
> ► ►http://www.flexrequest.co.uk

EXAMPLE

'**Telford and Wrekin Borough Council** won two Parents at Work Awards in 2003. Since introducing flexible working practices, it has been able to extend its hours of operation – and has seen dramatic reductions in staff turnover and sickness levels.

'The borough has one of the highest concentrations of single mothers in Europe and, as roughly 80 per cent of the council's workforce are female, HR supports a range of initiatives that enable mothers to return to work and generally help working parents. These include assistance with childcare costs, a workplace crèche, local shop discounts and a hot-line to a nursery for those needing emergency childcare. Most important are working hours that allow parents to combine careers with bringing up children.

'[The council] also stresses the need to help the wider community, especially the elderly and the young. For example, allowing an employee to work flexible hours so they can care for an elderly relative relives the council of some or all of the burden of caring for that person itself.

'Over the past three years, the composition of the council's workforce has changed dramatically, with 52 per cent working part-time. Many work from home, others opt for annualised hours, term-time working or a week-on, week-off working pattern. [The council's manager] believes a decentralised approach is best, with line managers handling individual requests. "We encourage managers to use their common sense and be caring in a practical way," he says.

'Managers are expected to initiate work-life balance conversations and act as a role models by looking after their own work-life balance. Senior managers are as eligible for flexible working as junior staff. To ensure consistency and fairness, managers are assessed on the work-life balance competencies in their department through a management development programme. An annual employee survey also looks at the issue, asking questions such as: "Is your manager flexible to your own personal circumstances?" ...'

(Woolnough, 2003)

Flexibility is clearly in line with the HRM approach to making the most effective and efficient use of the human resource. As we saw in Chapter 8, however, there are two ways of looking at HR issues: from a 'hard' perspective and from a 'soft' perspective. What does flexibility look like from each of these.

1.4 Hard or soft HRM?

There are two distinct orientations to flexibility, in accordance with the hard and soft views of HRM.

(a) Flexibility is a key goal of strategic HRM, with its hard emphasis on meeting business needs through **efficient deployment** of the labour resources. 'Hard' flexibility, in the words of Beardwell and Holden, means 'the ability to adjust the size and mix of labour inputs in response to changes in product demand so that excess labour is not carried by the organisation'. This approach has been popularised as '**lean production**': minimising overhead labour costs by reducing jobs not directly contributing to production, and minimising the cost of directly productive labour by raising productivity.

(b) Flexibility is consistent with the soft HRM emphasis on **empowerment and involvement** of employees for increased commitment, motivation and development. 'Soft' flexibility means creating an adaptable workforce, by involving employees in decision-making, broadening their skills individually and through teamworking and creating a culture of continuous learning and improvement focused on quality outcomes rather than adherence to procedures.

1.5 Mutual benefits

Depending whether a hard or soft flexibility approach is used, flexibility may have benefits for the employing organisation and for employees. We will discuss the advantages and disadvantages of specific flexible working practices, from both points of view, as we proceed through this chapter. In general, however, the intended benefits are as follows.

(a) For the **organisation**, it offers a cost-effective, efficient way of utilising the labour resource. Under competitive pressure, technological innovation and a variety of other changes, organisations need a flexible, 'lean' workforce for efficiency, control and predictability. The stability of the organisation in a volatile environment depends on its ability to adapt swiftly to meet changes, without incurring cost penalties or suffering waste. If employee flexibility can be achieved with the co-operation of the employees and their representatives, there may be an end to demarcation disputes, costly redundancy packages and other consequences of apparently rational organisation design.

(b) From the point of view of the **employee**, the erosion of rigid specialisation, the micro-division of labour and the inflexible working week can also offer benefits. For example, a higher quality of working life; an accommodation with non-work interests and demands (work-life balance); greater job satisfaction, through variety of work; and perhaps job security and material benefits, since a versatile, mobile, flexible employee is likely to be more attractive to employers and have a higher value in the current labour market climate.

FOR DISCUSSION

'The concept of flexible working has been at the top of the HR agenda for some time now. It is clear that many people (particularly women) feel unable to accept the old-style pattern of "full-time" commitment to a job – without any opportunity to spend time with small children, care for older relatives or even simply take time out. Employers have responded in a number of ways: from the bare legal minimum to packages that offer enormous flexibility.

'But it's equally clear that workplaces aren't always finding it easy to put these policies into practice. A study from the Institute for Employment Studies last year, *Work-Life Balance Beyond the Rhetoric*, demonstrated that employees wanted a work pattern that offered them flexibility for other commitments; and HR managers were generally convinced that this had definite business benefits. But the same study shows that few people actually move away from conventional work patterns.

'This is mainly because they think that doing so would affect their career prospects; and many managers, even if they would like to be supportive, simply don't know how to help. In practice, long working hours and heavy workloads (and, of course, the need to bring in a full-time wage) remain the norm for many.'

(Holmström, 2003)

How might work-life, family-friendly and flexible polices be undermined by corporate culture, management style and economic reality?

NOTES

You may have noticed from the preceding paragraph that there are a number of different types of flexibility, including not only the employer's ability to change the size of the workforce in response to demand, but the broadening of employees' skills and task variety, and the re-structuring of the working day or week. We will now summarise the flexibility approaches.

1.6   Types of flexibility

There are a number of possible approaches to flexibility.

Type of flexibility	Responding to:	HRM approach
• **Numerical**	Fluctuations in demand for staff numbers (seasonal, cyclical, task-related and so on)	Use of non-permanent, non-career labour: temporary staff, part-time staff, short-contract staff, consultants, sub-contractors
• **Temporal**	Fluctuations in working patterns, over 24 hours/week/year: fluctuations in demand for labour at particular times; the need for work-life balance and support for equal opportunity	Use of 'flexi-time' and variations: overtime, shift-working, annualised hours
• **Functional** (versatility)	Fluctuations in demand for particular skills – not necessarily related to staff numbers (since one person can be multi-skilled)	Deployment of staff across job/skill boundaries ('demarcation lines'): multi-skilling, multi-disciplinary teams, fewer or broader job descriptions
• **Financial**	The need for functional/temporal staff to be rewarded flexibly and fairly – since 'the job' is no longer a fixed basis for reward. The need for choice (eg in incentive and benefit schemes) to raise value of rewards in a diverse workforce	Performance – and/or profit-related pay; individual pay negotiation; broad-band pay schemes; flexible benefits
• **Locational**	Opportunities presented by information and communication technology (ICT) to reduce office costs and create 'virtual' (dispersed but interconnected) teams	Use of home-working, tele-working and networking; use of ICT to facilitate mobile working (eg for sales and service staff)

Type of flexibility	Responding to:	HRM approach
• **Cultural**	The need for a change of traditional attitudes towards jobs, careers, occupational identify: the need for a culture which embraces flexibility, variety, change, entrepreneurship	Recruitment and reward systems geared to employ and advance culturally flexible and versatile people; communication of flexibility and work-life balance as key values; counselling to help overcome fear of change

Activity 2 (no time limit)

Observe staff at a local supermarket and talk to friends who might work for one of the big supermarket chains. What evidence of flexibility can you see within organisations such as these? Which 'type' of flexibility is suggested by each of your examples?

We will now look in more detail at two key models for numerical flexibility.

2 MODELS OF THE FLEXIBLE FIRM

2.1 The core/periphery model

Fluctuations in the (numerical) demand for workers may be foreseeable: regular peaks due to daily, weekly or seasonal cycles (such as lunch and dinner times at an all-day restaurant, Saturdays at supermarkets, or Easter at a chocolate factory) or irregular peaks due to organisational activity (such as a product launch). Other fluctuations may be unforeseeable: industrial action affecting competitors; events or reports in the media which stimulate or 'kill' demand for the product/service and so on.

The organisation cannot afford to employ a full-time workforce based on the best-case scenario or greatest demand. Indeed, in times of pressure to downsize the workforce (or at least, not to expand it), organisations prefer to increase their proportion of non-permanent labour, to avoid redundancies and/or seasonal layoffs.

The **'flexible firm' or 'core periphery' model** (Atkinson, 1984; Atkinson & Meager, 1986) divides the workforce into 'core' and 'peripheral' groups: Figure 9.1.

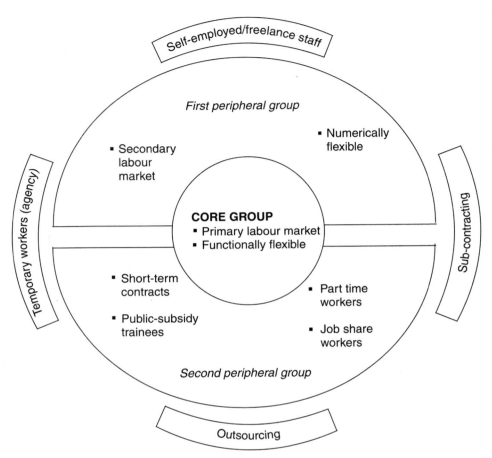

Figure 9.1: Atkinson's core-periphery model of the flexible firm (Atkinson, 1984)

The core

The **core** group is permanent and stable, and is based on:

(a) The lowest number of employees required by work activity at any time throughout the year and

(b) Core tasks which are specific to the firm and require firm-specific skills and experience.

The core group offers **functional** flexibility by virtue of re– or multi-skilling: training, retraining and redeployment within core tasks.

HR implications include:

(a) The need for training in core skills

(b) The need to offer employment security/continuity in order to facilitate skill/experience build-up and in order to protect the firm's investment in core workers' training

(c) The need for reward structures which reflect and support flexibility and multi-skilling by removing rigid grade or functional barriers

(d) The need to secure the commitment of the core workforce: this would usually foster commitment-based 'soft' HRM policies.

The periphery

The **peripheral** group is designed to offer numerical flexibility: the ability to meet short-term fluctuations in demand for skills which are not distinctive of the firm. It includes:

(a)   Full-time employees in areas where there is a high level of mobility and wastage/turnover (clerical/secretarial and so on), creating a relatively numerically flexible internal labour market: the *first peripheral group*

(b)   Workers on non-standard contracts: the *second peripheral group*

(c)   'Distance' workers not employed by the organisation but contracted to supply services

Core-periphery flexibility

By acting as a 'buffer' against the need to downsize the organisation in the face of fluctuating demand (Figure 9.2), the core-periphery model allows for:

(a)   Relatively 'hard' HR policies aimed at reducing labour costs, and avoiding labour excesses and shortages, applied at the periphery and

(b)   Relatively 'soft' HR policies aimed at increasing productivity and commitment, providing employment security and organisational stability, applied at the core.

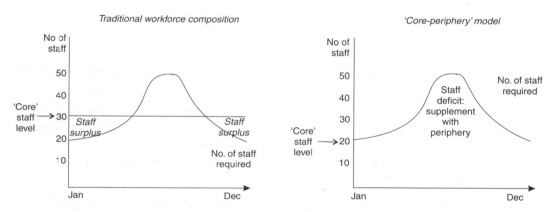

Figure 9.2: The flexible firm and HR planning

2.2   The Shamrock organisation

Charles Handy (1989) put forward the idea of the shamrock (or clover-leaf) organisation, giving examples such as Rank Xerox and IBM.

Mullins (1999) represents this as follows: Figure 9.3.

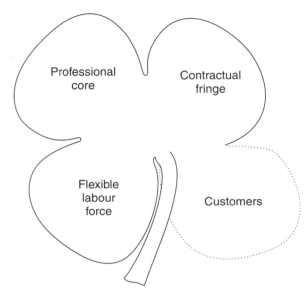

Figure 9.3: The Shamrock Organisation

- The **professional core** are permanently-employed people who represent the distinctive knowledge and competences of the firm. They are qualified professionals, technicians and managers. Their commitment is focused on their work and career within the organisation.

- The **flexible labour** *force* are temporary and part-time workers who can be brought in as and when needed – especially to meet peaks in the demand for services (since they have to be supplied in 'real time'). Their commitment is typically focused on the immediate job and work group, rather than career or the organisation. However, they are crucial in maintaining standards of service – so it is important for the firm not to treat them 'casually': they should receive fair and equitable treatment (now enshrined in employment law), adequate training and status.

- The **contractual fringe** are external providers (freelancers, consultants and sub-contractors) who are able to undertake non-core activities and/or provide specialist services, more economically than the firm could manage internally. Their commitment is typically to achieving specified results in return for fees.

These represent three distinct labour forces, each with its own type of psychological (and legal) contract with the firm.

Activity 3	**(5 minutes)**

What would you expect the key HRM issues to be in the case of each of Handy's 'leaves' discussed above?

In addition, Handy notes the 'lucky' fourth leaf of the clover: the organisation may be able to 'sub-contract' some sales, service and supply tasks – for free – to **customers**. Information and communication technology (ICT) has supported a wide range of 'self service' applications such as: Internet/phone banking and automated teller machines (ATMs); Internet/telephone reservations and ticketing, in entertainment and travel; on-line information services and so on – in addition to traditional self-service retail and catering outlets, self-assembly products and so on. This should allow labour savings in other 'leaves' of the organisation.

We will now look at other approaches to numerical, locational, functional and temporal flexibility.

3   FLEXIBLE WORKING METHODS

3.1   Part-time and temporary working

Definition

> Under the EU Directive on part-time work, a **part-time employee** is someone with a contract or employment relationship whose normal hours of work, averaged over a period of up to a year, are less than the normal hours of comparable full-timers.

> **Activity 4**   **(45 minutes)**
>
> Why do you think there has been an increase in part-time working?
>
> Consider the employer and employee points of view.

The thrust of legislation and court decisions has been to protect 'peripheral' employees from exploitation by 'hard' flexibility policies.

EU Directives on part-time and temporary work were incorporated into UK law by regulations and a Code of Practice under the *Employment Relations Act 1999*. Part-time and temporary or fixed-contract employees are now entitled to the same employment and health and safety protection as permanent full-time staff.

(a)   Part-timers (who work 8 hours or more per week) may not be treated less favourably because they work part time. They are entitled to the same hourly rate of pay, sick pay, access to training, selection for promotion, protection from unfair dismissal, and so on. They also have the same entitlements to annual leave and maternity/paternity leave but on a *pro rata* basis

(b)   Obstacles to part-time work should be removed: there should be opportunities for part-time work at all levels, and for transfer between full-time, part-time and job-sharing arrangements: part-time (and temporary) workers should be informed of permanent full-time vacancies, for example.

    (c)   The *Working Time Regulations 1998* give equal rights to part-time and temporary workers in respect of night working, minimum rest periods and Health and Safety protection services, since they are held to be particularly at risk.

    (d)   Temporary and fixed-contract workers are also entitled to the same social security benefits as permanent employees.

    (e)   Individuals engaged under temporary contracts must be informed of the reasons for their being employed on a temporary rather than a permanent contract.

    (f)   Health and safety legislation applies equally to full-time, part-time and temporary workers.

FOR DISCUSSION

Does the protection and extension of part-time and temporary workers' rights defeat the object of the core-periphery model? What does it suggest about the perceived advantages of the model to employers and its perceived disadvantages to peripheral employees?

INTERNATIONAL COMPARISONS

The **USA** has a comparatively free approach to part-time and temporary workers. Beardwell and Holden suggest that 'there are grounds for thinking that workers employed by temporary help agencies or contracting firms in the USA are denied the benefits of employment security, job progression and benefits such as pensions that go with internal labour markets.'

3.2   Job-sharing

Job-sharing is an approach to part-time job creation in which an existing full-time position is split in two, so that two people can share it, working part-time and paid pro-rata.

3.3   Tele-working and home-working

Definition

> **Tele-working** describes the process of working from home, or from a satellite office close to home, with the aid of networked or Internet-linked computers, fax machines and other ICT applications.

Tele-working offers:

(a)   Savings on overheads, particularly premises costs, in view of rising rents in many of the major cities in the UK

(b)   The opportunity to bring into employment skilled and experienced people for whom traditional working practices have hitherto been impracticable: single parents, mothers, the disabled, carers and so on

(c)   Elimination of the need to commute – with consequent reductions in traffic congestion, fuel consumption, travel costs, pollution, commuter stress

(d)   Better work-life balance: less stress; more employment opportunities for those with family responsibilities

Tele-working may take the form of:

(a)   **Homeworking**: traditional outworkers such as home typists, market-research/ tele-sales workers etc

(b)   **Freelancing**: working for a number of different clients from a home office, or in client offices

(c)   **Mobile working**: using laptop computers, the Internet and mobile phone technology to work 'on the road' (eg field sales staff)

(d)   **Call-centre working**: working in specialist centres providing helpline services, telesales, data entry and so on.

EXAMPLE: GOOD PRACTICE AT SOLAGLAS

Taking flexibility to the customer

Solaglas is a UK subsidiary of French multinational glassmaker Saint-Gobain employing glaziers and installation workers. Its 'Moving Forward' agreement on annualised hours with the GMB and AEEU is designed to focus its business on customer service, through flexibility in working hours. Features of the agreement include: single-status employment; annual salaries; flexible start times (between 7 am and 11 am, Monday to Saturday); computerised working for home-based glaziers using palm-tops for job allocation, progress reports and factory contact.

The benefits for the company are increased productivity, a single pay scheme, flexibility, profitability and significant reinvestment by the French parent company. Benefits for staff include enhanced terms and conditions, permanent status and greater choice in working time (of particular benefit for two men who were caring for wives with long-term illnesses). The work is also carried out at the customer's convenience.

(Bond, 2003)

NOTES

Barnes (1997) helpfully summarises how teleworking might be most effectively managed.

- Develop relationships of trust

- Have policies covering operational issues such as insurance, confidentiality, taxation (possible capital gains tax liability arising from the use of domestic property for business purpose), security and health and safety

- Use criteria when recruiting which enables the selection of those with self-discipline, good self-management skills and other attributes of effective teleworkers

- Have formal and informal channels of communication (social isolation is the major disadvantage of teleworking as reported by the workers themselves) with visits by supervisors, regular meetings at the office, use of telephone, newsletters, informal gatherings etc.

(We might add web-conferencing e-mail and instant messaging, ten years later!)

- Clearly define quantitative and qualitative targets to 'manage-by-results' and give thought to monitoring performance, making use of electronics whenever possible

- Have performance appraisal, career management and training policies which meet the needs of teleworkers

- Be open to part-time home and part-time office working and even 'occasional' teleworking if appropriate

- Maintain the voluntary principle and have a 'revolving door' policy whereby as circumstances change workers can return to full-time office working

- Evaluate outcomes against objective measures in productivity, quality of output, accommodation cost etc

3.4 Multi-skilling

Jobs are changing from simple, well-defined tasks (set out in job descriptions) to more flexible, multi-dimensional working recognition of the following.

(a) Performing a whole meaningful job is more satisfying to a worker than performing only one of its component tasks (as in 'scientific' job design)

(b) Allowing workers to see the big picture enables and encourages them to contribute information and ideas for improvements, which might not otherwise have come to light

(c) The focus on the task and overall objectives reduces the need for tight managerial control and supervision over work processes and practices

Definition

Multi-skilling is functional versatility: the opposite of specialisation, with its tendency towards rigid job descriptions and demarcation lines between one job and another. It involves the development of versatility in the labour force, so that individuals can perform more than one task if required to do so: workers are being encouraged, trained and organised to work across the boundaries of traditional jobs and crafts.

Multi-skilling has been difficult to achieve historically, because craft and occupational groups (such as trade unions) have supported demarcation in order to protect jobs and maintain special skills, standards and pay differentials. This situation is changing now that multi-skilled, flexible labour is highly prized in today's labour market.

EXAMPLE: SMITHKLINE BEECHAM

SmithKline Beecham introduced multi-skilling at its factory in Irvine in 1995 . This was accomplished across a great 'divide' of strict demarcation between **operators** (belonging to the Transport and General Workers' Union, TGWU) and **craftsmen** (represented by the Amalgamated Electrical and Engineering Union, AEEU). Further problems were posed by deeply-entrenched working practices, and the strong trade union traditions of western Scotland.

In the past, process operators faced with a blockage in the pipes (carrying materials from one stage of the process to another) have had to tell their supervisor, who would tell the engineering foreman, who would send a fitter to deal with it: meanwhile, production would grind to a halt. After multi-skilling, the job could be done by whoever was best placed to do it: craftsman or – more often – operator.

Analysis of such situations by working parties resulted in the concept of the 'best person': instead of jobs being 'owned' by particular groups, the most appropriate individual to do a particular job should be trained and skilled to do it!

'The intention was to increase efficiency across the whole site by cross-skilling electrical, mechanical and instrument engineers, while at the same time equipping operators with basic engineering, materials movement and analytical skills'.

Agreement was achieved after three years' consultation and negotiation with the unions.

The benefits of multi-skilling to the organisation are as follows.

(a) It is an efficient use of people resources.

    (i) It smoothes out fluctuations in demand for different skills or categories of worker.

    (ii) It may be possible to maintain a smaller staff, because specialists would not be needed in each skill area.

(b) It puts an end to potentially costly demarcation disputes, where one category of worker objects to others 'invading' their area of work, as defined by narrow job descriptions.

(c) On the other hand, it is less likely that a task will be left undone because it does not explicitly appear on anybody's job description.

Activity 5	(15 minutes)

What does multi-skilling offer the *employee*?

3.5 Flexible working groups

The basic work units of organisations have traditionally been specialised functional departments. In recent decades, organisations have moved towards small, functionally flexible working groups or teams. Teamworking allows work to be shared among a number of individuals, without the requirement for complex and lengthy co-ordination and communication mechanisms.

Teams may be:

(a) Temporally flexible: called together to achieve specific task objectives and then disbanded (project management), and/or

(b) Numerically flexible: co-opting members and advisers as different skills, attributes and expertise are required, and/or

(c) Virtual: consisting of individuals networking, data-sharing and collaborating as and when required, using ICT links.

In terms of functional flexibility, there are two basic types of flexible working groups.

(a) **Multi-disciplinary teams,** which bring together individuals with different skills and specialisms, so that their skills, experience and knowledge can be pooled or exchanged (like different pieces making up a jigsaw puzzle).

This is regarded as a useful mechanism for organisational communication and co-ordination. It is particularly useful in problem-solving and creative ideas generation, since it fosters awareness of overall objectives, allows the airing of wide-ranging organisational issues, and accesses different ideas which can 'hitchhike' or 'leapfrog' on one another.

(b) **Multi-skilled teams** which bring together a number of multi-skilled individuals who can each perform any of the group's tasks. These tasks can therefore be shared out in a more flexible way between group members, according to who is available and best placed to do a given job at the time it is required. (See the Smithkline Beecham example above.)

Activity 6   **(45 minutes)**

What may be the drawbacks to teamworking? (Your other studies in *Organisational Behaviour and Management* should furnish some ideas ...)

Finally, we will look at approaches to temporal flexibility.

3.6 Flexible contracts

Forms of flexible contracted hours of work include the following.

(a) **Overtime**: premium rates of pay for hours worked in excess of standard hours. A business may ask employees to work overtime:

    (i) To increase production to meet seasonal or ad hoc peaks in demand, without increasing the labour force

(ii) To maintain production (eg machine running) despite temporary shortages of labour. (Covering colleague absence is an example of this in the service section.)

Overtime can militate *against* efficiency where it is employee-driven, as a means of increasing outcome. Salaried workers are often not paid overtime, and some businesses negotiate higher basic pay rates for wage earners in lieu of overtime.

(b) **Zero hour contracts**: no guarantee of work (or pay) is given for the week. Staff may be called upon as and when required, on a full– or part-time basis, effectively imposing self-employed status. This is obviously highly flexible from the employer's point of view, but has been identified by the National Association of Citizens' Advice Bureaux (NACAB) as potentially abusive, since it creates financial insecurity and inability to plan commitments.

(c) **Annualised hours contracts**: agreeing a number of hours' work per year, rather than per week or month. Some or all of these hours may be committed to a rota schedule or roster while additional 'bank hours' may be held in reserve for unforeseen fluctuations (such as the need to cover for absences) plus 'reserve hours' designated for specific purposes other than normal working (such as training). Intensive hours can be called on during seasonal peaks in labour demand via longer working days or shifts, with time off in periods of low demand. This offers high flexibility for the employer, with employment security for the employee, although there is the danger of overwork during peak hours.

(d) **Term-time contracts**: similar to annualised-hours but allowing parents to maximise hours during school terms, so that family responsibilities can be met during holidays.

3.7 Flexi-time

There are many 'flexi-time' systems in operation providing freedom from the restriction of a '9 to 5' work-hours routine. The concept of flexi-time is that predetermined fixed times of arrival and departure at work are replaced by a working day split into two different time zones.

(a) The main part of the day is called 'core time' and is the only period when employees must be at their job (this is commonly 10.00 to 16.00 hours).

(b) The flexible time is at the beginning and the end of each day and during this time it is up to the individual to choose when he arrives and leaves. Arrival and departure times would be recorded by some form of 'clocking in' system. The total working week or month for each employee must add up to the prescribed number of hours, though he may go into 'debit' or 'credit' for hours from day to day, in some systems.

A flexi-time system may operate within the day – or within the span of a week or month.

Activity 7   **(20 minutes)**

Suggest three advantages to

(a) the organisation, and

(b) the worker,

of implementing a flexi-time system.

We have already covered some of the HR implications of flexible working on a method-by-method basis. Here, we will draw together some of the threads.

4 ISSUES IN FLEXIBILITY

4.1 HR issues

Some of the HR policy choices to be considered are as follows.

(a) **Recruitment and selection**. Flexibility will need to be reinforced by selection criteria, both in terms of temperament (adaptability, willingness to adopt flexible working) and skills (trainability, existing multiple skills). In return, flexible working practices may act as a boost to the recruitment and retention of staff (especially women returners, say).

(b) **Training and development**. Performance management, training needs analysis and career planning will have to be tailored to flexible working in terms of: broadening skills, fostering flexible attitudes, teamworking (where relevant: criteria may be different for isolated homeworkers), opportunities for promotion (with equal access for part-time and temporary workers).

(c) **Supervision and control**. Flexibility militates against the supervisor's traditional role as monitor/controller of performance – especially where outworking and/or self-managing teams are used. The supervisor is increasingly becoming a coach/mentor/facilitator to empowered teams and/or a co-ordinator/facilitator ensuring that communication is maintained with distant or part-time workers. (This change in role may itself require HR interventions in training and counselling support.) Control mechanisms must be developed to retain cohesion without rigidity: performance management, communication of cultural values, commitment-based policies and so on.

(d) **Motivation and reward**. Flexible payment structures will be required to reflect multi-skilling and team-working, while detailed administrative systems will have to support flexi-time and its variants. Attention will need to be given to employee morale and esprit-de-corps, particularly where people are only part-time or external members of the team: team-building will have to be broadened to include geographically separated 'virtual' teams.

(e) **Health and safety and other compliance aspects**. The employment environment is more highly regulated than ever before in terms of the protection of flexible workers. It places planning, administrative and employee relations duties on HR departments. In addition to compliance, there are the issues of social responsibility and employer branding/reputation, which dictate that 'soft' flexibility approaches may be more favourably regarded than 'hard' approaches such as zero hours contracting.

(f)   **Cultural reinforcement**. HRM will have an important role in developing a culture which accepts and celebrates flexibility in general, through integrated systems for recruiting, rewarding, promoting, developing and facilitating flexibility, change, innovation and so on.

(g)   **Problem-solving**. As we have seen, there are a number of drawbacks to flexibility from the point of view of the employee. HRM as a welfare function will have the task of minimising the impact of uncertainty, fluctuating earnings, isolation and so on, through supportive systems, compensations, safeguards and benefits. There may also be negative impacts on the firm's employer brand (and ability to attract and retain staff), if it is seen to abuse or exploit flexibility.

Activity 8   **(2 hours)**

Pick an organisation that you have worked for, or are familiar with, or can find out about. How flexible is the workforce in this organisation? Is it versatile, multi-skilled and happy to work unorthodox hours or without a strict job description? What does the human resource department in this organisation do to encourage, or to discourage, flexibility of labour? (Think about job descriptions, training and development, working hours and so on.)

4.2   New psychological contracts

According to the concept of '**job shift**' (Bridges, 1995), the workforce is increasingly made up of 'skill vendors' who sell their services to a variety of clients on a project basis, and who take responsibility for their own résumé management: skill development, experience, self-marketing and so on.

This amounts to the re-writing of the traditional psychological contract of employment. Many organisations are making this explicit, by spelling out the new contract, in which concepts such as 'lifetime employment' or even a 'career' within a company are no longer valid. There are compelling reasons why an organisation may wish to repudiate responsibility for the job security and career development of its employees, even where it is offering 'permanent' employment.

(a)   It may wish to discourage a culture of complacent performance based on job security and the fulfilment of job descriptions, and instead encourage the perception that competitive, value-adding performance is required in order to keep one's position.

(b) It may genuinely be unable to guarantee long-term, secure employment: in making this explicit, it is being socially responsible in encouraging employees to take ownership of their careers.

(c) It may wish to establish an attractive employer brand as an honest, open and realistic employer, in a market where educated employees are cynical about unrealistic recruitment offers.

On the other hand, there are risks to such an approach.

(a) There may be some loss of morale and performance, as the effects of newly-articulated insecurity are felt.

(b) There may be some loss of skilled labour, where individuals are alienated by the implication that they are not doing enough, or made uncomfortable by the uncertainty and responsibility of having to manage their own careers.

(c) There may be some loss of skilled labour, where individuals embrace the 'skill vendor' approach and career mobility to the point where they leave the organisation in order to develop their career portfolio.

One concept arising from the de-jobbing of employment is **'employability'**: a term which describes a portfolio of knowledge, skills and attributes that enhances an individual's marketability in the labour pool. Companies which have spelled out the new psychological contract may offer employability training in order to be socially responsible in facilitating employees' transition (if necessary) to other employment – while simultaneously benefiting from the resulting flexibility and versatility of employable individuals. (Employability and employability training are discussed further in Chapter 14.)

FOR DISCUSSION

'The TUC guide to work-life balance (*Changing Times*) argues that, without staff involvement and support, flexibility can mean management imposing forms of work organisation on employees who are given no opportunity to state their opinions or explain their needs. In contrast, "positive flexibility" gives people more autonomy and choice, with the employer investing in development and training and working in partnership with the workforce.'

(Bond, 2003)

What do you think are the 'exploitative' and 'positive' aspects of flexibility?

NOTES

EXAMPLE

People Management (28 September 2000) reported how **King's Healthcare NHS Trust**, London, used an innovative package of flexible working practices – called Kingsflex – to meet a serious shortage of nursing and midwifery professionals.

The Kingsflex 10-point package

- Part-time working.

- Job-sharing.

- Temporary reductions in hours for specific periods to help employees deal with special circumstances.

- Staggered working hours. Staff can determine their working patterns on a planned, weekly basis. Hours can be staggered – for example, 10am to 6pm instead of the standard 9am to 5pm – for the whole week or for one or two days.

- Annual hours. Work can be spread unevenly over the year, giving employees scope for reducing their hours during school holidays, for example.

- A phased return to work. Staff can build up the number of weekly hours over a period after an absence such as sickness or maternity leave.

- Special and parental leave. Staff can take paid time off for specific needs – fostering, for example.

- Working from home – an occasional option as long as normal work is fulfilled.

- Career breaks. Employees can take unpaid leave for up to two years in order to travel, pursue further education or fulfil their caring responsibilities.

- 'Personalised' annual leave. Individuals can buy or sell days of annual leave, adjusting their entitlement by up to 10 days and increasing or decreasing their salaries accordingly.

Although these options are open to everyone, they were recognised as offering a better work-life balance for working mothers in particular. The Trust was overall champion in the 2000 Parents at Work/Employer of the Year Awards.

NOTES

Chapter roundup

- Labour flexibility has been driven by demographic factors (notably the increased participation of women in the labour force) and the increasing focus on work-life balance. The rights of parents of small children to request flexible working arrangements have been enacted in law.

- Labour flexibility can be approached from a 'hard' HRM orientation (focused on reducing labour costs and unit costs of production and on minimising the organisation's exposure to 'excess' labour: an approach called 'lean production') or from a 'soft' HRM orientation (focused on enhancing the quality and adaptability of the labour resource through broadening skills and commitment).

- Flexibility may be numerical, temporal, locational and/or functional, and must be supported by cultural flexibility through integrated HRM systems. (A number of specific methods and techniques of flexibility were discussed in detail.)

- Two broadly similar models have been put forward for the flexible firm: Atkinson's core-periphery model and Handy's Shamrock model.

- Flexibility poses key HR issues for recruitment and selection, training and development, control and the role of the supervisor, motivation and reward and compliance with legal requirements.

- 'Flexible working arrangements used positively can benefit employees as well as being in the interests of the business ... but abusing them could make it more difficult to recruit people and could damage competitiveness in the long run.' (CIPD).

- The nature of the 'job' and the psychological contract of employment have changed with the emphasis on flexible working.

Quick quiz

1   What are the pressures that have led organisations to develop flexible working?

2   What kinds of flexible working arrangements are parents of small children entitled to request and what are the justified grounds for refusing such a request?

3   What are the five types of flexibility?

4   Outline (a) the core-periphery model and (b) the Shamrock organisation.

5   What are the rights of part-time workers under the Employment Rights Act 1999?

6   List three advantages of teleworking.

7   What are the two basic approaches to flexible group working?

8   List five methods of allowing flexibility in working hours.

9   How does flexibility affect the supervisor's role?

10   What is 'employability'?

Answers to quick quiz

1   Increased market uncertainty, increased competition, technological change, labour market demographics and the shift towards work-life balance.

(see paragraph 1.1)

2   See paragraph 1.3 for a full answer.

3   Numerical, temporal, functional, financial, locational, cultural.   (para 1.6)

4   For a full account, see paragraphs 2.1 and 2.2.

5   Rights to equal treatment in respect to access to training, selection for promotion, protection from unfair dismissal (and other statutory requirements); proportional entitlement to benefits (paid holiday, sick pay, maternity pay); access to pension schemes and parental leave, protection under all health and safety legislation.   (para 3.1)

6   Savings on overheads; employment access for home-bound workers; elimination of commuting; reduction in stress through better work/life balance.

(para 3.3)

7   Multi-disciplinary teams, multi-skilled teams.   (para 3.5)

8   Zero hours, annualised hours, overtime, flexi-time, term-time contracts.

(para 3.6)

9   Shift from monitor/controller to coach/facilitator and/or co-ordinator.

(para 4.1)

10 The development of a portfolio of knowledge, skills and experience that enhances a worker's marketability and mobility in the labour pool.

(para 4.2)

Answers to activities

1   This is a research activity, designed to get you explaining sources of information on the labour market and labour market trends. You may only have been able to find forecasts relevant to the data requested – since the gathering and analysis of statistics takes time: this should remind you that HRM is a forward-looking activity!

2   Examples of flexibility in a supermarket might include:

(a)   Extra staff employed for Christmas (numerical)

(b)   Adult staff with family responsibilities employed just during school term-times (numerical/temporal)

(c)   School-age staff employed just during school holidays (numerical/temporal)

(d)   Staff on zero hours contracts (only called in to work when needed) (numerical/temporal)

(e)   Staff paid according to their performance (financial)

(f)   All staff trained to use checkouts (functional)

(g)   Staff skilled enough to work in more than one department (functional)

3   *Professional core:* recruitment of high quality core people; retention, intrinsic rewards, career management; knowledge management. Possibly also delayering or downsizing: as the core is expensive, it makes sense to keep it as small as possible. This will take careful HR planning, to decide what core activities are and which people belong to the core group.

Flexible labour force: HR planning, management and control of work (to maintain standards), teambuilding, equitable treatment (while controlling costs), culture management and communication.

Contractual fringe: planned outsourcing, contracting (results and standard specification), relationship management, quality control, communication.

4   Connock (1991) gives seven main reasons for the increase in part-time working.

   (a)   Employers can match working hours to operational requirements better.

   (b)   The personal circumstances of key staff can be accommodated through part-time working. This will be particularly relevant to women returners.

   (c)   The productivity of part-timers is generally higher than that of full-timers (hardly surprising, since work is undertaken in more concentrated time periods).

   (d)   The absence levels of part-timers are generally lower: domestic requirements can more easily be fitted into the free periods in the part-time schedule.

   (e)   A pool of trained employees is available for switching to full-time work, or extending working time temporarily.

   (f)   Difficulties in recruiting full-time staff have prompted organisations to recruit and train part-time staff. Women returners are more likely to be attracted to an organisation if the hours of work are suitable, which will generally mean working part-time.

   (g)   Part-time working can cut overtime costs, since it makes it possible to avoid paying premium rates.

5   The erosion of rigid specialisation and fragmented job design can offer:

   (a)   A higher degree of job satisfaction, through variety of work and a greater understanding of its purpose and importance.

   (b)   Job security and material benefits, since a versatile, flexible employee is likely to be more attractive to employers, and have a higher value in the current labour market; and

   (c)   Personal skill development.

6   (a)   Teamworking is not suitable for all jobs: it does not always lead to superior or faster decision-making or performance than individuals working alone.

   (b)   Teams can delay decision-making in search of consensus (although consensus decisions do offer commitment and a rounded perspective).

   (c)   Social relationships might be maintained at the expense of other aspects of performance.

   (d)   Group norms may restrict individual personality and flair.

(e) Group think, or self-maintaining consensus, may prevent consideration of alternatives or constructive criticism.

(f) Personality clashes and political behaviour can get in the way of effective working.

7   Benefits to the organisation include: improved staff morale (because of flexibility); less stressed/distracted staff (because problems outside work can be solved without the guilt attached to lateness); less absenteeism (because of the 'I'm late for work: I'd better not go at all' syndrome).

Benefits to the workers include: less frustration in rush-hour commuting; less pressure over needs like the dentist or school sports days; time to shop, socialise etc in off-peak times; satisfaction of choice.

8   This allowed some space for your own research and reflection on your own experience. Plenty of sources of information: the HRM journals regularly report on flexibility initiatives, the currency of which is constantly renewed by fresh considerations like family-friendly policies for recruitment, EU Directives on worker rights and so on.

Chapter 10:
EQUAL OPPORTUNITIES

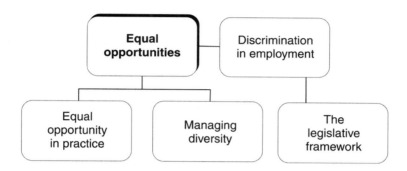

Introduction

In this chapter, we look at discrimination at work and the legal framework shaping HR policy in this area. As you read, be aware that while the law defines certain 'groups' against whom discrimination is illegal, discrimination can result from bias and prejudice of any kind. An ethical and cultural framework for justice and equality is as important as legislation and codes of practice: the 'management of diversity' concept is one development of this line of thought.

You may also note that discrimination can take subtle forms – classified as 'indirect' in current legislation: 'sexual harassment' is perhaps the most high-profile example of an issue which has emerged and been recognised as a form of discrimination.

Your objectives

In this chapter you will learn about the following.

(a) Forms of discrimination in employment

(b) The legislative framework on discrimination, including proposed changes

(c) Equal opportunities practices and initiatives in the workplace

(d) The move from equal opportunity to managing diversity

NOTES

1 DISCRIMINATION IN EMPLOYMENT

1.1 Equal opportunities

Definition

> **Equal opportunities** is an approach to the management of people at work based on equal access and fair treatment irrespective of gender, race, ethnicity, age, disability, sexual orientation or religious belief.

Equal opportunities employers will seek to redress imbalances based around differences, where they have no relevance to work performance. Certain aspects of equal opportunities are enshrined in law; others rely upon models of good practice and have no legislative foundation.

1.2 Women in employment

Despite the fact that women have contributed directly to the national product since medieval times – on the land and in home-based industries such as textiles – the acceptance of women in paid employment has been a slow process, which is even now having to be enforced by law.

The distribution of women in the UK workforce today is still heavily concentrated in categories such as textiles, footwear, clothing and leather, hotel and catering, retail distribution and repairs, professional and scientific services, and miscellaneous services. A significant percentage of the women employed in these categories work part-time.

Only in recent decades has there been a widespread challenge to gender segregation in employment – the idea that there are 'men's jobs' and 'women's jobs', with only a few genuinely 'unisex' categories of work.

> **Activity 1** (30 minutes)
>
> Why do you think women have been regarded as 'second-class citizens' in the work place? Consider social values, educational influences; the changing nature of work; the historical composition of the workforce and so on.

Many assumptions about women's attitudes to work, and capabilities for various types of work are being re-examined, and we will look a bit later at some of the measures being taken to remove the barriers to women in employment.

Meanwhile, pay differentials between men and women have remained an issue, despite equal pay legislation. The *Annual Survey of Hours and Earnings* (2006) reported that across all occupations, women earned 77% of male earnings in the same occupational group (based on median gross annual earnings in full-time employment).

Pregnant workers sill seem to be poorly treated. Research published in *People Management* (28 June 2007) reveals that they are frequently disadvantaged or bullied in ways ranging from being passed over for promotion or training, to not being given rest breaks, to being pressured to over-perform to make up for lost time – to being made redundant while on maternity leave.

Women's representation in top jobs also remains an issue. the EOC survey *Sex and Power = Who Runs Britain? 2007* found that women make up just 10% of directors of FTSE 100 companies – and barely 20% of members of parliament! According to the survey ethnic minority women are particularly poorly represented: 5.2% of the population 3.9% of the labour market – and just 0.4% of FTSE 100 directors...

Jenny Watson, chair of the EOC, stated that:

> We all pay the price when Britain's boardrooms and elected chambers are unrepresentative. Our democracy and local communities will be stronger if women from different backgrounds are able to enjoy an equal voice. In business, no one can afford to fish in half the talent pool in today's intensely competitive world. (www.hrmguide.co.uk/top-women)

1.3 Ethnic minorities in employment

The Ethnic Minority Advisory Group reported in 2006 (www.dwp.gov.uk – (Department for work and pensions) July 2006) that the employment rate for working age ethnic minorities is 59.2% compared to 74.8% for the UK population as a whole. While employment rates vary significantly between different minority groups, all have lower employment than the overall rate: people from ethnic minority backgrounds are twice as likely as white people to be unemployed – and are one and half times more likely to be economically inactive than the overall working age population.

There is also ethnic segregation in the labour market, with a concentration of minority (male) employees in manufacturing, hotel, catering, repairs and distribution sectors.

The proportion of ethnic minority employees falls sharply at higher levels of the organisation (only 1% of senior managers in FTSE 100 companies).

Reasons cited for adopting positive action plans on racial equality include:

Activity 2 **(5 minutes)**

Have you ever felt discriminated against (at school, work or training institution)? On what grounds: your sex, colour, age, social background/ beliefs/attitudes? What was the effect of the discrimination on your plans and attitudes?

(a) Good HR practice, in attracting and retaining the best people (not just ethnic minority employees, but all those who care about discrimination)

(b) Compliance with the Codes of Practice which are used by Employment Tribunals

(c) Widening the recruitment pool for access to more labour

(d)   Other potential benefits to the business, through its image as a socially responsible employer, and through the identification with customers, particularly in geographical areas of ethnic diversity.

EXAMPLE

Since 2004 the BBC has had **diversity targets** or 12.5% of the overall workforce to be from black and ethnic minorities (BME), with 7% BME staff at the senior management grade. It also set targets in 2005 of 4% for the presentation of disabled people within its workforce, to be met by December 2007.

Having failed to meet this diversity target (a key performance objective) BBC's senior management has waived its contractual bonuses! Understandably, they also plan to announce a programme of action on diversity later in 2007: watch this space...

Reported at www.cipd.co.uk/news, 26 June 2007

1.4   Disabled people in employment

Definition

Disability is 'a physical or mental impairment which has a substantial and long-term adverse effect on a person's ability to carry out normal day-to-day activities' (*Disability Discrimination Act 1995*).

Disability covers a wide range of impairments, including restricted mobility, speech impediment, poor hearing or eyesight, learning disability and disfigurement. It is estimated that this applies to one in five of the working age population (Torrington *et al*, 2002). The choice of jobs for the disabled is often restricted, resulting in higher and longer unemployment rates than the general population. Jobs are concentrated in plant/ machine operative jobs, which tend to be low-paid: disabled people are under-represented in professional and managerial jobs.

Attitudes towards the disabled in the workplace have been extremely negative, tending to focus on generalised and stereotypical problems such as:

(a)   Long periods off work for medical causes

(b)   Accident-proneness

(c)   Poor skill levels

(d)   Difficulties of adjusting the work environment for wheelchair access and other disability needs

(e)   Negative image to customers, who allegedly felt awkward in the presence of disabled people

(f)   The 'positive' association of certain jobs with disabled workers (eg lift attendants, switchboard operators, simple assembly tasks) stereotyping disabled roles and capabilities.

1.5   Age diversity in employment

Despite demographic and educational changes and associated skill shortages among the younger population, a certain amount of discrimination has continued to be directed at more mature workers.

The voluntary Code of Practice on Age Diversity in Employment (1999) appeared to have some impact on the number of recruitment advertisements specifying or implying age limits (Torrington *et al*, 2002). However, negative perceptions of older workers continued to impact on recruitment, selection for promotion, selection for redundancy, access to training opportunities and so on.

Activity 3   (10 minutes)

List some reasons – perhaps based on your own experience or prejudices! – why organisations might practise age discrimination.

The fact is that older workers:

(a)   Have developed experience and skills in the job that may counteract any age-related loss of performance.

(b)   Tend to stay in the job, reducing turnover and associated costs, and have better attendance and disciplinary records.

(c)   Do experience some loss of strength and stamina. However, this is unlikely to be relevant to performance in most modern jobs, and older workers typically understand and work within their physical limitations.

(d)   Do experience some loss of mental functioning (short term memory, for example) but retain – or even gain – in other cognitive functions.

(e)   Are no more likely to be flexible or inflexible in relation to learning and change than younger employees.

(f)   Do not necessarily cost the organisation more, as age-based reward systems are being replaced by performance-related ones.

INTERNATIONAL COMPARISON

In the Far-East, great value is placed on 'the wisdom of age'. In Japan, age is equated with long service, the acquisition of skill and experience, and hence the quality of the worker.

1.6 Other forms of discrimination

As we noted in our introduction to this chapter, there are many potential differences that may be used as a point of discrimination. Recent attention has particularly been drawn by legislation (see Section 2 below) in regard to:

(a) **Sexual orientation**. Gay, lesbian and bi-sexual people may experience discrimination in:

- The culture of the firm: behavioural norms and attitudes that may cause harassment, verbal abuse or isolation of 'outed' gay workers, or the need to hide sexual orientation for fear of discrimination.

- HR practices: discrimination in terms and benefits due to eligibility criteria which exclude same-sex partners, for example.

(b) **Religious belief**. Apart from direct religious (often related to ethnic) discrimination against adherents to particular faiths, there is indirect discrimination through work practices which affect some groups more than others. Dress codes, dietary laws, time off for religious holidays and available facilities to comply with prayer requirements, for example, have recently been highlighted as diversity issues.

EXAMPLE: OUT WITH DISCRIMINATION

'HBOS, the financial services group, is a member of Stonewall's employer champion network, which meets quarterly to discuss topical issues surrounding sexual orientation. The company has also established a joint working group from its lesbian and gay network, supported by its unions Accord and Unifi, explained Tyrone Jones, diversity manager for HBOS.

' "The group meets to support colleagues and helps ensure that discriminatory practices have no place in the organisation," he said. HBOS has equality-proofed its employment policies to ensure that staff are not disadvantaged by their sexual orientation. For example, its paternity leave applies to same-sex partners.

'In addition, the financial services group has raised awareness of sexual orientation among its staff through holding diversity roadshows, workshops and divisional diversity taskforces. "Our HR teams have received information on the impact of the new regulations and a presentation on sexual orientation is available to all staff on the company's intranet," said Jones.'

(Higginbottom, 2003 (b))

FOR DISCUSSION

What aspects of religion or belief and sexual orientation are most clearly subject to discrimination, harassment or lack of understanding in your own work or study environment?

Is the discrimination systematic/procedural – or cultural/personal?

We will now look at the laws passed to protect the rights of key disadvantaged groups, as well as some of the issues which are currently being worked out in European courts and professional Codes of Practice.

2 THE LEGISLATIVE FRAMEWORK

2.1 Sex Discrimination and Race Relations Acts

In Britain, two main pieces of legislation deal with inequality of opportunity by reason of sexual and racial discrimination.

- The **Sex Discrimination Act (SDA) 1975** (and amendments) outlawed certain types of discrimination on the grounds of sex, marital status, maternity or pregnancy. Subsequently amended by the Employment Equality (Sex Discrimination) Regulations 2005 (see also Paragraph 2.3 below.)

- The **Race Relations Act (RRA) 1976** (and amendment) outlawed, certain types of discrimination on the grounds of colour, race, nationality, or ethnic or national origin.

There are three types of discrimination, under the Acts, which are covered below. Harassment, which can take many forms, is also outlawed and its application was recently extended to sex and gender re-assignment and age.

Definitions

- **Direct discrimination** occurs when one interested group is treated less favourably than another (except for exempted cases).

- **Indirect discrimination** has recently been redefined by the *Employment Equality (Sex Discrimination) Regulations 2005*. Basically, it occurs when an employer applies a provision, criterion or practice to men and women equally, but it has the effect of putting one sex at a particular disadvantage, without justification.

- **Victimisation** occurs when an employer disadvantages workers because they have sought to exercise their legal rights or assisted others in doing so.

- **Harassment** occurs when an employee is subjected to conduct that violates his or her dignity, or creates an intimidating hostile, degrading, humiliating or offensive environment for him or her. (This now applies to conduct targeted at race, disability, sexual orientation, religious belief and – most recently – sex and gender reassignment, and age.)

An example of **direct** discrimination would be failing to select or promote a women because she is pregnant, or a person because they are of a particular nationality or race.

An example of **indirect** discrimination is changing shift patterns to include an early morning start, as women are more likely to be responsible for child care.

BPP
LEARNING MEDIA

An example of **victimisation** would be passing an employee over for promotion because (s)he had recently threatened to take the firm to an Employment Tribunal over discriminatory practices.

An example of **harassment** might be racial abuse, unwanted sexual advances – or even putting vital objects on a high shelf (as females are usually shorter).

The obligation of non-discrimination generally applies to all aspects of employment, including advertisements, recruitment and selection programmes, access to training, promotion, disciplinary procedures, selection for redundancy, grounds for dismissal and retirement ages for men and women.

Activity 4	(15 minutes)

Suggest four examples that would constitute **indirect** discrimination on the grounds of sex.

In each of the Acts, however, there are certain exceptions, in which discrimination of a sort may be permitted.

Permissible reasons for discriminating on grounds of gender (*genuine occupational qualifications*)	Permissible reasons for discriminating on racial grounds
• Physiology (not physical strength) • Decency or privacy (closely defined) • Special welfare consideration • Provision of personal services promoting welfare or education • Legal restrictions, particularly jobs likely to involve work outside the UK, where 'laws or customs are such that the duties could not, or could not effectively, be performed by a woman'	• Dramatic performances, where the *dramatis personae* requires a person of a particular racial group • Artists or photographic models for advertising purposes, for reasons of authenticity • Personal services rendered for the welfare of the particular group

Activity 5	(15 minutes)

Think of examples of **each** of the categories of exception listed above.

Despite these 'special cases', the legislation does *not* permit **positive discrimination** – actions which give preference to protected groups, regardless of genuine suitability and qualification for the job (eg by stating that the employer 'welcomes' applications from women or ethnic minorities). However, **training** may be given to particular groups exclusively, if the group has in the preceding year been substantially under-represented. It is also permissible to encourage such groups to:

(a)   Apply for jobs where such exclusive training is offered

(b)   Apply for jobs in which they are under-represented

Complaints of discrimination

Complaints of discrimination may be made to an Employment Tribunal within three months of the alleged offence. If conciliation is unsuccessful, the tribunal will hear the case, with the power to award:

(a)   An order declaiming the rights of both parties

(b)   A recommendation for action to redress discriminatory practices within a specified time and

(c)   An order requiring the discriminating employer to pay compensatory damages.

The *EU Reversal of Burden of Proof in Sex Discrimination Cases Directive* established the assumption that employers accused of sexual discrimination are guilty unless they can prove the contrary: a reversal of the previous system whereby the complainant had to prove that discrimination took place. (This has caused huge controversy in the UK.)

Public body requirements

Additional requirements are place on late public organisations.

- The **Race Relations (Amendment) Act 2000** requires them to draw up detailed plans for achieving racial equality in all employment practices.

- The **Equality Act 2006** requires them to eliminate all unlawful discrimination and harassment, and to actively promoter equality of opportunity between men and women (the '**gender duty**').

EXAMPLE

'BT has launched a female executive network as part of a drive to boost the number of women in senior management and on its board.

'Like many FTSE 100 companies, BT has no full-time female executives on its board. And while women make up 24 per cent of its workforce, they hold only 18 per cent of senior management positions.

'The first networking event was held this week and included 200 of BT's top female managers, both at executive level and just below. It was aimed at giving these senior women a chance to meet and exchange careers advice.

'There will be further events, both formal and informal, which will focus on helping women to move up through the top ranks. Senior women from outside the company will also be invited to participate in future events.

'There are a number of networks at BT, ranging from "Able To", a network for disabled employees, to "Kaleidoscope", for gay, lesbian and bisexual workers.'

(Roberts, 2003 (b))

The Commission for Equality and Human Rights

The **Equal Opportunities Commission** and **Commission for Racial Equality** (set up under the Acts) have had powers, subject to certain safeguards: to investigate alleged breach of the Acts; to serve a 'non-discrimination notice' on employers found guilty of contraventions; and to follow-up the investigation until satisfied that undertakings given (with regard to compliance and information of persons concerned) are carried out. Both bodies have also published **Codes of Practice** giving detailed guidance on how HR policies could be developed to avoid discrimination, how staff should be informed and trained, how practices should be monitored and so on.

Under the *Equality Act 2006*, these specialist bodies – together with the Disability Rights Commission – have been replaced by a single organisation: the **Commission for Equality and Human Rights** (CEHR). The umbrella body (launched in October 2007) assumes responsibility for all areas of discrimination law, and for promoting equal opportunities and access to services in society as a whole.

(It is worth noting in connection with this integration of responsibilities, that the **Discrimination Law Review** (June 2007) invites consultation on whether the nine pieces of legislation that currently make up UK discrimination law should be replaced by a single equality bill: watch this space!)

2.2 Equal Pay Act

The *Equal Pay Act 1970* was the first major attempt to tackle sexual discrimination. It was intended specifically 'to prevent discrimination as regards terms and conditions of employment between men and women'.

The *Equal (Amendment) Regulations* 1984 established the right to equal pay for 'work of **equal value**', so that a woman would no longer have to compare her work with that of a man in the same or broadly similar work, but could establish that her work had equal value to that of a man in the same establishment. These provisions were discussed in Chapter 5.

Equal pay questionnaires were launched in 2003, giving employees the right to request the pay details of a named colleague (subject to their consent under the Data Protection Act) to support claims that they are being paid less because of their race or sex. HR commentators have noted that if pay systems are open, fair and transparent, such questionnaires are less likely to be submitted.

2.3 The Employment Equality (Sex Discrimination) Regulations 2005

The Regulations made some significant changes to the Sex Discrimination Act including the following.

(a) **Redefinition of indirect discrimination**. Treatment used to have to be to the detriment of a larger proportion of members of one sex: now it merely has to put women at a particular disadvantage when compared with men (or *vice versa*), or single versus married (or *vice versa*). Employers must show that the treatment was a reasonable means to achieve a legitimate aim, in the light of its discriminatory effects.

(b) **Specific definition of sexual harassment,** in line with other discrimination legislation. A person subjects a women to sexual harassment if:

(i) On the grounds of sex, he engages in unwanted conduct which violates the dignity or creates an intimidating, hostile, degrading, humiliating or offensive environment for her

(ii) He engages in unwanted verbal, non-verbal or physical conduct of a sexual nature that violates her dignity or creates an intimidating, hostile, degrading, humiliating or offensive environment for her

(iii) On the grounds of her rejection of (or submission to) the conduct he treats her less favourably.

The conduct need not be intentional on the part of the man if it is felt to be offensive by the complainant. However, the complaint must be reasonable (as decided by tribunal) – not 'over-sensitive'.

(c) **Pregnancy and maternity**: unfavourable treatment on these grounds (in relation to employment and vocational training) is now explicitly unlawful.

Sexual harassment

Harassment has long been unlawful (as a form of direct discrimination), but the three types of harassment defined in the new Regulations make the position clear.

2007 recommendations to organisations for handling harassment from the CIPD include the following.

(a) The issuing of a clear policy statement or corporate Code of Conduct:

(i) Giving examples of what constitutes harassment, bullying and intimidating behaviours (as well as defining positioning and supportive behaviours).

(ii) Explaining the damaging effects, why it will not be tolerated – and that it will be treated as a disciplinary offence.

(iii) Undertaking that allegations will be treated speedily, seriously and confidentially.

(b) The implementation of training, education and discussion to increase awareness of all managers and staff.

(c) The implementation of counselling procedures, giving advice to victims, and hopefully resolving problems by informal means, but – if not – also planning further proceedings.

(d) The design and communication of complaints procedures.

(i) Informal procedures would include person-to-person reproof (a clear statement by the victim to the offender that the conduct is unwelcome) and intervention by a trusted third party.

(ii) Formal procedures should exist for confidentiality to be guaranteed, and for an investigator of the same sex as the victim to be available to follow up complaints.

(e) The implementation of disciplinary action. Rules should be defined, including protection of the complainant from further victimisation as a result of the action.

(f) Monitoring and evaluation of the process, and incidence of complaint.

FOR DISCUSSION

Come up with some examples of what might be defined as 'harassment': you may even have experienced some. Are these examples clear-cut? What issues are involved? How are your examples discriminatory? What forms might age, sexual orientation or religious harassment take? Do you think this is important – or just 'political correctness'?

2.4 Disability Discrimination Act 1995

Previous legislation on disability focused narrowly on securing employment (on a Quota Scheme) for disabled people, without addressing the issue of discrimination. This shortcoming was addressed when the *Disability Discrimination Act 1995* came into force in December 1996.

Definition

A **disabled person** is defined as a person who has a physical or mental impairment that has a substantial and long-term (more than 12 months) adverse effect on his ability to carry out normal day to day activities. The effect includes mobility, manual dexterity, physical co-ordination, and lack of ability to lift or speak, hear, see, remember, concentrate, learn or understand or to perceive the risk of physical danger. Severe disfigurement is included, as are progressive conditions such as HIV even though the current effect may not be substantial.

The Act contains provisions for disabled access to services, transport facilities and education and training opportunities. In the sphere of employment, it makes it unlawful for an employer with more than 20 employees to discriminate against a disabled person/employee:

(a) In deciding who to interview or who to employ or in the terms of an employment offer

(b) In the terms of employment and the opportunities for promotion, transfer, training or other benefits, or by refusing the same

(c) By dismissal or any other disadvantage.

The employer also has a duty to make reasonable adjustments to working arrangements or to the physical features of premises where these constitute a disadvantage to a disabled job applicant or employee. Examples of changes to working arrangements given in the Government's Code of Practice include the following.

(a) Altering working hours
(b) Acquiring or making changes to equipment
(c) Allocating some duties to another employee
(d) Providing supervision
(e) Making adjustments to premises
(f) Assigning the employee to a different place of work
(g) Training
(h) Providing a reader or interpreter.

A number of factors will be relevant in deciding whether a change is reasonable, chiefly its effectiveness, cost (both financially and in terms of disruption), and practicability in the light of the employer's resources and the availability of financial or other help.

A **Disability Rights Commission** was established to ensure that employers and disabled people are informed of their respective rights and duties but will now be replaced by the CEHR.

The Government has issued a Code of Practice on disability which gives advice to employers on how to avoid disability discrimination in employment. It does not itself impose legal obligations, but will be taken into account by Employment Tribunals. The Code provides many examples of good practice, as well as general principles.

(a) Be flexible
(b) Do not make assumptions
(c) Consider whether expert advice is needed
(d) Plan ahead
(e) Promote equal opportunities.

Activity 6   (30 minutes)

What arguments would you put forward as to why an organisation should consider employing people with disabilities?

2.5 Employment Equality Regulations 2003

The *Employment Equality Regulations 2003* outlawed discrimination on the basis of:

- Religious belief and
- Sexual orientation.

The Regulations outlaw both direct and indirect discrimination and harassment. They apply to private– and public-sector organisations and cover all aspects of employment, from recruitment to working conditions and terms, to dismissal. Compensation for successful claims is unlimited.

HR practitioners have had to review and monitor a wide range of existing policies to ensure that staff are not being treated less favourably on grounds of religious belief or sexual orientation: for example, equalising pension and benefit entitlements for same sex partners (particularly in the light of the *Civil Partnership Act 2006* which allows homosexual couples to have their relationship legally recognised)., imposing dress codes that infringe religious customs, or handling requests for time off to celebrate religious holidays.

The HR department will need to communicate policy changes and guidelines clearly to line managers. This will also present an opportunity to raise awareness of religious and sexual orientation issues. Cultural change will be important to control jokes and other forms of harassment: the regulations make employers liable for the acts of their employees, unless they can prove that they have taken steps to prevent them – for example, with clear anti-harassment policies and supporting awareness training.

NOTES

Weblinks

ACAS has issued guidelines for employers, and the CIPD has also released a 'change agenda'. You may like to check out or, if you are interested in this area.

▶▶ **http://www.acas.co.uk**

▶▶ **http://www.cipd.co.uk/changeagendas**

EXAMPLES

'The employers who are least likely to fall foul of the [Employment Equality (Religion or Belief) Regulations] are those with progressive HR policies. They include Croydon London Borough Council, which has moved from flexitime to a 'worksmart' system whereby staff don't have to work a core number of hours but can arrange job shares or to work from home. The move will, for example, make it easier for Muslims to choose not to work on Friday, their holy day.

'Transport for London is considering replacing bank holidays with a number of 'floating days' which will allow non-Christians to work through Christmas and Easter.

'Unilever has a casual dress policy which permits employees to wear what they like, including clothing associated with their religion, so long as this is within the bounds of reason and safety. BT has gone a step further by attaching flexible straps to its safety helmets so that Rastafarian employees can wear them above their religiously significant hats. …

'The Royal Mail is also thinking of introducing 'quiet rooms'. As well as providing prayer space, these could be used by all staff for quiet reflection. The organisation may also install foot basins to allow Muslim staff to wash their feet in preparation for prayers, but would need to discuss this with staff first, it says.

'In its canteens, BT provides kosher and halal meals on request, although most Jewish and Muslim employees bring their own or use the company's flexible working arrangements to go out for lunch.'

(Cooper, 2003)

Activity 7	**(10 minutes)**

Can you see any areas of potential conflict in practice between:

(a) Religious belief and sexual orientation regulations?
(b) Anti-discrimination regulations and privacy/data protection law?

2.6   Employment Equality (Age) Regulations 2006

Ageism is finally unlawful in the UK, after many years of voluntary (patchy) self-regulation.

The 2006 Regulations ban direct discrimination (eg refusing medical insurance to employees over 50) and indirect discrimination (eg requiring new employees to pass a fitness test) in recruitment promotion, training and terms and conditions. There are certain lawful exceptions, including objective justification, genuine occupational requirement and imminent retirement: discussed in Chapter 3. They also ban victimisation and harassment – including ageist jokes and nicknames.

As with other forms of discrimination a tribunal may award compensation for financial loss and injury to feelings.

The regulations also:

(a)   Remove the current age limit for unfair dismissal and redundancy rights (previously, age 65). Workers over 65 can now claim the same entitlement as younger workers (unless there is genuine retirement)

(b)   Set the default retirement age at 65. If an organisation's normal retirement age is below 65, this will need to be objectively justified

(c)   Give all employees the right to requires to work **beyond** the age of 65 or the company's normal retirement age. Such requests must be considered (and discussed with the employee), though not necessarily accepted

(d)   Give employees the right to be informed of their expected retirement date at least six months in advance of the planned retirement, in order to assist preparation (or requests to stay on).

Employers and vocational training providers may have to make significant changes (discussed with employees and/or their representatives) for full compliance in areas such as:

(a)   **Recruitment**: particularly applicable to recruitment; wording used; qualification requirements (eg asking for 'media studies' from older people for whom such subjects did not exist); removal of age/date of birth questions; requirements in job descriptions/person specification; asking for 'new graduates'; stereotyping (of young or old) and so on.

(b)   **Policies**. All employment contracts, rules and handbooks should avoid discrimination. Clear policy statements may be required (supported by education and training).

(c)   **Record-keeping**. Any policies or practices potentially considered discriminatory should have a written statement on file stating why they are objectively justified. Records of the workforce's age profile and turnover rate should be kept to check whether discrimination is occurring.

(d)   **Training, promotion and benefits**. Policies should be checked to ensure equal access for older workers – or objective justification of any age/service related limitations.

FOR DISCUSSION

- 'We required an enthusiastic person, flexible enough to fit in with our dynamic organisation culture and in touch with the latest thinking.'

- 'How would you feel about managing older people?'

- 'Don't you think someone like you should be looking for something with a little more responsibility?'

Are these ageist comments? If so, why – and to whom?

Weblinks

For more on equal opportunity and diversity:

Human Rights and Equal Opportunities Commission (Australia)
►► **http://www.hreoc.gov-au**

European union
►► **http://www.europa-eu.int Activity (a)(i)**

3   EQUAL OPPORTUNITIES IN PRACTICE

3.1   Formulating effective policies

In it often suggested that many organisations make minimal efforts to avoid discrimination. They pay lip-service to the idea, to the extent of claiming 'We are an Equal Opportunities Employer' in advertising literature or (more recently) adding the words 'religion', 'sexual orientation' and 'age' to discrimination policies. A number of measures are necessary to establish equal opportunity in reality.

Ingam (2003) suggests the following key steps in implementing a **diversity policy**, taking into account all the equal opportunity requirements.

Step 1.   **Analyse your business environment**

- Internally – does the diversity of the organisation reflect the population in its labour market?

- Externally – does the diversity of the workforce mirror that of the customer base?

Step 2.   **Define diversity and its business benefits**

- Legal, moral and social benefits

- Business benefits: better understanding of market segments; positive employer brand; attraction and retention of talent

- Employee benefits: more representative workforce; value and respect for people; opportunity to contribute fully; enhanced creativity

Step 3. **Introduce diversity policy into corporate strategy**

- Weave diversity into corporate values and mission

Step 4. **Embed diversity into core HR processes and system**

- Review and refocus recruitment and selection, induction, reward and recognition, career management and training and development

Step 5. **Ensure leaders implement policy**

- Leaders and top management need to provide long-term commitment and resources

- Use diversity as a key factor in coaching, awareness training and development of managers

Step 6. **Involve staff at all levels**

- Educate the workforce through awareness training
- Create a 'diversity handbook'
- Set up diversity working parties and councils
- Establish mentoring schemes

Step 7. **Communicate, communicate, communicate**

- Communicate diversity policy and initiatives clearly
- Internally: updates, briefings, training, intranet pages
- Externally: to boost employer brand and recruitment

Step 8. **Understand your company's needs**

- Match resources to the size of the organisation and the scale of change required

- Consider using diversity consultants or best practice representatives to provide advice, support and training

Step 9. **Evaluate**

- Benchmark progress at regular intervals
- Internally: diversity score cards, employee climate surveys
- Externally: focus groups, customer/supplier surveys

Monitoring will be a particularly important part of the implementation process. The numbers of female, disabled, ethnic minority and mature-age staff can easily be monitored using workforce statistics and 'Equal Opportunity Monitoring Forms' filled out by employees:

(a) On entering (and applying to enter) the organisation
(b) On leaving the organisation
(c) On applying for transfers, promotions or training schemes

Another area of particular sensitivity is recruitment and selection. There is always a risk that a disappointed job applicant, for example, will attribute his or her lack of success to discrimination, especially if the recruiting organisation's workforce is conspicuously lacking in representatives of the same ethnic minority, sex or age band.

BPP
LEARNING MEDIA

Activity 8 (1½ hours)

Outline a set of anti-discrimination policy points for the recruitment manager, covering:

(a) Job advertising
(b) Use of recruitment agencies
(c) Job application forms
(d) Job interviews
(e) Selection tests
(f) Record keeping

Bear in mind the need to avoid both *discrimination* and *allegations* of *discrimination*.

3.2 Positive action approaches

In addition to responding to legislative provisions, some employers have begun voluntarily to address the underlying problems, by taking active steps to encourage the recruitment, training and promotion of previously under-represented groups. The following are just some of the positive action measures that might be used.

(a) Putting equal opportunities higher on the agenda by appointing Equal Opportunities Managers (and even Directors) reporting directly to the HR Director.

(b) Flexible hours, childcare vouchers, 'term-time' or annual hours contracts (to allow for school holidays), career break and return-to-work schemes to help women to combine careers with family responsibilities.

(c) Posting managerial vacancies internally, giving more opportunities for movement up the ladder for groups currently over-represented at lower levels of the organisation.

(d) Assertiveness training and business networking to support various groups in managing their career potential.

(e) Awareness training for managers and staff to encourage them to think about issues of discrimination, harassment and diversity.

(f) Positive action to encourage job and training applications from minority groups: using ethnic languages and pictures showing a racial/ethnic mix of people in advertisements, for example. Another example is pre-recruitment or pre-training training for minority groups: the Metropolitan Police piloted a scheme of such courses, covering literacy, numeracy, current affairs, physical fitness and interpersonal skills, to allow ethnic minority applicants to compete on an equal basis for training places.

(g) Alteration of premises to accommodate wheelchair users: supplying Braille or large-print versions of documentation; supplying computerised text-based telephones or interpreters for hearing impaired people and so on.

We have illustrated other positive action approaches in our examples throughout this chapter.

Perhaps it is unfair to expect legislation to change deep-seated attitudes towards individual differences. Law may only change people's behaviour; *to change how we feel and what we know (ie our attitudes) requires long term education and actual experience of working with the affected groups. A new approach to the management of individual differences emerged in the USA and is beginning to capture the imagination of British employers.*

4 MANAGING DIVERSITY

4.1 Diversity

Definition

> **Managing diversity** is based on the belief that the individual differences we currently focus on under equal opportunities (gender, race, age etc) are crude and irrelevant classifications of the most obvious differences between people, and should be replaced by a genuine understanding of the ways in which individuals differ.

The ways in which people are *meaningfully* different in the workplace include personality, preferred working style and individual needs and drives. These things do not necessarily correlate with racial or gender differences in any way. For example, it would be a gross oversimplification to say that all women in your organisation require assertiveness training: it may be less appropriate for many women than for some men. Thus, effective managers seek to understand the job-relevant ways in which their staff differ and should seek to manage their performance in ways which recognise those differences as far as possible. Managers need to understand the unique contribution each person – not each 'category or person' – can make to the organisation.

A 'managing diversity' orientation implies the need to be proactive in managing the needs of a diverse workforce in areas (beyond equal opportunity and discrimination) such as:

(a) Tolerance of individual differences

(b) Communicating effectively with (and motivating) culturally diverse workforces. (We will address this issue further in Chapter 12.)

(c) Managing workers with diverse family structures and responsibility

(d) Managing the adjustments to be made by the ageing workforce

(e) Managing diverse career aspirations and paths

(f) Confronting literacy, numeracy and qualifications issues in an international workforce

(g) Managing co-operative working in ethnically diverse teams

EXAMPLE

Kramer, McGraw and Schuler (1997) describe the award-winning diversity strategy of USA multi-national, Pitney Bowes.

The vision statement on diversity reads

> Pitney Bowes will provide an open, flexible and supportive work environment that values the uniqueness of each of its employees. Through leadership, communication and training programs, Pitney Bowes will aggressively promote an understanding of individual difference, including (but not limited to) age, gender, race, religion, ethnicity, disability, sexual orientation and family circumstances.

The five goals of the Pitney Bowes strategic plan on diversity and examples of the actions the company has taken to achieve these are set out below.

- **Goal 1: Communications**: 'Our vision of diversity and its implications for the organisation will be clearly communicated to all of us'. Actions:

    – Formed diversity councils throughout the company

    – Engaged in widespread promotional activity to promote diversity

    – Development of diversity marketing guidelines for Pitney Bowes products and services.

- **Goal 2: Education and training**: 'We will become sensitive to and demonstrate an understanding of the value of differences through education and training'. Actions:

    – Provided multiple training opportunities for the stimulation of diversity awareness

    – Identified high profile minority customers to address employees on diversity issues.

- **Goal 3: Career development:** 'We will create a culture that enables and encourages the development and upward mobility of all of us'. Actions:

    – Introduced new succession planning process based on 'assessing competencies for tomorrow'

    – Published career networking directory

    – Increased opportunities for rotational assignments and cross-training

    – Increased participation in employee mentoring programme.

- **Goal 4: Recruitment and hiring**: 'We will further increase the diversity of our employees so that our organisation reflects the demographic changes in our labour force'. Actions:

    – Developed new minority recruitment campaigns including new promotional material and specific recruitment from schools with diverse populations

    – Supported minority scholarships and intern programs

    – Increased funding support for external organisations promoting the diversity agenda

    – Tied management bonuses to diversity recruitment goals.

- **Goal 5: Work/life balance**: 'We will provide a flexible and supportive work environment for employees in achieving a balance of work/life issues'. Actions:

    - Developed training to enhance flexible work environment for all employees
    - Expanded child care, elderly care and school referral programs
    - Supported emergency sick child care
    - Conducted employee surveys on work/life balance
    - Piloted telecommuting program.

In order to achieve the five goals of diversity, the business units at Pitney Bowes have tied the concept of diversity to management performance ratings. Part of the incentive compensation plan for the corporate management committee, for instance, includes a diversity component directly linked to the business unit's diversity action plan, and all managers are held accountable for diversity through the performance appraisal system.

4.2 Equal opportunities and management of diversity

Torrington *et al* (2002) sum up the major differences between an 'equal opportunities' approach and a 'management of diversity' approach as follows.

	Equal opportunities	Managing diversity
Purpose	Reduce discrimination	Utilise employee potential to maximum advantage
Case argued	Moral and ethical	Business objectives: improve profitability
Responsibility	HR/personnel function	All managers
Focuses on	Groups	Individuals
Benefits for employees	Improved opportunities for disadvantaged employees	Improved opportunities for all employees
Focus of management activity	Recruitment	Managing
Remedies	Changing systems and practices	Changing corporate culture

BPP
LEARNING MEDIA

NOTES

Chapter roundup

- Discrimination at work affects a number of different groups, including women, ethnic minorities, the disabled, gays and bisexuals, people of different religious beliefs and older workers – all are now protected in UK law.

- Discrimination can be either direct or indirect, or by implication. Victimisation and harassment should also be addressed by equal opportunities policies.

- Equal opportunities is not only concerned with access to employment but also the whole employment life cycle: training and development, appraisal, promotion, reward, employment protection and so on.

- Managing diversity means managing people in a way that respects their individuality and beliefs, instead of by crude stereotypes.

Quick quiz

1 List five major forms of discrimination covered by UK law.

2 What is meant by:
   - (a) Direct discrimination,
   - (b) Indirect discrimination, and
   - (c) Victimisation?

3 A woman may lawfully be turned down for promotion if she is pregnant, and intends to take maternity leave. True or false?

4 What is sexual harassment?

5 What are the three main provisions of the Disability Discrimination Act 1995?

6 What are the Employment Equality Regulations 2003?

7 What legislation covers discrimination on the basis of age in the UK?

8 Outline a nine-step plan for implementing diversity policy.

9 What is managing diversity?

10 How is an 'equal opportunities' approach different from a 'managing diversity' approach?

Answers to quick quiz

1 Direct and indirect discrimination (and victimisation), against women, ethnic minorities, older workers, disabled workers, gay/lesbian/bisexual workers and religious groups.   (see Section 1)

2 (a) Direct discrimination is where one group is treated less favourably than another.

   (b) Indirect discrimination is where a condition is applied which is not relevant to the job and which serves to disadvantage one group disproportionately.

(c) Victimisation is where an individual is penalised for seeking to assert legal rights. (para 2.1)

3 False. Pregnancy/maternity rights are protected regardless of circumstances. (para 2.1)

4 Sexual harassment is unwanted physical or verbal conduct with sexual connotations. (para 2.3)

5 (a) A 'disabled person' is defined as one who has a physical or mental impairment that has a substantial and long-term effect on his/her ability to carry out normal activity.

   (b) It is unlawful to discriminate against a disabled person in selection, and employment terms and conditions.

   (c) The employer must make reasonable adjustments to working arrangements and premises which disadvantage the disabled person. (para 2.4)

6 Anti-discrimination laws relating to religion and belief, and sexual orientation. (para 2.5)

7 The Employment Equality (Age) Regulations 2006. (para 2.6)

8 See paragraph 3.1 for a full answer.

9 It is an alternative to equal opportunities which seeks better performance from employees based on their individual differences in personality, style and needs, rather than cruder distinctions such as gender and ethnicity. (para 4.1)

10 See paragraph 4.2 for a full answer.

Answers to activities

1 Reasons for discrimination against women at work include the following.

   (a) Social pressures on the woman to bear and rear children, and on the man to make a lifetime commitment to paid work as the 'breadwinner'. Employers assumed – and sometimes still assume – that women's paid work would be short term or interrupted, and that training and development was therefore hardly worthwhile.

   (b) The nature of earlier industrial work, which was physically heavy: legal restrictions were placed on women's employment in areas such as mines, night work in factories etc.

   (c) Lack of organisation of women at work and influence in trade unions (except in industries like textiles), up until 1980s.

   (d) The reinforcing of segregation at home and at school: for example, lack of encouragement to girls to study mathematical and scientific subjects.

   (e) Career ladders which fail to fast-track women. Apprenticeships, for example, are rarely held by girls. A woman graduate starting as a secretary is less likely to advance than a male graduate who starts as a management trainee. In addition, organisations like banks, which have traditionally developed staff on the assumption of a lifetime career with the one employer, have tended to assume that women are unlikely to want a lifetime career. Commitments to geographical mobility are similarly assumed to be undesirable to women.

(f) Child-bearing and family responsibilities. Part-time work has enabled many women to continue in paid employment, but tends to apply to jobs which carry little prospect for promotion.

2 This is personal to you. Note, however, how pervasive, subtle and influential discrimination can be.

3 Organisations offer a variety of excuses for doing this:

(a) Cost (although performance-based pay systems are taking over from age-based ones in many companies).

(b) Fear that the pay-back period on training will be too short.

(c) A young customer base (on the supposition of an affinity between people of a common age).

(d) A 'young' organisational culture.

(e) In IT recruitment, lack of relevant experience among older workers.

(f) Stereotypes about older workers' assumed resistance to change, inability to learn (and 'unlearn') skills and reduced motivation.

(g) 'Image' – if this is the right word! Middle managers will often go for very young glamorous secretaries, particularly if they are recruiting themselves.

In addition, one of the principal reasons for discriminatory practices is that they have only recently been addressed in UK law.

4 (a) Advertising a vacancy in a primarily male environment, where women would be less likely to see it.

(b) Offering less favourable terms to part-time workers (given that most of them are women).

(c) Specifying age limits which would tend to exclude women who had taken time out of work for child-rearing.

(d) Asking in selection interviews about plans to have a family (since this might be to the detriment of a woman, but not a man).

5 (a) Examples of gender exception to the discrimination laws include:

(i) Specification of a male artist's model where male anatomy is required

(ii) Specification of a female changing room attendant for a women's lingerie shop

(iii) Specification of a same-sex employee in a private household, where the degree of contact and knowledge of intimate details may infringe privacy

(iv) Specification of women-only access to free breast cancer screening services

(v) Specification of women-only access to 'well women' clinics promoting women's health, or open days at college to encourage vocational education

(vi) Specifying a male driver in some Muslim countries

(b) Examples of ethnic minority exceptions include:

    (i)   A white actress to play the part of Queen Elizabeth

    (ii) Specifying an Afro-Caribbean model for the advertisement of Afro-Caribbean cosmetic products

    (iii) Inviting ethnic minority applicants only for a training course

6   (a)   Most people with disabilities have the same skills and abilities to offer as able-bodied people and are effective as employees without the need for any special help.

    (b)   Many other people with disabilities have as much to offer as able-bodied people, given the use of appropriate help which is readily available.

    (c)   When the abilities of workers with disabilities are overlooked, companies are missing out on the contribution of potentially valuable employees.

    (d)   Employers have obligations, along with the rest of the society, to ensure that people with disabilities are treated fairly.

    (*Code of Good Practice on the Employment of Disabled People*, Employment Service, 1984)

7   (a)   Potential conflict between religious beliefs and sexual orientation, eg if an employee is homophobic on the basis of religious belief. Policy will have to state clearly that the right not to be harassed has priority over the right to religious expression, and what this means in practice.

    (b)   Potential conflict between anti-discrimination law and privacy/data protection law; where questions of a potentially 'sensitive' nature may be asked to justify challenges. (The Employment Equality (Sexual Orientation) Regulations protect people who are 'perceived' to be lesbian, gay or bisexual, so they do not have to 'prove' their orientation to an Employment Tribunal.) Where employees request details of colleagues' pay, under Equal Pay Questionnaires.

8   (a)   **Advertising**

    (i)   Any wording that suggests preference for a particular group should be avoided (except for genuine occupational qualifications).

    (ii) Employers must not indicate or imply any 'intention to discriminate'.

    (iii) Recruitment literature should state that the organisation is an Equal Opportunities Employer.

    (iv) The placing of advertisements only where the readership is predominantly of one race or sex is construed as indirect discrimination.

    (b)   **Recruitment agencies.** Instructions to an agency should not suggest any preference.

    (c)   **Application forms**. These should include no questions which are not work-related (such as domestic details) and which only one group is asked to complete.

(d) **Interviews**

    (i)   Any non-work-related question must be asked of all interviewees, if any. Even then, some types of question may be construed as discriminatory. (You cannot, for example, ask only women about plans to have a family or care of dependants, or ask – in the worst case – about 'the pill' or PMT.)

    (ii) It may be advisable to have a witness at interviews, or at least to take detailed notes, in the event that a claim of discrimination is made.

(e) **Selection tests**. These must be wholly relevant, and should not favour any particular group. (Even personality tests have shown to favour white male applicants.)

(f) **Records**. Reasons for rejection, and interview notes, should be carefully recorded, so that in the event of investigation the details will be available.

Chapter 11:
WELFARE, HEALTH AND SAFETY

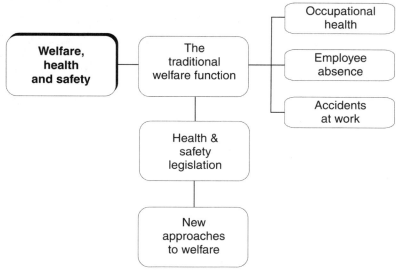

Introduction

Health, safety and well-being at work may be considered important for several reasons.

(a)   Employees should be protected from needless pain and suffering (obvious – we hope!)

(b)   Employers have legal obligations to take reasonable measures to protect the health and safety of their employees.

(c)   Accidents, illness and other causes of employee absence and/or impaired performance cost the employer money.

(d)   A business's employer brand and image in the market place may suffer if its health and safety record is bad.

This chapter looks at the law and best practice relating to health and safety at work, as well as broader welfare issues.

Your objectives

In this chapter you will learn about the following.

(a)   The traditional welfare function

(b)   Occupational health practices and policies

(c)   The management of employee absence and absenteeism

(d)   Accidents at work

(e)   Health and safety legislation and the role of the Health and Safety Commission

(f)   New approaches to welfare, ergonomics, substance abuse, stress, HIV/AIDS and workplace counselling

1 THE TRADITIONAL WELFARE FUNCTION

1.1 What is welfare?

Definition

> **Welfare** is 'a state of faring or doing well, freedom from calamity, enjoyment of health'. In HRM terms, this implies 'efforts to improve conditions of living for a group of employees or workers'.

In Chapter 1 of this Course Book, we described how the HR function grew out of industrial welfare work.

Employers might want to provide welfare:

(a) Because of a genuine sense of corporate social responsibility towards employees

(b) To improve the morale and loyalty of employees

(c) Because work (and non-work) problems impact on the 'steady state' performance of employees

(d) Because other companies and organisations are offering similar services/benefits, and they need to do the same in order to attract and retain the calibre of staff they require.

FOR DISCUSSION

Staff spend at least half their waking time at work or in getting to it or leaving it. They know they contribute to the organisation when they are reasonably free from worry, and they feel, perhaps inarticulately, that when they are in trouble they are due to get something back from the organisation. People are entitled to be treated as full human beings with personal needs, hopes and anxieties; they are employed as **people**, they bring themselves to work, not just their hands, and they cannot readily leave their troubles at home.'

(Martin, 1967)

Is this a 'soft' or a 'hard' HRM view? Is it a convincing argument for welfare?

Note that a case be made *against* the provision of discretionary welfare.

(a) Welfare is provided for by the state: why should other organisations duplicate services?

(b) Welfare is irrelevant or even counter to the strategic objectives of the business (notably, profit maximisation).

(c) Welfare services have not been shown to increase loyalty or motivation: they are largely taken for granted, and as such are more likely to be a source of disappointment and dissatisfaction at any shortcomings than a source of satisfaction. Even gratitude/or appreciation is not a prime motivator. Any positive effects are hard to measure: the whole concept is relentlessly 'soft'.

(d)   The non-work affairs and interests of employees are not the business of employers. If this attitude prevails in some situations (so that if the employee commits an offence outside work, this is not sufficient grounds for dismissal) it should prevail in others.

(e)   Business organisations are not equipped to deal with welfare issues. Line managers are not trained to do so, and cannot devote sufficient time to follow-up. Centralising welfare responsibilities places a burden on HR specialists who are struggling to get away from the 'nursemaid' role and into strategic management.

Welfare may not demonstrably have a *positive* effect on morale and productivity – but anxiety, stress and distress invariably have a *negative* effect which should be alleviated where possible in the interests of effectiveness. In other words, welfare is a **hygiene factor**.

The more recent orientation of HRM towards welfare is that the health of the individual (in the broadest sense) represents the health of the organisation: if employees can be proactively helped not just to avoid accidents and illnesses, but to become more resilient to stress, healthier, physically fitter, mentally more flexible, emotionally more stable, they are more likely to perform at a consistent and high level on behalf of the organisation. We will examine this orientation and its implications in Section 4 below. Here, we will look at some of the concerns of traditional welfare.

1.2   Occupational health

Occupational health programmes are concerned largely with the effects of the working environment on workers. This may involve:

(a)   Identifying substances, conditions or processes which are actually or potentially hazardous, and in what circumstances

(b)   Identifying the effect of methods and processes of work on the human body and mind

(c)   Exercising control over the working environment and substances used in the course of work, so as to minimise risk.

Thus, occupational health is concerned with toxic substances (such as lead oxide, chlorine, asbestos, and radiation) and with protective measures against all of these, as well as less obvious sources of ill health at work, including noise, fatigue and physical and mental stress (excessive demands on the body and mind). Increasingly, it is also concerned with personal substance abuse and other fitness and mental well-being factors that might have a direct or indirect affect on the workplace and work performance. We will discuss these factors in Section 4 below.

NOTES

Activity 1   **(30 minutes)**

Are there any aspects of your work or study environment that you would describe

(a) As a hindrance to your work

(b) As a source of stress or dissatisfaction

(c) As a hazard to your health?

Some of the key 'traditional' causes of ill-health at work, and the regulations applying to them, are as follows.

(a) **Noise**

Industrial hearing impairment has long been recognised as a problem for factory workers and machine operators, but the stressful and distracting effects of noise have more recently been identified. Continuous loud noise can be protected against by sound-proofing and personal ear protection. Sound-proofing (eg acoustic hoods over noisy office printers) and broadcast 'white noise' (soft, constant, featureless sound) are often used in office environments to reduce noise irritation. *(Noise at Work Regulation 1989)*

(b) **General environmental 'hygiene'**

The *Workplace (Health, Safety and Welfare) Regulations 1992* provides for health and hygiene in areas such as the following.

(i) **Ventilation**. Air should be fresh or purified.

(ii) **Temperature** levels must be 'reasonable' inside buildings during working hours: not less than 16°C where people are seated, or 13°C if moving about.

(iii) **Lighting** should be suitable and sufficient, and natural if practicable. Windows should be clear and unobstructed.

(iv) **Cleaning and decoration**. Premises must be kept clean.

(v) **Space**. Each person should have at least 11 cubic metres of space.

(vi) **Sanitary conveniences and washing facilities** must be suitable and sufficient: properly ventilated and lit, properly cleaned, separate for men and women – and enough of them to avoid undue delay!

(vii) **Drinking water** should be available in adequate supply, with suitable drinking vessels.

(viii) **Rest facilities and eating facilities** must be provided unless the employees' work stations are suitable.

(ix) **First aid** equipment should be provided, under the charge of a responsible person who should be trained in first aid.

(c) **Hazardous substances and work-related diseases**

Procedures will need to be in place for: warning signs and labels identifying toxic or hazardous chemicals and other substances; training of staff in handling and storing substances and in first aid treatment and reporting mechanisms in the event of exposure; secure storage of substances; protective clothing and equipment for handling substances and so on. *(Control of Substances Hazardous to Health Regulations 1994 (COSHH).)* Hazards include not only burning, blinding, respiratory dysfunction, poisoning and other 'immediate' effects of substances, but also **work-related diseases**.

(d)   **Manual handling operations**

Back injuries due to the incorrect lifting and carrying of heavy objects accounts for more than a quarter of the accidents reported each year in the UK. Employers should, as far as is reasonably practical, avoid the need for employees to undertake risky manual handling activity. All remaining operations must be assessed, and steps taken to reduce risks to the lowest level reasonably practicable: providing properly maintained equipment and procedures (back braces, conveyer belts etc) and training in their use. *(Manual Handling Operations Regulations 1992)*

(e)   **Use of computer workstations**

The workstation has become one of the potentially toxic hazards of the workplace. If you have ever worked for a long period at a VDU you may personally have experienced some discomfort: back ache, stiffness, eye-strain and muscular disorders are common effects. Referred to collectively as **'Repetitive Strain Injury'** or RSI, they now account for more than half of all work-related injuries in the USA and have reached epidemic proportions in Australia. Problems are due both to the ergonomics of the workstation and to working practices: poor posture, insufficient breaks for movement and so on. The *Health and Safety (Display Screen Equipment) Regulations 1992* provide for the adaptation of computer workstations and equipment so that: VDU screens do not flicker, are free from glare and are able to swivel and tilt; radiation is reduced to negligible levels; and desk, chair and keyboard arrangement allows for forearm rest and adjustment for improved posture. Additional policies should emphasise education in posture, stretching exercises and so on, and the provision of regular work breaks or changes in activity for VDU users.

(f)   **Pregnancy/maternity**

Pregnant women, those who have recently given birth and those who are breastfeeding are traditionally recognised as a special at-risk group by occupational health regulation and policy. The EC Directive on pregnancy and maternity was incorporated into the *Management of Health and Safety at Work (Amendment) Regulations 1994*.

Provisions include: risk assessment; adjustment or offers of alternative work to reduce the risk; suspension on full pay as a last resort.

Activity 2   **(30 minutes)**

Reassess your appraisal of the health of your workplace in answer to Activity 1 above, in the light of the specific issues and provisions discussed. Were any of the health hazards mentioned new to you – or easily overlooked in the course of work? If so, what does this say about the need for occupational health policies?

Occupational health policy

There will be several elements to occupational health policy in any given area.

(a) **Hazard minimisation**: removing hazards where possible. Assessing and reducing employees' exposure to risk.

(b) **Information about hazards**: education, warning signs and labels, consultation with employees and safety experts.

(c) **Equipment**: protective clothing, ergonomically-designed work-stations, sound-proofing, safety equipment, maintenance.

(d) **Training in the use of equipment**: systems and procedures for safe and healthy working, compulsory use of safety/protective equipment and clothing.

(e) **Employee responsibilities**: to co-operate with health and safety policies, use systems responsibly, inform the employer of conditions placing them at risk, inform the employer or health and safety officer of identified hazards.

(f) **Monitoring of occupational health**: reporting of illness and injury, identification of emerging health issues.

'Ill-health' and 'injury' are obviously closely related, and occupational health policies would consider issues relating to both. We will consider accidents as a particular workplace risk, in Section 2 of this chapter.

1.3 Absenteeism and employee absence

Employee absence

Ill-health and injury are major causes of long– and short-term employee absence from work. A 2006 survey by insurance firm AXA suggested that such absences cost UK business more than £12 billion a year (and estimated that £1.7 billion is due to staff 'pulling sickies' rather than absence resulting from genuine ill-health!).

Some other reasons for absence are covered by employment protection legislation, such as pregnancy, maternal/paternal leave, redundancy preparation, trade union activities and (most recently) time off for jury service.

Various legislation in the UK provides for:

(a) **Maternity leave** of 52 weeks in total.

(b) **Paternity leave**, whereby fathers may take two weeks' unpaid leave within 56 days of their child's birth. (In 2007, this is being extended by the *Work and Families Act 2006*.)

(c) **Right of return**, following maternity and paternity leave, to the same job on equivalent terms, provided that written notice of intention to return has been given prior to the absence.

(d) **Parental leave**, whereby parents, adoptive parents and legal guardians with one year's continuous service have the right to 13 weeks' unpaid leave during a child's first five years in order to care for that child. The time off in any one year is limited to four weeks, and leave has to be taken in blocks of at least one week.

(e) **'Reasonable' time off**, unpaid, to deal with 'family emergencies' involving a dependent, including sickness, accident, death or serious problems at a child's school.

As we suggested in Chapter 10, many companies are now pursuing 'family friendly' policies over and above the statutory minimum.

Absence procedure

An absence procedure should do the following.

(a) Require all employees to notify their manager as soon as possible on the first day of absence, giving as much information as possible about the nature and likely duration of the absence.

(b) Require all employees absent with prior consent to complete an absence form on their return to work.

(c) Require a medical certificate to be provided (where relevant) for absences of seven days or more.

(d) Discuss absences with employees and keep in touch with them, alerting them to the possibility of disciplinary action where appropriate.

(e) Ensure access to medical information and check this is up to date, prior to any disciplinary action being considered.

(f) Require the employee to notify management in the event of infectious or dangerous illness (so that other staff can be checked or warned).

(g) Look for suitable alternative work within the organisation for employees no longer able to perform their duties, and consider requests for flexible working where this might help.

(h) Check employees' entitlements to relevant benefits.

EXAMPLE

The state government of New South Wales, Australia, found a radical way of cutting 'sickies' (sick days) among ferry deckhands, with a deal which obliged fellow team-members to work extra shifts – unpaid – to cover for absent colleagues! Introduced as part of a wages package, the agreement was based on the 'mateship concept', applying peer pressure within the team. A report by Morgan and Banks revealed that most Australians took an average of six days' sick leave a year – with 12.4% admitting none of their 'sickies' were genuine! The new State Transit deal, however, saw the average number of sick days per employee per year plunge from 13.13 to 5.56...

(Australian *Daily Telegraph*)

'Absence' raises issues such as ill-health and injury and domestic problems. What might the organisation do to help its employees in such times?

1.4 Welfare benefits and services

Some of the key issues (from the traditional welfare perspective) are as follows.

(a) **Pension schemes**

Many firms set up occupational pension schemes for their employees, with various levels of employer and employee contributions.

Tight controls have been placed over the operation of pension funds, particularly with regard to the accountability of trustees, fund managers, auditors and advisers (Social Security Act 1985; Pensions Act 1995). Employees in occupational schemes which are contracted out of the State Earnings-Related Pension Scheme (SERPS) lose their future entitlements under the state scheme: occupational schemes are required to ensure that they provide adequate benefits, however, and are potentially much more generous than the state scheme.

(b) **Sick pay**

Statutory Sick Pay provides a basic income to employees who are incapable of attending their normal place of work due to illness. Employers are responsible for the first four weeks of SSP, after which they can claim payments back from the State through reduced National Insurance contributions.

Employers may also wish to offer discretionary Occupational Sick Pay, for example by maintaining full salary payment for a defined period of time. In order to minimise abuse of OSP, HR practitioners and line managers will need to monitor absence rates and periods carefully.

For motivational reasons, claims of sickness might be taken on trust as far as possible (unless there is positive proof of malingering). An illness or diagnosis may be confirmed by referring the employee to a company-approved doctor – but disciplinary action cannot be taken against an employee who refuses to be examined (unless there is a contractual agreement).

Welfare calls and visits may also be made during prolonged absence, in order to identify financial or practical help that may be offered, alleviate anxiety, offer counselling and so on.

(c) **Maternity**

Maternity leave and health and safety provisions for pregnant workers have already been mentioned above.

Statutory maternity pay is being extended in 2007 (under the *Work and Families Act 2006*) from 39 weeks to 52 weeks.

(d) **Domestic problems**

Situations such as marital breakdown or bereavement are essentially private, but their effects are likely to carry over into the workplace. The Employment Relations Act 1999 provides for what used to be called 'compassionate leave' (unpaid) to deal with 'family emergencies', but organisations may develop a policy on:

(i)   What constitutes 'reasonable' time off
(ii)   Whether time off will be paid to some degree
(iii) Whether additional welfare interventions will be offered.

Welfare services may include: access to the firm's own counsellors or referral to other support organisations; help with financial, legal and funeral arrangements arising from bereavement; and so on.

(e)   **Retirement/redundancy**

As discussed in Chapter 7, retirement and redundancy may be regarded as major adjustment crises in the lives of employees, and a variety of counselling, training and other services may be offered.

(f)   **Annual leave**

People need holidays! All employees are currently entitled to a minimum of 20 days' paid annual leave and under the *Work and Families Act*, public holidays will become additional entitlements. The basic entitlement is also expected to rise to 24 days in October 2007 and 28 days in October 2008: watch this space!

Activity 3   **(45 minutes)**

Does your college or workplace have provision for welfare services? What are they? How well publicised are they? Ask for information, if it is not available in the Student/Employee Handbook or on notice boards. List the issues which are highlighted by the counselling or welfare programme

---

We will now look at a major health and safety issue: workplace accidents.

2   ACCIDENTS AT WORK

2.1   Incidence of industrial accident

Newspapers frequently quote statistics showing large number of employee hours lost through accident and the associated cost to business. Torrington *et al* (2002) cite IRS figures of 1.3 million workers taken ill in the UK as a result of their work, resulting in the loss of 24.3 million working days at a total annual cost to employers of £2.5 billion. However, it should be noted that:

(a)   Accident rates vary substantially by industry. (A high proportion of deaths at work occur in the construction industry for example.)

(b)   Small and large organisations have lower incidence rates than medium-sized organisations (perhaps because supervision is closer in small organisations and investment in safety/accident prevention staff and systems is greater in large ones).

(c)   Working conditions (outdoor v indoor) and tools and technology (heavy machinery v PC) have the greatest impact on incident rates, followed by ...

(d)   The 'accident proneness' of individual workers. There are suggestions that some people are more prone to accidents than others (due to poor vision, stress, depression, alertness, immaturity and so on). However, accident proneness is also related to the working patterns, responsibility and safety-awareness of individual employees: horseplay, practical jokes, cutting corners on safety measures and so on are frequent causes of accident.

(e)   Death by homicide is, in fact, the biggest cause of death in the workplace in the USA (Filipczale, 1993)!

Activity 4   **(10 minutes)**

A scene from everyday office life is shown below: Figure 11.1. Note down anything that strikes you as being dangerous about this working environment.

Figure 11.1: Unsafe work practices!

Apart from obviously dangerous equipment in factories, construction sites and even offices, there are many hazards to be found in the modern working environment. Many accidents could be avoided by the simple application of common sense and consideration by employer and employee, and by safety consciousness encouraged or enforced by a widely acceptable and well published **safety policy**.

2.2   Cost of accidents

The **cost** of accidents to the employer consists of:

(a)   Time lost by the injured employee

(b)   Time lost by other employees whose work is interrupted by the accident

(c)   Time lost by supervision, management and technical staff as a result of the accident

(d)   A proportion of the cost of first aid materials, or even medical staff

(e)   The cost of disruption to operations at work

(f)   The cost of any damage and repairs and modification to the equipment

(g)   The cost of any compensation payments or fines resulting from legal action

(h)   The costs associated with increased insurance premiums

(i)   Reduced output from the injured employee on return to work

(j)   The cost of possible reduced morale, increased absenteeism, increased labour turnover among employees

(k)   The cost of recruiting and training a replacement for the injured worker

An employer may also be liable to an employee in tort if the employee is injured as a result of either:

(a)   The employer's failure to take reasonable care in providing safe premises and plant, a safe system of work and competent fellow employees, or

(b)   The employer's breach of a statutory duty – say, to fence dangerous machinery. Although the injured employee's damages may be reduced if the injury was partly a consequence of his/her own contributory negligence, due allowance is made for ordinary human failings, such as inattentiveness, tiredness and so on.

2.3   Accident prevention

The prevention of accidents requires integrated HR-led policies and practices, including attention to workplace design, communication of health and safety rules and values, training and so on. Some of the steps which might be taken to reduce the frequency and severity of accidents are as follows.

(a)   Developing safety awareness among staff and workers and encouraging departmental pride in a good safety record.

(b)   Developing effective consultative participation between management, workers and unions so that safety and health rules can be accepted and followed.

(c)   Giving adequate instruction in safety rules and measures as part of the training of new and transferred workers, or where working methods or speeds of operation are changed.

(d)   Minimising specific hazards. Materials handling, a major cause of accidents, should be minimised and designed as far as possible for safe working and operation.

(e)   Building and equipment maintenance – apart from making sound job repairs, temporary expedients to keep production going should not prejudice safety.

(f)   Safety inspections – carried out as a comprehensive audit, working through a checklist; or by using random spot checks or regular checks of particular risk points. Checklists used in the inspection process should identify corrective action to be taken, and allocate responsibility for that action.

(g) Compliance with legislation and industry/work environment codes of practice.

2.4 Accident reporting

An accident report is a management tool, designed to:

(a) Identify problems and
(b) Indicate corrective action.

Recurring accidents may suggest the need for special investigation, but only more serious incidents will have to be followed-up in depth. Follow-up should be clearly aimed at preventing recurrence – not placing blame.

The drawing below (Figure 11.2) shows the format of a **typical accident book** which should by law be kept by any organisation which employs more than 10 people. (The one used by your organisation may be laid out differently, or it might consist of loose-leaf sheets.)

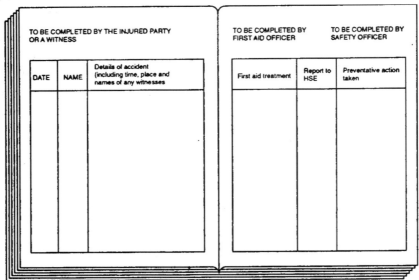

Figure 11.2: Accident Book

The *Reporting of Injuries, Diseases and Dangerous Occurrences Regulations 1995 (RIDDOR 95)* require employers to do the following.

(a) Notify the environmental health authority or the Health and Safety Executive *immediately* if one of the following occurs.

(i) There is an accident connected with work and either an employee or self-employed person working on the premises is killed or suffers a major injury (including as a result of physical violence) or a member of the public is killed or taken to hospital.

(ii) There is a dangerous occurrence.

(b) Send a completed **Accident report form** (see next page) to do the following.

(i) Confirm within ten days a telephone report of an accident or dangerous occurrence (as described in (a) above).

(ii)   Notify, within ten days of the accident, any injury which stops someone doing their normal job for more than three days.

(iii)   Report certain work-related diseases.

Definitions

Major injuries include things like fractures other than to fingers, thumbs or toes, amputation, temporary or permanent loss of sight and any other injury which results in the person being admitted to hospital for more than 24 hours.

Dangerous occurrences are 'near misses' that might well have caused major injuries. They include the collapse of a load bearing part of a lift, electrical short circuit or overload causing fire or explosion, the malfunction of breathing apparatus while in use or during testing immediately before use, and many others.

Notifiable diseases include certain poisonings, occupational asthma, asbestos, hepatitis and many others.

The standard for the notification of injuries and dangerous occurrences is reproduced on the next page: Figure 11.3.

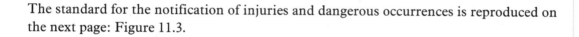

NOTES

Health and Safety at Work etc Act 1974
The Reporting of Injuries, Diseases and Dangerous Occurrences Regulations 1995

HSE
Health & Safety
Executive

Report of an injury or dangerous occurrence

Filling in this form
This form must be filled in by an employer or other responsible person.

Part A

About you
1 What is your full name?

2 What is your job title?

3 What is your telephone number?

About your organisation
4 What is the name of your organisation?

5 What is its address and postcode?

6 What type of work does your organisation do?

Part B

About the incident
1 On what date did the incident happen?

/ /

2 At what time did the incident happen?
(Please use the 24-hour clock eg 0600)

3 Did the incident happen at the above address?

Yes ☐ Go to question 4

No ☐ Where did the incident happen?

☐ elsewhere in your organisation - give the name, address and postcode

☐ at someone else's premises - give the name, address and postcode

☐ in a public place - give the details of where it happened

If you do not know the postcode, what is the name of the local authority?

4 In which department, or where on the premises, did the incident happen?

Part C

About the injured person
If you are reporting a dangerous occurrence, go to Part F.
If more than one person was injured in the same incident, please attach the details asked for in Part C and Part D for each injured person.

1 What is their full name?

2 What is their home address and postcode?

3 What is their home phone number?

4 How old are they?

5 Are they
☐ male?
☐ female?

6 What is their job title?

7 Was the injured person (tick only one box)
☐ one of your employees?
☐ on a training scheme? Give details:

☐ on work experience?
☐ employed by someone else? Give details of the employer:

☐ self-employed and at work?
☐ a member of the public?

Part D

About the injury
1 What was the injury? (eg fracture, laceration)

2 What part of the body was injured?

308

3 Was the injury (tick the one box that applies)

☐ a fatality?

☐ a major injury or condition? (see accompanying notes)

☐ an injury to an employee or self-employed person which prevented them doing their normal work for more than 3 days?

☐ an injury to a member of the public which meant they had to be taken from the scene of the accident to a hospital for treatment?

4 Did the injured person (tick all the boxes that apply)

☐ became unconscious?

☐ need resuscitation?

☐ remain in hospital for more than 24 hours?

☐ none of the above?

Part E

About the kind of accident
Please tick the one box that best describes what happened, then go to part G.

☐ Contact with moving machinery or material being machined

☐ Hit by a moving, flying or falling object

☐ Hit by a moving vehicle

☐ Hit by something fixed or stationary

☐ Injured while handling, lifting or carrying

☐ Slipped, tripped or fell on the same level

☐ Fell from a height
How high was the fall?

☐ _____ metres

☐ Trapped by something collapsing

☐ Drowned or asphyxiated

☐ Exposed to, or in contact with, a harmful substance

☐ Exposed to fire

☐ Exposed to an explosion

☐ Contact with electricity or an electrical discharge

☐ Injured by an animal

☐ Physically assaulted by a person

☐ Another kind of accident (describe it in part G)

Part F

Dangerous occurrences
Enter the number of the dangerous occurrence you are reporting. (The numbers are given in the Regulations and in the notes which accompany this form.)

Part G

Describing what happened
Give as much detail as you can. For instance
• the name of any substance involved
• the name and type of any machinery involved
• the events that led to the incident
• the part played by any people.

If it was a personal injury, give details of what the person was doing. Describe any action that has since been taken to prevent a similar incident. Use a separate piece of paper if you need to.

Part H

Your signature

Date

☐ / ☐ / ☐

Where to send the form
Please send it to the Enforcing Authority for the place where it happened. If you do not know the Enforcing Authority, send it to the nearest HSE office.

For official use

Client number   Location number   Event number

☐ INV   REP ☐ Y ☐ N

Figure 11.3: RIDDOR Report Form

NOTES

> **Activity 5**   **(30 minutes)**
>
> Invent (or carefully role-play) your own scenario for a typical (or unusual) workplace accident causing injury. Invent as many relevant details as you can. Now complete the specimen RIDDOR report reproduced here.

We will now look at some of the main legislation on Health and Safety at work. Much of it is refreshingly practical, with lots of measures to be taken and procedures to be put in place: we will only be able to summarise. Like other legal provisions we have discussed in this Course Book, the 'law is a floor': remember that these are minimum standards – not 'best practice'! Best practice among employers is likely to be:

- *More scrupulous in enforcing safeguards*

- *More committed to providing consultation, information and training on health and safety, and*

- *More wide-ranging in its attempt to promote positive health and well being and a culture of safety.*

3   HEALTH AND SAFETY LEGISLATION

3.1   Health and safety responsibilities

In the UK, the *Health and Safety at Work Act 1974* is the major piece of UK legislation on health and safety, together with Regulations and Codes of Practice implementing EU Directives. The 1974 Act provides for the introduction of a system of approved Codes of Practice, prepared in consultation with industry. Thus an employee, whatever his/her employment, should fund that his/her work is covered by an appropriate code of practice.

Employers also have specific duties under the 1974 Act.

- All systems (work practices) must be safe.

- The work environment must be safe and healthy (well-lit, warm, ventilated and hygienic).

- All plant and equipment must be kept up to the necessary standard.

The **employee** also has a duty under the 1974 Act.

- To take reasonable care to avoid injury to himself/herself and others

- To co-operate with his or her employers to help them comply with their legal obligations (including enforcing safety rules)

3.2   On-going risk management

Information, instruction, training and supervision should be directed towards safe working practices. Under the *Management of Health and Safety at Work Regulations 1992*, employers must:

- Carry out **risk assessment**, generally in writing, of all work hazards on a continuous basis.

- Introduce **controls** to reduce risks.

- Assess the **risks to anyone else** affected by their work activities (such as suppliers, customers, visitors)

- **Share hazard and risk information** with other employers, including those on adjoining premises, other site occupiers and all subcontractors coming onto the premises

- **Revise safety policies** in the light of the above – or initiate safety policies if none were in place previously

- Identify **employees who are especially at risk** (such as pregnant women or night shift workers)

- Provide up-to-date and appropriate **training in safety matters**

- Provide **information to employees** (including part-time and temporary workers) about health and safety

- Employ **competent health and safety advisers**

Employees also have specific responsibilities to:

- Use all equipment, safety devices, etc, provided by the employer **properly** and in accordance with the instructions and training received

- **Inform** the employer, or another employee with specific responsibility for health and safety, of any perceived shortcoming in safety arrangements or any serious and immediate dangers to health and safety.

Activity 6   **(no time limit)**

Consider the health and safety programme at your place of work (or study).

(a) How well *aware* are you of any rules, procedures and information regarding health and safety? (Who is responsible for *making* you more aware of such matters?)

(b) How well do the organisation's rules, procedures and information comply with the requirements of the Regulations?

3.3   Information and consultation

Under the *Health and Safety (Consultation with Employees) Regulations 1996*, employers must consult all of their employees on health and safety matters (such as the planning of health and safety training, any change in equipment or procedures which may substantially affect their health and safety at work or the health and safety consequences of introducing new technology). This involves giving information to employees *and* listening to and taking account of what they say before any health and safety decisions are taken.

Part B: HRM Issues

FOR DISCUSSION

'Developing countries are often so in need of economic development that they may accept any industry, even those that have the potential for significant harm ... Health hazards are still ignored: by having lax safety standards, developing countries can lure large multinational firms to their shores.'

(Kramer, McGraw Shuler, 1997)

What issues does this raise for HR pratitoners participaing in the outsourcing of organisational activitis to overseas economies?

3.4 Health and Safety authorities

The **Health and Safety Commission** was set up under the Health and Safety at Work Act 1974 to develop health and safety policies. It is made up of representatives of employers, employees, local government and relevant professional bodies. Responsibility for communicating, monitoring and enforcing the Commission's policies and relevant legislation falls to the Health and Safety Executive, which has powers of inspection and enforcement by:

(a) **Prohibition notice** requiring the shut down of hazardous processes until remedial action has been taken

(b) **Improvement notice** requiring compliance with a statutory provision within a certain time (subject to appeal to an industrial tribunal)

(c) **Seizure** of hazardous articles for destruction or rendering harmless, and /or

(d) **Prosecution** of offenders, who are liable to fine and even imprisonment in serious cases.

Weblink

The **Health & Safety Executive** has an extremely informative website, with an easy-to-use pull-down menu covering a wide range of 'health and safety topics' from Asbestos to Young people!

▶▶ http://www.hse.gov.uk

3.5 Health and safety policy

There will be several elements to a health and safety policy, whatever the specific needs and hazards of a particular workplace.

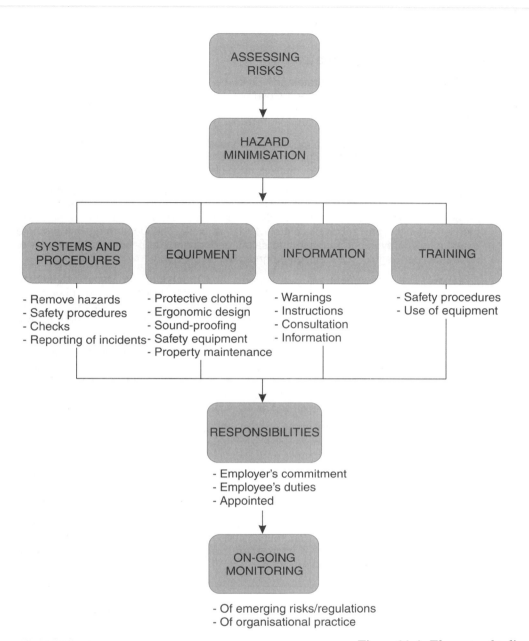

Figure 11.4: Elements of policy

The following is an **example of a Policy Statement** released by the former Department of Environment, Transport and the Regions (DETR), which used to have responsibility for the Health and Safety Commission (HSC) and the Health and Safety Executive (HSE). (In 2002, this responsibility was taken over by the Department for Work and Pensions.)

Health and safety policy statement

This Health and Safety Policy Statement is to be observed by staff throughout the Department (including the Agencies and Government Offices). It reflects the importance I attach to the health, safety and welfare of all staff and others who may be affected by our activities. That includes contractors and visitors to our premises.

I expect all managers to give similar importance to these issues in their operational area and when determining local priorities, plans and resource allocation. I also recognise the valuable role played by Safety Representatives appointed by Trade Unions.

1   **Objectives.** The Department will meet all current and proposed legal requirements in the Health and Safety at Work Act 1974 and relevant subordinate legislation. This will be achieved through effective risk assessment and the implementation of appropriate measures for the prevention or control of risks at work. The Department will promote continuous improvement in health and safety performance to become an exemplar of good practice. Regular feedback on progress will be provided.

2   **Systems.** The Department will put systems and procedures in place designed to ensure a safe system of work. As far as reasonably practicable, all equipment, vehicles, plant, premises, other work sites and work practices will be safe and free from any hazards to health and that employees, the public and other affected by our operations are not exposed to undue risk.

3   **Communication/Co-operation.** The policy will be brought to the attention of all employees and contractors. Legally all employees must co-operate in establishing and maintaining safe and healthy working conditions and avoid any actions which may adversely affect the health, safety and welfare of themselves, their colleagues, contractors or visitors. Consultation on Departmental health and safety issues will be undertaken...

4   **Monitoring and Auditing.** The Department will monitor and audit health and safety management systems and performance. An annual report on health and safety will be produced reflecting the Department's progress, forward plans and innovative initiatives.

5   **Review.** The policy will be continuously reviewed. A full review, including related management arrangements and performance, will be held in three years time, or earlier, following any major change in health and safety legislation or our organisation.

This policy is fully endorsed by the Board and will be implemented by management throughout the Department. Roles and responsibilities will be clearly defined to ensure effective communication, provision of information, training, and systems for reporting to those with delegated responsibilities.

| **Activity 7** | **(5 minutes)** |

Underline or highlight the key words and phrases in the above example of a Policy Statement, which seem to you to reflect the most important aspects of health and safety policy, as described so far.

This will help you to know what to look for when you appraise the health and safety policies of your own organisation.

FOR DISCUSSION

Safety policy must be implemented in detailed practice (such as fire drills and equipment checking) but it is less likely to be consistently observed if senior managers fail to set a good example, to discipline breaches of policy, or to reward health and safety suggestions. The aim is to create a culture in which health and safety are key values.

What are the cultural values in your nation, local community and organisation that:

(a) Promote health and safety?

(b) Promote risk-taking and ill-health?

3.6 Working hours

You should be aware that working hours are also a health and safety issue, under the Working Time Regulations 1998 (implementing the EU Working Time Directive).

(a) Working hours are limited to 48 hours per week, averaged over a standard reference period of 17 weeks (or 26 weeks, where continuity of work is necessary, as in health or essential services, 24-hour production or seasonal work). This can be extended to a year by collective workplace agreement – to preserve annual hours schemes, for example.

(b) An employee may agree individually, in writing, to work more than 48 hours per week, and a record of hours should be retained in case the Health and Safety Commission requires it.

(c) All employees are entitled to a daily rest of 11 consecutive hours in every 24, and a 24-hour rest in every seven days (averaged over 2 weeks) – subject to adjustment by collective agreement.

(d) If the working day exceeds six hours, the employee is entitled to a minimum of 20 minutes' break.

Activity 8 **(15 minutes)**

Since you have broadened your awareness of what constitutes a threat to health and safety, take some time to think through HR policies. Suggest five other areas for consideration. (If you are currently employed, check your organisation's manual on health and safety: use the real-life resources available to you.)

Now let's look at the 'new' welfare role of HRM, and some of the hazards of the new workplace.

4 NEW APPROACHES TO WELFARE

4.1 A shift in perspective

HRM specialists have tried to distance themselves from the traditional welfare tag with its legalistic/reactive and paternalistic associations.

The new orientation to welfare activities is based on the recognition that healthy and focused individuals are likely to perform better at work, to be more flexible (physically, mentally and emotionally) and adaptable to change: in short, that it is possible to take a business-strategic view of employee health and well-being.

The new model of welfare is therefore:

(a) **Pro-active** in its attempt to address potential health and safety issues, rather than reacting to regulation, complaint or crisis

(b) **Positive** in its attempt to promote health and well-being rather than focusing solely on ill-health, injury and crisis

(c) **Holistic** in its definition of health and well-being, including emotional and even spiritual factors

(d) **Wide-ranging** in its attention to diverse issues, rather than being led by legislative agendas

Goss (1994) summarised this new perspective as 'tough love': a hard-soft policy aimed at offering benefits and services which employees need and value, 'linked strategically with the needs of the organisation by enhancing performance'.

Issues in the new welfare model include:

(a) Work-life balance and the management of stress

(b) Ergonomics

(c) Promotion of positive health and fitness, and the management of substance abuse

(d) Confrontation of emerging health issues (such as HIV/AIDS) and other sources of distress

(e) Workplace counselling

(f) Employee Assistance Programmes (EAPs)

We will discuss each of these issues, briefly, in turn.

4.2 Work-life balance and control of stress

Overwork is frequently associated with poor diet, lack of exercise, inadequate relaxation, stress and relationship difficulties.

Despite the desire to increase productivity or enhance performance, many companies are realising that increasing workloads and working hours is in fact counter-productive, potentially encouraging absenteeism, ill-health, accidents and poor-quality work.

Elements in a **work-life balance programme** may include:

(a)   In-house or consultant-led awareness training: clarification of values and priorities and so on

(b)   In-house or consultant-led skills training: in time-management, delegation, work organisation, relaxation techniques and, say,

(c)   Flexible working arrangements to allow time for family and social activities within the working week (as discussed in Chapter 9).

Stress and stress management

Stress is a term which is often loosely used to describe feelings of tension – usually associated with too much, or overly demanding, work. In fact, stress is the product of demands made on an individual's physical *and mental* energies: monotony and feelings of failure or insecurity are sources of stress, as much as the conventionally-considered factors of pressure, overwork and so on.

It is worth remembering, too, that demands on an individual's energies may be stimulating as well as harmful: many people, especially those suited to managerial jobs, work well under pressure, and even require some form of stress to bring out their best performance. (It is excessive stress that can be damaging: this may be called strain.) This is why we talk about the management of stress, not about its elimination: it is a question of keeping stress to helpful proportions and avenues.

Harmful stress can be identified in symptoms such as nervous tension, irritability, sensitivity, sleeplessness, withdrawal (reluctance to communicate, absenteeism), depression, substance abuse and a variety of physical symptoms (such as skin and digestive disorders, tension headaches). Some symptoms of stress – say, absenteeism – may or may not be correctly identified with stress: there are many other possible causes of such problems, both at work (lack of motivation) and outside (personal problems).

All these things can, however, adversely affect performance, which is why stress management has become a major workplace issue.

Stress can be caused or aggravated by:

(a)   Personality: competitive, sensitive and insecure people feel stress more acutely

(b)   Ambiguity or conflict in the demands made on an individual in their various roles

(c)   Insecurity, risk and change

(d)   Management style including:

   (i)   Unpredictability
   (ii)   Destruction of workers' self esteem
   (iii)   Setting up win/lose situations.

NOTES

> **Activity 9** **(30 minutes)**
>
> What sources of stress are there in your own lifestyle? Are you aware of the symptoms of stress in yourself? What do you do (if anything) to control your stress?

Greater awareness of the nature and control of stress is a feature of the modern work environment. **Stress management techniques** are increasingly taught and encouraged by organisations, and include:

(a) Counselling (to air and resolve conflicts)

(b) Time off or regular rest breaks

(c) Relaxation techniques (breathing exercises, meditation)

(d) Physical exercise and creative self-expression (as a safety valve for tension)

(e) Delegation and planning (to avoid work-load related stress)

(f) Assertiveness (to control stress related to insecurity in interpersonal relations).

Ecological control can also be brought to bear on the problem of stress, creating conditions in which stress is less likely to be a problem: well designed jobs and environments, and an organisation culture built on meaningful work, mutual support, communication and teamwork.

Other causes of 'dis-ease' at work

Workplace intimidation, harassment and physical violence have been the subject of recent studies, suggesting that **bullying** is every bit as prevalent – and painful – in the workplace as it is in the school playground! 'Cyber-bullying', in particular, is on the increase, involving abusive or detrimental e-mails, website pests and mobile phone text messages. Employers may be liable for these, as for other forms of harassment at work.

Policies should take into account victim-side factors (grievance procedures, confidentiality, counselling, transfer) and perpetrator-side factors (disciplinary procedures, counselling, transfer, cultural change): see the sexual harassment guidelines in Chapter 10 for a good model.

Weblinks

> If you are interested in this area, check out or the Bully Online website
>
> The HSE's report *Beacons of Excellence in Stress Management* outlines a 'good practice model' for reducing stress.
>
> ▶▶ http://www.bullyonline.org
>
> ▶▶ http://www.peoplemanagement.co.uk/stressbusters
>
> ▶▶ http://www.hse.gov.uk/stress

Activity 10	(15 minutes)

Brainstorm a list of behaviours you would consider 'bullying' in the workplace.

EXAMPLES

- John Hamilton, head of group health and safety at Bradford & Bingley, has achieved a 75 per cent reduction in the number of stress-related absences since making **risk assessments** across the business.

  While it's not possible to cover every individual, you can assess each team as a whole, looking at the pressure they are under,' he told PM. 'It could be something fundamental – for instance a lack of resources – or it might be something more subtle. Because we talked about stress in terms of a natural response to pressure, a lot of managers thought about how they could mitigate the pressures on their teams and made immediate changes as a result.

  The initiative had saved the bank about £250,000 worth of working days.

- The London Borough of Brent has introduced a **mediation facility** to improve working relationships which is one of the biggest causes of stress at the council.

  Despite reducing our sickness absence significantly over the past few years stress still accounts for a significant proportion of referrals to our occupational health providers.

INTERNATIONAL COMPARISON

In extreme cases, stress is a killer. The Japanese, who work longer hours than people in the US and the UK, experience **karoshi** (death from overwork). This is a documented ailment in which people develop illnesses and die from high stress and the pressures of overtime. **Karoshi** was officially registered as a fatal illness in 1989.

4.3 Ergonomics

Definition

Ergonomics [(Greek: **ergos** (work) + **nomos** (natural laws)] is the scientific study of the relationship between people and their working environment. This sphere of scientific research explores the demands that can arise from a working environment and the capabilities of people to meet these demands.

Ergonomics supports the design of machines and working conditions which function well and are best suited to the capacities and health requirements of the human body. In old people's homes and hospitals, for example, switches are placed according to measurements of chair height and arm reach. In the same way, computer consoles and controls, office furniture, factory layout and so on can be designed so that the individual expends minimal energy and experiences minimal physical strain in any given task.

More recently ergonomics has developed into a field that embraces the whole range of psychological factors that affect people at work. Apart from purely mechanical considerations – in what position should a worker be sitting in order to exert maximum force over a long period of time without physical strain or fatigue? – the ergonomist must now take into account the increasing problems of the worker as information processor. The perceptual limitations of the worker can also be measured, and systems designed which do not make unreasonable demands on the worker's attention span or capacity to absorb information – for example, the use of sound signals to attract attention to visual displays or equipment.

4.4 Promoting positive health and fitness

Approaches to health promotion include the following.

(a) **Health monitoring and awareness campaigns**

Employees may be given regular health checks under occupational health regulations (hearing and eye tests, for example): this may be extended to heart and cholesterol checks, general fitness checks, skin cancer checks and so on, as part of a campaign to increase health awareness. Campaigns may be run to educate employees on nutritional guidelines, smoking and substance abuse hazards, the need for exercise and so on.

(b) **Nutritional support**

The link between motivation and health is well-documented. Employers can encourage healthy eating habits through education programmes and through access to nutritionally balanced food in staff canteens, voucher schemes linked to health food outlets or products, sponsorship of weight-loss (or gain) programmes and so on.

(c) **Anti-smoking programmes**

In 2007 new legislation in England and Wales placed an outright ban on smoking in enclosed public places including all work places. Organisations which had not done so already were encouraged (but not compelled) to take this further and adopt health-promoting thinking into their whole practice. Suggested supportive measures included consulting with staff in building smoke-free behaviour into health and safety policies and to support employees' or customers' attempts to quit smoking. For some organisations the benefits of being smoke-free – a fitter workforce, less downtime for cigarette breaks and the removal of the associated cleaning, ventilation and space – issues were outweighed by the detrimental effects to employee relations. On some premises a smoking culture has been enshrined in a 'smoking shelter' to continue the practice but within the terms of the law.

(d) **Fitness promotion**

Sedentary occupations erode physical strength, stamina and flexibility, interfere with sleep patterns and metabolic rate, reduce alertness and contribute to the long-term consequences of all the above in stress, heart disease and other serious ailments. Fitness promotion in the workplace may range from educating employees in basic stretching exercises during work

breaks to extensive facilities, accessed via discounted membership at health clubs and sports centres. In radical cases (considered the norm in Japan), whole staff exercise may be held at the start of each day.

EXAMPLE

'Companies have long offered healthcare and private medical insurance (PMI) schemes as part of employee benefits packages. But many have now switched focus from cure to prevention.

'In January, Standard Life teamed up with health management firm Vielife to create a package that combines PMI with health management programmes. Employees have access to a personalised, private online portal with email advice on topics including sleep, stress, nutrition and fitness.

'As for fitness, the British Heart Foundation (BHF) is so concerned about the predominance of 'desk potatoes' it has launched a workplace health activity toolkit to provide employers with ideas to increase staff activity levels and thus avoid ill health, stress and low morale. According to the BHF, physical activity programmes at work reduce absenteeism by up to 20 per cent and physically active employees take 27 per cent fewer days of sick leave than their less active colleagues. The Foundation recommends at least 30 minutes of moderately intense exercise, such as brisk walking, swimming or cycling, at least five times a week.

'Nicki Cooper, BHF head of education, says, "Researchers have found that employees who are more physically active can better manage stressful situations at work. These employees are also more likely to have less sick days for back problems and other health issues, making them more productive long-term employees." '

(Persaud, 2003)

4.5 Substance abuse

Substance abuse has become a major work-place issue with up to 17 million working days lost annually in the UK as a result of alcohol-related absences, including accidents at work.

Most estimates place the numbers of drug users slightly below these levels, taking into account the sheer variety of prescription and non-prescription drugs used, and the difficulties of gathering user information (given the illegality of most drug use).

Alcohol policy

Alcohol may be part of the culture of the workplace. Studies have found that:

(a) Workers who suffer from job stress and organisational frustration frequently turn to alcohol as a tool for unwinding.

(b) Organisations continue to encourage social drinking, despite the known effects of physical/psychological dependency. Company celebrations frequently revolve around alcohol, and little concern is shown for the heavy drinker until his or her work is adversely affected, which may not be for some time after the onset of dependency.

Activity 11 (30 minutes)

What would you expect to be the symptoms of alcohol abuse that might alert a supervisor or manager to the problem?

Most alcohol policies embrace the following areas.

(a) **Positive aims and objectives** – including statistics on alcohol-related harm and affirmation of successful treatment.

(b) **Restrictions on alcohol possession or consumption** during working hours, in certain areas or for certain at-risk employees

(c) **The links between the policy and disciplinary procedure**. This is a sensitive area, but random drunkenness and bad behaviour are usually treated under the heading of 'gross misconduct'.

(d) **Policy on testing**. Employers must be clear that the benefits of testing justify the privacy intrusion and tests should be restricted to jobs that pose safety risks, such as operating dangerous machinery.

(e) **Confidentiality** of all measures undertaken in relation to alcohol problems of individual employees.

(f) **Internal and external counselling services available**.

Drugs policy

Drug abuse policies are much more difficult to implement because:

(a) A significant number of workers may be legitimate short– or long-term users of prescription drugs and over the counter medicines which may impair performance in various ways (for example, by causing drowsiness)

(b) The illegality of the use of many drugs makes it difficult to gather information, and places drug use firmly within disciplinary as well as welfare policy frameworks

(c) Harm minimisation approaches (restricted use, risk avoidance and so on) may be interpreted as condoning drug use, although they do address the major workplace issues of safety risk and impaired performance

(d) It is difficult to distinguish fairly between 'acceptable' recreational drug use (of ecstasy or cannabis, say) and 'hard' drug use

(e) Random drug testing is fraught with industrial relations and legal issues (for example, under the Human Rights Act 1998), particularly since there are major problems of test reliability and privacy.

Counselling, harm-minimisation (avoiding heavy machinery, driving and so on if affected) and voluntary supported rehabilitation programmes may be used judiciously as the basis of a policy. Entry into a company treatment programme should not be compulsory, where an employee can show that (s)he is undertaking independent treatment. The disciplinary issues will (as with alcohol) have to be worked out in detail.

FOR DISCUSSION

- Alcohol and drug use are a private matter.
- Zero tolerance is the only approach to stopping alcohol and drug abuse.

Debate these two propositions, from the perspective of HR policy.

4.6 HIV/AIDS

The fear and prejudice surrounding the Acquired Immune Deficiency Syndrome and the Human Immunodeficiency Virus require positive policy commitments from employers. Guidelines on policy, followed by many major employers, include the following.

(a) People with AIDS or who are HIV positive are entitled to the same employment rights and quality of working life as people with other serious diseases.

(b) Employment policies should be based on the scientific evidence that people with AIDS or HIV do not pose a risk of transmitting the virus through normal workplace contact.

(c) Employers should provide all workers with up-to-date, sensitively-handled information about AIDS/HIV, safe practices and risk reduction.

(d) Employers must protect the confidentiality of employees' medical histories, test results and so on.

(e) Employers should not require HIV screening ('AIDS testing') as part of general pre-employment or workplace physical examinations; nor should particular groups (eg gay men) be unfairly targeted for screening (discriminatory practice).

(f) Education and counselling programmes are considered helpful, but should not replace rigorous equal opportunities policies.

The Health and Safety Executive booklet (*AIDS and the Workplace*, 1990) offers policy guidelines.

EXAMPLE

The Body Shop runs an education and counselling programme on HIV and AIDS. Its purpose is to give support to HIV-positive employees and employees with HIV-positive partners, and to prevent fear and discrimination by other employees, while promoting safe practices.

We have already suggested 'counselling' as part of many welfare policies. We will now go on to discuss counselling itself.

323

4.7 Workplace counselling

Definition

> 'Counselling can be defined as a purposeful relationship in which one person helps another to help himself. It is a way of relating and responding to another person so that that person is helped to explore his thoughts, feelings and behaviour with the aim of reaching a clearer understanding. The clearer understanding may be of himself or of a problem, or of the one in relation to the other.'
>
> (Rees, 1996)

Activity 12 (10 minutes)

Suggest five situations, already mentioned in this Course Book, in which workplace counselling may be helpful.

The CIPD's *Statement on Counselling in the Workplace* makes it clear that effective counselling is not merely a matter of pastoral care for individuals, but is very much in the organisation's interests.

(a) Appropriate use of counselling tools can prevent under performance, reduce labour turnover and absenteeism and increase commitment from employees. Unhappy employees are far more likely to seek employment elsewhere.

(b) Effective counselling demonstrates an organisation's commitment to and concern for its employees and so is liable to improve loyalty and enthusiasm among the workforce.

(c) The development of employees is of value to the organisation, and counselling can give employees the confidence and encouragement necessary to take responsibility for self and career development.

(d) Workplace counselling recognises that the organisation may be contributing to the employees' problems and therefore it provides an opportunity to reassess organisational policy and practice.

The counselling process

Managers may be called on to use their expertise to help others make informed decisions or solve problems by:

(a) **Advising:** offering information and recommendations on the best course of action. This is a relatively *directive* role, and may be called for in areas where you can make a key contribution to the *quality* of the decision: advising an employee about the best available training methods, say, or about behaviours which are considered inappropriate in the workplace.

(b) **Counselling:** facilitating others through the process of defining and exploring their own problems and coming up with their own solutions. This is a relatively *non-directive* role, and may be called for in areas where you can make a key contribution to the *ownership* of the decision: helping employees to formulate learning goals, for example, or to cope with work (and sometimes non-work) problems.

The counselling process has three broad stages (*Egan*).

Step 1 **Reviewing the current scenario**: helping people to identify, explore and clarify their problem situations and unused opportunities. This is done mostly by listening, encouraging them to tell their 'story', and questioning/probing to help them to see things more clearly.

Step 2 of clear goals and objectives. This is done mostly by encouraging them to envisage their desired outcome, and what it will mean for them (in order to motivate them to make the necessary changes).

Step 3 **Determining how to get there:** helping people to develop action strategies for accomplishing goals, for getting what they want. This is done mostly by encouraging them to explore options and available resources, select the best option and plan their next steps.

Confidentiality is central to the counselling process. There will be situations when an employee cannot be completely open unless he is sure that his comments will be treated confidentially. However, certain information, once obtained by the organisation (for example, about fraud or sexual harassment) calls for action. In spite of the drawbacks, therefore, the CIPD statement is clear that employees must be made aware when their comments will be passed on to the relevant authority, and when they will be treated completely confidentially.

EXAMPLE

'The findings of more than 80 studies on workplace counselling show that 90% of employees are highly satisfied with the process and outcome. Evidence suggests that counselling helps to relieve work-related stress and reduces sickness absence rates by up to half. That view is borne out by Mike Doig, medical director at Chevron Europe: "For every $1 spent on workplace counselling, $6–$10 was saved for our company, with the workforce receiving the direct benefit," ' he says. (*People Management*, May 2003)

4.8 Employee assistance programmes (EAPs)

Recognising the difficulty of providing an effective counselling service in-house and also the special skills involved, a notable modern trend is to use outsiders for employee support.

Companies such as EAR, Focus, and ICAS provide Employee Assistance Programmes (EAPs), offering a 24-hour telephone line with instant access to a trained counsellor. Meetings can be face-to-face if the employee wants, and their immediate families are also covered by the scheme. The providers offer thorough briefing on the scheme for all employees, and management information and consultancy for the employers.

NOTES

An article in *People Management* (12 October, 2000) laid out how to get the best from an EAP.

What to look for in an EAP

- Effective promotion of services

- Easy access – normally through a round-the-clock operations centre

- Expert consultation and training for managers, HR and occupational health professionals

- Confidential, appropriate and timely assessment of problems

- 'Brief-focused' professional counselling

- Referrals to long-term treatment

- Follow-up and monitoring of employees who access clinical services

- Crisis support after critical incidents

Dos and don'ts for the HR manager

Do   use the programme yourself

press for a dedicated EAP account manager

insist that complaints are fully investigated

check take-up figures each year

check the capabilities of the operations centre

check up on clinical procedures, counsellors' qualifications and supervision processes

intervene quickly during critical incidents and bigger crises

encourage managers and supervisors to use the EAP

Don't   expect your EAP provider to be proactive on all of these issues

imagine that your firm is receiving a high-quality EAP – verify it yourself.

Chapter roundup

- The traditional welfare function was legalistic/reactive or paternalist in its orientation, and regarded as entirely 'soft'. The new welfare model, while meeting its legal obligations (in traditional health and safety and welfare benefits and services) is more positive, pro-active, holistic, flexible and strategic in aiming to improve employee performance.

- Occupational health and safety are key areas of legislation and regulation. The Health and Safety at Work Act and regulations implementing EU Directives cover many areas of policy and practice.

- The modern workplace contains many potential hazards and particular attention must be given to accident prevention and reporting.

- Issues in the new welfare model include: work-life balance and stress management; ergonomics; positive health promotion; and meeting emerging health issues such as substance abuse and HIV/AIDS.

- Counselling in the workplace and Employee Assistance Programmes are two ways of accessing help.

Quick quiz

1   Give reasons for the importance of health and safety at work.

2   What are the health risks associated with VDU use?

3   What is the cost of accidents to an employer?

4   What preventative action could be taken to reduce the possibility of illness or accidents at the workplace?

5   What are the duties placed on an employee by the Health and Safety at Work Act 1974?

6   What additional duties have been placed on employers by recent regulations?

7   What are the major work-related causes of stress?

8   What is ergonomics?

9   What might be the components of an HIV/AIDS policy?

10 What is an Employee Assistance Programme?

Answers to quick quiz

1   To protect employees from pain and suffering; legal obligations; the cost of workplace accidents; to improve the company's image.   (see introduction)

2   Various manifestations of RSI.   (para 1.2)

3   Time lost by employees and management; cost of first aid and staff; cost of disrupted work.   (para 2.2)

4   Safety consciousness; consultation and participation; adequate instruction; minimal materials handling; safety devices on machines; good maintenance; codes of practice.   (para 2.3)

5   To take reasonable care of self and others; to allow employers to carry out their duties.   (para 3.1)

6   Risk assessment; risk control; information on risks and hazards; revise and initiate safety policies; identify 'at risk' employees; training; competence of advisers; consultation with employees.   (para 3.2)

7   Job demands; role conflict; role ambiguity; role overload and underload; responsibility for others; lack of social support; non-participation in decision making.   (para 4.2)

8   The study of the relationship between people and their working environment.   (para 4.3)

9   Equal opportunities for employees with HIV/AIDS; emphasis on low risk of infection; education on safe practices; counselling of employees with HIV (or HIV positive partners).   (para 4.6)

10 A contract for counselling services with an external service provider.   (para 4.8)

Answers to activities

1,2   Your own environment and experience – but the text in paragraph 1.2 should give you some ideas. If you spot any hazards: make a report and submit it to the relevant person in authority!

3   Again, your own research: learn to use the real-life resources you have available to you!

4   You should have spotted the following hazards.

(a) Heavy object on high shelf
(b) Standing on swivel chair
(c) Lifting heavy object incorrectly
(d) Open drawers blocking passageway
(e) Trailing wires
(f) Electric bar fire
(g) Smouldering cigarette unattended
(h) Overfull waste bin
(i) Overloaded socket
(j) Carrying too many cups of hot liquid
(k) Dangerous invoice 'spike'

If you can see others, you are probably right.

5   Up to you: have fun!

6   Your own research: do think the questions through, once you have gathered your data!

7   How about: risk assessment; feedback; systems and procedures; attention of all employees and contractors; monitor and audit; full review.

8   Some areas you might have thought of include:

(a) Alcohol on the premises
(b) Drug taking (including prescription drugs) on the premises
(c) Horse play and practical jokes
(d) Noise (or 'acoustic shock'), particularly from headset use.
(e) Workplace behaviour: running, throwing things, etc
(f) Tiredness (dangerous objects, dust, slippery objects etc)

9   Your own experience. Be as honest as you can. If you aren't doing much to control your stress, consider doing some further research on the list of techniques following the activity.

10   Some suggestions are: shouting, swearing; persistent public criticism; ridicule and name-calling; threats; physical intimidation (use of threatening body language or actual violence); sexual harassment; racial vilification; victimisation in applying work rules; deliberately allocating difficult or unpleasant tasks to an individual; sabotaging the individual's work complaining to other staff or supervisors about the individual; multiple grievance or disciplinary actions and so on.

11   Symptoms typically include: avoidance of supervisors and workmates; uncharacteristic aggression, mood swings and variations in work pace; sloppy appearance, signs of hangover; hand tremors, gastric upsets, insomnia; financial difficulties and relationship problems; bizarre excuses for work deficiencies; increased accidents and absences for ill health. (Similar

symptoms apply to drug abuse, with the addition of: dilated or contracted pupils in the eyes; sudden 'nodding off'; slurred speech; uncontrolled laughter or tears; sloppy appearance and unsteady movements but without the smell of alcohol.)

12   The need for workplace counselling can arise in many different situations. your answer should include five of the following.

(a)   During appraisal

(b)   In grievance or disciplinary situations

(c)   Following change, such as promotion or relocation

(d)   On redundancy or dismissal

(e)   As a result of domestic or personal difficulties, alcoholism, drug abuse, HIV/AIDS

(f)   In cases of sexual harassment or violence at work.

Chapter 12:
INTERNATIONAL HRM

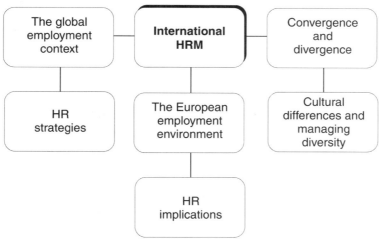

Introduction

We have already made some international comparisons in the context of specific HR policies and practices, in earlier chapters: similar comparisons will be made in Parts C and D of this Course Book with reference to employment development and employee relations. The key point, however, is that there are very many complex differences in the culture, law and practice relating to HRM from nation to nation.

In this chapter, we draw together the threads of an international perspective on HRM.

We begin by considering the implications of **cross-national transfer of people**: the impact of globalisation on the labour market and human resource planning, policy and practice.

We then go on to consider the implications of **cross-national transfer of HRM values and practices**: the extent to which there is (or should be) convergence or divergence.

Finally, we look at the ways in which **national cultures** differ, and the implications of this for the management of **diversity** in the workplace, following on from our discussion in Chapter 10.

This is clearly a vast area of study. We recommend that you use this brief overview to identify your own areas of interest and to guide you in follow-up reading (in the press, international HR journals and so on).

Your objectives

In this chapter you will learn about the following.

    (a)   The impact of globalisation on human resource planning and policy

    (b)   The HRM implications of European Union

    (c)   Areas of convergence and divergence in international HRM

    (d)   The impact of different national cultures, and ways of managing a culturally diverse workforce

NOTES

1 INTERNATIONAL HRM

Definition

> **International HRM** is 'the process of employing and developing people in international organisations... It means working across national boundaries to formulate and implement... strategies, policies and practices which can be applied to an international workforce.'
> (Armstrong, 2003)

1.1 The global employment context

People are increasingly likely to work in an organisation that has multinational or multiethnic elements, whether based in their own national culture, or in another culture at home or abroad. In some respects, a global labour market has developed in recent decades, because of such factors as:

- Domestic skill/education shortages, encouraging international recruitment – which in turn has been facilitated by social policy harmonisation (eg freedom of labour movement within the European Economic Area)

- The emergence, with political change, of new markets in areas such as Eastern Europe, South-East Asia and China.

- The development of integrated trading blocs such as NAFTA (North American Free Trade Agreement), the European Union, and the World Trade Organisation.

- The 'shrinking' of the world through Information and Communication Technology (ICT) developments and travel. There are now 'virtual organisations' scattered geographically around the globe, in which people work together via e-mail, the Internet, web-conferencing and so on.

- The pressures of globalised competition. Under the ethos of globalisation, local markets are considered too small to justify the costs of developing and marketing new products. This has encouraged the growth of multinational corporations operating outside national boundaries, and an increase in international mergers, acquisitions, joint ventures and strategic alliances.

At the same time, however, geo-political 'chunking' (the separatist aspirations of political/ethnic/religious movements, as in the Balkan states) is creating new and more culturally complex markets.

> **Activity 1** (15 minutes)
>
> What barriers to a common, global employment environment can you foresee? What, for example, might prevent a UK organisation from recruiting in China?

1.2 Characteristics and challenges of cross-national HRM

Torrington (1994) suggests that international personnel management has seven key characteristics.

1. **Cosmopolitan.** People who cope well with cross-national management tend to be culturally flexible, multi-lingual and geographically mobile.

2. **Culture.** Cross-national management faces major diversity in terms of cultural backgrounds and values.

3. **Compensation.** There are complex issues in the remuneration of people working outside their country of origin, and of ensuring a balance of equity and market rate across different national labour markets.

4. **Communication.** The flow of information and network of relationships must be maintained between geographically dispersed units of the business.

5. **Co-ordination.** Formal and informal methods must be used to ensure integration of the direction and effort.

6. **Competence.** Cross-national (and cross-cultural) working requires the definition, resourcing and development of a wider set of competences than intra-national working.

7. **Consultancy.** Where local requirements outstrip business competence in a given unit, there is a greater need to bring in expertise (from local partners or consultants, or from the parent company if the requirement is to transfer particular policies or practices from the 'home' nation).

Torrington suggests that international HRM is in many ways qualitatively similar to HRM within the borders of a single country – but on a wider scale, involving greater variety and complexity. However, Armstrong (2003) argues that international HRM is likely to be significantly more demanding than intra-national management for four reasons.

(a) **The complexity of the workforce mix.** International organisations may include 'home' country nationals working in subsidiaries abroad, as well as foreign nationals working in the 'home' country or a third 'host' country (eg Europeans working for a UK-owned firm in the US). This particularly impacts on HRM because of the legal complexities of labour mobility.

(b) **The management of diversity.** Different nations vary (as we see throughout this chapter) on a number of key dimensions, including cultural values and norms, social systems and legal requirements.

(c) **The need for communication.** International co-ordination poses huge information and communication challenges. In the field of HRM, face-to-face communication is particularly important – and not easily substituted.

(d) **Resourcing 'world-wide capabilities'.** International operations must recruit and retain people with the skills to deal with the complexities of cross-border and cross-cultural management.

NOTES

1.3 HR and internationalisation strategy

HR issues will have a key influence on the strategic management of multi-national organisations. The choice of a base of foreign operations, or the decision of whether to set up a foreign subsidiary or enter into a joint venture or strategic alliance with foreign partners, for example, might be influenced by a number of HR factors, including:

(a) Labour costs

(b) Skills available in the local or national labour market: government policy on education and training, available recruitment avenues and media and so on

(c) Employment legislation, controlling the employment relationships (eg health and safety regulation, minimum wage)

(d) Industrial relations culture, trade union power

(e) Language, cultural and social differences that would make transfer of HR practices (and/or the use of expatriate staff) difficult to implement.

1.4 Human resourcing strategy

Multi-nationals will have to develop specific human resourcing strategies about whether to use 'local' labour, or labour from the 'parent' (head office) country, especially in regard to:

(i) Managerial staff, in order to transfer consistent HR (and business) culture and practices to the international operation

(ii) Technical and professional staff, since equivalent skills or qualifications may not be available in all nations in which the firm wishes to operate.

The range of strategies may be broadly summarised as follows.

Strategy	Advantages	Disadvantages
Key positions are filled with nationals of the 'parent' country. Eg: a US multinational transfers US employees to key positions in foreign subsidiaries.	Facilitates the transfer of the distinctive culture and practices of the parent company to the overseas subsidiary (or project), especially where straight-forward overseas expansion is involved.	• Expatriates find it difficult to adjust to the environment and culture of work/management in the foreign country. • May alienate local employees, because of reward disparity or lack of promotion opportunities.
Key positions are filled by local nationals, although overall control is retained by senior management in the 'parent' country. Eg: a US multinational recruits within Italy to find managers for its Italian subsidiary.	Avoids difficulties of expatriate employment.	• May be cultural/linguistic/priority barriers to co-operation between local and 'parent' country management. • Little genuine cross-cultural experience on either side.

Strategy	Advantages	Disadvantages
Key positions are filled by the best available people, regardless of nationality. Eg: a US multinational recruits a German to manage a UK subsidiary.	Develops genuine cross-cultural experience.	• Difficult to implement, given 'protectionist' employment policies. • Requires strong corporate culture, communication and co-ordination.

'**Offshoring**' is a major trend of globalisation, whereby organisations in developed countries outsource functions to another group company or third party overseas, in order to take advantage of large, low-cost and increasingly well-educated labour forces in countries such as India and China. This has been traditional in areas such as manufacturing and printing, but has more recently spread to financial services and other service industries: call centres, research and 'back-office' operations are extensively off-shored, using ICT developments such as the Internet to co-ordinate and control operations.

EXAMPLE

As part of workforce restructuring, **IBM** recently 'offshored' a large number of highly-skilled IT jobs from developed economies – mainly the United States – to Bangalore in India, Shanghai and the north-eastern city of Dalian in China and to Sumare in Brazil.

'Where the IBM initiative differs from what has gone before is that it highlights the fact that developed countries are losing skilled service-sector jobs that have hitherto been seen as offering secure and well-paid employment opportunities. Such services have traditionally been seen as non-tradeable but increasingly more and more jobs in the sector have, thanks largely to the globalising power of the Internet, become internationally mobile. All knowledge-based activities – financial services, communications, health, education, architecture, the law, media – are discovering that the natural protection they have enjoyed in the past is fast diminishing...'

(Walsh, 2004)

Activity 2	**(10 minutes)**

What are the HRM implications raised by the example given above?

1.5 Human resource development

There may need to be strategies for developing required skills in overseas labour markets where they are currently underdeveloped, for example through the systematic education and training of employees, or the wider sponsorship of education and technical training in the community.

International HRM itself requires the organisation to recruit, retain and/or develop 'cognitively complex self-monitoring managers who have global perspectives and boundary spanning capabilities' (Huczynski & Buchanan, 2001).

- **Cognitively complex**: able to use multiple-solution models rather than 'one best way' approaches
- **Self-monitoring**: personally flexible, sensitive to verbal and non-verbal messages, and able to adjust their behaviour to the social demands of different cultures
- **Global perspectives**: having an understanding of the interrelated and systemic nature of the global community and economy
- **Boundary spanning capabilities**: able to act as interpreters between their own and other cultures

Schneider and Barsoux (1997) suggest that individual background impacts on cross-cultural competence: exposure to different cultures at an early age (via multi-cultural environments, travel or media) develops flexibility. However, these skills can also be enhanced by human resource development strategies which:

(a) Offer diversified work experience in international or multi-cultural settings

(b) Offer relevant awareness and skills training (language learning, cultural briefings, cross-cultural interpersonal skills training)

(c) Encourage networking with professionals of other relevant cultures

(d) Encourage learning through all cross-cultural interactions in the workplace.

1.6 Labour mobility issues

Article 48 of the Treaty of Rome protects the free movement of 'workers' (including part-time and economically-active self-employed workers) within the European Economic Area. The general principle is that people coming to the UK for the purposes of employment (excluding short 'business visits') require a **work permit**, but nationals from within the EEA have a right to work anywhere in the EEA *without* permits.

Work permits for non-EEA nationals are tightly controlled, but the Employment Department tends to require less information where the post is a transfer within an international group; is at board level (or equivalent); is in a skill area recognised to be scarce in the EU; or is essential to a project which will bring investment and jobs into the UK.

A combination of immigration rules and agreements within the EU have complicated the position on UK firms' employment of non-UK nationals. Under the new **Immigration, Asylum and Nationality Act 2006**, it is a criminal offence to employ an illegal migrant worker.

(a) Employers are required to view a number of official documents provided by a recruit prior to the first day of employment – with additional checking requirements, designed to prevent document fraud, set out in the *Immigration (Restrictions on Employment) Order 2004*. This in itself has been a source of concern to recruiters (particularly in the hospitality, catering and construction industries) who receive large numbers of job applications from candidates who do not have work permits, or who present forged or stolen documents.

(b) On the other hand, extensive background checks into the immigration or work permit status of foreign recruits 'suspected' of being illegal immigrants lay employers open to claims of discrimination under the *Race Relations Act*.

Additional proposals have been put forward by the Borders and Immigration Agency (BIA) for all working migrants to be sponsored by an employer. The BIA would maintain a register of accredited sponsors, from which a business could be removed if it failed to maintain a good practice/compliance rating. The EU is also considering measures to prevent illegal employment of foreign nationals. Watch this space...

FOR DISCUSSION

'The Commission for Racial Equality (CRE) has claimed that Internet job site **Monster.co.uk** could be acting unlawfully after it deleted the CVs of jobseekers with links to countries that are out of favour with the US.

'According to US legislation, US companies and their subsidiaries are prevented from trading goods, technology and services with Iran, Iraq, Syria, Sudan, Myanmar (Burma), Cuba, Libya and North Korea. As a result, Monster's European director of communications said, Monster had applied the policy to its UK arm...

'The CRE said that applying the rule to jobs based in the UK could be unlawful under the Race Relations Act 1976. Razia Karim, head of legal policy at the CRE, said: "... As a recruitment agency, Monster may be discriminating in preventing these nationalities from applying for jobs based in Britain." '

(Watkins & Staines, 2003)

What issues does this example raise for international HRM? What kinds of differences does it highlight?

2   THE EUROPEAN EMPLOYMENT ENVIRONMENT

2.1   The European labour market

Some of the key features of the European labour market are as follows.

(a) **General and vocational education**

About 23% of the EU's population is currently in full-time education (comparable to Japan, but slightly lower than in the USA) and 25% of people stay in education after the age of 19.

Vocational Education and Training (VET) varies widely in the extent of specialisation, financing, methods of testing competence and the status and role of VET in the national education system. VET begins at an earlier age in some nations than others, and in some EU countries, vocational

NOTES

qualifications obtained at school offer equal access to higher education as 'academic' qualifications.

Although the proportion of the UK workforce with higher skills (degree or equivalent and above) is similar to France and Germany, the UK compares less well by having a higher proportion of people with low skills and a low proportion with intermediate skills.

(b) **Age structure**

As in the UK, the EU workforce is ageing (and shrinking, due to accelerating retirements).

(c) **Non-permanent employment**

Some 15% of all EU workers are estimated to be on part-time contracts, most of them women – although the proportion of working women who are in part-time jobs varies from 10% (Italy, Portugal, Greece) to 80% (Netherlands). Some countries (including France and Germany) have statutory restrictions on the use of temporary employees.

2.2 HR implications of European Union

The implications for European HRM are still being worked out in detail, as EU directives are enacted in the law of member states, and other aspects of European social policy are still subject to negotiation and amendment. However, HR practitioners will need to be aware of the following issues.

(a) **Compliance with EU law** across a wide range of employment issues (as discussed in relevant chapters of this Course Book).

(b) **Differences in specific law and practice** in countries where the organisation may intend to recruit. The Posted Worker Directive provides that any employee posted to a foreign country for more than three months is entitled to the protection of the employment laws of the host country (minimum wage, working hours, notice periods and so on) rather than those of his or her home country, so that organisations cannot cut corners on employment protection by contracting labour from countries where the law is weaker.

(c) **The need for workers to be cross-educated in the languages and cultures of other states**: language is not an area amenable to harmonisation!

(d) **The mobility of labour within the EU**, allowing residence and permit-free working for full-time, part-time and economically active self-employed workers from all member states of the European Economic Area. The recognition and comparison of **qualifications** is a key related issue for recruitment, reward and development: harmonised standards for Higher Educational Diplomas (HEDs) in specific professions and industry-based 'Certificates of Experience' are designed to facilitate mobility of qualified workers.

(e) **Implications of European Monetary Union.** Although the UK has not joined the EMU, the 'euro' has been the accepted currency of business in the EU since 1999, and national currencies have been phased out. This raises issues such as: the prospect of pan-European pay bargaining and settlements; the increased importance of European Works Councils for such pay bargaining; the need to reassess corporate structures in view of their potential for mergers and acquisitions, and opportunities for central payroll administrations.

(f) **Potential pan-European HRM:** cross-border head-hunting and recruitment advertising, choice of international education and training avenues, management of expatriate management and staff, training in relevant EU markets (and product standards and other differences), management of diversity, welfare for dislocated staff and families, pan-European reward harmonisation and so on.

EXAMPLE

A feature in *People Management* (3 June 1999) described the Eurofighter programme, a four-nation exercise in political, technical, cultural and management integration between British Aerospace, Daimler Chrysler Aerospace (Dasa) of Germany, Alenia Aerospazio of Italy and Construcciones Aeronauticas of Spain, run by a German management company in Germany. Here are some soundbites on the HR issues (as identified by the German HR director) and the techniques used.

> The project's official language is English, and all the teams are multi-national, so fluency is essential. 'The southern Europeans feel disadvantaged... The Spanish especially will not admit that they haven't understood something – they simply agree. And you have to be sensitive to varying language skills.' Eurofighter has an open learning centre with language facilities...
>
> But cultural differences go deeper. 'The decision-making process is different... The Latins need consensus and aren't empowered to make decisions. The Germans come closer to the Anglo-Saxon model of responsibility, but the Latins need more social contact, which develops trust. It's something we can learn from them'...
>
> There is a handover period for new employees, who are coached by the previous incumbents. They are briefed on local law, including the formalities of registering with the town hall, their entitlement to state benefits, the availability of local services, and – vital to the British contingent, according to [the German HR director] – the fact that cycling drunk in Bavaria is an offence that could cost you your driving licence. Each partner company has a sponsor – a senior manager in Eurofighter – who looks after the welfare of its employees and their families while in Germany...
>
> Managers need extra training to comply with German employment laws such as the rigid agreements on working hours and the role of the works council. 'You can't do overtime without authorisation.' Through the 'right of co-determination' legislation, works councils have the right to negotiate on all terms and conditions. Everyone has to comply, right up to the managing director. Yet it's not a confrontational relationship. 'This is a nightmare for British managers, who are used to the union system.'
>
> 'People here are very experienced. If the organisation is limiting them, they need to be given permission to act. We threw away all the terms of reference from the old days. Job descriptions, for example, were sometimes years old and did not reflect reality... Managers were given responsibility for designing their own jobs, and the works council backed the changes... 'Everyone now has a dynamic job description that is updated twice a year. It is job enlargement. This does frighten people, but we try to support them.'
>
> Appraisals are a tradition familiar to BAE staff, but other people have had less experience of implementing them successfully. Dasa had an appraisal programme, but it had not provided effective feedback for junior staff. The Spanish had appraisals only for senior managers, while the Italians had no comparable system at all...'

2.3 Harmonisation and divergence between states

The intention of EU policy appears to be the convergence or harmonisation of employment law and practice in member states. However, the protection of common minimum standards and principles does not in itself create a 'pan-European' model for HRM. Member states still vary widely from each other (and from the UK) in:

(a) Their culture (discussed further in Section 6 below), which may dictate different approaches to motivation and reward, employee relations, discrimination issues and so on

(b) The extent of State intervention in employment practices, according to political ideology, and the extent to which regulation, prescription and bureaucratisation is accepted in national culture and systems

(c) Their economic, technical and social development: standard of living, rates of unemployment, pressures on public sector expenditure, communication systems and other infrastructures, taxation incentives and disincentives to particular practices and so on

(d) The specific issues that affect their labour markets: for example, the extent of immigration from non-EU countries, trade agreements with other trading blocs and so on.

(e) Their specific national laws and practices.

FOR DISCUSSION

'A French manager working in a subsidiary of an American corporation that insisted upon an open-door policy may well leave his office door open – thus adjusting to the behavioural requirements of the corporate culture – without any modification whatsoever to his basic concept of managerial authority.' (Laurent, cited by Beardwell & Holden, 1997)

What does this suggest about the 'transferability' of HRM approaches? Do you think there is any possibility of a truly international model of HRM – or is the model too hard to pin down even within one country?

Having already mentioned harmonisation and differences in HR policy and practice within the European Union, we will now go on to look more generally at issues of convergence and divergence in international HRM.

3 CONVERGENCE AND DIVERGENCE IN HRM

As we noted in relation to the European Union, there are attempts to 'harmonise' social and HRM policy for greater consistency and fairness across national borders, and to facilitate the free movement of labour: this process is known as '**convergence**'. However, there is also '**divergence**': differentiation in response to local conditions and requirements.

Individual trans-national organisations face the same pressures to standardise their HR policies as far as possible in the various countries in which they operate (in order to preserve their distinctive organisation culture, operating style and internal equity) while recognising the need for divergence in the face of environmental differences. The classic challenge is to **'think global, act local'**: to achieve consistency and equity in core activities and values, while allowing flexibility in non-core activities and values.

3.1 Convergence

It may be argued that the 'activities' of HRM – HR planning, recruitment and selection, appraisal and reward, training and development, welfare, discipline, employee exit and employee relations – are common to organisations everywhere. The need to attract, retain, motivate and develop employees (the 'aims' of HRM) are universal.

The globalisation of business and communications has also encouraged:

- The exchange and sharing of certain technical terms, theories and practices: for example, the widespread adoption of Swedish-style autonomous working groups or Japanese-style quality circles

- The standardisation of certain HR techniques, such as job evaluation and 360° appraisal

- The subordination of national culture and national employment practices to corporate culture and HRM practices, which is a recognised tendency of international HRM.

In this sense, there seems to be a convergence of HR policy and practice. Schneider and Barsoux (1997) suggest that alongside the 'convergence myth' of the global village, there is a belief in the convergence of management practice and competence. According to this belief, 'management is management': principles and techniques (such as performance management) can be effective anywhere. With economic, technological and managerial development, business cultures worldwide will be brought into line.

FOR DISCUSSION

How 'universal' should human rights standards (which affect the treatment of employees by multinational corporations) be? What other areas of HRM (if any) do you think should be subject to globally consistent standards?

Extensive international research does not, however, bear out this idea of a common culture of management. While structures and technologies may converge, there is still enough diversity to encourage divergence. The fact is that although everybody 'does' HRM – they seem to do it differently!

3.2 Divergence

Bratton & Gold (2007) point to comparative research suggesting that there are significant differences between Asian, European and North American companies with regard to HR strategies. They note that: 'The employment relationship is shaped by national systems of employment legislation and the cultural contexts in which it operates. Thus, as the world of business is becoming more globalised, variations in national regulatory systems, labour markets and institutional and cultural contexts are likely to constrain or shape any tendency towards "convergence" or a "universal" model of best HRM practice.'

A number of factors contribute to divergence.

(a) **Cultural factors**, arising from the history, traditions, language, social development and values and religious beliefs of different countries and ethnic groups. Culture amounts to a national way of doing and perceiving things. Cultural factors influence management/worker models, career expectations, perceptions and attitudes to work, education and training needs and so on, and are reflected in the culture of the organisation.

(b) **National legal frameworks.** Specific laws and regulations, and the systems by which they are derived, vary markedly from state to state. The extent of political/legal intervention in employment underscores the cultural dimension.

(c) **Structural factors.** Education and training systems influence the skills available in the labour pool, and therefore HRP, recruitment and development policies. Demographic factors likewise affect the structure of the labour market. Technological and communication infrastructures affect the way in which work is performed and structured, since work organisation and employment policies are different (as the UK experience has shown) in a fast-changing high-tech market than in a low-tech industrial market. Political factors also influence HRM via government intervention.

(d) **Employee relations traditions and ideologies**: the degree of state involvement in industrial conflict and regulation; government support for the unionisation or anti-unionisation of the workforce; collectivisation or individualisation of employment relationships; traditions of co-operation or conflict in industrial relations.

(e) **National economic development**: unemployment levels, rates of inflation, rate of economic growth, balance of trade: the extent of competition in the local product markets (encouraging HRM for competitive edge) and labour markets (encouraging HRM for attracting and retaining skills).

Activity 3 (30 minutes)

A Brainstorm a number of cultural dimensions or values on which societies might differ. (Think about all aspects of life that might impact on attitudes in employment.) Suggest examples where possible.

Weblinks

You might like to check out some HR professional bodies and journals around the world, for case studies and insights into HR law and practice in other cultures

HR Magazine (USA) and the Society for HRM
►► **hppt://www.shrm.org/hrmagazine**

HR Monthly (Australia) and the Australian HR Institute
►► **http://www.ahri.com.all**

Japan Society for Human Resource Management
►► **http://www.jshrm.org**

Hong Kong Institute of HRM
►► **http://hkihrm.Org**

3.3 Comparative HRM

Definition

Comparative HRM is 'a systematic method of investigation relating to two or more countries, which... seeks to explain the patterns and variations encountered in cross-national HRM.'   (Bratton & Gold, 2003)

We will now look in some detail at national culture, as one of the key factors in comparative HRM and the management of diversity.

4   CULTURAL DIFFERENCES AND MANAGING DIVERSITY

4.1   What is culture?

Schein (1985) defined culture as 'a set of basic assumptions – shared solutions to universal problems of external adaptation (how to survive) and internal integration (how to stay together) – which have evolved over time and are handed down from one generation to the next'.

Manifestations of culture include:

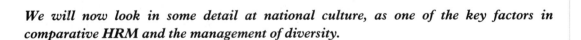

(a)   **Behaviour**: norms of personal and interpersonal behaviour including forms of address, communication styles, expression of emotion and so on

(b)   **Artefacts**: concrete expressions such as art and architecture, dress codes and symbols

(c)   **Rituals**: patterns of collective behaviour which have customary or symbolic value, such as business formalities and social courtesies

(d)   **Underlying values and beliefs**, which invest the behaviour, artefacts and rituals with meaning. For example, the size of a person's office may imply status and honour, or reflect the importance of privacy within a culture: it 'means' more than the surface suggests.

Activity 4   **(30 minutes)**

Select another culture with which you have had some contact (perhaps working or studying with someone from another culture).

What behaviours have you noticed that are different from the norms of your own culture?

What values do you think might underlie these behaviours?

How easy is it to interpret the cultural values underlying differences in behaviour?

4.2   Globalisation and cultural differences

There is a prevailing sense that 'the world is getting smaller'. Travel, migration, multiculturalism and globalised communications and commerce (especially e-commerce) have eroded national distinctives in what societies wear and eat, what they buy, and how they view themselves in relation to the world. National boundaries are being broken down and global concerns (not just free trade, but social and economic justice and the environment) have gained increasing profile.

Does this mean that cultures are converging? Or, as Guirdham (1999) puts it: 'Are cultural differences disappearing so fast that it is unnecessary to allow for them?' If we look at people wearing jeans, drinking Coke, watching CNN and eating McDonalds in Moscow – or eating sushi in London – we may be tempted to think so. But these are essentially the surface expressions of culture, not the 'deep' culture of worldview and social organisation.

Ethnic separatist movements, ethnic clusters in multicultural cities (eg a 'Chinatown' or 'Little Italy') and anti-globalisation movements testify to the enduring power of cultural distinctives. Moreover, these cultural distinctives have been identified as a source of:

- Competitive advantage or disadvantage in domestic and international markets

- Friction in cross-cultural business relationships and

- Success or failure in reaching cross-cultural markets

EXAMPLE

Consider a project on the scale of the London Olympics in 2012...

> Every service organisation around London needs to undertake **culture training** now and until 2012. However well the games are organised, there are huge benefits to be gained by ensuring that global visitors have a positive experience.

(*People Management*, 14 June 2007)

We will look at two influential models of national cultural differences.

4.3 The Hofstede Model

Hofstede (1984, 1991) carried out cross-cultural research at 66 national offices of IBM and formulated one of the most influential models of work-related cultural differences.

The Hofstede model describes four primary dimensions of differences (predominant traits) between national cultures, which impact on all aspects of organisational behaviour: motivation, team working, leadership style, conflict management, HR practices and so on.

Power distance: the extent to which unequal distribution of power is accepted.

High PD cultures accept greater centralisation, a top-down chain of command and closer supervision. Subordinates have little expectation of influencing decisions. White collar jobs are valued more than blue collar jobs.	*Low* PD cultures expect less centralisation and flatter organisational structures. Subordinates expect involvement and participation in decision-making. Clerical and manual jobs are equally valued.

Uncertainty avoidance: the extent to which security, order and control are preferred to ambiguity, uncertainty and change.

High UA cultures respect control, certainty and ritual. They value task structure, written rules and regulations, specialists and experts, and standardisation. There is a strong need for consensus: deviance and dissent are not tolerated. The work ethic is strong. People are risk-averse and experience more stress.	*Low* UA cultures respect flexibility and creativity. They have less task structure and written rules; more generalists and greater variability. There is more tolerance of risk, dissent, conflict and deviance from norms. People take each day as it comes: there is less stress.

Individualism: the extent to which people prefer to live and work in individualist (focusing on the 'I' identity) or collectivist (focusing on the 'we' identity) ways.

High Individualism cultures emphasise autonomy and individual choice and responsibility. They prize individual initiative. The organisation is impersonal and tends to defend business interests: task achievement is more important than relationships. Management is seen in an individual context.

Low Individualism (or Collectivist) cultures interdependence, reciprocal obligation and social acceptability. The organisation is seen as a 'family' and tends to defend employees' interests: relationships are more important than task achievement. Management is seen in a team context.

Masculinity: the extent to which social gender roles are distinct. (Note that this is different from the usual sense in which the terms 'masculine' and 'feminine' are used.)

High Masculinity cultures clearly differentiate gender roles. Masculine values of assertiveness, competition, decisiveness and material success are dominant. Feminine values of modesty, tenderness, consensus, focus on relationships and quality of working life are secondary (and confined to women).

Low Masculinity (or Femininity) cultures minimise gender roles. Feminine values are dominant and both men and women are allowed to behave accordingly.

Each of these dimensions is a continuum. Hofstede placed various cultures on the continuum as follows.

Cultural group		Power distance	Uncertainty avoidance	Individualism	Masculinity
I	More developed Latin (Belgium, France, Italy, Argentina, Brazil, Spain)	High	High	Medium to high	Medium
II	Less developed Latin (Portugal, Mexico, Peru)	High	High	Low	Whole range
III	More developed Asian (Japan)	Medium	High	Medium	High
IV	Less developed Asian (India, Taiwan, Thailand)	High	Low to medium	Low	Medium
V	Near Eastern (Greece, Iran, Turkey)	High	High	Low	Medium

Cultural group	Power distance	Uncertainty avoidance	Individualism	Masculinity
VI Germanic (Germany, Austria, German Swiss)	Low	Medium to high	Medium	Medium to high
VII Anglo (UK, US, Australia, Canada)	Low to medium	Low to medium	High	High
VIII Nordic (Scandinavia, Netherlands)	Low	Low to medium	Medium to high	Low

Activity 5   **(20 minutes)**

According to the Hofstede model, what issues might arise in the following cases?

(a) A Swedish company sets up a subsidiary in Brazil under a Swedish general manager, who wishes to import Scandinavian decision-making styles.

(b) The newly appointed Spanish HR manager of a UK firm asks to see the Rules and Procedures Manual for the HR department.

(c) A US-trained HR manager attempts to implement a system of Management By Objectives in Thailand.

(d) A Dutch HR manager of a US subsidiary in the Netherlands is instructed to implement downsizing measures.

4.4 The Trompenaars Model

Fons Trompenaars (1997) questioned 30,000 managers in 55 countries to identify cultural differences that may affect aspects of organisational behaviour. His findings suggested that certain cultures emphasise some values more than others, on seven key dimensions: cultures do not embody one value *or* another on each dimension, but differ in the amount of emphasis placed on each.

Universalism: behaviour is governed by the standards, rules and norms of the group Eg: North America, Switzerland, Scandinavia	**Particularism**: behaviour is governed by one's relationships with a particular individual Eg: Korea, China, Indonesia
Individualism: emphasis is on the individual and individual contribution, the 'I' identity and independence Eg: US, Eastern Europe, Denmark, Nigeria	**Collectivism**: emphasis is on the group/team contribution, the 'we' identity (firm, family) and interdependence Eg: Mexico, Indonesia, Japan, India
Affective: Issues are dealt with emotionally; emotions are openly expressed and displayed Eg: Middle East, Southern Europe	**Neutral**: issues are dealt with rationally and unemotionally, with a focus on goals Eg: Japan, Germany, UK, China, Korea
Specific: work and non-work roles and relationships are kept separate Eg: Netherlands, Sweden, US, UK	**Diffuse**: work and non-work roles and relationships are integrated and merged Eg: China, Singapore, Korea
Achievement: status is based on personal attainments and abilities Eg: North America, Norway, Austria	**Ascription**: status is based on attributes ascribed to age, gender, background etc. Eg: Egypt, Indonesia, Korea, Spain, South America
Past/present: the future is seen as growing from the past, history and tradition Eg: France, Japan, UK	**Future**: the future is seen as created fresh from a 'zero base' Eg: US, Netherlands
Internal control: individuals are in control of their own lives: they shape events Eg: North America, UK, Israel, Austria	**External control**: nature and other external forces control much of life: individuals adapt Eg: Japan, Egypt, China

Activity 6   **(no time limit)**

Prepare (and if possible, give) a 'cultural briefing' to someone of another culture, explaining what you think are the important points about your culture in a work/business setting. (You may like to use either the Hofstede or Trompenaars model as a guide.) What are the top 10 things a foreigner would need to know if doing business or working in your country? Describe it as you see it.

If possible, encourage the other person to give you a similar briefing and highlight the differences between his or her culture and your own. Consider any information that surprised you, or the other person: what does this say about cultural assumptions?

4.5 Managing cultural differences

We have already discussed some of the specific HRM policies involved in managing diversity, in Chapter 10. However, it is worth noting that cultural diversity in the workplace also requires:

- **Cultural sensitivity**: the awareness of the potential differences in perception and behaviour that arise from diversity

- **Cultural intentionality**: 'the ability to generate the thoughts, words and behaviours necessary to communicate and work effectively with a variety of diverse groups and individuals' (Ivey *et al*, 1993)

'Rather than knowing *what* to do in country X, or whether national or functional cultures are more important in multicultural teams, what is necessary is to know *how to assess the potential impact* of culture, national or otherwise, on performance.' (Schneider and Barsoux, 1997)

Attention may have to be given to cultural values and norms around:

(a) **Teambuilding**

(i) *Specificity/diffusion.* Forced camaraderie may violate the boundaries between work and non-work relationships

(ii) *Individualism/collectivism.* Team working and rewards may be more congenial to some cultures than to others.

(b) **Communication**

(i) *Language.* Language dominance may create a power or contribution imbalance in a team or negotiation.

(ii) *Communication patterns and styles.* Norms may have to be negotiated within a team or organisation in regard to: the balance of task and social communication; the style and pace of decision-making and negotiation; the nature of conflict and the style of conflict management; preferences for face-to-face or written media; the role of feedback and the style in which it is appropriately given and so on.

(iii) *Inclusive language:* ensuring that barriers to intercultural communication are not created by phrases that exclude or give offence. Biased language may reflect inappropriate or demeaning attitudes or stereotypes.

(iv) *Encouraging, integrating and balancing diverse contributions:* making sure that all members are heard and that their views are properly considered.

(v) *Different cultural values about interaction.* Some people may prefer to raise issues or ideas one-to-one rather than in a group; or in private rather than in public; or in social rather than formal settings.

(c) **Expectations of roles and relationships**

(i) Roles and styles of leadership and team member contribution

(ii) Appropriate degrees of formality and informality

(iii) The role of women, younger people and other (traditionally non-dominant) groups in business contexts.

Different expectations can be acknowledged by corporate 'diversity briefings' and awareness training. They should also be brought into the open and negotiated as part of a team 'contract' by line managers and team leaders.

The key aim is to avoid not only discrimination and harassment, but disempowerment of people from different cultures: to ensure that they are able to make a full contribution to the organisation.

Chapter roundup

- International HRM is the process of employing and developing people in international organisations. It means working across national boundaries to formulate and implement strategies, policies and practices which can be applied to an international workforce.

- Key challenges of international HRM include: the complexity of the workforce mix; the management of diversity; the need for communication; and the resourcing of 'world-wide capabilities'.

- Global HR issues will impact on the internationalisation, human resourcing and human resource development strategies of the organisation. Current practical issues affecting HR practitioners include: the trend towards offshoring and the legal ramifications of labour mobility.

- Issues in the European labour market relate to the mobility of labour, European Monetary Union, cultural and linguistic differences and continuing differences in national law and practice for companies exploring the possibilities of pan-European HRM.

- Despite some convergence in (or harmonisation of) the structure, technology and terminology of HRM across the 'global village', there is still enough diversity to support strategies of divergence. Certain aims and activities of HRM are international – but they are 'done' differently.

- Differences in policy and practice may arise from cultural factors, national law and regulation, structural factors (such as education, demographics, infrastructure, politics), employee relations traditions and ideologies, and economic and social development.

- Two influential models of the national cultural differences impacting on the workplace are the Hofstede model and the Trompenaars model.

- Managers need to exercise cultural sensitivity and intentionality, responding flexibly to cultural differences, in order to support organisational diversity policy.

Quick quiz

1   What are the seven key characteristics (7 Cs) of international HR management?

2   What is 'off-shoring'?

3   How can managers develop cross-cultural skills?

4   Outline the HR implications of European Union.

5   What aspects of HRM can be said to show 'convergence' across national boundaries?

6   What is 'comparative HRM'?

7   What are the manifestations of culture?

8   Explain the terms 'power distance, 'uncertainty avoidance', 'individualism' and 'masculinity' as they are used in the Hofstede model.

9   What are the seven dimensions on which Trompenaars distinguished national culture?

10 What is 'cultural intentionality'?

Answers to quick quiz

1   Cosmopolitan, culture, compensation, communication, co-ordination, competence, consultancy   (see paragraph 1.2)

2   Organisations in developed countries outsourcing functions to another group company or third party overseas.   (para 1.4)

3   Diversified work experience; awareness/skills training; networking; continuous learning through cross-cultural interactions.   (para 1.5)

4   See paragraph 2.2 for a full answer.

5   Basic HR activities (HRP, recruitment, selection, appraisal, training and so on); the broad aims of HRM (attract, retain, motivate, develop); technical terms and techniques (job evaluation, quality circles)   (para 3.1)

6   A systematic method of investigation relating to two or more countries, which seeks to explain the patterns and variations encountered in cross-national HRM.   (para 3.3)

7   Behaviour, artefacts, rituals, values and beliefs   (para 4.1)

8   See paragraph 4.3 for a full answer.

9   Universalism-particularism;   individualism-collectivism;   affective-neutral; specific-diffuse; achievement-ascription; past-present; internal control-external control.   (para 4.4)

10 The ability to generate the thoughts, words and behaviours necessary to communicate and work effectively with a variety of diverse groups and individuals.   (para 4.5)

Answers to activities

1   Barriers to a global labour market include: language; culture (eg the fact that women are discouraged from certain jobs in some cultures); differences in employment law and practice; recognition/equivalency of education/training qualifications; market rates of pay in different currencies (and cost of currency dealings); different expectations of working conditions; personal attachment of workers to family/country of origin.

2   Some of the issues you might have identified include:

(a)   The requirement to consult with employee representatives on redundancies, together with other redundancy procedures and compensation

(b)   Likely trade union resistance to the loss of jobs

(c)   Encouragement of trade union recruiting within the company, and potential loss of morale (because of the erosion of job security) in surviving employees

(d)   Claims of unfair dismissal by redundant employees, if relocation cannot be shown to be a justifiable 'economic, technical or organisational' reason

(e)   Impact on employer branding, given likely poor publicity, impacting on future recruitment

(f)   Poor PR in general, since off-shoring is a highly political issue

3   Here are just some of the many dimensions you may have come up with.

(a)   Attitudes to the balance of work, leisure and family life ('work ethic': traditionally more pronounced in northern/protestant countries of Europe than in Mediterranean cultures)

(b)   The importance attached to the individual vis-à-vis the group or society as a whole (individualistic like the USA; family-oriented like Latino cultures; team/organisation-oriented like Japan)

(c)   Concepts of justice, fairness and ethical dealing (definitions of 'gifts' and 'bribes', for example are fluid in eastern cultures)

(d)   The relative value of different forms of reward and incentive (money is high-value in the US: respect and belonging have high value in Asian cultures)

(e)   Attitudes towards gender roles (women in business are less accepted in Islamic and, to a lesser extent, Asian and 'macho' Latino cultures), age (the seniority culture of Asia or the youth culture of the US and Western Europe), diversity: attitude to disabled, ethnic minorities, sexual orientation, religious beliefs (including specific traditional conflicts eg in Northern Ireland and Islamic states)

(f)   Valued personal attributes and attainments (status attached to education; different styles of education and training)

(g)   Perceptions of continuity/stability/security (Japanese 'commitment' system) v mobility/risk/change (Western 'flexibility' model)

(h) Styles of interpersonal communication and decision-making (formality, reticence, consensus and hierarchy in Japan: informality, directness, authority in US: differences in eye contact and body language)

And so on...

4 Whichever specific behaviours you noted in your own experience, you may have found it difficult to interpret the values underpinning them. (Why is it more respectful in a Japanese business context to offer your business card with two hands rather than with one?) The behaviours you noted may have as much to do with the particular *individual's* personality or education or profession/occupation – or the *corporate* culture in which the behaviours were learned, as with his or her national culture.

The lesson is: beware making assumptions and interpretations. When attempting to manage a diverse workforce, it may be better to *ask* (respectfully) what people find helpful...

5 (a) A low-PD manager is likely to attempt consultative joint decision-making: high PD workers will be inexperienced and uncomfortable with such styles, preferring authoritative instruction.

(b) A high-UA manager, expecting to find detailed and generally adhered-to rules for everything, may be horrified by the adhocracy of a low-UA organisation: if (s)he attempts to impose a high-UA culture, there may be resistance from low-UA employees and management.

(c) A high-individuality manager may implement MBO on the basis of individual performance targets, results and rewards: this may fail to motivate low-individuality workers, for whom group processes and performance is more important.

(d) A low-masculinity manager may try to shelter the workforce from the effects of downsizing, taking time for consultation, retraining, voluntary measures and so on: this may seem unacceptably 'soft' to a high-masculinity parent firm.

6 Your own research.

PART C

HUMAN RESOURCE DEVELOPMENT

Chapter 13:
LEARNING AND THE LEARNING ORGANISATION

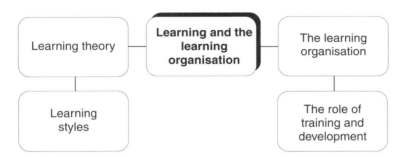

Introduction

Providing the organisation with the most suitable human resources for the task and environment is an on-going process. It involves not only recruitment and selection, as discussed in Chapters 2-4, but the training and development of employees in order to help them meet current and potential future requirements.

In recent years, there has been a shift in emphasis from **training**, as a separate activity aimed at improving competence in a particular job area, to **learning**, as the process by which individuals develop competence in *any* area, in response to changing requirements. Teaching people how to learn – and supporting their learning at and through their work – enables the organisation to develop human resources more flexibly: by fostering continuous learning to meet changing capability requirements *and* by adapting to the learning preferences and opportunities of individuals.

In this chapter we examine how people learn, and how learning might be built into organisational culture and practice. In the next chapter, we explore the systematic planning, design, implementation and evaluation of training and development. Finally, in Chapter 15, we survey a range of government-led initiatives aimed at developing life-long learning and development skills in the UK.

Your objectives

In this chapter you will learn about the following.

(a)   Learning theories

(b)   Different learning styles

(c)   The impact of the learning curve and transfer of learning

(d)   Implications of learning theories and styles for planning learning events

(e)   The learning organisation

(f)   How training contributes to the achievement of business objectives

(g)   The role of training and development policy within the organisation

1 LEARNING THEORY

1.1 Three theoretical approaches

It is not possible to put forward a simple definition of learning, because despite intensive scientific and practical work on the subject, there are different ways of understanding how the process works, what it involves, and what we mean when we say that a person 'knows' something (epistemology).

There are three basic theories of how learning works.

(a) **The behaviourist (or stimulus-response) approach.** Behaviourist psychology is based on 'empirical' epistemology (the belief that the human mind operates purely on information gained from the senses by experience) and concentrates on observable behaviour, since 'thought processes' are not amenable to scientific study. It therefore concentrates on the relationship between stimuli (input through the senses) and the organism's responses to those stimuli. The work of Pavlov (on dogs) and Skinner (on rats) suggested that learning is the formation of new connections between stimulus and response on the basis of experience, which they called **conditioning.** According to this theory, we modify our responses to a given stimulus according to whether the feedback on the results of our previous responses was good or bad: an incentive (positive reinforcement) or deterrent (negative reinforcement) to similar behaviour in future. Repetition of the stimulus-response sequence strengthens the conditioning, making us more likely to respond in the same way in future.

(b) **The cognitive (or information-processing) approach.** Cognitive psychology is based on 'rationalist' epistemology (the belief that the human mind imposes organisation and meaning on sensory raw material) and assumes that it is possible to make inferences about those thought processes. According to this theory, our behaviour is 'purposive': we make plans of action in pursuit of goals that we value. Learning is the way in which we process and interpret feedback on the results of past behaviour/experience, and make decisions about whether to maintain successful behaviours or modify unsuccessful behaviours in future, in pursuit of our goals. We do not simply learn new habits (as conditioning theories suggest) but ways of dealing with information and choosing alternative methods of reaching our goals: we learn to learn.

(c) **The social learning approach.** Studies of child development suggest that human beings are designed to learn by imitating other people who are significant to us: our behavioural and role models (who shift over time from our parents and caregivers in childhood, to peers in adolescence, to selected experts and mentors in adulthood). We define our social identity and behaviour by reflection from other people: how they respond to us. We learn to perform actions by 'modelling': watching and analysing the way others do them, and imitating the successful aspects of their performance.

Activity 1	(10 minutes)

Before reading on, pick out the aspects of the theoretical approaches above which might be important for the design of training programmes. (Think about your experiences of training/learning techniques as you read about each theory...)

Implications for training design

Whichever approach it is based on, learning theory offers certain useful propositions for the design of effective training programmes.

(a) The individual should be **motivated** to learn. The purpose and benefits of a learning activity should be made clear, according to the individual's motives or goals: reward, challenge, competence or whatever. Organisational support is critical to the effectiveness of its members' learning.

(b) Clear **goals and objectives** should be set, so that each task has some meaning. This will help trainees in the control process that leads to learning, providing targets against which performance will constantly be measured and adjusted. Motivation to learn will be enhanced if the individual has been involved in setting his or her own learning goals.

(c) Learning should be **structured** and **paced** to allow learning processes to take place effectively and progressively. Each stage of learning should present a challenge (motivation), without overloading trainees so that they lose confidence and the ability to assimilate information/experience.

(d) **Exposure to learning materials** and interactive input (from learning software and/or from coaches or facilitators) enriches the cognitive process and encourages the internalisation of learning. Case-studies, problem solving exercises and so on engage the purposive process of learning. Coaching, mentoring and team learning activities engage social earning.

(e) There should be timely, relevant **feedback** on performance and progress. This will usually be provided by the facilitator, and should be concurrent – or not long delayed. If progress reports or appraisals are given only at the course end, for example, there will be no opportunity for progressive behavioural adjustment.

(f) Positive and negative **reinforcement** should be judiciously used. Recognition and encouragement embeds correct learning and motivates further effort. Constructive criticism of errors is essential for learning, but must be used sensitively: 'punishing' error or slow progress may simply discourage the learner and create a culture of failure. (Even behaviourism notes that negative reinforcement merely conditions people to avoid error and punishment – not to find more constructive behaviours.) 'Failure' should be redefined as 'opportunity for learning'.

(g) Active **participation** in the learning experience (for example, in action learning or discovery learning) is generally more effective than passive reception (for example, in lectures or reading), because it enhances concentration and conditioning. Practice and repetition can be used to reinforce passive learning, but participation has the added effect of encouraging 'ownership' of the goals and process of change.

1.2 Stages of learning

The 'stages of learning' comprise a simple, intuitive model of the evolution of learned behaviour.

Stage 1. **Unconscious incompetence**. You aren't aware of what you don't know: you simply act in the way that seems best with the knowledge you have at the time.

Stage 2. **Conscious incompetence**. You become aware that you don't know. New information, feedback from others, or the results of your behaviour, suggest that there is something missing.

Stage 3. **Conscious competence**. You work at knowing. You research, analyse, practise, repeat, monitor, adjust. You may be competent – but it requires conscious thought and application.

Stage 4. **Unconscious competence**. You don't have to think about knowing. You have internalised the knowledge or skill and use it without having to think about it.

Think about the way a baby learns to walk, for example, and you will find that it corresponds to these four stages. The same goes for learning to type or to drive a car (remember how laborious the 'conscious competence' stage seemed?).

Activity 2	**(15 minutes)**

Illustrate the Stages of Learning with another example of learning a work-related skill.

1.3 The learning curve

Definition

A **learning curve** is a graph showing the relationship between the time spent in learning and the level of competence attained. Hence, it describes the progress and variable pace of learning. (It is common for people to say that they are 'on a steep learning curve' when they have to acquire a lot of new knowledge or skills in a short period of time.)

A learning curve may be used:

(a)   To suggest **typical patterns** in the acquisition of a given skill or type of skill: the pace of skill acquisition, the standard at which performance 'levels out' (does not improve further); the point at which performance 'plateaus' (levels out for a while and then improves further).

(b)   To illustrate the **progress of a given trainee's learning**/proficiency during the training process, in order to monitor the progress and pace of training – and to make allowances for different rates of learning and the 'steepness' of the curve where necessary.

(c)   To **plan** the size of the 'chunks' to be taught in one serving or stage of learning, the length of practice/consolidation periods before moving to the next stage and so on.

A 'standard' learning curve is initially steep, levelling out towards proficiency. However, in practice this will depend on the design of the learning programme (allowing for consolidation periods) and the motivation and aptitude of the learner. The curve for the acquisition of skills typically shows one or more plateaus, reflecting the trainee's need to consolidate what (s)he has learned so far, to correct some aspects of performance, to regain motivation and focus after the initial effort, or to establish habitual or unconscious competence in one skill prior to moving on to a new area. Momentum then gathers again, until the trainee reaches proficiency level, where the curve will level off – unless there is an injection of new equipment or methods, or fresh motivation, to lift output again. Such a learning curve is illustrated in Figure 13.1.

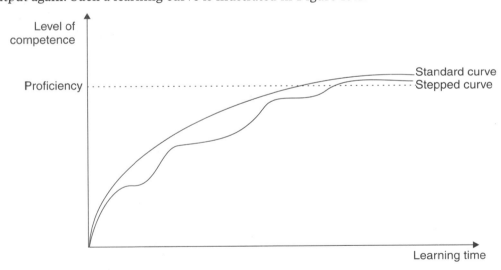

Figure 13.1: Learning curve

Note that learning curves can be quite complex, going down as well as up: for example, if the trainee is unable to practise or apply newly acquired skills and forgets, or refuses to accept new areas of conscious incompetence which emerge in the course of training. An up-and-down **'transition curve'** is common in cases where an individual changes jobs or work methods, or makes the transition from a non-managerial to a managerial position.

Activity 3	(20 minutes)

Draw a learning curve for:

(a) An easy task that takes two weeks to learn.

(b) A complex task that takes eight weeks to learn, but for which the training programme has been 'paced' to include consolidation and problem-solving time.

You may have noticed that the stages of learning and the learning curve appear to be linear or progressive, but in fact form part of an on-going cycle or control system: discovering further areas of conscious incompetence, starting further learning curves in order to adjust performance in response to feedback. This aspect of learning has been formulated as 'the learning cycle'.

1.4   The learning cycle

The best known model is the **experiential learning cycle** devised by David Kolb (1984) and popularised by Honey and Mumford (1992). Kolb suggested that effective learning could start from concrete experience, as well as from abstract concepts. It should not be 'a special activity cut off from the real world and unrelated to one's life', but should integrate concrete (involvement) and abstract (detachment), active (doing) and reflective (observing) elements. This could be conceived as a simple cyclical process, as follows: Figure 13.2.

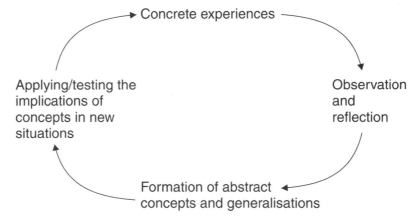

Figure 13.2: Experiential learning cycle

- **Having an experience**: being fully involved in an action or interaction, utilising your current knowledge and skills.

- **Reviewing the experience**: looking back at what happened, describing it, reflecting on the causes and effects of your behaviour.

- **Concluding from the experience**: forming generalisations, concepts and theories that will enable you to integrate your observations and reflections into your behaviour on future occasions or in other contexts.

- **Planning the next steps**: planning ways in which you can apply and test your conclusions in further action.

Suppose that an employee interviews a customer for the first time (concrete experience). He observes his own performance and the dynamics of the situation (observation) and afterwards, having failed to convince the customer to buy his product, the employee analyses what he did right and wrong (reflection). He comes to the conclusion that he failed to listen to what the customer really wanted and feared, underneath his general reluctance: he realises that the key to communication is active listening (abstraction/ generalisation). He decides to apply active listening techniques in his next interview (application/testing). This provides him with a new experience with which to start the cycle over again.

FOR DISCUSSION

Can you trace the phases of the learning cycle in the way your studies are structured? What phases are well provided for – and which might you require more opportunity for? Do some phases(s) of the cycle naturally appeal to you more than others?

Kolb recognised that people tend to have a preference for a particular phase of the cycle, which he identified as a preferred 'learning style'. We will discuss this aspect of learning theory in Section 2 of this chapter. Meanwhile, we will look at another issue raised by the experiential learning cycle: what is the relationship between theory and practice in learning? If you have read a book on how a car works, should you be able to drive it? If you can drive a car, do you need to be able to explain how it works? And if you have grasped both theory and practice of driving a car, should you also be able to drive a truck? The idea that we can learn something in one context and 'carry it across' to another context is called the **transfer of learning**.

1.5 Transfer of learning

Definition

> **Transfer of learning** refers to the extent to which newly learned information or skills have been transferred from the learning context to the application of a specific task.

Positive transfer refers to a situation in which learning has been successfully transferred to a task: negative transfer refers to a situation in which learning has not been transferred to the application of a task.

There are two basic approaches to the transfer of learning.

(a) **Transfer by specific correspondence of elements.**

If you were learning French, for example, you might listen to language tapes which feature the repetition and rehearsal of common phrases used in specific contexts: this would facilitate transfer of learning (use of these phrases) when you found yourself in those specific contexts. The workplace equivalent might be hands-on training in a specific administrative or technical procedure used by your employer.

The advantage of this approach, when the correspondences are strong, is that learning can be swiftly and effectively applied in the work context, where it will be further embedded and adapted. The danger with this approach is that if the context, procedure or equipment are not quite the same as the models used in your learning, you might not be able to 'generalise' in order to transfer learning to the new situation. Indeed, the attempt to transfer learning may have a detrimental effect on its application, if the techniques learned in one context are actively 'wrong' in another and have to be unlearned.

(b) **Transfer by principle.**

If you were learning French, for example, you might use a method which went through the grammatical rules of the language: this might facilitate transfer of learning to a range of situations, since you could simply slot in specific contextual vocabulary as you acquired it. The workplace equivalent would be training which covered:

(i) The desired outcomes of performing a procedure (why it is performed)

(ii) Under what conditions this procedure is likely to be the most appropriate strategy among available alternatives

(iii) How to perform the procedure

(iv) How the stages of the procedure follow and depend on one another and what other variables influence performance

(v) Possible problems during a procedure and how to 'troubleshoot'

(vi) Sources of information and help, should they be required

The advantage of this approach is that it generalises learning and facilitates its transfer across a wider range of contexts. The danger, however, is that it may be too generalised to allow immediate application to a particular work context, and the knowledge may be forgotten if it is not immediately applied.

There is no right or wrong approach to transfer of learning. The nature of the task and the uniqueness or otherwise of the organisation's systems and 'house style' may dictate one or the other. In addition, some people have a preference for learning exactly what they need to do, by doing it: others prefer to work through a conceptual framework and then to apply what they know to a specific context. ('Learning styles' again: we will discuss them below.)

Whichever approach is used, organisations must take into account the transferability of learning if they are not to waste their training efforts and budgets. The range of contexts and variables, and the preferences of trainees, should be taken into account in designing training programmes where possible, to ensure positive transfer. Modern approaches to training (such as competence definition, employability training and attitude and awareness training) are designed to be widely transferable within the organisational context and in the personal lives of trainees.

In addition, practical measures are required to support transfer of learning. The worksite and job context are important in enabling trainees to apply newly-learned skills. They require:

- Appropriate **systems, tools and resources** to be available to apply their learning on the job, and

- Support from **supervisors, peers and co-workers** (if whole-team learning has not been used).

Activity 4   **(30 minutes)**

We have already mentioned some situations in which the learning curve levels out or even goes downwards: loss of motivation and negative transfer, for example. Can you think of other factors that might hinder or block learning? (Consider your work or study situation. What factors – cultural, emotional, intellectual, motivational, situational, physical – make it more difficult for you to learn than it needs to be?)

1.6 Whole or part learning

Learning may be done in whole or in part. Whole learning occurs where tasks are taught or modelled in their entirety. In part learning, tasks are broken down and taught and practised stage by stage, building up to the complete task.

The various theories we have discussed so far encourage a contingency approach to learning: the appropriate strategy and techniques will depend on (among other things) the preferences of the individual for active or reflective, concrete or abstract learning experiences. Several theorists have classified these preferences as distinct 'learning styles': we will discuss them now.

2 LEARNING STYLES

2.1 Honey and Mumford

Kolb (1984) recognised that people tend to have a preference for a particular phase of the cycle, which he identified as a preferred **learning style**.

Honey and Mumford (1992) also noted that 'people vary not just in their learning skills but also in their learning styles. Why otherwise might two people, matched for age, intelligence and need, exposed to the *same* learning opportunity, react so differently?' Honey and Mumford formulated a popular classification of learning styles in terms of the attitudes and behaviours which determine an individual's preferred way of learning.

NOTES

Style	Characteristics	Learning preferences
ACTIVIST *'I'll try anything once'*	Activists involve themselves fully in new experiences. They are open-minded and enthusiastic about new things – but easily bored by long-term implementation and consolidation: act first and think about consequences later. They prefer to tackle problems by brainstorming. They easily get involved with others – but tend to centre activities on themselves.	Learn best from activities which: • present new experiences/ problems • involve short 'here and now' activities • offer excitement, drama and variety • have high visibility/ limelight • allow them to generate ideas without constraints of structure or feasibility • challenge/throw them in at the deep end • involve them with other people • allow them to 'have a go'
REFLECTOR *'Look before you leap'*	Reflectors like to stand back to observe and ponder new experiences, preferring to consider all angles and implications, and to analyse all available data, before reaching any conclusions or making any moves. When they do act, it is from awareness of the big picture. They tend to adopt a low profile, taking a back seat in meetings and discussions – though listening and observing others carefully – and tend to have a slightly distant, tolerant, unruffled air.	Learn best from activities which: • encourage observation and reflection • allow them to stand back from events • allow them to think before acting • involve painstaking research • offer an opportunity for review • help them to exchange views with others without risk, with structure • allow them to arrive in their own time
THEORIST *'If it's logical it's good'*	Theorists are keen on basic assumptions, principles, theories, models and systems thinking. They are detached and analytical and like to analyse and synthesise facts and observations into coherent theories. They think problems through systematically and logically. They are interested in maximising certainty, and so tend	Learn best from activities which: • relate to a system, model or theory • allow time to grasp underlying logic • display rationality or logic • have clear purpose and structure

Style	Characteristics	Learning preferences
	to be rigidly perfectionist and uncomfortable with subjectivity, ambiguity, lateral thinking and flippancy.	• allow analysis/generalisation of reasons for success/failure • stretch them intellectually
PRAGMATIST 'If it works, it's good *(but there is always a better way)'*	Reflectors are eager to try out ideas, theories and techniques to see if they work in practice. They like to get on with things, acting quickly and confidently on ideas that attract them – and tending to be impatient with ruminating and open-ended discussion. They are down to earth: enjoying practical decisions and responding to problems and opportunities 'as a challenge'.	Learn best from activities which: • relate to work problems/ opportunities • offer techniques with obvious practical applications/advantages • allow practise with coaching/feedback from a credible expert • expose them to role models to imitate • allows them to concentrate on practical issues (plans, tips etc) • are followed up with immediate opportunities to implement learning

Source: compiled from Honey and Mumford (1992)

Training should ideally be designed to accommodate the preferences of all four styles. This can often be overlooked, especially as the majority of training staff are activists!

Activity 5 **(15 minutes)**

John, Paula, Ringo and Georgette are learning French, as part of their firm's initiative to develop staff in European markets.

(a) John reckons that since he does not actually speak to clients, the whole scheme is a waste of time. He claims to be too busy to attend classes.

(b) Paula loves the classes, because they simulate real conversational situations. The trainees have to use whatever vocabulary they have to get their meaning across guided and corrected by the tutor: Paula doesn't like learning grammatical rules, she's happy to pick up the phrases to fit the situations.

(c) Ringo doesn't mind the teaching method either. He doesn't say anything for the first few minutes, though, just picks up what he can, gets it straight (allowing Paula to make the mistakes) and then comes out with a fluent response.

> (d)   Georgette is lost. She feels frustrated because, although she has learned the phrases for a given situation she is not sure it will apply in other contexts. She takes home a book of grammar at night, to bone up on the
>
> Who represents which learning style? What style has the course been designed for?

2.2   Kolb's Learning Styles Inventory

Kolb's Learning Styles Inventory is designed to identify the preferences of learners for particular phases of his experiential learning cycle (see Paragraph 1.4 above).

For copyright reasons, the inventory cannot be reproduced here, but the broad categories of preference identified by Kolb are as follows.

(a)   The '**converger**' (Abstracting/Generalising and Applying/Testing) prefers applying abstract generalisations in practical and specific ways.

(b)   The '**diverger**' (Concrete Experience and Reflective Observation) prefers to reflect 'laterally' on specific experience from different points of view.

(c)   The '**assimilator**' (Abstracting/Generalising and Reflective Observation) is comfortable with concepts and abstract ideas.

(d)   The '**accommodator**' (Concrete Experience and Applying/Testing) prefers to learn primarily from doing.

Now that we have surveyed some of the theoretical framework of training, let's move on to its organisational framework.

3   THE ROLE OF TRAINING AND DEVELOPMENT

3.1   Outcomes of training and development

We have talked about learning in terms of acquiring the knowledge or ability to do something. In fact, training and development activities may be directed towards a number of different outcomes.

Skill

Definition

> **Skill** may be defined as a learned pattern of operations, or responses to stimuli, which allow the successful, rapid and apparently confident performance of a complex task.

Manual work is often divided into categories according to varying degrees of perceptual-motor skill required: 'skilled' (like electricians and vehicle mechanics), 'semi-skilled' (like machine operators) and 'unskilled' (like road sweepers and canteen assistants). The degree of skill attributed to these jobs is clearly associated with:

(a)   The amount of learning required to master the necessary actions, techniques and methods

(b)   The sophistication of perception and response required (diagnosing a fault and repairing a machine is more skilled work than simply operating it in accordance with learned methods).

Non-manual work involves a wide range of what are classified as 'higher order' thinking skills: cognitive (including information-processing and decision-making), creative, perceptual, linguistic/expressive, social/interpersonal and so on.

Knowledge

Knowledge is a very complex concept, but in the training context may be divided into two areas which are sometimes referred to as 'know-that' and 'know-how'.

(a)   **'Know-that'** is knowledge *about* something or 'propositional knowledge': awareness of ideas, concepts, theories, methodologies and so on.

(b)   **'Know-how'** is knowledge *of* something, or the ability to do something: 'practical knowledge'. This may be based on underlying, unverbalised, untaught knowledge ('tacit knowledge'), but is typically acquired through imitation and experience.

Propositional knowledge is commonly associated with formal education, and has traditionally attracted high status in the social hierarchy of skills – while at the same time attracting the suspicion of those with practical knowledge, who see it as divorced from real-world competence. At the end of this course, you may know how HRM 'should' be done – but actually doing it in an organisational setting may be something else again! An organisation clearly needs to acquire and develop both propositional knowledge (understanding of management and technical processes) and practical knowledge (ability to make those processes work in practice).

FOR DISCUSSION

Which is more useful to an organisation: 'know-that' (propositional knowledge) or 'know-how?' (practical knowledge)? Do you agree that 'those who can, do: those who can't, teach'?

Competence

Definition

Competence may be defined as the skill, knowledge and behaviours that need to be applied for effective performance in a work context.

Competence represents one of the 'bundles' of practice which may contribute to the 'fit' or integration of HRM policies in an organisation. (See Chapter 8 if this does not ring a bell.) Competence frameworks may be used in HR planning, recruitment and selection, performance management, reward and training and development. There are two key elements in the concept.

(a) It integrates knowledge, skills and other attributes into the notion of overall ability.

(b) It defines and assesses ability in the context of workplace performance and proficiency.

Competency definition and testing have become a major element in the design of training and development in the UK: we will return to this theme in Chapter 16, where we trace the history of the competence movement.

Attitudes and awareness

Another recently-recognised area of training is aimed at encouraging trainees to gain insight into their own behaviour and to try to change the negative or restricting attitudes that prevent the individual from attaining more effective performance. Examples of training outcomes include:

(a) Assertiveness (a communication style which asserts one's rights, wishes and opinions in a straightforward, non-passive, yet non-aggressive manner which also respects the rights, wishes and opinions of others)

(b) Insight into the style and effectiveness of interpersonal relations and group dynamics (eg through encounter or 'T' groups)

(c) Insight into the motives underlying undesirable attitudes (racism, sexism, sexual harassment, bullying and so on)

(d) Self-awareness, social awareness, social skills and the ability to manage one's emotional responses (collectively called 'emotional intelligence').

Activity 6   **(10 minutes)**

Who do you think would benefit most from assertiveness training, and for what purpose?

Employability

Definition

Employability describes a portfolio of knowledge, skills, competences and attributes that enhances an individual's mobility and power in the labour marketplace. Employability training aims to equip employees with such a portfolio.

Traditionally, training has been seen as a way of improving an employee's performance in a particular job or career path for the benefit of the employing organisation. However, many organisations are no longer in a position to offer long-term job security to their employees. Socially responsible employers wish to classify this new psychological contract and facilitate employees' transition to other jobs by enhancing their employability portfolio – while simultaneously benefiting from the creation of a more flexible multi-skilled labour force.

What benefits can the organisation expect to gain from achieving the above outcomes? This is the first question in evaluating the role of training and development in the organisation.

3.2   Benefits of training and development activity

In so far as training and development activity (or a broader perception of learning) increases competency, skills, versatility, confidence, awareness, knowledge and further learning among employees, it may contribute to the business objectives of the organisation in a number of ways.

(a)   Increased efficiency and productivity, through faster, more skilled work and greater labour flexibility (eg through multi-skilling)

(b)   Reduction in costs, associated with the above, and with less wastage and fewer errors

(c)   Reduction in interpersonal and performance-related problems – both because of enhanced competence and greater confidence

(d)   Improved quality of work/service

(e)   Fewer accidents and problems with equipment and machinery

(f)   Enhanced ability to attract and retain high calibre employees

(g)   Improved job satisfaction, motivation and morale among developed employees since skill and career development are key intrinsic rewards which may further increase productivity and quality

(h)   Greater communication between employees on job-related issues, with potential for quality improvements and innovations

(i)   Greater potential for increased empowerment and involvement of employees, as they become more aware and more skilled (particularly if training goes beyond technical skills to embrace communication and interpersonal skills, delegation skills for managers, problem-solving and decision-making skills and so on)

(j)   The fostering of a culture of continuous learning and improvement, which promotes adaptability to change, organisational flexibility and a positive organisation culture

(k)   Compliance with legislation and regulation (where training is given in health and safety measures, non-discrimination and so on)

(l)   Better promotion and management succession planning, as employee potential is systematically developed

(m)   Fulfilling the future needs of the organisation for skills which may be subject to shortages or fluctuations in the external labour market

(n)   Corporate social responsibility (and enhanced employer/recruiter brand) through developing employees – particularly in general employability.

We will look at ways in which training and development activities can be evaluated (and justified in terms of their return on investment) in Chapter 14.

EXAMPLE: MOTOROLA

Motorola found itself trying to compete globally in a market of new technologies and changing demands, with people who, in many cases, had difficulty with reading and basic mathematics. It launched a wide-ranging scheme of education and training (its own 'University') for its employees – and for the employees of suppliers and key customers. Training was designed to develop the person, not just the company and the job. It was aimed at 'creating an environment for learning, a continuous openness to new ideas... We not only teach skills, we try to breathe the very spirit of creativity and flexibility into manufacturing and management.'

Activity 7   **(20 minutes)**

What might be the benefits of training to the trainee? (Think what you are getting out of doing this course, for example.)

List at least five benefits.

You might by now be thinking that training is obviously such a good thing that an organisation could not go wrong by simply providing some. If performance is poor: do some training! If morale is low: do some training! If empowerment is a foreign concept in your organisation: do some training! Let's get things into perspective ...

Realistic expectations

The HR function must recognise – and emphasise to line managers – that:

•   Training and development can improve performance
        but

•   There are many variables in job performance, not all of which may be addressed by training alone
        and

•   Even in areas susceptible to training, the training programme must be designed and implemented appropriately for the needs of the organisation and the specific group of trainees – or it will not be effective.

3.3 Stakeholders in human resource development

It is worth noting that there are a number of different stakeholders in organisational training and development. (Stakeholders are individuals or groups who have an interest or 'stake' in a given endeavour, because they have contributed to it and/or because they are affected by its outcomes.)

Potential stakeholders in training (in general, or particular training events) include:

(a)   The owners and senior mangers of the organisation, who invest in human resource development and determine training policy to reap certain returns on their investment

(b)   The line managers of trainees, whose units' performance will be affected by (positive or negative) changes in trainees' competence, behaviour and attitudes

(c)   The trainees, who invest time, effort and a range of psychological resources in learning and whose competence, employability and job satisfaction are affected by the organisation's development policies (or lack of them)

(d)   The training managers (planners, funders, providers, evaluators) who must develop and deliver successful training in order to meet their own objectives

(e)   The instructors, coaches and mentors within the work team, who likewise measure their success by the effectiveness of the learning they deliver and support

(f)   Training vendors (course providers, materials publishers, software developers, consultants) whose continued relationship with the firm, and business success, depends on positive evaluation by training managers and trainees

(g)   The training community in general, whose reputation, viability and methodology depends on the standard and effectiveness of members' offerings and feedback from customers.

The design, planning, delivery and evaluation of learning and training events must take the needs, requirements, preferences and priorities of some or all of these stakeholders into account. As we will see in Chapter 14, most models of training evaluation recognise stakeholder experience and feedback (from at least some constituent groups) as an important measure of success.

FOR DISCUSSION

What do you think are likely to be the key evaluation criteria of each of the stakeholder groups listed above, in measuring the 'success' of a training event or programme? What might be the implications if each of these stakeholder groups were dissatisfied with the experience or outcomes of training?

3.4 The role of training and development policy

Armstrong (2003) suggests that:

> The objective of an organisation's policies, processes and programmes for the delivery of learning and training is to achieve its human resource development strategies by ensuring that it has the skilled, knowledgeable and competent people required to meet its present and future needs.

A human resource development policy will therefore address the following issues.

- Why does the organisation train and develop people: how is human resource development envisaged as contributing to strategic objectives and the HR plan? How does investment in it benefit organisational stakeholders?

- What are the desired outcomes of HRD: skills, knowledge, competence, awareness/attitudes, employability? How do these support business and other HRM strategies?

- How will learning and development needs and objectives be determined? How will they relate individual, team and organisational performance and bottom-line results? What value is placed on employability and 'personal' development?

- Whom does the organisation intend to train and develop? What grades of employee will have access to training, of what type and at what level? What equal opportunity commitments should be made? (This may be part of a wider commitment to encouraging and supporting all members of the organisation to pursue continuous learning opportunities.)

- Who will be responsible for the initiation and control of training: HR specialists, line managers, employees themselves? What value is placed on the concept of 'self-development'?

- When, where and how will training activity take place? What mix of methods, formats and styles will be used?

- How much investment is the organisation prepared to put into training, development and organisational learning?

- How is training and development to be monitored and evaluated?

We will discuss various policy issues in detail in Chapter 14.

3.5 Learning, training and development

It may be worth distinguishing between these terms, although in practice they are often used interchangeably.

- **Learning** is the process whereby people acquire knowledge, capabilities and skills

- **Training** is the use of planned, systematic instruction and other learning events and programmes to promote learning, with the particular aim of enhancing competence in a work role

- **Development** is the growth of people's knowledge and capabilities and the increasing fulfilment of their potential, through a range of learning experiences.

Development is often linked to systems whereby people gain experience within an organisation and are offered increasing opportunities and challenges through lateral or vertical movements in the organisation structure. 'Management development', for example, often implies not only management education and training, but mentorship and career planning, promotion planning and planned managerial succession.

3.6 Management development

Definition

Management development is 'an attempt to improve managerial effectiveness through a planned and deliberate learning process'.

(Mumford, 1994)

Much of our discussion of learning and training in Chapter 14 will apply as well to managerial as to non-managerial grades of staff. However, organisations have a significant investment in their managers – and in the quality of their leadership and decisions – and in order to secure and maximise the managerial resource, attention is typically given to:

(a) Some form of management **education and training**. This may range from short skill-based training courses (eg in leadership or interpersonal skills) to on-going learning activities directed towards demonstrating competencies (as defined by in-house or nationally-accredited competency frameworks) to sponsorship/leave for studies towards formal qualifications such as an MBA degree.

(b) Planned **career management**, to enable managers to gain experience of different functions, units or areas of the business, different national cultures (if the organisation is international or internationalising) and increasing levels of responsibility.

(c) **Performance management** to develop and reinforce managerial competencies through on-going goal-setting and continuous improvement.

(d) **Self-managed and experiential learning**, encouraging managers to recognise and seek out opportunities to enhance their skills.

(e) **Guidance and mentoring** by effective motivators, success coaches and power sources in the organisation (usually more senior managers).

Activity 8 **(5 minutes)**

Suggest three reasons why an organisation should give attention to management training and development.

NOTES

INTERNATIONAL COMPARISONS

- **European** approaches have traditionally been less concerned with management development as a discrete activity. In France, the making of a manager begins within the higher education institutions and forms part of the development of a historical social elite. In Germany, the approach is more functional: managers tend to stay in functional roles longer, and specialist expertise is pre-developed within the vocational education system. Where there is training, it tends to be highly structured and specified. Despite this 'relatively weak tradition in explicitly focused forms of management', there has been an upsurge of interest in management education since European Union: the emergence of business schools, MBA activity, and EU-led initiatives promoting the exchange of European business and management students between nations.

- The development of managers in **Japan** (based on a system of commitment and seniority), is long-term, slow-progression, carefully planned and generalist in its scope. 'Whereas Anglo-Saxon models stress individualism and development through short, intensive bursts of training to prepare managers for assignments characterised by challenge and risk, Japanese development programmes are longer and more culturally reflective in focusing on collectivism and group/team effort … Unlike the US/UK where management development is in the hands of specialists, the Japanese view the relationship between the individual and the boss as a significant factor in developing the manager.'

(Beardwell & Holden, 1997)

So far, we have discussed learning theory mainly in terms of individual learning. We will now look briefly at organisational *learning.*

4   THE LEARNING ORGANISATION

4.1   The learning organisation

Definition

A **learning organisation** is one that facilitates the acquisition and sharing of knowledge, and the learning of all its members, in order continuously and strategically to transform itself in response to a rapidly changing and uncertain environment, and to develop and refine the capabilities required for future success.

A learning organisation values the process of learning – not just its specific outcomes. It learns how to learn: how to be open to new information; how to use feedback to adjust performance; how to view mistakes and failed experiments as opportunities for change; how to make decision-making flexible in order to accommodate learning.

Pedler *et al* (1991) define a learning organisation as one 'which facilitates the learning of all its members and continually transforms itself'.

This implies an underlying vision for organisational learning and flexibility, and the creation of a culture conducive to learning, via an integrated and mutually-reinforcing set of policies, processes and techniques.

4.2 Learning culture

The cultural mechanisms and characteristics of a learning organisation are as follows (Senge, 1990; Garvin, 1993).

(a) Decision-making procedures are continuously modified in the light of experience, avoiding rigid plans and procedures.

(b) Problem-solving is systematic and based on scientific method rather than guesswork: insisting on data rather than assumptions, generating and testing hypotheses.

(c) Experimentation – the systematic search for and testing of new knowledge – is encouraged, in order to generate new insights. Continuous improvement programmes (based on the Japanese concept of 'kaizen') are a feature of learning organisation.

(d) Risk-taking, failures and mistakes are regarded as useful input to the learning process, to avoid problems in future. (This has been called the 'Santayana principle' after the philosopher who said: 'Those who cannot remember the past are condemned to repeat it'.) In any case it is better to experiment with something new than stick with what you know for fear of failure.

(e) Information and feedback is encouraged from all possible sources (notably customers and competitors): opportunities to learn from others should be sought out. This includes the process of benchmarking: identifying best practice in other organisations and transferring appropriately adapted elements of their practice to one's own organisation. (Also known as 'SIS' – 'steal ideas shamelessly'!)

(f) Knowledge is disseminated throughout the organisation by formal communication and informal networking. Everyone operates with the knowledge of environmental changes and challenges and customer demands. Open-channel upward, downward and lateral communication is encouraged.

(g) Everything is open to challenge and questioning: no body of knowledge or procedure becomes 'enshrined' by habitual acceptance. Management actively supports questioning by subordinates.

(h) Selection, training and development, appraisal and reward are based not on existing goals and attainments but on flexibility, continuous improvement, initiative and ability to identify and exploit new areas of activity.

(i) Flexibility of decision-making is supported by self-managed team-working and the role of the manager/supervisor as coach/facilitator.

(j) Training focuses on 'learning how to learn': how to obtain, use and adapt to new information.

Activity 9   **(45 minutes)**

From what you know of how organisational culture is developed and reinforced, and building on the characteristics listed above, what would you expect to be the potential **barriers** to the creation of a successful learning culture?

4.3 The organisational learning cycle

According to the New Learning for New Work Consortium's report *Managing Learning for Added Value* the goal of the new learning paradigm is a workforce capable of taking responsibility for adding value. This amounts to a new learning cycle, which may be illustrated as follows (Figure 13.3)

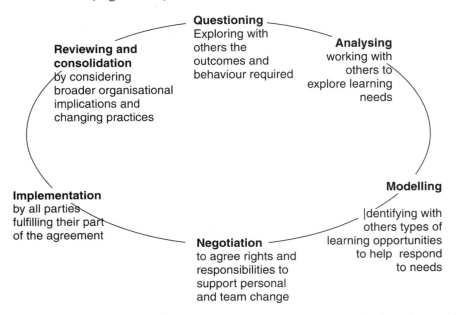

Figure 13.3: A new learning cycle – managing learning to add value

4.4 Individual ownership of organisational learning

Definition

Personal development plans are action plans for individuals' skill and career development which put the onus on the individuals themselves to seek out and organise training and development opportunities

---

The number of Negotiated Personal Development Plans (PDPs) or **learning contracts** are often the basis of mentoring and continuous development programmes. A PDP is usually prepared by the individual and his or her line manger (although they may ask a mentor or learning and development adviser for guidance); they retain responsibility for the plan and for the learner's performance.

Parsloe & Wray (2000) suggest that the role of the mentor or HR adviser will be to:

- **Confirm the PDP**: providing guidance in its preparation, checking that learning goals are realistic and effective, and helping to identify learning needs

- **Encourage the self-management of learning**: offering information about learning opportunities and encouraging learner in accessing them

- **Provide support during implementation**: providing guidance, feedback and resources as required

- **Assist in evaluation**: encouraging the learner to arrange formal evaluation with the time manager or qualification supervisor, and encouraging on-going development planning.

The most popular PDP schemes take account of people's wider needs and aspirations, rather than focusing on skills required for present job performance.

This trend is also reflected in **employee development programmes** which offer employees a wide range or 'menu' of development opportunities, not necessarily related to the job. The effect of such schemes is to develop a culture in which learning and adaptability is valued, as well as to attract, retain and motivate skilled employees.

EXAMPLE

- A National Health Service development programme for unit general managers includes a budget for each individual to spend – as he or she wishes – on personal development. This can be spent on courses, seminars or books, or on 'buying in' a coach or instructor, or visiting other organisations to observe their methods – whatever. This approach empowers would-be learners, and encourages creative thinking about development needs and opportunities.

FOR DISCUSSION

Why might an organisation wish to give control of the development agenda to the individual employees? What might the drawbacks be? Who controls your learning objectives and opportunities?

Chapter roundup

- There are three basic theoretical approaches to learning: the behaviourist, cognitive and social learning approaches.

- Learning has been modelled as:

  - Four stages (unconscious incompetence, conscious incompetence, conscious competence, unconscious competence

  - A curve, showing the relationship between learning time and level of competence: training must take account of the steepness of the curve and the need for consolidating plateaux or steps.

  - A cycle, such as the experiential learning cycle of David Kolb (concrete experience, reflective observation, abstract conceptualisation, active experimentation): this can be used as an aid to self-managed learning.

- Transfer of work learning to the work context may be achieved in various ways, depending on the nature of the learning, the motivation and preferences of the learners and the support given by the worksite and work group.

- Honey and Mumford identified four learning styles: theorist, reflector, activist, pragmatist. Learning programmes should take into account the strengths and weaknesses of each style, as well as challenging learners to increase their learning repertoire and flexibility.

- Training may be directed at the acquisition of skill, knowledge, competence, attitudes/awareness or employability.

- The planning, design, implementation and evaluating of learning events and training programmes will have to take into account:

  - The organisation's philosophy and expectations of human resource development, as set out in the HRD policy.

  - The needs, requirements and preferences of various stakeholders in development.

  - The implications of learning theories and styles.

- The learning organisation is one that is skilled at creating, acquiring and transferring knowledge, and at modifying its behaviour to reflect new knowledge and insights.

Quick quiz

1   What is an 'empirical' epistemology and a 'rational' epistemology?

2   What are 'whole' and 'part' learning?

3   Define the four stages of learning.

4   What is a 'plateau' in a learning curve?

5   What are the two approaches to transfer of learning, and what other elements are needed to support transfer to the work context?

6   Which of Honey and Mumford's learning styles shows a preference for the 'generalising/abstracting' stage of the learning cycle?

    A   Pragmatist
    B   Activist
    C   Theorist
    D   Reflector

7   Distinguish between skill, 'know-that', 'know-how' and competence.

8   List the potential stakeholders in a training event.

9   Outline an approach to management development.

10   List five methods of creating a learning organisation/culture.

Answers to quick quiz

1   *Empirical*: a theory of how people know things based on the belief that the human mind operates purely on information gained from the senses by experience. *'Rational'*: a theory of how people know things based on the belief that the human mind imposes organisation and meaning on sensory raw material.   (see paragraph 1.1)

2   Whole learning: tasks are taught or modelled in their entirety. Part learning: tasks are broken down and taught and practised stage by stage, building up to the whole task.   (para 1.6)

3   See paragraph 1.2.

4   The point at which progress levels off, due to the trainee's need to consolidate, correct, regain motivation or establish unconscious competence before moving on further.   (para 1.3)

5   Correspondence of elements between the learning situation and applied context *or* transfer by principle, which allows general learning to be transferred to specific contexts. Worksite systems, tools and resources and support from the manager and work group.   (para 1.5)

6   C   (paras 1.4, 2.1)

7   See paragraph 3.1 for a full account.

8   Owners/managers of the firm; line managers of trainees; training managers; instructors/coaches; external training providers; training community.   (para 3.3)

9   See paragraph 3.6.

10   See paragraph 4.2 for a full account.

NOTES

Answers to activities

1   A full account of the implications of learning theory for training design, is given in the text following the exercise.

2   We have used the example of assertiveness training: you may have come up with others.

Stage 1.   You have not heard of assertiveness, so you are not aware that you relate to people in a way that is either aggressive or passive: you simply relate in the way that seems natural to you.

Stage 2.   You read about assertiveness, or someone feeds back to you that your style of relating is unhelpfully unassertive, or you realise that you hardly ever get your needs met without damaging relationships: you realise that your behaviour is unassertive.

Stage 3.   You research and think about the principles of assertiveness, and remind yourself of them by sticking positive affirmation messages around your home and office. You apply the techniques of assertion consciously, having to remind yourself of the principles, using scripted responses, monitoring their effectiveness.

Stage 4.   You naturally react in an assertive manner, without having to remind yourself or plan to do so.

3   (a)

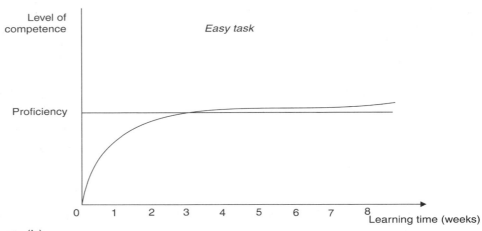

(b)

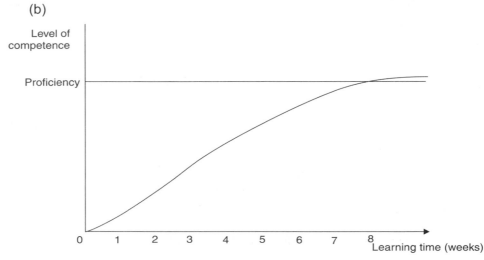

4   Some of the factors you may have identified include the following.

   (a) Perceptual factors: unconscious incompetence, not seeing that there is a need; not receiving honest feedback from others

   (b) Emotional factors: fear or insecurity about performance (not wanting to be a 'beginner' or 'learner'), fear of being judged, discomfort of conscious incompetence, frustration

   (c) Motivational factors: lack of goals/incentives, unwillingness to take risks or make mistakes, no positive reinforcement for progress, previous bad experience with training

   (d) Cultural factors: values about 'not getting above yourself', 'the way we do things here' frustrating application of learning; boss/colleagues/family unsupportive

   (e) Physical factors: no suitable space or time to study, practise

   (f) Situational factors: lack of training opportunities; poorly designed training courses (negative transfer, unsuited to learning styles of trainees)

   (g) Skill factors: poor learning skills (never learned to learn), limited learning styles, poor communication skills

5   John is a pragmatist: Paula an activist: Ringo a reflector: Georgette a theorist. The course seems tailored to activists: reflectors would probably cope, but might not contribute enough to keep the classes going.

6   Assertiveness training is popularly seen as a prime means of remedying under-achievement in women, or of helping women to avoid exploitation at work. It is likely to be part of a 'Women Into Management' programme. The techniques and insights involved are likely to be of benefit to men as well, but it has been recognised that it is primarily women who are disadvantaged in western society by the failure to distinguish between assertion and aggression, submission and conflict-avoidance. Assertiveness training may help women to criticise, confront and direct male subordinates and colleagues non-aggressively. The failure of victims of sexual harassment to come forward may indicate another area in which assertiveness could be of value.

7   (a) It demonstrates that the individual is valued and believed to have potential.

   (b) It gives the individual an enhanced sense of security (that he or she is and will be useful to the organisation).

   (c) It can enhance a person's portfolio of skills, and hence a person's ability to take responsibility.

   (d) It can motivate employees, because they see opportunities for advancement, or to make a difference to quality or innovation.

   (e) Training and development sessions enable employees to mix with people from other business functions, and so develop networks and contacts.

   (f) Training in areas such as assertiveness, communication or interpersonal skills can enhance personal effectiveness and self-esteem outside the work context.

8   (a) The prime objective of management development is improved performance capacity – both from the managers *and* from those they manage.

(b) Management development secures management succession: a pool of promotable individuals in the organisation.

(c) The organisation's showing an interest in the career development of staff may motivate them and encourage loyalty. (This will be especially important if the firm intends to rely on management succession to fill senior management positions.)

9   Some problems you may have identified include the following.

(a) Inadequate organisation mechanisms for multi-directional communication, training in learning, selection according to flexibility etc: these will have to be established, and old machinery (reporting channels, job descriptions etc) dismantled or adapted.

(b) Lack of commitment and example-setting by top management (essential to the development of culture).

(c) Poor communication and/or learning skills in some existing employees: they would need to be developed or the employees would need to be 'weeded out'. (This may happen through 'accelerated wastage', since the learning culture would be highly uncomfortable for them.)

(d) Organisational politics, discouraging the open sharing of information and acceptance of challenge.

(e) Fear/insecurity on the part of managers (required to open their decision-making to challenge) and all employees (fear of risk-taking, never secure in sense of competence under continuous improvement).

(f) Previous management style: punishing mistakes, avoiding risks etc.

(g) Lack of motivation to learn at all levels: inadequate perception of the need to be constantly learning, flexible – when it would be much easier to settle into established routines.

Chapter 14:
TRAINING AND DEVELOPMENT

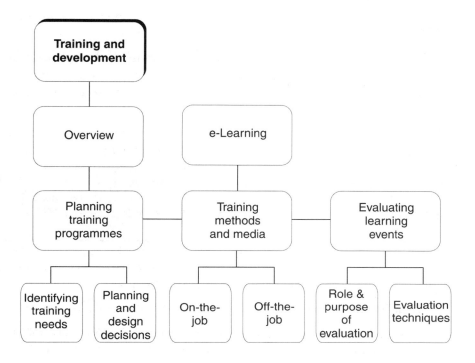

Introduction

In this chapter, we examine the practical application of the principles discussed in Chapter 13, starting with an overview of the systematic approach to training and development.

We discuss the key issues, resources and techniques of each stage of this approach, from the identification of training and development needs to the planning and design of learning events and programmes – and finally, the systematic evaluation of their success and contribution. This is a long chapter: take it at your own pace, and use the activities to consolidate your learning.

Your objectives

In this chapter you will learn about the following.

(a)   The systematic approach to training

(b)   The identification of training and development needs

(c)   The setting of training objectives

(d)   Planning issues in devising training programmes

(e)   The advantages and disadvantages of on-the-job and off-the-job training and development methods

(f)   The use of a variety of on-the-job and off-the-job methods

    (g)   The 'what, why, when and who' of evaluating learning events

    (h)   A range of models and techniques of evaluation

    (i)   How to investigate a vocational training scheme

    (j)   Implementation of (training) practice in the UK and one other country

1 OVERVIEW

If training is to make a impact on performance at an individual level, let alone at a strategic level, it must be carefully designed to suit the **need for training** and the **needs of the trainee.**

Definition

> According to the Department of Employment, **training** is 'the systematic development of the attitude/knowledge/skill/behaviour pattern required by an individual in order to perform adequately a given task or job.'

A systematic approach to training encompasses four basic stages.

Stage 1.   Identify and define training needs

Stage 2.   Design learning and development programmes which meet those needs, selecting relevant methods and media

Stage 3.   Implement learning events and programmes

Stage 4.   Systematically evaluate training (although this will not necessarily be a one-off, after-the-event exercise, as we will see in Section 4 of this chapter).

We will now look at each of these stages in turn.

2 IDENTIFYING TRAINING NEEDS

2.1 Whose needs and objectives?

Training needs and outcomes should be evaluated in terms of their potential contribution to the key objectives of the organisation, which could include the following.

    (a)   Profitability; by increasing productivity/revenue or reducing costs

    (b)   The cost-effective provision of services, customer retention, ethical compliance, technical innovation, market standing and other measures of added value

    (c)   The survival or growth of the business, which may be based on profitability, return on investment for shareholders, retention of market share and so on

    (d)   Increased employee loyalty (with a knock-on effect in decreased labour turnover and smoother management succession)

(e) Enhanced corporate image (which may impact favourably on consumer attitudes and the ability to attract skilled labour)

(f) Enhanced potential for quality, innovation, flexibility in the face of change and acceptable risk-taking, through a culture of broad-based competence and support of learning

There is no intrinsic incompatibility between a **business's** strategic goals for training, and the developmental aspirations of **individuals**. The desire for learning, skill development and self-actualisation by the individual have long been recognised (Maslow, Herzberg) as incentives to motivated performance at work, as well as offering personal satisfaction.

Activity 1   **(20 minutes)**

When might fulfilling employee aspirations for training become incompatible with business objectives?

The training needs of individuals and groups vary enormously, according to the nature of the job and particular tasks, and the abilities and experience of the employees.

2.2 Training needs recognition

Some training requirements will be obvious and 'automatic'.

(a) If a piece of legislation is enacted which affects the organisation's operations, training in its provisions will automatically be indicated. Thus, for example, HR staff will need to be trained as and when various EU Directives are enacted in UK law.

(b) The introduction of new technology similarly implies a training need: for relevant employees to learn how to use it.

(c) An organisation seeking accreditation for its training scheme, or seeking a British Standard or International Standard (say, for quality systems, ISO 9000), will have certain training requirements imposed on it by the approving body.

Other training requirements may emerge in response to **critical incidents**: problems or events which affect a key area of the organisation's activity and effectiveness. A service organisation may, for example, receive bad press coverage because of a number of complaints about the rudeness of its customer service staff on the telephone. This might prompt an investigation which might in turn highlight the need for training in telephone skills, customer care, scheduling (for the team manager, if the rudeness was a result not of lack of skill but pressure of unmanageable workloads) and so on.

Some **qualitative indicators** might be taken as symptoms of a need for training: absenteeism, high labour turnover, grievance and disciplinary actions, crises, conflict, poor motivation and performance. Such factors will need to be investigated to see what the root causes are, and whether training will solve the problem.

Another alternative is **self-assessment** by the employee. This may be highly informal (a list of in-house or sponsored courses is posted on the notice board or intranet and interested employees are invited to apply) or more systematic (employees complete surveys on training needs). An example of a self-administered needs survey for managerial staff (suggested by Kramer *et al*, 1997) is as follows.

Self assessment of training needs

Please indicate in the blanks the extent to which you have a training need in each specific area. Use the following scale

Scale

1 ———— 2 ———— 3 ———— 4 ———— 5

(To no extent)   (To a very large extent)

To what extent do you need training in the following areas?

Basic management skills (organising, planning, delegating, problem-solving)

———— A   Setting goals and objectives
———— B   Developing realistic time schedules to meet work requirements
———— C   Identifying and weighing alternative solutions
———— D   Organising work activities

Interpersonal skills

———— A   Resolving interpersonal conflicts
———— B   Creating a development plan for employees
———— C   Identifying and understanding individual employee needs
———— D   Conducting performance appraisal reviews
———— E   Conducting a disciplinary interview

Administrative skills

———— A   Maintaining equipment, tools and safety controls
———— B   Understanding local agreements and shop rules
———— C   Preparing work flowcharts
———— D   Developing departmental budgets

Quality control

———— A   Analysing and interpreting statistical data
———— B   Constructing and analysing charts, tables and graphs
———— C   Using statistical software on the computer

The advantage of self-assessment, or self-nomination for training, is that it pre-supposes motivation on the part of the trainee and harnesses employees' knowledge of their own job requirements and skill weaknesses. The drawback, however, is that employees may be reluctant to admit to performance deficiencies.

A further alternative, therefore, is the use of **attitude surveys** and **360° feedback appraisal reports,** since the employee's superiors, subordinates, colleagues and customer contacts will be in a good position to identify performance deficiencies in areas that affect them: this will be particularly important in the case of customers.

Activity 2 **(15 minutes)**

Complete the above self-assessment for yourself. For any areas which are not applicable to your job, put NA (not applicable).

FOR DISCUSSION

How did you become aware of this gap in your skills or knowledge? Was it an immediate need or because of something you desired in the future? Were you helped in identifying your training needs? Did you define them (or had them defined for you) in a helpful, systematic way?

Other training requirements may only emerge as a result of systematic learning gap (or training need) analysis.

2.3 Training needs analysis

Definition

Training needs may be defined as the gap between what people should be achieving and what they actually are achieving. In other words:

Required level of competence *minus* present level of competence = training need.

Training needs analysis may be carried out at the **corporate level** as part of the human resource planning process, through:

(a) Analysis of corporate objectives and business plans and their human resource requirements.

(b) Analysis of existing human resource records and appraisals (training evaluations, performance management reports, surveys and so on).

(c) A **human resources audit** or **skills audit** may also be conducted for a more comprehensive accounting of the current level of competence, skill, knowledge (and so on) in the workforce.

At **group/team and individual level**, a similar exercise will be carried out, to identify where the corporate needs can best be met.

LEARNING MEDIA

The required level of competence for the job can be determined by:

(a)   **Job analysis**, identifying the elements of the task in terms of key activities and outcomes

(b)   **Skills analysis**, identifying the skill elements of the task, such as:

(i)   What senses (vision, touch, hearing etc) are involved?
(ii)   What left-hand/right-hand/foot operations are required?
(iii)   What interactions with other operatives are required?

(c)   **Role analysis,** for managerial and administrative jobs requiring a high degree of co-ordination and interaction with others

(d)   **Existing records**, such as job specifications and descriptions, person specifications, the organisation chart (depicting roles and relationships) and so on

(e)   **Competence analysis** or existing competence frameworks, such as NVQs relevant to the job, to define the skills, knowledge and competencies required to meet performance standards.

The present level of employees' competence (which includes not only skill and knowledge, but the employee's inclination or willingness to work competently as well) can be measured by an appropriate **pre-training test** of skills, knowledge, performance, attitude and so on. Performance appraisals and past training reports will furnish some of this information. It should be noted that training needs analysis need not have a reactive or problem-solving focus aimed solely at meeting shortfalls in competence in the current job.

The **future development needs** of the organisation, team and individuals should also be taken into account, by considering employment, consumer and technological trends (such as the need to increase flexibility, improve e-commerce or customer service skills, or encourage innovation) and employees' potential for promotion, empowerment, multi-skilling and so on. Training and development needs analysis should be part of the pro-active process of performance management, whereby managers and team leaders guide people in setting performance improvement and learning targets for the forthcoming planning period.

The training manager will have to investigate any gap between current and required performance/competence to see whether training might be the solution. (Remember, there are alternative solutions: machinery may need repairing or upgrading, poor motivation might need to be addressed through pay and incentives, and so on.)

If training is identified as the way to close the gap, a **learning or training specification** should be drawn up. This will include specific learning objectives, perhaps with action plans as to:

- Methods of learning that may be used

- Timescales within which learning should be undertaken and

- Methods by which achievement of the objectives will be monitored and measured.

2.4 Setting training objectives

Objectives should be clear, specific and related to observable, measurable targets. Ideally, there should be detailed definitions of:

(a) **Knowledge** – what the trainee should understand
(b) **Behaviour** – what the trainee should be able to do
(c) **Standard** – to what level of performance
(d) **Environment** – under what conditions.

The advantage of competence frameworks is that they typically define competent performance in exactly this specific and quantifiable way.

Objectives are the yardsticks that will allow the trainer (and trainees) to see clearly whether and how far training has been successful. They are usually best expressed in terms of active verbs: at the end of the course the trainee should be able to describe... , or identify... or distinguish X from Y... or calculate... or assemble... and so on.

It is insufficient to define the objectives of training as 'to give trainees a grounding in... or 'to encourage trainees in a better appreciation of...': this offers no target achievement which can be objectively measured. Where possible, a **quantifiable** measure should be added: time taken to perform a task, percentage of questions answered correctly, percentage of errors acceptable, and so on.

Activity 3   **(30 minutes)**

Translate the following training needs into specific learning objectives. Begin each objective with the words: 'the employee will…'

Training need

(a) To know more about the Data Protection Act
(b) To establish a better rapport with customers
(c) To assemble clocks more quickly

Having defined what a training programme should be able to do, the training manager needs to evaluate different options for how training is to be delivered, and how the desired outcomes are to be achieved. We will outline some of the methods and media available in Sections 4 and 5 below. Here, we will just highlight some of the decisions to be made.

3 PLANNING AND DESIGN DECISIONS

3.1 Training programmes and learning plans

Once organisational, job/role related and individual learning needs have been established, training managers must make plans as to the best route for implementation.

(a)   **Training programmes** – a menu or 'core curriculum' of training initiatives which will be offered in the forthcoming planning period, which will be open to relevant categories of staff. Examples (Hargreaves and Jarvis, 2000) include:

- Finance training for project managers

- Management skills for all management staff

- Presentation and interpersonal skills for trainers, interviewers and customer service staff

- Teambuilding and teamworking for all departments

- Basic health and safety training for all staff

- Intra-departmental seminars and in-house discussion groups.

It may be necessary to design full-scale formal training programmes, if a suitably-tailored programme is not available 'off the shelf', or if large numbers of staff are regularly involved, making programmes more cost-effective.

Once these have been prioritised, they can be designed and timetabled.

(b)   **Learning plans** – individual or team plans for accessing training courses/ resources and/or for taking advantage of learning opportunities at work. These may be more flexibly adapted to individual and team needs. Coaching, mentoring, reading and e-learning, for example, would not require formally designed programmes: learning targets, timescales and monitoring/ evaluation procedures would still need to be planned.

3.2   Type of learning

As we will see in Sections 4 and 5 below, learning experiences may be of different types, which will variously suit particular learning needs.

(a)   **Formal and informal learning**

Formal learning often takes place away from the work setting, and involves techniques such as classroom teaching and instruction. It is driven by the teacher or trainer, often to a pre-set curriculum or agenda which may or may not be adapted to all members of the learning group. Transfer of learning may be difficult, although theorists may prefer this method.

Informal learning occurs in the workplace, in response to immediate, job-relevant needs. The learner essentially drives the process by asking questions and accessing opportunities for coaching, advice and instruction. Since it is largely unplanned, it may not systematically meet training needs. However, some learners will find this method more relevant, more suited to their learning style and easier to apply in practice.

(b)   **On-the-job and off-the-job learning**

On-the-job or workplace learning may use the workplace as a training environment (eg for briefings, demonstrations or site visits) or may use actual work processes and tasks as learning events. On-the-job training methods include: systematic job instruction; working with experienced colleagues or trainers; coaching or mentoring; and various guided challenges such as project or committee work.

Off-the-job training methods include: formal taught or self-administered courses (eg by computer-based training); outdoor training; research assignments and so on.

We discuss methods – and their advantages and disadvantages – in Sections 4 and 5 below.

(c)   **Self-managed learning**

Individuals are encouraged to define their own learning objectives and create action plans (or Personal Development Plans) to meet them. Managers, mentors or trainers may jointly agree learning objectives, in the form of a **learning contract**. They may also guide the learner in accessing resources and learning opportunities, provide coaching, offer feedback as part of the evaluation process and so on.

(d)   **Programmed learning**

The trainee works at his or her own pace through a carefully ordered sequence of learning modules and assessments. This is a feature of many distance learning and computer-based training programmes.

(e)   **Blended learning**

Blended learning is a recognition that a mix of learning types, styles and technologies may be most effective in order to meet individual needs and learning preferences. This might be applied to a training course or programme: for example, using instruction on basic principles, group exercises for practice, e-learning for consolidation and coaching and mentoring for follow-up back in the workplace. Similarly, an individual's personal development plan might include a blend of reading, e-learning, experiential learning (using mentor feedback), coaching where required, and formal courses for certification.

Alan Mumford suggests that trainers should ask the following questions of any method proposed.

(a)   What is the contribution of the method to the development of knowledge, skills and insight?

(b)   What is the impact of individual learning-style preferences on the acceptability of the method?

(c)   What are the particular features of this method that make it more appropriate than a method I have used previously?

(d)   In what way is the method more appropriate than any other method for a particular need?

In addition, there is the need for cost-benefit analysis on any given method: are the outcomes to be gained worth the cost involved?

NOTES

> **Activity 4** (20 minutes)
>
> What methods of learning and training have you encountered in your job? What methods are you using now to study for your qualification? What do *you* think are the advantages and disadvantages of this 'blend' for you as a learner?

3.3 Timing and duration of training

If generic programmes, involving staff from different departments, are being planned, training managers there are additional considerations.

(a) Negotiation with line managers as to the length of time staff can be available for training, when, and how the time could most conveniently be structured (day release, several-day blocks) to minimise the impact on the department.

(b) Consideration of the availability of training facilities and personnel (especially if external training partners are used): large-scale, specialist programmes may need to be booked up to a year in advance.

(c) Consideration of the learning curve and learning style preferences of trainees. Programme timetabling will have to take into account the need for icebreakers and participant teambuilding; refreshment and relaxation breaks; variations in 'pace' of learning activity to allow for consolidation, practice, reflection and so on.

There is a noticeable trend towards short-course or **'bite size' learning**, led by the Learning and Skills Council's (LSC) Bite Size campaign. Surveys suggest that training courses are increasingly modularised into 1-3 hour blocks – with two days considered a larger training course.

Key advantages of bite-sized learning are cost, time, the speed with which learning can be transferred to the job, and ease of learning. However, this is another area in which *blended* strategies may be required.

EXAMPLE

'There is widespread agreement that much of the demand for bite size is coming from employees. "Our courses are aimed at giving employees a few pragmatic techniques that they can use immediately. This was certainly an area where we found a demand and we knew that our employees were looking for more accessible learning," says [Louise Prashad, capability development manager at drinks company, Diageo].

'She says the training department has found that delivering shorter courses has enabled them to offer a wider range of topics. It has also eased some of the pressures on the training department. "Over 18 months ago we were struggling with the cost of the three-day training courses, as well as trying to get people available for them." ...

'But the experience for the training department wishing to introduce modularisation can be challenging ...

BPP
LEARNING MEDIA

' "One of the biggest challenges is getting the pitch right because of the short duration. There are restrictions on both the topic and the extent to which you can explore it in the short time allocated," [Prashad] told *PM*.

'In addition, it can sometimes be easier to get staff off-site for the whole day rather than an hour. "In some respects it is easier to arrange cover for one day than one hour. In a hospital, the loss of a person for an hour can be very evident in an emergency," says Simon Tisdale, head of training and development, Salford Royal Hospitals NHS Trust. ...'

(Roberts, 2003 (c))

3.4 Training providers

There is a wide range of options open to the HR or training department: see Figure 14.1 on the following page.

3.5 Programme administration

A number of administrative matters will occupy the training department, including:

(a) Selecting participants for planned courses, according to preferences for schedule, content, learning style, location and training need priorities identified by line managers.

(b) Negotiating course content, time-tables and costs with external training providers.

(c) Booking external (and internal) training facilities and personnel.

(d) Sourcing relevant training materials and resources.

(e) Compiling calendars of training events, participant information briefings and other supporting materials.

(f) Marketing training programmes within the organisation.

	Advantages	Disadvantages	Factors to be taken into account
In-house options • 'On-the-job' vocational training (eg coaching) • In-house seminars, workshops, mentoring and job exchange for skill development • Participation in national initiatives, eg NVQs or Modern Apprenticeships • Call in a consultant to design and run specialist courses in-house	• May be cost-effective for large trainee numbers • Matching to specific organisational needs • Control over standards, accommodation etc • Ready transfer of learning to work context • Employer brand as corporate trainer	• Distractions from work task/context • Limited space, facilities, expertise? • Training department required to co-ordinate details (catering etc)	• Availability of suitably expert, trained instructors • Number of participants: cost of provision • Other alternatives • External advice and resources available
External options • Contract external training providers to run programmes externally	• Specialist facilities and expertise available • Less distraction from work tasks/ contexts • Greater freedom to raise work problems • Less demands on training department	• Expense • Planning/booking time required • May involve travel/ disruption for participants	• Cost – and resources available • Standard of training facilities • Qualifications, credibility and track record of trainers • Degree of specialism required • Location/travel/ access
Distance-learning options • Published resources • CD-ROM/video resources • Software and web-based (e-learning) resources	• Learner-paced • Can be undertaken in own time/work or home • Cost advantages	• Lack of social interaction and support • Perception of 'own time' v 'work'	• Quality, interactivity and relevance of resources • Learning style preferences of trainees

Figure 14.1: Training and development options
Source: Hargreaves and Jarvis, 2000

FOR DISCUSSION

Beardwell and Holden (1997) quote the sad but familiar story of Del the Delegate, who returns from a course full of new ideas, anxious to implement them. He is confronted with scepticism and cynicism from both his bosses and fellow employees. 'The friction set up between Del and his company undermines his enthusiasm and exhausts all his energy. Del's behaviour reverts to what is (and always was) reinforced by the company.

Is there an alternative ending to this tragic parable?

We will now go back and look at some of the available training methods and media in more detail. We will classify these under on-the-job training (Section 4) and off-the-job training (Section 5), but you should be aware that some methods may be used in either setting.

4 ON-THE-JOB TRAINING AND DEVELOPMENT

4.1 'Sitting with Nellie'

This is the traditional method of skill training. The trainee is placed beside an experienced worker (Nellie) and learns by observing him or her work and by imitating his or her operations and methods under close instruction and supervision, working with the actual materials and equipment that are involved in the job.

Advantages

- High transfer of learning (because learning in context)
- Effective and economical (where task amenable to observation-imitation)
- Immediate feedback and adjustment
- Establishes working relationships as well as skills

Disadvantages

- Ineffective if 'Nellie' uses poor work technique, or skill not amenable to observation

- Ineffective if 'Nellie' lacks training/instruction skills and job requires explanation

- Trainee socialised into shop floor culture of work: not necessarily methods or attitudes desired by management

4.2 Job instruction training

This is a technique which can be added to the 'sitting with Nellie' approach to minimise the disadvantages cited above. It was developed as a guide to systematic on-the-job training.

(a) Careful selection and preparation of trainer/'Nellie' and trainee: goals and objectives of learning outlined etc.

(b) Full explanation and demonstration of skill/task by the trainer/'Nellie'.

(c) Trial on-the-job practice/performance by the trainee.

(d) Thorough feedback session between trainer/'Nellie' and trainee to appraise and adjust trainee's performance and set further improvement goals. (Repeat (b) – (d) as required.)

4.3 Coaching

Coaching is one element of the 'sitting with Nellie' approach, but may be used flexibly in a wide range of training situations, and at any time during performance on an on-going basis.

Coaching is on-the-job guidance, advice, correction and feedback-giving with a view to improving performance in specific skill areas. A coach should:

(a) Demonstrate how areas of a job are performed, and guide the trainee's own performance of the same tasks, by advice and correction

(b) Help the trainee to identify and resolve problems in his or her work

(c) Seek out or identify opportunities for the trainee to develop, through doing new things at work

(d) Give feedback on progress and results, to guide learning

(e) Encourage the trainee to assess his or her own progress and performance, and to formulate further plans for improvement in an ongoing cycle.

Essentially, coaching is a **collaboration** between the coach and the trainee, in which the coach's special role is encouragement and guidance as the trainee develops on the job.

Advantages

- Flexible and interactive: pace and content of learning suited to trainee needs and trainer analysis

- Collaborative: involves trainee in problem-solving

- High transfer of learning (connected to live job performance)

Disadvantage

- Requires coaching skills

4.4 Mentoring

Definition

A **mentor** is a guide, ideally both more experienced and more powerful in the organisation, whose concern is the trainee's long-term personal development. The role is varied: counsellor, role model, champion/sponsor, spur to action or improvement, critical friend, encourager and so on.

While coaching is directed at short-term, skill-based development, mentoring is a longer-term relationship focused on broader career and personal development

A mentor should assist the mentored as follows.

(a)   Help the trainee to greater self-awareness, by listening to, questioning and challenging his or her ideas, and feeding back on his or her behaviour

(b)   Help the trainee to formulate and clarify his or her needs and ambitions in life, and to identify where events and opportunities at work fit into those plans

(c)   Encourage the trainee to take responsibility for his or her development, while offering support – personally and within the organisation – if required

(d)   Help the trainee to reconcile his or her non-work needs, interests and circumstances with the demands of work (or vice versa)

(e)   Help the trainee to plan specific development and career paths or directions, offering opportunities where appropriate and possible

4.5   Action learning

Action learning was developed by Reg Revans in the 1970s. It is described (Pedler *et al*, 2003) as a method for individual and organisational development in which 'working in small groups, people tackle important organisational issues or problems and learn from their attempts to change things'.

The key elements of action learning programmes are as follows.

(a)   A small group of four or five people (usually managers) meet together regularly, on a wholly voluntary basis, for the programme period (perhaps several months).

(b)   Each participant brings a managerial or organisational problem they want to deal with.

(c)   Group members support and learn from one another, acting as a mentoring, consulting and problem-solving network. (An external advisor may sit in and facilitate.)

(d)   The group both generates and examines options in response to member issues/problems *and* learns about the interpersonal and managerial processes involved as they do so.

(e)   Group members take action – and the group learns further from feedback on that action (in a learning cycle).

Pedlar *et al* note that many organisational project teams, self-help groups, productivity improvement meetings and quality circles are in fact reflecting action learning processes.

So far we have looked at ways in which employees can acquire and improve skills in a particular job or task through guided imitation and practice. A slightly different approach is to give employees a 'taste' of different jobs and functions.

4.6 Training by switching or 'shadowing' roles

This may be accomplished by a number of methods.

(a) **Job rotation** or **'shadowing'**: the trainee is given several jobs in succession, to gain experience of a wide range of activities and departments. (Even experienced managers may rotate their jobs to gain wider experience; this method is commonly applied in the Civil Service.)

(b) **Temporary promotion:** an individual is promoted into a superior's position while the superior is absent. This gives the individual a chance to experience the demands of a more senior position.

(c) **'Assistant to' positions:** an individual with management potential may be appointed as assistant to a manager. In this way, the individual gains experience of management, without a risky level of responsibility.

(d) **Project or committee work:** trainees might be included in the membership of a project team or committee, to obtain an understanding of inter-departmental relationships, problem-solving and particular areas of the organisation's activity.

(e) **Assignments:** trainees may be delegated to a particular task or project by a superior.

Advantages

- Employees gain experience without risking immediate responsibility.
- Task/role variety may increase job satisfaction and awareness of organisational processes.
- Aids career/management/succession planning.

Disadvantages

- May be perceived as perpetual traineeship: not real work
- May be perceived as a 'nuisance' in departments having to 'carry' trainees

4.7 Apprenticeship and traineeship training

Apprenticeships and traineeships involve a combination of on-the-job training (using any of the above methods) and off-the-job training (one or two days a week, or a number of weeks in the year, at a college or university). The trainees earn while they learn, but at a lesser rate than full-time employees of the organisation in which they are placed to gain their work experience.

4.8 Advantages and disadvantages of on-the-job training and development

On-the-job training is very common, especially when the work involved is not complex, but will only be successful under the following circumstances.

(a) **Assignments must have a specific purpose** from which the trainee can learn and gain experience; otherwise, it can be unfocused and overwhelming

(b) **It works best where the trainee is a practical type,** who prefers to learn by doing and can tolerate the process of trial and error. (Other people might need to get away from the pressures of the workplace to think through issues and understand the underlying principles before applying new techniques: remember Honey and Mumford's learning styles: how would they describe this type of learner?)

(c) **Trainers are themselves trained** in instruction and coaching techniques (as well as modelling efficient and effective work practices)

(d) **The organisation is tolerant of mistakes.** Mistakes are an inevitable part of on-the-job learning, and if they are punished or frowned on, the trainee will be reluctant to take further risks and will be de-motivated to learn.

There may be real risks involved in throwing people in at the deep-end: the cost of mistakes or inefficiencies may be high and the pressure on learners great. (Would you want medical procedures, or air traffic control procedures to be learned on-the-job?)

The key **advantage** of on-the-job training, however, is that it takes place in the environment of the job itself, and in the context of the work group in which the trainee will have to operate. The style of supervision, personal relations with colleagues, working conditions and pressures, the culture of the office/shop floor and so on will be absorbed as part of the training process.

Activity 5 (20 minutes)

If you have had work experience, list the advantages you experienced through on-the-job training. If you have not worked, think about this course and list the disadvantages of the different methods of study you are given.

4.9 Self-development approaches

There are a number of techniques for informal, self-managed experiential learning at work.

- **Informal** – arising from the job and work context

- **Self-managed** – planned, implemented and evaluated primarily by the learner

- **Experiential** – using the learning cycle to turn any work event or action in to a learning opportunity

There are various methods for self development.

(a) **Personal Development Plans** and **learning contracts** formulated with line managers or mentors: formal commitment to work towards specified learning goals, with action plans.

(b) **Personal Development Journals** or **learning logs**: a structured approach to the learning cycle. The learner selects a critical incident at work which illustrates a learning need: (s)he describes what happened, reflects on the event and its consequences, draws conclusions, and identifies future actions to reinforce successful behaviours and/or change unsuccessful behaviours.

(c) **Self-development groups**: groups which meet to discuss personal development and work issues, give each other feedback and information and so on – like a flexible action learning group.

Activity 6   **(no time limit)**

Keep a Personal Development Journal for a week.

(a) Select a particular skill area you want to develop: say, interviewing, presentation, assertiveness or team working.

(b) Each day, reflect on your day at work. What incidents demonstrate something to you about your competence (good or bad) in your chosen area?

(c) Describe the incident. What did you and others do or say? How did you feel?

(d) Reflect on the incident. What could you have done differently to get a better result? (Or what did you do *well,* to get a good result?)

(e) How can you put your insights into action? Plan to access whatever information, advice, feedback or help you need. (What will you need? Who will you ask? When?) Plan a specific 'next time' to try your better solution.

We will now look briefly at a particular kind of training programme, involving both off– and on-the-job elements: induction.

4.10 Induction training

From the first day in a job, a new recruit must be helped to find his or her bearings. There are limits to what any person can pick up in a short time, so the process of 'getting one's feet under the table' will be a gradual one. Induction is an ongoing process.

On the first day, a manager or HR officer should welcome the new recruit. The manager might discuss in broad terms what he requires from people at work, working conditions, pay and benefits, training opportunities and career opportunities. He should then introduce the new recruit to the person who will be his immediate supervisor.

The immediate supervisor should then take over the process of induction. Here is a general checklist.

(a) Pinpoint the areas that the recruit will have to learn about in order to start work. Some things (such as detailed technical knowledge) may be identified as areas for later study or training, while others (say, some of the procedures and systems with which the recruit will have to deal) will have to be explained immediately. A list of learning priorities should be drawn up, so that the recruit, and the supervisor, are clear about the rate and direction of progress required.

(b) Explain first of all the nature of the job, and the goals of each task, of the recruit's job and of the department as a whole. This will help the recruit to work to specific targets and to understand how each task relates to the overall objectives of the department – or even the organisation as a whole.

(c) Explain about hours of work and stress the importance of time-keeping. If flexitime is operated, explain how it works. Any other work practices, customs and rules should be explained clearly.

(d) Explain the structure of the department: to whom the recruit will report, to whom (s)he can go with complaints or queries and so on.

(e) Introduce the recruit to people in the workplace. (S)he should meet the departmental manager and all the members of the immediate work team (and perhaps be given the opportunity to get to know them informally). One particular colleague may be assigned to the recruit as a **mentor** for the first few days, to answer routine queries and 'show him (or her) the ropes'. The layout of the premises, procedures for lunch hours or holidays, rules about smoking or eating at work and so on will then be taught informally.

(f) Plan and implement an appropriate training programme for whatever technical or practical knowledge is required. Again, the programme should have a clear schedule and set of goals so that the recruit has a sense of purpose, and so that the programme can be efficiently organised to fit in with the activities of the department.

(g) Coach and/or train the recruit; check regularly on his progress, as demonstrated by performance, reported by the mentor, and/or as perceived by the recruit. Feedback information will be essential to the learning process, correcting any faults at an early stage and building the confidence of the recruit.

(h) Integrate the recruit into the culture of the workplace. Much of this may be done informally: (s)he will pick up the prevailing norms of dress, degree of formality, attitude to customers etc. However, the supervisor should try to 'sell' the values and style of the organisation and should reinforce commitment to those values by rewarding evidence of loyalty, hard work and desired behaviour.

After three months, six months and/or one year the performance of a new recruit should be formally appraised and discussed. This should dovetail into a regular employee appraisal programme.

Activity 7   (5 minutes)

Did you have any form of induction into student life?

Compare your experience to the checklist given above. How effective did you feel your induction was? What difference did it make to your confidence in your studies?'

We will now move on to off-the-job training.

5 OFF-THE-JOB TRAINING

5.1 Training providers

Off-the-job training providers include:

(a) Universities and colleges

(b) Private-sector colleges and training organisations including assessment centres for group training exercises

(c) Training consultancies, which may help the organisation locate or develop courses to meet its needs

(d) Publishers of training materials (texts and workbooks, videos, computer-based training packages), or

(e) The in-house education and training department of the organisation itself (large organisations).

Internal courses are sometimes run by the training departments of larger organisations. Skills may be taught at a technical level, related to the organisation's particular product and market, or to aspects such as marketing, teambuilding, interviewing or information technology management. Some organisations also encourage the wider development of staff by offering opportunities to learn languages or other skills.

One convenient and popular method of in-house education is **computer-based training** (CBT), **Interactive Video** (IV) or **e-learning** (Internet-based) using equipment in offices or even trainees' homes. Training programmes may be developed by the organisation or by outside consultants – or bought 'off the shelf': the software (or 'courseware') can then be distributed, so that large numbers of dispersed staff can learn about new products or procedures quickly and simultaneously.

EXAMPLE

'For years universities have been urged to become more businesslike. But the boot, it seems, is on the other foot as a growing number of employers attempt to emulate academia by setting up in-house 'universities'

'Corporate universities take a variety of forms. While some are little more than revamped training departments, others represent ambitious attempts to co-ordinate learning and share knowledge across organisations. A few have even begun to imitate real universities to the extent of investing in academic research. But a common feature of many of these institutions is their use of academic terminology to describe, and raise the status of, corporate training and development activities.

'Although the University for Lloyds TSB was launched only last year, the corporate university concept is far from new. Pioneered in the US in the 1950s, it was not widely known in this country until the arrival of McDonald's Hamburger University.

'The fast-food giant has now quietly dropped this title in the UK and these days refers – more accurately – to its nationwide network of "training centres". But the Hamburger University is still going strong on the other side of the Atlantic, where corporate universities are set to outnumber traditional higher educational establishments by the year 2010, according to a report by the US Department of Labor.

'In the UK, the first homegrown corporate university was set up in 1993 by Unipart, followed two years later by Anglian Water's University of Water. But it is only in the past couple of years that the idea has really taken off. According to research by Ray Wild and Colin Carnall of Henley Management College, there are around 200 corporate universities in the UK, and this number is likely to increase over the next few years.'

Anat Arkin, *People Management* (12 October 2000)

5.2 Training methods

Some methods of off-the-job training include the following.

(a) **Training room instruction.** Similar to on-the-job job instruction training (see Paragraph 4.2 above), but in a dedicated training environment. Instruction is given using presentation techniques and/or a simulation of workplace equipment and methods.

(b) **Lectures** or **taught classes.** These are useful for knowledge or theory/principle-based learning. They may incorporate elements of instruction, case-study, role-play and other techniques to overcome the limitations of passive learning. They suit large numbers of trainees requiring the same basic body of knowledge. Drawbacks include their passivity and the difficulty of absorbing more than three or four key points per session, and their relative inflexibility to individual trainees' learning styles and needs.

(c) **Case study.** Using a description of a real-life scenario or example for analysis, providing insights and opportunities to exercise problem-solving skills, which can be transferred to the work context. Case-studies are a kind of on-paper simulation of work scenarios, allowing experimentation and exploration without risk. They are particularly useful for problem-solving and decision-making in a wide rage of specific contexts.

(d) **Role play.** The simulation of an interpersonal scenario, allowing trainees to experiment with learned behaviours and skills and to observe their effects in interpersonal encounters. This is particularly helpful in training for customer service, interviewing, conflict resolution and so on. It suits small groups, allowing for all-member participation.

(e) **Simulation.** In technical training, this may involve the mocking-up of equipment and environments so that trainees can experiment with technical skills and observe results in a safe, progressively-staged and controlled manner. (Flight simulators for pilots is one example.) In other forms of training, simulation may involve case studies, role plays, assignments of 'in-tray' exercises, which mock up typical tasks and scenarios to test trainees' organisational and problem-solving skills.

(f) **Open** or **distance learning.** Employees access technology-assisted instruction where and when it suits them, using training manuals, workbooks, video (and video conferencing for group sessions), tapes, computer-based packages and so on. Some face-to-face tuition may be used periodically to assess or reinforce learning, or to add more interactive and group work. This can be a highly economical method, especially where trainees are geographically dispersed.

(g) **Discovery learning.** A method by which trainees explore a task or concept for themselves, with relatively little initial instruction or demonstration. Trainees are thus encouraged to find out the key principles, constraints and methods of the task, and to ask the questions that are relevant to them. This is a highly trainee-centred technique which is tailored to the learning styles and needs of the trainees and fosters problem-solving and learning skills alongside specific technical competencies. It is, however, time-, labour– and cost-intensive.

(h) **Programmed learning.** A structure of learning by which a trainee, working at his or her own pace, works through a carefully ordered sequence of units or operations, each with objectives, instruction, testing and consolidation which allow the trainee to master one unit before progressing to the next. This is a feature of many distance learning and computer-based learning programmes.

(i) **Visits and tours**. Trainees are given opportunities to observe other sites, departments, operations and so on. This may be helpful in demonstrating: how skills learned in the classroom are applied in practice; different types of machinery and work organisation; stages of operation before and after that in which the trainee will be involved; application of products/services by customers or end users; and so on.

(j) **Outdoor training**. Physical tasks and activities in challenging environments, designed to help trainees learn about themselves and their motivations, leadership skills, group dynamics and co-operation and so on. This is increasingly used in team-building and leadership training. Another growth area is corporate social responsibility (Allen, 2003), with teams being sent to renovate inner-city residential hostels and similar experiences, to encourage awareness of the wider community's needs. Learning takes place through the process of working out a group solution to a problem or challenge, with a facilitator aiding reflection and analysis afterwards. Outdoor training specialists are increasingly looking to target their offering more accurately, keeping courses short and making sure that they are useful (and clear) metaphors for the workplace.

(k) **Computer-based training.** Using computer software for instruction and assessment. (This will be discussed further below.)

(l) **E-learning**: learning or training delivered by electronic technology, particularly ICT developments such as the Internet and company intranets – in support of (rather than instead of) traditional training methods. This is a major development, and we will discuss it separately in Paragraph 5.4 below.

EXAMPLE

'Jaded employees? Perhaps its time to unleash the dogs of motivation. In fact, the Virgin Experience's "Thinking Like Canines" programme is not quite as barking as it sounds. Far from instilling dog-like obedience among staff, the basic aim is to strip bare the essentials of workplace – that occupied by working border collies.

'Professional dog trainer Barbara Sykes, along with her team of canine consultants, takes participants through a variety of sheepdog trials – showing them their own communication foibles and how to get the best from individual team members. There is a strong focus on body language and presenting a clear message. "A dog will only respond to clearly defined body language, so each 'shepherd' learns to use their natural communication in different circumstances, with different recipients and under pressure," says Sykes.

'Within day-long programmes emphasising either leadership or teamwork, participants have to assess different dogs correctly and react to their personalities in order to realise each dog's full potential. Starting off in a training ring, they eventually graduate to the open field, where they are handed a variety of tasks with workplace parallels.

' "The dogs work together in harmony for the good of the pack," Sykes says. "They don't argue about their position and don't waste time scoring points off each other. They accept and respect leadership but use their initiative whenever the need arises." '

(Allen, 2003)

Activity 8 **(20 minutes)**

Suggest a suitable training method for each of the following situations.

(a) A worker is transferred onto a new machine and needs to learn its operation.

(b) An accounts clerk wishes to work towards becoming qualified with the relevant professional body.

(c) An organisation decides that its supervisors would benefit from 'picking up some ideas' on participative management and democratic leadership.

(d) A new member of staff is about to join the organisation.

(e) A supervisor allows himself to be intimidated by his workteam and ends up carrying most of the workload himself. Occasionally, he tries to throw his weight around, but this never lasts.

5.3 Advantages and disadvantages of off-the-job training

Advantages	Disadvantages
• It allows exploration and experimentation by inexperienced employees without risking negative consequences for live performance	• If the subject matter of the training course is not felt to relate directly to the individual's job and organisation culture, the learning will not be applied afterwards, and will quickly be forgotten.
• It allows trainees to be away from the work environment where interruptions, distractions and performance pressure may interfere with learning.	• Individuals may feel that courses are, in general, a waste of time. They will not benefit from the training unless they are motivated to learn.
• It allows training to be standardised and distributed across a geographically dispersed workforce (eg via video, CBT or distance learning).	• Immediate and relevant feedback on performance and progress may not be available from the learning process, especially if knowledge is tested by unrealistic methods (such as exams) or at wide intervals. This will lower the learner's incentive and sense of direction.
• It allows for self-study at the trainee's own pace (eg via distance learning).	• It does not suit some people, who may not have much experience of (or taste for) classroom learning since school. Some people simply prefer a 'hands-on' type of learning: learning by doing.
• It may have organisational status as a reward or peak: being sent on a course is a sign of potential.	• Some organisational cultures encourage fear and insecurity around training courses, with the perception that a person sent on a course must be performing inadequately.

5.4 E-learning

Armstrong (2003) calls it 'perhaps the most important recent development in approaches to the delivery and support of learning'. Surveys suggest that it is showing fast growth world-wide, with the UK becoming a major European market.

Definition

> **E-learning** is: 'Learning that is delivered, enabled or mediated by electronic technology for the explicit purposes of training in organisations. It does not include stand-alone technology-based training such as the use of CD-ROMs in isolation.' (CIPD)

This places e-learning firmly in the context of ICT networks, including:

- Networked computers forming a corporate intranet
- The Internet and World Wide Web.

E-learning systems typically include:

(a) **Software packages** – purchased 'off-the-shelf' from providers, or designed and developed in-house – which provide e-learning programmes and facilities: course content, navigation tools, interactive testing and feedback mechanisms and so on.

(b) **Learning support** from online tutors and/or 'e-moderators', who track participation, co-ordinate information-sharing and interactions with other learners (discussion boards, chat sessions, student blogs, web seminars and so on) and provide guidance as appropriate.

In addition, **informal e-learning** may take place through everyday information-sharing and interaction over the Internet or intranet in the course of work.

Advantages and disadvantages of e-learning

Advantages cited for e-learning include:

- Learning at the learner's pace and convenience
- Flexible delivery, with access from home, work, libraries etc
- Reduction in delivery costs
- Potential for collaborative learning in 'virtual learning groups' for employees (and others) spread over wide geographical distances: chat, web conferencing and other technologies allow real time support and interaction
- High degree of interactivity, for immediate feedback (eg test scoring), question and answer and so on
- Potential for multi-media, high-interest presentation of learning material (not just 'e-reading') for enhanced learning motivation

Disadvantages cited include:

- The need for Internet or network connection, which may not be available to all employees – and may be complex and expensive to set up
- The need for culture and attitude change to support e-learning, since it represents (for many people) a radically new way to work and learn
- The poor quality or relevance of some off-the-shelf e-learning programmes
- Limitations in the applications for which e-learning is suited, notably in the area of interpersonal skills. Over-reliance on e-learning alone has led to disappointed expectations.

Applications of e-learning

There are several areas in which e-learning might be particularly appropriate, because there are easily identifiable knowledge/learning needs which can be effectively met by electronic means.

(a) **Training in IT skills**. Learners can be led through relevant programmes, shown what to do, given opportunities to practise, tested and given competence feedback and records with little need for interpersonal or face-to-face support. Online support usually takes the form of e-mail contact and response.

(b) **Information/awareness-based learning**: induction briefings, health and safety awareness programmes, job-related information briefings/updates, new product/service information, company policy/rule changes and so on. E-learning does information transfer efficiently and with potential for greater creativity, interest and user-friendliness than oral briefings or printed manuals. Face-to-face methods might be used to follow-up or reinforce learning: emphasising the importance of compliance, say, or getting a team together to discuss the new product they've been informed about.

E-learning is not an optimal stand-alone solution for training needs such as 'soft' people management and interpersonal skills: negotiating, giving presentations, team-building, interviewing, leadership and so on. Instructor-led training, coaching, practice and feedback are required. E-learning may still be used to provide pre-course instruction and orientation, to reduce face-to-face time requirements. It may also be used where necessary to reach geographically dispersed learners: webcasts and video-conferencing can be used to stage virtual meetings and presentations, for example.

However, the limitations of e-learning in these areas gave rise to the concept of blended learning: supporting e-learning with the right mix of face-to-face training methods (and *vice versa*).

EXAMPLE

'Over 2,500 **Royal & Sun Alliance** (R&SA) staff will undertake up to 35 hours of e-learning this year developing the IT and people skills that will support their customer facing role. As Katherine Plant, training manager at R&SA, explained: "In the past, with the numbers of people who need training, we would probably have implemented a classroom-based roll-out. My remit, however, has been to look at alternative methods of delivering this training and clearly e-learning is the best solution. We can ensure a consistent, high quality training message every time, wherever our people are located. It's also available to people when they need it and this latest learning technology shows them how much we are investing in their development; it sends the message that as a company we believe in both our people and our customers."

'The first of the three Customer Relationship Management (CRM) training programmes focuses on communication skills and includes the theory of how people communicate. It then looks at the practical skills required to put people at their ease such as how staff can match their pace and their language to that of customers.

'The second e-learning programme considers the rationale behind CRM at R&SA ... This programme recognises that the real experts in the business are its front-line staff and it encourages them to contribute their ideas and make the case for how these ideas could make a difference to their customers.

'The third e-learning programme will educate users on the new single view system which R&SA is implementing and which will underpin all customer contact. This is the system that maps and records all customer enquiries and interactions and ensures that all R&SA's staff have the latest customer details at their fingertips.

'Throughout the programmes R&SA is supporting its people with coaching and role-play exercises. This is the important 'blended solution' aspect of the programme where staff can build their skills, get the objective feedback they need and learn from one another. With such people skills it is seldom a matter of right and wrong; people have their own ways of communicating and they need to develop their own style. The coaching input enables them to build awareness of what they currently do and develop the 'best practice' skills and techniques that they have learned to ensure that their customers get a great service. This is what ongoing coaching and support is really about – helping people to develop their confidence and competence in their role.'

(Clague, 2004)

Activity 9   **(no time limit)**

Check out some e-learning related websites and browse through the links and resources.

▶▶ www.e-learningcentre.co.uk

▶▶ www.e-learningnetwork.org

▶▶ www.smartforce.com

How easy was this information to access and use? What does this say about e-learning?

We will now go on to the 'final' stage of systematic training: evaluation.

6   EVALUATING LEARNING EVENTS

6.1   Purposes of evaluation

Evaluation is the process whereby feedback is gathered on the progress and outcomes of training events or programmes, in order to support further planning and decision-making. It may fulfil a number of purposes.

(a)   To **determine the effectiveness of training**: measuring whether each training programme is meeting its intended objectives (in terms of learning outcomes, stakeholder satisfaction, impact on performance and a range of other criteria). Effective evaluation is important to validate training as a business tool for improving organisational performance and profitability.

(b)   To **help improve the design of training**: asking 'Are we training the right people in the right things, in the right way, with the right materials, at the right time?'

(i)   Identifying the strengths and weaknesses of specific training approaches, activities, materials and providers, so that programmes can be revised or modified for improved value and benefits.

(ii)   Identifying what types of staff benefit the most or the least from a given training approach, in order to adjust and develop future programmes and select appropriate participants

Effective evaluation enables training designers and providers to make objective comparisons and decisions.

(c)   To **support accountability:** determining the cost-benefit ratio or return on investment of each training event (and of training activity as a whole), in order to justify expenditure – and gain the support of management and other training sponsors, in the face of competition for scarce resources.

(d)   To gather information on the nature, experience and outcomes of training programmes so that they can be effectively **marketed within the organisation**

(e)   To allow **stakeholders** in the training process to express their needs and preferences and to have their feedback heard, in order to improve the relevance and acceptability of training

(f)   To provide **management information**: on skills and competences (for HR planning), training costs, benefits and resources (for HRD planning) and so on.

6.2   What should be evaluated?

In one sense, the 'what' of evaluation refers to the **criteria** for measuring training success: what are evaluators looking *for*? There are various models suggesting specific sets of criteria, which we will discuss in Paragraph 6.6. However, the full range of criteria selected for evaluation might include the following.

(a)   **Participant reactions**: trainees' satisfaction with the course or activity, its relevance to their work and so on. This can be measured using feedback forms, attitude surveys or 'happy sheets' (and also, as a rough guide, numbers of trainees applying for and attending training events). It is important, because a negative experience may inhibit transfer of learning, cause negative word-of-mouth and impact on future take-up of training opportunities.

(b)   **Learning outcomes**: new or enhanced knowledge, skills and attitudes. This can be measured using post-training tests or assessments (and follow-up tests to see how much has been retained after the training is over). The effectiveness of a training event may be measured by the number of participants achieving learning objectives.

(c)   **Behaviour change**: new work behaviours which reflect learning outcomes, by applying new skills or awareness on the job. This can be measured using observation and performance monitoring, both before and after training (for comparison). It is important in order to evaluate transfer of learning.

(d)   **Performance change**: the outflow of behaviour change into impact on individual, unit and organisational performance. This can be measured using feedback from the performance management system (on key performance indicators), and comparing groups who have and have not been through the training. (Otherwise, it is hard to verify that training has made the difference, rather than a number of other variables.) This is important to make a business case for training.

(e) **Other desired outcomes**: for example, whether training has been effective in encouraging networking and co-operation between participants (particularly if they have been brought together from different units or dispersed teams); or whether training is perceived as a valued benefit or reward (if this is part of the organisation's reward management plans).

(f) **Costs of training**: in order to compare the cost-effectiveness of different approaches and providers, and to provide data for cost-benefit (or return on investment) analysis. The organisation should measure both:

- **Direct** costs, which would not be incurred if the particular training did not take place: the cost of learning resources and materials; external training facilities and trainer/consultant fees; travel expenses and so on *and*

- **Indirect** costs, which would be incurred whether or not the particular programme was held: training department salaries and costs, participant salaries for the duration of the training, in-house training facilities and equipment.

(g) **Efficiency**: the amount of learning achieved relative to the amount of time and effort expended. This is an important element in cost-effectiveness.

(h) **Performance to schedule and specification**: the performance of the training provider in relation to agreed criteria for training completion dates, support services, quality of materials and facilities and so on.

In another sense, the 'what' of evaluation refers to the activities and attributes to be assessed: what are evaluators looking *at*?

Activity 10   **(5 minutes)**

What areas would you look at in order to evaluate the quality and suitability of a training course – both as a learner and as training manager?

6.3 When should evaluation take place?

Evaluation is a decision-making tool. It should lead to decisions about which programmes will be continued or discontinued; which learning methods and activities will be incorporated; which materials and technologies will be used; which course providers and learning facilitators will be used; who should be encouraged to participate and so on. In a sense, therefore, the four 'stages' of systematic training should really be seen as a **cycle** (Bramley, 1986), whereby information from the evaluation stage is fed back into further analysis of training needs, design decisions and programme plans: Figure 14.2.

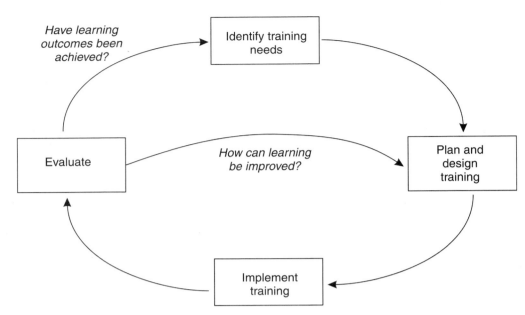

Figure 14.2: Systematic training cycle

There are two basic types of evaluation.

(a)   **Formative** (or process) evaluation focuses on appraisal as a source of data which will be fed back into the planning process, in order to refine or improve training. It may be carried out:

- At the development stage, in order to check that the planned approach, activities, content and materials are likely to achieve the desired training outcomes and justify their anticipated costs.

- On an on-going or periodical basis throughout the training programme, in order to highlight any problems or shortcomings which need adjustment.

(b)   **Summative** (or product) evaluation focuses on appraisal of the effectiveness of the completed event or programme, at its conclusion. The 'product' or results of the programme are analysed and recommendations made as to whether the programme should be continued and/or modified in future.

Both types of evaluation are necessary. Formative feedback is particularly beneficial because it helps training providers to get things right *this* time – not just next time! This in turn helps to ensure the least possible waste of time and resources.

6.4   Who should evaluate training?

We noted in Chapter 13 that there are a number of stakeholders in training. All of them will want to carry out some level of evaluation in order to justify their particular 'investment' in the training. The roles of key stakeholders in the evaluation process may be summarised as follows.

(a)   **Senior management** will undertake a strategic-level evaluation of training as a whole, both formative (in order to approve the human resource development plan and resources) and summative (in order consider the business case for further or adjusted plans). Information about the impact of training on overall organisational performance and culture may only be available at this level.

(b) **Training/development specialists** will have the primary responsibility for evaluating particular training programmes and events, in order to design and manage programmes effectively, justify past and future expenditure, and supply management information for the higher level. Evaluation criteria, methods and schedules should be built into all training plans.

(c) **Trainees** have an important role in evaluating training events in which they have participated: trainee satisfaction is a key criterion, because it supports effective learning and transfer of learning. Trainee feedback *during* training is particularly valuable, as it helps trainers to adapt activities as far as possible to the needs and preferences of the current participants: trainees should be encouraged to co-operate with trainers in improving their experience and outcomes – rather than complaining at the end. In addition, feedback may be sought on the wider perception of training by employees, which will influence its take-up (where voluntary), effectiveness (which depends on learner motivation) and usefulness as part of the total reward package.

(d) **Trainees' line managers** have a strong interest in the transfer of learning to the workplace. Their main role in evaluation will be to assess the impact of training on work behaviour and individual/group performance, as a key criterion of training effectiveness.

(e) **External training providers** will need to evaluate their own performance in relation to desired outcomes: number of courses run, number of students, income, profitability, reputation, client/trainee satisfaction and so on. They should make use of feedback from their customers (both training managers and trainees) and should provide feedback to them (eg trainee test and assessment results, and perhaps also a report on the conduct or motivation of trainees).

6.5   How is evaluation data gathered?

A number of formal and informal evaluation techniques may be used.

Method	Advantages	Limitations
Interviews		
• With participants, line managers, team members • To assess satisfaction, learning, impact on work performance	Flexible focus and style Opportunity for clarification, probing Face-to-face: may encourage personal feedback (eg on aspirations, problems)	Time/labour-intensive Costly May be unstructured Face-to-face: may inhibit honest feedback May 'lead'/influence responses
Questionnaires		
• 'Happy Sheets' (reaction or satisfaction focused) • Systematic evaluation instruments (reaction, outcome and improvement focused)	Low cost to administer May be tailored to specific events May allow anonymity, more honest responses Respondents control pace and depth of feedback	If badly designed or managed: poor data quality and return rate Data may be too general Questions may focus on 'likes/dislikes' rather than learning achieved, content relevance and how

Method	Advantages	Limitations
		trainers/materials/facilities supported learning (or not).
Direct observation • Of training (eg by assessors 'sitting in') • Of post-training behaviour	Good way to measure behavioural change Non-intrusive on personal responses	May be disruptive May be subjective: requires trained observers May influence behaviour
Written tests • Knowledge test (eg by multiple choice) • Case study analysis	Low-cost development Ease of administration Ease of processing/scoring (objective testing) Allows wide sampling	May not relate to directly to work: only measures cognitive learning May not reflect learning (eg due to test stress or literacy/language problems)
Performance tests • Competence assessment • Simulation/in-tray exercises/role plays	Relevance to work and performance Includes cognitive and skill-based learning Allows evaluation of 'soft' (interpersonal) skills	Time consuming to create, administer and score May require external development/assessment High cost
Performance data • Individual performance and training records • Archived unit results	Job-based Easy to review Historical: not influenced by evaluation process	Relevant records may not be available Records prepared for other purposes may not contain usable data

FOR DISCUSSION

Have you ever been asked to fill in a feedback or review sheet for training events or materials? How seriously did you take this exercise? What might prevent students or trainees from taking the feedback process seriously (or engaging in it at all)? What kinds of questions could be asked to give planners and providers *meaningful* feedback to help them improve training?

6.6 Evaluation models

There are a number of models of evaluation. The most influential is The Kirkpatrick Model, originally devised in 1959.

The Kirkpatrick Model

Kirkpatrick sets out four levels of evaluation.

Level	Evaluation of	Measure	Methodology
1	**Reaction**	Trainee satisfaction: 'Were participants pleased with the programme?'	Post-training forms, quantifying reactions as far as possible, and encouraging written comments and suggestions
2	**Learning**	The extent to which learning objectives were met: 'What did participants learn in the programme'?	Pre– and post-training written or performance-based tests of the materials covered in the training
3	**Behaviour**	Transfer of learning to the workplace: 'Did the participants change their behaviour based on what was learned'?	Various: eg observation, work/output sampling, follow-up training audit, competence assessment
4	**Results**	Impact on the organisation: 'Did the change in behaviour positively affect the organisation?'	Monitoring comparable pre– and post-training data: sales or productivity, accidents, customer satisfaction

The Kirkpatrick model is widely known and accepted. It usefully highlights key outcomes of training, the link between them and the need to evaluate all four of them. As Armstrong (2003) notes: 'Training produces reactions, which lead to learning, which leads to changes in job behaviour, which lead to results at unit and organisational level Trainees can react favourably to a course... but learn little or nothing. They might learn something, but be unable or unwilling to apply it. They might apply it but it does no good within their own areas, or it does some good in their function, but does not improve organisational effectiveness'.

However, there are some well-recognised issues in applying this model.

(a) It can be interpreted as focusing on post-training or summative evaluation, rather than formative evaluation, for the purposes of programme design and inter-stage adjustments and improvements. Kaufman (1994), for example, separates Level 1 into 'enabling' (the availability of inputs for the training programme) and 'reaction' (participants' satisfaction).

(b) Many organisations evaluate only at the easiest and least costly Level 1: using 'smiles tests' which are meaningless in terms of justifying training's contribution (Level 4). Nor does enjoyment imply that trainees will apply what they have learned to their jobs: it may be seen as irrelevant, or may not be backed by managerial or resource support. Phillips (1997) adds a useful strand at Level 1 called 'intent to apply'.

(c) Level 4 is particularly difficult in practice: it is not always easy to prove that improved results are attributable to training, let alone to quantify its contribution.

(d)   Evaluation at all levels for all programmes may not be necessary or cost-effective. Training planners may find information Levels 1-2 feedback more useful in designing training events: obtaining information at higher levels of evaluation may appear both more costly and less valuable.

(e)   Despite the widespread neglect of Level 4, the model in some respects falls short. Kaufman (1994) adds a Level 5 which addresses the broader societal outcomes of training (adding the wider community to the list of stakeholders). Phillips (1997) adds a Level 5 for Return on Investment (ROI) assessment, calculating a monetary value for the impact of the instructional programme.

FOR DISCUSSION

'The evaluation of training, like motherhood and apple pie, is inherently a good thing. but, because short-term priorities always crowd out their longer-term competitors, it's typically something we plan to do better next year – after all, we've got away with it so far, so another year won't hurt!'   (Shepherd, 2004)

Why does a firm really *need* to evaluate its training programmes?

The CIRO model

The CIRO model (Warr, Bird and Rackham) sets out four evaluation categories.

Context   Identify:

- the performance need/deficiency or desired outcome at which the instructional programme is aimed

- the specific changes in work behaviour that will overcome the deficiency

- the knowledge, skill or attitudes needed to change behaviour

Input   Identify the resources to be used in conducting the programme

Reaction   Measure the participants' satisfaction with the programme

Outcome   Measure the results of the programme in terms of context requirements.

This more formative model uses similar *outcome* measures to the Kirkpatrick model, but broadens the scope of evaluation to include planning *inputs* including need analysis and resourcing. It does not offer an extensive framework for assessment (like the Kirkpatrick model or ROI) but it provides a strong linkage between the objectives of the training programme and its eventual outcomes, creating an objective basis for validation of the programme: did it achieve what it was intended to achieve?

Return on Investment (ROI) model

Definition

> **'Return on investment** (ROI) is a measure of the monetary benefits obtained by an organisation over a specified time period in return for a given investment in a training programme. Looking at it another way, ROI is the extent to which the benefits (outputs) of training exceed the costs (inputs).' (Shepherd, 2004)

Phillips (1997) put forward ROI as a quantitative measurement of training impact, stressing its use in justifying expenditure on a planned training programme (or training activity as a whole) and evaluating the extent to which the planned/desired return was achieved. It is seen as a 'Level 5' evaluation, not a substitute for measuring learner satisfaction, learning outcomes or learning transfer.

ROI is a complex process of data gathering and analysis. Phillips suggested that programmes suitable for ROI evaluation are those which:

- (a) Involve large target audiences
- (b) Are expected to have a long life cycle
- (c) Are important to the strategic objectives of the business
- (d) Require significant investment
- (e) Have high visibility
- (f) Are developed through systematic and comprehensive needs assessment.

A (deceptively simple) approach to calculating ROI (Shepherd, 2004) involves:

- (a) Forecasting and/or measuring the **total costs** associated with a training programme (including evaluation costs).

- (b) Forecasting and/or measuring the **total financial benefits** of the training programme. This is not easy, as many of the benefits of training are non-quantifiable and difficult to measure, some may take time to emerge to the point where they offer a measurable return on investment: paradigm shifts and cultural changes, employee satisfaction and commitment, increased flexibility and ideas generation and so on. However, quantifiable categories include:

  - (i) Labour savings

  - (ii) Productivity increases

  - (iii) Other cost savings (eg fewer machine breakdowns and accidents, lower staff turnover)

  - (iv) Other income generation (eg higher sales success rates, new product ideas)

- (c) **Calculating return on investment:**

  % ROI (over a specified period) = (benefits/costs) × 100

- (d) **Calculating the 'packback' period**: how long it will take before the benefits of the training match the costs and the training pays for itself. This is a powerful tool in marketing a training proposal to senior management – as long as the figure is relatively low!

  Payback period = costs/monthly benefits

Activity 11 (no time limit)

Find out how training is evaluated in your own work organisation, or another organisation of your choice. (You may use published sources or personal contacts to obtain this information.) What model of evaluation is used (if any)? How effective is the method perceived to be? What limitations or difficulties are experienced in practice?

Chapter roundup

A systematic approach to training can be illustrated as follows.

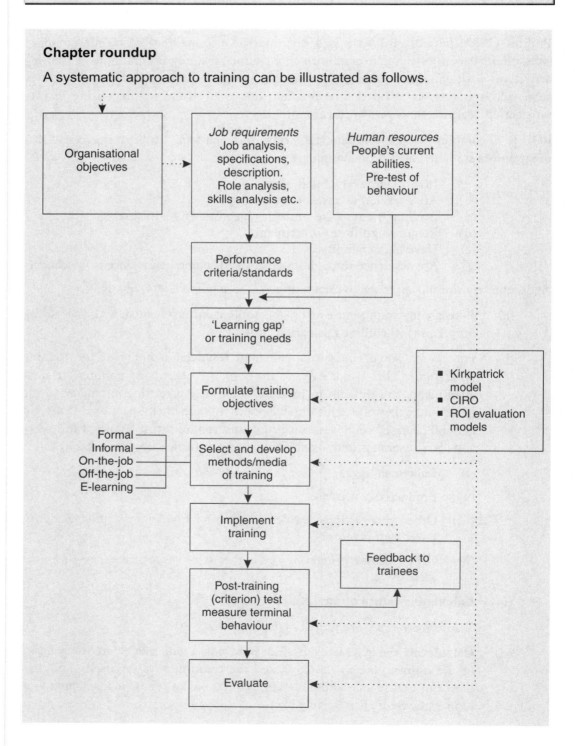

BPP LEARNING MEDIA

Quick quiz

1 How do 'training needs' arise in an organisation and how would you carry out a 'training needs analysis' if required to do so?

2 What is 'blended learning'?

3 List three methods of 'on-the-job' training.

4 What are the advantages and disadvantages of 'on-the job' training methods?

5 What is induction?

6 Training using physical challenges in unfamiliar environments is called 'Action Learning'. True or false?

7 Outline the advantages and disadvantages of e-learning.

8 Suggest three key reasons for evaluating training.

9 What criteria should be evaluated?

10 What do TKM, CIRO and ROI stand for?

Answers to quick quiz

1 The answer depends on the job or tasks and the abilities and experience of individuals or groups. Training needs analysis entails finding the difference between the required level of competence and the present level.
(see paragraphs 2.2-2.3)

2 Using a mix of learning types, styles and technologies in order to meet needs and preferences of trainees. (para 3.2)

3 Coaching, job rotation, 'assistant to' positions. (paras 4.1-4.7)

4 The main advantage is that it is relevant to the job. It takes place within the job environment, so that the style of supervision, personal relations and working conditions are absorbed. The main disadvantages are pressure and the cost of mistakes. (para 4.8)

5 Introducing new recruits to the job and environment. (para 4.10)

6 False. (paras 4.5, 5.2)

7 See paragraph 5.4 for a full answer.

8 Determining effectiveness, improving design, supporting accountability.
(para 6.1)

9 See paragraph 6.2 for a full answer.

10 The Kirkpatrick Model; Context, Input, Reaction, Outcome; Return on Investment. (para 6.6)

Answers to activities

1   Fulfilling such aspirations may become incompatible with business objectives if:

    (a) Specific training outcomes become divorced from the strategic aims of the business, and become focused on purely personal development for its own sake

    (b) Training outcomes serve to increase employee mobility, by giving them transferable skills and self-confidence

    (c) Training outcomes encourage the employee to 'outgrow' the organisation's culture and leadership style, creating expectations and capabilities that the organisation may not (yet) be in a position to utilise or even tolerate

2   Your own needs assessment: you might make this the basis for Activity 11, later.

3   The answer offered by Torrington and Hall (1991) is as follows.

Training needs	Learning objectives
(a) To know more about	The employee will be able to answer four
	the Data Protection Act out of every five queries about the Data Protection Act without having to search for details.
(b) To establish a better	The employee will immediately attend to a rapport with customers customer unless already engaged with another customer.
	The employee will greet each customer using the customer's name where known.
	The employee will apologise to every customer who has had to wait to be attended to.
(c) To assemble clocks	The employee will be able to assemble more quickly each clock correctly within thirty minutes.

4   Your own experience. Note particularly how the *blend* of approaches gives you variety, suits your learning style and so on. Disadvantages may include inconsistent messages, extra time/cost and so on.

5   You have probably covered most of the following points.

    Advantages include working for a specific purpose, carrying out practical work, the feeling of achievement when a task is completed successfully, knowing you have made a contribution to the organisation's objectives, learning to work with others. If mistakes are made they are rectified and do not affect your overall performance (unless you make too many or keep making the same mistakes).

    Disadvantages could include the difficulty of relating exercises or assignments to the 'real work' situation, working mainly on your own and the few practical applications for your studies. Unlike work, you only have one chance to get things right: the marking system means that if you make a mistake there is little you can do once the work is handed in and marked.

6   We highly recommend this exercise: it may become a (very useful) habit!

7   Your own experience (NB: important source of learning!)

8   Training methods for the various workers indicated are as follows.

    (a) Worker on a new machine: on-the-job training, coaching.

    (b) Accounts clerk working for professional qualification: external course – evening class or day-release.

    (c) Supervisors wishing to benefit from participative management and democratic leadership: internal or external seminar, or group training exercise. Careful attention will need to be given to how these 'ideas' will be integrated into practice on the job.

    (d) New staff: induction training.

    (e) Intimidated supervisor: assertiveness training.

9   Note that this activity was in itself an exercise in e-learning!

10   Evaluation would typically cover areas such as: the learning and teaching processes used; course content; materials and teacher aids; credibility and competence of trainers/facilitators; training premises and amenities; flexibility and quality of service; costs; and outcomes of training (according to the criteria discussed earlier).

11   Your research: good evidence of competence in this area!

Chapter 15:
LEARNING AND SKILLING INITIATIVES

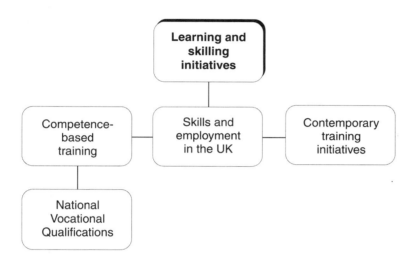

Introduction

One of the key resources of HR planners and developers will be contacts with other organisations dedicated to assessing, developing and mobilising employable skills. A wide range of schemes is sponsored in the UK by the Department for Education and Skills (DfES) and the Qualification and Curriculum Authority (QCA) to support vocational education and training both in and out of the workplace, aimed primarily at:

- Helping redundant and other unemployed individuals to develop (or re-develop) vocational skills in order to find work; and

- Increasing the knowledge and skill base of the UK labour pool to support economic growth.

All these schemes will be relevant to HR practitioners looking to forecast skill supply in the local labour market; recruit suitably skilled individuals; demonstrate corporate social responsibility by creating employment and development opportunities; support the development and employability of existing employees; and/or ease the impact of redundancy on staff, where required.

In this chapter, we will look briefly at a range of UK training initiatives and their sponsors. Many initiatives and structures are still under development or being reviewed. Use this chapter to orient your own on-going research and awareness, as the picture changes!

Your objectives

In this chapter you will learn about the following.

(a)   The context influencing government approaches to training and development

(b)   The competency movement and the development of NVQs

(c)   The role of the Qualifications and Curriculum Authority (QCA)

(d)   The role of Learning and Skills Councils (LSC)

(e)   Specific general and vocational training initiatives, including: modern apprenticeships, Investors in People, New Deal and the University for Industry

(f)   The role of Union Learning Representatives in employee development

1   SKILLS AND EMPLOYMENT IN THE UK

1.1   Vocational education and training in the UK

Research over some decades has highlighted poor levels of organisational investment in education and training in the UK, compared to its key competitors (Constable and McCormick, 1987; National Skills Task Force, 1998). Bolton (1997) summarises the position as follows.

> Study after study… has repeated the assertion that at the top end of training and education, the United Kingdom does as well as any other nation with, for instance, the proportion of young people achieving university degrees. It is at the intermediate level of qualification, the technician, the apprenticeship, secretarial and clerical training, that we do so poorly. It is generally recognised that the UK trains about half the number of young people with these skills as do many of our competitors.

This has been attributed to a number of factors.

(a)   Entrenched philosophies of organisation and management which maximise managerial control through the micro-design of jobs, automation and close supervision. Such systems devalue the role of employee development, other than at a basic competence level.

(b)   The emergence of human capital theory, which views HRD as an investment. While positive in supporting a business case for HRD, this viewpoint may cause a narrow focus on return on investment (direct contribution to profits). Development activities with less quantifiable or longer-term benefits may be seen as a cost to be minimised or cut, particularly in the face of competition for scarce resources and pressures to meet short-term financial targets.

(c)   Lack of systematic human resource planning, in the face of changing labour markets, so that skill requirements and shortages are not identified as an impetus to HRD.

(d)   A voluntarist or market-led approach to skill development, whereby responsibility for HRD decisions and funding lies primarily with employers, rather than with government. Many employers will choose to minimise their investment in training, where demand for skills is not perceived to be pressing.

(e) Self-limitation to low-skilled product and service markets. The deputy director of SKOPE (Skills, Knowledge and Organisational Performance) has been quoted as saying: 'Employers can happily ignore the government's warning about the effects of globalisation. In today's climate many firms can and do compete successfully on low skills and by producing goods at the low end of product specialisation. There is no impetus for them to change.'

(Manocha, 2003)

FOR DISCUSSION

Why do you think UK employers have been so reluctant to develop their people?

INTERNATIONAL COMPARISONS

	UK	Germany	US	Japan
Extent of State intervention	Voluntarist (left to employers)	Directed (laws and guidelines require employers to provide training funding and resources)	Voluntarist (anti-federalist, with wide variation)	Voluntarist/directed (voluntary, provision, but strong directives setting and enforcing high-quality training standards)
Orientation to development	Finance (rather than industry) oriented. Individualist development. Development largely extraneous to corporate culture: seen in context of performance improvement or management succession	Industry oriented (eg engineering) Functionally specific	Individualist: trainee aspirations, effort, reward. Excellent training by leading companies – otherwise unco-ordinated.	Collectivist view of development. On-going long-term training within employment: structured development for individual/organis-ation benefit. Development embedded in corporate culture, open to all employees

In the 1980s, recognition of the UK's poor skill base in relation to global competitors, supported by growing business/employer influence, led policy makers and educationalists to seek ways to shift the emphasis in education towards vocational skills. Competence approaches (aimed at defining, developing and assessing competent performance of specific job-related tasks) were introduced along side other aspects of change in education – including the National Curriculum, GCSEs, General National Vocational Qualifications (GNVQs) and the use of problem-based and experiential learning – which focus on learners' development of skills and abilities, rather than on purely theoretical knowledge.

The 1990s saw the development of a broader agenda, responding to the challenges of global competition, developments in ICT and the transition from industrial to knowledge-based economies. The Department for Education and Employment – and its successor, the Department for Education and Skills – engaged in intensive research, strategy and standard development.

A Skills Task Force was set up in 1998 to develop a National Skills Agenda to 'ensure that Britain has the skills needed to sustain high levels of employment, compete in the global marketplace and provide opportunity for all' (National Skills Task Force, 1998). The Task Force conducted a series of major research reports, case studies and skills surveys which revealed a number of issues.

(a)   Mismatch between skill supply and demand (notably in technical jobs)

(b)   Lack of systematic analysis of future skill requirements

(c)   Lack of training for lower-level and flexible workers, particularly in small organisations

(d)   Lack of qualified adults in the workforce, especially compared with major European competitors such as France and Germany.

The Government's 2003 White Paper *21st Century Skills: Realising Our Potential* argued that despite extensive intervention, the UK still had gaps in basic skills (including literacy, numeracy and ICT); intermediate skills (such as at professional, apprenticeship and technician level) and higher-level leadership and management skills.

EXAMPLE

The National Employers Skills Survey 2005

Over 74,000 employers in different sectors and localities in England took part in the National Employers Skills Survey (NESS), which was commissioned by the LSC in partnership with the Sector Skills Development Agency and the Department for Education and Skills.

Among their key findings were the following.

(a)   7% of establishments reported having hard-to-fill vacancies, and 4% cited skill shortages among applications as the reason.

(b)   Employers, once prompted on the issue said they experienced skill shortages among applicants for a quarter of all vacancies.

(c)   The proportion of the total workforce regarded as lacking proficiency is lower now than at any time since 2001 (at 6%).

(d)   Occupationally, lack of proficiency is more common in lower level occupations than in managerial and professional positions.

(e)   65% of employers had funded or arranged any training or development for any of their workforce in the previous 12 months (compared to 59% in 2003).

(f)   Employers funded or arranged 162 million days of training over the past 12 months (equivalent to 7.5 days per annum for every worker the country).

(g)   Employers spent approximately £33.3 billion on training over the past 12 months, the bulk of which was spent on the labour cost of those being trained (48%) and the management of training and delivery costs (35%).

(Learning and Skills Council, June 2006)

For more details, go to: http://research.Isc.gov.uk/latest+updates

1.2   Skills, employment and competitiveness

Low training and skill levels raised concerns about national economic performance, due to:

(a)   The potential inability of many UK firms to respond to changing world economic conditions and technological developments

(b)   Poor productivity and competitiveness compared with other countries

(c)   Self-limitation to competing in relatively low-skilled product and service markets

(d)   The social costs of having a rising proportion of the potential labour force condemned to long-term economic inactivity because of inadequate skills (including literacy and numeracy).

Bratton and Gold (2007) note that the economic case for investment in human resource development can be made at different levels.

(a)   At the individual level, there is a close relationships between learning (in various forms) and job prospects, especially in terms of minimising unemployment and increasing overall earnings.

(b)   At the organisational level, HRD is a central feature of a 'bundle' of HRM practices which have been shown to impact on corporate performance. HRD itself may offer measurable financial returns on investment – and may also contribute less readily quantifiable benefits, such as employee commitment and organisational flexibility.

(c)   At the level of the national economy and society as a whole, there is a demonstrable connection between school enrolments, the proportion of the labour force in higher education and the level and growth of the nation's gross domestic product (GDP). Skill levels are argued to be important for future national competitiveness. Low qualifications also prevent entry into the labour market and contribute to the emerging problems of **social exclusion**. *Bridging the Gap*, the 1999 social exclusion unit report, found that 9% of 16-18 year olds were not in education, training or work, creating a mix of educational, health and social welfare problems. This has become a key focus of government policy-making in recent years.

Activity 1	(20 minutes)

'Michael Porter, in his recent DTI-sponsored review of UK competitiveness, said that labour force skills continue to be an area of competitive disadvantage for the UK. It has been estimated that poor skills levels account for up to a fifth of the productivity gap. All of which provides compelling support for the official line that the country needs to upskill to boost the economy.

'But do raised skill levels directly equate to increased productivity?' (Manocha, 2003)

From our discussion in this and the previous chapter, suggest two reasons why raising skill *levels* might not directly equate to increased *productivity*.

1.3 Government policy on training and development

Interventionist approaches to HRD seek to influence organisational decision-making in the interests of the economy as a whole. In France, for example, there is a highly-developed concept of 'social partnership' between government and organisations, supported by tax levies on organisations to fund training grants.

Under the UK's voluntarist approach, the role of government (and related agencies) is seen primarily as encouraging and facilitating organisational training.

(a) **Stimulating employer demand** for skills and investment in education and training: researching and promoting the business case for learning and development, and promoting benchmark HRD standards such as Investors in People (discussed in Section 3 below).

(b) **Developing the national training infrastructure**, including:

   (i) The establishment of an integrated **framework of vocational qualifications** based on national standards: National Vocational Qualifications (NVQs) in England and Wales, and SVQs (Scottish Vocational Qualifications) in Scotland (discussed in Section 2 of this chapter)

   (ii) The establishment of a national **network of regionally-based institutions** to co-ordinate, finance and administer delivery of national training programmes. This was previously the role of Training and Enterprise Councils (TECs) and Local Enterprise Councils (LECs) in Scotland. The regional basis of the network allowed links with local authorities and chambers of commerce, careers services in schools, local Job Centres and so on, fostering business support and community awareness. In the interests of greater clarity and co-ordination, these were replaced in 2001 by the Learning Skills Council (LSC) and its local delivery units (discussed in Section 3 of this chapter).

(c) Providing funding for specific **initiatives to support HRD**, where the market alone fails to maintain sufficient levels of demand and investment. A number of national initiatives are aimed at enhancing the employability of young people and their access to training, including New Deal (formerly Youth Training), Connexions and Modern Apprenticeships (discussed in Section 3 of this chapter.)

(d)   Stimulating **demand for learning**. The Green Paper, *The Learning Age: a Renaissance for a New Britain* (DfEE, 1998) set out the government's vision for 'lifelong learning' and the 'learning society'. A key policy goal of the Lifelong Learning agenda is to drive up the demand for learning, of any kind, among individuals. The theory is that if individuals can be encouraged to engage in learning activities, this will improve their employability *and* their openness to further learning within organisations, creating the impetus for continuous improvement that is a key to competitive advantage. This particularly applies to unqualified adults who have previously been excluded from the training market. Initiatives launched to support individual education and learning include the University for Industry (UfI) and learndirect (discussed in Section 3 below).

Activity 2   **(5 minutes)**

What sources of information can you monitor regularly, in order to keep up to date with government policy on skills, training, life-long learning and other aspects of HRD?

We will now look at some of the key areas of training infrastructure discussed above, starting with the development of competence-based training.

2   COMPETENCE-BASED TRAINING

2.1   The competence movement

Historically, the UK has shown an educational bias towards knowledge – and educational institutions and occupations which deal in knowledge – rather than practical skills. The poor performance of British industry and management (as discussed earlier) provided political impetus towards the definition and development of more practical, demonstrable workplace competences.

> The concept of training for competence is that it should be criterion related, directed at developing the ability of trainees to perform specific tasks directly related to the job they are in, or for which they are preparing, expressed in terms of performance outcomes and specific indicators. It is a reaction against the confetti-scattering approach to training as being a good thing in its own right, concerned with the general education of people dealing with general matters.
> (Torrington *et al*, 2002)

The idea has been around for some time, having its roots in teacher education in the US, but only gained currency in the UK in the 1980s. The Review of Vocational Qualifications in England and Wales (RVQ) Working Group report in April 1986 recommended the introduction of NVQs, to address weaknesses in the then current system, including (www.qca.org.uk/TheStoryOfNVQ):

- Assessment methods biased towards testing of knowledge rather than skill or competence

- Insufficient recognition of learning gained outside formal education and training

- Many barriers to accessing vocational qualifications and inadequate arrangements for progression and transfer of credit

- Limited take-up of vocational qualifications.

The National Council for Vocational Qualifications (NCVQ) – now the Qualification and Curriculum Authority – was formed to develop a criteria for a clear, coherent and comprehensive system of vocational qualifications. This led to National Vocational Qualifications (NVQs, discussed below) and a wide range of other vocational qualifications (VQs) accredited within the framework.

Competence-based training and assessment has been enthusiastically promoted by the government, proponents of management development (such as the Management Charter Initiative) and professional bodies, as a way of:

(a) Supporting the career and development aspirations of learners without the historical bias towards formal academic achievement: NVQs, for example, have no formal pre-entry qualifications.

(b) Supporting flexible and job-relevant learning, through on-going training and assessment in the workplace, with no pre-determined time-frame for completion, and potentially minimal inputs from education providers.

(c) Supporting employers' objectives for HRD, by focusing on relevant job skills. Competence frameworks and assessments also support a range of HR planning and performance management applications.

(d) Supporting employees' employability objectives. NVQs, for example, are modularised, so that learning can be transferred freely between providers and elements can be tackled in any order (to suit job– and employer-related priorities).

2.2 The Qualifications and Curriculum Authority

The QCA (ACCAC in Wales and SQA in Scotland) developed the National Qualification Framework, which creates a coherent classification for NVQs. It is the regulatory authority in charge of the formal recognition of all standards and qualifications in education and training, including the National Curriculum, GNVQs, NVQs and technical certificates awarded under Modern Apprenticeship schemes.

The QCA also shares with the Learning and Skills Council (LSC) and the Sector Skills Development Agency (SSDA) a remit to:

- Extend the take-up of vocational qualifications, including their use by more 14-19 year olds

- Develop a more flexible VQ system. A proposed programme of work, with a seven-year workplan, was endorsed in 2003: watch this space!

2.3 National Vocational Qualifications (NVQs)

NVQs and SVQs are part of the National Qualifications Framework in the UK. They are work-related, competence-based qualifications, reflecting the skills and knowledge needed to do a job effectively.

'NVQs are based on national occupational standards: statements of performance that describe what competent people in a particular occupation are expected to be able to do. They cover all the main aspects of an occupation, including current best practice, the ability to adapt to future requirements and the knowledge and understanding that underpin competent performance' (www.qca.org.uk).

Competence frameworks are developed by Standards Setting Bodies made up of representatives of an occupation or profession nationwide. Qualifications are **delivered** through a network of training centres (eg local colleges) which are approved by one of several **awarding** bodies (eg EdExcel, City and Guilds and professional bodies) which in turn must be **accredited** by the Qualifications and Curriculum Authority (or its equivalents).

Standards of competence identify the key roles of a given occupation and break them down into areas or units of competence. These in turn are formulated as statements describing what a competent person should be able to do at different levels, including:

- The specific activities concerned (elements of competence)
- To what standard (performance criteria)
- In what contexts and conditions (listed in a range statement)
- With what underpinning knowledge and understanding.

Activity 3   **(30 minutes)**

Use your existing knowledge (eg of the HNC/HND qualification) or research skills to find out how the five levels of competence for NVQs are defined.

Torrington *et al* (2002) note that NVQs have had a 'rough ride' since the concept was first introduced. There have been reservations in relation to:

(a) **Standards.** Employers inevitably care more about fulfilling their own skill requirements then those of the national employment base – and may find occupational standards too general and/or over-onerous for their own needs. In some areas – such as management – competence frameworks inevitably oversimplify the complexity and need for flexibility of the work.

(b) **Assessment.** The assessment process is time-consuming, particularly in view of the bureaucracy (and specialist terminology) involved. The need to collect acceptable evidence of competence may distract attention from learning, work requirements and other development needs. The quality of assessment also depends heavily on individual assessors: there has been some pressure to re-introduce written examinations in some settings.

(c) **Educational issues.** Since the training agenda is set by the demonstration of job performance, there may be a lack (and future loss) of training in cognitive (thinking) skills. The framework does not address the difficulties

BPP
LEARNING MEDIA

of defining higher-level competencies (eg creative conceptual skills) or underlying issues such as the reluctance of UK employers to invest in training.

However, NVQs and SVQs have certainly added to the number of vocational qualifications offered and attained in the UK. They are also (as we noted earlier) an important part of the national infrastructure and the basis of training targets.

2.4 The Management Charter Initiative

The MCI was set up in 1988, as the operating arm of the National Forum for Management Education and Development. Its aims were to:

(a) Define generic standards of assessment for management competence

(b) Promote 'best practice' in management education, training and development

(c) Develop ethical and qualification standards with a view to the eventual 'professionalising' of management under a chartered body.

The **Management Standards Centre** is now the government-recognised Standards Setting Body for management and leadership.

Managerial qualifications were originally developed by the MCI, as the basis for NVQs and SVQs in Management and Team Leading. However, the **Management Standards Centre,** now the government-recognised Standards Setting Body for Management and Leadership, has developed a new set of National Occupational Standards (NOS) for management and leadership, launched in 2005.

The Standards cover six functional areas within the management and leadership fields.

A Managing Self and Personal Skills
B Proving Direction
C Facilitating Change
D Working with People
E Using Resources, and
F Achieving Results.

Each function has a list of Units of Competence, which combined in a modular approach lead to:

• Level 2 NVQ/SVQ in Team Leading

• Levels 3, 4 or 5 NVQ/SVQ in Management (depending on different levels at which the functions are exercised)

Weblink

The full 2005 Standards can be downloaded from the Management Standards Centre.

▶▶ **http://www.management-standards.org**

The competence-based approach to management development appears to have taken hold in the UK. Some observers, however, note that organisations are beginning to move away from the standard model and towards:

    (a)   **In-house frameworks**, reflecting specific organisational culture and context

    (b)   The use of more '**holistic**' forms of development, underpinning specific competences with a wider skill base, employability training, mentoring, self-managed and experiential learning, learning to learn and so on.

FOR DISCUSSION

How far can managerial work be defined or assessed as competences? For which particular aspects of a manager's job would it be hard to demonstrate 'outputs'? What other approaches to management qualifications would you propose?

3   CONTEMPORARY TRAINING INITIATIVES

3.1   Learning and Skills Councils

The Learning and Skills Council was set up in April 2001, bringing various learning providers together under a single funding regime. It is responsible for funding and planning all education and training for over 16-year-olds in England, other than in universities.

The LSC's website states its vision as follows: 'By 2010, young people and adults in England will have knowledge and productive skills matching the best in the world.' Its main tasks are as follows.

- Raising participation in training by young people
- Increasing demand for learning by adults and increasing the supply of flexible, high-quality learning opportunities for adults
- Raising the quality of education and training delivery
- Equalising opportunity by facilitating access to learning
- Developing education-business links.

In April 2002, 47 local LSCs were established to deliver outcomes at a regional and sub-regional level, replacing the old Training and Enterprise Councils (TECs). Each local Council includes representatives of employers, trades unions, learning providers and community groups. They work in partnership with each other (Local Strategic Partnerships) to develop shared community strategies, particular in deprived areas. The LSC also seeks to work alongside the Employment Service, the Small Business Service ('Business Link'), Connexions, the University for Industry and other stakeholders (eg on the Skills Alliance initiative).

3.2 Train To Gain

Train to Gain is a service linking employers with an experienced **Skills Broker** (trained by the LSC) whose role is to offer impartial and independent advice to businesses; match identified training needs with appropriate training providers and ensure that training is delivered to meet business needs. According to the programme's website: 'This marks a cultural shift in how skills training will be delivered, and will ensure that the delivery of training is much more flexible and responds to business needs.' (www.traintogain.gov.uk)

Skills Brokers:

- Help employers to identify skilling needs in response to business goals and constraints

- Make recommendations based on the skills analysis in order to help businesses pinpoint the types of training required, appropriate providers, qualification schemes and so on

- Agree a training package with the employer and selected training provider

- Recommend funding options or provide access to funding (eg wage compensation for firms with fewer than 50 employees)

- Provide support and progress review as the training package is delivered.

Train To Gain also funds training initiated under the **Skills Pledge**. The pledge, recommended by the 2006 Leitch Review of Skills, is a voluntary commitment by firms to help staff develop basic literacy and numeracy skills and work towards Level 2 qualifications. Arriva, EDF Energy and First Group are among early signatories along with all central government departments.

3.3 Modern Apprenticeship schemes

The UK government launched Modern Apprenticeship in 1994 in an attempt to involve industry more closely in the process of vocational training. Apprenticeships (traditionally available in crafts and engineering sectors) are available in childcare, tourism, travel, retail and a range of other industries.

The apprenticeship model combines vocational education (towards NVQ Level 3) including core skills development (literacy, numeracy, communication and so on) with hands-on experience in a sponsoring organisation. Apprentices are attached to a particular employer (as contracted between the administering LSC and the employer) for the purposes of training: there is no guarantee of employment at the end of the training period.

Foundation modern apprenticeships (FMA) normally consist of approximately 180 guided learning hours, equivalent to one-day-a-week of off-the-job learning over a period of one year, or 30 weeks. The NVQ component is at Level 2.

Advanced modern apprenticeships (AMA) normally consist of approximately 360 guided learning hours, equivalent to one-day-a-week of off-the-job learning over a period of two years, or 60 weeks. The NVQ component is at Level 3: technical certificates are mandatory to support the knowledge and understanding required.

Technical certificates are qualifications that support structured off-the-job teaching and assessment of the knowledge and understanding required by an NVQ. They have recently been introduced to modern apprenticeships to improve the quality of the

programmes and to form the basis for apprentices to progress, either within the workplace or to further or higher education (www.qca.org.uk/Modernapprenticeship). Sector Skills Councils are responsible for the development of modern apprenticeships in their sectors, working with awarding bodies, providers and employers to identify suitable qualifications for use as technical certificates.

EXAMPLE

ASDA announces major workplace training pilot including Modern apprenticeships: 18/02/04)

'ASDA today announced a workplace training pilot for 1,000 employees following the validation of the company's own in-house training programme. Colleagues will be offered the chance to train toward National Vocational Qualifications (NVQ) in retail and Modern Apprenticeships.

'In a trial commencing in March, 1,000 ASDA employees in eight North London stores will train toward fully transferable retail qualifications. Employees over the age of 25 will work toward NVQ Level 2 qualifications and younger employees, aged 16-24, will work toward Modern Apprenticeships.

'Also commencing in March, 1,000 employees will train toward voluntary, paid, basic skills qualifications, following a successful basic skills pilot in 2003. ASDA expects the pilot and the basic skills implementation to deliver benefits including: increasing productivity, improved staff morale and retention and a higher level of internal promotion.

'The Learning and Skills Council, the organisation responsible for developing skills in England, has contributed over £500,000 to the pilot and the first stage of the basic skills roll out. ASDA's goal is to use the NVQ and Modern Apprenticeship trial to offer company-wide accredited workforce development...

'David Smith, People Director at ASDA, said: "It's been great to work so closely with the Learning and Skills Council and City & Guilds to extend our adult learning offering, and in the future to create a well thought-out and relevant Retail Modern Apprenticeship for our stores. Their flexibility and can-do approach has meant that over a thousand colleagues will benefit from training programmes that offer a transferable qualification and life-changing basic skills".'

(Learning and Skills Council, 2004 (b))

FOR DISCUSSION

The Adult Learning Inspectorate (ALI) failed 46% of work-based training schemes in inspections throughout 2002/2003, although this was an improvement on the year before (www.ali.gov.uk). The Association of Learning Providers countered that judgements on performance were made on incorrectly defined measures: for example, a person leaving a modern apprenticeship for a better paid, better skilled job constituted a 'failure'.

What do you think is a 'successful' outcome for a Modern Apprenticeship, for all the stakeholders concerned?

3.4 Investors in People

The Investors in People scheme (IiP) was launched in 1991 by the National Training Taskforce, together with the Confederation of British Industry (CBI), Trades Union Congress (TUC), the Institute of Personnel and Development (IPD) (now the CIPD) and leading national businesses. It was designed to provide a national benchmark standard for investment in employee training and development. IiP is delivered in the UK by local Learning and Skills Councils and 'Business Links' (the Small Business Service), which have targets for the number of organisations committing to the scheme and attaining the standard.

Organisations seeking accreditation must audit their current training practice and provision (with the aid of survey instruments provided) and bring them into line with published standards. They are required to produce evidence of their training objectives and standards, which are assessed by the LSC. The programme is not intended to be a prescriptive set of rules and procedures: organisations are encouraged to develop their own solutions and methods towards benchmark standards. The key principles are set out on the IiP website.

- (a) **Commitment** to invest in people to achieve business goals

- (b) **Planning** how skills, individuals and teams are to be developed to achieve these goals

- (c) **Action** to develop and use necessary skills in a well defined and continuing programme directly tied to business objectives

- (d) **Evaluating** outcomes of training and development for individuals' progress towards goals, the value achieved and future needs.

Commitment to IiP requires significant time, effort and investment – potentially including major cultural change. The benefits of IiP status have been debated. Some studies have shown an increase in commitment to HR development, a belief in the value of the process and perceived performance gains, particularly where it was used to assess performance and implement continuous improvement (Alberga *et al*, 1997) The IiP website devotes a whole page to the standard's benefits, and a library of successful case studies.

EXAMPLE

'Although the Pontin's name is well known to British holiday makers, the Pontin's of the 21ˢᵗ Century is very different from the traditional 'holiday camp' of the past. New managing director Colin Homer is turning a loss-making organisation into a profitable one, using Investors in People to improve the core area of the business... namely its employees.

'This is a human resources challenge most managers would baulk at: 300 full-time employees are joined each Spring by 1,600 seasonal workers whose turnover has meant that, in past years, Pontin's has had to employ over 5,000 people during the summer season to fill the 1,600 positions... But as a staunch advocate of the business benefits that Investors in People recognition brings, Colin Homer is already seeing improved employee retention – which will in turn result in greater productivity and reduced costs.

'Pontin's can now give employees more and better reasons for staying with the company... Following the guidance of Investors in People, Pontin's is now putting in place a structure whereby every employee will have:

- a personal development file with job descriptions and aims
- access to NVQs
- access to funding for vocational training
- assistance with professional qualifications
- assessment of aims and goals and help in achieving them

'Even if someone only stays for a matter of months, they should still have a new qualification to take to their next job.

(Investors in People, 2004)

Some organisations have struggled to find real benefits through the process.

(a)   There can be difficulties administering the process

(b)   It encourages organisations to underrate the importance of informal development methods

(c)   It does not imply genuine commitment to improving development, since organisations may seek IiP status purely as a rubber stamp for their employer brand

(d)   It is a 'spurious' tool for stimulating the demand for organisational HRD, because many of the organisations achieving the standard were already convinced of its benefits and doing what was required (Bratton and Gold, 2007).

Activity 4   **(no time limit)**

Check out the Investors in People website (www.investorsinpeople.co.uk) and view the Investors in People Standard itself. Use it as a checklist to do a quick appraisal of your own organisation: would it (broadly) qualify as an 'Investor in People'? What areas would have to be brought in line with the Standard?

3.5   New Deal

New Deal is delivered by Jobcentre Plus, through its network of Jobcentres. It is a key part of the Government's strategy to:

(a)   Get people off benefits and into work, giving long-term unemployed people the opportunity to develop or upgrade their skills

(b)   Improve the overall skills base and employability of the UK workforce.

The **New Deal for Young People** programme is mandatory for jobseekers aged 18 to 24 who have been unemployed for 6 months or more and are claiming Jobseeker's Allowance. The initial part of the programme is a concentrated period of help and advice in order to help them to find work. The government offers subsidies to employers who take on a full-time or part-time New Deal employee, plus a grant towards certified vocational training. Candidates become employees under normal terms and conditions, and training arrangements must be agreed with a New Deal personal adviser.

The **New Deal 25 Plus** programme is also mandatory for those claiming Jobseeker's Allowance for 18 months or more. Jobseekers undertake short courses to refresh existing skills or learn new skills. Employers are given the option of taking candidates on Work Trial. They are also offered subsidies to take candidates on for six months, full-time or part-time, allowing long-term unemployed people to gain work experience and show what they can do.

There are also a number of voluntary programmes, including:

- **New Deal for Lone Parents**: advice on childcare, access to training and help with applications for in-work benefits.

- **New Deal 50 Plus**: advice and assistance with job search, and access to retraining.

- **New Deal for Disabled People**: advice and support from Job Brokers, who can also work with employers to adapt the workplace for disabled people.

The new sector-specific **Ambition Programme** works with business leaders in sectors with skills shortages that would not ordinarily recruit jobless people (IT, retail, construction and energy) to:

(a) Improve placement and retention rates of New Deal participants in jobs with good career potential, not usually accessible to unemployed people

(b) Meet employer HR and skill shortages.

Employers' hiring requirements are used to define training needs and standards of job readiness of New Deal candidates, with a steering group of business leaders from each sector overseeing the programme.

Activity 5 (5 minutes)

What would be the potential benefits to employers of taking on people who join New Deal 25 Plus, voluntary programmes or Ambition Programme?

3.6 University for Industry and learndirect

Ufi Ltd is one of the Government's key partners in delivering its workforce development and lifelong learning agendas. It 'aims to drive up demand for learning, help adults improve their employability by acquiring new knowledge and skills, and help businesses become more competitive.' (www.ufi.com)

Ufi works with a broad range of public and private providers in local, employer and sector-based 'hubs', to deliver mainly online courses and information through a network of e-learning centres. One of its priorities is meeting the training needs of small and medium-sized enterprises (SMEs), although it also works with many large employers, including Barclays, Nissan, Tesco and Remploy. Ufi also works with the Adult Basic Skills Strategy Unit and awarding bodies to offer the National Certificate in Adult Literacy and Numeracy, through online tests. Further links with further and higher education establishments should develop further e-learning routes to accredited qualifications, while a pilot scheme is currently working with 14 – 16 year olds who have been excluded from mainstream schooling.

As the world's largest supported e-learning network, Ufi plays a key part in delivering the government's recently-launched e-learning strategy (*Towards a Unified e-Learning*, July 2003): 'E-learning should become a standard feature of learning and teaching for all ages, from school children to pensioners, throughout the education system, in the workplace and beyond.' (UfI, 2003).

learndirect is a government-sponsored network of online learning and information services, developed by Ufi in 2000 to help deliver workforce development and lifelong learning. In particular, it aims to support the government's vision of a 'learning society' where people can access learning opportunities and upgrade their skills throughout their lives, whether they are

- employees seeking to improve their workplace skills
- job seekers wishing to improve their employability
- people who feel excluded from the world of education or IT or
- interest learners.

learndirect offers supported flexible learning courses in three main categories: skills for life (literacy, numeracy and ESOL); business and management; and IT skills. Over 80% of courses are online, while others are delivered via workbooks or CD-ROM.

learndirect's free information and advice service (delivered by phone helpline and web site) offers guidance to adults wanting to access learning opportunities.

earndirect can be accessed via over 2,000 e-learning centres located throughout England, Wales and Northern Ireland in high street locations, libraries colleges and workplaces. There are also 'virtual learning centres' run completely online, allowing enrolment and learning from home, libraries or wherever users wish.

Activity 6 (no time limit)

Check out the learndirect website at

www.learndirect.co.uk and www.learndirect-advice.co.uk. Also check out www.learndirect.co.uk/personal/freestuff/tasters to experiment with free 'taster' courses.

How might you use learndirect as part of your own self-managed learning? How might you use it to develop Human Resources?

3.7 Connexions

Connexions is the government's support service for young people aged 13 – 19 in England, joining up the work of six government Departments and their agencies, together with private and voluntary sector groups and youth and careers services.

Launched in April 2003, it offers practical help with choosing and accessing courses and careers – as well as personal counselling on issues like drug abuse and homelessness. Connexions is delivered through local Partnerships – based on LSC areas, working to national planning guidelines and managed and monitored by local management committees.

'Connexions is the government's ambitious attempt to stop young people bouncing from pillar to post for support during their transition to adulthood. The previous services geared towards young people formed a patchwork of provision, with too many teenagers falling through the gaps and joining the drop-out generation.' (Prasad, 2003)

A 'Connexions Card' encourages young people to stay in learning after the age of 16, by accumulating points for attending school, college or work-based training: points can be redeemed for goods and services, or VIP passes at sports events, concerts and fashion shows.

Personal advisers are deployed in schools, colleges and the community, available on an outreach basis to provide support and guidance on formulating goals and accessing relevant services.

FOR DISCUSSION

How is Connexions relevant to employers?

3.8 Union learning representatives

Increasing employee demand for training and development is a feature of the new psychological contract of employment. Trade unions have for some years worked for the development of their members, developing learning provision and creating demand from sections of the workforce that had little access to employer-provided training: manual workers, part-timers, older and ethnic minority workers and so on.

In 1998, the TUC set up a task group to examine how to improve the role of trade unions in learning. It proposed a network of Union Learning Representatives (ULRs) in workplaces to: analyse members' training needs; provide members with information and advice on learning matters; arrange learning and training and promote its value to members; and consult with the employer on union members' learning and training. The Union Learning Fund provides training for union learning reps and contributes to the costs of developing and co-ordinating learning programmes.

The government has supported ULRs as important contributors to its basic skills, social inclusion and lifelong learning agendas. The network has grown rapidly: The TUC hopes to have 22,000 reps in place by 2010. The *Employment Protection Act 2002* awarded ULRs paid time off for reps to perform their duties.

The benefit of having union learning representatives (ULRs) in the workplace are said to be as follows.

(a)   They are a trained and inexpensive source of training advice for employers

(b)   They are trusted by, and have access to, workers who might not otherwise engage in learning. This contributes to equal opportunities and inclusion, 'reaching out in particular to people who do not do well in formal education or who need help with English as a second language' (Margolis, 2003)

(c)   They support learning focused on the employees' development needs – not just immediate job training – and this has benefits to employers, through increased openness to learning, continuous improvement, confidence, improvement in basic skills, employability and so on.

(d)   They are advocates for training, ensuring that line managers follow through with agreed time off, resources and so on, against pressures to side-line development activities.

EXAMPLE

Although the law does not provide for paid time off for workers to study, ACAS reckons some companies are already doing this. One example is Sainsbury's, which has encouraged the ULR initiative and allows learning to happen in working time.

It all started in 2001, when a deputy shop steward made an approach to the company to introduce a lifelong learning project. He devised a plan that involved sending learner reps on a 10-day course promoting basic skills awareness. In April 2002, a successful bid was made to the LSC for £100,000 of funding for courses in Sainsbury's depots in Hertfordshire... Sainsbury's now has 73 learner reps. The project has grown so fast that there is a rep in each region... ULRs deliver courses when they are needed to suit shift work. 'In a climate of multi-racial employment, we found huge demand for courses in English as a second language, in particular', [Sarah Lacey, learning rep for the Union of Shop, Distributive and Allied Workers] explains. 'Sainsbury's has done a marvellous job in recognising a basic skills need and allows two hours paid time off a week, she says. 'People do not have to give up their own time to attend. For the company, the benefits have been phenomenal too.'

(Margolis, 2003)

FOR DISCUSSION

What does the example above suggest about the impact of HRD on employee relations?

NOTES

Weblinks

You will need to use your research skills and awareness to keep up-to-date on consultations and reviews, new proposals, body name changes and so on. Some useful information sources include:

The Dfes Skills Strategy home page
▶▶ **htpp://www.Dfes.gov.uk/skills**

Investors in People, UK
▶▶ **http://www.iipuk.co.uk**

The Learning and Skills Council
▶▶ **http://www.lsc.gov.uk**

University for Industry learndirect
▶▶ **http://www.learndirect.co.uk**

New Deal
▶▶ **http://www.newdeal.gov.uk**

The Qualifications and Curriculum Authority
▶▶ **http://www.qca.org.uk**

Train to Gain
▶▶ **http://www.traintogain.gov.uk**

Chapter roundup

- Vocational education and training in the UK has traditionally suffered from low levels of employer commitment and investment, leading to skill gaps, lack of competitiveness and social exclusion of people lacking basic skills.

- Government policy on VET has focused on: stimulating employer demand for skills; developing the national qualifications framework (including NVQs); establishing regionally-based institutions to deliver training programmes; initiatives for employability training; and stimulating a demand for life-long learning and basic skill development.

- The competency movement has supported training for competence as a way of focusing attention on transferable, employable, competitive vocational skills. NVQs are based on national occupation standards. Management competencies were first developed by the Management Charter Initiative.

- The Learning and Skills Council is responsible for planning and funding all education and training for over-16 year olds in England, other than in universities. The Qualifications and Curriculum Authority is responsible for the formal recognition of all standards and qualifications in education and training.

- A range of training initiatives has been launched to involve industry in education and training (Modern Apprenticeships); define benchmark standards in HRD (Investors in People); improve the employability of unemployed people (New Deal); encourage lifelong, flexible and e-learning (Ufl/learndirect); and support young people in accessing learning (Connexions).

- Union Learning Representatives contribute to the basic skills, social inclusion and lifelong learning agendas by supporting workplace learning.

Quick quiz

1 What are some of the causes of poor investment in training in the UK?

2 What is the theory behind the Lifelong Learning Agenda?

3 What are the advantages and disadvantages of NVQs?

4 What do QCA, MCI and LSC stand for?

5 An Advanced Modern Apprenticeship includes a Level 2 NVQ component. True or false?

6 What are the four principles of Investors in People?

7 Which government programme is mandatory for a 24-year old who has been unemployed for six months or more and is claiming Jobseeker's Allowance?

8   The world's largest supported e-learning network is:

A   Connexions

B   Ufl

C   SVQ

D   The Ambition Programme

9   What are the advantages of having Union learning representatives in the workplace?

Answers to quick quiz

1   Philosophies of organisation and management; human capital theory; lack of HRP; voluntarist framework; self limitation to low-skill markets   (para 1.1)

2   Encouraging individuals to engage in learning of any kind improves their employability and openness to learning, creating a culture of continuous improvement.   (para 1.3)

3   See paragraphs 2.1 and 2.3 for a full answer.

4   Qualifications and Curriculum Authority; Management Charter Initiative; Learning and Skills Council   (paras 2.2, 2.4, 3.1)

5   False: Level 3.   (para 3.3)

6   Commitment, planning, action, evaluation   (para 3.4)

7   New Deal for Young people   (para 3.5)

8   B   (para 3.6)

9   See paragraph 3.8 for a full answer

Answers to activities

1   Manocha himself identifies two problems with the more-training-equals-higher-productivity equation.

(a)   'The UK doesn't simply need higher-level skills: it needs the *right* skills. As many a dinner party conversation has recorded, while the UK pushes for more graduates, we are short of plumbers...' The government is addressing this by matching skills output with industry requirements (as we see later in the chapter).

(b)   'What happens to the higher-skilled people? Many commentators point out that the productivity gap will not be closed by training people and then sending them back to an unreceptive workplace, where new skills are wasted through lack of opportunity.' We noted the need for transfer of learning in Chapter 13.

2   Suggestions include: quality national press; HRM and HRD journals; web sites of relevant organisations (starting with the Department of Education & Skills).

3   As set out at www.dfes.gov.uk/nvq/what (although you could have used a number of other information sources) the five levels are as follows.

Level 1   Competence which involves the application of knowledge in the performance of a range of varied work activities, most of which may be routine and predictable

Level 2   Competence which involves the application of knowledge in a significant range of varied work activities, performed in a variety of context. Some of these activities are complex or non-routine and there is some individual responsibility or autonomy. Collaboration with others, perhaps through membership of a work group or team, may often be a requirement.

Level 3   Competence which involves the application of knowledge in a broad range of varied work activities performed in a wide variety of contexts, most of which are complex and non-routine. There is considerable responsibility and autonomy and control or guidance of others is often required.

Level 4   Competence which involves the application of knowledge in a broad range of complex, technical or professional work activities performed in a variety of contexts and with a substantial degree of personal responsibility and autonomy. Responsibility for the work of others and the allocations of resources is often present.

Level 5   Competence which involves the application of a range of fundamental principles across a wide and often unpredictable variety of contexts. Very substantial personal autonomy and often significant responsibility for the work of others and for the allocation of substantial resources feature strongly, as do personal accountabilities for analysis, diagnosis, design, planning, execution and evaluation.

4   Your own research and application.

5   The key benefit to employers is ease of access to potential employees who may already have the skills and experience required, and who have had guidance in training to meet employer requirements (especially in the Ambition programme). In the case of voluntary programmes, it may also support equal opportunity programmes. The financial incentives should not be the primary benefit – but may help to reduce the risk.

6   Your own research. If you had trouble accessing the information, what does this say about the programme?

PART D

EMPLOYEE RELATIONS

Chapter 16:
THE CONTEXT OF EMPLOYEE RELATIONS

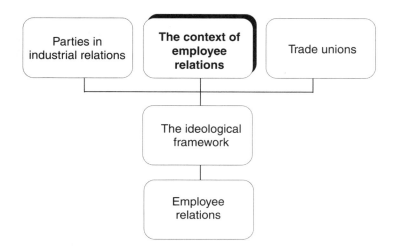

Introduction

Thanks largely to its turbulent history and tainting with political colours, industrial relations is an emotive subject which requires careful handling in study and professional contexts: as you read, try to appreciate both sides of the debate.

Traditionally, industrial relations are the dealings and co-operation (or lack of it) between management and workers, usually via their representatives in a trade union or staff association. However, trade unionism has been on the decline in the UK (and USA) and a high proportion of employees do not now belong to unions. Nevertheless, industrial relations still exist in organisations. A shift to the term 'employee relations' reflects a broader orientation towards communication with and involvement of employees, and a more unitarist perspective in which co-operation is regarded as both possible and desirable in order for business' and employees' needs to be met.

In this chapter we will consider the players and ideologies involved in industrial relations and the shift towards 'employee relations'. In Chapters 17 and 18 we will examine more closely some of the processes involved in the management of employee relations.

Your objectives

In this chapter you will learn about the following.

    (a)   The unitary and pluralistic frames of reference

    (b)   The development of trade unions and the nature of industrial relations

    (c)   The role of a trade union and its contribution to effective industrial relations

    (d)   The ideological framework of industrial relations

    (e)   The roles taken by the main actors in employee relations

    (f)   The impact of human resource management on employee relations

1 PARTIES IN INDUSTRIAL RELATIONS

1.1 What are industrial relations?

Definition

Industrial relations (IR) comprises 'all the rules, practices and conventions governing interactions between managements and their workforces, normally involving collective employee representation and bargaining.'

(Graham and Bennett, 1998)

Industrial relations policy and practice covers these areas.

(a) Procedures for setting terms and conditions of work, profit-sharing, training targets, equal opportunities policy and so on

(b) Disciplinary and grievance procedures, both individual and collective, including external arbitration and conciliation. (Individual disciplinary and grievance procedures were discussed in Chapter 6.)

(c) Recognition of trade unions (if applicable) to represent worker interests through the processes of collective bargaining and consultation

(d) Development of added or alternative mechanisms for employee representation and consultation (such as works councils, joint consultation committees and employee forums)

(e) Determination of the structure and scope of consultation and employee involvement in decision-making, within the framework of collective bargaining, partnership agreements, works councils, general HRM policies and so on.

1.2 Workers and their organisations

Trade unions

Definitions

A **trade union** is an organised association of employees who 'consist wholly or mainly of workers of one or more description and whose principal purposes include the regulation of relations between workers and employers' *(Trade Unions and Labour Relations (Consolidation) Act.)*

An **independent trade union** is one which has been certified as being autonomous and financially self-supporting: not dominated by an employer because of the provision or withdrawal of financial or other support.

A single trade union might include members from different organisations in the same industry, and a single organisation might employ workers who belong to a number of different trade unions. Employees may be members of various unions, but the employer is not compelled to deal with a union unless it is 'recognised' for the purposes of collective bargaining or negotiation. Until recently, there was no statutory provision for obtaining or enforcing recognition: that was changed by the *Employment Relations Act 1999* (Paragraph 2.6 below).

A firm may recognise a number of different unions in the workplace, to represent different categories of employees. Multi-unionism has significant drawbacks, however: encouraging demarcation disputes and the proliferation of work rules; competitive and therefore escalating pay settlements; and the cost and complexity of multiple bargaining time and machinery.

Firms desiring to simplify bargaining arrangements and secure greater flexibility and integration will often seek to negotiate a **sole recognition** or **single union agreement**, whereby only one union is recognised for the purpose of collective bargaining: workers who want representation must join this union. Sole recognition – and even more, the de-recognition of one union in favour of another – is, however, fraught with inter-union competition, and may not be perceived as genuinely representative of the interests of all staff. It is frequently achieved by a 'beauty contest approach', which arguably creates a situation in which unions must offer to fulfil the expectations of management in order to be granted recognition (and access to a fresh pool of members) rather than fulfilling the expectations of their members.

The primary functions carried out by a trade union are directly related to its objectives of improving the collective pay, conditions and job security of its members. Trade unions pursue their objectives through the processes of:

(a)   **Collective bargaining** and negotiation (discussed in Chapter 17), which determines minimum standards to be applied to members covered by the resulting agreement

(b)   **Joint consultation**: discussing, with representatives of management, issues of mutual concern (such as re-organisations, redundancies, health and safety).

(c)   **Member services**: representation in grievance and disciplinary matters; obtaining sickness and accident benefits; advising on, and arranging access to, basic skills and workplace training (through Union Learning Representatives, as discussed in Chapter 15); legal advice and assistance.

Activity 1   **(15 minutes)**

What other activities of unions are you aware of, which are not directly connected to the achievement of its goals, but which might indirectly be effective in protecting members' rights?

The Trades Union Congress (TUC)

The TUC is a voluntary association of unions originally established in 1868. It holds an annual week-long congress or conference, for the purpose of debate, policy formation and the election of its general council. The TUC's purpose is:

(a) To formulate and express policy for the UK trade union movement as a whole

(b) To consult with industry and government bodies on issues affecting the trade union movement, and to lobby for relevant legislation

(c) To manage disputes between affiliated unions (eg over membership 'poaching' or job demarcation) through a Disputes Committee

(d) To intervene and try to effect a settlement in an industrial dispute, if invited to do so by the union involved

(e) To investigate complaints that an affiliated union's conduct is against the interest or policy of the congress.

The TUC has limited influence over its affiliates, however, through the threat of suspension or expulsion from the Congress. The autonomy of affiliates is still a key value.

We will discuss trade unions in more detail in Section 2 below. However, trade unions are not the only employee representatives with whom management may deal, formally or informally. There has been a trend towards non-unionised forums for consultation and participation. Again, these will be discussed in detail later (in Chapter 18), but we will survey some of the possibilities briefly here.

Staff associations represent the employees (or groups of employees) within a particular organisation. They have been particularly popular among white-collar workers (eg in banking and insurance), for whom trade unionism was less socially acceptable. The main reasons for employees to form a staff association are the desire for collective representation and/or negotiating powers (eg to respond to a specific threat, such as redundancies) – *without* the formality and ideological baggage of a trade union. The majority of staff associations are recognised by employers for the purposes of consultation and negotiation. However, their narrow membership base and lack of funding limits their bargaining power.

Management generally prefer to deal with staff associations because they are less subject to third-party external interests: mutuality of interests may therefore be expected to be easier to achieve, with less external exposure, and staff associations may offer sufficient representation to head off demands for unionisation. Most staff associations, however, are independent of the employer and provide a genuine alternative to trade unions in terms of employee representation.

Professional bodies and associations (eg the British Medical Association) may also represent the interests of their members in negotiation with employers, alongside their role as guardians of professional ethics and standards, educators and certifiers of practitioners and so on.

1.3 Employers and their organisations

Employers' associations and federations

Employers' associations are voluntary private groups of employers founded to facilitate trade, communication and representation in areas of common interest. Some are national bodies covering a whole industry (for example, the Engineering Employers Federation), while others are regional or specialised in their scope.

The largest UK employers' associations include the Engineering Employers' Federation, the Chemical Industries Association, the Road Haulage Association, the Federation of Master Builders, the Newspaper Society and the British Clothing Industry Association.

Employers' associations consist of companies of different sizes and organise themselves in different ways: most are consultative, rather than decision-making, bodies. Some give priority to trade matters, others to employee relations.

They were initially developed on an ad hoc basis in response to specific industrial disputes with the early trade unions, but by the end of the nineteenth century, in response to the growing influence of unionism, adopted the federated approach to organisation at an industry/national level.

The role of the associations has declined with the increasing decentralisation of industrial relations processes: the growth in company– or plant-level bargaining, for example, and the decline of industry-wide agreements. Nevertheless, employers' associations still negotiate agreements at national level, especially in industries (such as electrical contracting and printing) which are dominated by small companies in competitive labour markets: national agreements provide industry frameworks and reduce price competition for skills. Moreover, employers wishing to influence EU policy must be part of an employers' association, which in turn may be affiliated to one of the EU-wide employer voices recognised by the EU Commission for the purposes of consultation and negotiation.

The main purposes of employers associations are:

(a) To give general help and advice on employee relations issues

(b) To represent members' views to political influencers and decision-making bodies (eg lobbying parliament)

(c) To assist member firms in the resolution of disputes (including representation at Employment Tribunals)

(d) To negotiate sectoral collective agreements (where applicable) with trade unions.

The Confederation of British Industry (CBI)

The Confederation of British Industry (CBI) was formed in 1965 as the main national federation of employers' associations in the UK, with the purpose of promoting British industry through political lobbying. Its main function is to influence policy on industry-related issues: it is not directly involved in employee relations processes, although it does maintain working relationships with the TUC, ACAS and other bodies.

1.4 Third parties

Third parties, such as government, arbitrators and judges (including the European Court of Justice) have an important bearing on industrial relations, because they set a framework for what employers and employees can and cannot do.

The UK government has established agencies such as the Advisory, Conciliation and Arbitration Service (ACAS) and Employment Tribunals, to assist or act as go-betweens in employment and industrial relations matters.

ACAS

According to the Employment Protection Act 1975, ACAS was designed to 'promote the improvement of industrial relations'. It is an independent body, governed by a Council whose members are appointed after consultation with worker and employer organisations.

ACAS has the ability to intervene at the request of employers and/or trade unions in the event of a possible or actual trade dispute. It may enquire into a complaint by a recognised trade union that insufficient information has been disclosed for collective bargaining purposes. It may also enquire on its own initiative into any industrial relations matter and publish its findings. It prepares and publishes Codes of Practice giving guidance for improving industrial relations (in areas such as disciplinary procedure).

ACAS may also be involved in individual conciliation cases, prior to hearing by tribunal. (It is frequently called in, for example, over equal opportunity and unfair dismissal complaints.)

Activity 2   **(10 minutes)**

Look up some definitions: what is the meaning of (a) conciliation (b) mediation and (c) arbitration? (Add the ways in which ACAS accomplishes these things, briefly, if you know.)

The Central Arbitration Committee

This body acts as arbitrator in disputes referred to it by ACAS. Under the Employment Relations Act 1999, it is called upon to make a ruling in cases where a union and an employer fail to reach agreement on union recognition or on the conduct of collective bargaining or on the establishment and operation of European Works Councils.

Employment Tribunals

Employment Tribunals (formed under the Employment Tribunals Act 1996) deal with most cases brought under employment law. They consist of an independent, legally-qualified chairperson, and two representative members, from the employer and the union. Their constitution is informal, but their decisions are legally binding. Evidence is given on oath, witnesses are called and legal representation is permitted as in a court of law. Appeals may be made (on points of law only) to the Employment Appeals Tribunal:

this is a formal court, consisting of a judge and lay members representing both sides of industry, and its decisions establish legal precedent.

Tribunals – and proposed changes to the system – were discussed in Chapter 7.

INTERNATIONAL COMPARISON

In the **USA**, although the government plays a limited role in influencing collective agreements, third party intervention in negotiation and mediation (eg via the Federal Mediation and Conciliation Service) is widespread.

1.5   Other stakeholders

There is increasing public awareness of Corporate Social Responsibility (CSR) in relation to labour-related globalisation issues such as the use of child labour and sweatshops in developing nations, and the widening gap between 'fat cat' managerial pay and that of workers. These issues have been brought to the public's attention not by trade unions, but by pressure groups (non-government organisations, or NGOs) such as Oxfam, Anti-Slavery International and Clean Clothes.

Pressure groups have arguably become lead players in employment-related issues. Industries in sporting goods, and apparel, fashion and food retail are among the targets of widespread PR pressure, consumer protest and boycott in relation to labour practices.

'The challenges for unions and HR practitioners are different. Some unions are starting to form alliances with pressure groups. HR needs to take the initiative to defend its company's interests on employment-related issues as a whole and not to focus too closely on relations with the company's own employees. HR is also best placed to understand the new risks associated with the employment-related behaviour of contractors or companies that form part of the supply chain' (Wild, 2003).

EXAMPLE

Appreciate the irony of this story...

'Oxfam is to continue sourcing anti-poverty wristbands from China, despite concerns about ethical standards. But the charity has stopped supplies from one manufacturer whose staff were found to be working under poor conditions.

'The move follows national media reports that some 'Make Poverty History' bands had been manufactured at the Tat Shing Rubber Mfg Company, which forces new workers to pay 'financial deposits'. The coverage also reported how employees worked in unsuitable conditions and raised concerns over health and safety. Each of these points breach Oxfam's own Ethical Trading Initiative guidelines.

'The charity has stressed how the 'mistake' highlights the importance for buyers to ensure goods are sourced at plants where conditions meet minimum standards.

'This should not mean a blanket rejection of sourcing in China. Instead we can work with the local company or factory to improve conditions. It is important that we engage to have a positive impact.'

(Supply Management, 23 June 2005)

FOR DISCUSSION

Whose 'business' is it how corporations treat their workers?

1.6   The role of the HR department

As in many other areas of HRM, it is often the line managers who have responsibility on a day-to-day basis for the implementation of industrial relations policy in regard to:

(a)   Exchanging information with office representatives – say, to discuss changes in work procedures or newly-introduced rules

(b)   Conducting disciplinary and grievance measures

(c)   Implementing collective agreements on working procedures and conditions

(d)   Managing interpersonal and team relations in such a way as to minimise potential conflict and preserve organisational authority in the face of collective labour strength

However, there is a continuing role of HR specialists in developing policies which promote consistent decisions on industrial relations issues, especially since line managers may resist employee relations techniques in the belief that they will hamper their work and limit their flexibility.

We will discuss in Section 4 below how HR policy affects industrial relations, and how the HRM approach ('employee relations') differs from the traditional approach ('industrial relations'). Here, we will look in more detail at the major player in traditional industrial relations: the trade unions.

2   TRADE UNIONS

2.1   Types of trade union

Unions are often distinguished as follows.

(a)   **Craft and occupational unions**, which recruit employees who perform certain jobs. These include:

(i)   White collar unions (employees in office work or desk jobs), and
(ii)   Craft unions (manual workers skilled at a particular craft)

Examples include the British Airline Pilots Association (Balpa) and the National Union of Teachers.

(b) **Industrial unions**, which recruit all grades of employees employed in a particular industry. Examples include the National Union of Mineworkers and the Iron and Steel Trades Confederation.

(c) **General unions**, which organise workers from a variety of different jobs and industries. Examples include the Transport and General Workers Union (T&G) and GMB, the 'general' trade union.

Despite these different types, the UK system is essentially 'job-centred': the job an individual performs largely determines which union (s)he will join.

INTERNATIONAL COMPARISONS

- In **Germany**, trade unions are organised on industrial lines: one trade union represents all organised employees at a workplace, irrespective of their individual occupation. The German Trade Union Federation (DGB) is a non-political affiliation based on industrial unionism.

- In **Japan**, unions are mostly organised by company or establishment: an enterprise union consists of regular employees of a single firm, both white– and blue-collar. This has traditionally been supported by long-term career stability.

- In **France**, unions are mostly general unions, organised into five major confederations with broad divisions along politico-religious lines: socialist, communist, social democratic, Christian.

- Job- or occupation-centred unionism is a feature of **Anglo-Saxon countries** such as the UK, USA and Australasia.

2.2 Trade union representatives

Trade union representatives include:

(a) **Full-time paid officials**: 'organisers' or 'officers', employed by the union at district or regional level to carry out its policies under the direction of its national executive committee; and headquarters staff (financial, legal and administrative, under a 'general secretary')

(b) **Part-time voluntary officials**, elected to be branch officers of the union in a particular area

(c) **Workplace representatives** (shop stewards or staff representatives) who are employed by the organisation, but act on behalf of their fellow employees as their recognised representative. (Some very large firms with sensitive industrial relations may retain one or two employees on full pay to act in their union capacity full time.) **Shop stewards** are the link between the work group, the union officials and management: they require extensive knowledge of the union's service, employment and industrial relations law, ACAS and tribunal machinery, the policies and practices of the organisation, the role of managers and so on.

The structure of a union is **democratic**: local branch members elect representatives to a district or regional committee, which elect a national committee. The policy of the union is (theoretically) representative of the views of members, not of its leadership. However, the potential divergence between the goals and values of individual members and those of the organisation is just as great for a trade union as for a business. This view was given a political edge by the 1980s Conservative government's legislative support for the rights of individual union members (for example, secret balloting on use of union funds and industrial action). Its Industrial Relations Code of Practice stated that it should be the responsibility of the union to ensure that:

(a)   Its members understand the organisation, policy and rules of the union

(b)   Its members understand the powers and duties of the members themselves and those of their union representatives

(c)   Its officials are adequately trained to look after their members' interest in an efficient and responsible way.

2.3   The rise, fall and rise of trade unionism

Early development

The UK trade union movement is the oldest in the world. Trade unions developed in the mid-nineteenth century, mainly as organisations of skilled workers in craft-dominated industries seeking to secure employment. In the latter half of the century, labourers and other unskilled workers also organised.

The first attempt to unite skilled and unskilled workers was Robert Owen's Grand National Consolidated Trades Union (1834). This collapsed following the transportation to Australia of the so-called 'Tolpuddle Martyrs': six members of the Friendly Society of Agricultural Labourers of Tolpuddle, Dorset, founded in 1833 to secure fair wages for its members, who were charged with administering unlawful oaths, and became the founding heroes of the trades union movement.

In 1851, the first successful national trade union, the Amalgamated Society of **Engineers**, was formed, and the Trades Union Congress (TUC) met for the first time in 1868.

Trade unions were finally granted legal status in 1871.

Rise...

Following legal status, more trades unions began to be formed, particularly by unskilled workers. The London dockers successfully struck in 1889 (for a wage of sixpence, ie 2 ½ pence, per hour!), encouraging others.

During the 1890s, the trades union movement supported the formation of the Labour Party, supplying funding (as it continues to do today). The Labour Representation Committee was formed in 1900 and renamed the Labour Party in 1906.

1926 saw a national strike by workers in Britain's major industries, lasting from 3-12 May: The General Strike. The TUC called out its members in support of the miners, who had refused to accept a reduction in wages. The strike involved over two million workers in transport, iron and steel, building, printing, gas and electricity. However, the government was able to keep essential services going, and the strike was forced to fold.

In 1945, however, Labour won a huge majority in the first post-war general election, and was able to introduce a programme of radical policies under Clement Attlee. The unions became increasingly powerful during the Labour term(s) in government. Trade union membership in the UK reached a peak of 13.29 million in 1979, also the year in which the number, duration and severity of strike actions reached their peak.

And fall…

During the 1980s and early '90s, the power of trade unions in the UK was affected by a number of factors.

(a)   Declining membership and the increase in non-unionised organisations. This was partly due to the decline in manufacturing and the growth in the service sector where membership has traditionally been low. Meanwhile, competitive pressures resulted in employers' de-recognising of trade unions in order to end restrictive work rules and collective bargaining. Falling membership creates a vicious circle: weakening union effectiveness, which further depresses membership, and so on.

(b)   Union concerns such as collective negotiation, occupational demarcations and work rules were being marginalised by HRM trends such as: negotiation of individual contracts; individual performance management and performance– or merit-related pay awards; multi-skilling and flexible working; direct communication policies; worker empowerment, involvement and participation schemes; the introduction of Japanese management and production techniques (collectivist, participative, low-conflict) and so on. The whole trend towards 'commitment'-based HRM, with a unitary perspective, suggested that the adversarial industrial relations model, associated with unionism, could be by-passed.

(c)   The unions' power was intentionally weakened by Conservative governments from 1979 – 1997, through legislation such as:

(i)   The abolition of the 'closed shop', under which membership of a union could be made a condition of employment

(ii)   The requirement for secret balloting of union members when proposing industrial action, which gave support to the more moderate elements of the trade union movement

(iii) The protection of individual union members' rights (including the right to refuse to participate in or support a strike)

(iv)   The right of employers to dismiss employees taking unofficial strike or other industrial action.

And rise…?

There has been a significant turnaround in the last few years in the number of union recognition agreements in force in the UK and the number and proportion of workers covered by such agreements.

This has been accelerated by:

(a) New recognition laws (see Paragraph 2.6 below)

(b) The Labour government's support for an industrial relations climate in which employers are less inclined to behave unilaterally, thus legitimising the union role in organisations

(c) Employer recognition that there is a positive business case for dealing with the workforce through unions, as a more efficient, positive and democratic method. Trade unions may be argued to fulfil a number of key managerial functions (Sisson & Storey, 2000):

   (i) An **agency** function, acting on behalf of large numbers of employees in their dealing with management, with benefits for consistency and management time/cost savings.

   (ii) A **feedback** function, voicing the complaints and grievances of employees – which management need to be aware of

   (iii) A **stabilising** function, helping to manage workforce discontent by legitimising procedures and managerial prerogatives.

(d) Concerted recruitment drives, often supported by employers who have signed voluntary and partnership agreements with a union. 'At a workplace level, partnership means employers and trade unions working together to achieve common goals such as fairness and competitiveness. This more co-operative attitude on the part of trade unions, it is argued, has made employers more willing to recognise them and have a relationship with them' (Gennard & Judge, 2003).

The picture for unions is not all rosy, however. In 2006, trade union membership for employees in the UK fell to 28.4% – and shows the largest percentage point decline since 1998 ('Trade Union Membership 2006', DTI).

2.4 The sources of trade union power

The power of a given trade union in bargaining and negotiating with employers will depend on a complex of factors.

(a) The **degree of support** for union actions from its members, and its ability to attract and maintain membership. This in turn may depend on a number of factors:

   (i) The conditions pertaining in the industry or organisation, the aspirations of members and hence the perceived advantages of trade union membership.

   (ii) Employment issues such as recessionary downsizing, or the introduction of new technology, which enhance the perceived importance of worker representation.

   (iii) Competition for members between unions, or between a union and a staff association.

(b) The **perceived success or failure** of the union in obtaining beneficial agreements for its members.

(c)   The **bargaining environment**, including:

   (i)   The **employer's HRM policies**. If terms and conditions are felt to be fair, good in comparison to market rates and so on, there will be little impetus for bargaining.

   (ii)   The **local labour market**. If there is a local shortage of the skill groups represented by the union, it will have greater bargaining power, but the reverse is also true: in time of high unemployment, the union movement is weakened. 'There is less talk about the quality of working life when there is little work to be had' (Huczynski & Buchanan, 2001).

(d)   The culture of the union, and in particular its willingness to use industrial muscle. This resides primarily in the threat of withdrawal of labour in disputes (discussed in Chapter 17).

Activity 3   **(5 minutes)**

Why do you think the **size of the union** (number of members) has been left out of our account?

2.5   The law on trade union membership and activities

The **closed shop** (whereby an employee had to be a member of a relevant union in order to obtain or retain a job) was stripped of all legal protection under the Employment Acts 1988: dismissal for non-membership of a union was automatically to be deemed unfair, and industrial action to create or maintain closed shop practices lost its legal immunity.

On the other hand, further legislation has protected the freedom of individuals to join the union of their choice. No action may be taken to compel people to be members of a union, nor to deter them. Nor can employees be prevented from participation in union activities at an appropriate time: if the union is both independent and recognised by the employer, there is a further right to reasonable time off for union activities.

Individual union members' rights (*Employment Act 1988, Employment Relations Acts 1999 and 2004*) include the following.

(a)   Individuals have the right not to be unjustifiably disciplined by a union (eg by fines, expulsion, withdrawal of benefits or blacklisting) for refusing to strike, for crossing a picket line or for initiating or inciting legal actions against the union.

(b)   Individual's cannot be dismissed for taking official, lawfully-organised industrial action in the first 12 weeks.

(c)   Employees covered by a collective workplace agreement cannot be forced to sign an individual contract.

(d)   Blacklisting of, or discrimination against, trade union members is outlawed.

(e)   Improper campaigning activity by unions and employers, in relation to recognition/de-recognition ballots, is defined (to prevent intimidation).

Activity 4	(15 minutes)

Why do you think the closed shop existed, and why was it abolished?

The law on strikes is discussed in Chapter 17. The **Employment Relations Act 1999** *also introduced major new provisions for statutory trade union recognition, the first time this has been subject to UK law. We will look at the implications for industrial relations.*

2.6   Trade union recognition

Under the *Employment Relations Act 1999*, independent trade unions can apply in writing to an employer to be granted recognition. Recognition may be:

(a)   **Voluntary**, if a ballot (triggered by 10% union membership within the proposed bargaining unit) returned a 40% 'yes' vote, or

(b)   **Automatic**, if more than 50% (plus one person) of the bargaining unit are 'full and conscious' members of the union.

If the union and the employer fail to reach agreement on recognition or on the conduct of collective bargaining, the Central Arbitration Committee (CAC) can make a ruling.

Reports from the CAC suggest that trade unions are using applications for statutory recognition as bargaining tools to win voluntary agreements from employers. Several hundred new recognition deals per year have been signed since 1999. High-profile 'scalps' include Virgin Atlantic, which after many years of refusal entered discussions on recognition with the pilots' union Balpa. The overwhelming majority of trade union agreements have been voluntary agreements for recognition, covering at least pay, hours and holidays.

There are also a small but significant number of **non-traditional deals** stipulating that bargaining should be conducted through company councils or staff forums, on which there may also be representation for union members. This usually happens where union recognition is added to existing consultation procedures: examples include Monarch Airlines' agreement with the AEEU and Eurotunnel's with the T&G.

> The proposition unions are putting to employers is different from what it was a generation ago. More are approaching companies with an offer that seeks to provide workforce representation in a way that's not necessarily going to make life disruptive for the employer. They are asking: 'How can we work with you?' We've been surprised at the extent to which the voluntary approach seems to be the dominant one.   *(People Management,* September 2000)

The *Employment Rights Act 2004* has made some amendments to the 1999 Act, including the following.

- Improving the operation of the statutory recognition procedures. This includes clarifying 'appropriate bargaining units' and 'topics' appropriate for collective bargaining and allowing unions to communicate with workers earlier in the process.

- Tackling intimidation of workers during recognition and de-recognition ballots.

- Extending the protection of employees taking official and lawfully organised industrial action: extending the 'protected period' (during which dismissal is automatically unfair) to 12 weeks, and exempting 'lock out' days from this period (so employers can't justify dismissals by preventing employees from returning to work for 12 weeks!).

Weblinks

You may like to explore some trade-union related sites.

The TUC
▶▶ http://www.tuc.org.uk

Unions 21, the trade union 'think tank'
▶▶ http://www.unions21.org.uk

Aslef (the main train drivers union)
▶▶ http://www.aslef-org.uk

The Communication Workers Union
▶▶ http://cwu.org

The GMB ('Britain's General Union')
▶▶ http://www.gmb.org.uk

The Commonwealth Trade Union Council
▶▶ http://www.commonwealthtuc.ord

International Centre for Trade Union Rights
▶▶ http://ictur.labournet.org

Industrial relations can be contentious, with both legitimate differences and ingrained prejudices on either side. We will now look briefly at the ideological framework underlying industrial relations.

3 THE IDEOLOGICAL FRAMEWORK

3.1 Unitary and pluralist frames of reference

Fox (1975) identified three broad ideologies which are involved in industrial relations.

(a) **Unitary ideology.** All members of the organisation, despite their different roles, have common objectives and values which unite their efforts. Workers are loyal, and the prerogative of management is accepted as paternal, and in everyone's best interests. Unions are a useful channel of communication, but are no longer strictly necessary: they can indeed be counterproductive in offering support to potentially disruptive elements.

Any business must mould a true team and weld individual efforts into a common effort. Each member of the enterprise contributes something different, but they must all contribute towards a common goal. Their efforts must all pull in the same direction, without friction, without unnecessary duplication of effort.

(Drucker, 1955)

(b) **Pluralist ideology.** Organisations are political coalitions of individuals and groups which have their own interests. Management has to create a workable structure for collaboration, taking into account the objectives of all the various interest groups or stakeholders in the organisation. A mutual survival strategy, involving the control of conflict through compromise, can be made acceptable in varying degrees to all concerned.

(c) **Radical ideology.** This primarily Marxist ideology argues that there is an inequality of power between the controllers of economic resources (shareholders and managers) and those who depend on access to those resources (wage earners). Those in power exploit the others by indoctrinating them to accept the legitimacy of their rights to power, and thus perpetuate the system. Conflict between these strata of society – the proletariat and the bourgeoisie – does not aim for mutual survival, but for revolutionary change: bringing down the system.

> The history of all societies hitherto is the history of class struggles. Freeman and slave, patrician and plebeian, lord and serf, guildmaster and journeyman, in a word, oppressor and oppressed, stood in constant opposition to one another, carried on an uninterrupted, now hidden, now open fight.

(Marx and Engels, *The Communist Manifesto*, 1888)

FOR DISCUSSION

Which of the above views do you subscribe to?

3.2 Different stakeholder interests

'Them and us' attitudes have traditionally been ingrained in UK industry, partly because of class-consciousness. You should be aware that they are to an extent inevitable, given the tendency of people to draw boundaries round any group they are in. It should be remembered that there are different interest groups *within* both management and employees as well as *between* them. For example, there may be a clash of interests between HR managers aiming for the stability, quality and flexibility of the workforce, in accordance with ethical HR practice, and production operations managers aiming for immediate efficiency gains through 'lean production'. The interests of white-collar, craft and unskilled workers may clash over differentials, status and demarcation boundaries.

However, the root of union-management conflict, as we have seen, frequently lies in genuine inequities and artificial status distinctions. We have already discussed ways in which less divisive systems (such as single status agreements, salaried status for all grades and Japanese management practices) are available to emphasise a unitary rather than a pluralistic perspective.

According to Gennard and Judge (2003), 'the rationale for employee relations is to solve the problem that in a labour market the buyers (employers) and sellers (employees) have an endemic conflict of interests over the 'prices' at which they wish to exchange their services.' In this view, there is a perpetual **trade off** between what the employer wants (productivity, quality, functional flexibility, numerical flexibility and/or labour stability according to circumstance and so on) and what the employee wants in return (a certain level of pay and incentives, family-friendly policies, opportunities for development, job security and/or mobility according to circumstances and so on).

Employee relations therefore recognises differences (if not conflicts) of interest. Gennard and Judge quote a Recognition Procedural Agreement involving the Scottish Carpet Workers Union which includes the following general principles.

The Union recognises management's responsibility to plan, organise and manage the company's operation.

The company recognises the Union's responsibility to represent the interests of their [sic] members and to maintain or improve their terms and conditions of employment and work within the constraints imposed on the plant by corporate policy and finance.

3.3 Shared stakeholder interests

Trade unions have a vested interest in the success of the organisation to which their members belong because unless the organisation prospers, the job security, pay and benefits of their members will be compromised. Likewise, employers have a vested interest in the continuing commitment and welfare of employees, in order to maintain the viability of the business through the availability, quality and competitiveness of goods and services.

Sir Ken Jackson (*People Management*, September 2000) writes:

It is clear that unions need to improve their ability to support their members. Our aim is to secure a better deal for them by adding value to their employers. We want to contribute to the success of the company by applying our representational talents with honesty, passion and industrial knowledge... It is only when managers are given intelligent, coherent criticism that they think through all the implications of their decisions. Equally, on many occasions, an informed union organisation will support managers' decisions and give them added credibility with the workforce.

3.4 Co-operation

According to the radical perspective, co-operation is merely collaboration in perpetuating oppression. According to the pluralist perspective, however, it is a negotiated process of mutual survival, taking into account the needs of the various stakeholders in the organisation. And according to the unitary perspective, it is the natural mode of business relations and achieves greater productivity and satisfaction for all parties than conflict or competition. Whatever your opinion, it is worth bearing in mind the following points.

(a) **Co-operation has a rational appeal.** It is demonstrable that a suitable number of people co-operating on a task will achieve a better result than one person doing the same task (synergy may enable 2+2 to equal 5) and that groups of co-operating individuals have higher productivity than groups of competing individuals. *However*, it has also been demonstrated that this is not always the case: collaboration can adversely affect individual and group performance, because of group norms, the distraction of group maintenance processes and the tendency of cohesive groups to become blinkered, self-protecting and risky in their decision-making.

(b) **Co-operation has an emotional appeal**. It incorporates values about unity, teamwork, comradeship and belonging: as such, it is a useful cornerstone to the communication of corporate culture. *However*, Charles Handy (among others) has suggested that organisations are too quick to label and discourage differences, argument and competition as 'conflict': these are not only natural and inevitable (pluralist perspective) but potentially beneficial and fruitful (Handy, 1993).

(c) **Co-operation is a common cultural value-cluster**: collectivist cultures such as Japan and Sweden emphasise inter-dependence. *However*, individualist cultures such as the UK and USA value independence more highly.

Activity 5   **(15 minutes)**

How might conflict in the form of differences, argument and competition be beneficial and fruitful for an organisation?

---

4 EMPLOYEE RELATIONS

4.1 HRM and industrial relations

Guest (2001) described four possible orientations to industrial relations strategy as follows.

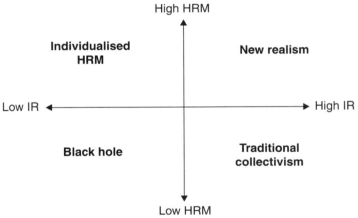

Figure 16.1: Guest's orientations for industries relations strategy

(a) **The new realism:** *high emphasis on HRM and industrial relations.* Companies such as Rover, Nissan and Toshiba have initiated collaborative arrangements, extended consultation processes and moves towards single status, in order to facilitate greater flexibility, more multi-skilling, the removal of demarcations and improvements in quality.

(b) **Traditional collectivism:** *emphasis on industrial relations without HRM.* Unions provide useful, well-established channels for communication and the handling of grievance/discipline/safety issues: it is easier to continue to operate a traditional pluralist industrial relations arrangement.

(c) **Individualised HRM:** *emphasis on HRM without industrial relations.* This is an 'essentially piecemeal and opportunistic' approach which is only common among North-American firms.

(d) **The black hole:** *no industrial relations.* HRM is not considered a policy priority for management, but neither is there seen to be a need for a traditional industrial relations system.

It has been argued that a thorough-going 'HRM' approach – with its unitary perspective and commitment-based strategies renders the traditional 'industrial relations' approach irrelevant and marginalises the traditional roles of the trade union.

Activity 6 (15 minutes)

(a) What are the features of employee relations in the 'industrial relations' model and the 'HRM' model (see Chapter 8 if necessary)?

(b) What kinds of HRM policies, discussed in this Course Book, would reduce the perceived need for trade union representation?

The TUC's HRM Taskforce reported in 1994 that it found no direct relationship between HRM techniques and anti-unionism. In fact, HRM was most prevalent in unionised workplaces. Taskforce chair Bernadette Hillan said: 'If an employer is really trying to improve business performance, is committed to involving workers in the running of the organisation and is seeking to develop a real partnership with recognised trade unions, then HRM and collective bargaining can work in harmony.' She did, however, admit that some employers were using at least the language of HRM as an excuse to de-recognise unions.

The 2000 TUC conference was likewise told by its general secretary, John Monks, that: 'The most successful companies in the UK have the very best management practice, where unions are strong and working in partnership with management.'

FOR DISCUSSION

'One of the unsubstantiated myths in employee relations has been the idea that non-unionism is the panacea for business success, for which organisations such as Marks & Spencer and IBM are put forward as prime examples. There will always be a debate between those who see trade unions as a negative influence and those, like most of our European partners, who see rights at work (including trade union membership and collective bargaining) as part of an important social dimension to working relationships. 'Although the debate about unionism versus non-unionism continues, the real question tends to be ignored. That is – is it easier to manage with unions or without unions? ... 'How many of the companies who yearn for non-union status would be prepared to make the investment in people management that the organisations that they envy have done?'

(Gennard & Judge, 2003)

Debate the issues raised here, justifying your views.

4.2 From 'industrial relations' to 'employee relations'

The Industrial Relations Services have identified four approaches to industrial relations (as cited by Armstrong, 2003).

(a) **Adversarial**: the organisation decides what it wants to do and employees are expected to fit in. Employees only exercise power by refusing to co-operate.

(b) **Traditional**: a good day-to-day working relationship, but management proposes and the workforce reacts through its elected representatives.

(c) **Partnership**: the organisation involves employees in the drawing up and execution of organisation policies, but retains the right to manage.

(d) **Power sharing**: employees are involved in both day-to-day and strategic decision-making.

Definition

Employee relations 'consist of all those areas of HRM that involve general relationships with employees, through collective agreements where trade unions are recognised [industrial relations] and/or through commonly applied policies for employee involvement and communications.' (Armstrong, 2000)

According to Armstrong, employee relations strategy will be concerned with how to:

(a) Build **stable and co-operative relationships** with employees that minimise conflict

(b) Achieve **commitment** through employee involvement and communications processes

(c) Develop **mutuality** – a common interest in achieving the organisation's goals through the development of organisational cultures based on shared values between management and employees

He suggests that such strategies will result in the following kinds of policies.

(a) Changing forms of recognition, including single union recognition or de-recognition

(b) New bargaining structures, including decentralisation or single-table bargaining (discussed in Chapter 17)

(c) The achievement of increased levels of commitment through involvement or participation – giving employees a voice

(d) Deliberately by-passing trade union representatives to communicate directly with employees

(e) Increasing the extent to which management controls operations in such areas as flexibility

(f) Generally improving the employee relations climate in order to produce more harmonious and co-operative relationships

(g)   Developing a 'partnership' with trade unions (discussed in Chapter 18), recognising that employees are stakeholders and that it is to the advantage of both parties to work together.

EXAMPLE 1

Strike Free: New Industrial Relations in Britain by Philip Bassett (1986) illustrated the height of the 'anti-union' phase of HRM in the UK. The following was the experience of the (then) leading-edge computer company, IBM.

Company management attribute the good employee relations to IBM's belief in respect for the individual. One aspect of this philosophy is that IBM does not recognise trade unions for collective bargaining purposes. To do so, they believe, would imply that without trade unions employees' interests would be neglected. Management are convinced that the company's record disproves such a belief.

IBM does not discourage its employees from becoming members of trade unions, but very few of them do so. Even of those who do, a significant minority are against collective bargaining. Pay in IBM is not a collective matter for employees; instead, the company conducts its own confidential survey of comparable companies and determines salary ranges centrally. There is scope for line managers to recommend increases for specific individuals based on merit.

The other traditional function of trade unions at plant level is to assist their members over the hurdles of the employer's grievance system. IBM believe that their own internal complaints procedures, which allow an individual to take a grievance to the very highest levels of management, remove the need for any union involvement.

Other companies, looking at IBM's industrially harmonious, strike-free, non-union record, have asked how they could emulate it. The answer given by a former personnel director of the company is simple: 'You start 30 years ago.'

EXAMPLE 2

Canadian-owned Sheerness Steel, Kent, is the first company in its industry to have de-recognised unions, led by the Iron and Steel Trades Confederation (ISTC), as part of a change to a single status company. According to the personnel director: 'We have become a single status company with personal contracts, salaries, performance-related pay and no defined jobs – people do whatever they are trained to do. We realised that we no longer had anything to debate or discuss with the unions and that they were no longer necessary.'

However, according to the ISTC, the workforce is not happy. Local conditions of high unemployment 'had made it difficult for members to withstand company pressure to take personal contracts'. The change to salaried work means that employees have lost overtime payments which, according to the ISTC, has severely affected their earnings. On the other hand, many of the old disciplinary problems, such as being late, are no longer a problem: just as well, perhaps, since the unions are no longer even allowed to represent individual members in disciplinary cases...'

(*Personnel Management Plus*, September 1992)

NOTES

FOR DISCUSSION

Do the examples cited above reflect an HRM approach to employee relations?

Chapter roundup

- Industrial relations comprises all the rules, practices and conventions governing interactions between managements and their workforces, normally involving collective employee representation and bargaining.

- Employee relations consist of all these areas of HRM that involve general relationships with employees, including industrial relations and employee involvement and communication.

- The stakeholders in industrial relations include: management and/or employers' associations, worker representatives (trade unions, staff associations or other forms of representation) and third parties, such as ACAS, Employment Tribunals and a range of non-government organisations.

- Trade unions may be craft/occupational, general or industrial. After a period of declining membership (accelerated by HRM policies, the decline of manufacturing and Conservative government policy) the political climate and statutory recognition laws have shown an upswing in unionism.

- There are three basic perspectives on industrial relations: unitary, pluralist and radical.

Quick quiz

1 What is an independent trade union?

2 What are the purposes of employers' associations?

3 How might wider society be involved in employee relations in a firm?

4 Distinguish between craft, industrial and general unions.

5 What is a shop steward?

6 Give four reasons for the recent turnaround in the number of workers covered by union recognition agreements.

7 What was the closed shop and what happened to it?

8 Distinguish between the unitary and pluralist frames of reference.

9 In what ways might management and workers be said to have:

   (a) Different interests, and
   (b) Common interests

10 Outline Guest's four orientations to industrial relations strategy.

Answers to quick quiz

1 One which has been certified as being autonomous and financially self-supporting, not dominated by an employer. (see paragraph 1.2)

2 To give help and advice on employee relations issues; to represent members' views to political influencers; to assist in dispute resolution; to negotiate sectoral agreements. (para 1.3)

3 Through pressure groups seeking to oppose exploitative labour relations. In a wider sense, in demanding corporate social responsibility. (para 1.5)

4 Craft unions recruit employees who perform certain jobs. Industrial unions recruit all grades of employees in a particular industry. General unions organise workers from a variety of different jobs and industries. (para 2.1)

5 A workplace union representative: the link between the work group, union officials and management. (para 2.2)

6 Statutory recognition; Labour government support for partnership; recognition of unions as a useful and efficient mechanism for employee relations; increasing recruitment, supported by single union and partnership agreements. (para 2.3)

7 An employee had to be a member of a particular union to secure or retain employment. The closed shop was stripped of legal support: dismissal for non-membership was made automatically unfair, selection on membership discriminatory and industrial action in support of a closed shop unlawful. (para 2.5)

8 Unitary: all members of the organisation, despite their different roles, have common interests and objectives which unites their efforts. The management prerogative is recognised as being in everyone's best interests.

Pluralist: organisations are political coalitions of individuals and groups which inevitably have their own interests. Management has to take into account the objectives of all the various stakeholders in the organisation, to develop a strategy of mutual compromise and survival. (para 3.1)

9 Basically, differences arise from the labour market: trading off the objectives of buyers (management) and sellers (workers) of labour. Common interests arise from both sides' vested interest in the survival and prosperity of the organisation. (see paragraphs 3.2 and 3.3)

10 New realism: high emphasis on HRM and industrial relations eg through partnership agreements.

Traditional collectivism: emphasis on industrial relations without HRM eg through collective bargaining.

Individualised HRM: HRM without industrial relations eg through individual contracts.

Black hole: no HRM or industrial relations eg authoritarian management. (para 4.1)

Answers to activities

1   (a)   Lobbying politicians to obtain legislation to improve conditions of work (eg the minimum wage)

    (b)   Developing political affiliations with other trade unions, to create a power base for achieving political influence

    (c)   Providing financial support for a sympathetic political party (traditionally, the Labour Party)

    (d)   Establishing non-negotiatory processes for sharing management decision-making: eg by joint consultative committees or partnership agreements.

    (e)   Providing welfare help and support for members: funding during industrial action, say.

2   (a)   Conciliation (getting conflicting parties together for informal discussion to resolve a dispute)

    (b)   Mediation (providing a mediator or mediation board, which hears arguments and makes proposals and recommendations as a basis for settlement)

    (c)   Arbitration (assisting in the appointment of independent arbitrators who make a binding ruling)

3   Size is a variable insignificant in itself: the Union's credibility rests on size as a proportion of potential membership. The threat of industrial action even by a large union would be hollow if its membership represented a very small proportion of workers in the relevant organisation or sector. A union which is small in terms of membership numbers may still have a very strong negotiating position if its members are of an occupational category which is significant to the organisation or national life (eg nurses, firemen).

4   The closed shop was encouraged by unions as a means of increasing their membership and bargaining power within a company. It was supported by some managements as a way of facilitating single-union agreements. Closed shops were criticised for interfering with individual rights of choice; constraining management decision-making on recruitment and retention; and strengthening the bargaining power of unions to the detriment of industrial relations.

5   (a)   Differences allow for diversity of talents, viewpoints, ideas: necessary for innovation, problem-solving, understanding human dynamics, flexibility. Differences reflect the diversity of the customer base: conformity may blinker the organisation to potential needs or problems. Suppression of diversity may cause stress and resentment.

    (b)   Argument is useful to clear the air, help divergent viewpoints to emerge, encourage empathy with different viewpoints: extremely helpful in conflict resolution, in change management (bringing resistance into the open), in encouraging emotional intelligence.

    (c)   Controlled competition between teams has been demonstrated to increase team cohesion/co-operation and motivation and improve performance. Competition tied to incentives is a powerful energiser of performance (particularly in individualistic cultures).

6   (a)   IR = low trust, collectivist, pluralist. HRM = high trust, individualist, unitarist.

         (b)   Examples include: direct voluntary communication and consultation on matters which will affect employees; worker involvement techniques; fair, consistent and transparent discipline and grievance handling; equitable and non-discriminatory recruitment, selection, appraisal and reward systems; health, safety and welfare policies clearly aimed at problem-solving and worker protection; programmes at improving the work environment; flexible remuneration packages (such as cafeteria benefits) encouraging individual aspirations and priorities.

Chapter 17:
INDUSTRIAL RELATIONS PROCESSES

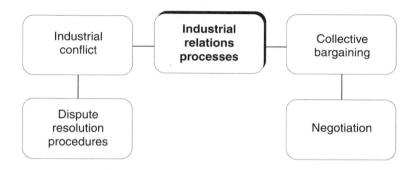

Introduction

In this chapter we explore some of the key processes in industrial relations: collective bargaining, and the related strategies and skills of negotiation and the management of industrial disputes.

In each of these areas, we will see signs of the shift towards a unitarist perspective discussed in Chapter 16, while at the same time recognising the differing interests of stakeholders in the organisation. Even industrial conflict must be managed in the context of an on-going relationship. This perspective is typified in the various measures taken to involve employees in decision-making, under the general banner of 'participation' and 'involvement': it will be covered in Chapter 18.

Your objectives

In this chapter you will learn about the following.

- (a) Different types of collective dispute
- (b) Dispute procedures and the resolution of conflict
- (c) The nature and scope of collective bargaining
- (d) Negotiation processes and strategy

1 INDUSTRIAL CONFLICT

1.1 Types of collective dispute

Individual disputes against employers are covered by disciplinary and grievance procedures (see Chapter 6).

We have already seen in Chapter 16 that there are deep-rooted ideologies of conflict embedded in industrial relations in the UK. **Collective disputes** typically involve pay, conditions of employment, job security or breach of contracts and negotiated agreements.

According to the *Employment Act 1982*, a 'lawful trade dispute' is one between workers and their own employers, wholly or mainly about work related matters, and *not*:

- Demarcation and other inter-union disputes
- Disputes between workers and employers other than their own
- Disputes other than those mainly connected with pay and conditions or
- Disputes overseas.

1.2 Industrial action

Industrial action in pursuance of a dispute may take a number of forms (discussed below), but are classified on four basic dimensions.

(a) **Official** action is supported by the trade union representatives of the employees in dispute, and conducted according to union procedure, including secret balloting of members.

(b) **Unofficial** action is taken by a part of the workforce without recognition and support from union officials and without balloting and approval procedures.

(c) **Primary** action is aimed at the employer with whom the participating union is in dispute.

(d) **Secondary** action is aimed at employers who trade with firms in dispute, but who are not directly involved in the dispute themselves.

Activity 1 (15 minutes)

What do you think might be the purpose of threatening or implementing industrial action?

EXAMPLE

In September 2003, members of the Communication Workers Union (CWU) voted against a national strike against Royal Mail following a pay deal which offered a productivity-linked 14.5% pay rise. (Even so, Royal Mail workers in London subsequently staged a series of 24 hour strikes over the London Weighting allowance.)

In May 2007, the postal group offered a pay freeze for the year (amidst planned cost cuts of £350 million), cutting weekend and night-shift working at many mail centres. The

CWU referred to the moves as a 'cost cutting frenzy' and accused Royal Mail of blaming competition in the postal market for a 'slash and burn' approach to pay and working conditions.

Royal Mail countered that its workers were paid too highly compared with the industry average – although in 2006 it signed an agreement to improve pay. The CWU is fighting for pay to be brought into line with the national average – which would require a 27% increase.

In June 2007, the CWU called a one-day national strike accusing **Royal Mail** of not taking their grievances seriously. Post Office staff as well as Royal Mail staff would be called out, following a 77% vote of support from union members.

Royal Mail was 'astonished' and 'disappointed' by the threat.

(*People Management*, 26 April & 22 June 2007)

Definition

> **Strike action** is the withholding of labour in the course of a dispute with management.

Various forms of primary industrial action by union members (in order of severity) include the following.

(a) **Withdrawal of co-operation** by the union (eg refusal to participate in disciplinary procedures).

(b) **Insistence on formal rights** by the union (eg raising trivial infringements as grievance issues, insistence on taking time off or limiting overtime, where there would normally be informal flexibility).

(c) A **work-to-rule or go-slow**: employees follow official work procedures and rules to the letter, thereby reducing productivity without doing anything to justify disciplinary action by management. This also highlights the extent to which management take for granted the commitment and voluntary contribution of employees.

(d) A **ban on overtime** and weekend working to restrict productivity, often highlighting issues of work organisation.

(e) A **token withdrawal of labour**: for example, a one-day strike by the union membership in the workforce, as a protest against management's unwillingness to make further concessions in negotiation. These may be repeated over a period of time, in order to provide a recurring disruption to the organisation's operations without a complete loss of pay: 24-hour strikes by Royal Mail workers in 2003 is one example.

(f) **Indefinite strike action** by the entire union membership in the workforce, either at national level, company level or plant level: the 1984 miners' strike is a historic example.

(g) **Picketing**: striking workers maintain a presence outside the employer's premises (a 'picket line'). The aim of the picket line is to highlight the protest and to inform and solicit the support of workers attempting to enter the workplace. In practice, this often takes the form of active discouragement and intimidation of strike-breakers, replacement workers and others. The Employment Act 1982 protects unions and their members against most civil and criminal actions 'in contemplation or furtherance of a trade dispute', including picketing at or near the place of work with a purpose that is 'peacefully to obtain or communicate information, or peacefully to persuade a person to work or not to work'. Secondary picketing (of organisations not involved in the dispute) is not protected, however.

Activity 2 (5 minutes)

What are the corresponding 'industrial sanctions' which might be used by management in furtherance of an industrial dispute? Why might these be used as a 'last resort'?

The **threat** of applying industrial sanctions may be sufficient to make either or both of the parties adjust their position in a dispute, it being in the interests of neither party to incur the heavy costs of such sanctions – particularly if there is unlikely to be a successful outcome.

1.3 Statistics on strikes

Official statistics on the use of industrial sanctions in the UK only cover strikes. They measure:

(a) The frequency (number) of strikes

(b) The size of strikes (that is, the number of workers involved)

(c) The duration of strikes (that is, the number of working days lost) – since this figure on its own may give a distorted impression if there are a few very long strikes. For example, the 1984 miners' strike accounted for 83% of the total number of working days lost to strikes in that year!

All three measures peaked in 1979 (2,125 stoppages in progress, 4.6 million workers involved, and 29.4 million working days lost – of which 54% were accounted for by a strike of engineering workers). All three measures have since been steadily falling.

- In the year 2000, there were 212 stoppages, involving 182,000 workers and a loss of 499,000 lost working days.

- In 2006, there were 116 stoppages, involving 92,000 workers and a loss of 157,000 working days.

(*Labour Market Trends, 2006*)

1.4 The law on strikes

Relevant provisions include the following.

(a) Official industrial action requires the **secret balloting** of all affected members. Seven days' notice must be given to an employer of a union's intention to ballot its members on industrial action.

(b) In the course of a lawful and duly balloted trade dispute, the trade union, its officials and participants in the dispute are immune from legal action. However, members of the public have the right to apply for a court order restraining a union from taking *unlawful* industrial action.

(c) **Picketing** carries legal immunity only if the pickets consist of employees who normally work at the premises, former employees (if the dispute concerns their termination), and employees who have no fixed place of work or who cannot picket their own place of work (and who therefore picket the premises from which their work is administered). Picketing solely to obtain or communicate information is not unlawful, but may become so if it involves obstruction of the public highway or breach of the peace. Secondary action of any kind is unlawful.

(d) An individual may not be unjustifiably disciplined by a union (eg by fines, expulsion, withdrawal of benefits or blacklisting) for **refusing** to strike or go slow if by so doing (s)he would be in breach of contract, or for crossing a picket line.

(e) It is unlawful to **dismiss strikers** for the first twelve weeks of a strike.

EXAMPLE

'The 250 **British Airways** staff who staged an unofficial walkout [in July 2003] certainly achieved the profile they would have wished for.

'The dispute provoked furore among customers left stranded at Heathrow airport, cost BA £40 million and also marked the beginning of days of deadlock in talks between management and staff.

'Many have been unsympathetic to the reason for the strike, which centred around the introduction of an electronic clocking-in system.

'While members of the public remained largely indifferent, some fellow colleagues described it as a 'piffling issue'.

'But analysts and experts have warned the significance of this strike should not be undermined. What is critical, they have said, is that in this era of partnership working and general lack of rebellion, staff reached a point of such desperation they were willing to take the drastic action of staging a strike without their unions' backing. It demonstrates the severity of the breakdown in relations between management and staff. ...

'Mike Emmott, the CIPD's head of employee relations, agrees that this raises questions about people management practices at BA.

' "Workers do not take such drastic action as to walk out when they feel that they have trust in their management, when they feel listened to and when they feel that their best interests are at heart," he says.

' "Management has been saying that the scheme is simply about turning the paper-based system into an electronic one and that the workforce should trust them, but the simple fact is that the workforce doesn't believe them," he adds.'

(Watkins, 2003 (d))

1.5 No strike agreements

The 'right to strike' in enshrined in employment law. However, no-strike agreements may be made by voluntary agreement between employers and unions. The Trade Union and Labour Relations Act 1974 states that a no-strike clause in a collective agreement can only be made part of individual contracts of employment when the agreement provides expressly and in writing for its inclusion, and when the agreement is made reasonably accessible to employees at the workplace.

No-strike clauses effectively deprive union negotiators of the threat of strike action in the event of breakdown in bargaining, and arguably deprive workers of one of their only sources of power in the employment relationship. They therefore tend to be attached to collective agreements which support the managerial prerogative, such as single-union and partnership agreements.

FOR DISCUSSION

Do you think certain categories of worker should be deprived of the right to strike, in the national interest? If so, which? (Think of times when your own life was disrupted by strike action.)

Having seen how industrial disputes arise, we will now consider how they may be resolved.

2 DISPUTE RESOLUTION PROCEDURES

2.1 Dispute procedures

Detailed procedural agreements on disputes are generally made during collective bargaining or other (non-union) negotiated agreements. A typical dispute procedure would provide for the 'escalating' involvement of more senior representatives of both sides, with a guarantee of new industrial action until all stages have been followed through.

(a)   Meeting of union representative and middle management

(b)   Meeting of district union officer and senior management

(c)   Meeting of regional and then national officials of the union and employers' association (in national disputes)

(d)   Conciliation (if required)

(e)   Mediation (if required)

(f)   Agreement to abide by the decision of an independent arbitrator (as a last resort, since the decision then passes out of the hands of the parties involved)

If dispute procedures fail to re-open negotiation or resolve conflict, the parties may consider calling in ACAS to offer the services of conciliation, mediation and arbitration.

2.2   The role of ACAS

Conciliation is a voluntary process of discussion, facilitated by ACAS conciliators whose role is to make constructive suggestions, provide information and manage the process. At this stage, ACAS has no power to impose or recommend settlements. ACAS will only agree to conciliate where internal dispute resolution procedures have been exhausted without result. The conciliation process typically involves:

(a)   **Fact-finding**, to explore the reasons for the dispute, often through separate meetings of the conciliator with each side.

(b)   **Explanation** of each side's position in joint meetings, often facilitated by side meetings between the conciliator and the parties separately, to encourage parties to keep talking and to consider potential areas of movement towards settlement (which parties may not wish to consider openly in full session at first).

(c)   **Negotiation** towards a mutually acceptable position, finalised in a joint agreement between the two sides.

If a voluntary settlement is not reached through conciliation, ACAS can arrange for **mediation**. This involves the appointment of an independent person or Board of Mediation, who will consider the case of both sides (set out in writing) and then hear both sides' evidence and arguments at a hearing. The mediator makes a formal proposal or recommendation as a basis for settlement of the dispute, but this is not legally binding on either party.

If both parties agree to **arbitration**:

(a)   Terms of reference must be defined, setting limits to the arbitrator's powers and to the issues to be considered.

(b)   Parties may select the independent arbitrator from the ACAS panel, or may let ACAS appoint an arbitrator.

(c)   A date and venue are set for the arbitration hearing. Prior to the hearing, both sides exchange and submit to the arbitrator a written statement of their case and arguments, supporting documents, and a list of those attending (usually the negotiators). The arbitrator may also request a site

BPP LEARNING MEDIA

visit, for example if the dispute concerns the conditions under which work is done or the level of skill required.

(d) An informal, private and confidential hearing is held, at which the arbitrator hears arguments from both sides. A typical procedure would allow each side an uninterrupted opportunity to state its case and critique the opposing case (as set out in the written submission), prior to questioning by the other side and by the arbitrator. The arbitrator then ensures that both parties have said or asked everything they wish to, and invites closing statements.

(e) The arbitrator considers the arguments after the hearing and delivers an award via ACAS, usually within two to three weeks.

FOR DISCUSSION

Why might employers and trade unions regard arbitration as a little-used instrument of last resort?

What more effective ways might each seek to resolve disputes?

2.3 Conflict resolution

The rationale behind the collaborative approach is explored in the win-win model of conflict resolution. Cornelius and Faire (1989) suggest that there are three basic ways in which a conflict or disagreement can be worked out.

(a) **Win-lose**: one party gets what he wants at the expense of the other party. However well justified such a solution is, there is often lingering resentment on the part of the 'losing' party, which may begin to damage working relationships.

(b) **Lose-lose**: neither party gets what he really wants. Compromise comes into this category. However logical such a solution is, there is often resentment and dissatisfaction on both sides: even positive compromises only result in half-satisfied needs.

(c) **Win-win**: both parties get as close as possible to what they really want. Whether or not such an outcome is possible, the attempt to find it invariably generates more options, more creative and collaborative problem-solving, more open communication and a greater likelihood of preserved working relationships.

A basic win-win approach may be outlined as follows.

(a) **Find out why each party *needs* what they say they *want*.** Probing for, and mapping, both party's fears/concerns and needs in the situation facilitates meaningful problem-solving. It also encourages communication, supports other people's values, and separates the problem from the personalities involved.

(b) **Find out where the differences dovetail.** Diverging needs may seem like the cause of conflict – but they also offer potential for more creative problem-solving, since the different needs may not be mutually exclusive: there may be opportunities for both sets of needs to be satisfied by different means.

(c) **Design more options**, where everyone gets more of what they need. Techniques for doing this include:

    (i) Brainstorming, which temporarily (and by agreement) allows the generation of options temporarily *uncensored* and *uncriticised* by viewpoints which by definition are limited by the conflict;

    (ii) Chunking (breaking a big problem down into manageable chunks and seeking solutions to each); and

    (iii) Devising usable 'currencies' (suggestions and concessions which are easy or low-cost for both parties, and can be traded in negotiation). The aim is *mutual gain*.

(d) **Co-operate**. Treat the other party as a partner in problem-solving, not as an opponent in competition.

EXAMPLE

Dispute resolution procedure: the British Airways walkout

18 July	250 BA staff take part in unofficial walkout after BA announces it is to introduce an electronic swipe-card system.
19 July	Staff return after unions announce talks with BA.
23 July	Talks break down, with unions accusing BA of 'failing to move an inch'.
24 July	GMB and Amicus say that they will ballot staff over strike action.
26 July	Talks resume at conciliation service ACAS after BA chief executive Rod Eddington agrees to attend the talks.
28 July	TUC joins the talks in a 'peace broker' role.
31 July	Unions say the dispute has been resolved, after BA agrees to make scheme voluntary until September, and to separate the issue from ongoing pay negotiations.

(Watkins, 2003 (d))

Activity 3   **(30 minutes)**

From the elements, timetable and result listed in the above example, how successful do you think this dispute resolution was?

2.4 Coping with industrial action

While managerial focus is likely to be on avoiding industrial action, (dispute resolution procedures, threat of sanctions) there should be **contingency plans** in place to minimise the disruptions caused by industrial action if, and when, it occurs.

Depending on the nature of the business, and the group of workers involved, key considerations may be:

(a) **To maintain incoming deliveries** of materials and supplies: eg for a retail organisation, or a factory threatened with picketing.

(b) **To maintain production output or service levels**: eg by finding suitable alternative labour (transfers of staff from other sites, or jobs, use of short-contract and casual staff), or re-organising and prioritising(using up existing overstocks, transferring stock from other plans, transferring production to other plants, encouraging overtime working prior to strike).

(c) **To maintain supply of goods and services to the customer**: eg through picket lines, by subcontracting distribution, or encouraging customer self-service.

3 COLLECTIVE BARGAINING

3.1 The nature and scope of collective bargaining

Definition

> **Collective bargaining** is the process whereby employers and employee representatives negotiate agreements by which terms and conditions of employment (and related matters) are determined for groups of represented employees.

Collective bargaining is basically concerned with reaching two types of agreement.

(a) **Substantive agreements,** which determine the terms and conditions of employment. A substantive agreement between a union and employer might cover areas such as: rates of pay for various categories of worker; premium rates of pay; working hours, breaks and holidays; benefits; access to training programmes and so on.

(b) **Procedural agreements,** which determine the methods and procedures for:

(i) Arriving at substantive agreements. (What negotiating machinery should be set up? Should a particular issue be discussed at national level, company level, local plant/branch level – or not at all?)

(ii) Settling any disagreements or disputes which cannot be resolved by normal negotiation. There might be arrangements to refer disputes at plant level to regional or national level, or to arbitration. Procedural rules would determine what the arbitration arrangements should be (eg involving ACAS).

In practice, there are likely to be a range of procedural arrangements and agreements, in areas such as: employee grievances; disciplinary action; redundancy; health and safety; staff development; pay grading; union recognition and so on. Procedural arrangements and agreements basically provide 'law and order' in the workplace: a definition of fair and reasonable behaviour by employers, and the rights and obligations of employees, in a given set of circumstances.

A '**workforce agreement**' is a particular arrangement, under the *Working Time Regulations 1998*, which allows employers to fix working-time arrangements with workers who do not have collectively-agreed terms or conditions. This allows flexibility in taking account of the needs of local workforces or workgroups in applying the regulations.

Note that non-unionised, as well as unionised, organisations have substantive and procedural arrangements (pay grades, dispute procedures etc) in place: employers may (or may not) have drawn these up in consultation with workers.

Gennard & Judge (2003) note that even the outcome of collective bargaining is not, in practice, confined to union members.

(a)   Unionised companies apply collectively-bargained terms and conditions to non-union staff as well.

(b)   Non-unionised companies partly determine their terms and conditions with regard to market rates – which take into account collectively-bargained terms elsewhere.

3.2   Levels and parties in collective bargaining

Collective bargaining may take place at different levels.

(a)   Some issues are discussed at **national (or multi-employer) level**, between *representatives of employers* for the industry or sector and *national trade union officials*. In France, Holland, Italy, Sweden, Finland, Belgium and Spain, for example, sectoral collective agreements are common. These may provide only a basic outline and floor of conditions (for example, minimum rates of pay, maximum weekly and overtime hours, paid holiday entitlements) which trade unions expect to elaborate and improve through company-level agreements.

(b)   Other issues will be settled at **company level**, by *representatives of management* and the *unions or staff associations* recognised by the company. Ford, for example, have their own company-wide pay agreements, and do not join in national negotiations with an employers' federation. This allows pay and conditions to be related to the economic and competitive circumstances, and internal equity considerations, of the particular firm.

(c)   Other issues will be settled at more local level by '**domestic' (or enterprise) bargaining**, involving representatives of *plant or business unit management* and *local shop stewards*. Phillips Electronics in the UK, for example, has abandoned its national bargaining structure in favour of plant by plant negotiations. This reflects the decentralisation of industrial relations (among other HRM functions) within organisations. Enterprise bargaining may be autonomous, or co-ordinated across all plans/unit, by taking place within centrally-set parameters.

Decentralised bargaining has increased in recent years, because it provides greater flexibility than national agreements. This applies both to the employer (allowing for greater labour flexibility by tailoring work rules and pay agreements to the needs of specific plants) and to the employee (reflecting the desire for more direct influence in employment terms and conditions, which has created a further trend towards individualised contracts). It is also more easily changed, if necessary, because there is less (and more accessible) negotiating machinery. This relative flexibility may have drawbacks, however, if it results in fragmented and inequitable pay structures, inflationary 'leapfrogging' of settlements, and freedom to break or re-negotiate agreements at will. It also relies on competent negotiations by plant-level management.

3.3 Single-table bargaining

Definition

> **Single-table bargaining** describes a situation in which the terms and conditions of all represented workers employed by an establishment are determined in a single set of negotiations. This could involve a single union representing different types and grades of employees (manual and non-manual), or several unions which negotiate a bargaining position amongst themselves prior to negotiating with management as a single bargaining unit.

> **Activity 4**   **(45 minutes)**
>
> What would you anticipate to be the advantages and disadvantages of single-table bargaining?

Beardwell and Holden (1997) argue that the significance of single-table bargaining is not primarily its advantages in simplifying and integrating bargaining processes, but the opportunity to extend consultation beyond the basic negotiation forum, to include matters which affect all employees: training and development, fringe benefits, the future direction of the business, change management and so on.

We will be covering employee consultation in Chapter 18, but you should be aware that trade unions recognised for the purpose of collective bargaining are entitled to certain information.

3.4 Disclosure of information

An employer must provide information in response to a written request by a union representative, as long as:

(a) It relates to his (or an associated employer's) undertaking

(b) It is in his possession

(c) It is in accordance with good practice (as laid down in an ACAS Code of Practice)

(d) Lack of the information would materially impede the representative in collective bargaining.

The ACAS Code of Practice recommends that information should be disclosed on pay and benefits, conditions of service, human resources, performance (eg productivity, sales/order forecasts) and financial matters. It suggests that unions should define and request the information before negotiations begin, stating why they consider it relevant. A union may apply to the Central Arbitration Committee if it believes disclosable information has been withheld. If an employer refuses to comply with a Committee declaration that information should be disclosed, the CAC may make an enforceable award of terms and conditions, at the request of the trade union.

There is no obligation to give information relating to:

(a) Information given in confidence

(b) Information relating to particular individuals

(c) Information which – in any context other than collective bargaining – would cause injury to the undertaking

(d) Information protected by statute (say, in the interests of national security) or subject to legal proceedings.

3.5 Attitudes to collective bargaining

Chamberlain and Kuhn *(1965)* traced a historical development in attitudes towards collective bargaining.

(a) At first, there was a **marketing theory**, in which collective bargaining was seen as pay bargaining for the supply of labour. Rates of pay would be settled on the basis of supply and demand.

(b) Later, a **governmental (or control) theory** developed. Collective bargaining was seen as a way of making rules of conduct and enforcing those rules in addition to pay bargaining.

(c) Finally, a **managerial theory** emerged, on the basis that decisions about matters in which both management and employees have a vital interest should be discussed and decided by collective negotiation.

A greater range of matters theoretically now come within the sphere of collective bargaining arrangements. Negotiations might cover not only pay, conditions of employment (holidays, hours of work etc) and demarcation lines, but also promotion and training opportunities, fringe benefits, health and safety, equal opportunities and so on. In practice, the Workplace Employee Relations surveys suggest that the number of non-pay items subject to collective bargaining has actually fallen in the private sector.

As we saw in Chapter 16 on union recognition, a managerial approach to collective bargaining is arguably a systematic, efficient, relationship-building and equitable method of conducting industrial relations. It encourages a collectivist orientation which is suited to some cultures of employment and may encourage teamworking and identification with the organisation in others.

> **Activity 5** (20 minutes)
>
> There has been a decline in collective bargaining in recent decades. From what you know of the development of trade unionism during this period, why might this be so?

3.6 The status of collective agreements

In most democratic societies, collective agreements are legally binding: if either party breaks the terms of the agreement, the other can pursue its rights through the courts. This is not the case in the UK! UK collective agreements are only binding in 'honour'. This means that agreements are generally not as comprehensive or precise as legal contracts; they are often reviewed and renegotiated annually. It is, however, important to have rigorous procedural arrangements in place, to define acceptable behaviour and dispute/appeal mechanisms.

4 NEGOTIATION

Definition

> **Negotiation** is a process whereby two parties come together to confer with a view to concluding a jointly acceptable agreement.

4.1 The purpose of negotiation

The general purpose of such a process is for interest groups to attempt to resolve differences between and within themselves, in order to **maintain co-operation** in the pursuit of shared or superordinate goals. Such an approach may be applied in a number of different situations, including collective (and individual) bargaining, conflict resolution and group decision making. Negotiation is basically a **problem-solving** *technique*, enabling parties to meet their own needs (as far as possible) without breaking the relationship or co-operation between them. This is obviously essential where management and workers are concerned!

Gennard & Judge (2003) suggest that this process requires:

- **Purposeful persuasion**: whereby each party attempts to persuade the other to accept its case by marshalling arguments, backed by factual information and analysis.

- **Constructive compromise**: whereby both parties accept the need to move closer towards each other's position, identifying the parameters of common ground within and between their positions, where there is room for concessions to be made while still meeting the needs of both parties.

Fisher *et al* (1999) suggest three criteria for effective negotiation.

- It should produce a wise agreement: 'one which meets the legitimate interests of each side to the extent possible, resolves conflicting interests fairly, is durable and takes community interests into account'.

- It should be efficient.

- It should improve (or at least not damage) the relationship between the parties.

FOR DISCUSSION

How important is the assumption of on-going relationship in your dealings with other people at work (or in your studies)? What does this encourage you to do, and what does it *prevent* you from doing, in the informal 'negotiations' you conduct every day?

4.2 Approaches to negotiation

There are two approaches to negotiation, which involve different methodologies and outcomes.

(a) **Distributive bargaining**, where negotiation is about the distribution of finite resources. One party's gain is another's loss: a 'win-lose' or 'zero sum' equation. If a pay increase of, say, 10% is gained, where the management budget was 5%, the extra has to be funded from elsewhere – profits, investments, other groups (such as shareholders), increased prices, increased productivity, cuts in training or whatever.

(b) **Integrative bargaining**, based on joint problem-solving, where negotiations aim to find a mutually satisfying solution to problems. This has emerged in recent years in a technique called the 'win-win' approach, a process of exploring and defining the needs and fears of all parties with a view not just to getting the best outcome for one's own party ('win-lose') or even compromise ('lose-lose') but to fulfilling the needs of all parties: a 'win-win' solution may not be available, but the process makes it possible. 'Win-win' negotiation is based on the desire to preserve a constructive relationship between the negotiating parties. 'Win-lose' outcomes can cause resentment or under-motivated performance by the 'losing' party, and perpetuates underlying conflict.

NOTES

We will be outlining a negotiation process based on concessions and the attempt to find 'middle ground'. However, you should be aware of an alternative approach to collective bargaining, called 'pendulum arbitration'.

Definition

> **Pendulum arbitration** is a system whereby a third party will arbitrate on behalf of the two principals in collective bargaining, should they fail to reach agreement, by awarding the final position of one side or the other: either the employer's final offer or the employees' final claim.

Traditional arbitration draws from both sides of the negotiation in an attempt to find 'middle ground', and this may encourage principals to exaggerate their demands, knowing that they will eventually have to compromise or 'split the difference'. Pendulum arbitration encourages principals to moderate their final positions and to attempt to settle in good faith, knowing that an extreme position will rebound on them if the decision goes to the other side. It avoids the drawing out of the negotiation process by each side holding back from their final position during bargaining.

In practice, however, it is a difficult process, since disputes may involve complex multiple issues, and the final positions of each side on each issue may not be clear.

FOR DISCUSSION

What kind of industrial relations atmosphere is created by a concept such as 'pendulum arbitration'?

Do you think that a 'win-win' solution is possible in collective bargaining?

4.3   The negotiating process

The following (Figure 17.1) is a general overview of the negotiation process. Any negotiation will involve the stages illustrated, although the duration and approach of each will vary according to the particular situation.

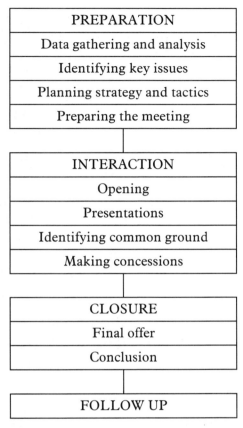

| PREPARATION |
| Data gathering and analysis |
| Identifying key issues |
| Planning strategy and tactics |
| Preparing the meeting |

| INTERACTION |
| Opening |
| Presentations |
| Identifying common ground |
| Making concessions |

| CLOSURE |
| Final offer |
| Conclusion |

| FOLLOW UP |

Figure 17.1 The negotiation process

4.4 Preparing a negotiation and negotiation strategy

Formal negotiations, as opposed to informal 'arrangements', should follow broad guidelines.

(a) **Set objectives, parameters and priorities** which are achievable and consistent with industrial relations policy. These are likely to be couched in optimum, most likely and fall-back terms (see (e) below).

(b) **Research the background** of issues over which negotiations are to be conducted: trends in union responses, market pay rates, case studies from similar organisations/sectors, relevant legislation and court decisions and so on.

(c) **Recognise potential for conflict.** In an integrative framework, each side accepts that the objectives and perspectives of the other side are as genuine and legitimate as their own. Even in a distributive framework, it must be recognised that the outcome will have to be 'sold' to all parties, and the consequences of resistance, resentment and lost relationship managed. Recognition of the needs, wants and fears of the other party helps in managing expectations and in the process of devising a workable trade-off between divergent interests.

(d) **Identify tradable items and bargaining power.**

Each party identifies the key issues or items likely to be on the bargaining agenda, and decides on which of these it will be willing to trade or make concessions. It also tries to anticipate the items on which the other party will be willing to trade or make concessions. Some items will be non-tradable: others may be amenable to movement on both sides, especially if some items are identified as being relatively 'cheap' for one party to give up and relatively valuable for the other party to receive.

Each party may also attempt to evaluate its bargaining power, relative to the other party. A frequently used formula for this is:

$$\text{Bargaining power of A} = \frac{\text{Costs to B of disagreement with A's terms}}{\text{Costs to A of disagreement with B's terms}}$$

If the cost of disagreeing is greater than the cost of agreeing, the bargaining power lies with the other side.

Activity 6   (10 minutes)

This bargaining power model provides a quantitative measure of relative bargaining power. What other, more qualitative factors are there that might enhance or detract from the bargaining power of one side or the other?

(e) **Determine negotiating strategy**. Given a fair idea of what the other side's position and bargaining power are likely to be, the party in question should be able to predict any demands the other side will make, or what kind of offer is likely to be accepted. Each side should look for potential counter-arguments to its own case, without underestimating the potential gap between the parties.

There are basically three possible outcomes for either side:

(i) If we were to achieve all our objectives, what would be the *ideal settlement* or outcome?

(ii) If we were to make progress, but being realistic about the power of the other side, what is a *realistic settlement* or outcome?

(iii) If we were to concede, what is an acceptable *fall-back position*: the least favourable outcome that can be accepted without failing to meet our objectives?

A position for each side should be estimated for each of the above situations, and areas of agreement concentrated on, as potential *middle ground*.

John Sawbridge (*People Management* 14 September 2000) suggests that:

The union will move only if it believes that:

- there is no other option
- its members will benefit
- it will be painful not to do so.

(f) **Determine the agenda** ('terms of reference') of the meeting. The agenda for negotiation should be accepted (or acceptable) in advance by both sides. The order of items may have tactical significance: imposing time pressures for agreement on issues raised late in the day, say, or gaining momentum on related issues by placing them after a major point of agreement.

(g) **Issue prior information**. This may be done:

(i) As pre-conditioning: for example, advance announcement of poor trading results and intense competition as a prelude to negotiating pay awards, redundancies or productivity agreements.

(ii) As a matter of legal obligation. Information relevant to collective bargaining must be disclosed to trade union representatives (see above).

(iii) To allow all parties to do their homework, for better quality decision-making, (unless there is any assumed advantage in surprise disclosures).

(h) **Select participants.** Representatives of management must be articulate, persuasive, acceptable to employee representatives and authoritative enough to implement agreed decisions. Face-to-face negotiations require particular skills in persuasion, personal rapport, reading of verbal and non-verbal signals and so on.

4.5 Conduct of negotiation

During the conduct of the negotiations themselves, participants should consider the following.

(a) **Opening presentation**: a broad statement of each side's ideal position or opening offer, explaining the rationale (and strength of feeling) behind the proposals and supporting them with relevant data. This will be a clue to strategy – and may also be an opportunity for broad general agreement. It is recommended that the party seeking change be invited to state its case first.

(b) **Fact-finding**: each party should use the other party's presentation as an opportunity for fact-finding, rather than point scoring or unconsidered ('knee-jerk') opposition. Active listening should be used to clarify or expand on proposals, or to probe for supporting data. During the fact-finding process, the negotiator should gain a better understanding of the other party's ideal position or proposal *and* its strengths and weaknesses (Dobler *et al*, 1990). At the end of this session, there may be a recess or adjournment to allow negotiators to reassess their positions and strategies.

(c) **Identifying common ground**: having established each others' ideal positions (potentially polarised differences) the emphasis switches to exploring the territory *within* the bargaining range in which agreement might be reached; the room for manoeuvre offered by both parties' (possibly dovetailed) realistic and fall-back positions should be explored.

(d) **Use of the negotiating strategy and bargaining power.** Items should be linked and packaged to achieve two-way momentum, so that no party gives away anything without getting something in return. Be firm on principles and flexible on details, so that there is room to move without compromising strategic priorities.

(e) **Making concessions**. A concession is 'a revision of a position you have held previously and justified publicly' (Guirdham, 1995). Concessions are not easy to make without undermining credibility – but *must* be made in order to bring both parties progressively closer together. They should be made only in response to pressure – or to offers-in-exchange from the other party – and in small increments. **Reciprocal concessions** can be promoted by negatively reinforcing the other side's present position (eg emphasising that it will not work) and positively reinforcing movement (eg offering options for them to move without losing face).

The meeting should be facilitated by an experienced chairperson, who will ensure that the meeting is conducted in a courteous and effective manner: sticking to the point of the agenda reached; giving alternating opportunities to speak (rather than a 'free for all'); and so on.

Activity 7	**(30 minutes)**

From your study or awareness of communication and persuasion techniques, suggest some techniques which you might use in negotiation.

Adjournments may be used to give parties time to review progress, consider proposals, enter informal 'off-the-table' discussions which might help break an impasse, or just 'cool off' when negotiation reaches a heated stage.

All relevant details of the discussion should be recorded by a minute-taker, stenographer or sound recorder, in order to furnish minutes which can be used in formulating final agreements.

4.6 Settlement and follow-up

At the conclusion of negotiations, both parties must be satisfied that all issues have been discussed and that they understand exactly what has been agreed: the proceedings should be summarised and agreements 'played back' for confirmation by both sides. If there is any misunderstanding or ambiguity which raises objections, negotiations should recommence.

Once there is oral agreement, the points should be written up as a signed 'draft agreement', stating:

- (a) Who made the agreement and on what date

- (b) Who is to be covered by the agreement (groups and grades of employee, for example)

- (c) When the agreement is to take effect, how long it is to run, and whether and how it may be amended or terminated prior to this date

- (d) The contents (or 'clauses') of the agreement and any exceptions that may apply

- (e) How disagreements and appeals will be dealt with once the negotiated settlement is implemented.

The draft agreement should be circulated and checked by both sides, and clauses initialled once their wording is accepted. When all clauses have been approved by both sides, the agreement can be printed, formally signed and communicated to those affected by its provisions.

Activity 8   **(1 hour)**

In an example cited by Gennard and Judge (2003), the annual pay negotiations between a trade union and a manufacturing company started with the following sets of demands.

Trade Union	**Manufacturer**
• Substantial increase on all basic rates of pay	• Wage increase of 1.5%
• Holiday pay to be improved, to include all earnings in the 12 weeks prior to the holiday period	• No changes to the basis of calculation of holiday pay
• Shift premiums payable at weekends to be raised to double-time and for nightwork to time-and-a-third	• No changes to shift premiums
• Overtime payments to be time-and-a-half (standard) and double-time plus time in lieu (customary holidays)	• No changes to overtime payments
• Drivers' overnight allowance increased to £20 per occasion	• Drivers' overnight allowance increased to £18 per occasion
	• Any additional costs of the settlement to be recovered in full by efficiency and productivity improvements at plant levels

Consider which items are most important, and which most tradable, for each side. (If possible, role play a negotiation with a fellow student.) Come up with a 'trade' of terms that you think might be acceptable to both parties.

NOTES

Chapter roundup

- A lawful trade dispute is one between workers and their own employers, wholly or mainly about work-related matters. Various forms of sanctions are available to workers in pursuance of an industrial dispute, including strikes. Strike action has been strictly controlled by legislation and has correspondingly declined in severity and frequency.

- Collective bargaining is the process whereby employee and employer representatives negotiate agreements on terms and conditions of employment (and related matters) for groups of represented employees. There has been a tendency to decentralise bargaining to plant level, in order to retain flexibility.

- Negotiating is a bargaining process through which commitments and compromises are reached, using the relative power of the parties involved.

Quick quiz

1   Distinguish between primary and secondary industrial action.

2   List five areas of industrial action that are subject to UK legislation.

3   Outline the process of arbitration of a trade dispute and the role of ACAS.

4   What are procedural agreements in collective bargaining?

5   What is single-table bargaining?

6   What does the ACAS Code of Practice recommend on the disclosure of information for collective bargaining?

7   What is pendulum arbitration?

8   What three outcomes of negotiation should negotiators plan in advance, as the basis of negotiating strategy?

9   What is the 'win-win' approach?

10 Draw an overview of the process of negotiation.

Answers to quick quiz

1   Primary: aimed at the employer with whom the participating union is in dispute. Secondary (unlawful): aimed at employers who trade with firms in dispute.

(para 1.2)

2   Balloting of members; legal immunity for lawful dispute; outlawing of secondary action; individual member rights not to participate; unlawful dismissal of strikers in first eight weeks of dispute.

(para 1.4)

3   See paragraph 2.2 for a full answer.

4   Agreements which determine methods and procedures for arriving at substantive agreements (on pay, conditions and so on) and for settling disputes.

(para 3.1)

5   Terms and conditions of all workers (manual and non-manual) are determined in a single negotiation. This may be achieved by multiple unions pre-negotiating a bargaining proposal prior to collective bargaining with management.   (para 3.3)

6   Information should be disclosed on pay and benefits, conditions of service, human resources, performance (productivity, sales, orders) and financial matters. Unions should define and request specific information before negotiations begin.   (para 3.4)

7   Instead of the arbitrator finding 'middle ground' between the final offer/claim of each side, (s)he awards for one side's final position over the other: **either** the employer's final offer **or** the employees' final claim.   (para 4.2)

8   Ideal settlement, realistic settlement, fall-back position.   (para 4.4)

9   An approach to conflict resolution and distributive bargaining/negotiation which seeks to meet the needs of both parties as far as possible.   (paras 2.3, 4.2)

10   See paragraph 4.3 (Figure 17.1).

Answers to activities

1   Industrial action may be used as:

(a)   A demonstration of bargaining strength, by the threatened or actual withdrawal of labour and/or restriction of productivity, aimed at forcing management to enter negotiations or make concessions, or

(b)   A gesture of protest to highlight a grievance issue, aimed at management, government and other influential bodies, or at the general public. (For example, a literal 'go-slow' was staged by a transport union in Sydney, Australia in November 2000. Bus drivers drove at a crawl during the rush hour to highlight the failure of state government and policy to enforce city-centre bus lane rules, exposing drivers to stress, risk and commuter frustration: passengers and the media were handed leaflets explaining the purpose of the action and urged to support the protest.)

2   The main industrial sanctions available to the *employer* are:

●   Locking out some, or all, of the workforce from the worksite

●   Closing the worksite and/or relocating operations elsewhere

●   Dismissing employees who participate in industrial action

The main reasons why these are 'last resort measures' is because:

(a)   They are costly, involving lost production/service. Without alternative arrangements this may mean lost orders and lost customers.

(b)   They risk escalating the conflict, hardening attitudes on both sides.

(c)   They risk long-term damage to the loyalty and commitment of staff after the particular dispute is over.

(d)   They need to be carefully checked for legality, with regard to detail (eg if it is unlawful to dismiss within the first eight weeks of a strike).

3   The dispute was effectively resolved within two weeks.

The unions successfully got together to bring staff to the discussion table with BA initially, and persuaded them to return to work on this basis.

First-round talks appear not to have been successful. However, this may have been a bargaining strategy by BA, determined not to give way initially, given the unofficial nature of the original worker action. Positive use is made of third-party conciliation, both through ACAS and the TUC.

The involvement of the chief executive is a positive gesture of willingness by BA to come to the table seriously.

The outcome is relatively satisfactory to both sides. It appears that the swipe-card system may in itself be not the prime cause of the dispute, but worker fears about the erosion of their flexible working arrangements (work-life balance), lack of managerial trust and so on. The procedure will only have been truly successful insofar as these matters were brought into the open and discussed.

4   **Advantages**

(a)   Less time and resources spent on negotiations than with multiple bargaining.

(b)   Takes account of more viewpoints, more representative: enhances likelihood of acceptance of decisions. (Particularly helpful for change management affecting multiple groups of employees.)

(c)   Encourages resolution of inter-union disputes as part of preparation for negotiation: saves wasted time and energy in harmonising separate agreements.

(d)   May help avoid demarcations and inflexible work rules, with overall bargaining perspective (needs for flexibility, quality etc).

Disadvantages

(a)   Agenda may be overcrowded by concerns of multiple groups.

(b)   Requires higher levels of negotiating and relationship management skills.

(c)   Inflexibility: management may be less able to differentiate and change agreements with different segments of the workforce.

(d)   Inter-union disputes may not be resolved prior to negotiation.

(e)   May hamper individual union attempts to recruit members.

5   Decline in collective bargaining, due to:

(a)   The decline in union membership, and therefore the number of workers covered by collective bargaining

(b)   The rise of individual– and team-based systems, with new emphasis on employees' responsibility for self-management and self-development: individual contracts, learning plans and career mobility; team-centred performance management, performance-related pay and so on

(c)   The rise of workforce flexibility, with the erosion of job descriptions, occupational demarcations and associated work rules

(d)   The decentralisation of employee relations (and other HRM) processes to line managers

(e) The introduction of non-negotiatory consultation and involvement techniques

As we saw in Chapter 16, however, union recognition in the UK may be on the upturn: watch this space!

6   Quantitative elements of bargaining power include:

- The intrinsic merit of each party's case or argument (the stronger your case, the better the prospect of achieving agreement on your terms)

- The skill and ability of the negotiator

- The potential for coercion (the power of underlying sanctions or 'threat' eg to close a plant, or initiate industrial action)

Note that bargaining power may be actual or 'real' and/or perceived, and that the one may be much higher or lower than the other…

7   (a) Gain agreements or commitments from the other side that can be used as a stepping stone for the logical progression of your argument.

(b) Summarise periodically, especially to highlight common ground and consolidate progress.

(c) Sell the benefits of your proposals to the other side: allow them to agree with you, without loss of face, whenever possible.

(d) Preserve a tone of commitment, belief, even emotion: make your cause human.

(e) Use questions. Positive, joint-problem-solving questions: 'What would it take to make this work?'. Probing, challenging questions: 'Where would the money for that proposal come from?' Push for answers where necessary.

(f) Release information with a tactical awareness of its affects on negotiating position.

(g) Use all interpersonal and communication skills: listening, empathy, accessible language, giving non-verbal cues (eg confident body-language) and interpreting non-verbal cues (eg signs of hesitation, tentative phrasing, suggestions of readiness to move).

8   In the example cited, the agreed settlement was as follows.

Company conceded	*Company gained*
• Wage increase of 1.5%	• No changes to holiday pay
• Increase in drivers' overnight allowance to £20 per occasion	• No change to weekend shift premiums
• Shiftwork premiums (nightwork) increased to time-and-a-third	• No change to overtime premiums
	• Additional costs of the agreement fully covered by efficiency/productivity improvements

Chapter 18:
EMPLOYEE PARTICIPATION AND INVOLVEMENT

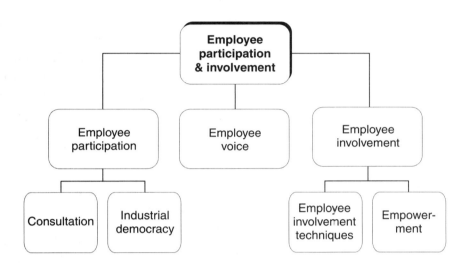

Introduction

The concept of 'employee voice' embraces 'a whole variety of processes and structures which enable, and sometimes empower employees, directly and indirectly, to contribute to decision-making in the firm' (Boxall & Purcell, 2003). The term has come to embrace a wide range of mechanisms for:

- **Employee involvement**: informing and consulting employees about aspects of decision making

- **Employee participation**: involving employees (often via their representatives) in the decision making machinery of the organisation

In this chapter, we look at both of these key aspects of employee relations, drawing together coverage in other chapters (especially Chapters 8 and 15) of the role of HRM and line management in shifting focus from 'industrial relations' to 'employee relations', and from a unitarist towards a pluralist frame of reference.

Your objectives

In this chapter you will learn about the following.

(a) Different forms of employee consultation and participation

(b) Industrial democracy and its European roots

(c) Employee involvement techniques

(d) Empowerment

(e) Employee voice

1 EMPLOYEE VOICE

1.1 What is employee voice?

Armstrong (2003) summarises 'employee voice' as 'the say employees have in matters of concern to them in their organisation'. He suggests that this is closer to **participation** ('ensuring that employees are given the opportunity to influence management decisions and to contribute to the improvement of organisations performance') than to **involvement** (where 'management allows employees to discuss with it issues that affect them but management retains the right to manage'). However, employee voice may be seen as a framework for both processes.

Employee voice is both an individual concept and a collective concept: it includes, for example, individual grievances and suggestions as well as collective bargaining and industrial democracy agreements made with trade unions and/or other employee representatives.

Marchington *et al* (2001) model the territory of employee voice as follows: Figure 18.1.

- Involvement may be **direct** (where management deal with individuals/teams) or **indirect** (where management deal with trade unions or other representative groups)

- Involvement may be based on a **shared agenda** (directed at improving organisational performance and the quality of working life) or on a **contested agenda** (directed at addressing areas of conflict, dissatisfaction or competition)

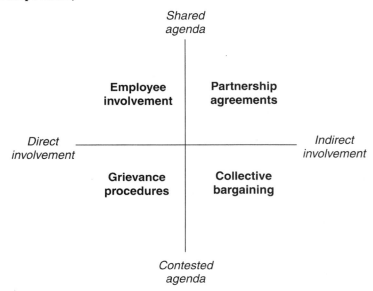

Figure 18.1: Employee voice matrix

In practice, an organisation's approach will be a mixture of direct and indirect, and focus on both shared and contested agendas (weighted according to whether HRM policies take a pluralistic or unitarist viewpoint, as discussed in Chapter 16). If there is an anti-union culture of management, the balance will shift towards direct involvement. If there is a co-operative or unitarist culture of management, the balance will shift towards shared agenda.

1.2 Purposes of employee voice

Marchington *et al* (2001) suggest that employee voice offers:

- The ability for individual employees to express dissatisfaction, solve problems with management and preserve working relationships

- The ability for employees collectively to express their needs and wishes in matters that affect them, providing a counterbalance to managerial power

- The ability for employees to contribute to management decisions, allowing the organisation to harness the expertise and commitment of workers to improve quality, productivity and work organisation

- The ability for employers and employees to demonstrate their intention to focus on shared goals, mutual interests and co-operative working relations, for the long-term benefit of the organisation and its people.

Employee voice thus involves both 'soft' HRM elements (fairness, relationship, mutual commitment) and 'hard' HRM elements (problem-solving, conflict/grievance management and performance improvement).

1.3 Mechanisms of employee voice

Marchington *et al* (1992, 2001) classify the main approaches to implementing employee voice as 'representative participation' (which we call 'participation' in this chapter) and 'upward problem-solving' (which we include among techniques for 'involvement').

(a) **Representative participation** includes:

- **Collective representation**: grievance procedures, collective bargaining, collective dispute resolution and other settings in which trade unions, staff associations or elected employee representatives represent the interests of individual employees or groups of employees (as discussed in Chapters 16-17).

- **Joint consultation**: formal non-negotiatory meetings between management and employee representatives to discuss matters of shared interest or concern (discussed in Section 2 below).

- **European Works Councils**: joint consultation machinery for organisations with sites in two or more member states of the European Union (discussed in Section 2 below).

- **Partnership schemes**: formal agreements between management and employee representatives to work together for mutual benefit, in a non-adversarial climate (discussed in Section 2 below).

(b) **Upward problem-solving** includes:

- **Two-way communication**: encouraging upward communication (from staff to management) as well as downward, eg through briefing groups, team meetings and corporate intranets.

- **Upward communication**: seeking staff feedback, opinions and suggestions, eg through attitude surveys, suggestion schemes and employee intranet discussion groups.

- **Project teams**: getting staff and management together to solve problems, discuss issues or generate ideas (eg quality circles, customer care task forces).

FOR DISCUSSION

'What institution embodying the employee voice might be appropriate? Is it a trade union? A works council? Or should employee voice not be viewed any longer in terms of collective representation?'. (Gennard & Judge, 2003)

What do you think?

We will now go on to look at some of the mechanisms of employee voice in more detail.

2 EMPLOYEE PARTICIPATION AND CONSULTATION

2.1 What is participation?

Definition

> **Employee participation** 'concerns the extent to which employees, often via their representatives, are involved in the decision-making machinery of the organisation. This includes joint consultation, collective bargaining and worker representation on the board'. (Gennard & Judge, 2003)

As noted in Section 1, there are different degrees and methods of participation, reflecting the extent to which organisations wish to involve employees in decision-making.

> **Activity 1** (30 minutes)
>
> Outline four general reasons why an organisation may consider it desirable or necessary to work towards employee participation.

2.2 Information and consultation

We have already encountered some of the circumstances in which recognised trade unions (or other employee representatives) are legally entitled to information and consultation, including:

- **Redundancy**, where more than 20 people are affected (see Chapter 7)
- **Health and safety** (see Chapter 11)
- **Collective bargaining** (see Chapter 17)

FOR DISCUSSION

The general secretary of the GMB told the 2000 TUC conference: 'We need better rights to consultation and information. I look forward to the day when British workers hear about the changes in their employment from the lips of their managers and not from the pages of the *Financial Times* or the early morning news bulletins of the BBC'.

Do workers have a 'right' to information and consultation in a moral sense?

Consultation, from a legal point of view, means talking formally to employee representatives on a matter which will affect employees or their work, with a view to seeking agreement. There is no obligation on employees to negotiate or take employee views into account in any specific way – but there must be dialogue entered into 'in good faith'.

Under the Companies Act 1989, an organisation employing more than 250 employees is required to include a statement in its Directors' Report describing the action taken in the previous financial year to introduce, maintain or develop arrangements for:

(a) Information/consultation of employees on matters affecting their employment

(b) Consultation with employee representatives to canvass their views on matters affecting them

(c) Financial participation of employees in the company's performance

(d) Extending employees' awareness of financial and economic factors affecting the company's performance.

Activity 2 (no time limit)

Get hold of the Directors' Report (found as part of the Annual Report and Accounts) of any public limited company of your choice. Examine the statements made in regard to the above matters. Do they reflect genuine involvement or participation, from what you can gather?

2.3 Joint consultation and works councils

Definition

Joint consultation is a process by which management and employee representatives jointly examine and discuss issues of mutual concern.

Joint consultation is the main form of representative participation in the UK. Gennard and Judge (2003) distinguish between 'employee communication' (similarly concerned with the interchange of information and ideas within an organisation) and 'consultation', which involves managers actively seeking and taking account of the views of employees before making a decision. Consultation 'affects the process through which decisions are made in so far as it commits management first to the disclosure of information at an early stage in the decision-making process and second to take into account the collective views of the employees.'

Joint Consultative Committees (JCCs) – sometimes called '**Works Councils**' – are composed of managers and employee representatives who come together on a regular basis to discuss matters of mutual interest. Members should include senior managers (in order to demonstrate commitment and mobilise authority where required) and representatives of all significant employee groups (in order to be regarded as genuinely representative). Committees usually have a well defined constitution and terms of reference.

Like any committee or group meeting, a JCC meeting will need a skilled Chairperson to facilitate and control discussion, and a clear and manageable agenda, circulated in advance for member preparation. Minutes will need to be taken for feeding back to the parties represented (via briefing groups, noticeboards, intranet and so on). Management needs to demonstrate its commitment to genuine consultation by giving appropriate facilities, time off and training to committee members. In unionised organisations, issues such as pay bargaining are generally left to collective bargaining, so JCCs must also be given something of perceived importance to deal with if they are not to be marginalised as ineffectual 'talk shops'.

Activity 3	(no time limit)

What are the structures for joint consultation in your work organisation (or one you know well or can find out about). What issues are consultations designed to cover? What influence do they have on organisational policy? How are they regarded by employees in general?

Bratton & Gold (2007) suggest that there are arguments both for **integrating** consultative machinery with negotiating (collective bargaining) machinery in an organisation and for **separating** the two activities.

Arguments for integration	Arguments for separation
• Communicating, consulting and negotiation are interlinked processes	• May reduce organisational complexity
• Union reps must be involved in consultation anyway	• Collective bargaining deals with substantive/procedural matters: consultation addresses other matters
• As collective bargaining's scope expands, remaining issues are less important	• Regular JCC meetings ensure that consultation is (and is seen to be) a managerial commitment

2.4 European Works Councils

While JCCs are voluntary works councils, the term 'European Works Council' is specifically used to describe mandatory meetings between management and elected employee representatives (independent of trade unions) under the 1994 European Works Council Directive, which became law in the UK in 1999.

A **European Works Council** must be set up in all organisations with more than 1,000 employees in Member States and employing more than 150 people in each of two or more of these. A **Pan-European Works Council** (or alternative) has to be agreed between central management and a Special Negotiating Body of employee representatives from the countries involved.

If no agreement is reached, a fallback system requires the establishment of a **European Works Council** of employee representatives with the right to meet central management at least once a year for information and consultation about the progress and prospects of the company. It may also request further or special meetings on transnational ('community scale') issues of concern, defined as 'measures significantly affecting employees' interests': large scale redundancies, for example.

EXAMPLE

Electrics giant Panasonic decided in 1994 to adopt a proactive view of the European Works Council Directive and to conclude a voluntary agreement with employee representatives, resulting in the establishment of:

(a) A 'Panasonic European Congress' (PEC), meeting yearly for consultation on transnational issues. The congress involves representatives from different nations; different types of operations (sales, manufacturing, R & D) and both unionised and non-unionised companies.

(b) Two representative committees: an Employee Representative Committee and a Management Representative Committee, which meet three or four times a year to discuss the agenda for the annual meeting, agree the minutes and be informed and consulted on transnational issues.

(c) A Panasonic UK Consultative Committee (PUCC), with 11 employee representatives from the different divisions of Panasonic UK Ltd. (The UK company was non-union and non-works-council, so there was no existing formal structure for information and consultation with elected employee representatives.) The PUCC meets with company directors every two months to discuss company performance, sales figures, health and safety, canteen and sports facilities, technological and structural changes and training and education.

Note that EWCs do not represent industrial democracy or co-determination such as operates in countries such as Germany or Sweden (discussed later in this section). They are only for the purposes of consultation.

(a) Councils have the right to be informed and consulted about 'any measure likely to have a considerable effect on employees' interests'.

Part D: Employee Relations

(b) Matters for discussion must be transnational or 'community scale': this is not an alternative forum to discuss matters affecting a single group of employees.

The European Commission is reviewing the operation of the original EWC Directive: watch this space!

FOR DISCUSSION

Running costs for an EWC have been reported as running as high as £150,000 a year, because of training, travel and transportation costs, and the entitlement to 'assistance' from an expert paid for by the employer.

How might developments in Information and Communications Technology (ICT) be used to reduce the cost of meetings – and/or keep the wider employee body better informed in general?

2.5 Information and Consultation of Employees Regulations 2005

Under the ICE Regulations employers must:

(a) Inform representatives about recent and foreseeable developments concerning the enterprise's activity and economic and financial situation

(b) Consult representatives on any restructuring of employment (particularly, threat to jobs) with a view to exchanging views

(c) Consult representatives on decisions that are likely to lead to substantial changes in work organisation and contractual relations (eg collective redundancies or business transfers) 'with a view to reaching agreement'.

The practical arrangements used for information and consultation must be agreed by the workforce. If current structures do not meet the requirements of the Regulations, management will have to negotiate new machinery with employee representatives. The procedures may be triggered by a formal request from employees or by the initiative of the employer.

The ICE provisions currently apply to businesses with 100 or more employees: from 6 April 2008, it will apply to businesses with 50 or more employees...

EXAMPLE

In 2003, 13 people from all walks of life and all levels of Marks & Spencer participated in the first meeting of its national business involvement group (Big), the company's body for information and consultation. Their role was to debate business decisions and HR policies face-to-face with their chief executive.

These types of staff council are being established in companies across the UK in response to the European directive on information and consultation... But for M&S, the new group was the culmination of a series of measures aimed at improving employee communications.

NOTES

510

There have been discussion groups in the stores for some years. But during the firm's financial difficulties in 1999, staff were involved in a consultative process called Clearview, which moved communications up a gear. It involved brainstorming sessions between employees and managers to consider what was wrong with the structure, processes and culture of the business.

M&S recognised the contribution that such a process made to the organisation's recovery. A review of the staff focus groups in Spring 2001 indicated that they wanted a structure that enabled issues to be represented at a more senior level and wanted managers and staff to sit in a combined forum. This led to the creation of Bigs at a local and area level in September 2001.

Local Bigs were set up in 309 shops, head office locations, the financial services unit and its distribution centres. Area Bigs provided a forum for issues that affected more than one store or business area. The company also had a European council, established in 1995 in line with EU legislation. But discussions were confined to issues affecting more than two countries. This was despite the closure of continental European stores in 2001, leaving the European council with members from only the UK and the Republic of Ireland. A review in March 2002 highlighted the need for a national forum.

(Higginbottom, 2003 (c))

2.6 Information and consultation: summary

The following (Figure 18.2) is a helpful schematic showing various methods of employee information and consultation (*source unknown*).

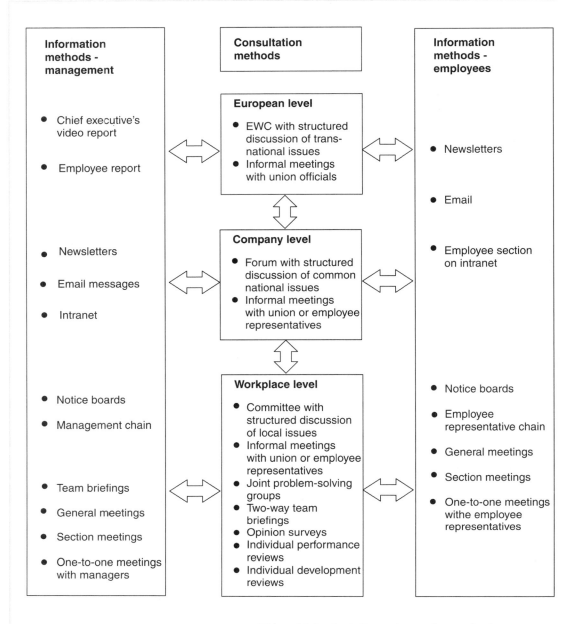

Figure 18.2: An information and consultation structure

2.7 Partnership agreements

Definition

Partnership agreements are negotiated arrangements 'in which both parties (management and the trade union) agree to work together to their mutual advantage and to achieve a climate of more co-operative and therefore less adversarial industrial relations.' (Armstrong, 2003)

Partnership agreements generally include undertakings from both sides, linking job security, pay awards or participation (in the control of management) to productivity gains or greater flexibility in work organisation (in the control of unions).

Gennard & Judge (2003) identify six key principles underpinning partnership agreements in the workplace.

Principle	Comment
1 Commitment to success of the enterprise	Partnership depends on shared understanding and commitment in regard to the business goals of the organisation
2 Recognising legitimate interests	A recognition that interests and priorities will not always coincide: parties must respect each others' responsibility to do their best for their stakeholders
3 Commitment to employment security	Measures to maximise employment security (eg limit redundancies) and improve staff employability (eg through transferable skills training)
4 Focus on the quality of working life	Recognition of the need to develop employees and create opportunities for personal growth
5 Transparency	Real sharing of information and early discussion of plans for the future
6 Adding value	Partnership should access and deploy commitment/resources not available through previous employees relations machinery

Activity 4 (30 minutes)

What advantages might parties in a partnership agreement be aiming for?

Note that partnership also has its critics!

> There are critics who see partnership as an illusory concept. Those on the left of the political spectrum… fear that unions, far from gaining influence, will be co-opted by management into their projects, effectively neutralising any chance of opposition. Critics from the right would argue that partnership hampers management's ability to manage, or, as the president of the CBI… believes, that it may even provide a 'Trojan horse' through which unions could gain more influence.

(*People Management,* 14 September 2000)

We will now look briefly at European models of employee participation, which are closer to 'industrial democracy'.

3 EMPLOYEE PARTICIPATION AND INDUSTRIAL DEMOCRACY

3.1 Social dimensions of the European Union

The European Union was partly developed as a 'Single Market' or trading bloc, removing barriers to trade and competitive bias, standardising technical regulations and creating a convergence of conditions between European markets. However, it also has a sociopolitical dimension which embraces employment issues, since it is believed that the success of the Single Market depends on the united efforts of employers and labour.

The main statement of European social policy is the 'Community Charter of the Fundamental Social Rights of Workers'– commonly known as the 'Social Charter' – which was ratified by 11 of the (then) 12 member states: the UK opted out. The Charter is based on the desire to improve living and working conditions and to ensure effective use of human resources across the EU. It is a statement of intent to guarantee individual rights in areas such as: freedom of movement; fair remuneration; improvement of living and working conditions (including working time); freedom of association and collective bargaining (the right to join, or not to join, a trade union; the right to negotiate and conclude collective agreements and the right to collective action such as strikes); access to vocational training; equal treatment for men and women; health and safety in the workplace; and the protection of children, adolescents and the disabled in the workplace.

Additional rights are guaranteed in respect of the information, consultation and participation of workers. Changes that affect the workforce such as new technology, working practices, mergers, restructuring and collective redundancy should involve prior consultation with employees.

All members of the EU have since agreed that the Social Charter be implemented by directive: member states will be bound to legislate and 'mobilise all the resources necessary' to implement its provisions. Some have already been covered by EU Directives, while others are still subject to negotiation and amendment.

3.2   The European Company Statute

The European Company Statute (2001) gives companies the option of forming a European company which can operate on a Europe-wide basis and be governed by Community law. An accompanying Directive requires employee involvement arrangements in all such companies, including:

(a)   Collective bargaining on decisions or

(b)   A two-tier board structure, with elected worker representatives on the senior or 'supervisory' board to which the management or 'executive' board is responsible, or

(c)   A unitary board structure with worker representatives as non-executive directors, or

(d)   A sub-board level company council, solely comprised of worker representation.

3.3   National cultural differences in regard to participation

In **Germany,** the concept of consultation and participation is based on a system called **co-determination**, formally involving employees and their representatives in nearly all decisions relating to personnel and other aspects of company policy. Co-determination is supported by specific legislation. There are three methods by which workers can participate: by Works Councils, Supervisory Boards and Management Boards.

(a) In workplaces with more than five employees, the workforce elects a **works council** consisting solely of workers' representatives. This council has the right:

   (i) To receive information on health and safety, work organisation, jobs, work environment, the hiring of executives and planned changes which could adversely affect employees

   (ii) To make suggestions during the formulation and implementation of HR plans, and specifically regarding vocational training (eg apprenticeships) and other training and development opportunities.

   The views and suggestions of the council must be considered, although they are not binding on managerial decision-making.

(b) In companies employing more than 500 people, elected worker representatives sit on the **supervisory board** which meets four times a year. Worker representatives make up one-third to one-half of this policy-making body (depending on size), with other board members elected by the shareholders, under a 'neutral' chairperson. The supervisory board is responsible for deciding the overall direction of the enterprise; matters concerning corporate finance and structure (including mergers and takeovers); and the appointment, dismissal and remuneration of members of the executive or management board.

(c) The executive or **management board** is the full-time body responsible for the day-to-day running of operations.

Sweden also operates a co-determination system based on consultation with employees and the participation of representatives in decision making at both board and shop floor levels. Industrial democracy was developed early in Sweden, and techniques such as job enrichment, autonomous working groups and 'quality of working life' programmes were developed by companies such as Volvo back in the 1970s. The Swedish model is more highly unionised that the German model, with union membership over 80%.

Belgium, France, Italy, Spain and the Netherlands also have works councils supported by legislation, but the range of issues open to employee approval is smaller than in the German or Swedish co-determination models. Belgium and the Netherlands have an additional legal requirement for large companies to operate a two-tier (supervisory and executive) board of directors.

In **Japan,** employee involvement practices are deeply embedded in the collectivist and commitment-based culture of employment, in techniques such as quality circles, teamworking, consensus decision-making and long-term employee development. There is a unitarist assumption of the value of participation, supported by the training of group leaders and workers in the skills of participative working. However, observers note that employee involvement techniques are not primarily used as decision-making mechanisms or channels of communication (as in Europe) but as a cultural mechanism reinforcing identification with shared aims and goals.

NOTES

Activity 5 **(5 minutes)**

From your knowledge of national cultural differences (Chapter 12) what characteristics would you expect to be most relevant to a country's acceptance of industrial democracy?

We will now look at employee involvement. We have already covered many employee involvement techniques in other contexts (such as reward, quality management, flexibility and development), and have discussed issues of involvement and empowerment of employees in our exploration of the HRM approach in Chapter 8. As you review such topics, bear in mind that they are part of the overall relationship of employees and management in the organisation.

4   EMPLOYEE INVOLVEMENT TECHNIQUES

4.1   Employee involvement

Definition

Employee involvement describes a wide range of policies and techniques for 'informing and consulting employees about, or associating them with, one or more aspects of running an organisation.'   (Gennard & Judge, 2003)

Employee involvement concentrates mainly on individual employees and the degree to which they can be encouraged to identify with the goals of the organisation. It can be distinguished from employee participation (discussed earlier), which concerns the extent to which employees are involved (via their representatives) in management decision-making.

The aims of involvement may be:

(a)   To generate commitment to the organisation

(b)   To help the organisation improve performance, especially in the face of change

(c)   To enable the organisation to better meet changing customer requirements

(d)   To improve the challenge and satisfaction of the work experience

(e)   To aid the organisation in attracting and retaining skilled labour

(f)   To develop the business awareness of labour at all levels

(g)   To increase employee incentives and accountabilities through tying reward to company performance and profitability, and/or

(h)   To marginalise trade unions.

BPP
LEARNING MEDIA

Guest (2001) describes five ways to get employees involved.

- By improving the provision of information to employees

- By improving the provision of information from employees

- By changing the structure and arrangement of work

- By changing the incentives

- By changing relationships, through more participative leadership and informality.

Activity 6   **(15 minutes)**

Suggest three techniques (already encountered in this Course Book) by which each of the above could be implemented.

Marchington *et al* (1992) similarly divide employee involvement schemes into four categories.

(a) **Downwards communications:** from managers to other employees and so on. This includes house journals, employee reports and briefings.

(b) **Upwards problem-solving forms:** designed to tap into individual and team knowledge and expertise. This includes suggestion schemes, attitude surveys, quality circles, customer care programmes and so on.

(c) **Financial participation:** linking rewards of individuals to the performance of the unit or business. This includes profit sharing, employee share ownership and factory-wide or value added bonus schemes (discussed in Chapter 5).

(d) **Representative participation:** employees are involved in decision-making through their representatives on JCCs, advisory councils, works councils, or collective bargaining. (This may operate at different levels of involvement, from consultation and dialogue to co-determination and even to control, eg in worker-managed teams or co-operatives.)

In addition, involvement may be encouraged by:

(a) **Empowerment**: the devolving of control and responsibility to individuals or teams at the workplace or 'front line' customer-service level. Empowerment may be 'soft' (providing enhanced opportunities for involvement in decision-making, fewer status barriers, more open communication, greater flexibility) or 'hard' (devolution of responsibility and accountability: standards and targets, monitoring and control)

(b) **Inclusion in the cultural and strategic priorities of the business**. Employees are invited and encouraged to share in commitment to quality, customer care, continuous improvement, learning and so on. This is frequently linked to empowerment as a set of guiding values and objectives within which teams can be more or less self-managing.

We will look at some of these techniques in more detail, where they have not been covered elsewhere in this Course Book.

4.2 Downward communication

Downward communication is usually well established in an organisation in the form of instructions, job briefings, rules and policies and announcement of plans by managers to staff.

There may, however, be potential for more empowering downward information flow about a wider range of matters, including: company strategy and future plans; positive performance feedback, celebrating individual, team and company achievements; competitor and other environmental factors that may influence work (or stimulating problem-solving); and so on.

Examples of mechanisms for downward communication of this type (see also Figure 18.2, earlier) include:

(a) **In-house journals,** bulletins and newsheets (and their electronic equivalents by e-mail or intranet pages). This is commonly used to foster a sense of involvement and belonging, but may be made a tool for greater participation by including various mechanisms for feedback and interaction: suggestion schemes, 'letter' pages, discussion forums, noticeboards and so on.

(b) **Team briefings**, where management pass information face-to-face to team members, on a regular basis. This enables people to feel that they know what is going on, and have access to the information required to do their work. Briefing meetings can also be used for interactive question-and-answer and problem-solving, however, for a more participative element.

(c) **Management by Walking Around**. The managerial culture of some organisations will need to be changed in order to increase information flow to employees. The hoarding of information as a source of power by managers, or the withholding of information on a 'need to know' basis are a feature of command-and-control cultures rather than facilitate-and-empower organisations.

FOR DISCUSSION

Is there too much information flowing around organisations – or does keeping employees 'in the loop' meaningfully contribute to employee relations?

4.3 Upward communication

Upward communication is rarer than downward – but vital to many modern organisations in:

(a) Providing feedback on progress and performance, so that plans can be adjusted where necessary

(b)   Harnessing the experience and know-how of employees for innovation, problem-solving and decision-making

(c)   Giving management insight into employees' needs, interests and problems, to help them manage better

(d)   Demonstrating the value management places on employees, establishing the mutual trust and commitment that underpins constructive employee relations.

Mechanisms for upward communication include the following.

Attitude surveys

Surveys of employee opinions are a useful source of feedback (especially if there are no other direct avenues for employees to express their satisfactions and dissatisfactions). Attitude surveys may be carried out via:

(a)   **Questionnaires,** whether standardised or tailored to the particular organisation or issue concerned. These may be paper-based or (increasingly) posted online on a company intranet. Questionnaires have the advantage of being quick and relatively cost-effective to administer, although they must be carefully designed if they are to elicit honest, meaningful and comparable responses.

(b)   **Interviews,** either completely free-flowing or structured to a specific agenda of issues. Interviews are time-consuming and costly, but may also be more revealing, allowing a skilled interviewer to probe.

(c)   **Focus groups,** allowing a structured response to interview questions by a representative sample of employees on specific issues

The CIPD has produced the following checklist for conducting an employee attitude survey.

(a)   Gain the commitment of senior management, clarify objectives and define areas where the company is prepared to take action.

(b)   Decide between a census of employees – probably paper-based – and a random sample – maybe face-to-face interviews.

(c)   Conduct a pilot survey.

(d)   Design a questionnaire – this needs experienced help.

(e)   Tell employees what is being done: the more internal publicity, the greater the chances of success.

(f)   Guarantee confidentiality.

(g)   Consider measures to improve the response rate, for example by holding supervised completion sessions in company time.

(h)   If the survey involves face-to-face interviews, conduct them with one or two employees at a time. Avoid group discussions – it is difficult to maintain confidentiality in groups and to enable everyone to have a say.

(i)   Produce the final report. Distil the evidence, reach conclusions and put forward recommendations. Present the report to top management.

(j)   Report back to employees with a summary of the main findings.

(k)   An individual or a group should be made responsible for action following the survey findings; progress should be monitored.

Activity 7   **(15 minutes)**

How would you respond to the following objections from a management traditionalist to employee surveys?

(a) Good managers already know their staff's opinions.

(b) Surveys are superficial, impersonal and bureaucratic.

(c) Surveys open cans of worms and raise false hopes.

(d) Surveys contain built in bias because of the unknown opinions of the many who do not respond.

Suggestion schemes

Suggestion schemes were discussed in Chapter 5 as a way of offering performance rewards and incentives. However, they are also an important mechanisms for upward communication.

EXAMPLE

'What's the big idea, Vodafone?

'Vodafone is running a campaign to promote innovation: in the workforce. "My big idea" has already generated 500 ideas from employees aimed at improving customer experience, products and services.

'The ideas amassed so far will be whittled down to five with the finalists presenting their suggestions to the board later this month. The winning idea will be assessed for feasibility and rolled out next year.

'Dawn McIntyre, an HR business partner at Vodafone, told PM: "It's important to encourage staff to come up with ideas, and firms that don't do that are missing out as it's key to employee satisfaction."'

(*People Management*, 9 November 2006)

Quality circles

Definition

> **Quality circles** are groups of six to ten employees from different levels and/or disciplines within an organisation, who meet regularly to discuss problems of quality, quality control, customer care or related issues in their area of work.

Quality circles emerged first in the US but were most enthusiastically adopted in Japan. They are still used to get employees involved in organisational quality values, but some commentators suggest that they have been superseded by other team-based working methods and a wider orientation to quality in organisations (such as a Total Quality Management orientation).

The circle is facilitated by a leader who directs the discussion and helps to orient and develop members (as required) in quality control and problem-solving techniques. It is important that the group is made up of volunteers, in order to harness genuine commitment and enthusiasm.

Quality circles do not generally have responsibility for making, implementing or following up recommendations. Even as discussion groups, however, they may have significant benefits, as members return to their departments as ambassadors for quality, customer care and employee involvement.

FOR DISCUSSION

Why might values such as quality or customer care be a powerful focus for attempts to involve employees?

4.4 Empowerment

Empowerment has two key aspects. It involves giving workers discretion to make decisions about how to organise work in order to achieve task goals *and* making workers responsible for achieving production and quality targets. (The French word for empowerment is 'responsibilisation'.)

The purpose of empowerment is:

(a) To free employees from rigorous control by instructions and orders, which contributes to job satisfaction *and* learning and flexibility

(b) To give employees opportunities for growth and job satisfaction through taking responsibility for their ideas and actions

(c) To release and develop resources in the workforce that would otherwise remain inaccessible, including creativity and initiative

(d) To harness employee commitment by allowing them to share in the process of target-setting and work organisation

(e)   To decentralise decision-making and problem-solving initiative to 'front line' customer-facing roles, to enhance the flexibility and responsiveness of customer service.

Empowerment goes hand in hand with:

(a)   **Delayering,** or a cut in the number of levels in the organisation hierarchy: responsibility previously held by managers is, in effect, being given to operational workers

(b)   **Flexibility,** since giving responsibility to the people closest to the product or customer encourages responsiveness

(c)   **New technology,** since skilled knowledge workers need less supervision, being better equipped to identify and control the means to clearly understood ends

(d)   **Employee development,** since the personal and interpersonal skills needed to meet the challenges of responsibility and participation in decision-making need to be developed

(e)   **Unitarist employee relations,** since empowerment rests on the belief that employees will recognise and commit themselves to the business goals of their unit and organisation.

Empowerment implies a shift in the role of both **line managers** (who effectively become 'coaches' and 'facilitators' in team decision-making processes, setting parameters and providing information and guidance where required) and **HR practitioners** (who increasingly share responsibility for delivering HR policy outcomes not only with line managers but with employees themselves).

EXAMPLE

The validity of this view and its relevance to modern trends appears to be borne out by the approach to empowerment adopted by **Harvester restaurants,** as described in *Personnel Management.* The management structure comprises a branch manager and a 'coach', while everyone else is a team member. Everyone within a team has one or more 'accountabilities' (these include recruitment, drawing up rotas, keeping track of sales targets and so on) which are shared out by the team members at their weekly team meetings. All the team members at different times act as 'co-ordinator' – the person responsible for taking the snap decisions that are frequently necessary in a busy restaurant. Apparently, all the staff involved agree that empowerment has made their jobs more interesting and had hugely increased their motivation and sense of involvement.

We will look briefly at two approaches to empowerment: self-managed teamworking and total quality management (TQM).

4.5 Self-managed teams

Self-managed teams are the most highly-developed form of team working. They are permanent structures in which team members collaboratively decide all the major issues affecting their work: work processes and schedules, task allocation, the selection and development of team members, the distribution of rewards and the management of group processes (problem-solving, conflict management, internal discipline and so on). The team leader is a member of the team, acting in the role of coach and facilitator: leadership roles may be shared or rotated as appropriate.

Self managed teams generally have the following features (Harrington-Mackin, 1994).

(a) They contract with management to assume various degrees of **managerial responsibility** for planning, organising, directing and monitoring (which may increase as the team develops). Team members learn and share the jobs usually performed by a manager: no 'visible' immediate manager is present. They often report to 'absentee' managers with broad responsibilities for several functions, whose role is to act as integrators/facilitators.

(b) They perform **day-to-day planning and control functions**: scheduling and co-ordinating the daily and occasional tasks of the team and individuals; setting performance goals and standards; formulating and adopting budgets; collecting performance data and reviewing results.

(c) They perform **internal people management functions**: screening and interviewing candidates to join the team, and contributing to selection/hiring decisions; providing orientation for new members; coaching and providing feedback on member performance; designing and conducting cross-training on all tasks.

(d) Team members **cross-train** in all the tasks necessary for a particular process, and members rotate flexibly from job to job.

(e) **Weekly team meetings** are used to identify, analyse and solve task and relationship problems within the team: reviewing team working and progress; getting team members to research and present team issues and so on.

Activity 8 **(20 minutes)**

What do you think are likely to be the advantages of self-managed teamworking for the organisation?

4.6 Total quality management (TQM)

TQM is a Japanese-inspired orientation to quality in which quality values and aspirations are applied to the management of *all* resources and relationships within the firm and throughout the value chain (from suppliers to distributors), in order to seek continuous improvement and excellence in all aspects of performance.

Mullins (1999) synthesises various definitions of TQM as expressing: 'a way of life for an organisation as an whole, committed to total customer satisfaction through a continuous process of improvement, and the contribution and involvement of people'.

Two key aspects of TQM are:

- **Quality chains**. The quality chain extends from suppliers through to customers, via the 'internal customers' of each department within the organisation. The chain may be broken at any point where people or processes fail to fulfil the quality requirements of their immediate customer.

- **Total involvement**. Quality requires the commitment of all staff, and needs to be modelled from the top by senior management. It needs to be supported and reinforced by HRM policies for recruitment, training, appraisal, reward and development. It also emphasises the importance of people: communication, awareness and problem-solving are more important than mere systems.

FOR DISCUSSION

On a scale from 'no voice' through involvement and participation to full empowerment or democracy, where would you place the orgnisation you currently work for, or one you know well?

Chapter roundup

- Employee voice embraces 'a whole variety of processes and structures which enable, and sometimes empower employees, directly and indirectly, to contribute to decision-making in the firm.

- Employee participation concerns the extent to which employees, often via their representatives, are involved with management in the decision-making machinery of the organisation. It includes joint consultation, works councils, European Works Councils and worker representation on the board.

- Employee involvement is the process of informing and consulting employees about, or associating them with, one or more aspects of running an organisation. It may be accomplished by two-way communication, financial participation, representative participation, empowerment and inclusion in cultural programmes such as quality management and organisational learning

Quick quiz

1   Distinguish between the terms 'employee voice', 'employee participation' and 'employee involvement'.

2   Draw Marchington *et al*'s matrix model of employee voice.

3   Give three examples of 'representative participation'.

4   What is joint consultation?

5   What is an EWC and when is it compulsory to have one?

6   A partnership agreement reflects a pluralist approach to employee relations. True or false?

7   Outline the German model of co-determination.

8   Give five examples of employee involvement techniques.

9   What is TQM?

10   What are the purposes of empowerment?

Answers to quick quiz

1   Employee voice covers the range of possibilities from no voice through to full participation. Involvement is consultation/communication where management retains the right to manage. Participation allows employees to influence organisational decisions.   (para 1.1)

2   See figure 18.1.

3   Collective representation, joint consultation, European Works Council, partnership agreements.   (para 1.3)

4   Formal non-negotiatory meetings between management and employee representatives to discuss matters of shared interest.   (para 2.3)

5   A Pan-European body of employee representatives with the right to meet central management at least once a year for information and consultation about the progress and prospects of the company. All organisations with more than 1,000 employees in the EU member states, with more than 150 people in each of two or more states, must establish some form of Europe-wide consultational system: an EWC is the fallback system if unions and employee negotiators fail to agree on an alternative.   (para 2.4)

6   False: unitarist.   (para 2.7)

7   See paragraph 3.3 for a full answer.

8   Communication (eg briefings, journals)

Up-down communication (eg suggestion schemes, quality circles)

Financial participation (eg profit-sharing, share ownership)

Representative participation (eg joint consultation, works councils)

Empowerment (eg self-managed teamworking, delegation)

Cultural programmes (eg TQM, customer care, learning organisation)
(**Note:** the activity only required five).   (para 4.1)

BPP
LEARNING MEDIA

9   Total Quality Management: a whole-organisation approach to managing quality through the application of quality values, continuous improvement and total involvement.   (para 4.3)

10   See paragraph 4.4 for a full answer.

Answers to activities

1   Participation may be desirable or necessary because of the following factors.

(a) **Commitment**: the perceived need to obtain a higher level of identification with organisational goals and a higher degree of acceptance and support of strategies for change.

(b) **Quality of decision-making**: the perceived need to involve employees with 'front-line' knowledge, experience and influence in areas such as quality management and customer care. Quality circles and empowered teams are developed on this basis.

(c) **Trade union pressure.** Collective bargaining has been extended into areas traditionally considered as management concerns: human resource levels, training and so on. Joint consultation is another prevalent form of worker participation, where management discuss matters of concern regularly with union representatives, on Joint Consultative Committees (JCCs) or non-negotiatory staff forums. A more radical approach is the formation of partnership agreements with worker representatives.

(d) **Legal requirements.** Participation and consultation have occupied a high profile in employment protection and – most recently – in the social policy of the European Union, with provision for employee representation in decision-sharing structures such as Works Councils and Supervisory Boards.

2   Your own research.

3   Your own research (and opinion).

4   Some advantages (identified by Legal & General and MSF in their partnership agreement) include:

(a) Increased flexibility, honesty and trust in relationships

(b) Better quality, faster decision-making, with decisions that were more likely to be readily accepted within the company

(c) Positive public relations for the company – and for the union ('rebranded' to attract new members)

(d) Having the right people focused on the right issues

(e) The development of an 'adult' relationship in which company and union could move in the same direction

5   Low power-distance and collectivist cultures are particularly likely to accept employee participation at a deep level.

6   (a) Briefing groups and meetings, Joint Consultation Committees or works councils, open direct communication from managers, encouraging informal networking, 360° feedback, consultation policy, noticeboards/memos etc.

     (b) Suggestion schemes, quality circles, upward appraisal, JCCs or works councils, attitude surveys

     (c) Increased delegation (empowerment), self-managed and/or multi-skilled teamworking, horizontal structures focused on the customer, job design based on whole meaningful tasks

     (d) Financial participation through profit-related pay, employee share ownership schemes; cafeteria benefits; learning/development opportunities

     (e) Participative management style; single status agreements; culture of informality (Management By Walking Around); role of supervisor as coach/facilitator.

7   Nigel Nicholson (*Financial Times*, January 1993) gave the following answers (briefly summarised).

     (a) How do managers know if their reading of opinions is correct?

     (b) Yes, they are no substitute for good personal communications, but 'Thanks for asking us' is a common response.

     (c) Cans of worms probably should be opened. 'Management's commitment, clearly communicated at the outset, should be not only to take action where feasible, but also to be frank about reasons for not acting when this would be unreasonably difficult, contentious or costly.

     (d) Bias is modest when return rates of over 50% are achieved, and a well-designed and carefully introduced survey can expect returns of 65% or more.

8   Self-managed teamworking is said to have advantages in:

     •   Savings in managerial costs

     •   Gains in quality and productivity, by harnessing the commitment of those who perform work

     •   Encouraging individual initiative and responsibility, enhancing organisational responsiveness (particularly in front-line customer service units)

     •   Gains in efficiency, through multi-skilling, the involvement of fewer functions in decision-making and co-ordinating work, and (often) the streamlining of working methods by groups

     However, self-managed teams are a comparatively recent (and rare) phenomenon, and require skilled leadership and culture change (particularly in former 'command and control' organisations) in order to be effective.

BPP
LEARNING MEDIA

APPENDIX

Edexcel Guidelines for the HND/HNC Qualification in Business

This book is designed to be of value to anyone who is studying Human Resource Management, whether as a subject in its own right or as a module forming part of any business-related degree or diploma.

However, it provides complete coverage of the topics listed in the Edexcel guidelines for Units 21 to 24 of the HRM endorsed title route. We include the Edexcel Guidelines here for your reference, mapped to the topics covered in this book.

EDEXCEL GUIDELINES FOR UNIT 21: HUMAN RESOURCES MANAGEMENT

Description of the Unit

This unit provides an introduction to the concepts and practices of human resources management within the United Kingdom. The aim of the unit is to provide an understanding of the human resources management role and function within the key areas of resourcing, reward, development and relations.

Summary of learning outcomes

Outcomes and assessment criteria

Outcomes	Assessment criteria **To achieve each outcome a learner must demonstrate an ability to:**
1 Investigate the traditional view of **personnel management and the new approach of human resource management**	• distinguish between 'personnel management' and 'human resource management' and discuss the historical development and changing context in which they operate • assess the role, tasks and activities of the human resource practitioner • evaluate the role and responsibilities of line managers in human resource practices
2 Evaluate the **procedures and practices used for recruiting and selecting suitable employees**	• analyse the need for human resource planning, the information required and the stages involved in this process • compare the structured process for recruitment in two organisations and evaluate the methods and media that can be used • evaluate the interview as a selection technique and discuss a range of alternative selection methods available • evaluate selection practices and procedures in two organisations comparing these to 'best practice'

Outcomes		Assessment criteria
		To achieve each outcome a learner must demonstrate an ability to:
3	Establish the effectiveness of **principles and procedures for monitoring and rewarding the employee**	• evaluate the process of job evaluation and the main factors determining pay • identify a range of rewards systems, eg performance-related pay and its benefits and limitations • explain the link between motivational theory and reward • explore organisational approaches to monitoring performance
4	Explore **rights and procedures** on exit from an organisation	• evaluate exit procedures used by two organisations, comparing these to best practice • analyse selection criteria for redundancy

Covered in chapter(s)

Content

1 **Personnel management and the new approach of human resources management**

The nature and development of personnel management and human resource management: historical development of personnel management; the change in context which has led to the term human resources management

1, 8

The roles and tasks of the human resources management function: the range of tasks and activities of the human resource management practitioner, eg recruitment and selection, payroll administration and reward management, training and development and performance management and employee relations; the changing roles of human resource specialists, eg the move from reactive/welfare to proactive/ strategic and increasing requirement to work in partnership with the business; the involvement of line managers in human resource practices, eg selection, disciplinary handling, absence management, coaching and appraising

1

2 **Procedures and practices used for recruiting and selecting suitable employees**

Human resource planning: definition, purpose, processes and stages involved; the types of data needed as a basis for human resource planning; limiting factors, eg supply and demand for labour

2

	Covered in chapter(s)

The systematic approach to recruitment: recruitment policies, recruitment procedure, job analysis, job description, personnel specification, recruitment methods and media including design of application form — 3

The systematic approach to selection: aims and objectives of the selection process; the interview – advantages and disadvantages, interviewer skills and questioning techniques; alternative selection methods to supplement the interview, eg assessment centres, psychological testing, work simulations, references — 4

The legislative framework and benchmark evidence guiding the recruitment and selection process: reference to Sex Discrimination Act (1975), Race Relations Act (1976), Equal Pay Act (1970), Disability Discrimination Act (1995); exploration of a range of organisational approaches to recruitment and selection highlighting 'best practice' — 3–5

3   Principles and procedures for monitoring and rewarding the employee

Reward management: the process of job evaluation and the main factors determining pay, different types of reward systems, the relationship between motivation theories and reward, approaches to monitoring and managing performance — 5, 6

4   Exit rights and procedures

Tribunals: role, composition, powers and procedure — 7, 11

Dismissal: wrongful, unfair, justified

Termination of employment: resignation, retirement, termination of contract

Redundancy: definition, procedure, selection, redeployment, retraining

Management of exit: procedures, notice, counselling, training

Guidance

Delivery

Learners' understanding of human resources management can be developed through the use of a variety of learning methods including lectures, discussions, seminars, videos, role plays, case studies and learner-led presentations.

Investigations of human resources management policies and practices within organisations and talks from human resources management practitioners can both develop understanding and provide support for the knowledge and skill base established within the unit.

Assessment

Evidence of outcomes may be assessed as follows:

- use of presentations as a context for conveying understanding of human resource management issues; learners could use their own experiences and commercial contacts as a basis for collection and analysis of human resource management policies and practices

- use of role plays to simulate interview practice

- case studies to assess learners' understanding of human resource management issues, eg disciplinary and grievance handling, reward systems, training interventions

- written assignments to test knowledge and understanding

Links

The unit is part of the HN Human Resource Management pathway and forms a direct link with other human resource units in the programme such as Unit 3: Organisations and Behaviour, Unit 22: Managing Human Resources Issues, Unit 23: Human Resource Development and Unit 24: Employee Relations.

Links are also to be found within *Unit 25: English Legal System,* which covers employment protection legislation.

The unit covers some of the underpinning knowledge and understanding for the following units of the NVQ in Operational Personnel Level 4:

- Mandatory units
- Area A – Resourcing and Retention

Resources

Sufficient library resources should be available to enable learners to achieve this unit. Texts that are particularly relevant are:

Armstrong M – *A Handbook of Human Resources Practice* (Kogan Page, 2001)

Business Basics Human Resource Management – 2nd Ed (London, BPP Publishing, 1997)

Corbridge M and Pilbeam S – *Employment Resourcing* (FT Prentice Hall, 1998)

Dransfield R, Howkins S, Hudson F and Davies W– *Human Resource Management for Higher Awards* (Heinemann, 1996)

Foot M and Hook C – *Introducing Human Resource Management* – 3rd Ed (Harlow, FT: Prentice Hall, 2002)

Torrington D, Hall L and Taylor S – *Human Resource Management* – 5th Ed (Harlow, FT: Prentice Hall, 2002)

Journals/Newspapers

- *People Management*
- *Personnel Review*
- *Personnel Today*
- *Human Resource Management Journal*
- *Training*
- *Any quality broadsheet newspapers – eg The Guardian*

Videos

Companies such as Video Arts and Melrose produce a variety of videos which may be useful in covering human resource management topics. Television current affairs programmes can also provide a useful additional resource.

Websites

See the list relating to all four Units at the end of this appendix.

BPP
LEARNING MEDIA

EDEXCEL GUIDELINES FOR UNIT 22: MANAGING HUMAN RESOURCES ISSUES

Description of the Unit

The aim of this unit is to build upon the knowledge and understanding developed in the human resource management unit.

A broader and wider perspective is developed in relation to the application of human resource management practices. A comparative approach is also introduced to consider HRM policy and practice in a global context.

Summary of learning outcomes

Outcomes and assessment criteria

Outcomes	Assessment criteria
	To achieve each outcome a learner must demonstrate the ability to:
1 Examine the **differing perspectives of human resource management**	• explain Guest's model of hard-soft, loose-tight dimensions of HRM • review the differences between Storey's definitions of HRM and personnel and IR practices • analyse HRM from a strategic perspective and its implications for the role of the line manager and employees
2 Review ways of developing **flexibility within the workplace**	• review and explain a model of flexibility and show how this might be applied in practice • describe the need for flexibility and the types of flexibility which may be developed by an organisation and give examples of how they can be implemented • evaluate the advantages and disadvantages of flexible working practices from both the employee and the employer perspective

Outcomes	Assessment criteria
	To achieve each outcome a learner must demonstrate the ability to:
3 Determine the need for **equal opportunities within the workplace**	• describe the forms of discrimination that take place • review how the legislative framework and any proposed changes relating to discrimination in the workplace can be applied by an organisation • explain a range of current initiatives and practices which focus on equal opportunities in employment • compare and contrast equal opportunities and managing diversity
4 Explore **topical human resource practices and issues**	• explain performance management in practice • critically evaluate different human resource practices in the workplace • evaluate the impact of globalisation on issues such as human resource planning • review the impact of different national cultures and practices human resource professionals can employ to manage a culturally diverse workforce

*Covered in
chapter(s)*

Content

1   Differing perspectives of human resource management

The different perspectives of human resource management (HRM): 'soft'   8
and 'hard' human resource management, 'loose' and 'tight' human
resource management; differences between HRM and IR and
personnel practices, eg use could be made of Storey's research, 1992
highlighting twenty seven points of difference; strategic approaches
to HRM

2   Flexibility within the workplace

Flexible working models: the core and periphery workforce model   9
(Atkinson 1984); Handy's (1989) Shamrock Organisation

Types of flexibility: eg numerical, functional, temporal, locational,   9
financial

Flexible working methods: eg employment of part-time and temporary   9
staff, teleworking, homeworking, job sharing, zero hours contracts,
annual hours

BPP
LEARNING MEDIA

	Covered in chapter(s)

Labour market and the need for flexibility: labour market demographics, employment statistics, local, regional and national labour markets and the growing recognition of the importance of work-life balance — 9

3 Equal opportunities within the workplace

Discrimination in employment: forms of discrimination, eg gender, ethnicity, religion, disability, age, sexual orientation, education — 10

The legislative framework: direct and indirect discrimination; current legislation and proposed changes to the law, eg age, temporary workers — 10

Equal opportunities in employment: equal opportunities practices and initiatives in the workplace including initiatives such as Opportunity 2000 and positive action approaches, codes of practice, implementing policy, training within the law and monitoring; the move from equal opportunities to managing diversity — 3, 10

4 Topical human resource practices and issues

Learners should explore a range of topical HRM issues to evaluate how they are applied in practice. Examples of some of the topical issues are detailed below.

Performance management: the role, purpose and types of appraisal, 360 degree feedback, the skills of carrying out appraisals and giving feedback, the link of appraisals to reward management — 6

Counselling and employee welfare: the traditional welfare function – occupational health practices and policies, the management of ill health at work, costs and absenteeism, accidents at work (statistics) — 11

Health and safety legislation: Health and Safety at Work Act (1974) and the role of the Health and Safety Commission, European Community Directives, eg Working Time Regulations (1998), Parental Leave (2000) — 11

New approaches to welfare: ergonomics, alcohol and drug abuse, HIV and AIDS, stress and stress management, workplace counselling — 11

Other topical issues: e-recruitment, e-learning, flexible benefits, work-life balance, employee voice — 3, 5, 9–11, 14–18

Guidance

Delivery

Learners' understanding of human resources management can be developed through the use of a variety of learning methods including lectures, discussions, seminars, videos, role plays, case studies and learner-led presentations.

Investigations of human resources management policies and practices within organisations and talks from human resources management practitioners can both develop understanding and provide support for the knowledge and skill-base established within the unit.

Assessment

Evidence of outcomes may be assessed as follows:

- use of presentations as a context for conveying understanding of human resource management issues. Learners could use their own experience and commercial contacts as a basis for collection and analysis of human resource management policies and practices

- use of role plays to simulate appraisal practice

- case studies to assess learners' understanding of human resource management issues, eg stress management, flexibility, equal opportunities and performance management

- written assignments to test knowledge and understanding

Links

The unit has particular links with the other units in the Human Resource Management pathway. It also has links with NVQ Level 4 in Personnel.

Resources

Suggested reading

Sufficient library resources should be available to enable learners to achieve this unit. Texts that are particularly relevant are:

Armstrong M – *A Handbook of Human Resources Practice* (Kogan Page, 2001)

Corbridge M and Pilbeam S – *Employment Resourcing* (FT Prentice Hall, 1998)

Dransfield R, Howkins S, Hudson F and Davies W– *Human Resource Management for Higher Awards* (Heinemann, 1996)

Foot M and Hook C – *Introducing Human Resource Management* – 3rd Ed (Harlow, FT: Prentice Hall, 2002)

Torrington D, Hall L and Taylor S – *Human Resource Management* – 5th Ed (Harlow, FT: Prentice Hall, 2002)

Newspapers/Newspapers

- *People Management*
- *Personnel Review*
- *Personnel Today*
- *Human Resource Management Journal*
- *Training*
- *The Economist*
- *Any quality broadsheet newspapers – eg The Guardian*

Videos

Companies such as Video Arts and Melrose produce a variety of videos, which may be useful in covering human resource management topics. Television current affairs programmes can also provide a useful additional resource.

Websites

See the list relating to all four Units at the end of this appendix.

EDEXCEL GUIDELINES FOR UNIT 23: HUMAN RESOURCES DEVELOPMENT

Description of the Unit

This unit will develop students' understanding of the nature and role of training and employee development. The unit provides an introduction to the range of government initiatives aimed at developing skills within the labour market. It explores how people learn as well as developing a systematic approach to the design and delivery of training. Consideration is given as to how to measure the effectiveness of training and development in practice.

Summary of learning outcomes

Outcomes and assessment criteria

Outcomes	Assessment criteria
	To achieve each outcome a learner must demonstrate the ability to:
1 Explore a range of **differing learning theories and learning styles**	• differentiate between different learning styles • analyse learning theories and explain their contribution to the planning and design of learning events • explain the implications of the learning curve and the importance of ensuring the transfer of learning to the workplace
2 Critically evaluate the **planning and design of training and development**	• explain how training contributes to the achievement of business objectives and the role of a training and development policy • explain and describe a systematic approach to training and development using a model and outline each stage of the training cycle • critically evaluate the factors to take into account when planning a training and development event • evaluate an organisation's approach to training

Outcomes	Assessment criteria
	To achieve each outcome a learner must demonstrate the ability to:
3 Explore the **role and purpose of evaluation and evaluation techniques**	• examine the importance of evaluation and how it can help to market the contribution of training and development to the business
	• explore the way that evaluation needs to be on-going and systematically planned for at each stage of the training cycle
	• review the key stakeholders in the evaluation process and the roles that they play
	• compare and contrast a range of evaluation techniques and the pros and cons of these
	• analyse the contribution of evaluation models and the difficulties that these can pose in practice
4 Examine a range of **government-led initiatives** aimed at developing skills in the labour market	• analyse the context influencing the role of government in training and development and the growing emphasis on lifelong learning and continuous development
	• review the development of NVQs, MCI and the competency movement
	• examine a range of contemporary training initiatives introduced by the UK government

Covered in chapter(s)

Content

1   **Learning theories and learning styles**

Learning theories and learning styles: activists, reflectors, theorists, pragmatists (Honey and Mumford 1982), and Kolb's (1979) learning style inventory; learning theories, eg behaviourist, cognitive; impact of the learning curve and transfer of learning to the work place; impact of learning theories and styles when planning and designing a learning event

13

NOTES

2   The planning and design of training and development

The systematic approach: the role of training and development policy   13
within the organisation, identification of training and development
needs, setting training objectives, planning issues, eg numbers,
location, content, internal/external trainers, administration;
designing and using a range of training and development methods,
eg advantages and disadvantages of a range of on- and off-the-job
methods, eg 'sitting next to Nellie', mentoring, coaching, action
learning, assignments, projects, shadowing, secondments, training
courses, seminars, e-learning and outdoor development; delivery of
the learning event

3   The role and purpose of evaluation and evaluation techniques

The 'what, why, when and who' of evaluation: exploration of what   14
evaluation involves and what can be measured, the importance of
evaluating learning events and measuring the contribution, the need
for continuous evaluation at every stage in the training cycle, the
key stakeholders in the evaluation process and their roles within it

A range of evaluation techniques: eg 'Happy Sheets', pre/post tests, and   14
the benefits and limitations of these; different evaluation models
and the difficulties that these pose in practice, eg Kirkpatrick, CIRO

4   Government-led initiatives

General and vocational training schemes and initiatives: context   15
influencing government approaches to training and development in
the UK; development of NVQs, MCI and the competency
movement; national training targets and the role of the
Qualifications and Curriculum Authority (QCA); specific
initiatives, eg modern apprenticeship schemes, Investors in People,
New Deal, University for Industry – learndirect, Learning and
Skills Councils, Connexions

Guidance

Delivery

Learners' understanding of human resources development can be developed through the
use of a variety of learning methods including lectures, discussions, seminars, videos,
role plays, case studies and learner-led presentations.

Investigations of human resource development practices within organisations and talks
from training and development practitioners can both develop understanding and
provide support for the knowledge and skill base established within the unit.

Assessment

Evidence of outcomes may be assessed as follows:

- use of presentations as a means of demonstrating understanding of how to design and deliver a learning event. Learners could use their own experience and commercial contacts as a basis for collection and analysis of human resource development practices

- case studies and the review of current journal articles to assess learners' understanding of human resource development issues, eg e-learning, outdoor development and evaluation

- written assignments to test knowledge and understanding

Links

The unit has particular links with the other units in the Human Resource Management pathway. It also has links with NVQ Level 4 in Personnel.

Resources

Suggested reading

Sufficient library resources should be available to enable learners to achieve this unit. Texts that are particularly relevant are:

Barrington H and Reid M A – *Training Interventions* – 6th Ed (CIPD, 1999)

Moorby E – *How to Succeed in Employee Development* – 2nd Ed (McGraw-Hill, 1996)

Redman T and Wilkinson A – *Contemporary Human Resource Management* – (Harlow, FT: Prentice Hall, 2001)

Foot M and Hook C – *Introducing Human Resource Management* – 3rd Ed (Harlow, FT: Prentice Hall, 2002)

Newspapers/Newspapers

- *People Management*
- *Personnel Review*
- *Personnel Today*
- *Training*
- Any quality broadsheet newspapers – eg *The Guardian*

Videos

Companies such as Video Arts and Melrose produce a variety of videos, which may be useful in covering human resource development topics. Television current affairs programmes can also provide a useful additional resource.

Websites

See the list relating to all four Units at the end of this appendix.

EDEXCEL GUIDELINES FOR UNIT 24: EMPLOYEE RELATIONS

Description of the Unit

The main aim of this unit is to provide a general introduction to employee relations and develop knowledge and understanding of the changes which have taken place over the years with respect to the employment relationship in the UK. The unit considers the nature of industrial conflict and the resolution of collective disputes. The processes of collective bargaining and negotiation are also explored.

Summary of learning outcomes

Outcomes and assessment criteria

Outcomes	Assessment criteria
	To achieve each outcome a learner must demonstrate the ability to:
1 Explore the **context of employee relations against a changing background**	<ul><li>explain the unitary and pluralistic frames of reference</li><li>review the development of trade unions and nature of industrial relations</li><li>determine the role of a trade union and its contribution to effective employee relations</li><li>differentiate the roles taken by the main actors in employee relations</li></ul>
2 Examine the nature of **industrial conflict and the resolution of collective disputes**	<ul><li>explain the ideological framework of industrial relations</li><li>investigate the different types of collective dispute</li><li>review dispute procedures and the resolution of conflict</li><li>critically evaluate the effectiveness of dispute procedures in resolving conflict in a given situation</li></ul>
3 Explore the processes of **collective bargaining and negotiation**	<ul><li>explore the nature and scope of collective bargaining</li><li>describe the processes of negotiation</li><li>prepare and apply negotiation strategy for a given situation</li></ul>

Outcomes	Assessment criteria
	To achieve each outcome a learner must demonstrate the ability to:
4 Investigate the concept of **employee participation and involvement**	• investigate the effectiveness of arrangements made by two organisations to involve their employees in decision-making
	• analyse the influence of the EU on democracy in the UK
	• distinguish between industrial relations and employee relations
	• assess the effectiveness of employee involvement techniques
	• establish the impact of human resource management on employee relations

Covered in chapter(s)

Content

*Covered in
chapter(s)*

3   Collective bargaining and negotiation

The nature and scope of collective bargaining: role of shop stewards,   17
union officials, employer associations and management

The collective bargaining process: institutional agreements for   17
collective bargaining, local workplace bargaining, single-table
bargaining

Negotiation processes: negotiation strategy, preparation for   17
negotiation, conducting the case-settlement, disclosure of
information

4   Employee participation and involvement

Consultation and employee participation: different forms of employee
consultation and participation, joint consultation committees,
upward-downward forms of communication

Industrial democracy and employee participation: European Works   18
Councils (European Objectives), the social dimensions of the
European Union and supervisory boards, national cultural
differences towards democracy and employee participation

Employee involvement techniques: sharing information, consultation,   18
financial participation, commitment to quality, developing the
individual, involvement of other stakeholders

Empowerment: devolution of responsibility/authority to line   18
managers/employees, the role of human resource management,
approach to employee relations (link to unitarist and pluralist
perspectives)

Guidance

Delivery

Learners' understanding of employee relations can be developed through the use of a
variety of learning methods including lectures, discussions, seminars, videos, role plays,
case studies and learner-led presentations.

Investigations of employee relations policies and practices within organisations and talks
from union officials and human resource management practitioners can both develop
understanding and provide support for the knowledge and skill base established within
the unit.

Assessment

Evidence of outcomes may be assessed as follows:

- use of presentations as a context for conveying understanding of employee
  relations

- use of role plays for exploring the processes of collective bargaining and
  negotiation

- case studies to assess learners' understanding of the nature of industrial conflict and the resolution of collective action

- written assignments to test knowledge and understanding

Links

This unit is part of the HN Personnel pathway and forms a direct link with other personnel units in the programme: Unit 3: Organisations and Behaviour, Unit 21: Human Resource Management, Unit 22: Managing Human Resources Issues *and* Unit 23: Human Resource Development.

Links may also be found with Unit 4: Organisations, Competition and Environment, Unit 6: Business Decision Making, Unit 26: English Legal System *and* Unit 39: Quality Management.

This unit covers some of the underpinning knowledge and understanding for units of the NVQ in Personnel at Level 4.

Resources

Sufficient library resources should be available to enable learners to achieve this unit. Texts that are particularly relevant are:

Blyton P and Turnbull P – *The Dynamics of Employee Relations* – 2nd Ed (Palgrave, 1998)

Farnham D – *Employee Relations in Context* – 2nd Ed (London, CIPD, 2000)

Gennard J and Judge G C – *Employee Relations* – 3rd Ed (London, CIPD, 2002)

Newspapers/Newspapers

- *British Journal of Industrial Relations*
- *Employment Gazette*
- *Industrial Relations Journal*
- *Industrial Relations Review and Report*
- *People Management*
- *Personnel Review*
- *Personnel Today*
- *European Journal of Industrial Relations*
- *Labour History Review*
- *Labour Research*
- Any quality broadsheet newspapers – eg *The Guardian*

Videos

Companies such as Video Arts and Melrose produce a variety of videos, which may be useful in covering employee relations topics. Television current affairs programmes can also provide a useful additional resource.

Websites

See the list relating to all four Units at the end of this appendix.

WEBSITES

The Edexcel Guidelines provide a comprehensive list of websites relevant to the four HRM Units.

These are:

• www.acas.org.uk	Advisory, Conciliation and Arbitration Service
• www.berr.gov.uk	Department for Business enterprise and Regulatory Reform
• www.bized.ac.uk	which provides business case studies appropriate for educational purposes
• www.cipd.co.uk	Chartered Institute of Personnel and Development website with a range of learning resources
• www.compactlaw.co.uk	Employment questions and answers
• www.cre.org.uk	Commission for Racial Equality
• www.drc-gb.org.uk	Disability Rights Commission
• www.dfes.gov.uk	Department for Education and Skills
• www.dti.gov.uk	Department of Trade and Industry
• www.employment-studies.co.uk	Institute for Employment Studies
• www.eoc.org.uk	Equal Opportunities Commission
• www.guardian.co.uk	Provides links to news items and reports
• www.hse.gov.uk	Health and Safety Executive
• www.iipuk.co.uk	Investors in People UK
• www.ilo.org	International Labour Organisation
• www.incomesdata.co.uk	up-to-date intelligence on employment issues (Incomes Data Service)
• www.isma.org.uk	International Stress Management Association (UK)
• www.learndirect.co.uk	UK learndirect
• www.lsc.gov.uk	The Learning and Skills Council
• www.peoplemanagement.co.uk	bi-monthly journal of the Chartered Institute of Personnel and Development
• www.newdeal.gov.uk	New Deal
• www.nto-nc.org	The National Training Organisational National Council
• www.personneltoday.com	Relevant articles and statistics
• www.qca.org.uk	Qualifications and Curriculum Authority
• www.successunlimited.co.uk	Site on bullying in the workplace
• www.trainingjournal.com	Relevant articles on current training and development topics
• www.wfpma.com.br	A journal with articles on international aspects of managing people at work
• www.wto.org	World Trade Organisation

NOTES

For recruitment and selection learners could access websites such as:

- www.bbc.co.uk/jobs
- www.jobability.com
- www.monster.co.uk
- www.totaljobs.com

BPP
LEARNING MEDIA

BIBLIOGRAPHY

Adair, J & Allen, M (1999) *Time Management and Personal Development*. London: Hawksmere

Adams, J S (1963), 'Toward an understanding of inequity' *Journal of Abnormal & Social Psychology* 64/4.

Alberga, T, Tyson, S & Parsons, D (1997) 'An evaluation of the Investors in People Standard', *Human Resource Management Journal* 7 (2)

Albrecht, K & Albrecht, S (1993) 'Added Value Negotiating', *Training*, April pp 26-29

Armstrong, M (2000) *Strategic Human Resource Management: A Guide to Action* (2nd edition). London: Kogan Page

Allen, A (2003) 'Out of the ordinary', *People Management*, 4 December

Armstrong, M (2003) *A Handbook of Human Resource Management Practice* (9th edition). London: Kogan Page

Arnold, J, Copper, C & Robertson, I (1995) *Work Psychology: Understanding Human Behaviour in the Workplace* (2nd edition). London: Pitman

Atkinson, J (1984) 'Manpower strategies for flexible organisations' *Personnel Management*, August

Atkinson, J & Meager, N (1986) *Changing patterns of Work*. London: IMS/OECD

Barnes, P (1997) 'Teleworking'. *Chartered Secretary*, May

Beardwell, I & Holden, L (1997) *Human Resource Management* (2nd edition). London: Pitman

Beer, M, Spector B, Laurence P, Quinn Mills, D & Walton, K (1984) *Managing Human Assets*. New York: Free Press

Beer, M & Spector, B (1985) 'Corporate transformations in human resource management', *HRM Trends and Challenges* (ed Walton & Lawrence). Boston, Mass: Harvard University Press

Blyth, A (2003) 'The art of survival', *People Management*, 1 May

Blyton, P & Turnbull, P (1992) *Reassessing HRM*. London: Sage

Bolton, T (1997) *Human Resource Management: An Introduction*. Oxford: Blackwell

Bond, S (2003) 'How to effect changes in working hours', *People Management*, 10 July

Bottomley, C (1998) in *People Management*, 9 September

Boxall, P F (1995) 'Building the theory of comparative HRM', *HRM Journal*, 5 (5)

Boxall, P F & Purcell, J (2003) *Strategy and Human Resource Management*. Basingstoke: Palgrave Macmillan

Bramley, P (1986) *Evaluation of Training: A practical guide*. London: BASIE

Bratton, J & Gold, J (2007) *Human Resource Management: Theory and Practice* (4th edition). Basingstoke: Palgrave Macmillan

Brewster, C (1999) 'Strategic HRM: the value of different paradigms', *Strategic Human Resource Management* (ed Schuler, Jackson). Oxford: Blackwell

Bridges, W (1994) *Jobshift: How to Prosper in a Workplace Without Jobs*. London: Allen & Unwin

Bronstein, M (2003), 'A life less ordinary', *People Management*, 17 April

Brown, D & Baron, A (2003) 'A capital idea' *People Management*, 26 June

Budhwar, P S and Mellahi (2006) *Managing Human Resources in the Middle East.* Abingdon, Oxon: Routledge

Burgoyne, J (1999) *Developing Yourself, Your Career and Your Organisation.* London: Lemos & Crane

Burns, J M (1978) *Leadership.* London: Harper & Row

Cartright, A (2003) 'How to deal with requests for flexible working', *People Management*, 6 November

Chamberlain, N W & Kuhn, J (1965) *Collective Bargaining.* New York: McGraw Hill

CIPD (1994) *Statement on Counselling in the Workplace.* London: CIPD

Clague, I (2004) 'Soft touch strategies', posted at www.learningtechnologies.co/article on 02/03/04

Clarke, K (2003) 'Show me the money' *People Management*, 1 May

Clegg, H (1976) *The System of Industrial Relations in Great Britain.* Oxford: Blackwell

Clutterbuck, D (1991) *Everyone Needs a Mentor: How to Foster Talent Within the Organisation* (2nd edition). London: IPM

Connock, S (1991) *HR Vision: Managing a Quality Workforce.* London: IPM

Constable, R & McCormick, R J (1987) *The Making of British Managers.* London: BIM

Cooper, C (2003) 'Minority report', *People Management*, 4 December

Cornelius & Faire, S (1989) *Everyone Can Win: How to Resolve Conflict.* Sydney: Simon & Schuster Australia

Critchley, R (1996). 'New paradigms for "sustainable employability"', *HR Monthly*, April, pp 22-23

Cuming, M W (1993) *The Theory and Practice of Personnel Management.* London: Butterworth Heinemann

Cushway, B & Lodge, D (1994) *Human Resource Management.* Nichols

Dalgamo, D & Davies, P (2003) 'How to consult on collective redundancies', *People Management*, 11 September

Department for Education and Employment (1998) *The Learning Age: a renaissance for a new Britain.* Sheffield: DfEE

Department for Education and Employment (1999) *Learning to Succeed: a new framework for post-16 education.* Sheffield: DfEE

Department for Education and Employment (2000) *Labour Market and Skill Trends.* Sheffield: DfEE

Dobler, D W, Burt D N & Lee, L (1990) *Purchasing and Materials Management.* (5th edition) New York: McGraw Hill

Drucker, P (1955). *The Practice of Management.* London: Heinemann

Equal Opportunities Commission (2000) *Good Practice Guide: Job evaluation schemes free of sex bias.* Manchester: EOC

Evans, J (2003) 'DTI official hints at tougher law', *People Management*, 10 July

Fisher, R, Ury, W & Patton, B (1999) *Getting to Yes: Negotiating an Agreement Without Giving In* (2nd edition). London: Random House

Fombrun, C J, Tichy, N M & Devanno, M A (1984) *Strategic Human Resource Management.* New York: Wiley

Fox, A (1975) *Industrial Relations and a Wider Society: Aspects of Interaction.* London: Faber & Faber

Gardenswartz, L & Rowe, A (1993) *Managing Diversity: A Complete Desk Reference and Planning Guide.* Homewood, IL: Irwin

Garvin, M (1993) 'Building a Learning Organisation', *Harvard Business Review*, July-August

Gennard, J and Judge, G *Employee Relations* (3rd edition). London: CIPD

Goldthorpe, J H, Lockwood, D C, Bechofer, F & Platt, J (1968) *The Affluent Worker: Industrial Attitudes and Behaviour.* Cambridge: CUP

Goleman, D C (1998) Working with Emotional Intelligence. London: Bloomsbury

Goss, D (1994) *Principles of Human Resource Management.* London: International Thomson Business Press

Graham, H T & Bennett, R (1998) *Human Resources Management* (9th edition). London: Pitman

Gratton, L, Haily, V H, Stile, P & Truss, C (1999) *Strategic HRM.* Oxford: OUP

Guest, D E (1989) 'Personnel & HRM: Can you tell the difference?' *Personnel Management*, January pp 48-51

Guest, D E (1991) 'Personnel management: the end of orthodoxy', *British Journal of Industrial Relations* 29 (2)

Guest, D E (1999) 'Human Resource Management: the workers' verdict', *Human Resource Management Journal* 9 (2)

Guest, D E (2001) 'Industrial relations and HRM', *Human Resource Management: A Critical Text* (2nd edition) (ed Storey). London: Thomson

Guest, D E, Michie, J, Sheehan, M & Conway, N (2000) *Employment Relations, HRM & Business Performance.* London: CIPD

Guirdham, M (1999) *Communicating Across Cultures.* Basingstoke: Palgrave

Handy, C B (1989) *The Age of Unreason.* London: Business Books

Handy, C B (1993) *Understanding Organisations.* Harmondsworth: Penguin

Hargreaves, P & Jarvis, P (2000) *The Human Resource Development Handbook* (revised edition). London: Kogan Page

Hersey, P & Blanchard, K H (1988) *Management of Organisational Behaviour: Utilising Human Resources* (5th edition). New Jersey: Prentice Hall

Herzberg, F W (1966) *Work and the Nature of Man.* New York: Staples

Higginbottom, K (2003 (a)) 'More than lip service' *People Management*, 4 December

Higginbottom, K (2003 (b)) 'HR in the spotlight' *People Management*, 20 November

Higginbottom, K (2003 (c)) 'Mind your own business', *People Management*, 1 May

Hofstede, G (1989) *Cultures Consequences.* Beverley Hills, CA: Sage

Hofstede, G (1991) *Cultures and Organisations.* London: McGraw Hill

Holmstrom, R (2003) 'Time well spent', *People Management*, 28 August

Honey, P & Mumford, A (1990) *The Opportunist Learner.* Maidenhead: Peter Honey

Honey, P & Mumford, A (1992) *A Manual of Learning Styles* (3rd edition). Maidenhead: Peter Honey

Huczynski, A & Buchanan, D (2001) *Organisational Behaviour: An Introductory Text.* Harlow, Essex: FT Prentice Hall

Hunt, J (1982) *Managing People in Organisations.* NY: McGraw Hill

Huthwaite Inc (2000) *Behaviour of Successful Negotiators.* Percellville, VI: Huthwaite Inc.

Ingham, J (2003) 'How to implement a diversity policy', *People Management*, 24 July

Investors in People (2004) posted at www.investorsinpeople.co.uk/IIP/...CaseStudies, 12.02.04

IPD (1998) *The IPD Guide to Outsourcing.* London: IPD

IPM (1992) *Statement on Counselling in the Workplace.* London: IPM

Ivey, A, Ivey, M & Simek Morgan, L (1993) *Counselling and Psychotherapy: a Multicultural Perspective* (3rd edition). Boston, Mass: Allyn & Bacon

Johns, E (1994) *Perfect Customer Care.* London: Random House

Jones, B (1982) *Sleepers, Wake!: Technology and the Future of Work.* Oxford: OUP

Kane & Stanton (1994) *Human Resource Planning in a Changing Environment.*

Katz, R (ed) *Career Issues in Human Resource Management.* New Jersey: Prentice Hall

Kaufman, R & Keller, J M (1994) 'Levels of Evaluation: Beyond Kirkpatrick', *HRP Quarterly* (5)

Kirkpatrick, D L (1998) *Evaluating Training Programmes: the Four Levels.* San Francisco: Berrett-Koehler

Kohn, A (1993) 'Why incentive plans cannot work', *Harvard Business Review*, Sep-Oct pp 54-63

Kolb, D (1984) *Experiential Learning.* New York: Prentice Hall

Kramar, R, McGraw, P & Schuler, R (1997), *Human Resource Management in Australia* (3rd edition). Melbourne: Addison Wesley Longman

Leat, M (2007) *Exploring Employee Relations* (2nd edition) Oxford: Butterworth-Heinemann

Legge, K (1989) 'Human Resource Management: a critical analysis', *New Perspectives in HRM* (ed Storey). London: Routledge

Legge, K (1998) 'The morality of HRM', *Experiencing HRM* (ed Mabey, Skinner & Clark). Cambridge

Liff, S (2000) 'Manpower or HR planning: what's in a name?' *Personnel Management* (3rd edition) eds Bach & Sisson. Oxford: Blackwell

Livy, B (1988) *Corporate Personnel Management.* London: Pitman

Lockett, J (1992) *Effective Performance Management.* Kogan Page

LSC (2004 (a)), posted at www.lsc.gov.uk/National/media/News/Nationalemployersurvey on 02/02/04

LSC (2004 (b)), posted at www.lsc.gov.uk/National/media/PressReleases/ASDAMA on 18.02.04

Lupton, T (1974) *Wages and Salaries.* London: Penguin

Maier, N (1958) *The Appraisal Interview.* New York: Wiley

Manocha, R (2003) 'Catch 22', *People Management,* 9 October

Marchington, M, Goodman, J, Wilkinson, A & Ackers, P (1992) *New Developments in Employee Involvement.* London: HMSO

Marchington, M, Wilkinson, A, Ackers, P & Dundon, A (2001) *Management Choice and Employee Voice.* London: CIPD

Margolis, A (2003) 'Licenced to skill', *People Management,* 26 June

Martin, A O (1967) *Welfare at Work.* London: Batsford

Maslow, A (1954) *Motivation and Personality.* New York: Harper & Row

McGregor, D (1987) *The Human Side of Enterprise.* London: Penguin

Mowdray, R, Porter, L & Steers, R (1982) *Employee-Organisation Linkages* London: Academic Press

Moxon, G R (1958) *Functions of a Personnel Department.* London: IPM

Mullins, L (1985) 'The personnel function: a shared responsibility' *The Administrator,* May

Mullins, L (1999) *Management and Organisational Behaviour* (5th edition). Harlow, Essex: FT Prentice Hall

Mumford, A (1994) *Management Development: Strategies for Action.* London: IPM

Munro Fraser, J (1971) *Psychology: General, Industrial, Social.* London: Pitman

National Skills Task Force (1998) *Towards a National Skills Agenda.* London: DfEE

National Skills Task Force (2000) *Skills for All: research report from the NSTK.* London: DfEE

Ouchi, W (1981) *Theory Z*. Reading, Mass: Addison Wesley

Overman, S (2003) 'HR drives change at Levis', *People Management*, 6 November

Oxford Institute of International Finance (2002) *Managing Self Development*. London: OITF

Parsloe, E & Wray, M (2000) *Coaching and Mentoring: Practical Methods to Improve Learning*. London: Kogan Page

Pedler, M Burgoyne, J & Boydell, T (1991) *The Learning Company*. Maidenhead: McGraw Hill

Pedler, M, Burgoyne, J & Boydell, T (2001) *A Manager's Guide to Self Development* (4th edition) Maidenhead: McGraw Hill

Pedler, M, Brook, C & Burgoyne, J (2003) 'Motion Pictures', *People Management*, 17 April

Persaud, J (2003) 'Fitness First', *People Management*, 11 September

Personnel Standards Lead Body (1993) *A Perspective on Personnel*. London: PSLB

Peters, T J & Waterman, R (1982) *In Search of Excellence*. New York: Harper & Row

Peters, T J (1989) *Thriving on Chaos*. New York: Pan

Peters, T J (1994) *Liberation Management*. New York: Pan

Phillips, J (1997) *Return on Investment in Training and Performance Improvement Programs*. Houston, TX: Gulf

Pickard, J (2003) 'Joint effort', *People Management*, 24 July

Plumbley, P (1991) *Recruitment and Selection* (5th edition). Hyperion

Prasad, R (2003) Connexions Special Supplement, *The Guardian*, January 29

Purcell, J, Kinnie, N & Hutchinson, S (2003) 'Inside the black box' *People Management*, 15 May

Ream, B (1984) *Personnel Administration*. London: ICSA

Rees, W D (1996) *The Skills of Management* (4th edition). London: Thomson Business Press

Roberts, Z (2003 (a)) 'Barclays banks on older staff', *People Management*, 29 May

Roberts, Z (2003 (b)) 'BT drive for top women', *People Management*, 11 September

Roberts, Z (2003 (c)) 'Fast-track learning', *People Management*, 10 July

Rodger, A (1970) *The Seven Point Plan* (3rd edition) London: NFER

Rosenberg, M (2003) 'Best laid plans', *People Management*, 3 April

Schein, E H (1985) *Organisational Culture and Leadership*. San Francisco: Jossey Bass

Schneider, S & Barsoux, J (1997) *Managing Across Cultures*. Harlow, Essex: FT Prentice Hall

Schuler, R S (1995) *Managing Human Resources*. St Paul, Minn: West Publishing

Senge, P (1990) *The Fifth Discipline: the Art and Practice of the Learning Organisation*. New York: Random Century

Shepherd, C (2004) 'Assessing the ROI of training', www.fastrak-consulting.co.uk/tactix/features on 02/03/2004

Sisson, K & Storey, J (2000) *The Realities of HRM: Managing the employment relationship*. Buckingham: OUP

Sloman, M (2001) *The e-Learning Revolution*. London: CIPD

Sloman, M (2003) 'Learning Curve', *People Management,* 25 September

Solomon, C M (2001) 'Managing Virtual Teams', *Workforce,* June

Stone, F M (1999) *Coaching, Counselling and Mentoring*. New York: AMACOM

Storey, J (1989) 'From personnel management to human resource management', *New Perspective on HRM* (ed Storey). London: Routledge

Storey, J (1992) *New Developments in the Management of Human Resources*. London: Routledge

Taylor, S (1998) *Employee Resourcing*. London: IPD

Torrington, D (1994) *International Personnel Management*. Englewood Cliffs, NJ: Prentice Hall

Torrington, D & Hall, L (1991) *Personnel Management: A New Approach*. Englewood Cliffs, NJ: Prentice Hall

Torrington, D, Hall, L, Taylor, S (2002) *Human Resource Management* (5th edition). London: Pearson Education

Townsend, R (1985) *Further up the organisation*. London: Hodder & Stoughton

Trades Union Congress (2000) *Qualifying for Racism*. London: TUC

Trompenaars, F (1993) *Riding the Waves of Culture*. London: Nicholas Brealey

Tulip, S (2003 (a)) 'Just rewards', *People Management,* 25 September

Tyson S (2006) *Essentials of Human Resource Management* (5th Edition) Oxford: Butterworth-Heinemann

Tyson, S & Fell, A (1986) *Evaluating the Personnel Function*. London: Hutchinson

University for Industry (2003) 'UfI/learndirect well placed to deliver Government's e-learning vision', posted at www.ufi.com/press/releases on 08/07/03

Upton, R (2003) 'Star gazers', *People Management,* 26 June

Vroom, V (1964) *Work and motivation*. New York: Wiley

Walsh, M (2004) 'Ill winds offshore', *The Bulletin,* February 3

Watkins, J (2003 (a)) 'Staff turnover hits four-year low', *People Management,* 4 December

NOTES

Watkins, J (2003 (b)) 'Tests cut EA turnover', *People Management*, 25 September

Watkins, J (2003 (c)) 'Stress busters', *People Management*, 25 September

Watkins, J (2003 (d)) 'Serious turbulence', *People Management*, 7 August

Watkins, J & Staines, K (2003) 'Job firm risks discrimination', *People Management*, 15 May

Welch, J (2003) 'In the hiring line', *People Management*, 26 June

Whetten, D, & Cameron, K (2002) *Developing Management Skills* (5th edition). New Jersey: Prentice Hall

Whetten, D, Cameron, K & Woods, M (2000) *Developing Management Skills for Europe* (2nd edition). Harlow, Essex: FT Prentice Hall

Wild, A (2003) 'Pressure point', *People Management*, 10 July

Wood, R and Payne, T (1998) *Competency-based Recruitment and Selection.* Chichester: Wiley

Woodruffe, C (1992) 'What is meant by a competency?' *Designing and Achieving Competency* (ed Boam & Sparrow). Maidenhead: McGraw Hill

Woolnough, R (2003) 'Child benefits', *People Management*, 4 December

BPP
LEARNING MEDIA

INDEX

NOTES

Definitions are highlighted in **bold**

NOTES

564

NOTES

NOTES

Review Form – Business Essentials – Human Resource Management (9/07)

BPP Learning Media always appreciates feedback from the students who use our books. We would be very grateful if you would take the time to complete this feedback form, and return it to the address below.

Name: _____   Address: _____

_____

_____

How have you used this Course Book?
(Tick one box only)

☐ Home study (book only)

☐ On a course: college _____

☐ Other _____

Why did you decide to purchase this Course book? *(Tick one box only)*

☐ Have used BPP Learning Media Texts in the past

☐ Recommendation by friend/colleague

☐ Recommendation by a lecturer at college

☐ Saw advertising

☐ Other _____

During the past six months do you recall seeing/receiving any of the following?
(Tick as many boxes as are relevant)

☐ Our advertisement

☐ Our brochure with a letter through the post

Your ratings, comments and suggestions would be appreciated on the following areas

	Very useful	Useful	Not useful
Introductory pages	☐	☐	☐
Topic coverage	☐	☐	☐
Summary diagrams	☐	☐	☐
Chapter roundups	☐	☐	☐
Quick quizzes	☐	☐	☐
Activities	☐	☐	☐
Discussion points	☐	☐	☐

	Excellent	Good	Adequate	Poor
Overall opinion of this Course book	☐	☐	☐	☐

Do you intend to continue using BPP Learning Media Business Essentials Course books?   ☐ Yes   ☐ No

Please note any further comments and suggestions/errors on the reverse of this page.

The BPP author of this edition can be e-mailed at: pippariley@bpp.com

Please return this form to: Pippa Riley, BPP Learning Media Ltd, FREEPOST, London, W12 8BR

Review Form (continued)

Please note any further comments and suggestions/errors below